The Legacy of Herbert Simon in Economic Analysis
Volume I

Intellectual Legacies in Modern Economics

Series Editor: Steven G. Medema
Professor, University of Colorado at Denver, USA

Associate Editors: Roger Backhouse
Professor of the History and Philosophy of Economics
University of Birmingham, UK

A.W. Coats
Professor Emeritus of Economic and Social History
University of Nottingham, UK

Wherever possible, the articles in these volumes have been reproduced as originally published using facsimile reproduction, inclusive of footnotes and pagination to facilitate ease of reference.

For a list of all Edward Elgar published titles visit our site on the World Wide Web at
http://www.e-elgar.co.uk

The Legacy of Herbert Simon in Economic Analysis Volume I

Edited by

Peter E. Earl

Senior Lecturer in Business Economics
University of Queensland, Australia

INTELLECTUAL LEGACIES IN MODERN ECONOMICS

An Elgar Reference Collection
Cheltenham, UK • Northampton, MA, USA

Published by
Edward Elgar Publishing Limited
Glensanda House
Montpellier Parade
Cheltenham
Glos GL50 1UA
UK

Edward Elgar Publishing, Inc.
136 West Street, Suite 202
Northampton
Massachusetts 01060
USA

A catalogue record for this book
is available from the British Library

Library of Congress Cataloguing in Publication Data

The legacy of Herbert Simon in Economic analysis / edited by Peter E. Earl.
     p. cm. — (Intellectual legacies in modern economics ; 8)
   Includes bibliographical references and index.
   1. Simon, Herbert Alexander, 1916– 2. Economists—United States—Biography. I. Earl,
Peter E. II. Series.

HB119.S47 L44 2001
330'.092—dc21   200104031

ISBN   1 85898 526 9 (2 volume set)

Printed and bound in Great Britain by MPG Books Ltd, Bodmin, Cornwall

Contents

---

[1]   References provided by Peter Earl
[2]   References provided by Peter Earl

---

[3]   References provided by Peter Earl

Acknowledgements

The editor and publishers wish to thank the authors and the following publishers who have kindly given permission for the use of copyright material.

Academic Press, Inc. for articles: Robert J. Aumann (1997), 'Rationality and Bounded Rationality', *Games and Economic Behavior*, **21** (1/2), October/November, 2–14; Reinhard Selten (1998), 'Aspiration Adaptation Theory', *Journal of Mathematical Psychology*, **42** (2/3), June/September, 191–214.

American Economic Association for articles: Herbert A. Simon (1979), 'Rational Decision Making in Business Organizations', *American Economic Review*, **69** (4), September, 493–513; Roy Radner (1992), 'Hierarchy: The Economics of Managing', *Journal of Economic Literature*, **XXX** (3), September, 1382–415.

American Philosophical Society for article: Herbert A. Simon (1962), 'The Architecture of Complexity', *Proceedings of the American Philosophical Society*, **106** (6), December, 467–82.

American Psychological Association for article: Gerd Gigerenzer and Daniel G. Goldstein (1996), 'Reasoning the Fast and Frugal Way: Models of Bounded Rationality', *Psychological Review*, **103** (4), 650–69.

Blackwell Publishers, Inc. for article: Barton L. Lipman (1995), 'Information Processing and Bounded Rationality: A Survey', *Canadian Journal of Economics*, **XXVIII** (1), February, 42–67.

Blackwell Publishers Ltd for articles: The Royal Swedish Academy of Sciences (1979), 'The Nobel Memorial Prize in Economics 1978: The Official Announcement of the Royal Academy of Sciences', *Scandinavian Journal of Economics*, **81** (1), 72–3; William J. Baumol (1979) 'On the Contributions of Herbert A. Simon to Economics', *Scandinavian Journal of Economics*, **81** (1), 74–82, references; Albert Ando (1979), 'On the Contributions of Herbert A. Simon to Economics', *Scandinavian Journal of Economics*, **81** (1), 83–93, references; Pamela S. Barr and Anne S. Huff (1997), 'Seeing isn't Believing: Understanding Diversity in the Timing of Strategic Response', *Journal of Management Studies*, **34** (3), May, 337–70.

John Conlisk for his own article: (1996), 'Why Bounded Rationality: The Much Too Long Version' [previously unpublished extended version of an article of the same title published in the *Journal of Economic Literature*, **34**, June, 1–64].

Elsevier Science for articles: Roy Radner (1975), 'Satisficing', *Journal of Mathematical Economics*, **2** (2), 253–62; Cristiano Antonelli (1989), 'A Failure-Inducement Model of Research and Development Expenditure', *Journal of Economic Behavior and Organization*, **12** (2), October, 159–80; Eric von Hippel and Marcie I. Tyre (1995), 'How Learning by Doing is Done: Problem Identification in Novel Process Equipment', *Research Policy*, **24** (1), January, 1–12; Arnold C. Cooper, Timothy B. Folta and Carolyn Woo (1995), 'Entrepreneurial Information Search', *Journal of Business Venturing*, **10**, 107–20; Mark Pingle and Richard H. Day (1996), 'Modes of Economizing Behavior: Experimental Evidence', *Journal of Economic Behavior and Organization*, **29** (2), March, 191–209; Andrew L. Zacharakis and G. Dale Meyer (1998), 'A Lack of Insight: Do Venture Capitalists Really Understand their own Decision Process?', *Journal of Business Venturing*, **13** (1), 57–76; Bruce E. Kaufman (1999), 'Emotional Arousal as a Source of Bounded Rationality', *Journal of Economic Behavior and Organization*, **38** (2), February, 135–44.

Institute for Operations Research and the Management Sciences for article: Kenneth W. Koput (1997), 'A Chaotic Model of Innovative Search: Some Answers, Many Questions', *Organization Science*, **8** (5), September–October, 528–42.

Brian J. Loasby for his own excerpt: (1989), 'Herbert Simon's Human Rationality', in *The Mind and The Method of the Economist: A Critical Appraisal of Major Economists in the 20th Century*, Chapter 9, 140–54, references.

Oxford University Press for articles: Esther-Mirjam Sent (1997), 'Sargent versus Simon: Bounded Rationality Unbound', *Cambridge Journal of Economics*, **21**, May, 323–38; Geoffrey M. Hodgson (1997), 'The Ubiquity of Habits and Rules', *Cambridge Journal of Economics*, **21**, 663–84.

Herbert A. Simon for his own excerpt: (1972), 'Theories of Bounded Rationality', in C.B. McGuire and Roy Radner (eds), *Decision and Organization: A Volume in Honor of Jacob Marschak*, Chapter 8, 161–76.

Taylor and Francis Ltd (http://www.tandf/co.uk/journals/) for articles: Marina Bianchi (1990), 'The Unsatisfactoriness of Satisficing: From Bounded Rationality to Innovative Rationality', *Review of Political Economy*, **2** (2), July, 149–67; Neil M. Kay (1995), 'Alchian and "the Alchian Thesis"', *Journal of Economic Methodology*, **2** (2), December, 281–6.

University of Chicago Press for articles: Denis A. Lussier and Richard W. Olshavsky (1979), 'Task Complexity and Contingent Processing in Brand Choice', *Journal of Consumer Research*, **6** (2), September, 154–65; Steven M. Shugan (1980), 'The Cost of Thinking', *Journal of Consumer Research*, **7** (2), September, 99–111.

John Wiley & Sons Limited for article: Ron Sanchez and Joseph T. Mahoney (1996), 'Modularity, Flexibility, and Knowledge Management in Product and Organization Design', *Strategic Management Journal*, **17**, Winter Special Issue, 63–76.

Every effort has been made to trace all the copyright holders but if any have been inadvertently overlooked the publishers will be pleased to make the necessary arrangement at the first opportunity.

In addition the publishers wish to thank the Marshall Library of Economics, Cambridge University, the Library of the London School of Economics and Political Science, B&N Microfilm, London, and the Library of Indiana University at Bloomington, USA, for their assistance in obtaining these articles.

Introduction: Part I

Peter E. Earl

Herbert Simon was born on 15 June 1916 in Milwaukee, Wisconsin and died in Pittsburgh, Pennsylvania on 9 February 2001 from complications following surgery a few weeks earlier. He was the second son of a migrant German father, who was a successful electrical engineer. His mother was also of German descent. After an accelerated path through school, he graduated with his first degree at the University of Chicago in 1936 and before he reached 21 he had begun graduate assistant work there and achieved his first publications. Though he studied economics extensively, he actually majored in political science and his doctoral dissertation, when eventually published in 1947 as the book *Administrative Behavior*, became one of the most influential management texts of the 20th century. After short periods at Berkeley University in California and back in Chicago at the Illinois Institute of Technology (where, at the tender age of 30, he became chairman of the department of political and social science), Simon moved to Pittsburgh in 1949 to the Carnegie Institute of Technology, subsequently Carnegie Mellon University. There he was to work for the rest of his life. Initially he played a leading role in the development of Carnegie's Graduate School of Industrial Administration, but he then became the Richard King Mellon University Professor of Computer Science and Psychology, and a member also of the Departments of Philosophy and of Social and Decision Sciences. Simon never really retired. He celebrated his first three-quarters of a century with the publication of his (1991) autobiography *Models of my Life* and continued his teaching and research activities for a further decade, until his final illness.

In this collection, we focus on just one facet of Simon's intellectual legacy, his significance in economics. He published extensively in the most prestigious US economics journals and economics is the field in which he was awarded the 1978 Nobel Prize. However, Simon was a polymath who also made major contributions to political science, management, cognitive psychology and statistics, and who, with Allen Newell, played the seminal role in establishing artificial intelligence as a field of research. At the time of his Nobel Prize, when he was close to the normal age of retirement, his publications list already ran to around 475 items, but by the time of his death it had almost doubled, to 959 entries, involving collaboration with over 80 other researchers. Volume II of this Collection includes a select bibliography extracted from the complete list that is available at http://kungfu.psy.cmu.edu/psy/faculty/hsimon/hsimon.html.

He was awarded many other honours in addition to the Nobel Prize. These included honorary doctorates from 24 universities and colleges, the A.M. Turing Award in 1975 for his work in computer science and the National Medal of Science in 1986. In 1993, he won the American Psychological Association Award for Outstanding Lifetime Contributions to Psychology and in the following year he was inducted into the Chinese Academy of Sciences, one of only 14 foreign scholars ever to be accorded this status. His pioneering work in the field of artificial intelligence led to his induction into the Automation Hall of Fame in Chicago, which recognizes individuals who have made major contributions to the practice and philosophy of manufacturing technology. There were also major national awards from the Association for Computing Machinery, the American Political Science Association, the Academy of Management, the Operations Research Society and the Institute of Management Science, and many others.

Throughout his long and fruitful academic career Herbert Simon sought to understand and model the processes by which decision-makers try to cope with problems in the face of *bounded rationality*. By this he meant a situation in which there is a mismatch between the scale of the task at hand and the decision-maker's information-processing and linguistic capabilities. There is something of an irony here: despite his ability to make brilliant contributions across many disciplines, Simon (1991) was keen to emphasize that his life had been akin to a journey through a maze. Most economists clearly suffer from bounded rationality to a far greater extent than Simon did and yet they have been less willing than he to grapple with it.

In mainstream economics, the decision-maker is commonly presumed to have information about what might be chosen and the consequences attached to each feasible choice, and a well-defined objective function. Computation of the optimal choice is presumed to be a simple matter. From Simon's standpoint, the standard economic approach to choice fails to capture its essence as an activity involving the *perception* of problems, *search* for potential solutions, *evaluation* of options, the *complexity* of deciding what to do and the barriers to putting a decision into practice. Throughout the decision-maker's life there is the problem of allocating *attention* in the midst of potential foci and solutions (see Berger, 1989, for an endorsement of Simon's work as the basis for a hermeneutic approach to economics). Hence he consistently emphasized selective perception and attention, scope for individuals to interpret given pieces of information in different ways depending on their mental models, and action-based learning. In doing so, Simon displayed affinities with subjectivist economists such as G.L.S. Shackle who were less wedded than he to evolutionary thinking and empirically based modeling. For evolutionary economists, his work has signaled a need to accept that the knowledge on which decisions are based is always conditional on the temporal and spatial experiences of decision-makers (see Tamborini, 1997).

Bounded Rationality and the Determination of Simon's Legacy in Economics

In principle, the task of editing a collection such as this is quite straightforward. First, the editor uses library resources to discover all the contributions to economics that have been influenced by the writings of Herbert Simon. Having done this, the editor then chooses the most significant ones based on a combination of evidence of their past citation rates and an expert assessment of their likely impact in the future, given trends in economic research.[1] It is merely a problem of defining the optimal collection subject to the length constraints imposed by the publisher's commercial judgements. The reality of the task is, however, rather different.

The problem is that modern academic superstar economists such as Herbert Simon or Robert Lucas (whose citations are analysed by Hoover, 1999) can notch up more than an entire page of the hardcopy version of the *Social Sciences Citation Index* (SSCI) in a single year. That is to say, they achieve 500 or more 'hits' per year. The electronic version of the SSCI (at http://wos.isiglobalnet.com) permits those whose libraries have access to it the chance to study the total citation of individual articles since 1973, but though this reduces the risk of oversight, it also adds to the problem of information overload. For example, Simon's articles in the *American*

Economic Review in 1978 and 1979 each log around 300 'hits' but even this looks insignificant compared with the scores achieved by his books *Administrative Behavior* and *The Sciences of the Artificial*. My experience was that when a single edition recorded over 800 citations, there were problems in downloading more than the first 400 of them. But even a 'complete' downloading from the SSCI is incomplete, for it does not list *all* relevant journal articles and does not record which books cite Simon, even though there are potentially numerous chapters in edited books or extracts from single-author books that might be worth considering for inclusion. To judge the impact of an author by direct citations may be unwise given that, as the author's ideas achieve common currency, they may increasingly be employed without reference: a search under 'bounded rationality' reveals many articles that do not cite Herbert Simon despite using his key concept. In any case, no editor assessing the intellectual legacy of a superstar scholar can spend decades – during which the citations would explode further – going painstakingly though *all* the works that a citation search uncovers. In short, once the constraints of the editor's time and library resources are included, it becomes clear that the task of editing this collection has an unnerving reflexive aspect. In other words, it illustrates only too well the essence of Simon's concerns: the best one can hope for is a collection that will serve as a *satisfactory* research tool, without unacceptably large numbers of oversights (cf. Earl, 1983, Akin, 1998).

In assessing Simon's legacy in economics, I found it difficult to escape the fact that his impact might not be turning out in the manner that Simon might have hoped despite his formidable citation rates. There are two main reasons for this, in addition to many academics simply being ignorant of what he has written because their search processes have led them to miss his work or spend little time trying to get to grips with it. The first is that those who read his work carefully might not pick up the messages that he sought to convey: what they see is determined by their personal ways of making sense of what they read.[2] Second, academic economists have their careers to think about as well as the growth of economic knowledge and, in career terms, it can be dangerous to do the kinds of economics that Simon advocated, based on studies of *actual* behaviour. Such research is very time-consuming, unless aided by large research grants, but these can be difficult to obtain when the research method goes against the philosophy of those who allocate funds. Worse still, it is difficult to publish fieldwork-based research in top-ranking journals dominated by mainstream gatekeepers. The disincentive to follow Simon's philosophy is even stronger nowadays because of the prevalence of research audits associated with the managerial reforms that have swept the university sector.[3] Readers should bear this in mind when they look at the articles in these volumes: those from the 'core' economics journals are, by and large, theoretical pieces and those that are empirically based mainly come from sub-disciplinary journals or from outside of economics as it is conventionally defined.

These considerations led me to recognize that as an editor I was in a position akin to an executor of a will, with a degree of license to make choices that might have some impact on the subsequent use of Simon's ideas. I could use my choice of articles and the introduction to correct misperceptions and try to point research in particular directions that might better mirror Simon's view of the significance of his contributions. Given the sheer range of his writings in economics, it would have been possible to produce a far larger work than the present two-volume compilation. To keep the project within the constraints set by the publisher and within my own range of competence, I opted to focus editorial attention on contributions related to his work on decision making and organizations, which was emphasized in his Nobel Prize citation. The essays by Ando and Baumol in Part I of this volume provide useful overviews of some works by Simon in other contexts (for example, inventory management) that have also proved influential.

In order to show where Simon-inspired economics had traveled by the end of the 20th century, and because citations in recent papers provide a good, but by no means foolproof, way of getting back to earlier users of his thinking, I have skewed the collection in favour of recent works. In the 1990s, Simon's significance became recognized in economics on a scale far in excess of previous decades (see Cleaver, 1999). Furthermore, the remarkable survey essay by John Conlisk reproduced in Part II of this volume should reduce the risk of oversights in terms of pertinent pre-1996 writings.

This collection should be read in conjunction with the Elgar reference collection on behavioural economics (Earl, ed., 1988) to set his work among the broader literature in this genre. This is also a convenient source of some other papers which bear the stamp of Simon's influence (such as Mosley's 1976 satisficing analysis of macroeconomic policy making) and which would otherwise have been candidates for inclusion here. Ideally this collection should also be read when armed with the major volumes of Simon's collected economic writings (Simon, 1982a, 1982b, 1997), for I have chosen to let Simon's legacy become apparent through a focus on the use made of his work, only reproducing a handful of his original contributions. This strategy enables a bigger coverage of what has been done with Simon's thinking. It also seems sensible because, from my own experience and from studying contributions that refer to Simon, my impression is that the way that Simon's work has had an impact is essentially via scholars getting a broad-brush picture of how he sees things. This often comes via only a few of his writings, rather than from a comprehensive and painstaking reading of his work. It is sometimes rather difficult to disentangle this broad-brush impact from the influence of James March and Richard Cyert, his co-workers in pioneering the Carnegie approach to behavioural economics (especially Cyert and March, 1963). Within this remarkable trio, however, Simon was the mastermind.

The remaining sections of this introduction provide overviews of the literatures that include the articles collected under the respective headings. The introduction is partitioned across the two volumes to facilitate flexibility in their use. Volume I is concerned primarily with the impact of Simon's work on research into decision making and complex systems. Though we can think of this as the impact of his work on the core of the subject, quite a lot of the articles in this volume entail empirical work in particular contexts, that demonstrates its significance for the broader realm of the subject. The papers in Volume II are intended to show how his contributions have been affecting research in some of the major economics sub-disciplines, such as industrial organization, ecological economics, and law and economics.

The Nobel Laureate

A convenient way to get an overview of Simon's contribution to economics is by focusing on articles related to his 1978 Nobel Prize in Economics. This was marked in the 1979 *Scandinavian Journal of Economics* by an official citation for the award, a pair of tribute articles by William Baumol and Albert Ando, and a comprehensive bibliography of Simon's writings up to 1978.

In this section the citation and the articles are reproduced, minus the bibliography, followed by Simon's Nobel address which presents a convenient guide to his work on decision making, for which the prize was awarded. Both Baumol and Ando are careful to highlight the fact that Simon's work extends beyond the economics of bounded rationality. Ando notes at some length his contributions to the literature on skew distributions (which have been very heavily cited indeed),[4] and to econometric modeling, most notably on causal ordering. Hoover (1990) has further commented on the significance of Simon's work on causality, the later contributions to which are reprinted in Simon (1997, Part 1).

Bounded Rationality (1): Overview

A natural place to commence a comprehensive overview of the literature on bounded rationality spawned by Simon's work is with his own summary paper on theories of bounded rationality, written for a festschrift for his long-time friend Jacob (Jascha) Marschak. Like Simon, Marschak was very much concerned with the economics of information and decision making but throughout their long friendship Simon was never able to convince him that complexity and information problems implied a need to abandon optimization for satisficing concepts (see Simon, 1991, p. 105). Their differences over method are echoed by much of what follows in this section and the two that follow: mainstream uses of the notion of bounded rationality are remarkably different from those by economists and other researchers on decision making outside the mainstream neoclassical fraternity. Simon hoped that economics would take the path of basing models on behavioural research or pertinent empirical findings from other disciplines such as psychology. Mainstream writers, however, have continued to do axiomatic economics and continued to assume that actions are optimal despite being formed in the face of bounded rationality. In Simon's own words:

> I continue to get a stream of letters from folks who are doing something they label 'behavioral economics' whether it be the genuine kind or (as in the case of Sargent and Aumann) neoclassical model building carried on by other means. ... Many economists are learning that they can add 'limits of rationality' to their models, but most of them are doing it without any concern for the empirical validity of the assumptions they are making (Simon, e-mail message to Earl, 23 June 1997).

Given his own competence as a formal model builder, it should be no surprise that Simon is nonetheless receptive to mathematical models of choice that capture the essence of his analysis. These are models in which (i) choice entails satisficing rather than optimization, and (ii) satisfactory outcomes are defined in terms of aspiration levels which are adjusted, with something of a lag, in the direction of what experience demonstrates to be feasible. The articles by Radner and Selten deal, respectively, with these topics in a formal style. Selten is, incidentally, one of the modern writers whom Simon most admired. He described Selten as 'doubly impressive' (*ibid.*) for displaying thoughtfulness and a love of formal work, combined with a willingness to do empirical research as part of the business of being a serious scientist. Much the same could be said of Simon himself.

This section ends with a previously unpublished extended version of a well-known survey paper by John Conlisk, which examines a wide range of literatures associated with the notion of bounded rationality and argues forcefully the case for making the concept an essential part of economic thinking. Conlisk's paper is well complemented by a subsequent critical overview of the bounded rationality literature by Cleaver (1999).

Bounded Rationality (2): In Neoclassical Economics

The comments by Simon reproduced in the previous section call to mind the fate of Keynes' macroeconomics in the hands of neoclassical writers, a fate that led Joan Robinson to coin the term 'bastard Keynesians' and to Leijonhufvud's (1968) book *On Keynesian Economics and the Economics of Keynes*. It is hard to examine the economics literature that cites Simon, or refers to bounded rationality, without becoming conscious of the risk that illegitimate use of his thinking might dominate in terms of shaping his legacy in economics. This section is relatively short but it should contain enough to give a flavour of what is going on, while ensuring that the bulk of this collection can be devoted to work that properly reflects Simon's approach.

In the past, most neoclassical economists rejected the concept of satisficing via two main lines of argument. The first, which remains implied in the modern neoclassical applications of bounded rationality is that all Simon was really arguing is that choice entails optimization *with an extra constraint*, the finite rate at which decision-makers could process information. This perspective is very similar to Stigler's (1961) analysis of search in terms of the marginal costs and expected benefits of devoting resources to gathering information. That analysis begs the question of how choice can possibly be optimal if choosers cannot know whether their search has missed any fundamental pieces of information. Day (1967) opened up further scope for satisficing to be absorbed within the optimizing framework by arguing that decision-makers might eventually find optimal positions by a process of trial and error. This argument is not well suited to a turbulent world of innovation (see Nelson and Winter, 1982). It also presumes that decision-makers can correctly judge trials as successes or failures and can correctly infer whether they are at a local or global maximum position when small movements in either direction fail to yield improvements in performance (a point originally raised by Alchian, 1950, p. 219).

Second, neoclassical theorists have tended to maintain, via Friedman's (1953) discussion of Alchian's (1950) work on economic natural selection, that firms which failed to maximize profits would be driven out of the market by those that did so. This line of argument was challenged by Winter (1964), who recognized that a fleet-footed business using simple decision rules might outmanoeuvre a firm which took time to gather and process information carefully. What few economists (not even Simon) seemed to notice was that Friedman had misrepresented Alchian's original article. (There is a decision rule implied in all this: do not rely upon secondary sources.) The paper in which Neil Kay recently drew attention to this is included at the start of this section to alert readers to the muddled nature of critical discussion of the case for and against abandoning descriptively unrealistic maximizing models in favour of empirically-grounded satisficing analysis. It is followed by two papers (Lipman and Aumann) that epitomize the modern neoclassical approach but which do so mainly in words rather than the more common formal style. The section ends with Esther-Mirjam Sent's critical discussion of how the neoclassical rational expectations literature, like the bounded rationality literature, originated at Carnegie Mellon University, and of flaws in Sargent's claims to be offering a bounded rationality approach to economics.

Lipman's work is extended in several other papers (for example, Lipman, 1991, 1999), while those who share Aumann's interest in game theory might wish to explore the satisficing treatment of games in Stirling and Goodrich (1999). Game theorists in general need to go beyond recognizing that game playing might involve satisficing. One of the big problems faced in real-life economic games is that of working out exactly what the nature of the game is, rather than guessing what an opponent might do in terms of a given menu of possibilities.

Within the neoclassical bounded rationality literature there is an increasing trend favouring the construction of models of interacting computing automata that constitute completely artificial economies which are judged in terms of how well they mimic aspects of the real economy. In other words, we now have artificial economics as an offshoot of artificial intelligence. Sent's critique of Sargent is worth supplementing with the review of the 'artificial worlds' economics by Boumans (1997), which includes a critical examination of the work of Robert Lucas in this genre. In typical neoclassical style, Lucas builds his artificial worlds around representative agents. In the process he loses sight of the coordination problem. A properly Simon-inspired approach would recognize that economic systems are complex and populated by individuals who see the world differently and who experiment without necessarily converging on rational expectations. Volume II includes some examples (the articles by Krider and Weinberg, and Mirowski and Somefun) of how evolutionary economists have used a computational view of markets, with an eye to potential for chaos rather than equilibrium.

Bounded Rationality (3): Behavioural Approaches

Most of the articles in this section do not come from the kinds of journals that mainstream economists read, but the source journals will be relatively familiar to those who work in economic psychology or on the intersection between economics and management. The first half of the section consists of articles that give a taste of Simon-inspired consumer research. In contrast to the mainstream literature that focuses on indifference curves and equilibrium conditions for the representative consumer, and on the econometric estimation of demand systems, the literature here focuses on the use of simplifying decision rules that do not always obey the Axiom of Gross Substitution. Here, empirical methods involve experimentation and techniques such as protocol analysis, that concentrate on individuals rather than market demand (see also Bettman, 1979, Earl, 1986a, 1986b, and Payne, Bettman and Johnson, 1993). Although this literature reveals that satisficing via non-compensatory decision rules *need* not produce behaviour that looks grotesquely dysfunctional, the literature does also depart from neoclassical analysis in emphasizing that boundedly rational consumers *may* be prone to suffer from dysfunctional cognitive biases. It also suggests that their emotional states may have both helpful and unfortunate impacts on choice. (See also Earl, 1990a, Luce, Bettman and Payne, 1997, and Elster, 1999.)

The second half of this section consists of papers on decision making in organizations in the face of bounded rationality, beginning with research on processes of search and judgement, before going on to learning and adaptation to changed circumstances. The material here is complemented by many of the papers previously reprinted in Earl (ed.) (1988, Volume I) and books by Cyert and March (1963), Loasby (1976), Kay (1979) and Earl (1984), the last of which examines the dysfunctional behaviour of firms.

Bounded Rationality (4): Sympathetic Critics

Prior to the neoclassical wave of interest in bounded rationality, Simon had a difficult time with mainstream economists, both colleagues and in the profession at large, which contributed to his switch to psychology and computing science. As he observed (1991, pp. 270–1):

> The first hostilities took the form of counterattacks from the opponents of bounded rationality: from Edward S. Mason (1952) and Fritz Machlup (1946), the former claiming that my revisions of the theory of the firm were not very relevant to economic theory, the latter that people, what ever the appearances, really maximized. ... Jack Muth in his announcement of rational expectations in 1961, explicitly labeled his theory a reply to my doctrine of bounded rationality. Lunchtime debates with my colleagues and disputes about personnel decisions in the economics faculty undoubtedly contributed to the gradual escalation of my conflict with the profession. By the time I returned to a concern with economics in the 1970s, the war was open and declared.

In addition to these attacks and the arguments I reviewed in introducing neoclassical work with bounded rationality, Simon has also had to contend with criticism from heterodox economists who are sympathetic to much of his work. This section contains three papers (by Loasby, Bianchi and Hodgson) that give a flavour of the kind of critical comment that Simon's work provokes from behavioural, Post Keynesian and institutional economics. (See also Langlois, 1990, Schlicht, 1990, Dunn, 1999, and, for a critical view from the public administration literature, see the closing reading in Volume II of this collection.)

These critics have been uncomfortable with Simon's tendency to write as if fundamental (non-probabilistic) uncertainty is something that would not exist in the absence of cognitive constraints on choice. Innovative thinking is especially problematic: does it involve creating something truly new and incapable of anticipation, or does it merely entail removing a veil of ignorance? Moreover, even if one accepts that decision rules are widely employed in everyday life, their origins need to be considered carefully, as do processes by which people change the rules according to which they run their lives. Not all rules are a consequence of bounded rationality; rather, they may reflect moral bounds and the willingness of decision-makers to have standards imposed upon them by others.

The extent to which one regards these critiques as valid may depend in part on one's willingness to view creativity in terms of the splicing together of *existing* concepts, which then opens up further splicing opportunities. Discussions of how choice might be shaped by issues such as personal integrity rather than mere problems of handling information can be shifted to a different level of analysis in the light of Simon's work on parallels between computing and mental processes. We may think of the mind as being like a computer in the sense that there are some programmes which it simply will not run, or which it will only run as part of a specific sequence of programmes. This may mean that some actions or the admission of certain new rules of thought are unthinkable. Although the set of potential rules for thought that we encounter may depend on the social and institutional contexts in which we develop as people, our minds still have to deem them admissible and a degree of cognitive maturity is required before moral sense is developed. We may *have* to be hard-wired at birth in terms of a basic set of tacit judgmental rules that allow us to choose further rules for coping with life, gradually building up a system including rules for modifying rules. Such core rules could include self-denying clauses which specified the circumstances under which they would be displaced by new core principles. (This meta-level view of the evolution of decision rules can also be framed in terms of constitutional systems involving appeals to different levels of authority: see Earl, 1986b, pp. 145–7.)

Decomposability and Hierarchy

The comments just made about the multi-level nature of the human mind were in part inspired by the paper by Simon reproduced at the start of this section and which is often referred to via his (1969) book *The Sciences of the Artificial* in which it also appeared. The task of coping with complexity is made much easier if problems can be broken down into sub-problems, each of which can be tackled separately without the lower-level solutions operating against each other. If the system can be decomposed in a modular fashion, then it may enjoy resilience in the face of a changing external environment or when it suffers the failure of one of its components.

Prior to the appearance of this contribution by Simon, most economists had shown little interest in the structural architecture of the systems about which they wrote. Simon's work implied that structure has economic significance (see also Potts, 2000). It may be costly to have an integral structure in a context where shocks are common, but if the system is not naturally decomposable, attempts to carve it into sub-units to make it manageable may also be costly, the size of the cost depending on how it is segmented. These issues can arise within individual organizations or in respect of systems of interacting organizations.

In the second article in this section Radner surveys the economic analysis of management that has been greatly influenced by Simon's thinking. The context of Radner's paper is noteworthy: his Marshall Lectures in Cambridge. In many respects Alfred Marshall may be said to be the first behavioural economist, well before Simon. This is because Marshall spent much time studying the actual operations of business and his analysis of the firm was dominated by a concern with how problems of knowledge, such as those associated with the development of a bureaucratic structure and changes in products and production methods. This volume ends with a paper by Sanchez and Mahoney, which focuses on the use of standardized interfaces to facilitate coordination in processes of product design.

The decomposability theme comes up a number of times in Volume II of this collection. This section might have included more articles were it not for the irony that some of the heaviest users of this aspect of Simon's thinking have made their contributions in a non-modular manner, in books. One of the most extensive initial discussions of the significance of decomposability is in Loasby (1976), influential in the work of Kay (1982, 1984, 1997), on the evolution of business strategy and organizational structure, and, in turn, Earl (1986b), on strategic aspects of consumer behaviour. The focus here is on a trade-off that would be of little interest in a world of perfect insurance markets and limited complementarities. On the one hand, there are the advantages of 'hedging one's bets' or 'not putting all one's eggs in the same basket' in a world prone to unpleasant, non-probabilistic surprises (such as the catastrophic demise of a product technology). On the other hand, there are the synergy advantages of exploiting externalities or shared inputs across potentially separable production or consumption activities. The Sanchez and Mahoney article at the end of this volume overlaps with an important book by Langlois and Robertson (1995), who relate changes in the extent of modularity to the product life cycle and the division of labour among firms in a market. (Oddly, they make no explicit reference to Simon's work.) They include a series of case studies that show how modular systems tend to predominate when there is technological uncertainty. A prerequisite, however, is the development of institutional standards: these permit specialization in the supply of modules (such as loudspeakers, record player turntables, amplifiers and tuners in the audio equipment market, or subassemblies for these modules) that can be bolted together interchangeably in a mix-and-match fashion. But as the dominant technology becomes established, final products may increasingly be supplied in integrated form as 'appliances', thereby achieving economies of packaging and wiring modules together, as well as providing simplicity for the customers. At the appliance stage, the interior components may be supplied by a variety of subcontractors, with the integrating firm in effect acting as broker and orchestrating agent on behalf of the consumers.

There is also scope for applying the notion of decomposability in the context of macroeconomics. Simon's thinking links very well with Minsky's (1975) theory of systemic financial fragility, which focuses on inter-linked balance sheets in a multi-layered financial system. The resilience of such a system may depend crucially on the decomposability of the matrix of financial claims. Fragility is reduced if speculative activity is confined only to a subset of economic actors and only focuses on particular sectors (for example, real estate), and to the extent that financial reserves provide buffering in the event of defaults. Policy makers may be unable to predict the timing of collapses of confidence, but at least they might develop sets of rules of the game that enhance the decomposability of the financial system and thereby limit the explosiveness of any multiplier effects. I have commented on this at slightly greater length in Earl (1998), also noting the dependence of the volume of aggregate demand on network effects among consumers, including features such as transaction chains in markets for housing. So far, however, little work is evident along these lines but macroeconomists from several research programmes are getting quite close. For example, one might usefully read Bomfim and Diebold's (1997) New Keynesian paper on bounded rationality and strategic complementarity in a macroeconomic model mindful of Simon and decomposability.

The biggest hope for a structurally based macroeconomics probably lies with the Post Keynesians, who are the main users of Minsky's work. Members of this group are increasingly adopting Simon-inspired consumer theory for their micro-foundations (see, for example, Lavoie, 1993) and have periodically noted similarities between Simon's approach and Keynes' thinking on the role of decision rules in coping with ignorance about the future (a recent contribution is Marchionatti, 1999). Their route to the architecture of complexity seems likely to be via Sraffa's (1960) work on production matrices, which introduced the concept of 'basic commodities'. In the light of Sraffa, the Post Keynesians recognize that, for example, the 1970s OPEC-related oil crises in part achieved their status because oil is used directly or indirectly in so many products. Other elements of a structurally based approach to macroeconomics are considered in Earl (1990b).

Finally, it may be noted that within development economics there is a long tradition of debate between heterodox economists who think that structure matters and neoclassical economists who take a reductionist approach, focusing on freeing up markets and tending to downplay complications caused by links between different system elements. Simon's perspective clearly augments that of structuralist development economists, but again there is little sign of attempts at analysis in this area explicitly in terms of hierarchy, modularity and bounded rationality. However, at least Simon's writing on decision making has been used in critical discussions of the philosophy and practice of development planning in a world of complexity and uncertainty (see Killick, 1976; Leff, 1985).

Acknowledgements

This collection was prepared during the second half of 1999 when the editor was Visiting Professor of Economics at the University of Queensland, St Lucia, Brisbane, Queensland, Australia. I am grateful to my then-employer, Lincoln University, New Zealand, for granting me overseas study leave to engage in this work. I am grateful to Professor John Foster for inviting me to join his department for this period of study leave and for the facilities provided. In particular, the library facilities were absolutely first class and it was a pleasure to be among enthusiastic young staff working at the leading edge of complexity theory and evolutionary economics. I am also grateful for perceptive refereeing comments from Steven Medema, Bob Coats and Roger Backhouse.

Notes

1. There is considerable scope to use the electronic version of the *Social Sciences Citation Index*, in conjunction with techniques from network theory (cf. Zeggelink, 1994), to model patterns of influence of particular scholars and their ideas, as well as social links among communities of scholars.
2. Historians of economic thought would do well to consider using the kinds of mental mapping techniques that have been employed in studies of organizational behaviour by writers such as Swan (1995).
3. It is perhaps also worth noting that, in career terms, editing collections such as the present one is a rather dangerous activity in the present audit climate that insists on a focus on writing articles for core journals. Fortunately, for the progress of economics, the academic system has pockets of slack in it that can be exploited by those whose sub-goals include 'doing their own thing'.
4. Given that Simon's research output was so prolific and appeared frequently in the top US journals, it is interesting to note that Cox and Chung (1991) have attempted to model patterns of research output in economics journals with reference to Simon's (1955) work on skew distributions. (His work focused in particular on Lotka's law of distribution and its origins are explained by Simon (1991, pp. 372–5) in his autobiography.) Simon himself evidently is in the very select band of superstar economists who manage to publish multiple articles in many of the top-ranking economics journals, but it is hard to think of anyone else who has performed the same feat across the élite journals of a multiplicity of disciplines.

References

Akin, L. (1998), 'Methods for Examining Small Literatures: Explication, Physical Analysis and Citation Patterns', *Library and Information Science Research*, **20** (3), 251–70.
Alchian, A.A. (1950), 'Uncertainty, Evolution and Economic Theory', *Journal of Political Economy*, **57**, 211–21.
Berger, L.A. (1989), 'Economics and Hermeneutics', *Economics and Philosophy*, **5** (2), 209–33.
Bettman, J.R. (1979), *An Information Processing Theory of Consumer Choice*, Reading, MA, Addison-Wesley.

Bomfim, A.N. and Diebold, F.X. (1997), 'Bounded Rationality and Strategic Complementarity in a Macroeconomic Model: Policy Effects, Persistence and Multipliers', *Economic Journal*, **107**, September, 1358–74.

Boumans, M. (1997), 'Lucas and Artificial Worlds', *History of Political Economy*, **29** (annual supplement, edited by J.B. Davis), 63–88.

Cleaver, K.C. (1999), 'The Bounds of Rationality: Reflections on the Economic Representation of Rationality in the Late Twentieth Century', 178–98 in Dow, S.C. and Earl, P.E. (eds), *Complexity, Contingency and the Theory of the Firm: Essays in Honour of Brian J. Loasby, Volume II*, Cheltenham, Edward Elgar.

Cox, R.A.K. and Chung, K.H. (1991), 'Patterns of Research Output and Author Concentration in the Economics Literature', *Review of Economics and Statistics*, **73** (4), 740–47.

Cyert, R.M. and March, J.G. (1963), *A Behavioral Theory of the Firm*, Englewood Cliffs, NJ, Prentice-Hall.

Day, R.H. (1967), 'Profits, Learning and the Convergence of Satisficing to Marginalism', *Quarterly Journal of Economics*, **81**, 302–11 (reprinted in Earl, ed. 1988, Volume I, 149–58).

Dunn, S.P. (1999), 'Bounded Rationality, "Fundamental" Uncertainty and the Firm in the Long Run', 199–217 in Dow, S.C. and Earl, P.E. (eds) *Complexity, Contingency and the Theory of the Firm: Essays in Honour of Brian J. Loasby, Volume II*, Cheltenham, Edward Elgar.

Earl, P.E. (1983), 'A Behavioral Theory of Economists' Behavior', 90–125 in Eichner, A.S. (ed.), *Why Economics is Not Yet a Science*, Armonk, NY, M.E. Sharpe, Inc.

Earl, P.E. (1984), *The Corporate Imagination: How Big Companies Make Mistakes*, Brighton, Wheatsheaf/Armonk, NY, M.E. Sharpe, Inc.

Earl, P.E. (1986a), 'A Behavioural Analysis of Demand Elasticities', *Journal of Economic Studies*, **13** (3), 20–37 (reprinted in Earl, P.E. (ed.), 1988, Volume II).

Earl, P.E. (1986b), *Lifestyle Economics: Consumer Behaviour in a Turbulent World*, New York, St Martin's Press.

Earl, P.E. (ed.) (1988), *Behavioural Economics*, Aldershot, Edward Elgar.

Earl, P.E. (1990a), 'Economics and Psychology: A Survey', *Economic Journal*, **100**, September: 718–55.

Earl, P.E. (1990b), *Monetary Scenarios: A Modern Approach to Financial Systems*, Aldershot, Edward Elgar.

Earl, P.E. (1998), 'Information, Coordination and Macroeconomics', *Information Economics and Policy*, **10** (3), 331–42.

Elster, J. (1999), *Alchemies of the Mind: Rationality and the Emotions*, Cambridge, Cambridge University Press.

Friedman, M. (1953), 'The Methodology of Positive Economics', 3–43 in his *Essays in Positive Economics*, Chicago, IL, University of Chicago Press.

Hoover, K.D. (1990), 'The Logic of Causal Inference: Econometrics and the Conditional Analysis of Causation', *Economics and Philosophy*, **6** (2), 207–34.

Hoover, K.D. (1999), *The Legacy of Robert Lucas, Jr. (Intellectual Legacies in Modern Economics Series, No. 3)*, Cheltenham, Edward Elgar.

Kay, N.M. (1979), *The Innovating Firm: A Behavioural Theory of Corporate R&D*, London, Macmillan.

Kay, N.M. (1982), *The Evolving Firm*, London, Macmillan.

Kay, N.M. (1984), *The Emergent Firm: Knowledge, Ignorance and Surprise in Economic Organization*, London, Macmillan.

Kay, N.M. (1997), *Pattern In Corporate Evolution*, Oxford, Oxford University Press.

Killick, T. (1976), 'The Possibilities of Development Planning', *Oxford Economic Papers*, **28**, 161–84.

Langlois, R.N. (1990), 'Bounded Rationality and Behavioralism: A Clarification and Critique', *Journal of Institutional and Theoretical Economics*, **146** (4), 691–5.

Langlois, R.H. and Robertson, P.L. (1995), *Firms, Markets and Economic Change*, London, Routledge.

Lavoie, M. (1993), *Foundations of Post-Keynesian Economic Analysis*, Aldershot, Edward Elgar.

Leff, N.H. (1985), 'Optimal Investment Choice for Developing Countries', *Journal of Development Economics*, **18**, 335–60.

Leijonhufvud, A. (1968), *On Keynesian Economics and the Economics of Keynes*, New York, Oxford University Press.

Lipman, B.L. (1991), 'How to Decide How to Decide How to: Modeling Bounded Rationality', *Econometrica*, **59** (4), 1105–25.

Lipman, B.L. (1999), 'Decision Theory Without Logical Omniscience: Toward an Axiomatic Framework for Bounded Rationality', *Review of Economic Studies*, **66** (2), 339–61.

Loasby, B.J. (1976), *Choice, Complexity and Ignorance*, Cambridge, Cambridge University Press.

Luce, M.F., Bettman, J.R. and Payne, J.W. (1997), 'Choice Processing in Emotionally Difficult Decisions', *Journal of Experimental Psychology: Learning, Memory and Cognition*, **23** (2), 384–405.

Machlup, F. (1946), 'Marginal Analysis and Empirical Research', *American Economic Review*, **36**, 519–54.

Marchionatti, R. (1999), 'On Keynes' Animal Spirits', *Kyklos*, **52** (3), 415–39.

Mason, E.S. (1952), 'Comment', in Haley, B.F. (ed.), *A Survey of Contemporary Economics, II*, Homewood, IL, Irwin.

Minsky, H.P. (1975), *John Maynard Keynes*, New York, Columbia University Press.

Mosley, P. (1976), 'Towards a "Satisficing" Theory of Economic Policy', *Economic Journal*, **86**, March, 59–72 (reprinted in Earl, P.E. (ed.) (1988) Volume II, 319–32).

Nelson, R.R. and Winter, S.G. (1982), *An Evolutionary Theory of Economic Change*, Cambridge, MA: The Belknap Press of Harvard University Press.

Payne, J.W., Bettman, J.R. and Johnson, E.J. (1993), *The Adaptive Decision Maker*, Cambridge, Cambridge University Press.

Potts, J. (2000), *The New Evolutionary Microeconomics: Complexity, Competence and Adaptive Behaviour*, Cheltenham, Edward Elgar.

Schlicht, E. (1990), Rationality, Bounded or Not, and Institutional Analysis', *Journal of Institutional and Theoretical Economics*, **146** (4), 703–19.

Simon, H.A. (1947), *Administrative Behavior*, New York, Macmillan.

Simon, H.A. (1955), 'On a Class of Skew Distribution Functions', *Biometrika*, **42**, 425–40.

Simon, H.A. (1969), *The Sciences of the Artificial*, Cambridge, MA, MIT Press.

Simon, H.A. (1978), 'Rationality as Process and as Product of Thought' [Richard T. Ely lecture], *American Economic Review*, **68** (2), 1–16.

Simon, H.A. (1979), 'Rational Decision Making in Business Organizations' [The 1978 Nobel Memorial Prize in Economics lecture] *American Economic Review*, **69**, 493–513.

Simon, H.A. (1982a), *Models of Bounded Rationality, Volume I: Economic Analysis and Public Policy*, Cambridge, MA, MIT Press.

Simon, H.A. (1982a), *Models of Bounded Rationality, Volume II: Behavioral Economics and Business Organization*, Cambridge, MA, MIT Press.

Simon, H.A. (1991), *Models of My Life*, New York, Basic Books.

Simon, H.A. (1997), *Models of Bounded Rationality, Volume III: Empirically Grounded Economic Reason*, Cambridge, MA, MIT Press.

Sraffa, P. (1960), *Production of Commodities by Means of Commodities*, Cambridge, Cambridge University Press.

Stigler, G.J. (1961), 'The Economics of Information', *Journal of Political Economy*, **69** (3), 213–25.

Stirling, W.C. and Goodrich, M.A. (1999), 'Satisficing Games', *Information Sciences*, **114** (1–4), 255–80.

Swan, J.A. (1995), 'Exploring Knowledge and Cognition in Decisions About Technological Innovation: Mapping Managerial Cognitions', *Human Relations*, **48** (11), 1241–70.

Tamborini, R. (1997), Knowledge and Economic Behaviour: A Constructivist Approach', *Journal of Evolutionary Economics*, **7** (1), 49–72.

Winter, S.G. (1964), 'Economic "Natural Selection" and the Theory of the Firm', *Yale Economic Essays*, **4**, 225–72 (reprinted in Earl, ed., 1988, Volume I, 104–48).

Zeggelink, E. (1994), 'Dynamics of Structure: An Individual Oriented Approach', *Social Networks*, **16** (4), 295–333.

Part I
The Nobel Laureate

[1]

THE NOBEL MEMORIAL PRIZE IN ECONOMICS 1978

The Official Announcement of the Royal Academy of Sciences

The Royal Swedish Academy of Sciences has decided to award the 1978 Alfred Nobel Memorial Prize in Economic Sciences to Professor Herbert A. Simon, Carnegie-Mellon University, Pittsburgh, Pennsylvania, USA, for his pioneering research into the decision-making process within economic organizations.

Herbert A. Simon's scientific output goes far beyond the disciplines in which he has held professorships—political science, administration, psychology and information sciences. He has made contributions in the fields of science theory, applied mathematics, statistics, operations analysis, economics and business administration. In all areas in which he has conducted research, Simon has had something of importance to say; and, as a rule, he has developed his ideas to such an extent that it has been possible to use them as a basis for empirical studies. But he is, first and foremost, an economist—in the widest sense of the word—and his name is associated, most of all, with publications on structure and decision-making within economic organizations, a relatively new area of economic research.

In older, traditional economic studies, no distinction was made between enterprises and entrepreneurs, and it was assumed that entrepreneurs had only one goal: profit-maximizing. The primary purpose of this classic and rather rudimentary theory of the firm was to serve as a basis for studies of total market behavior and not of the behavior of individual firms. As long as these companies consisted of small, patriarchally run units, their activities remained relatively uninteresting. However, as companies grew in size, as operating them became more and more separated from owning them, as employees began to form labor unions, as the rate of expansion increased and as price competition between many was replaced by competition in regard to quality and service between few, the behavior of individual companies attained quite another degree of interest.

Influenced by the organizational research that was being conducted in other social sciences in the 1930s, economists began to look at the structure of companies and at the decision-making process in an entirely new way. Simon's work was of the utmost importance for this new line of development. In his epoch-making book *Administrative Behavior* (1947), and in a number of subsequent works, he described the company as an adaptive system of physical, personal and social components that are held together by a network of intercom munications and by the willingness of its members to cooperate and to strive towards a common goal. What is new in Simon's ideas is, most of all, that he rejects the assumption made in the classic theory of the firm of an omniscient, rational, profit-maximizing entrepreneur. He replaces this entrepreneur by a number of cooperating decision-makers, whose capacities for rational action are limited both by a lack of knowledge about the total consequences of their decisions and by personal and social ties. Since these decision-makers cannot choose a *best* alternative, as can the classic entrepreneur, they have to be content with a *satisfactory* alternative. Individual companies, therefore, strive not to maximize profits but to find acceptable solutions to acute problems. This might mean that a number of partly contradictory goals have to be reached at the same time. Each decision-maker in such a company attempts to find a satisfactory solution to his own set of problems, and takes into consideration how others are solving theirs.

Simon's theories and observations about decision-making in organizations apply very well to the systems and techniques of planning, budgeting and control that are used in modern business and public administration. These theories may be less elegant and less suited to overall economic analysis than the classic profit-maximizing theory, but they provide greater possibilities for understanding and prediction in a number of areas. They have been used successfully to explain and predict such diverse activities as the distribution of access to information and decision-making within companies, market adjustment to limited competition, choosing investment portfolios and choosing a country in which to establish a foreign investment. Modern business economics and administrative research are largely based on Simon's ideas.

Simon has been awarded this year's prize in economics for his research into the decision-making process within economic organizations, but he has also made other important contributions to the science of economics. For example, his interest in simplifying and understanding complex decision-making situations led him, at an early stage, to the problem of breaking down complex equation systems. His studies of "causal order" in such systems have been of particular importance.

[2]

ON THE CONTRIBUTIONS OF
HERBERT A. SIMON TO ECONOMICS

William J. Baumol

New York University, New York, N.Y. and Princeton University,
Princeton, N.J., USA

I. Introduction

Herbert Simon has made a number of profound contributions to economic
analysis and its applications. Both in depth and in volume his work is
remarkable, and this is all the more extraordinary since economics is not
his primary field. His work is used constantly in the economic literature.
His writings on human rationality have given rise to a new school of
investigation, the behavioral study of firms and other organizations—a
school which has produced a number of important books and articles. His
contributions to mathematical economics include a theorem (about which
more will be said later) that continues to serve as a key element in areas as
diverse as input–output analysis, comparative statics and its relations to
dynamics and the modern interpretation of the Ricardian and Marxian models.

He has also made contributions in a variety of other areas, such as the theory
of causal ordering and the analysis of the identification problem in econometrics. He has published applied econometric studies relating to organizational behavior. He has written a number of significant reports on important
economic issues in public policy. He has also contributed to the foundation
of the new field of operations research (management science) which consists,
to a considerable extent , in the adaptation of the more rigorous tools of
economic analysis to the analysis of governmental and business decisions,
that is, into means for more effective decision making.

Simon's productivity has continued undiminished throughout his career
(which still has a long time to go!). His recent publications continue to add to
his earlier work along lines of natural development.

This review will be devoted primarily to a discussion of Simon's two most
crucial contributions to economics. Wherever possible, his most recent work
will be noted.

II. Organizational Behavior: Satisficing vs. Maximization

Even since Cournot, the basic premise of microeconomic theory has been
maximization of some objective function by the decision-maker. Even most

of those who have suggested some alternative to profit maximization as the objective of the managerially dominated firm have retained the hypothesis that management is seeking to maximize *something*—whether it be total revenue (sales), rate of growth of assets, probability of survival or pleasant personal amenities for those who control the firm. Recently, at Chicago things have been pushed even further in this direction with decisions such as marriage, divorce, child-bearing, suicide and philanthropy all subjected to analysis basing itself on the premise that there is a more or less definable utility function whose value is maximized by the decisions made on these non-economic matters.

It would seem that if the utility function is suitably defined, utility maximization becomes little more than a tautology, and that one might perhaps choose to argue with this approach by claiming that it is not very illuminating but not by asserting that it is in conflict with the facts of human behavior.

But that is precisely what Simon has succeeded in doing. Moreover, he has done so in a constructive way. Obviously, he is not the first who has questioned the neoclasical model of rational human behavior. Even in the nineteenth century there were economists who argued on the basis of evidence from psychology that people simply do not behave as the neoclassical models assume. But this sort of criticism is not very helpful if it offers no usable alternative, and, incidentally, if it fails to show convincingly that even with suitable reinterpretation, the maximization model cannot be made to fit the facts.

How is it possible for people to behave in a way that fails to maximize *some* utility function? The answer is that maximization, by definition, requires a process of *comparison* of the available alternatives, explicit or implicit. We cannot, for example, be sure a particular quantity of fertilizer, x, will maximize agricultural output on the available quantity of land unless one has first studied the likely effects of every other possible quantity of fertilizer. One cannot know that the product of 300 000 kilos is maximal unless one has compared the likely product of 290 000 and 280 000, etc.; for otherwise, unbeknown to the decision-maker, there may be some other quantity which yields an output that is greater. Thus, if such comparisons do not occur then the decision-maker cannot be said to be *maximizing* anything— not production, or profit, or even utility.

Two questions arise immediately: First, is it not in some sense irrational to fail to maximize? Second, if it is rational is this not because the cost of information collection and calculation is too high, and, in light of this, may not the decision-maker who limits the comparison of available alternatives simply be maximizing his probable net benefits after making suitable allowance for decision costs? Is he not then making what I have once termed "optimally imperfect decisions"?

76   *W. J. Baumol*

Simon rejects the views implicit in both of these questions.[1] He makes his point by examples. Two of the most striking are the following: Among the experimental work of interest to students of so-called artificial intelligence or computer learning is the programming of computers to play chess. No one has yet succeeded in doing so to a degree of sophistication that premits the electronic equipment to beat the world's greatest players, but the computers now win rather consistently over players of very great skill. Surely, what the computer is being taught to do must represent rational behavior, in some sense; that is, it must involve "reasoned" decisions that are effective in getting the machine toward its goal (or, rather, that of the programmer). Yet, as Simon keeps reminding us, nowhere in any of the chess playing computer programs is there any step in any way involving a maximization process. There is no process of comparison of alternatives to determine which of them moves matters *closest* to the goal.

What is involved is brought out by Simon's second example—the search for a needle in a haystack. Here he modifies the old cliché by thinking of a haystack which is known to contain a considerable number of needles. He then contrasts two different search processes. The first seeks to locate *the sharpest* needle in the haystack (a maximization process). The second is a search for the first needle which can be found and which happens to be sharp enough for the searcher to complete some sewing. This second process Simon describes as "satisficing". Here two observations are pertinent: (*a*) different search procedures are appropriate for the two objectives and (*b*) there is nothing irrational about the satisficing objective; indeed, for most of us there is little to be gained by looking further once we have found the first good, usable needle.

An economic analogy is the business firm whose management is willing to stick to a set of decisions that bring 25 % return on investment to the firm even if aware that there may be alternative decisions of a character unknown to them which might raise profits still higher.

Satisficing can be described in linear programming terms as a decision process which involves a feasible region determined by a set of acceptability constraints (e.g., profits must be sufficiently high to prevent a stockholder revolt or a take-over bid). But it involves no objective function. The firm makes its decisions by trying possible courses of action chosen on the basis of experience or *a priori* reasoning. But the decision process does not consist of comparison of the outcomes of alternative decisions. Rather, any candidate decision is tested in terms of the acceptability constraints. The *first* decision encountered which passes the acceptability test is then adopted. That is the hallmark of satisficing. The decision-maker rests content with the first

---

[1] For the latest of Simon's statements on this subject see his "Rationality as Process and as Product of Thought", Richard T. Ely lecture delivered before the American Economic Association, New York, December 1977.

acceptable decision he happens to stumble upon and makes no further attempt to see if there exists something even better.

This may all seem reasonable enough, but is it not a dead-end? Can one go beyond these observations to formulate a usable analysis on their basis? The answer is that it is possible and that such analyses have in fact been carried out. They have been of two general types.

The first, for which the path-breaking work is that of Cyert and March,[1] which itself built on Simon's two fundamental writings in this area,[2] is behavioral economic analysis. Essentially, what this consists of is a combination of empirical observation, followed, by computer simulation. Data are collected to document systematically the actions of some decision-making unit. For example, Cyert and March systematically collected information about the pricing decisions of a department store in Pittsburgh, encompassing the prices of a very large number of goods. Simultaneously, interviews were used to determine the decisionmaker's own views of the process by which the prices were decided upon. Third, a computer program was designed on the basis of these two sorts of information. This program was intended to be capable of replicating (predicting) the decisions in question. Using data not employed in constructing the program, its predictions could then be tested independently for accuracy. In fact, Cyert and March's results turned out to perform remarkably well in this respect. Having constructed such a program which is capable of simulating actual decisions, one can then hope to go on to the next step—the counterpart of standard comparative statics. One can investigate how a change in circumstances, that is, a change in values of the parameters, will affect the ultimate decisions. Thus, at least potentially, this form of inquiry may be able to achieve as illuminating an analysis as is usually provided by more conventional maximization models.

The second direction toward operational satisficing analysis has been pursued most notably by Simon himself. As already noted, he points out that the principles of efficient search for a satisficing solution are fundamentally different from those that work in the calculation of a maximum. Simon has written a number of papers analyzing the search process and describing procedures that can be used to increase its efficiency by taking advantage of observed characteristics of the phenomena in question, to reduce the size of the region of candidate solutions in which the search must be conducted. Highly fruitful and sophisticated work in this area, which may be compared to the search for a solution process in linear programming by Kanterovich and Danzig, still continues.[3]

Using these general approaches Simon has carried out a long series of

---

[1] R. M. Cyert & J. G. March, *A Behavioral Theory of the Firm* (Englewood Cliffs, N. J.: Prentice-Hall, 1963).
[2] H. A. Simon (1956) and (1957), listed in the Bibliography.
[3] Two recent pieces are H. A. Simon (1972) and (1976), listed in the Bibliography.

78   *W. J. Baumol*

theoretical and empirical studies dealing with the issue of rationality and examining how man behaves in fact and what his options are. Using information processing systems and programming them to employ a satisficing approach, he has shown them to be capable of solving difficult problems and to be able to respond in a manner that must be considered to be "rational" even though not optimal. He has also shown empirically that such systems can be used to explain a considerable range of human rational behavior in situations requiring the solution of problems.

III. On the Criterion for Positive Valued Solutions

In the solution to an input–output process one of the fundamental requirements is that none of the outputs be assigned a negative value. This sounds like a trivial and uninteresting requirement, but in fact, it is neither easy to judge *a priori* from the data in an input–output table, nor does it turn out to be devoid of implications beyond the arithmetic of the input–output calculation.

The basic contribution dealing with this issue is called the Hawkins-Simon theorem.[1] Though its operational form is expressed in terms of the signs of a sequence of determinants which permit it to deal with a system of simultaneous relationships in a multiplicity of variables, its logic is, as usual, made clearest if described in terms of the simplest applicable model. For this purpose let us deal with an input–output structure involving two interdependent industries, and whose respective outputs satisfy the trivial input–output equations

$$X_a = k_{ab} X_b + t_a$$
$$X_b = k_{ba} X_a + t_b$$

where

X_a = output of good a
k_{ab} = quantity of good a used as input per unit of good b
t_a = target of net output of good a

and X_b, k_{ba} and t_b are defined similarly. Three possible relationships of the graphs of these equations are depicted in Fig. 1.

In all three cases the line labelled X_a represents the equation $X_a = k_{ab} X_b \times t_a$, and the line labelled X_b is to be interpreted similarly. All six curves have positive slopes and have intercepts yielding positive values of t_a and t_b, as one should expect. But only the configuration shown in Fig. 1a has a solution involving positive values of X_a and X_b. That is, only the curves in Fig. 1a can satisfy the Hawkins-Simon conditions.

---

[1] See D. Hawkins & H. A. Simon (1949), listed in the Bibliography.

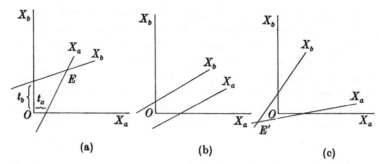

Fig. 1

The graph can be used to tell us what those conditions are. Obviously, they require that the slope of the X_b curve, k_{ab}, be smaller than the slope of the X_a curve; for otherwise, they will either have no solution (Fig. 1b) or a solution outside the positive quadrant. One more step is needed to yield the actual Hawkins-Simon condition for this simple case. Since our graph has X_b on the vertical axis and X_a on the horizontal axis, to find the slope of the X_a curve we must take its equation $X_a = k_{ab} X_b + t_a$ and rewrite it with X_b as a function of X_a, i.e. as

$$X_b = X_a/k_{ab} - t_a/k_{ab}.$$

Thus, we see that in Fig. 1 the slope of the X_a line is not k_{ab}, but rather, its reciprocal. Thus, the Hawkins-Simon requirement for a solution wth positive elements is

slope of X_b curve $<$ slope of X_a curve, i.e.,

$$k_{ba} < 1/k_{ab}$$
$$k_{ab}k_{ba} < 1. \qquad\qquad (1)$$

This, then, is the condition we are seeking in our trivial two-variable case. The conditions in the n variable case are, naturally, much more complex, but their logic, their interpretation and their implications are perfectly analogous to those of inequality (1).

Next, let us see what their interpretation is. X_{ab} is the quantity of good a used up in producing a unit of commodity b, and the interpretation of k_{ba} is analogous. The product $k_{ab}k_{ba}$ may be interpreted as follows: to produce one unit of good a we need k_{ba} units of b which, in turn, uses up k_{ab} units of good a. Thus, to manufacture one unit of a, the quantity $k_{ab}k_{ba}$ of good a must be used up *indirectly* in the interindustry relationships of the production process. Thus, if $k_{ab}k_{ba} > 1$ it means that to produce one unit of output a (gross—not net), *more* than one unit of a must be used up in the production process. It is

80   W. J. Baumol

like the allegation that has been made about certain types of solar energy apparatus whose manufacture is said to use up more energy than the unit can be expected to produce during its lifetime. In other words, an economy which fails the Hawkins-Simon test cannot survive over the long run because it must live off its own capital forever.

The Hawkins-Simon conditions have many other implications, some of them of fundamental importance. For example, as suggested by the Samuelson correspondence principle, an economy with the sort of misbehavior in its production system which was just described will also run into misbehavior in the dynamics of its structure.

Some of the power and wide applicability of the Hawkins-Simon conditions is brought out by Samuelson's ruminations on the formal structure of "Ricardo-like models".[1] Dealing only with Samuelson's simplest case, take x to represent quantity of labor, y to represent output in a one product economy, c =required (subsistence) consumption per unit of labor. Then with fixed coefficients, the labor input requirement is given by

$$x = ay.$$

Moreover. the subsistence requirement for the entire population is

$$cx \leqslant y.$$

These two relationships can be treated as an input–output model which together imply

$$\frac{y}{x} = \frac{1}{a} \geqslant c \quad \text{or} \quad 1 - ac \geqslant 0.$$

Now, as Samuelson points out, this requirement "is precisely the Hawkins-Simon condition". But this condition tells us a good deal more here. Suppose we follow Ricardo and assume that labor is (re)producible while land is not. Then Samuelson makes the remarkable observation that in the long run only land will have a positive shadow price, and labor and all outputs must be treated as congealed land rather than congealed labor, contrary to the usual interpretation of Ricardo.

To make this explicit we assume a fixed labor input–output coefficient a, and a fixed land coefficient b. Let w =wage and r =rent, then with pure competition and zero profit the price, p, of the community's one product must be

$$p = wa + rb$$

---

[1] P. A. Samuelson, "A Modern Treatment of the Ricardian Economy", *Quarterly Journal of Economics* 73 (February 1959): 1–35.

where a subsistence wage permits the purchase of c units of output at price p so that

$$w = pc$$

or substituting into the previous relation

$$p = pca + rb$$

so that

$$p/r = b/(1 - ac).$$

This will be positive only if the Hawkins-Simon condition $1 - ac > 0$ is satisfied. Moreover, if this condition holds, the expression for p/r can be expanded into the multiplier series

$$p/r = b(1 + ac + (ac)^2 + (ac)^3 + ...).$$

This last form is useful for calculation purposes (particularly in large input–output systems) where, if the sequence converges, as the Hawkins-Simon condition assures, it can be used to approximate the solution of the system to any desired degree of accuracy. For our purposes it can also be used to confirm Samuelson's "congealed land" interpretation since

$b =$ the quantity of land needed to produce a unit of y,

$bac =$ the quantity of land needed to produce subsistence for the labor going into a unit of y,

$b(ac)^2 =$ the quantity of land needed to produce subsistence for the labor needed to produce subsistence for the labor needed to produce a unit of y, etc.

Thus, $b(1 + ac + (ac)^2 + ...)$ is the sum of the quantities of land that had to be tied up directly, at first remove, at second remove, etc., etc. to produce a unit of y. So, the value (price) of y is indeed composed of all the congealed land going into the output of y. And this calculation is legitimate only if the Hawkins-Simon conditions are satisfied.

It must be emphasized that these conditions are not important only in the simple models that have been described here to make their application clear. The conditions achieve their full powers in large Leontief models where such conditions really become essential for interpretation and analysis.

IV. Concluding Comment

Herbert Simon certainly has an original and creative mind. Measured in sheer volume his contribution over the yers has been enormous. Measured in sub-

82   *W. J. Baumol*

stance it is no less impressive. Add to this the fact that he is not an economist but a professor of computer sciences and psychology, and the magnitude of his contribution to our discipline becomes all the more remarkable. Surely, if ever there was a case where interdisciplinary strengths have borne fruit in economics, this is it.

Works by Herbert Simon referred to by W.J. Baumol in 'On the Contributions of Herbert A. Simon to Economics'

Hawkins, D., and Simon, H.A. (1949), 'Note: Some Conditions of Macroeconomic Stability', *Econometrica*, **17**: 245–8.

Simon, H.A. (1956), 'Rational Choice and the Structure of the Environment', *Psychological Review*, **63**, March: 129–38.

Simon, H.A. (1957), *Models of Man*, New York, Wiley.

Simon, H.A. (1972), 'Theories of Bounded Rationality', 161–76 of McGuire, C.B. and Radner, R. (eds) *Decision and Organization: A Volume in Honor of Jacob Marschak*, Amsterdam, North-Holland Publishing Company.

Simon, H.A. (1976), 'From Substantive to Procedural Rationality', 129–48 of Latsis, S.J. (ed.) *Method and Appraisal in Economics*, Cambridge, Cambridge University Press.

[3]

ON THE CONTRIBUTIONS OF
HERBERT A. SIMON TO ECONOMICS

Albert Ando

University of Pennsylvania, Philadelqhia, Pa., USA

I. Introduction

The contributions of Herbert A. Simon are extremely vast and diverse, ranging from philosophy and methodology of science, applied mathematics, through various aspects of economics, computer science, management science, political science, cognitive psychology to the study of human problem-solving behavior. What makes his work truly remarkable is that he not only has had something fundamental and original to say in almost all of these areas, but he developed almost all of his many ideas precisely and far enough to serve as a basis for empirical work, which he himself has undertaken on many occasions. Today, in many of these areas, we can recognize the characteristic stamp of Simon's work imbedded in their basic body of knowledge.

Given this vastness and diversity of Simon's contribution, it is obviously impossible to summarize it in a few pages. Throughout his writings, however, there runs a consistent theme: to construct a comprehensive framework for modelling and analyzing the behavior of man and his organizations faced with a complex environment, recognizing the limitation of his ability to comprehend, describe, analyze and to act, while allowing for his ability to learn and to adopt. This limitation of human abilities is crucial not only in determining the behavior of many and his society, but also in formulating the methodology of science becaause the scientist is also a man with limited intellectual capacity.[1]

In this review of Simon's work, I shall attempt to illustrate how the application of this theme to four quite different areas has led Simon to critical contributions in each of these topics. The first is the problem of describing the goals and criteria of the decision maker in some approximate manner which makes it possible to solve the decision problem. The second is a discussion of the relationship between the dynamic adjustment processes in economics and the study of the limits of man's capacity to adapt to complex changes in

---

[1] In his Karl Taylor Compton Lectures at MIT, which was later published as *The Sciences of the Artificial*, Simon stated his basic view of human behavior as a hypothesis: "A man, viewed as a behavioral system, is quite simple. The apparent complexity of his behavior over time is largely a reflection of the complexity of the environment in which he finds himself" (p. 25).

84   *A. Ando*

environment. The third is the strategy of how approximately to describe the environment so that it is both comprehensible and manageable for decision makers. The fourth is the validation and discovery of scientific hypotheses, with an example taken from Simon's work on the size distribution of firms, income, city sizes, and other social entities.

It should be emphasized that these four topics are not meant to cover most of Simon's work, not even the most important ones. They are, instead, illustrations of Simon's work with his characteristic originality and his view of human behavior, taken from areas that are most familiar to economists.[1]

II. A Simplified Criterion Function and its Implications: Certainty Equivalent Theorem

In the well-known work by Simon and his coauthors, a solution to the problem of scheduling production, the work force, and inventories to meet uncertain and fluctuating demand over time is decsribed in detail.[2] For an abstract theorist, the problem is a fairly simple one. Information about sales for future periods can be summarized as a joint probability distribution. The cost function is assumed to be known, however complex. Thus the problem becomes one of dynamic programming, in which the total expected cost is minimized subject to the probability distribution of sales, the relation between production and the work force, and the identity among sales, inventory and production. The theorist can then write down a set of conditions under which a solution to this problem would exist, and perhaps characterize the nature of the solution.

But the manager who is faced with the problem of deciding how many workers to hire and at what level production should be maintained for the initial period must go beyond the mere existence and qualitative characterization of the solution. He needs a concrete decision rule which translates the initial conditions and information about future sales into employment and production with reasonable effort within reasonable time. In general, the dynamic programming problem arising from the situation of this sort involves, at best, such an enormous amount of computation that it cannot easily be solved for all practical purposes, even with the aid of today's most powerful computer, or any computer that may become available in the foreseeable future.

---

[1] The work of Simon best known to economists, that on the logic of rational decision and of heuristic decision making, sometimes referred to as the theory of bounded rationality, is summarized in the companion review article by William Baumol. Probably the most ambitious undertaking by Simon to model human problem solving behavior is reported in his monumental book with Allen Newell entitled *Human Problem Solving*. Although his findings reported in this book are of major potential importance to economists, they are at such a micro level that most economists are likely to find them somewhat remote from their everyday concern. See also Simon (1976), listed in the Bibliography.

[2] Holt, Modigliani, Muth & Simon (1960) and (1956), listed in the Bibliography.

In this situation, Simon saw that, if the cost function can be approximated by a quadratic function, the probability distribution of the future sales can be replaced by its first moments and the problem can be enormously simplified. This proposition has become known as the "Certainty Equivalent Theorem". Given this particular feature of the problem, the remaining problem is whether or not some quadratic function can serve as a satisfactory approximation of the true cost function. Since the true cost function is not known with certainty, the manager and researchers must answer this question through a variety of informal analysis.

Once the certainty equivalent theorem was understood and the decision was made that a particular quadratic function is a "satisfactory" approximation, then the minimization of this "approximate" cost subject to the constraints mentioned earlier can be carried out relatively easily. The desired decision rule can then be formulated.

In this example, the final result appears as though it is an application of the maximizing principle, but in a very critical way it is not. We do not know how good the quadratic approximation to cost really is. We do not even know that a particular quadratic function chosen by the team of researchers is the "best" among all possible quadratic functions. Hence, in spite of a maximization technique used to complete the solution, the solution described by Holt, Modigliani, Muth and Simon is not a solution ot the maximization problem in the sense of classical economics, but a "satisficing" solution. Hence, Simon and his colleagues stressed the importance of continually checking how satisfactorily the decision rule is performing in each practical application of this procedure.

The crucial point of this example, however, is that the decision maker could not have obtained a straight maximizing solution even if he tried. First, he would not have been able to write out the exact cost function and the exact description of constraints (probability distribution of all future sales). Secondly, even if he succeeded in writing out the "true" problem, the maximization of the "true" problem would have been beyond his computational capacity however augmented by, say, the most powerful computer that may become available in the foreseeable future.

Hence, in order either to describe the behavior of a decision maker faced with the problem like the one in the above example, or to assist him in improving his performance, the researcher must understand, in addition to the formal theory of maximization proper (the choice among known alternatives), the process by which alternative decisions to be considered are generated as well as the characteristics of efficient and feasible computational procedure involved. This is one aspect of the basic message of Simon, one that most economists, particularly those who have attempted to serve and advise businessmen and government officials, can readily appreciate.

III. Adaptive Behavior and the Dynamic Adjustment Process

If the ability of individuals and organizations to comprehend, describe, and respond to their environment is without limit, then their behavior reflects nothing but their goals and the characteristics of their environment. If any change occurs in the environment, such a change will be instantaneously and completely reflected in the behavior of the decision makers concerned. The comparative static analysis of economics clearly depends on this assumption, and discussion of growth paths described in the literature of neoclassical economics also takes this assumption for granted. But we know that, at least some of the time, economic agents do not respond to changes in the environment instantaneously and completely. While some of these delays may reflect the proper maximizing response to uncertain signals of the environment, at least some of these delays simply reflect the inability of decision makers to comprehend the change in enivronment accurately, to compute the new maximizing response, and then to act immediately. This last type of delay is the prime cause of the dynamic adjustment process of economics, and it is the type of behavior which applied econometricians are forced to deal with often, without much guidance from economic theory for its proper formulation.

Because economists are accustomed to formulating all behavior of decision makers as a constrained maximization problem, the initial inclination of economic theorists in their attempt to deal with the dynamic adjustment responses of decision makers is to formulate a new, more complex constained maximization problem in which the cost of adjustment depends on the speed and other details of adjustment. We have just noted, however, that at least some of the delays in decision makers' response to changes in environment are simply the reflection of the inability on the part of decision makers to comprehend the change in the environment, to carry out the necessary computations to select the new maximum, and to act promptly upon the new decision. Then any attempt to describe dynamic adjustment behavior in general as the consequence of solving an augmented constrained maximization problem incorporating adjustment costs is doomed to failure. This is because the maximization problem incorporating the adjustment costs by definition must be substantially more complex than the original one. Surely, we cannot suppose that decision makers get around the difficulty of their inability to solve a maximization problem by solving another, much more difficult one.

Simon not only recognized this problem but also went on to formulate a very different theory of human problem solving behavior that explicitly recognizes the limitation of human ability to adapt to changes in environment. His findings and theory, reported in his book with Allen Newell, *Human Problem Solving*, is formulated for the behavior of individuals in the context of laboratory experiments, and therefore it cannot be directly used to handle behavior of economic agents in real markets or other very complex situations. The task of extracting implications about market and nationwide economic behavior from such micro findings through complex processes of aggregation will be extremely difficult, and will not be accomplished overnight. Even for this purpose, however, Simon has made some beginning in organizing an analytical framework, as I shall indicate in the next section. Thus, his work can serve as the starting point for our understanding of the basic characteristics of partial and delayed responses of economic agents to complex changes in their environment. Simon's work in this area, therefore, is a unique and singularly important contribution to the understanding of dynamic adjustment processes in society.

IV. Simplified Description of Environment; Near Decomposability, Hierarchical Structure, and Causal Relationships[1]

As we have indicated earlier, Simon visualizes the study of man's adaptation to a very complex environment as the central issue of the social sciences. Given this vision, it is natural that he is concerned with the problem of describing man's environment approximately, and as simply as possible, while retaining its critical features. It is important for descriptive purposes since man's behavior obviously depends on his understanding of the environment; and for normative purposes because an accurate enough description of the environment is the first step in prescribing "optimal" or "satisfactory" decision rules.

Very early in his career Simon noted that the description and analysis of very complex systems can be enormously simplified if the whole system can be divided into a number of subsystems in such a way that each subsystem can be analyzed independently of one another. For the purpose of understanding more macro relationships, each subsystem may be represented by an aggregate variable so that the relationships among the subsystems can be analyzed without explicit attention being given to the internal structures of the subsystems. He observed that this type of simplification is quite common in the natural sciences, where an analysis of a macro structure often takes micro structures as given elements, while in an analysis of micro structures the interactions among very distant objects are ignored.

He then recognized that the possibility of this simplification depends on our ability to arrange elementary variables of the system in such a way that each elementary variable belongs to one, and only one, group of these variables. Relationships among the variables within a group are then very much stronger than relationships between any pair of variables not belonging to the same

---

[1] See Simon (1952), Simon (1953), Simon & Ando (1961), and Simon (1962), listed in the Bibliography. For another, somewhat related idea on causality among economic relationships, see Wold (1949).

88   *A. Ando*

group. Simon initially considered the limiting case in which weaker relationships among elementary variables are exactly zero's. This led him to a
definition of causality among variables in scientific discussion and a reinterpretation of identification conditions in simultaneous equations estimation
procedures.

A few years later, Simon took the critical step of replacing zero's for
relations between any pair of elementary variables belonging to two separate
subsystems by epsilon's (ε's) representing a very small interaction between
them compared with interactions among variables belonging to the same
subsystem. He also understood more explicitly the system under consideration as a dynamic one.

Let us call the earlier, exactly decomposable system A, and the second, only
approximately decomposable system B. Simon was then able to prove several
propositions, the most important of which are the following: (1) Provided that
the ε's are small enough, if the subsystems of A are stable, then the subsystems
of B are also stable, and the subsystems of B will reach internal equilibria
which are approximately the same as those of A in the short run; and (2) over
a much longer period, subsystems of B will interact with each other and
gradually approach the overall equilibrium position of the whole System B,
while maintaining the internal equilibrium position of each subsystem.

These results serve as the justification for a particular way of approximately
describing the complex environment faced by human problem solvers. In the
short run (depending on the size of the ε's), we can approximate the more
complex system B by system A, and treat each subsystem as though it were
independent of the others. In the longer run (again depending on the size of
the ε's), we can represent each subsystem of B by an aggregate variable and
consider relations among these aggregate variables without paying explicit
attention to the internal structure of each subsystem. We should note that this
hierarchical structure of the world need not be limited to two tiers, but can
be of many layers for a very complex system.

Hence, if man's environment is indeed capable of being described as nearly
decomposable, then, as the system becomes more and more complex, the
number of variables that the decision maker must deal with at any one
time need not necessarily increase. A greater complexity of the system can
be viewed as a larger number of layers, and hence would not necessarily
results in much greater complexity of the problem with which the decision
maker must be concerned at any one point in time.

Simon believes that man's environment does indeed have a nearly decomposable representation most of the time, and speculates on reasons why
nature and society naturally tend to form such a structure.[1] While this is a
strong hypothesis, it does enable ordinary decision makers to cope with their

---

[1] Simon (1962) and (1969), listed in the Bibliography.

environment, and scientists to proceed with their task of describing and analyzing both natural phenomena and human behavior. Indeed, scientists have almost always acted as though they believed in this hypothesis. Simon's contribution, therefore, is to have made explicit conditions under which this very common way of approximating the environment can be justified. He has thereby provided important guidance for future theorizing not only in the social sciences but also in the natural sciences.

V. Validation and Discovery of Scientific Hypotheses, with an Illustration from Studies of Size Distribution

A sciensific hypothesis does not arise from a complete vacuum. Usually, a scientist, or a generation of scientists, notice some regularity in the data generated by nature, and summarize it as a simple generalization (hypothesis). Such a generalization is seldom exactly true, but a rough approximation to the reality. With such a hypothesis in hand, the scientist is interested in a number of questions, such as "is the degree of approximation of the hypothesis to the reality good enough for the purpose at hand?" and "what causes the discrepancies between the hypothesis and observed facts?" The importance of the former in evaluating the value of scientific propositions is obvious, while the endeavor to answer the second, by finding limiting conditions under which the deviations of facts from the hypothesis might be expected to decrease, occupies the most of the scientist's time, and the progress of our scientific knowledge depends heavily on the success of this endeavor.

At this point, if the scientist applies the standard statistical testing procedure to his hypothesis, it is certain that any hypothesis of this type will eventually be rejected at any level of significance as the sample size increases, however close the original approximation may have been. For, the standard statistical testing procedure is designed to answer the question: "how likely is it that the deviations between the hypothesis and the observed data have arisen by chance alone?". Answering this question does not contribute much to our ability to judge whether the hypothesis is a satisfactory enough approximation, nor does it suggest limiting conditions under which the deviations between observed facts and hypothesis might become smaller.

This methodological problem has been well known to mathematical statisticians and to experienced scientist.[1] Natural scientists faced with this problem often resort to two sources of information that have proved helpful in suggesting limiting conditions. One is to perform more carefully controlled experiments, with more accurate measuring instruments. The second is to organize an "explanation" why the hypothesis should fit the observed facts under a set of ideal conditions. For economists, however, the first of these

---

[1] See, for example, Savage (1954), pp. 254–256.

alternatives is usually not available, because controlled experiments are difficult to perform in economics, certainly in practice and often even conceptually. Thus, the problem of making initial empirical generalizations and then systematically improving them in the light of observed facts is a particularly difficult one for economists. Yet, economists have not paid as much attention to the logical structure of this process as they should have, and their failure to understand this logical structure is one of the most important reasons for current confusion about interpretation of econometric studies, and for the lack of communication between econometricians and economic theorists.

Simon not only saw this problem clearly beginning in 1943 before the great advances in econometrics took place, and articulted the nature of the difficulty, but he also laid out informal guidelines that social scientists can observe in their empirical researches in the absence of a major development in statistical theory to remedy this difficulty.[1] His thinking on these questions is summarized in his essay, "On Judging the Plausibility of Theories".[2] While Simon's statement in this essay is no more than a summary of principles followed by the best empirical scientists (both natural and social) implicitly or explicitly over several centuries, it is probably one of the best and briefest statements of the principles available in the literature, particularly for social scientists. It should be noted that Simon's concern with this problem and his ideas on how to resolve it is consistent with his basic view of how a human problem solver would describe his complex environment, applied to scientists. Therefore, it is also closely related to his discussion of complexity summarized in the preceding section of this review.

Beginning in the mid 1950's, Simon undertook a research project on size distributions of, among other things, firm sizes, city sizes, income of individuals, and word counts which has served to illustrate the methodological point discussed above.[3] Physical nature as we observe it contains many well defined patterns, providing natural scientists with obvious starting points for their theorizing about nature. Such well-defined patterns are quite rare in data generated by social phenomena.

The observation that the size distribution of many things can be very accurately described by certain types of skew distributions is one of very few exceptions. That is, suppose one ranks many things, such as the income or wealth of individuals in a given population, the size of firms in an economy or an industry, the frequency of words used in a book, the size of cities in a given geographical area, etc., and plot the logarithm of the size on the vertical axis against the logarithm of the rank on the horizontal axis. We then find that

---

[1] Most of Simon's work on this subject is collected in Simon (1977); see in particular Section I of this volume.
[2] Simon (1968), listed in the Bibliography.
[3] Simon (1955) and Ijiri & Simon (1977), listed in the Bibliography.

On the contributions of Herbert A. Simon to economics   91

the observations line up very closely on the linear line with the slope of negative unity.

That the relationship is linear and has extremely close fit in many cases is striking enough, but the additional fact that the slope is very close to negative unity makes this observation an obvious and striking candidate for an empirical generalization. Yet it is not an exact relationship, and hence it also calls for specifying some limiting, ideal set of conditions under which the deviation of observed data from this distribution would tend to vanish. For this purpose, Simon sought to construct an "explanation" of why the size distribution of so many different phenomena should take this particular form. Because the same regularity of patterns appears among so diverse phenomena having no obvious common mechanism, Simon suggested chance operating through the laws of probability as a plausible candidate for explaining this regularity.

It was known for some time, due to the work of Yule and others, that the simplest kind of stochastic process that will yield skew distributions described above as the steady state distribution is based on the following assumption, known as the strong Gibrat assumption (taking the case of the distribution of the size of firms as our example):

Year to year changes in firm sizes are goverend by a simple Markoff process in which the probabilities of the size changes of any specified percentage magnitudes are independent of a firm's present absolute size.

In this strong form, it is fairly easy to point out instances in which the actual growth behavior of firms contradict this assumption. In a series of articles beginning in 1955, Simon was able, for purposes of deriving the Yule distribution as the steady state distribution, to replace the above assumption by a much weaker one in which the expected percentage change in the size of *the totality of firms in each size stratum* is assumed to be independent of stratum. This "explanation" or theory enabled Simon and his later collaborator, Injiri, to look for situations in which the basic distribution would fit particularly well, and to predict specific departures of data from the basic distributions when the underlying assumptions are known to be violated in a certain way.[1]

Simon began his work on the size distribution as that of identifying a striking regularity of empirical observations and providing scientific explana-

---

[1] In the case of word counts, Benoit Mandelbrot proposed an entirely different explanation for its observed skew frequency. It involved the assumption that the frequencies are determined so as to maximize the number of bits of information, in the sense of Shannon, transmitted per symbol. It seems that Mandelbrot's assumption is open to a number of serious doubts and in any case it cannot be generalized to phenomena other than word counts, and therefore of no interest to economists. I mention Mendelbrot's work here only because the controversy between Simon and Mandelbrot on the subject of word counts was rather famous in the 1950's. See Mandelbrot (1959) and Simon (1960), listed in the Bibliography.

tion (defining exact conditions under which such a regularity should be observed). But we can easily imagine that, particularly in the case of the size distribution of business firms, he found this particular line of inquiry congenial. For one thing, his theory does not require, although it is consistent with, any sort of maximizing behavior on the part of agents whose size distribution Simon's theory describes so well. In the second place, this theory can be viewed as the confirmation of the constant returns to scale for firms (as distinct from plants), and yet still manages to describe the size distribution among firms in each industry as well as in the whole economy. This contrasts very sharply with the classical theory of perfectly competitive markets. In the classical theory, in order to determine firm sizes, one must assume that decreasing returns to scale sets in at some point for firms. While most economists would agree that there are any number of reasons why plants may be subject to decreasing returns, it is not easy to identifiy acceptable reasons for decreasing returns for firms. Furthermore, even if we are prepared to accept that decreasing return does set in at some point, classical theory would imply that the distribution of the size of firms in any industry should be, if anything, of even shape, and certainly not that it should be skewed. It is therefore not surprising that Simon's is the only theory for the explanation of observed skew distribution of size frequencies that seems both plausible and is internally consistent.

VI. Conclusions

Simon's scientific contribution, from the point of view of economics, has been to work out the implications of recognizing the limitation of man to comprehend, to adapt to, and to affect his environment completely and instantaneously, as largely assumed in classical economics.[1] In this sense, Simon has not tried to replace the existing economic theory with something alien to it, but rather he has attempted to modify and to generalize it so that it fits better the real behavior of man and his organizations. In the process, Simon has exhibited almost unparalleled originality, profound analytical insight, and an extraordinary ability to extract information from a vast quantity of data. Among hundreds of items in his bibliography, there are necessarily some duplications, but there is no item that is either trivial or otherwise unworthy of a true scientist.

Before him, J. M. Keynes introduced into economics an explicit recognition that equilibration of markets does not take place instantaneously, that some price and quantity responses are slow and imperfect, and thus reformulated economic theory—with a macroeconomic emphasis. We can recognize

---

[1] His name is often associated with the notion of "bounded rationality" but his contribution is far broader than this term indicates, as I have tried to indicate in this review.

On the contributions of Herbert A. Simon to economics　93

some parallel between the works of these two men. Simon, however, starts his reformulation as well as his empirical work at a much more micro level of individuals, small groups, and organizations such as business firms. Because at these micro levels theoretical structure is almost necessarily more tedious, Simon's influence has been slower to penetrate the works of others than Keynes' was. Also, Simon has not been as active in the formulation of economic and social policy as Keynes was, and hence he is less well known publicly.

On the other hand, Simon has paid much closer attention and devoted a great deal more time and energy to the development of methodology and to actual empirical work, and therefore it is much easier for serious economists to take advantage of Simon's initiative and build on it than it was in the case of Keynes. Simon has not shown any sign of slowing down in his serious work, and it will be many years before we can evaluate his work in its entirety. But even now it is already clear that his contribution has been and will be, directly or indirectly, an important ingredient in every future economist's knowledge. It will become more and more important and more and more explicitly recognized as time goes on.

References

Champernowne, D. G.: A model of income distribution. *Economic Journal*, June, 1953.

Mandelbrot, B.: A note in a class of skew distribution functions. *Information and Control*, pp. 90–99, 1959.

Savage, L. J.: *The Foundations of Statistics*. John Wiley & Sons, New York, 1954.

Simon, H. A.: See the following Bibliography.

Wold, H. O. A.: Statistical estimation of economic relationships. *Econometrica*, Suppl. July, 1949.

Yule, C. U.: A mathematical theory of evolution, based on the conclusions of Dr J. C. Willis, F.R.S., *Philosophical Transactions*, B. 213, pp. 21–83, 1924.

Works by Herbert Simon referred to by Albert Ando in 'On the Contributions of Herbert A. Simon to Economics'

Holt, C.C., Modigliani, F., Muth, J., and Simon, H.A. (1960), *Planning Production, Inventories, and Workforce*, Englewood Cliffs, NJ, Prentice-Hall.

Ijiri, Y., and Simon, H.A. (1977), *Skew Distributions and the Sizes of Business Firms*, Amsterdam, North-Holland.

Newell, A. and Simon, H.A. (1972), *Human Problem Solving*, Englewood Cliffs, NJ, Prentice-Hall.

Simon, H.A. (1952), 'On the Definition of the Causal Relation', *Journal of Philosophy*, **49**: 517–28 (Cowles Commission New Series Reprint, No. 70).

Simon, H.A. (1953), 'Causal Ordering and Identifiability', chapter 3 of Hood, W.C. and Koopmans, T.C. (eds) *Studies in Econometric Method*, New York, Wiley.

Simon, H.A. (1955), 'On a Class of Skew Distribution Functions', *Biometrika*, **42**: 425–40.

Simon, H.A. (1960), 'Some Further Notes on a Class of Skew Distribution Functions', *Information and Control*, **3**, March: 80–88.

Simon, H.A. (1962), 'The Architecture of Complexity', *Proceedings of the American Philosophical Society*, **106**: 467–82.

Simon, H.A. (1968), 'On Judging the Plausibility of Theories', 439–59 in van Rootselaar, B. and Staal, J.F. (eds) *Logic, Methodology and Philosophy of Science III*, Amsterdam, North-Holland.

Simon, H.A. (1969), *The Sciences of the Artificial*, Cambridge, MA, MIT Press.

Simon, H.A. (1976), 'From Substantive to Procedural Rationality', 129–48 of Latsis, S.J. (ed.) *Method and Appraisal in Economics*, Cambridge, Cambridge University Press.

Simon, H.A. (1977), *The New Sciences of Management Decision* (rev. edn), Englewood Cliffs, NJ, Prentice-Hall.

Simon, H.A. and Ando, A. (1961), 'Aggregation of Variables in Dynamic Systems', *Econometrica*, **29**: 111–38.

[4]

Rational Decision Making in Business Organizations

By HERBERT A. SIMON*

In the opening words of his *Principles*, Alfred Marshall proclaimed economics to be a psychological science:

> Political Economy or Economics is a study of mankind in the ordinary business of life; it examines that part of individual and social action which is most closely connected with the attainment and with the use of the material requisites of wellbeing.
>
> Thus it is on the one side a study of wealth; and on the other, and more important side, a part of the study of man. For man's character has been moulded by his every-day work, and the material resources which he thereby procures, more than by any other influence unless it be that of his religious ideals.

In its actual development, however, economic science has focused on just one aspect of man's character, his reason, and particularly on the application of that reason to problems of allocation in the face of scarcity. Still, modern definitions of the economic sciences, whether phrased in terms of allocating scarce resources or in terms of rational decision making, mark out a vast domain for conquest and settlement. In recent years there has been considerable exploration by economists even of parts of this domain that were thought traditionally to belong to the disciplines of political science, sociology, and psychology.

*Carnegie-Mellon University. This article is the lecture Herbert Simon delivered in Stockholm, Sweden, December 8, 1978, when he received the Nobel Prize in Economic Science. The article is copyright © the Nobel Foundation 1978. It is published here with the permission of the Nobel Foundation.

The author is indebted to Albert Ando, Otto A. Davis, and Benjamin M. Friedman for valuable comments on an earlier draft of this paper.

I. Decision Theory as Economic Science

The density of settlement of economists over the whole empire of economic science is very uneven, with a few areas of modest size holding the bulk of the population. The economic Heartland is the normative study of the international and national economies and their markets, with its triple main concerns of full employment of resources, the efficient allocation of resources, and equity in distribution of the economic product. Instead of the ambiguous and over-general term "economics," I will use "political economy" to designate this Heartland, and "economic sciences" to denote the whole empire, including its most remote colonies. Our principal concern in this paper will be with the important colonial territory known as decision theory. I will have something to say about its normative and descriptive aspects, and particularly about its applications to the theory of the firm. It is through the latter topic that the discussion will be linked back to the Heartland of political economy.

Underpinning the corpus of policy-oriented normative economics, there is, of course, an impressive body of descriptive or "positive" theory which rivals in its mathematical beauty and elegance some of the finest theories in the physical sciences. As examples I need only remind you of Walrasian general equilibrium theories and their modern descendants in the works of Henry Schultz, Samuelson, Hicks, and others; or the subtle and impressive body of theory created by Arrow, Hurwicz, Debreu, Malinvaud, and their colleagues showing the equivalence, under certain conditions, of competitive equilibrium with Pareto optimality.

The relevance of some of the more refined parts of this work to the real world can be, and has been, questioned. Perhaps some of these intellectual mountains have been

494   THE AMERICAN ECONOMIC REVIEW   SEPTEMBER 1979

climbed simply because they were there—because of the sheer challenge and joy of scaling them. That is as it should be in any human scientific or artistic effort. But regardless of the motives of the climbers, regardless of real world veridicality, there is no question but that positive political economy has been strongly shaped by the demands of economic policy for advice on basic public issues.

This too is as it should be. It is a vulgar fallacy to suppose that scientific inquiry cannot be fundamental if it threatens to become useful, or if it arises in response to problems posed by the everyday world. The real world, in fact, is perhaps the most fertile of all sources of good research questions calling for basic scientific inquiry.

A. Decision Theory in the Service of Political Economy

There is, however, a converse fallacy that deserves equal condemnation: the fallacy of supposing that fundamental inquiry is worth pursuing only if its relevance to questions of policy is immediate and obvious. In the contemporary world, this fallacy is perhaps not widely accepted, at least as far as the natural sciences are concerned. We have now lived through three centuries or more of vigorous and highly successful inquiry into the laws of nature. Much of that inquiry has been driven by the simple urge to understand, to find the beauty of order hidden in complexity. Time and again, we have found the "idle" truths arrived at through the process of inquiry to be of the greatest moment for practical human affairs. I need not take time here to argue the point. Scientists know it, engineers and physicians know it, congressmen and members of parliaments know it, the man on the street knows it.

But I am not sure that this truth is as widely known in economics as it ought to be. I cannot otherwise explain the rather weak and backward development of the descriptive theory of decision making including the theory of the firm, the sparse and scattered settlement of its terrain, and the fact that many, if not most, of its investigators are drawn from outside economics—from sociolo-

gy, from psychology, and from political science. Respected and distinguished figures in economics—Edward Mason, Fritz Machlup, and Milton Friedman, for example—have placed it outside the Pale (more accurately, have placed economics outside *its* Pale), and have offered it full autonomy provided that it did not claim close kinship with genuine economic inquiry.

Thus, Mason, commenting on Papandreou's 1952 survey of research on the behavioral theory of the firm, mused aloud:

> ... has the contribution of this literature to economic analysis really been a large one? ... The writer of this critique must confess a lack of confidence in the marked superiority, *for purposes of economic analysis*, of this newer concept of the firm, over the older conception of the entrepreneur. [pp. 221–22]

And, in a similar vein, Friedman sums up his celebrated polemic against realism in theory:

> Complete "realism" is clearly unattainable, and the question whether a theory is realistic "enough" can be settled only by seeing whether it yields predictions that are good enough *for the purpose in hand* or that are better than predictions from alternative theories.
> [p. 41, emphasis added]

The "purpose in hand" that is implicit in both of these quotations is providing decision-theoretic foundations for positive, and then for normative, political economy. In the views of Mason and Friedman, fundamental inquiry into rational human behavior in the context of business organizations is simply not (by definition) economics—that is to say, political economy—unless it contributes in a major way to that purpose. This is sometimes even interpreted to mean that economic theories of decision making are not falsified in any interesting or relevant sense when their empirical predictions of *microphenomena* are found to be grossly incompatible with the observed data. Such theories, we are told, are still realistic "enough" provided that they do not contradict aggregate observations of concern to political economy. Thus economists who are zealous in insisting that economic actors maximize turn around and become satisficers when the evaluation of their own theories is concerned. They believe that businessmen maximize, but they know that economic theorists satisfice.

The application of the principle of satisficing to theories is sometimes defended as an application of Occam's Razor: accept the simplest theory that works.[1] But Occam's Razor has a double edge. Succinctness of statement is not the only measure of a theory's simplicity. Occam understood his rule as recommending theories that make no more assumptions than necessary to account for the phenomena (*Essentia non sunt multiplicanda praeter necessitatem*). A theory of profit or utility maximization can be stated more briefly than a satisficing theory of the sort I shall discuss later. But the former makes much stronger assumptions than the latter about the human cognitive system. Hence, in the case before us, the two edges of the razor cut in opposite directions.

In whichever way we interpret Occam's principle, parsimony can be only a secondary consideration in choosing between theories, unless those theories make identical predictions. Hence, we must come back to a consideration of the phenomena that positive decision theory is supposed to handle. These may include both phenomena at the microscopic level of the decision-making agents, or aggregative phenomena of concern to political economy.

---

[1]The phrase "that works" refutes, out of hand, Friedman's celebrated paean of praise for lack of realism in assumptions. Consider his example of falling bodies (pp. 16–19). His valid point is that it is advantageous to use the simple law, ignoring air resistance, when it gives a "good enough" approximation. But of course the conditions under which it gives a good approximation are not at all the conditions under which it is unrealistic or a "wildly inaccurate descriptive representation of reality." We can use it to predict the path of a body falling in a vacuum, but not the path of one falling through the Earth's atmosphere. I cannot in this brief space mention, much less discuss, all of the numerous logical fallacies that can be found in Friedman's 40-page essay. For additional criticism, see Simon (1963) and Samuelson (1963).

B. *Decision Theory Pursued for its Intrinsic Interest*

Of course the definition of the word "economics" is not important. Like Humpty Dumpty, we can make words mean anything we want them to mean. But the professional training and range of concern of economists does have importance. Acceptance of the narrow view that economics is concerned only with the aggregative phenomena of political economy defines away a whole rich domain of rational human behavior as inappropriate for economic research.

I do not wish to appear to be admitting that the behavioral theory of the firm *has been* irrelevant to the construction of political economy. I will have more to say about its relevance in a moment. My present argument is counterfactual in form: *even if* there were no present evidence of such relevance, human behavior in business firms constitutes a highly interesting body of empirical phenomena that calls out for explanation as do all bodies of phenomena. And if we may extrapolate from the history of the other sciences, there is every reason to expect that as explanations emerge, relevance for important areas of practical application will not be long delayed.

It has sometimes been implied (Friedman, p. 14) that the correctness of the assumptions of rational behavior underlying the classical theory of the firm is not merely irrelevant, but is not even empirically testable in any direct way, the only valid test being whether these assumptions lead to tolerably correct predictions at the macroscopic level. That would be true, of course, if we had no microscopes, so that the micro-level behavior was not directly observable. But we do have microscopes. There are many techniques for observing decision-making behavior, even at second-by-second intervals if that is wanted. In testing our economic theories, we do not have to depend on the rough aggregate time-series that are the main grist for the econometric mill, or even upon company financial statements.

The classical theories of economic decision making and of the business firm make very specific testable predictions about the concrete behavior of decision-making agents. Behavioral theories make quite different predictions. Since these predictions can be tested directly by observation, either theory (or both) may be falsified as readily when such predictions fail as when predictions about aggregate phenomena are in error.

C. *Aggregative Tests of Decision Theory: Marginalism*

If some economists have erroneously supposed that micro-economic theory can only be tested by its predictions of aggregate phenomena, we should avoid the converse error of supposing that aggregate phenomena are irrelevant to testing decision theory. In particular, are there important, *empirically verified,* aggregate predictions that follow from the theory of perfect rationality but that do not follow from behavioral theories of rationality?

The classical theory of omniscient rationality is strikingly simple and beautiful. Moreover, it allows us to predict (correctly or not) human behavior without stirring out of our armchairs to observe what such behavior is like. All the predictive power comes from characterizing the shape of the environment in which the behavior takes place. The environment, combined with the assumptions of perfect rationality, fully determines the behavior. Behavioral theories of rational choice—theories of bounded rationality—do not have this kind of simplicity. But, by way of compensation, their assumptions about human capabilities are far weaker than those of the classical theory. Thus, they make modest and realistic demands on the knowledge and computational abilities of the human agents, but they also fail to predict that those agents will equate costs and returns at the margin.

D. *Have the Marginalist Predictions Been Tested?*

A number of empirical phenomena have been cited as providing more or less conclusive support for the classical theory of the firm as against its behavioral competitors (see Dale Jorgensen and Calvin Siebert). But

there are no direct observations that individuals or firms do actually equate marginal costs and revenues. The empirically verified consequences of the classical theory are almost always weaker than this. Let us look at four of the most important of them: the fact that demand curves generally have negative slopes; the fact that fitted Cobb-Douglas functions are approximately homogeneous of the first degree; the fact of decreasing returns to scale; and the fact that executive salaries vary with the logarithm of company size. Are these indeed facts? And does the evidence support a maximizing theory against a satisficing theory?

Negatively Sloping Demand Curves. Evidence that consumers actually distribute their purchases in such a way as to maximize their utilities, and hence to equate marginal utilities, is nonexistent. What the empirical data do confirm is that demand curves generally have negative slopes. (Even this "obvious" fact is tricky to verify, as Henry Schultz showed long years ago.) But negatively sloping demand curves could result from a wide range of behaviors satisfying the assumptions of bounded rationality rather than those of utility maximization. Gary Becker, who can scarcely be regarded as a hostile witness for the classical theory, states the case very well:

> Economists have long been aware that some changes in the feasible or opportunity sets of households would lead to the same response *regardless of the decision rule used.* For example, a decrease in real income necessarily decreases the amount spent on at least one commodity... It has seldom been realized, however, that the change in opportunities resulting from a change in relative prices also tends to produce a systematic response, regardless of the decision rule. In particular, the fundamental theorem of traditional theory—that demand curves are negatively inclined—largely results from the change in opportunities alone and is largely independent of the decision rule. [p. 4]

Later, Becker is even more explicit, saying, "Not only utility maximization but also many other decision rules, incorporating a wide

VOL. 69 NO. 4   SIMON: RATIONAL DECISION MAKING   497

variety of irrational behavior, lead to negatively inclined demand curves because of the effect of a change in prices on opportunities" (p. 5).[2]

First-Degree Homogeneity of Production Functions. Another example of an observed phenomenon for which the classical assumptions provide sufficient, but not necessary, conditions is the equality between labor's share of product and the exponent of the labor factor in fitted Cobb-Douglas production functions (see Simon and Ferdinand Levy). Fitted Cobb-Douglas functions are homogeneous, generally of degree close to unity and with a labor exponent of about the right magnitude. These findings, however, cannot be taken as strong evidence for the classical theory, for the identical results can readily be produced by mistakenly fitting a Cobb-Douglas function to data that were in fact generated by a linear accounting identity (value of goods equals labor cost plus capital cost), (see E. H. Phelps-Brown). The same comment applies to the SMAC production function (see Richard Cyert and Simon). Hence, the empirical findings do not allow us to draw any particular conclusions about the relative plausibility of classical and behavioral theories, both of which are equally compatible with the data.

The Long-Run Cost Curve. Somewhat different is the case of the firm's long-run cost curve, which classical theory requires to be U shaped if competitive equilibrium is to be stable. Theories of bounded rationality do not predict this—fortunately, for the observed data make it exceedingly doubtful that the cost curves are in fact generally U shaped. The evidence for many industries shows costs at the high-scale ends of the curves to be essentially constant or even declining (see Alan Walters). This finding is compatible with stochastic models of business firm growth and size (see Y. Ijiri and Simon), but not with the static equilibrium model of classical theory.

Executive Salaries. Average salaries of

top corporate executives grow with the logarithm of corporate size (see David Roberts). This finding has been derived from the assumptions of the classical theory of profit maximization only with the help of very particular *ad hoc* assumptions about the distribution of managerial ability (see Robert Lucas, 1978). The observed relation is implied by a simple behavioral theory that assumes only that there is a single, culturally determined, parameter which fixes the average ratio of the salaries of managers to the salaries of their immediate subordinates (see Simon, 1957). In the case of the executive salary data, the behavioral model that explains the observations is substantially more parsimonious (in terms of assumptions about exogenous variables) than the classical model that explains the same observations.

Summary: Phenomena that Fail to Discriminate. It would take a much more extensive review than is provided here to establish the point conclusively, but I believe it is the case that specific phenomena requiring a theory of utility or profit maximization for their explanation rather than a theory of bounded rationality simply have not been observed in aggregate data. In fact, as my last two examples indicate, it is the classical rather than the behavioral form of the theory that faces real difficulties in handling some of the empirical observations.

Failures of Classical Theory. It may well be that classical theory can be patched up sufficiently to handle a wide range of situations where uncertainty and outguessing phenomena do not play a central role—that is, to handle the behavior of economies that are relatively stable and not too distant from a competitive equilibrium. However, a strong positive case for replacing the classical theory by a model of bounded rationality begins to emerge when we examine situations involving decision making under uncertainty and imperfect competition. These situations the classical theory was never designed to handle, and has never handled satisfactorily. Statistical decision theory employing the idea of subjective expected utility, on the one hand, and game theory, on the other, have contributed enormous conceptual clarification to these kinds of situations without providing

---

[2]In a footnote, Becker indicates that he denotes as irrational "[A]ny deviation from utility maximization." Thus, what I have called "bounded rationality" is "irrationality" in Becker's terminology.

498 THE AMERICAN ECONOMIC REVIEW SEPTEMBER 1979

satisfactory descriptions of actual human behavior, or even, for most cases, normative theories that are actually usable in the face of the limited computational powers of men and computers.

I shall have more to say later about the positive case for a descriptive theory of bounded rationality, but I would like to turn first to another territory within economic science that has gained rapidly in population since World War II, the domain of normative decision theory.

E. *Normative Decision Theory*

Decision theory can be pursued not only for the purposes of building foundations for political economy, or of understanding and explaining phenomena that are in themselves intrinsically interesting, but also for the purpose of offering direct advice to business and governmental decision makers. For reasons not clear to me, this territory was very sparsely settled prior to World War II. Such inhabitants as it had were mainly industrial engineers, students of public administration, and specialists in business functions, none of whom especially identified themselves with the economic sciences. Prominent pioneers included the mathematician, Charles Babbage, inventor of the digital computer, the engineer, Frederick Taylor, and the administrator, Henri Fayol.

During World War II, this territory, almost abandoned, was rediscovered by scientists, mathematicians, and statisticians concerned with military management and logistics, and was renamed "operations research" or "operations analysis." So remote were the operations researchers from the social science community that economists wishing to enter the territory had to establish their own colony, which they called "management science." The two professional organizations thus engendered still retain their separate identities, though they are now amicably federated in a number of common endeavors.

Optimization techniques were transported into management science from economics, and new optimization techniques, notably linear programming, were invented and devel-

oped, the names of Dantzig, Kantorovich, and Koopmans being prominent in the early development of that tool.

Now the salient characteristic of the decision tools employed in management science is that they have to be capable of actually making or recommending decisions, taking as their inputs the kinds of empirical data that are available in the real world, and performing only such computations as can reasonably be performed by existing desk calculators or, a little later, electronic computers. For these domains, idealized models of optimizing entrepreneurs, equipped with complete certainty about the world—or, at worst, having full probability distributions for uncertain events—are of little use. Models have to be fashioned with an eye to practical computability, no matter how severe the approximations and simplifications that are thereby imposed on them.

Model construction under these stringent conditions has taken two directions. The first is to retain optimization, but to simplify sufficiently so that the optimum (in the simplified world!) is computable. The second is to construct satisficing models that provide good enough decisions with reasonable costs of computation. By giving up optimization, a richer set of properties of the real world can be retained in the models. Stated otherwise, decision makers can satisfice either by finding optimum solutions for a simplified world, or by finding satisfactory solutions for a more realistic world. Neither approach, in general, dominates the other, and both have continued to co-exist in the world of management science.

Thus, the body of theory that has developed in management science shares with the body of theory in descriptive decision theory a central concern with the *ways* in which decisions are made, and not just with the decision outcomes. As I have suggested elsewhere (1978b), these are theories of *how* to decide rather than theories of *what* to decide.

Let me cite one example, from work in which I participated, of how model building in normative economics is shaped by computational considerations (see Charles Holt, Franco Modigliani, John Muth, and Simon).

In face of uncertain and fluctuating production demands, a company can smooth and stabilize its production and employment levels at the cost of holding buffer inventories. What kind of decision rule will secure a reasonable balance of costs? Formally, we are faced with a dynamic programming problem, and these generally pose formidable and often intolerable computational burdens for their solution.

One way out of this difficulty is to seek a special case of the problem that will be computationally tractable. If we assume the cost functions facing the company all to be quadratic in form, the optimal decision rule will then be a linear function of the decision variables, which can readily be computed in terms of the cost parameters. Equally important, under uncertainty about future sales, only the expected values, and not the higher moments, of the probability distributions enter into the decision rule (Simon, 1956b). Hence the assumption of quadratic costs reduces the original problem to one that is readily solved. Of course the solution, though it provides optimal decisions for the simplified world of our assumptions, provides, at best, satisfactory solutions for the real-world decision problem that the quadratic function approximates. In-principle, unattainable optimization is sacrificed for in-practice, attainable satisfaction.

If human decision makers are as rational as their limited computational capabilities and their incomplete information permit them to be, then there will be a close relation between normative and descriptive decision theory. Both areas of inquiry are concerned primarily with procedural rather than substantive rationality (Simon, 1978a). As new mathematical tools for computing optimal and satisfactory decisions are discovered, and as computers become more and more powerful, the recommendations of normative decision theory will change. But as the new recommendations are diffused, the actual, observed, practice of decision making in business firms will change also. And these changes may have macro-economic consequences. For example, there is some agreement that average inventory holdings of American firms have been

reduced significantly by the introduction of formal procedures for calculating reorder points and quantities.

II. Characterizing Bounded Rationality

The principal forerunner of a behavioral theory of the firm is the tradition usually called Institutionalism. It is not clear that all of the writings, European and American, usually lumped under this rubric have much in common, or that their authors would agree with each other's views. At best, they share a conviction that economic theory must be reformulated to take account of the social and legal structures amidst which market transactions are carried out. Today, we even find a vigorous development within economics that seeks to achieve institutionalist goals within the context of neoclassical price theory. I will have more to say about that a little later.

The name of John R. Commons is prominent—perhaps the most prominent—among American Institutionalists. Commons' difficult writings (for example, *Institutional Economics*) borrow their language heavily from the law, and seek to use the *transaction* as their basic unit of behavior. I will not undertake to review Commons' ideas here, but simply remark that they provided me with many insights in my initial studies of organizational decision making (see my *Administrative Behavior*, p. 136).

Commons also had a substantial influence on the thinking of Chester I. Barnard, an intellectually curious business executive who distilled from his experience as president of the New Jersey Bell Telephone Company, and as executive of other business, governmental, and nonprofit organizations, a profound book on decision making titled *The Functions of the Executive*. Barnard proposed original theories, which have stood up well under empirical scrutiny, of the nature of the authority mechanism in organizations, and of the motivational bases for employee acceptance of organizational goals (the so-called "inducements-contributions" theory); and he provided a realistic description of organizational decision making, which he characterized as "opportunistic." The numerous references to Barnard's work in *Administrative Behavior* attest, though inadequately, to the impact he had on my own thinking about organizations.

A. *In Search of a Descriptive Theory*

In 1934–35, in the course of a field study of the administration of public recreational facilities in Milwaukee, which were managed jointly by the school board and the city public works department, I encountered a puzzling phenomenon. Although the heads of the two agencies appeared to agree as to the objectives of the recreation program, and did not appear to be competing for empire, there was continual disagreement and tension between them with respect to the allocation of funds between physical maintenance, on the one hand, and play supervision on the other. Why did they not, as my economics books suggested, simply balance off the marginal return of the one activity against that of the other?

Further exploration made it apparent that they didn't equate expenditures at the margin because, intellectually, they couldn't. There was no measurable production function from which quantitative inferences about marginal productivities could be drawn; and such qualitative notions of a production function as the two managers possessed were mutually incompatible. To the public works administrator, a playground was a physical facility, serving as a green oasis in the crowded gray city. To the recreation administrator, a playground was a social facility, where children could play together with adult help and guidance.

How can human beings make rational decisions in circumstances like these? How are they to apply the marginal calculus? Or, if it does not apply, what do they substitute for it?

The phenomenon observed in Milwaukee is ubiquitous in human decision making. In organization theory it is usually referred to as *subgoal identification*. When the goals of an organization cannot be connected operationally with actions (when the production function can't be formulated in concrete terms),

then decisions will be judged against subordinate goals that can be so connected. There is no unique determination of these subordinate goals. Their formulation will depend on the knowledge, experience, and organizational environment of the decision maker. In the face of this ambiguity, the formulation can also be influenced in subtle, and not so subtle, ways by his self-interest and power drives.

The phenomenon arises as frequently in individual as in social decision making and problem solving. Today, under the rubric of *problem representation*, it is a central research interest of cognitive psychology. Given a particular environment of stimuli, and a particular background of previous knowledge, how will a person organize this complex mass of information into a problem formulation that will facilitate his solution efforts? How did Newton's experience of the apple, if he had one, get represented as an instance of attraction of apple by Earth?

Phenomena like these provided the central theme for *Administrative Behavior*. That study represented "an attempt to construct tools useful in my own research in the field of public administration." The product was actually not so much a theory as prolegomena to a theory, stemming from the conviction "that decision making is the heart of administration, and that the vocabulary of administrative theory must be derived from the logic and psychology of human choice." It was, if you please, an exercise in problem representation.

On examination, the phenomenon of subgoal identification proved to be the visible tip of a very large iceberg. The shape of the iceberg is best appreciated by contrasting it with classical models of rational choice. The classical model calls for knowledge of all the alternatives that are open to choice. It calls for complete knowledge of, or ability to compute, the consequences that will follow on each of the alternatives. It calls for certainty in the decision maker's present and future evaluation of these consequences. It calls for the ability to compare consequences, no matter how diverse and heterogeneous, in terms of some consistent measure of utility. The task, then, was to replace the classical model with one that would describe how decisions could be (and probably actually were) made when the alternatives of search had to be sought out, the consequences of choosing particular alternatives were only very imperfectly known both because of limited computational power and because of uncertainty in the external world, and the decision maker did not possess a general and consistent utility function for comparing heterogeneous alternatives.

Several procedures of rather general applicability and wide use have been discovered that transform intractable decision problems into tractable ones. One procedure already mentioned is to look for satisfactory choices instead of optimal ones. Another is to replace abstract, global goals with tangible subgoals, whose achievement can be observed and measured. A third is to divide up the decision-making task among many specialists, coordinating their work by means of a structure of communications and authority relations. All of these, and others, fit the general rubric of "bounded rationality," and it is now clear that the elaborate organizations that human beings have constructed in the modern world to carry out the work of production and government can only be understood as machinery for coping with the limits of man's abilities to comprehend and compute in the face of complexity and uncertainty.

This rather vague and general initial formulation of the idea of bounded rationality called for elaboration in two directions: greater formalization of the theory, and empirical verification of its main claims. During the decade that followed the publication of *Administrative Behavior*, substantial progress was made in both directions, some of it through the efforts of my colleagues and myself, much of it by other research groups that shared the same Zeitgeist.

B. *Empirical Studies*

The principal source of empirical data about organizational decision making has been straightforward "anthropological" field study, eliciting descriptions of decision-making procedures and observing the course

of specific decision-making episodes. Examples are my study, with Guetzkow, Kozmetsky, and Tyndall (1954), of the ways in which accounting data were used in decision making in large corporations; and a series of studies, with Richard Cyert, James March, and others, of specific nonprogrammed policy decisions in a number of different companies (see Cyert, Simon, and Donald Trow). The latter line of work was greatly developed and expanded by Cyert and March and its theoretical implications for economics explored in their important work, *A Behavioral Theory of the Firm*.

At about the same time, the fortuitous availability of some data on businessmen's perceptions of a problem situation described in a business policy casebook enabled DeWitt Dearborn and me to demonstrate empirically the cognitive basis for identification with subgoals, the phenomenon that had so impressed me in the Milwaukee recreation study. The businessmen's perceptions of the principal problems facing the company described in the case were mostly determined by their own business experiences—sales and accounting executives identified a sales problem, manufacturing executives, a problem of internal organization.

Of course there is vastly more to be learned and tested about organizational decision making than can be dealt with in a handful of studies. Although many subsequent studies have been carried out in Europe and the United States, this domain is still grossly undercultivated (for references, see March, 1965; E. Johnsen, 1968; G. Eliasson, 1976). Among the reasons for the relative neglect of such studies, as contrasted, say, with laboratory experiments in social psychology, is that they are extremely costly and time consuming, with a high grist-to-grain ratio, the methodology for carrying them out is primitive, and satisfactory access to decision-making behavior is hard to secure. This part of economics has not yet acquired the habits of patience and persistence in the pursuit of facts that is exemplified in other domains by the work, say, of Simon Kuznets or of the architects of the MIT-SSRC-Penn econometric models.

502   THE AMERICAN ECONOMIC REVIEW   SEPTEMBER 1979

C. Theoretical Inquiries

On the theoretical side, three questions seemed especially to call for clarification: what are the circumstances under which an employment relation will be preferred to some other form of contract as the arrangement for securing the performance of work; what is the relation between the classical theory of the firm and theories of organizational equilibrium first proposed by Chester Barnard; and what are the main characteristics of human rational choice in situations where complexity precludes omniscience?

The Employment Relation. A fundamental characteristic of modern industrial society is that most work is performed, not by individuals who produce products for sale, nor by individual contractors, but by persons who have accepted employment in a business firm and the authority relation with the employer that employment entails. Acceptance of authority means willingness to permit one's behavior to be determined by the employer, at least within some zone of indifference or acceptance. What is the advantage of this arrangement over a contract for specified goods or services? Why is so much of the world's work performed in large, hierarchic organizations?

Analysis showed (Simon, 1951) that a combination of two factors could account for preference for the employment contract over other forms of contracts: uncertainty as to which future behaviors would be advantageous to the employer, and a greater indifference of the employee as compared with the employer (within the former's area of acceptance) as to which of these behaviors he carried out. When the secretary is hired, the employer does not know what letters he will want her to type, and the secretary has no great preference for typing one letter rather than another. The employment contract permits the choice to be postponed until the uncertainty is resolved, with little cost to the employee and great advantage to the employer. The explanation is closely analogous to one Jacob Marschak had proposed for liquidity preference. Under conditions of uncertainty it is advantageous to hold resources in liquid, flexible form.

Organizational Equilibrium. Barnard had described the survival of organizations in terms of the motivations that make their participants (employees, investors, customers, suppliers) willing to remain in the system. In *Administrative Behavior*, I had developed this notion further into a motivational theory of the balance between the inducements that were provided by organizations to their participants, and the contributions those participants made to the organizations' resources.

A formalization of this theory (Simon, 1952; 1953) showed its close affinity to the classical theory of the firm, but with an important and instructive difference. In comparing the two theories, each inducement-contribution relation became a supply schedule for the firm. The survival conditions became the conditions for positive profit. But while the classical theory of the firm assumes that all profits accrue to a particular set of participants, the owners, the organization theory treats the surplus more symmetrically, and does not predict how it will be distributed. Hence the latter theory leaves room, under conditions of monopoly and imperfect competition, for bargaining among the participants (for example, between labor and owners) for the surplus. The survival conditions—positive profits rather than maximum profits—also permit a departure from the assumptions of perfect rationality.

Mechanisms of Bounded Rationality. In *Administrative Behavior*, bounded rationality is largely characterized as a residual category—rationality is bounded when it falls short of omniscience. And the failures of omniscience are largely failures of knowing all the alternatives, uncertainty about relevant exogenous events, and inability to calculate consequences. There was needed a more positive and formal characterization of the mechanisms of choice under conditions of bounded rationality. Two papers (Simon, 1955; 1956a) undertook first steps in that direction.

Two concepts are central to the characterization: *search* and *satisficing*. If the alternatives for choice are not given initially to the decision maker, then he must search for them. Hence, a theory of bounded rationality must incorporate a theory of search. This idea was

VOL. 69 NO. 4   SIMON: RATIONAL DECISION MAKING   503

later developed independently by George Stigler in a very influential paper that took as its example of a decision situation the purchase of a second-hand automobile. Stigler poured the search theory back into the old bottle of classical utility maximization, the cost of search being equated with its marginal return. In my 1956 paper, I had demonstrated the same formal equivalence, using as my example a dynamic programming formulation of the process of selling a house.

But utility maximization, as I showed, was not essential to the search scheme—fortunately, for it would have required the decision maker to be able to estimate the marginal costs and returns of search in a decision situation that was already too complex for the exercise of global rationality. As an alternative, one could postulate that the decision maker had formed some *aspiration* as to how good an alternative he should find. As soon as he discovered an alternative for choice meeting his level of aspiration, he would terminate the search and choose that alternative. I called this mode of selection *satisficing*. It had its roots in the empirically based psychological theories, due to Lewin and others, of aspiration levels. As psychological inquiry had shown, aspiration levels are not static, but tend to rise and fall in consonance with changing experiences. In a benign environment that provides many good alternatives, aspirations rise; in a harsher enviornment, they fall.

In long-run equilibrium it might even be the case that choice with dynamically adapting aspiration levels would be equivalent to optimal choice, taking the costs of search into account. But the important thing about the search and satisficing theory is that it showed how choice could actually be made with reasonable amounts of calculation, and using very incomplete information, without the need of performing the impossible—of carrying out this optimizing procedure.

D. *Summary*

Thus, by the middle 1950's, a theory of bounded rationality had been proposed as an alternative to classical omniscient rationality,

a significant number of empirical studies had been carried out that showed actual business decision making to conform reasonably well with the assumptions of bounded rationality but not with the assumptions of perfect rationality, and key components of the theory—the nature of the authority and employment relations, organizational equilibrium, and the mechanisms of search and satisficing—had been elucidated formally. In the remaining parts of this paper, I should like to trace subsequent developments of decision-making theory, including developments competitive with the theory of bounded rationality, and then to comment on the implications (and potential implications) of the new descriptive theory of decision for political economy.

III. The Neoclassical Revival

Peering forward from the late 1950's, it would not have been unreasonable to predict that theories of bounded rationality would soon find a large place in the mainstream of economic thought. Substantial progress had been made in providing the theories with some formal structure, and an increasing body of empirical evidence showed them to provide a far more veridical picture of decision making in business organizations than did the classical concepts of perfect rationality.

History has not followed any such simple course, even though many aspects of the Zeitgeist were favorable to movement in this direction. During and after World War II, a large number of academic economists were exposed directly to business life, and had more or less extensive opportunities to observe how decisions were actually made in business organizations. Moreover, those who became active in the development of the new management science were faced with the necessity of developing decision-making procedures that could actually be applied in practical situations. Surely these trends would be conducive to moving the basic assumptions of economic rationality in the direction of greater realism.

But these were not the only things that were happening in economics in the postwar period. First, there was a vigorous reaction that sought to defend classical theory from behavioralism on methodological grounds. I have already commented on these methodological arguments in the first part of my talk. However deeply one may disagree with them, they were stated persuasively and are still influential among academic economists.

Second, the rapid spread of mathematical knowledge and competence in the economics profession permitted the classical theory, especially when combined with statistical decision theory and the theory of games due to von Neumann and Morgenstern, to develop to new heights of sophistication and elegance, and to expand to embrace, albeit in highly stylized form, some of the phenomena of uncertainty and imperfect information. The flowering of mathematical economics and econometrics has provided two generations of economic theorists with a vast garden of formal and technical problems that have absorbed their energies and postponed encounters with the inelegancies of the real world.

If I sound mildly critical of these developments, I should confess that I have also been a part of them, admire them, and would be decidedly unhappy to return to the premathematical world they have replaced. My concern is that the economics profession has exhibited some of the serial one-thing-at-a-time character of human rationality, and has seemed sometimes to be unable to distribute its attention in a balanced fashion among neoclassical theory, macroeconometrics, and descriptive decision theory. As a result, not as much professional effort has been devoted to the latter two, and especially the third, as one might have hoped and expected. The Heartland is more overpopulated than ever, while rich lands in other parts of the empire go untilled.

A. Search and Information Transfer

Let me allude to just three of the ways in which classical theory has sought to cope with some of its traditional limitations, and has even sought to make the development of a behavioral theory, incorporating psychological assumptions, unnecessary. The first was to introduce search and information transfer explicitly as economic activities, with associated costs and outputs, that could be inserted into the classical production function. I have already referred to Stigler's 1961 paper on the economics of information, and my own venture in the same direction in the 1956 essay cited earlier.

In theory of this genre, the decision maker is still an individual. A very important new direction, in which decisions are made by groups of individuals, in teams or organizations, is the economic theory of teams developed by Jacob Marschak and Roy Radner. Here we see genuine organizational phenomena—specialization of decision making as a consequence of the costs of transmitting information—emerge from the rational calculus. Because the mathematical difficulties are formidable, the theory remains largely illustrative and limited to very simple situations in miniature organizations. Nevertheless, it has greatly broadened our understanding of the economics of information.

In none of these theories—any more than in statistical decision theory or the theory of games—is the assumption of perfect maximization abandoned. Limits and costs of information are introduced, not as psychological characteristics of the decision maker, but as part of his technological environment. Hence, the new theories do nothing to alleviate the computational complexities facing the decision maker—do not see him coping with them by heroic approximation, simplifying and satisficing, but simply magnify and multiply them. Now he needs to compute not merely the shapes of his supply and demand curves, but, in addition, the costs and benefits of computing those shapes to greater accuracy as well. Hence, to some extent, the impression that these new theories deal with the hitherto ignored phenomena of uncertainty and information transmission is illusory. For many economists, however, the illusion has been persuasive.

B. Rational Expectations Theory

A second development in neoclassical theory on which I wish to comment is the so-called "rational expectations" theory.

There is a bit of historical irony surrounding its origins. I have already described the management science inquiry of Holt, Modigliani, Muth, and myself that developed a dynamic programming algorithm for the special (and easily computed) case of quadratic cost functions. In this case, the decision rules are linear, and the probability distributions of future events can be replaced by their expected values, which serve as certainty equivalents (see Simon, 1956; Henri Theil, 1957).

Muth imaginatively saw in this special case a paradigm for rational behavior under uncertainty. What to some of us in the HMMS research team was an approximating, satisficing simplification, served for him as a major line of defense for perfect rationality. He said in his seminal 1961 *Econometrica* article, "It is sometimes argued that the assumption of rationality in economics leads to theories inconsistent with, or inadequate to explain, observed phenomena, especially changes over time... Our hypothesis is based on exactly the opposite point of view: that dynamic economic models do not assume enough rationality" (p. 316).

The new increment of rationality that Muth proposed was that "expectations, since they are informed predictions of future events, are essentially the same as the predictions of the relevant economic theory" (p. 316). He would cut the Gordian knot. Instead of dealing with uncertainty by elaborating the model of the decision process, he would once and for all—if his hypothesis were correct—make process irrelevant. The subsequent vigorous development of rational expectations theory, in the hands of Sargent, Lucas, Prescott, and others, is well known to most readers (see, for example, Lucas, 1975).

It is too early to render a final verdict on the rational expectations theory. The issue will ultimately be decided, as all scientific debates should be, by a gradual winnowing of the empirical evidence, and that winnowing process has just begun. Meanwhile, certain grave theoretical difficulties have already been noticed. As Muth himself has pointed out, it is rational (i.e., profit maximizing) to use the "rational expectations" decision rule if the relevant cost equations are in fact quadratic. I have suggested elsewhere (1978a) that it might therefore be less misleading to call the rule a "consistent expectations" rule.

Perhaps even more important, Albert Ando and Benjamin Friedman (1978, 1979) have shown that the policy implications of the rational expectations rule are quite different under conditions where new information continually becomes available to the system, structural changes occur, and the decision maker learns, than they are under steady-state conditions. For example, under the more dynamic conditions, monetary neutrality—which in general holds for the static consistent expectations models—is no longer guaranteed for any finite time horizon.

In the recent "revisionist" versions of consistent expectations theory, moreover, where account is taken of a changing environment of information, various behavioral assumptions reappear to explain how expectations are formed—what information decision makers will consider, and what they will ignore. But unless these assumptions are to be made on a wholly *ad hoc* and arbitrary basis, they create again the need for an explicit and valid theory of the decision-making *process* (see Simon, 1958a; B. Friedman, 1979).

C. *Statistical Decision Theory and Game Theory*

Statistical decision theory and game theory are two other important components of the neoclassical revival. The former addresses itself to the question of incorporating uncertainty (or more properly, risk) into the decision-making models. It requires heroic assumptions about the information the decision maker has concerning the probability distributions of the relevant variables, and simply increases by orders of magnitude the computational problems he faces.

Game theory addresses itself to the "outguessing" problem that arises whenever an economic actor takes into account the possible reactions to his own decisions of the other actors. To my mind, the main product of the very elegant apparatus of game theory has been to demonstrate quite clearly that it is virtually impossible to define an unambiguous criterion of rationality for this class of situations (or, what amounts to the same thing, a definitive definition of the "solution" of a game). Hence, game theory has not brought to the theories of oligopoly and imperfect competition the relief from their contradictions and complexities that was originally hoped for it. Rather, it has shown that these difficulties are ineradicable. We may be able to reach consensus that a certain criterion of rationality is appropriate to a particular game, but if someone challenges the consensus, preferring a different criterion, we will have no logical basis for persuading him that he is wrong.

D. *Conclusion*

Perhaps I have said enough about the neoclassical revival to suggest why it has been a highly attractive commodity in competition with the behavioral theories. To some economists at least, it has held open the possibility and hope that important questions that had been troublesome for classical economics could now be addressed without sacrifice of the central assumption of perfect rationality, and hence also with a maximum of a priori inference and a minimum of tiresome grubbing with empirical data. I have perhaps said enough also with respect to the limitations of these new constructs to indicate why I do not believe that they solve the problems that motivated their development.

IV. Advances in the Behavioral Theory

Although they have played a muted role in the total economic research activity during the past two decades, theories of bounded rationality and the behavioral theory of the business firm have undergone steady development during that period. Since surveying the whole body of work would be a major undertaking, I shall have to be satisfied here with suggesting the flavor of the whole by citing a few samples of different kinds of important research falling in this domain. Where surveys on particular topics have been published, I will limit myself to references to them.

First, there has been work in the psychological laboratory and the field to test whether people in relatively simple choice situations behave as statistical decision theory (maximization of expected utilities) say they do. Second, there has been extensive psychological research, in which Allen Newell and I have been heavily involved, to discover the actual microprocesses of human decision making and problem solving. Third, there have been numerous empirical observations—most of them in the form of "case studies"—of the actual processes of decision making in organizational and business contexts. Fourth, there have been reformulations and extensions of the theory of the firm replacing classical maximization with behavioral decision postulates.

A. *Utility Theory and Human Choice*

The axiomatization of utility and probability after World War II and the revival of Bayesian statistics opened the way to testing empirically whether people behaved in choice situations so as to maximize subjective expected utility (SEU). In early studies, using extremely simple choice situations, it appeared that perhaps they did. When even small complications were introduced into the situations, wide departures of behavior from the predictions of SEU theory soon became evident. Some of the most dramatic and convincing empirical refutations of the theory have been reported by D. Kahneman and A. Tversky, who showed that under one set of circumstances, decision makers gave far too little weight to prior knowledge and based their choices almost entirely on new evidence, while in other circumstances new evidence had little influence on opinions already formed. Equally large and striking departures from the behavior predicted by the SEU theories were found by Howard Kunreuther and his colleagues in their studies of individual decisions to purchase or not to purchase flood insurance. On the basis of these and other pieces of evidence, the conclusion seems unavoidable that the SEU theory does not provide a good prediction—not even a good approximation—of actual behavior.

Notice that the refutation of the theory has to do with the *substance* of the decisions, and not just the process by which they are reached. It is not that people do not go through the calculations that would be required to reach the *SEU* decision—neoclassical thought has never claimed that they did. What has been shown is that they do not even behave *as if* they had carried out those calculations, and that result is a direct refutation of the neoclassical assumptions.

B. *Psychology of Problem Solving*

The evidence on rational decision making is largely negative evidence, evidence of what people do *not* do. In the past twenty years a large body of positive evidence has also accumulated about the processes that people use to make difficult decisions and solve complex problems. The body of theory that has been built up around this evidence is called information processing psychology, and is usually expressed formally in computer programming languages. Newell and I have summed up our own version of this theory in our book, *Human Problem Solving*, which is part of a large and rapidly growing literature that assumes an information processing framework and makes use of computer simulation as a central tool for expressing and testing theories.

Information processing theories envisage problem solving as involving very selective search through problem spaces that are often immense. Selectivity, based on rules of thumb or "heuristics," tends to guide the search into promising regions, so that solutions will generally be found after search of only a tiny part of the total space. Satisficing criteria terminate search when satisfactory problem solutions have been found. Thus, these theories of problem solving clearly fit within the framework of bounded rationality that I have been expounding here.

By now the empirical evidence for this general picture of the problem solving process is extensive. Most of the evidence pertains to relatively simple, puzzle-like situations of the sort that can be brought into the psychological laboratory for controlled study, but a great deal has been learned, also, about professional level human tasks like making medical diagnoses, investing in portfolios of stocks and bonds, and playing chess. In tasks of these kinds, the general search mechanisms operate in a rich context of information stored in human long-term memory, but the general organization of the process is substantially the same as for the simpler, more specific tasks.

At the present time, research in information processing psychology is proceeding in several directions. Exploration of professional level skills continues. A good deal of effort is now being devoted also to determining how initial representations for new problems are acquired. Even in simple problem domains, the problem solver has much latitude in the way he formulates the problem space in which he will search, a finding that underlines again how far the actual process is from a search for a uniquely determined optimum (see J. R. Hayes and Simon).

The main import for economic theory of the research in information processing psychology is to provide rather conclusive empirical evidence that the decision-making process in problem situations conforms closely to the models of bounded rationality described earlier. This finding implies, in turn, that choice is not determined uniquely by the objective characteristics of the problem situation, but depends also on the particular heuristic process that is used to reach the decision. It would appear, therefore, that a model of process is an essential component in any positive theory of decision making that purports to describe the real world, and that the neoclassical ambition of avoiding the necessity for such a model is unrealizable (Simon, 1978a).

C. *Organizational Decision Making*

It would be desirable to have, in addition to the evidence from the psychological research just described, empirical studies of the process of decision making in organizational contexts. The studies of individual problem solving and decision making do not touch on the many social-psychological factors that enter into the decision process in organizations. A substantial number of investigations have been carried out in the past twenty years of the decision-making process in organizations, but they are not easily summarized. The difficulty is that most of these investigations have taken the form of case studies of specific decisions or particular classes of decisions in individual organizations. To the best of my knowledge, no good review of this literature has been published, so that it is difficult even to locate and identify the studies that have been carried out.[3] Nor have any systematic methods been developed and tested for distilling out from these individual case studies their implications for the general theory of the decision-making process.

The case studies of organizational decision making, therefore, represent the natural history stage of scientific inquiry. They provide us with a multitude of facts about the decision-making process—facts that are almost uniformly consistent with the kind of behavioral model that has been proposed here. But we do not yet know how to use these facts to test the model in any formal way. Nor do we quite know what to do with the observation that the specific decision-making procedures used by organizations differ from one organization to another, and within each organization, even from one situation to another. We must not expect from these data generalizations as neat and precise as those incorporated in neoclassical theory.

Perhaps the closest approach to a method for extracting theoretically relevant information from case studies is computer simulation. By converting empirical evidence about a decision-making process into a computer program, a path is opened both for testing the adequacy of the program mechanisms for explaining the data, and for discovering the key features of the program that account, qualitatively, for the interesting and important characteristics of its behavior. Examples

of the use of this technique are G.P.E. Clarkson's simulation of the decision making of an investment trust officer, Cyert, E. A. Feigenbaum, and March's simulation of the history of a duopoly, and C. P. Bonini's model of the effects of accounting information and supervisory pressures in altering employee motivations in a business firm. The simulation methodology is discussed from a variety of viewpoints in Dutton and Starbuck.[4]

D. *Theories of the Business Firm*

The general features of bounded rationality—selective search, satisficing, and so on—have been taken as the starting points for a number of attempts to build theories of the business firm incorporating behavioral assumptions. Examples of such theories would include the theory of Cyert and March, already mentioned; William Baumol's theory of sales maximization subject to minimum profit constraints; Robin Marris' models of firms whose goals are stated in terms of rates of growth; Harvey Leibenstein's theory of "X-inefficiency" that depresses production below the theoretically attainable; Janos Kornai's dichotomy between supply-driven and demand-driven management; Oliver Williamson's theory of transactional costs; the evolutionary models of Richard Nelson and Sidney Winter (1973); Cyert and Morris DeGroot's (1974) models incorporating adaptive learning; Radner's (1975a,b) explicit satisficing models; and others.

Characterized in this way, there seems to be little commonality among all of these theories and models, except that they depart in one way or another from the classical assumption of perfect rationality in firm decision making. A closer look, however, and a more abstract description of their assumptions, shows that they share several basic characteristics. Most of them depart from the assumption of profit maximization in the short run, and replace it with an assumption

---

[3] For leads into the literature, see March and Simon; March; Johnsen; J. M. Dutton and W. H. Starbuck. However, there are large numbers of specific case studies, some of them carried out as thesis projects, some concerned with particular fields of business application, which have never been recorded in these reference sources (for example, Eliasson, 1976).

[4] In addition to simulations of the firm, there are very interesting and potentially important efforts to use simulation to build bridges directly from decision theory to political economy. See G. Orcutt and R. Caldwell-Wertheimer, and Eliasson (1978).

of goals defined in terms of targets—that is, they are to greater or lesser degree satisficing theories. If they do retain maximizing assumptions, they contain some kind of mechanism that prevents the maximum from being attained, at least in the short run. In the Cyert-March theory, and that of Leibenstein, this mechanism can be viewed as producing "organizational slack," the magnitude of which may itself be a function of motivational and environmental variables.

Finally, a number of these theories assume that organizational learning takes place, so that if the environment were stationary for a sufficient length of time, the system equilibrium would approach closer and closer to the classical profit-maximizing equilibrium. Of course they generally also assume that the environmental disturbances will generally be large enough to prevent the classical solution from being an adequate approximation to the actual behavior.

The presence of something like organizational slack in a model of the business firm introduces complexity in the firm's behavior in the short run. Since the firm may operate very far from any optimum, the slack serves as a buffer between the environment and the firm's decisions. Responses to environmental events can no longer be predicted simply by analyzing the "requirements of the situation," but depend on the specific decision processes that the firm employs. However well this characteristic of a business firm model corresponds to reality, it reduces the attractiveness of the model for many economists, who are reluctant to give up the process-independent predictions of classical theory, and who do not feel at home with the kind of empirical investigation that is required for disclosing actual real world decision processes.

But there is another side to the matter. If, in the face of identical environmental conditions, different decision mechanisms can produce different firm behaviors, this sensitivity of outcomes to process can have important consequences for analysis at the level of markets and the economy. Political economy, whether descriptive or normative, cannot remain indifferent to this source of variability in response. At the very least it demands

that—before we draw policy conclusions from our theories, and particularly before we act on those policy conclusions—we carry out sensitivity analyses to test how far our conclusions would be changed if we made different assumptions about the decision mechanisms at the micro level.

If our conclusions are robust—if they are not changed materially by substituting one or another variant of the behavioral model for the classical model—we will gain confidence in our predictions and recommendations; if the conclusions are sensitive to such substitutions, we will use them warily until we can determine which micro theory is the correct one.

As reference to the literature cited earlier in this section will verify, our predictions of the operations of markets and of the economy *are* sensitive to our assumptions about mechanisms at the level of decision processes. Moreover, the assumptions of the behavioral theories are almost certainly closer to reality than those of the classical theory. These two facts, in combination, constitute a direct refutation of the argument that the unrealism of the assumptions of the classical theory is harmless. We cannot use the *in vacua* version of the law of falling bodies to predict the sinking of a heavy body in molasses. The predictions of the classical and neoclassical theories and the policy recommendations derived from them must be treated with the greatest caution.

V. Conclusion

There is a saying in politics that "you can't beat something with nothing." You can't defeat a measure or a candidate simply by pointing to defects and inadequacies. You must offer an alternative.

The same principle applies to scientific theory. Once a theory is well entrenched, it will survive many assaults of empirical evidence that purports to refute it unless an alternative theory, consistent with the evidence, stands ready to replace it. Such conservative protectiveness of established beliefs is, indeed, not unreasonable. In the first place, in empirical science we aspire only to approximate truths; we are under no illusion that we can find a single formula, or even a moderately complex one, that captures the whole truth and nothing else. We are committed to a strategy of successive approximations, and when we find discrepancies between theory and data, our first impulse is to patch rather than to rebuild from the foundations.

In the second place, when discrepancies appear, it is seldom immediately obvious where the trouble lies. It may be located in the fundamental assumptions of the theory, but it may as well be merely a defect in the auxiliary hypotheses and measurement postulates we have had to assume in order to connect theory with observations. Revisions in these latter parts of the structure may be sufficient to save the remainder.

What then is the present status of the classical theory of the firm? There can no longer be any doubt that the micro assumptions of the theory—the assumptions of perfect rationality—are contrary to fact. It is not a question of approximation; they do not even remotely describe the processes that human beings use for making decisions in complex situations.

Moreover, there is an alternative. If anything, there is an embarrassing richness of alternatives. Today, we have a large mass of descriptive data, from both laboratory and field, that show how human problem solving and decision making actually take place in a wide variety of situations. A number of theories have been constructed to account for these data, and while these theories certainly do not yet constitute a single coherent whole, there is much in common among them. In one way or another, they incorporate the notions of bounded rationality: the need to search for decision alternatives, the replacement of optimization by targets and satisficing goals, and mechanisms of learning and adaptation. If our interest lies in descriptive decision theory (or even normative decision theory), it is now entirely clear that the classical and neoclassical theories have been replaced by a superior alternative that provides us with a much closer approximation to what is actually going on.

But what if our interest lies primarily in normative political economy rather than in the more remote regions of the economic sciences? Is there then any reason why we should give up the familiar theories? Have the newer concepts of decision making and the firm shown their superiority "for purposes of economic analysis"?

If the classical and neoclassical theories were, as is sometimes argued, simply powerful tools for deriving aggregative consequences that held alike for both perfect and bounded rationality, we would have every reason to retain them for this purpose. But we have seen, on the contrary, that neoclassical theory does not always lead to the same conclusions at the level of aggregate phenomena and policy as are implied by the postulate of bounded rationality, in any of its variants. Hence, we cannot defend an uncritical use of these contrary-to-fact assumptions by the argument that their veridicality is unimportant. In many cases, in fact, this veridicality may be crucial to reaching correct conclusions about the central questions of political economy. Only a comparison of predictions can tell us whether a case before us is one of these.

The social sciences have been accustomed to look for models in the most spectacular successes of the natural sciences. There is no harm in that, provided that it is not done in a spirit of slavish imitation. In economics, it has been common enough to admire Newtonian mechanics (or, as we have seen, the Law of Falling Bodies), and to search for the economic equivalent of the laws of motion. But this is not the only model for a science, and it seems, indeed, not to be the right one for our purposes.

Human behavior, even rational human behavior, is not to be accounted for by a handful of invariants. It is certainly not to be accounted for by assuming perfect adaptation to the environment. Its basic mechanisms may be relatively simple, and I believe they are, but that simplicity operates in interaction with extremely complex boundary conditions imposed by the environment and by the very facts of human long-term memory and of the capacity of human beings, individually and collectively, to learn.

If we wish to be guided by a natural science metaphor, I suggest one drawn from biology rather than physics (see Newell and Simon, 1976). Obvious lessons are to be learned from evolutionary biology, and rather less obvious ones from molecular biology. From molecular biology, in particular, we can glimpse a picture of how a few basic mechanisms—the DNA of the Double Helix, for example, or the energy transfer mechanisms elucidated so elegantly by Peter Mitchell—can account for a wide range of complex phenomena. We can see the role in science of laws of qualitative structure, and the power of qualitative as well as quantitative explanation.

I am always reluctant to end a talk about the sciences of man in the future tense. It conveys too much the impression that these are potential sciences which may some day be actualized, but that do not really exist at the present time. Of course that is not the case at all. However much our knowledge of human behavior falls short of our need for such knowledge, still it is enormous. Sometimes we tend to discount it because so many of the phenomena are accessible to us in the very activity of living as human beings among human beings that it seems commonplace to us. Moreover, it does not always answer the questions for which we need answers. We cannot predict very well the course of the business cycle nor manage the employment rate. (We cannot, it might be added, predict very well the time of the next thunderstorm in Stockholm, or manage the earth's climates.)

With all these qualifications and reservations, we do understand today many of the mechanisms of human rational choice. We do know how the information processing system called Man, faced with complexity beyond his ken, uses his information processing capacities to seek out alternatives, to calculate consequences, to resolve uncertainties, and thereby—sometimes, not always—to find ways of action that are sufficient unto the day, that satisfice.

REFERENCES

A. A. Alchian, "Uncertainty, Evolution, and Economic Theory," *J. Polit. Econ.*, June 1950, *58*, 211-21.

A. Ando, "On a Theoretical and Empirical Basis of Macroeconometric Models," paper presented to the NSF-NBER Conference on Macroeconomic Modeling, Ann Arbor, Oct. 1978.

Chester I. Barnard, *The Functions of the Executive*, Cambridge, Mass. 1938.

William Baumol, *Business Behavior, Value and Growth*, New York 1959.

G. S. Becker, "Irrational Behavior and Economic Theory," *J. Polit. Econ.*, Feb. 1962, *70*, 1–13.

Charles P. Bonini, *Simulation of Information and Decision Systems in the Firm*, Englewood Cliffs 1963.

Alfred Chandler, *Strategy and Structure*, Cambridge, Mass. 1962.

N. C. Churchill, W. W. Cooper, and T. Sainsbury, "Laboratory and Field Studies of the Behavioral Effects of Audits," in C. P. Bonini et al., eds., *Management Controls*, New York 1964.

G. P. E. Clarkson, "A Model of the Trust Investment Process," in E. A. Feigenbaum and J. Feldman, eds., *Computers and Thought*, New York 1963.

John R. Commons, *Institutional Economics*, Madison 1934.

R. M. Cyert, E. A. Feigenbaum, and J. G. March, "Models in a Behavioral Theory of the Firm," *Behav. Sci.*, Apr. 1959, *4*, 81–95.

_____ and M. H. DeGroot, "Rational Expectations and Bayesian Analysis," *J. Polit. Econ.*, May/June 1974, *82*, 521–36.

_____ and _____ "Adaptive Utility," in R. H. Day and T. Groves, eds., *Adaptive Economic Models*, New York 1975, 233–46.

_____ and James G. March, *A Behavioral Theory of the Firm*, Englewood Cliffs 1963.

_____ and H. A. Simon, "Theory of the Firm: Behavioralism and Marginalism," unpublished work. paper, Carnegie-Mellon Univ. 1971.

_____, _____, and D. B. Trow, "Observation of a Business Decision," *J. Bus., Univ. Chicago*, Oct. 1956, *29*, 237–48.

D. C. Dearborn and H. A. Simon, "Selective Perception: The Identifications of Executives," *Sociometry*, 1958, *21*, 140–144; reprinted in *Administrative Behavior*, ch. 15, 3d ed., New York 1976.

512   THE AMERICAN ECONOMIC REVIEW   SEPTEMBER 1979

J. M. Dutton and W. H. Starbuck, *Computer Simulation of Human Behavior*, New York 1971.

G. Eliasson, *Business Economic Planning*, New York 1976.

———, *A Micro-to-Macro Model of the Swedish Economy*, Stockholm 1978.

B. M. Friedman, "Optimal Expectations and the Extreme Information Assumptions of 'Rational Expectations' Macromodels," *J. Monet. Econ.*, Jan. 1979 *5*, 23–41.

———, "A Discussion of the Methodological Premises of Professors Lucas and Sargent," in *After the Phillips Curve: The Persistence of High Inflation and High Unemployment*, Boston 1978.

Milton Friedman, *Essays in Positive Economics*, Chicago 1953.

J. R. Hayes and H. A. Simon, "Understanding Written Problem Instructions," in W. Gregg, ed., *Knowledge and Cognition*, Potomac 1974, 167–200.

A. O. Hirschman, *Exit, Voice and Loyalty*, Cambridge, Mass. 1970.

Charles C. Holt, Franco Modigliani, John F. Muth, and Herbert A. Simon, *Planning Production, Inventories and Work Force*, Englewood Cliffs 1960.

Y. Ijiri and H. A. Simon, *Skew Distributions and the Sizes of Business Firms*, Amsterdam 1977.

E. Johnsen, *Studies in Multiobjective Decision Models*, Lund 1968.

D. W. Jorgenson and C. D. Siebert, "A Comparison of Alternative Theories of Corporate Investment Behavior," *Amer. Econ. Rev.*, Sept. 1968, *58*, 681–712.

D. Kahneman and A. Tversky, "On the Psychology of Prediction," *Psychol. Rev.*, July 1973, *80*, 237–51.

Janos Kornai, *Anti-Equilibrium*, Amsterdam 1971.

Howard Kunreuther et al., *Disaster Insurance Protection: Public Policy Lessons*, New York 1978.

Harvey Leibenstein, *Beyond Economic Man*, Cambridge, Mass. 1976.

J. Lesourne, *A Theory of the Individual for Economic Analysis*, Vol. 1, Amsterdam 1977.

R. E. Lucas, Jr., "An Equilibrium Model of the Business Cycle," *J. Polit. Econ.*, Dec. 1975, *83*, 1113–44.

———, "On the Size Distribution of Business Firms," *Bell J. Econ.*, Autumn 1978, *9*, 508–23.

James G. March, *Handbook of Organizations*, Chicago 1965.

——— and H. A. Simon, *Organizations*, New York 1958.

Robin Marris, *The Economic Theory of "Managerial" Capitalism*, London 1964.

Jacob Marschak, "Role of Liquidity under Complete and Incomplete Information," *Amer. Econ. Rev. Proc.*, May 1949, *39*, 182–95.

——— and Roy Radner, *Economic Theory of Teams*, New Haven 1972.

Alfred Marshall, *Principles of Economics*, 8th ed., New York 1920.

E. S. Mason, "Comment," in Bernard T. Haley, ed., *A Survey of Contemporary Economics*, Vol. II, Homewood 1952, 221–22.

J. M. Montias, *The Structure of Economic Systems*, New Haven 1976.

J. F. Muth, "Rational Expectations and the Theory of Price Movements," *Econometrica*, July 1961, *29*, 315–53.

———, "Optimal Properties of Exponentially Weighted Forecasts," *J. Amer. Statist. Assn.*, June 1960, *55*, 299–306.

R. R. Nelson, and S. Winter, "Toward an Evolutionary Theory of Economic Capabilities," *Amer. Econ. Rev. Proc.*, May 1973, *63*, 440–49.

——— and ———, "Neoclassical vs. Evolutionary Theories of Economic Growth," *Econ. J.*, Dec. 1974, *84*, 886–905.

Allen Newell and Herbert A. Simon, *Human Problem Solving*, Englewood Cliffs, 1972.

——— and ———, "Computer Science as Empirical Inquiry: Symbols and Search," *Communications of the ACM*, Mar. 1976, *19*, 113–26.

G. Orcutt, and R. Caldwells-Wertheimer II, *Policy Exploration through Microanalytic Simulation*, Washington 1976.

A. Papandreou, "Some Basic Problems in the Theory of the Firm," in Bernard F. Haley, ed., *A Survey of Contemporary Economics*, Vol. II, Homewood 1952.

E. H. Phelps-Brown, "The Meaning of the Fitted Cobb-Douglas Function," *Quart. J. Econ.*, Nov. 1957, *71*, 546–60.

R. Radner, (1975a) "A Behavioral Model of Cost Reduction," *Bell J. Econ.*, Spring 1975, *6*, 196–215.

——, (1975b) "Satisficing," *J. Math. Econ.*, June–Sept. 1975, *2*, 253–62.

David R. Roberts, *Executive Compensation*, Glencoe 1959.

P. A. Samuelson, "Discussion: Problems of Methodology," *Amer. Econ. Rev. Proc.*, May 1963, *53*, 231–36.

Henry Schultz, *The Theory and Measurement of Demand*, Chicago 1938.

Herbert A. Simon, *Administrative Behavior*, New York 1947; 3d ed. 1976.

——, "A Formal Theory of the Employment Relation," *Econometrica*, July 1951, *19*, 293–305

——, "A Comparison of Organization Theories," *Rev. Econ. Stud.*, No. 1, 1952, *20*, 40–48.

——, "A Behavioral Model of Rational Choice," *Quart. J. Econ.*, Feb. 1955, *69*, 99–118.

——, "Rational Choice and the Structure of the Environment," *Psychol. Rev.*, Mar. 1956, *63*, 129–38.

——, "Dynamic Programming under Uncertainty with a Quadratic Criterion Function," *Econometrica*, Jan. 1956, *24*, 74–81.

——, *Models of Man*, New York 1957.

——, "The Compensation of Executives," *Sociometry*, 1957, *20*, 32–35.

——, "Theories of Decision Making in Economics and Behavioral Science," *Amer.*

Econ. Rev., June 1959, *49*, 223–83.

——, "Discussion: Problems of Methodology," *Amer. Econ. Rev. Proc.*, May 1963, *53*, 229–31.

——, "From Substantive to Procedural Rationality," in Spiro J. Latsis, ed., *Methodological Appraisal in Economics*, Cambridge 1976.

——, (1978a) "Rationality as Process and as Product of Thought," *Amer. Econ. Rev. Proc.*, May 1978, *68*, 1–16.

——, (1978b) "On How to Decide What to Do," *Bell J. Econ.*, Autumn 1978, *9*, 494–507.

——, G. Kozmetsky, H. Guetzkow, and G. Tyndall, *Centralization vs. Decentralization in Organizing the Controller's Department*, New York 1954; reprinted Houston 1978.

—— and F. K. Levy, "A Note on the Cobb-Douglas Function," *Rev. Econ. Stud.*, June 1963, *30*, 93–94.

G. J. Stigler, "The Economics of Information," *J. Polit. Econ.*, June 1961, *69*, 213–15.

H. Theil, "A Note on Certainty Equivalence in Dynamic Planning," *Econometrica*, Apr. 1957, *25*, 346–49.

John von Neumann and Oscar Morgenstern, *Theory of Games and Economic Behavior*, Princeton 1944.

A. A. Walters, "Production and Cost Functions: An Econometric Survey," *Econometrica*, Jan.–Apr. 1963, *31*, 1–66.

Oliver Williamson, *Markets and Hierarchies: Analysis and Antitrust Implications*, New York 1975.

S. Winter, "Satisficing, Selection, and the Innovating Remnant," *Quart. J. Econ.*, May 1971, *85*, 237–61.

Part II
Bounded Rationality (1): Overview

[5]

THEORIES OF BOUNDED RATIONALITY

HERBERT A. SIMON

1. Introduction. – 2. Approaches to rational choice in chess. – 3. Bounded rationality in design. – 4. Bounded rationality in management science. – 5. Conclusion.

1. Introduction

Rationality denotes a style of behavior that is appropriate to the achievement of given goals, within the limits imposed by given conditions and constraints. Theories of rational behavior may be normative or descriptive – that is, they may prescribe how people or organizations should behave in order to achieve certain goals under certain conditions, or they may purport to describe how people or organizations do, in fact, behave. This essay will be concerned with the structure of theories of rational behavior, whether they are intended prescriptively or descriptively.

Individual and organizational rationality. A theory of rational behavior may be concerned with the rationality of individuals or the rationality of organizations. In fact, the two bodies of theory are not wholly distinct.[1] One plausible distinction between them is that a theory of organizational rationality must treat the phenomena of goal conflict, while a theory of individual rationality need not. This is only partly correct, for goal conflict may be important in individual as in group behavior – it is a major theme of so-called "dissonance theory" in psychology. (See N. P. CHAPANIS and J. A. CHAPANIS (1964).) A theory of individual behavior microscopic enough to concern itself with the internal organization (neurological or functional) of the central nervous system will have a significant organizational component. A theory of organizational behavior macroscopic enough to treat the organization as a monolith will be a theory of an "individual." Although this chapter will be aimed primarily at understanding individual rationality, I shall not hesitate to use the theory of the firm – classically, the theory of a

---

[1] This point was made by J. MARSCHAK (1955) in his first paper on teams, "Elements for a Theory of Teams." I shall follow his good precedent.

monolithic entrepreneur – as a convenient and enlightening illustrative example.

From the standpoint of this chapter, then, the distinction between individual and organization will not be very important. A more significant taxonomy of theories of rational behavior, for our purposes, differentiates them by the assumptions they make about the "givens" – the given goals and given conditions. Particularly important is the distinction between those theories that locate all the conditions and constraints in the environment, outside the skin of the rational actor, and those theories that postulate important constraints arising from the limitations of the actor himself as an information processor. Theories that incorporate constraints on the information-processing capacities of the actor may be called *theories of bounded rationality*.

Rationality in the classical theory of the firm. The classical theory of the firm in its simplest form provides a useful standard for comparing and differentiating theories of rationality. In the theory of the firm, the given objective is to maximize profits, where profit is defined as the difference between gross receipts from sales and cost of production. The given conditions are two in number:

(I) *the demand function*: the quantity demanded is a function of price:

(1) $$q_d = D(p), \text{ or } p = D^{-1}(q_d).$$

Since gross receipts equal price times quantity, the demand function determines gross receipts:

(2) $$R = pq_d.$$

(II) *the cost function*: the cost of production is a function of the quantity produced:

(3) $$C = C(q_s).$$

If the quantity produced equals the quantity demanded,

(4) $$q_s = q_d,$$

then the profit, to be maximized, is simply the difference between gross receipts and the cost of production:

(5) $$\text{Profit} = R - C = pq - C(q),$$

and, under appropriate assumptions regarding differentiability, we will

§1.   INTRODUCTION   163

have for the maximum profit:

(6) $d(R - C)/dq = p + qd(D^{-1}(q))/dq - dC(q)/dq = 0$.

The constraints in this theory, the demand and cost functions, D and C, are both located in the actor's environment. He is assumed to find the solution of equation (6). To do this, he must have perfect knowledge of these constraints, and must be able to perform the necessary calculations – to set the derivative of profit with respect to quantity equal to zero and to solve the resulting algebraic equation.

The limits of rationality. Theories of bounded rationality can be constructed by modifying these assumptions in a variety of ways. *Risk and uncertainty* can be introduced into the demand function, the cost function, or both. For example, certain parameters of one or both of these functions can be assumed to be random variables with known distributions. Then the assumption of the actor's perfect knowledge of these functions has been replaced by the assumption that he has perfect knowledge of their distributions. This change in assumptions may, in turn, make it easier or more difficult to carry out the calculations for finding the optimum – usually it becomes much more difficult than in the corresponding case of certainty.

Another way in which rationality can be bounded is by assuming that the actor has only *incomplete information about alternatives*. Fewer models have been constructed to deal with this situation than with the situation in which he has incomplete information about consequences. However, in certain search models it is assumed that the actor knows the probability distribution of profits in a population of possible alternative actions. Specific actions become available to him – say, by random sampling from this population – as a function of the amount of resources he devotes to search. His task is to find the alternative that maximizes his expected profit net of the search cost. In this class of models, selecting the best alternative from among those already discovered is assumed to be a trivial problem; the decision question has been switched to the question of how much of the actor's resources should be allocated to search.[2]

---

[2] For an example, see STIGLER (1961). Theories of the allocation of resources to search can also be constructed to deal with incomplete information about consequences. Sequential sampling theory falls into this category, for it answers the question: shall I make a decision now, or wait until I have gathered additional information? The question is answered by comparing the incremental cost of enlarging the sample with the expected gain through the resulting average improvement in the decision.

164   THEORIES OF BOUNDED RATIONALITY

Finally, rationality can be bounded by assuming *complexity* in the cost function or other environmental constraints so great as to prevent the actor from calculating the best course of action. Limits on rationality stemming from this source have not been prominent in classical theories of rational behavior. However, in numerical analysis, the theory of approximation provides analogues, for it is concerned with the rate at which an approximation can be expected to improve as a function of amount of computational effort. By introducing explicitly into that theory the cost of computational effort, it can be transformed into a theory of optimal approximation.

Alternatives to the classical goals. The classical theory can be modified not only by altering the nature of the conditions and constraints, but also by altering the nature of the given goals. Some modern theories of the firm depart from the classical theory, not along any of the dimensions mentioned above, but by postulating different goals from the classical goal of profit maximization.

BAUMOL (1959, pp. 45–53), for example, has developed a model in which the firm maximizes sales subject to the constraint that profit should not be less than a specified "satisfactory" level. According to this theory of Baumol, equation (6) in the classical model should be replaced by:

(6') $$dR/dq = p + qd(D^{-1}(q))/dq = 0,$$

subject to the constraint that

(7) $$P = R - C \geq P^*.$$

It may be observed that the informational and computational requirements for applying Baumol's theory to concrete situations are not very different from the requirements of the classical model.

This essay will not be concerned with variants of the theory of rationality that assume goals different from profit or utility maximization, except to the extent that there is significant interaction between the assumptions about goals and the assumptions about conditions and constraints. We shall see, however, that this is a very important exception. In actual fact, most of the variants of the theory that make significant modifications in the assumptions about conditions and constraints also call for assumptions about goals that are different from the classical assumptions of profit or utility maximization. The reasons for this interaction will appear as we proceed.

2. Approaches to Rational Choice in Chess

A number of the persons who have engaged in research on rational decision-making have taken the game of chess as a microcosm that mirrors interesting properties of decision-making situations in the real world. The research on rational choice in chess provides some useful illustrations of alternative approaches to rationality.

The problem confronting a chess player whose turn it is to move can be interpreted in either of two ways. First, it can be interpreted as a problem of finding a good (or the best) strategy – where "strategy" means a conditional sequence of moves, defining what move will be made at each successive stage after each possible response of the opponent.

Second, the problem can be interpreted as one of finding a set of accurate evaluations for the alternative moves immediately before the player.

From a classical standpoint, these two problems are not distinguishable. If the player has unlimited computational power, it does not matter whether he selects a complete strategy for his future behavior in the game, or selects each of his moves, one at a time, when it is his turn to play. For the way in which he goes about evaluating the next move is by constructing alternative complete strategies for the entire future play of the game, and selecting the one that promises the best return (i.e., the best return under the assumption that the opponent will also do *his* best to win). This is the approach taken in the von Neumann-Morgenstern theory of games (VON NEUMANN and MORGENSTERN (1953)).

The game-theoretical definition of rationality in chess. As von Neumann and Morgenstern observed, chess is a trivial game. "... if the theory of Chess (i.e., the complete tree of possible games) were really fully known there would be nothing left to play" (*ibid.*, p. 125). Each terminus of the tree of possible games represents a win, loss, or draw for White. Moving backward one branch on the tree, the player whose move it is at that branch can examine the termini to which it could lead by his choice of move, and can choose the move having the preferred terminus. The value of that terminus becomes, then, the value of the branch that leads to it. Working backward in this way, a value – win, lose, or draw for White – can be assigned to each position, and ultimately to each of the initial legal moves for White. Now each player can specify an optimal strategy – a strategy that will guarantee him at least as good an outcome as any other – by specifying which move he would select at each branch point in the tree whenever it is his move.

Unfortunately, as von Neumann and Morgenstern also observed, the triviality of chess offers no practical help to a player in actually choosing a move. "But our proof, which guarantees the validity of one (and only one) of these three alternatives [that the game must have the value of win lose or draw for White], gives no practically usable method to determine the true one. This relative, human difficulty necessitates the use of those incomplete, heuristic methods of playing, which constitute 'good' Chess; and without it there would be no element of 'struggle' and 'surprise' in that game" (*ibid.*).

What "impracticality" means becomes more vivid when we calculate how much search would be involved in finding the game-theoretically correct strategy in chess. On the average, at any given position in a game of chess, there are about 30 legal moves – in round numbers, for a move and its replies, an average of about 10^3 continuations. Forty moves would be a not unreasonable estimate of the average length of a game. Then there would be perhaps 10^{120} possible games of chess. Obviously the exact number does not matter: a number like 10^{40} would be less spectacular, but quite large enough to support the conclusions of the present argument.

Studies of the decision-making of chess players indicate strongly that strong players seldom look at as many as one hundred possibilities – that is one hundred continuations from the given position – in selecting a move or strategy. One hundred is a reasonably large number, by some standards, but somewhat smaller than 10^{120}! Chess players do not consider all possible strategies and pick the best, but generate and examine a rather small number, making a choice as soon as they discover one that they regard as satisfactory (see DE GROOT (1965)).

Before we consider in detail how they do it, let us return to the classical model and ask whether there is any way in which we could make it relevant to the practical choice problem, taking account of the size of the problem space, in a game like chess. One possible way would be to replace the actual problem space with a very much smaller space that approximates the actual one in some appropriate sense, and then apply the classical theory to the smaller approximate space.

This approach was taken in some of the early computer programs for playing chess and checkers. In the Los Alamos program, for example, the computer generated all legal moves, all legal replies to each, and so on, two moves deep. Each of the terminal positions thus generated (about a million in a two-move analysis) was evaluated, and the minimax procedure applied, working backwards, to find the best first move. Thus, a space of about

§2.   RATIONAL CHOICE IN CHESS   167

10^6 elements was substituted for the space of 10^{120} elements that represents the "real" world of chess.

The scheme was approximate, because the actual chess values of the million terminal positions were not known, and could not be known accurately without returning to the space of 10^{120} elements – that is, returning to the game-theoretical analysis of the full game. In place of these unknown true values, approximate values were computed, using rules of thumb that are commonly employed by chess players – conventional numerical values for the pieces, and measures of mobility. Thus, the approximate scheme was not guaranteed to select the objectively best move, but only the move leading to the positions that appeared best, in terms of these heuristic criteria, after an analysis two moves deep. Experience indicates that it is not possible to make such approximate evaluations accurately enough to enable the program to play good chess. The optimal decision in the approximated world is not necessarily even a good decision in the real world.

Satisficing processes in chess thinking. Chess programs now exist that take the alternative course, trying to emulate the human chess player in looking at only a very few continuations. The effectiveness of such a scheme depends critically on three components: the *move generators*, processes that select the continuations to be explored; the *evaluators*, processes that determine how good each continuation is; and the *stop rules*, criteria that determine when the search should be terminated and a move selected.

By scanning a chess position, features of the position can be detected that suggest appropriate moves. To take an extreme case, suppose a chess player discovers, when it is his move, that one of his Pawns attacks the opponent's Queen. Obviously, the capture of the Queen by the Pawn is one move that deserves consideration. It may turn out to be a poor move – another piece will checkmate him, say, if he captures the Queen – but its superficial merits are obvious, and its deficiencies can only be detected by considering it and evaluating it dynamically. A simple process that would generate this move, and others like it, would consist in determining which of the opponent's pieces were attacked by a piece of lesser value, or were undefended and attacked by any piece. Thus, a suitable set of move-generating processes might identify for further analysis all or most of the moves deserving serious consideration. If the generators were ordered appropriately, they might usually identify first the most promising moves, then the ones slightly less promising, and so on.

Possible moves, produced by the move generators, can be evaluated by a combination of static and dynamic criteria. Static criteria are features of the position, or differences between successive positions. Thus, one of the important static evaluators used by all chess players is the piece count: each piece is assigned a conventional value (say, Pawn = 1, Knight and Bishop = 3, Rook = 5, Queen = 9), and the sums of the values for the two players are compared. In general, if the piece count of one player exceeds that of the other by more than one point (or even, in many cases, by a single point), the player with the higher count can find a winning continuation *unless* the balance is very quickly redressed by a sequence of forceful moves. (Thus, it does not matter being 5 points down if you can capture the opponent's Queen on the next move without further reprisals.)

The short-run tactical considerations are handled by carrying out dynamic analysis of plausible continuations until a position is reached that is sufficiently quiet or "dead" that it can safely be evaluated by means of the static evaluators. These static evaluators are then propagated backwards to the move under consideration by the familiar minimax procedure.

Two kinds of stop rules are needed in a program having this structure: rules to stop exploration at dead positions that can be evaluated statically, and rules to stop the entire process and select a move when a satisfactory one has been found. The former class of stop rules has already been discussed; the latter needs to be examined more closely. If the alternatives in a choice situation are not given, but have to be discovered or invented, and if the number of possible alternatives is very large, then a choice has to be made before all or most of them have been looked at. It was precisely this difficulty in the classical requirement of comparing all alternatives that led to the approach described here. But if all alternatives are not to be examined, some criterion must be used to determine that an adequate, or satisfactory, one has been found. In the psychological literature, criteria that perform this function in decision processes are called *aspiration levels*. The Scottish word "satisficing" (= satisfying) has been revived to denote problem solving and decision making that sets an aspiration level, searches until an alternative is found that is satisfactory by the aspiration level criterion, and selects that alternative (SIMON (1957), Part IV).

In satisficing procedures, the existence of a satisfactory alternative is made likely by dynamic mechanisms that adjust the aspiration levels to reality on the basis of information about the environment. Thus, in a chess-playing program, the initial aspiration level can be set (preferably with a little upward bias) on the basis of a static evaluation of the position. As alternative moves are considered and evaluated by dynamic and static analysis, the evaluation of the position can gradually be reduced until the best move discovered so far reaches or exceeds in value the aspiration level.

The limits of rationality in chess. In the introductory section of this paper, three limits on perfect rationality were listed: uncertainty about the consequences that would follow from each alternative, incomplete information about the set of alternatives, and complexity preventing the necessary computations from being carried out. Chess illustrates how, in real world problem-solving situations, these three categories tend to merge.

If we describe the chess player as choosing a *strategy*, then his difficulty in behaving rationally – and the impossibility of his behaving as game theory says he should – resides in the fact that he has incomplete information as to what alternatives (strategies) are open to him. He has time to discover only a minute fraction of these strategies, and to specify the ones he discovers only incompletely.

Alternatively, if we describe the chess player as choosing a *move*, his difficulty in behaving rationally lies in the fact that he has only rough information about the consequences of adopting each of the alternatives (moves) that is open to him. It would not be impossible for him to generate the whole set of his legal moves, for they seldom number more than about thirty. However, he can evaluate them, even approximately, only by carrying out further analysis through the immense, branching, move tree. Since only a limited amount of processing time is available for the evaluation, he must allocate the time among the alternative moves. The practical facts of the matter are that it is usually better to generate only a few of the entire set of legal moves, evaluating these rather thoroughly, than it is to generate all of them, evaluating them superficially. Hence the good chess player does not examine all the moves open to him, but only a small fraction of them. (Data presented by DE GROOT (1965) suggest that typically a half dozen to a dozen of a set of thirty legal moves may be generated and explored by the chess player.)

From still a third standpoint, the chess player's difficulty in behaving rationally has nothing to do with uncertainty – whether of consequences or alternatives – but is a matter of complexity. For there is no risk or uncertainty, in the sense in which those terms are used in economics or statistical decision theory, in the game of chess. As von Neumann and Morgenstern observe, it is a game of perfect information. No probabilities of future events need enter the calculations, and no contingencies, in a statistical sense, arise.

From a game-theoretical standpoint, the presence of the opponent does not introduce contingencies. The opponent can always be counted on to do his worst. The point becomes clear if we replace the task of playing chess with the task of proving theorems. In the latter task, there is no opponent. Nor are there contingencies: the true and the derivable theorems reside eternally in Plato's heaven. Rationality in theorem proving is a problem only because the maze of possible proof paths is vast and complex.

What we refer to as "uncertainty" in chess or theorem proving, therefore, is uncertainty introduced into a perfectly certain environment by inability – computational inability – to ascertain the structure of that environment. But the result of the uncertainty, whatever its source, is the same: approximation must replace exactness in reaching a decision. In particular, when the uncertainty takes the form of an unwieldy problem space to be explored, the problem-solving process must incorporate mechanisms for determining when the search or evaluation will stop and an alternative will be chosen.

Satisficing and optimizing. The terms satisficing and optimizing, which we have already introduced, are labels for two broad approaches to rational behavior in situations where complexity and uncertainty make global rationality impossible. In these situations, optimization becomes approximate optimization – the description of the real-world situation is radically simplified until reduced to a degree of complication that the decision maker can handle. Satisficing approaches seek this simplification in a somewhat different direction, retaining more of the detail of the real-world situation, but settling for a satisfactory, rather than an approximate-best, decision. One cannot predict in general which approach will lead to the better decisions as measured by their real-world consequences. In chess at least, good players have clearly found satisficing more useful than approximating-and-optimizing.

A satisficing decision procedure can often be turned into a procedure for optimizing by introducing a rule for optimal amount of search, or, what amounts to the same thing, a rule for fixing the aspiration level optimally. Thus, the aspiration level in chess might be adjusted, dynamically, to such a level that the expected improvement in the move chosen, per minute of additional search, would just balance the incremental cost of the search.

Although such a translation is formally possible, to carry it out in practice requires additional information and assumptions beyond those needed for satisficing. First, the values of alternatives must be measured in units comparable with the units for measuring search cost, in order to permit comparison at the margins. Second, the marginal productivity of search – the expected increase in the value per unit of search time – must be estimated on some basis or other. If one were designing a chess-playing program, it is doubtful whether effort spent in attempting to imbed the program in such a dynamic optimizing framework would be nearly as worthwhile as equivalent effort spent in improving the selectivity of the program's move-generating and move-evaluating heuristics.

Another quite different translation between optimizing and satisficing schemes has also been suggested from time to time. A chess program of the "classical" type, which makes optimal decisions in an approximated world, can be regarded as a particular kind of satisficing program, in which "satisfactory" is defined by the approximating procedure that is used. Hence, it is difficult to draw a formal distinction between optimizing and satisficing procedures that is so iron-clad as to prevent either from being reinterpreted in the frame of the other. The practical difference, however – the difference in emphasis that results from adopting one viewpoint or the other – is often very great.

In research on optimizing procedures, considerable attention has been paid to the formal properties of the evaluation functions, to the existence and efficiency of procedures for computing the optimum, and to procedures for reducing uncertainty (e.g., forecasting methods). The nature of the approximations that are necessary to cast real-world problems into forms suitable for optimization, and the means for choosing among alternative approximations, have been less fully and less systematically studied. Much effort, for example, has gone into the discovery of efficient algorithms for solving linear programming problems. Finding an appropriate way of formulating a concrete real-world decision problem as a linear-programming problem remains largely an art.[3]

Research on satisficing procedures has focussed primarily on the efficiency of search – on the nature of the heuristic methods that enable the rare solutions in enormous spaces of possibilities to be sought and found with moderate amounts of search effort. Since moderate changes in heuristics often make order-of-magnitude changes in search effectiveness, highly accurate means for assessing the quality of solutions or the effort required to find them may be relatively unimportant. It probably does not require delicate evaluation functions or stop rules to change a duffer's chess play to a reasonably effective move-choosing program.

---

[3] The work of A. CHARNES and W. W. COOPER (1961) is full of sophisticated examples of this art. See, for instances, Appendix B and Chapter 11 of Volume I.

3. Bounded Rationality in Design

The engineering activities usually called "design" have not been much discussed under the heading of rational decision-making. The reason for this should be clear from the foregoing discussion: classical decision theory has been concerned with choice among *given* alternatives; design is concerned with the discovery and elaboration of alternatives. Our exploration of the microcosm of chess has indicated, however, how the theory of design can be assimilated to a satisficing theory of rational choice. Let me spell the point out a little more fully.

Consider that interpretation of chess which views the task as one of choosing a strategy, and not just a single move. Specifically, consider a situation where a player is searching for a combination (a strategy) that will definitely checkmate his opponent, even though it may require sacrifices of pieces along the way. A chess player will ordinarily not enter into such a course of action unless he can see it through to the end – unless he can *design*, that is, a water-tight mating combination.

As we have seen already, the evaluations and comparisons that take place during this design process are not, in general, comparisons among complete designs. Evaluations take place, first of all, to guide the search – the elaboration of the design itself. They provide the basis for decisions that the design should be elaborated in one direction rather than another. Complete designs (in this case, mating combinations), when they are finally arrived at, are not generally evaluated by comparing them with alternative designs, but by comparing them with standards defined by aspiration levels. In the chess situation, as soon as the player discovers a strategy that guarantees a checkmate, he adopts it. He does not look for all possible checkmating strategies and adopt the best (H. A. SIMON and P. A. SIMON (1962)).

In the design of complex objects – a bridge, say, or an airplane – the process has an even more involved search structure. Here, the early stages of search take place in highly simplified spaces that abstract most of the detail from the real-world problem, leaving only its most important elements in summarized form. When a plan, a schematized and aggregated design, has been elaborated in the planning space, the detail of the problem can be reintroduced, and the plan used as a guide in the search for a complete design.

More than two spaces may be used, of course; there may be a whole hierarchy of planning spaces, leading from a highly abstract and global design to successive specification of detail. At each of these levels of abstraction, the design process, too, may be differently structured. Since the more abstract spaces tend to be "smoother," it is often possible to use optimization models for planning purposes, reverting to satisficing search models to fill in the detail of the design. Thus, linear programming or dynamic programming may be used for general planning of factory operations, while more heuristic techniques are used for scheduling of individual jobs. In other situations, the overall design process may employ satisficing search procedures, while optimizing techniques may be used to set parameters once the general design has been fixed.[4]

4. Bounded Rationality in Management Science

Most of the formal techniques that constitute the technical backbone of management science and operations research are procedures for finding the best of a set of alternatives in terms of some criterion – that is, they fall in our category of "classical" procedures. Linear and dynamic programming are among the most powerful of these techniques. The dominant approach to problems in this sphere has been to simplify the real-world problems to the point where the formal optimizing models can be used as approximations.

Some industrial problems of a combinatorial sort have not yielded easily to this approach. Typically, the recalcitrant problems involve integer solutions, or, what usually amounts to the same thing, the consideration of possible permutations and combinations of a substantial number of elements. Warehouse location is a problem of this kind. The task is to "determine the geographical pattern of warehouse locations which will be most profitable to the company by equating the marginal cost of warehouse operation with the transportation cost savings and incremental profits resulting from more rapid delivery" (KUEHN and HAMBURGER (1963), p. 643).

A heuristic program devised by KUEHN and HAMBURGER (1963) for locating warehouses has two parts: "(1) the main program, which locates warehouses one at a time until no additional warehouses can be added to the distribution network without increasing total costs, and (2) the bump and shift routine, ..., which attempts to modify solutions ... by evaluating the profit implications of dropping individual warehouses or of shifting them from one location to another" (ibid., p. 645).

---

[4] Some modern semi-automated procedures for the design of chemical processing plants proceed from heuristic techniques for selecting the unit operations and their flow, then employ linear programming to determine the parameters of the system so specified.

This program fits our earlier characterization of design procedures. A possible plan is gradually built up, step by step, through a search procedure, and then possible local modifications are investigated before the final plan is settled upon. In building up the initial plan, locations are tried that are near concentrations of demand, adding at each step the warehouse that produces the greatest cost savings for the entire system. Only a fraction of the possible warehouse sites, which preliminary screening selects as "promising," are evaluated in detail at each stage. Finally, a so-called "bump-shift" routine modifies the programs tentatively arrived at by (1) eliminating warehouses no longer economical because new warehouses have been introduced at later steps of the program, (2) considering shifting warehouses to alternative sites within their territories. The flow diagram of the warehouse location programs, which will serve to illustrate the typical structure of heuristic programs when they are formalized, is shown in Fig. 1.

Kuehn and Hamburger have carried out some detailed comparisons of the heuristic program with optimizing techniques. They conclude that "in theory, a linear programming approach ... could be used to solve the problem. In practice, however, the size and nonlinearities involved in many problems are such that application is not currently feasible" (*ibid.*, p. 658). They attribute the superior performance of the heuristic program to two main causes: "(1) computational simplicity, which results in substantial reductions in solution times and permits the treatment of large-scale problems, and (2) flexibility with respect to the underlying cost functions, eliminating the need for restrictive assumptions" (*ibid.*, p. 656).

Perhaps the technique most widely used in management science to deal with situations too complex for the application of known optimization methods is simulation. The amount of detail incorporated in the simulation of a large system is limited only by computational feasibility. On the other hand, simulation, unaided by other formal tools of analysis, provides no direct means for discovering and evaluating alternative plans of action. In simulation, the trial and error is supplied by the human investigators rather than by the technique of analysis itself (see FORRESTER (1961)).

5. Conclusion

The theory of rational decision has undergone extremely rapid development in the past thirty years. A considerable part of the impetus for this development came, during and since World War II, from the attempt to use formal decision procedures in actual real-world situations of considerable

A HEURISTIC PROGRAM FOR LOCATING WAREHOUSES

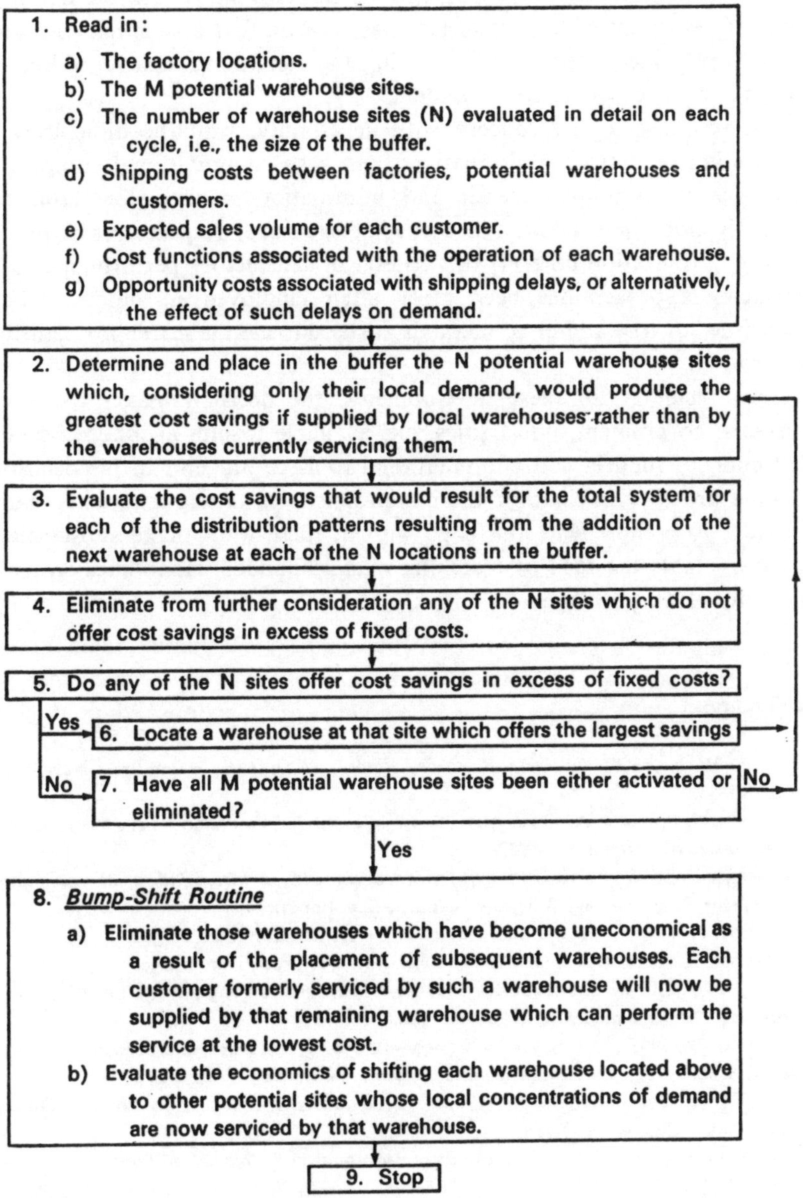

1. Read in:
   a) The factory locations.
   b) The M potential warehouse sites.
   c) The number of warehouse sites (N) evaluated in detail on each cycle, i.e., the size of the buffer.
   d) Shipping costs between factories, potential warehouses and customers.
   e) Expected sales volume for each customer.
   f) Cost functions associated with the operation of each warehouse.
   g) Opportunity costs associated with shipping delays, or alternatively, the effect of such delays on demand.

2. Determine and place in the buffer the N potential warehouse sites which, considering only their local demand, would produce the greatest cost savings if supplied by local warehouses rather than by the warehouses currently servicing them.

3. Evaluate the cost savings that would result for the total system for each of the distribution patterns resulting from the addition of the next warehouse at each of the N locations in the buffer.

4. Eliminate from further consideration any of the N sites which do not offer cost savings in excess of fixed costs.

5. Do any of the N sites offer cost savings in excess of fixed costs?

   Yes → 6. Locate a warehouse at that site which offers the largest savings

   No → 7. Have all M potential warehouse sites been either activated or eliminated? → No

   Yes ↓

8. *Bump-Shift Routine*
   a) Eliminate those warehouses which have become uneconomical as a result of the placement of subsequent warehouses. Each customer formerly serviced by such a warehouse will now be supplied by that remaining warehouse which can perform the service at the lowest cost.
   b) Evaluate the economics of shifting each warehouse located above to other potential sites whose local concentrations of demand are now serviced by that warehouse.

9. Stop

Fig. 1.   Flow diagram

176   THEORIES OF BOUNDED RATIONALITY

complexity. To deal with this complexity the formal models have grown in power and sophistication. But complexity has also stimulated the development of new kinds of models of rational decision that take special account of the very limited information-gathering and computing capacity of human beings and their associated computers.

One response to the concern with uncertainty, with the difficulties of discovering or designing alternatives, and with computational complexity has been to introduce search and information transmission processes explicitly into the models. Another (not exclusive) response has been to replace optimization criteria with criteria of satisfactory performance. The satisficing approach has been most often employed in models where "heuristic" or trial-and-error methods are used to aid the search for plausible alternatives.

As a result of all these developments, the decision maker today, in business, government, universities, has available to him an unprecedented collection of models and computational tools to aid him in his decision-making processes. Whatever the compromises he must make with reality in order to comprehend and cope with it, these tools make substantially more tractable the task of matching man's bounded capabilities with the difficulty of his problems.

References

BAUMOL, W. J. (1959), *Business Behavior, Value and Growth*, Macmillan, New York, pp. 45–53.

CHAPANIS, N. P. and J. A. CHAPANIS (1964), "Cognitive Dissonance: Five Years Later," *Psychological Bulletin*, *61*, 1023.

CHARNES, A. and W. W. COOPER (1961), *Management Models and Industrial Applications of Linear Programming*, Wiley, New York, (2 volumes).

DE GROOT, A. (1965), *Thought and Choice in Chess*, Mouton, The Hague.

FORRESTER, J. W. (1961), *Industrial Dynamics*, M.I.T. Press, Cambridge.

KUEHN, A. A. and M. J. HAMBURGER (1963), "A Heuristic Program for Locating Warehouses," *Management Science*, *9*, 643-666.

MARSCHAK, J. (1955), "Elements for a Theory of Teams," *Management Science*, *1*, 127–137

SIMON, H. A. (1957), Part IV in *Models of Man*, Wiley, New York, pp. 196–279.

SIMON, H. A. and P. A. SIMON (1962), "Trial and Error Search in Solving Difficult Problems," *Behavioral Science*, *7*, 425–429.

STIGLER, G. J. (1961), "The Economics of Information," *Journal of Political Economy*, *69*, 213–225.

VON NEUMANN, J. and O. MORGENSTERN (1953), *Theory of Games and Economic Behavior*, (3rd ed.), Princeton University Press, Princeton, pp. 125.

[6]

Journal of Mathematical Economics 2 (1975) 253–262. © North-Holland Publishing Company

SATISFICING*

Roy RADNER

University of California, Berkeley, Calif., U.S.A.

1. Introduction

As decision theorists have succeeded in extending their analyses into new domains, and have aspired to new levels of both realism and rigor, they have attempted to apply the rationality postulate to more and more complicated decision problems. In particular, decision theorists have become more concerned with the complexities associated with time, uncertainty, and interpersonal conflict and cooperation; and advances in mathematical theories of optimization, statistical decision-making, and games have provided new concepts and tools for the study of rational behavior in the face of such complexities.

Nevertheless, the very success and expansion of these theories have brought into sharper focus a deep problem for the widespread application of the rationality postulate in decision theory. It is now clear that specialists are far from finding 'optimal solutions' to such restricted problems as (1) the management of a network of warehouses under general conditions of uncertain demand, (2) winning a game of chess, or (3) administering a department of mathematics. It is probably not good positive theory to take very seriously an assumption that anyone behaves according to a sequential strategy that maximizes an expected lifetime (or infinite horizon) utility, nor is it good advice to a manager to recommend adoption of the solution of an optimization problem that there is no prospect of solving in the next hundred years.

In other words, decision theory is facing more and more clearly the problem of *the limits of rationality*. I am not speaking here simply of what is often described as the cost of information, but rather of the limited capacities of humans (and machines) for imagination and computation. These limits create theoretical problems on at least two levels. First, there is the profound logical or philosophical problem of defining what one means by 'rationality' in the

*Presented at the Mathematical Social Science Board Colloquium on Mathematical Economics in August 1974 at the University of California, Berkeley. This paper is based on research supported by the National Science Foundation, U.S.A.

L

presence of such limits;[1] I shall not discuss this problem here. Second, there is the problem of describing, in terms amenable to theoretical analysis, the different ways humans do behave in complex decision-making situations, and of deducing the consequences of different modes of behavior.

If we are not to discard entirely the rationality postulate in economic theory, then we must elaborate more sophisticated and empirically relevant concepts of rational behavior, which nevertheless retain the important insights provided by the notion of 'economic man'. Simon has used the term *bounded rationality* to describe such behavior.[2] I shall not attempt here to give a precise definition of bounded rationality. However, three aspects of bounded rationality do seem important for decision theory: (1) existence of goals, (2) search for improvement, and (3) long-run success.

It is no doubt useful to explain much of economic behavior in terms of 'goals' or 'motives', and normative economics would appear to be meaningless without reference to goals. On the other hand, an individual economic agent may have 'conflicting' goals, and it may be bad psychology in many instances to assume that these conflicts are resolved in terms of a single transitive preference ordering. Such conflicts may be 'resolved' in a dynamic way by various mechanisms for switching attention and effort, with results that do not appear to be transitive. (There are, perhaps, useful analogies between individuals with conflicting goals and groups of individuals with conflicting interests.) Also, the set of goals may be endogenous, so that, through time, some goals may be dropped and others added to the list.

Even if the theorist draws back from assuming that economic agents behave according to optimal lifetime strategies, it is no doubt useful to postulate that they search for improvements, at least from time to time, and that they take advantage of perceived improvements. How, and under what circumstances, agents search for improvements, and how these improvements are perceived, is, of course, an important subject of study. If repeated improvements can be made in the solution of the same problem, then we have a situation of 'expanding rationality'. On the other hand, an environment that changes at unpredictable times and in unpredictable directions may make past improvements obsolete, so that the individual is engaged in a race between improvement and obsolescence.

A strategy of search may itself be the object of an improvement effort (as in the planning of research and development), but this leads to a 'regression' in the model of decision-making; one eventually reaches a level of behavior at which it is no longer fruitful to assume that the search for improvement is itself being conducted 'optimally'.

---

[1]See, for example, Savage (1954, pp. 8–17, 59, 83) and Marschak and Radner (1972, pp. 314–317).

[2]Simon's description is somewhat more general: 'Theories that incorporate constraints on the information-processing capacities of the actor may be called *theories of bounded rationality*.' [See H.A. Simon, Chapter 8 of McGuire and Radner (1972); see, also, Simon (1959).]

The notion of 'adjustment', as it has commonly been used in economic theory, is in the spirit of bounded rationality in the following sense. At a given date the economic agent adopts a particular action (or strategy) that is optimal with respect to the agent's formulation of the decision problem and the agent's 'expectations'. At the next date, the agent receives new information, which causes him to revise his expectations in *a way that was not anticipated at the previous date*, or even causes him to revise his formulation of the decision problem. This revision of expectations or of problem formulation is to be distinguished from the behavior of a Bayesian statistician with an optimal sequential decision rule, who periodically revises his a posteriori probability distribution on the states of the environment in response to new information, according to a well-defined and completely anticipated (optimal) transformation.

In a similar spirit, a realistic treatment of the search for improvement in a theory of bounded rationality would not follow the present lines of development of the theory of optimal search.[3] Optimal search theory began with a few interesting theorems showing that for some simple search problems the optimal policies could be described in terms of 'aspiration levels' and 'satisficing'. To take a well-known example, suppose that one is searching for larger values in a sequence of independent and identically distributed random variables (with known probability distribution), but there is a constant cost per observation. If one's objective is to maximize the expected value of the difference between the largest value observed and the total cost of observation, then the optimal sequential stopping rule is characterized by an 'aspiration level', i.e., there exists a number, the aspiration level, such that one stops searching as soon as one observes a value that is greater than or equal to the aspiration level. However, there are fairly simple (and plausible) examples of search problems in which the optimal policy cannot be characterized by an aspiration level, or even by a rule that determines the aspiration level at each date as a function of the past history of observations. Rather than attempt to characterize optimal search in a greater variety of more and more complicated problems, the theorist following the approach of bounded rationality would observe that aspiration-level and satisficing behavior is common, even in complicated problems, and would endeavor to understand the implications of such behavior in a variety of situations.

In this lecture, I shall explore the consequences of satisficing in the context of a simple model of the allocation of an agent's effort to the search for improvement in one or more activities. For any fixed allocation of effort, the performance of each activity is assumed to be a random walk, or more generally, a semi-martingale. The expected rate of change per unit time for each activity depends on the effort allocated to it. This expected rate of change is positive if all of the agent's effort is allocated to the activity, and negative if none is. A behavior is

[3]See, for example, MacQueen (1964) and Rothschild (1974).

a rule that determines, at each date, the current allocation of effort among the activities as a function of the past history of performance up to that date.

In such a model, performance of the several activities will typically not approach a steady state, even in a stochastic sense, except for very special values of the parameters. In these notes, I examine 'long-run success' (i.e., asymptotic performance) with respect to two criteria: (1) the probability of survival, i.e., the probability that performance on one or more activities never falls below certain prescribed levels, and (2) the long-run average rate of growth per unit time.

2. Single objective

2.1. General formulation of a satisficing process

I start with a general formulation of a process of intermittent search for improvement with respect to a single objective. Consider a basic probability space (X, F, P), where F is a sigma-field of subsets of X, and P is a probability measure on F. Let F_t, $t = 0, 1, 2, \ldots$, be an increasing sequence of sub-fields of F; F_t is to be interpreted as the set of observable events through date t. Let $\{U(t)\}$ be a corresponding sequence of integer-valued random variables on X, such that $U(t)$ is F_t-measurable; $U(t)$ will be called the *performance at* t, relative to a given single objective. Finally, let T_n, $n = 0, 1, 2, \ldots$, be a non-decreasing sequence of random times, possibly taking on the value plus infinity, such that $T_n < T_{n+1}$ if T_n is finite; for n odd, T_n is to be interpreted as a date at which a period of search for improvement begins, and T_{n+1} as the date at which that period ends. [A random time T is an integer-valued random variable, possibly equal to plus infinity, such that the event $(T = t)$ is F_t-measurable.] Take $T_0 = 0$.

An interval $(T_n \leq t < T_{n+1})$ will be called a *search period* if n is odd and a *rest period* if n is even. To capture the idea of intermittent search for improvement I assume, for $T_n \leq t < T_{n+1}$,

$$E[U(t+1) \mid F_t] \geq U(t), \qquad \text{if } n \text{ is odd},$$
$$E[U(t+1) \mid F_t] \leq U(t), \qquad \text{if } n \text{ is even}. \tag{1}$$

In other words, $U(t)$ is a sub-martingale during the search periods, and a super-martingale during the rest periods.

To capture the idea of 'satisficing', let $\{S(t)\}$ be a sequence of random variables such that $S(t)$ is F_t-measurable; $S(t)$ is to be interpreted as the 'satisfactory level of performance' at date t. The random times T_n are determined by, for n even,

$$T_{n+1} \text{ is the first } t > T_n \quad \text{such that } U(t) < S(t),$$
$$T_{n+2} \text{ is the first } t > T_{n+1} \text{ such that } U(t) \geq S(t); \tag{2}$$

this is qualified by the convention that, for any n, if T_n is infinite, then so is T_m for every $m > n$.

In the next sections, more specific assumptions will be made about the processes $U(t)$ and $S(t)$.

2.2. A favorable satisficing process

Let $Z(t)$ be the successive increments of the process $U(t)$; thus $Z(t+1) = U(t+1) - U(t)$. Let ξ, η, and β be given positive numbers. For $T_n \leq t < T_{n+1}$, assume, for n even (rest),

$$E[Z(t+1) \mid F_t] \leq -\xi,$$
$$S(t) = U(T_n) - \beta + 1; \tag{3a}$$

for n odd (search),

$$E[Z(t+1) \mid F_t] \geq \eta,$$
$$S(t) = U(T_{n-1}). \tag{3b}$$

This, if a search period ends with $U(T_n) = u$, then the next search period begins as soon as $U(t)$ reaches or falls below $(u - \beta)$, and ends thereafter as soon as $U(t)$ reaches or exceeds u again. During such a search period, u may be called the 'aspiration level'. For technical reasons, assume further that there is a number b such that

$$|Z(t)| \leq b, \qquad \text{for all } t. \tag{3c}$$

Using an inequality of Freedman (1973), one can prove:

Proposition 1. The random times T_n have finite expectations; indeed, there are numbers μ_0 and μ_1 such that, for all n,

$$E[T_{n+1} - T_n \mid F_{T_n}] \leq \begin{cases} \mu_0, & \text{if } n \text{ is even,} \\ \mu_1, & \text{if } n \text{ is odd.} \end{cases} \tag{4}$$

For any non-negative integer k, let $V_k = U(T_{2k})$. The V_k are the performance levels at which successive search periods end, and each V_k is the aspiration level for the next succeeding search period. It is clear that the V_k form a non-decreasing sequence. If, during search, performance can (with positive probability) increase by more than one unit at a time, then V_k will actually increase from time to time. I shall say that the process is *strictly favorable* if there is a (strictly) positive number v such that, for every k,

$$E[V_{k+1} \mid F_{2k}] \geq V_k + v. \tag{5}$$

Again using Freedman (1973), one can prove:

Proposition 2. *If the process is strictly favorable, then*

$$\liminf_{k \to \infty} \frac{V_k}{k} \geq v, \quad \text{almost surely.}$$

2.3. Random-walk search and rest

In the model of section 2.2, assume further that, during rest the increments $Z(t+1)$ are independent and identically distributed, with mean $-\xi$, and during search they are also independent and identically distributed, with mean η. In other words, during rest the performance process is a random walk with negative drift, and during search it is a random walk with positive drift. To minimize technical complications, assume further that these random walks are integer-valued and aperiodic.

Let $a(t) = 1$ during search, and 0 during rest. The process $\{a(t-1), U(t), S(t)\}$ is a Markov chain with countably many states and a single class. Let $D(t) = U(t) - S(t)$. The process $\{a(t-1), D(t)\}$ is also Markovian, with a single class.

Proposition 3. *The process $\{a(t-1), D(t)\}$ is positive recurrent. Let $\bar{a}$ denote the long-run frequency with which $a(t) = 1$, and let $\zeta = \bar{a}\eta - (1-\bar{a})\xi$; then, almost surely,*

$$\lim_{t \to \infty} \frac{U(t)}{t} = \zeta. \tag{6}$$

If $\zeta > 0$, then the process is strictly favorable, in the sense of Proposition 2. In the present case, the sequence (V_k) is a random walk. However, *the sequence $U(t)$ is not a random walk, nor even a sub-martingale.* Nevertheless, one can prove for $\{U(t)\}$ the following result:

Proposition 4. *If the process is strictly favorable ($\zeta > 0$), then there exist positive numbers H and K such that, if $U(0) \equiv u > \beta + b$, then*

$$\text{Prob } \{U(t) \leq 0 \text{ for some } t \mid F_0\} \leq He^{-Ku}.$$

If $\zeta = 0$, then the above probability is 1.

Let us say that the process *survives* if the performance $U(t)$ remains positive for all t. Taken together, Propositions 3 and 4 assert that, for a strictly favorable process, with random-walk rest and search, in the long-run performance increases at a positive average rate per unit time, and the probability of survival approaches unity exponentially as a function of the initial performance level, $U(0)$. This implies further that, if the process has 'survived' for a long time, then the performance level is probably very high, and therefore the conditional probability of subsequent survival is close to unity. If the process is not strictly favorable, then the probability of survival is zero.

3. 'Putting out fires'

A manager usually supervises more than one activity. For any given level of search effort per unit time, the opportunity cost of searching for improvement in one activity is the neglect of others. Consider a stochastic process $\{U(t), F_t\}$, as in the first paragraph of section 2.1, but let $U(t)$ be a vector with coordinates $U_i(t)$, $i = 1, \ldots, I$, where $U_i(t)$ is a measure of performance of activity i at date t. An *allocation behavior* is a sequence, $\{a(t)\}$, where $a(t)$ is an F_t-measurable random vector with coordinates $a_i(t)$, $i = 1, \ldots, I$, such that, for any date t, exactly one coordinate of $a(t)$ is 1, and the other coordinates are 0. If $a_i(t) = 1$, this is interpreted as a search for improvement in activity i at date t.

Concerning the process $U(t)$, I shall make assumptions analogous to those of section 2.3. As before, let

$$Z(t+1) = U(t+1) - U(t). \tag{7}$$

For the conditional distribution of $Z(t+1)$, given F_t, assume:

> The distribution of $Z(t+1)$ depends only on $a(t)$. $\hspace{2em}$ (8a)

> $EZ_i(t+1) = a_i(t)\eta_i - [1-a_i(t)]\xi_i$, where ξ_i and η_i are given positive parameters. (8b)

> $\text{Var } Z_i(t+1) = s_i(a_i[t])$, where $s_i(0)$ and $s_i(1)$ are given positive parameters. (8c)

> The coordinates of $Z(t+1)$ are mutually independent. $\hspace{2em}$ (8d)

To minimize technical complications, I also assume:

> The coordinates of $Z(t+1)$ are integer-valued and uniformly bounded by b. $\hspace{2em}$ (8e)

A common managerial behavior is to pay attention only to those activities that are giving the most trouble; this is colloquially called 'putting out fires'. Formally, let

$$M(t) = \underset{i}{\text{Min}} \, U_i(t), \tag{9}$$

and define *putting out fires* by

$$\text{if } U_i(t) > M(t), \quad \text{then } a_i(t) = 0; \tag{10a}$$

$$\text{if } U_i(t) = M(t) \quad \text{and} \quad a_i(t-1) = 1, \quad \text{then } a_i(t) = 1; \tag{10b}$$

if neither (a) nor (b) holds, then $a_i(t) = 1$ for

$$i = \text{the smallest } j, \quad \text{such that} \quad U_j(t) = M(t). \tag{10c}$$

To compare putting out fires with the satisficing model of section 2, roughly speaking, the satisfactory level of performance of any activity is here defined to be equal to $M(t)+1$.

To describe the properties of the performance process under putting out fires, I first define

$$\zeta = \left(1 - \sum_i \frac{\xi_i}{\eta_i + \xi_i}\right) \bigg/ \left(\sum_i \frac{1}{\eta_i + \xi_i}\right). \tag{11}$$

$$\bar{a}_i = \frac{\zeta + \xi_i}{\eta_i + \xi_i}, \qquad i = 1, \ldots, I. \tag{12}$$

If the limit, as t increases, of $U_i(t)/t$ exists, I shall call this limit the *rate of growth of activity i*. If $M(t) > 0$ for all t, I shall say that the performance process *survives*. Define $W(t) = U(t) - M(t)$.

Proposition 5.   Under putting-out-fires behavior, if $\zeta > 0$, and if

$$\text{Prob } \{Z_i(t+1) = 0 \,|\, a_i(t)\} > 0,$$

$$\text{Prob } \{Z_i(t+1) = 1 \,|\, a_i(t) = 1\} > 0,$$

$$\text{Prob } \{Z_i(t+1) = -1 \,|\, a_i(t) = 0\} > 0,$$

then the Markov chain $\{a(t-1), W(t)\}$ is ergodic, and for each activity i,

(a)   *the long-run frequency with which $a_i(t) = 1$ is almost surely equal to $\bar{a}_i$;*
(b)   *the rate of growth of $U_i(t)$ is almost surely ζ (the same for all activities);*

furthermore, if $M(0) > 0$, then

(c) *the probability of survival is positive.*

In the context of the model defined by (8a)–(8e) one could explore other allocation behaviors, but the limitation of space does not permit that here. I mention, however, that a necessary and sufficient condition that there exist *any* allocation behavior with positive probability of survival is $\zeta > 0$. In other words, *survival is possible with positive probability if and only if it is possible with putting out fires.*

In the special case of two activities ($I = 2$) the conclusions (a) and (b) of Proposition 5 are true also if $\zeta \leq 0$.

For proofs of the facts mentioned in this section and for an analysis of other allocation behaviors, see Radner and Rothschild (1975).

4. Bibliographic note

The material of this lecture is adapted from Radner (1973 and 1975) and Radner and Rothschild (1975). Proposition 5, on putting out fires, has been significantly generalized by Rothschild (1974) in two directions. First, he has obtained an analogous result without the random-walk, or even Markovian, assumption, essentially relying only on the semi-martingale property (8b). Second, he has generalized the analysis to the case in which there may be increasing returns to uninterrupted effort allocated to any single activity. Satisficing plays an important role in the models of stochastic equilibrium and evolution in Winter (1971), Nelson and Winter (1972), and Nelson, Winter and Schuette (1973). Stochastic search for improvement is a key element of a decentralized resource allocation process that converges to Pareto optimal allocations in the presence of nonconvexities, as described in Hurwicz, Radner and Reiter (1975). Related stochastic adjustment processes for reaching the core of a game are described in Green (1974) and in Neuefeind (1974).

References

Freedman, D., 1973, Another note on the Borel–Cantelli lemma and the strong law, Ann. Probability 1, no. 6, 910–925.
Green, J., 1974, The stability of Edgeworth's recontracting process, Econometrica 42, no. 1, 21–34.
Hurwicz, L., R. Radner and S. Reiter, 1975, A stochastic decentralized resource allocation process: Parts I and II, Econometrica 43, no. 2, 187–221, and no. 3, 363–393.
MacQueen, J.B., 1964, Optimal policies for a class of search and evaluation problems, Management Science 10, no. 4, 746–759.
Marschak, J. and R. Radner, 1972, Economic theory of teams (Yale University Press, New Haven).
McGuire, C.B. and R. Radner, eds., 1972, Decision and organization (North-Holland, Amsterdam).

Nelson, R.R. and S.G. Winter, 1972, Toward an evolutionary theory of economic capabilities, Discussion Paper no. 44 (Institute of Public Policy Studies, University of Michigan, Ann Arbor).

Nelson, R.R., S.G. Winter and H.L. Schuette, 1973, Technical change in an evolutionary model, Discussion Paper no. 45 (Institute of Public Policy Studies, University of Michigan, Ann Arbor).

Neuefeind, W., 1974, A stochastic bargaining process for n-person games, Journal of Mathematical Economics 1, no. 2, 175–191.

Radner, R., 1973, Aspiration, bounded rationality, and control, Presidential Address, Oslo Meeting of the Econometric Society, Aug. 1973, unpublished manuscript.

Radner, R., 1975, A behavioral model of cost reduction, Bell Journal of Economics and Management Science 6, no. 1, 196–215.

Radner, R. and M. Rothschild, 1975, On the allocation of effort, Journal of Economic Theory 10, 358–376.

Rothschild, M., 1974, Searching for the lowest price when the distribution of prices is unknown, Journal of Political Economy 82, 689–712.

Rothschild, M., 1974, Further notes on the allocation of effort, Econometric Research Program Memorandum no. 171 (Department of Economics, Princeton University); forthcoming in: Proceedings of the Symposium on Adaptive Economics (University of Wisconsin, Madison).

Savage, L.J., 1954, The foundations of statistics (Wiley, New York).

Simon H.A., 1959, Theories of decision-making in economics and behavioral science, American Economic Review 49, no. 3, 253–283.

Simon, H.A., 1972, Theories of bounded rationality, ch. 8 in: C.B. McGuire and R. Radner, eds., Decision and organization (North-Holland, Amsterdam).

Winter, S.G., 1971, Satisficing, selection, and the innovating remnant, Quarterly Journal of Economics 85, 237–261.

[7]

Journal of Mathematical Psychology 42, 191–214 (1998)
Article No. MP971205

Aspiration Adaptation Theory

Reinhard Selten*

Rheinische-Friedrich-Wilhelms-Universität, Bonn, Germany

Aspiration adaptation theory, not available in English up to now, is a general model of nonoptimizing boundedly rational behavior. The theory is presented in a more formal fashion than in the original paper. Moreover, the presentation is complemented by remarks on decision resources as goal variables and the way in which aspiration adaptation copes with uncertainty by risk-related goal variables. Finally, possible modifications in the light of experimental evidence are discussed.   © 1998 Academic Press

Key Words: aspiration adaptation; bounded rationality.

1. INTRODUCTION

Most of the material presented in this paper is not new. However, aspiration adaptation theory (Sauermann & Selten, 1962) never has been presented in English before. It often happened to me that people to whom I explained some of the basic ideas expressed interest in reading more about the theory. The paper is written mainly for those who share this curiosity and cannot read German.

It seems to me that the basic ideas of aspiration adaptation theory are still useful as a point of departure for theory construction. The theory as it stands cannot claim to be a definite answer to the problem of modelling bounded rationality. Probably, one would need extensive experimental research in order to modify it in a way which fits observed behavior.

There is a body of experimental literature on two-person bargaining which is loosely connected with aspiration adaptation theory (Tietz & Weber, 1972, 1978; Tietz, 1975; Scholz, 1980; Scholz, Fleischer, & Bentrup, 1983; Tietz & Bartos, 1983; Crössmann & Tietz, 1983; Tietz, Daus, Lautsch, & Lotz, 1988). This literature is concerned with the principle of aspiration balance in two-person bargaining which will not be discussed here. Up to now there are no experiments which directly address the question to what extent aspiration adaptation theory is an adequate description of observed behavior.

* I am greatly indebted to Axel Ockenfels who helped me to prepare this paper on the basis of my notes for a chapter of my course on bounded rationality. He made many valuable suggestions and did all the technical work involved in the presentation of the material. Correspondence and reprint requests should be sent to Prof. Dr. Dr. h. c. Reinhard Selten, Hardtweg 23, D-53639 Koeningswinter, Germany.

0022-2496/98 $25.00

Students trained in game theory and neoclassical economics often have difficulties to understand how behavior can be nonoptimal. "There must be something which is optimized!", one of them once insisted in a discussion. Aspiration adaptation theory shows that it is possible to construct theories of bounded rationality in which behavior is non-optimizing but not irrational. Aspiration adaptation theory is rational in the sense that it is based on reasonable systematic procedures. The structure of the theory is very different from that of Bayesian decision theory. Aspiration adaptation theory is not a modified optimization approach. It does not proceed from a principle of optimality but directly exhibits a procedure of search and adaptation.

In my course on bounded rationality, aspiration adaptation theory serves the purpose to introduce the students to the spirit of modelling non-optimizing boundedly rational behavior. For some time I think of the possibility of writing a book on bounded rationality based on this course. If I ever succeed to realize this plan the material of this paper will be one of the first chapters.

The original paper by Heinz Sauermann and myself was completely verbal. It was our intention to reach a wide readership. Knowledge of mathematics was not' widespread among German economists in this time. A completely verbal text easily leads to misunderstandings if definitions are not read sufficiently carefully. Therefore, a more formal presentation is chosen here.

After some preliminary explanations two structural elements will be introduced, the influence scheme and the aspiration adaptation scheme. The influence scheme describes expectations on the direction of causal effects. The aspiration adaptation scheme takes the place of preferences in optimization theory. It guides the search for and the selection of alternatives.

2. INSTRUMENT VARIABLES, PLANS, AND ACTIONS

For the sake of having something definite in mind, we shall always speak about the case that the decision maker is a firm. However, the theory is also applicable in other contexts.

The firm has s instrument variables $X_1, ..., X_s$, e.g. price, advertising expenditures, quality etc. A *plan* $x = (x_1, ..., x_s)$ is a combination of values for the instrument variables. x_i is a possible value of X_i.

An *action* A is a rule for the change of a plan. Formally, it is a function which assigns a changed plan $x' = A(x)$ to every plan $x = (x_1, ..., x_s)$. The following examples illustrate the concept:

- price reduction by 5%,

- increase of advertising expenditures by 10%,

- price increase by 10% together with an increase of advertising expenditures by 20%,

- no change of the plan.

It is assumed that only finitely many actions $A_1. ..., A_n$ are considered. The decision maker takes one and only one action. Combinations of several measures like a price increase by 10% together with an increase of advertising expenditures by 20% are modelled as one composite action.

3. GOAL VARIABLES AND ASPIRATION LEVELS

The firm has m *goal variables* $G_1, ..., G_m$. As an example consider the case of the following three goal variables: rentability, market share, owned capital ratio (owned capital as a ratio of total capital).

Several goals are pursued simultaneously. The goals are incomparable. There is no aggregated goal function which assigns an index to a combination of values for the m goal variables. Such an aggregated goal function would be needed for a multigoal optimization theory. Aspiration adaptation theory takes the difficulties of comparing heterogeneous goals seriously. Therefore, it does not make use of aggregated goal functions.

It will always be assumed that goal variables are *upward directed* in the sense that ceteris paribus a higher value is preferred to a lower value. This, of course, is only a formality. If, e.g. one wants to keep costs low, one can do this by keeping negative costs high. The upward directedness entails no loss of generality.

It is assumed that aspirations on goal variables are adapted in discrete steps only, from one value on an aspiration scale to a neighboring one. The *aspiration scale L* for a goal variable G specifies an ascending sequence of *aspiration values* for the concerning variables. An aspiration scale L is associated to every goal variable G. We can distinguish four possible cases with respect of the structure of an aspiration scale:

(1) $L = (S_1, ..., S_\alpha)$,   finite,

(2) $L = (S_1, S_2, ...)$,   upward open,

(3) $L = (..., S_1, ..., S_\alpha)$,   downward open,

(4) $L = (..., S_i, S_{i+1}, ...)$,   open in both directions.

The values are increasing from left to right.

Let $L_1, ..., L_m$ be the aspiration scales of $G_1, ..., G_m$, respectively.

An *aspiration level* is a vector $a = (a_1, ..., a_m)$ with $a_j \in L_j$. We call a_j the partial aspiration level for G_j. Depending on the structure of the aspiration scales, one may or may not find extreme aspiration levels. $\underline{a} = (\underline{a}_1, ..., \underline{a}_m)$ is the *minimal aspiration level* if all components of $\underline{a}$ are minimal on their scales.

$$\bar{a} = (\bar{a}_1, ..., \bar{a}_m)$$

is the *maximun aspiration level* if all components of $\bar{a}$ are maximal on their scales.

4. THE INFLUENCE SCHEME

The decision maker is assumed to have expectations on the directions of the influences exerted by the actions $A_1, ..., A_n$ on the goal variables $G_1, ..., G_m$.

TABLE 1

Example of an Influence Scheme

	G_1	G_2	G_3
A_1	0	−	+
A_2	+	−	−
A_3	0	+	−
A_4	−	0	+

Formally, this is expressed by the *influence scheme*, a $n \times m$ matrix B whose entries b_{ij} stand for the expected direction of the influence of A_i on G_j. b_{ij} can take the values "−", "0", or "+", where minus stands for an expected decrease, plus for an expected increase, and zero for the lack of a significant influence (see Table 1).

5. THE ASPIRATION SCHEME

In the case of the adaptation of an aspiration level $a = a_1, ..., a_m$ one of the partial aspiration levels a_j is shifted by one step on the concerning aspiration scale. It is assumed that the decision maker feels that the possible upward aspiration adaptations are of different urgency. At every aspiration level the way in which the goal variables are ordered with respect to their urgencies may be different. Formally, this is expressed by an *urgency order function p* which assigns a permutation

$$p(a) = (p_1(a), ..., p_m(a))$$

of the ordered set $(G_1, ..., G_m)$ to every non-maximal aspiration level $a = (a_1, ..., a_m)$ such that the following condition is satisfied: Variables whose partial aspiration levels are maximal on their scales do not precede variables for which this is not the case. $p_1(a)$ is the most urgent variable, $p_2(a)$ is the second most urgent one, etc. We call $p(a)$ the *urgency order* at a. Thus, in the case of three goal variables G_1, G_2, G_3, the urgency order at an aspiration level a may have the value (G_2, G_3, G_1).

It is not necessary to assign an urgency order to a maximal aspiration level. In the case of spiration levels which are not maximal but nevertheless do have some components maximal on their scale one might consider not to include these goal variables into the urgency order. It is only a mathematical convenience that urgencies are specified for such goal variables, too. It is natural to require that all goal variables with maximal aspiration values are at the end of the urgency order.

It is important that the urgency order may depend on the aspiration level. Thus, if profits are low, rentability may be more urgent than market share, but for high levels of rentability this may be different.

It may happen that it is not possible to raise one's aspirations on the most urgent goal variable but that nevertheless an upward adaptation of aspirations on the second most urgent variable is feasible. Therefore, it is necessary not only to say what is the most urgent variable but to specify the whole urgency order.

We now look at downward aspiration adaptation. Here, the decision maker has to lower the partial aspiration level of one of his goal variables. We call the variables for which he does this the *retreat variable*. We do not need something similar to the urgency order for downward aspiration adaptations. For upward adaptations one needs an urgency order because a lack of available decision alternatives may exclude the upward adaptation in the most urgent direction. However, a downward adaptation always enlarges the space for decision alternatives satisfying the aspiration level. Upward adaptations may make it too difficult or even impossible to satisfice whereas downward adaptations always make it more easy or at least not more difficult to satisfice. Therefore, upward and downward adaptations are very different from each other. Whereas in the upward case one needs a preference over directions of adaptation one can always choose what hurts least in the downward direction.

A *retreat function* v is a function which assigns a retreat variable $v(a)$ to every non-minimal aspiration level $a = (a_1, ..., a_m)$ in such a way that the following condition is satisfied: The component a_j with $G_j = v(a)$ is not minimal on the aspiration scale for G_j.

It is not necessary to assign a retreat variable to a minimal aspiration level. When a minimal value on the aspiration scale is reached, no downward adaptation is possible anymore for that goal variable. Therefore, we require that the retreat variable is a goal variable with a partial aspiration level not minimal on its aspiration scale.

An *aspiration adaptation scheme* $S = (G_1, ..., G_m, L_1, ..., L_m, p, v)$ has the following constituents:

$G_1, ..., G_m$ are the goal variables,

$L_1, ..., L_m$ are the aspiration scales for $G_1, ..., G_m$, respectively,

p is an urgency order function for $L_1, ..., L_m$,

v is a retreat variable function for $L_1, ..., L_m$.

In the case of only two goal variables, an aspiration adaptation scheme can be represented graphically by a grid with arrows indicating the most urgent and the retreat variable. An example is shown in Fig. 1. An arrow to the left or to the below

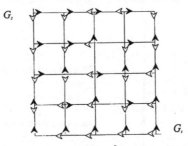

$\blacktriangleright$ most urgent variable $\triangleright$ retreat variable

FIG. 1. An aspiration adaptation scheme in the case of only two goal variables.

at a grid point indicates the retreat variable for the corresponding aspiration level. Similarly, an arrow to the right or in the upward direction at a grid point indicates the most urgent goal variable at the corresponding aspiration level.

In aspiration adaptation theory the aspiration adaptation scheme has a similar role as preferences in optimization theory. However, it does not only serve as an instrument for the selection of one alternative out of a given set but it also guides the search for new alternatives.

6. ASPIRATION ADAPTATION IN THE CASE OF A GIVEN FEASIBLE SET

In order to explain the process of aspiration adaptation, we shall now look at a simple situation in which the decision maker knows which aspiration levels can be reached by the alternatives among which she can choose. We call this set of aspiration levels the *feasible set*. If we say that an aspiration level can be reached by an alternative we mean that for every goal variable the choice of the alternative is connected with a value not below the corresponding partial aspiration level. This has the consequence that the feasible set always is *comprehensive* in the sense that with each aspiration level it also contains all other aspiration levels with equal or lower components.

Aspiration level adaptation always begins with an initial aspiration level. One may think of this initial level as taken over from the past. Fig. 2 shows an example of an aspiration adaptation process in a situation in which starting from the initial aspiration level an upward adaptation is possible. The feasible set consists of all aspiration levels in the shaded area including the border points. The aspiration adaptation scheme is that of Fig. 1. From the initial aspiration level indicated by a circle an upward adaptation in the most urgent direction is possible. This adaptation shifts the aspiration on G_1 by one step to the right. From there again an upward adaptation in the most urgent direction is possible. Thereby, the aspiration level shifts the partial aspiration on G_2 by one step. At the new aspiration level reached in this way an upward adaptation in the most urgent direction is not possible. However, an upward adaptation in the second most urgent direction is possible. This adaptation leads to the final aspiration level indicated by a square from which no further upward adaptation is possible. If the initial aspiration level

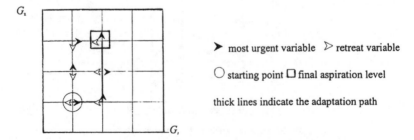

FIG. 2.   Upward aspiration adapatation in the case of a given feasible set.

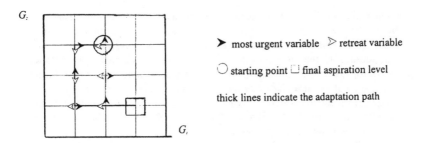

FIG. 3. Downward aspiration adaptation in the case of a given feasible set.

is in the feasible set then the process of aspiration adaptation will always proceed by steps in the most urgent feasible direction until a final aspiration level is reached in which no further upward adaptation is possible.

Figure 3 shows the case in which the initial aspiration level is outside the feasible set indicated by the shaded area as in Fig. 2. Again, the aspiration adaptation scheme is the one of Fig. 1. At the initial aspiration level indicated by a circle the retreat variable is G_1. The retreat variable at the new aspiration variable reached by the first adaptation step is G_2. After the second adaptation step the retreat variable again is G_2. After the third adaptation step a point in the feasible set is reached. The adaptation process does not stop there because an upward adaptation is possible. The aspiration level is adapted to the above in the most urgent direction. Thereby, a new aspiration level is reached from which the best feasible upward adaptation is in the second most urgent direction. This adaptation finally reaches an aspiration level from which no further upward adaptation is possible.

In the case of an initial aspiration level outside of the feasible set the process first proceeds by downward adaptations in the direction indicated by the retreat variable until a point in the feasible set is reached. From there the process proceeds in the same way as a process of upward adaptation starting with an aspiration level in the feasible set.

It can be seen immediately that the adaptation process never leaves the feasible set once it has entered it. Moreover, the final aspiration level is always Pareto-optimal in the sense that within the feasible set no goal variable can be increased without lowering another one. These properties are a consequence of the comprehensiveness of the feasible set.

The final aspiration level depends on the initial one. This shows that aspiration adaptation is not an optimization process. Of course, it is possible to define preferences as depending on the initial aspiration level. But this would be a rather artificial way of looking at aspiration adaptation as a special case of utility maximization.

7. TWO BEHAVIORAL MODELS

In the following we shall first discuss a behavioral model based on aspiration adaptation which we call the *routine model*. Later we shall also look at the

198   REINHARD SELTEN

possibility of modelling a more sophisticated behavior by a *planning model*. As far as beliefs are concerned, the routine model exclusively relies on the qualitative expectations expressed by the influence scheme. In the planning model it is assumed that in addition to this the decision maker also has a quantitative computational procedure of expectation formation which makes it possible to calculate expected values of all goal variables for every plan. We imagine that this procedure is a complex algorithm—e.g. a simulation model. This means that it is possible to compute expectations for every plan but that the function which connects plans and expectations cannot be handled analytically.

Both models operate in discrete time. In a sequence of periods $t = 1, 2, ...$ the results of period t determine the initial situation of period $t + 1$ and the decisions which are taken there.

Both models will be pure descriptions of behavior, i.e. the connection between decisions and results is not modelled. It is, of course, possible to complement the description of behavior by a model of the response of the environment. This is necessary if one wants to investigate the development of a firm over time. Here, we shall restrict ourselves to the description of behavior.

8. THE ROUTINE MODEL

Figure 4 shows a flow chart for the routine model. This flow chart is not very detailed; it only gives a rough overview over the steps in the decision process.

8.1. Correction of the Influence Scheme

The correction of the influence scheme is modelled in the simplest possible way; those directional expectations which have not been confirmed by the result of the last period are changed to the actually observed direction of change. This means that after the correction the entries in the row corresponding to the chosen action are the observed directions of change. Nothing is changed in rows corresponding to other actions.

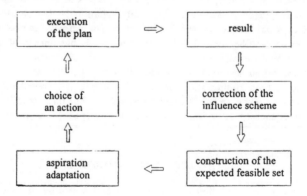

FIG. 4.   The routine model.

We may say that the correction rule attributes changes of the goal variables always to the action which has been taken. Of course, this is not always justified. Changes may be due to exogenous influences, too. A correction rule which takes this into account would have to be based on a much more elaborate picture of the decision maker's qualitative beliefs about his environment.

We shall make use of the following notation:

$g = (g_1, ..., g_m)$,   combination of the realized values of the goal variables $G_1, ..., G_m$ at the end of the last period;

$g^- = (g_1^-, ..., g_m^-)$,   combination of the realized values of the goal variables $G_1, ..., G_m$ in the second last period;

b_{ij},   corrected elements of the influence scheme matrix, $i = 1, ..., n$, $j = 1, ..., m$;

b_{ij}^-,   value of b_{ij} in the last period, $i = 1, ..., n$, $j = 1, ..., m$;

If A_k has been chosen in the last period then after the correction of the influence scheme we have:

$$b_{kj} = + \qquad \text{for} \quad g_j > g_j^-; \quad j = 1, ..., m;$$
$$b_{kj} = - \qquad \text{for} \quad g_j < g_j^-; \quad j = 1, ..., m;$$
$$b_{kj} = 0 \qquad \text{for} \quad g_j = g_j^-; \quad j = 1, ..., m;$$
$$b_{ij} = b_{ij}^- \qquad \text{for} \quad i \neq k; \quad j = 1, ..., m.$$

8.2. Construction of the Expected Feasible Set

Unlike in Section 6, in the routine model the decision maker cannot base aspiration adaptation on a known feasible set of aspiration levels. He has to form expectations about the aspiration levels which can be reached by his actions $A_1, ..., A_n$. Before we describe how this is done, we introduce some additional notation. As in 8.1, we assume that $g = (g_1, ..., g_m)$ is the combination of the realized values of the goal variables $G_1, ..., G_m$ at the end of the last period. For every value of the goal variable G_j we define a *just reached* partial aspiration level $\alpha_j(g_j)$. The level $\alpha_j(g_j)$ is the highest level on the aspiration scale L_j which is not greater than g_j. Moreover,

$$\alpha(g) = (\alpha_1(g_1), ..., \alpha_m(g_m))$$

is the aspiration level just reached by $g = (g_1, ..., g_m)$. The next higher level above $\alpha_j(g_j)$ on L_j, if there is one, is denoted by $\alpha_{j+}(g_j)$. For the case that $\alpha_j(g_j)$ is maximal on L_j, we define $\alpha_{j+}(g_j)$ as equal to $\alpha_j(g_j)$.

If the last realization was g_j and the influence scheme shows $b_{ij} = +$, then the decision maker expects that $\alpha_{j+}(g_j)$ will be just reached by A_i. This expectation is optimistic since one cannot say that a positive influence necessarily raises the goal variable above the next level. On the other hand, the expectation is not too optimistic because an increase of a_j by more than one step on the aspiration scale is not envisioned.

For $\alpha_j(g_j) = g_j$ we define $\alpha_{j-}(g_j)$ as the next lower level below $\alpha_j(g_j)$ on the aspiration scale L_j, if there is one. If $\alpha_j(g_j)$ is minimal on L_j or if $g_j > \alpha_j(g_j)$, then $\alpha_{j-}(g_j)$ is defined as equal to $\alpha_j(g_j)$. The partial aspiration level $\alpha_{j-}(g_j)$ is the level which is expected to be just reached by an action A_i with $b_{ij} = -$. This expectation is optimistic since in the case $g_j = \alpha_j(g_j)$ it does not envision a decrease by more than one step on the aspiration scale, and since in the case $g_j > \alpha_j(g_j)$ it assumes that the influence will not be strong enough to push g_j below $\alpha_j(g_j)$. Figure 5 shows two situations which may arise. In the case shown above, g_j is between two aspiration levels on the scale, whereas in the case shown below, g_j is exactly on one of the levels. The figure makes clear how $\alpha_{j+}(g_j)$ and $\alpha_{j-}(g_j)$ are defined differently in both cases. Of course, further cases arise if $\alpha_j(g_j)$ is maximal or minimal on L_j, but it can be seen easily how the corresponding figures would look like.

We now define an expected feasible aspiration level $\eta(A_i, g) = (\eta_1(A_i, g), \ldots, \eta_m(A_i, g))$:

$$\eta_j(A_i, g) = \begin{cases} \alpha_{j+}(g_j) & \text{for} \quad b_{ij} = + \\ \alpha_j(g_j) & \text{for} \quad b_{ij} = 0 \\ \alpha_{j-}(g_j) & \text{for} \quad b_{ij} = - \end{cases}$$

for $i = 1, \ldots, n$ and $j = 1, \ldots, m$.

Before we define the expected feasible set, we must first introduce the notion of a comprehensive hull. Let N be a set of aspiration levels $a = (a_1, \ldots, a_m)$. Then, the comprehensive hull of N consists of all elements of N together with all aspiration levels $a' = (a_1', \ldots, a_m')$ such that N contains at least one $a = (a_1, \ldots, a_m)$ with $a_j' \leqslant a_j$ for $j = 1, \ldots, m$. We use the symbol "comp$N$" for the comprehensive hull of N.

The *expected feasible set* $R(g)$ is defined as the comprehensive hull of the union of all expected feasible aspiration levels:

$$R(g) = comp \bigcup_{i=1}^{n} \eta(A_i, g)$$

Figure 6 shows an example for the construction of the expected feasible set. The right-hand side of the figure shows an influence scheme. In the figure, arrows

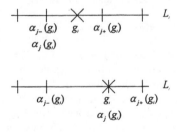

FIG. 5. Definitions of $\alpha_{j+}(g_j)$ and $\alpha_{j-}(g_j)$.

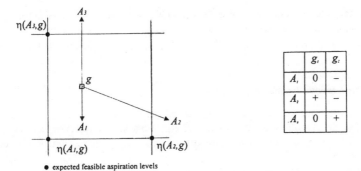

FIG. 6. Construction of the expected feasible set.

pointing away from the realization point g indicate in which areas the next realization is expected to lie for each of the actions. Accordingly, the three expected feasible aspiration levels are also shown by the figure.

8.3. Aspiration Adaptation and Choice of the Action

In the routine model aspiration adaptation starts with the aspiration level $a = (a_1, ..., a_m)$ at the end of the last period. From there, it proceeds in the same way as in the beginning of Section 6 with the only difference that now the expected feasible set $R(g)$ takes the place of the given feasible set.

Suppose that $a' = (a'_1, ..., a'_m)$ is the final aspiration level. The decision maker now selects an action with $a' = \eta(A_i, g)$. However, there may be several actions A_i with this property. If this is the case, the set of candidate actions is successively narrowed by the following two criteria if this is possible:

(1) the number of b_{ij} with $b_{ij} = -$ should be as small as possible;

(2) the number of b_{ij} with $b_{ij} = +$ should be as great as possible.

Of course, after the successive application of these two selection criteria, there still may be several actions connected to the final aspiration level a. If this is the case, one of them has to be selected arbitrarily, e.g. the first one in the list.

As has been pointed out before, the construction of the expected feasible set is optimistic. However, this should not be interpreted as a lack of realism. The decision maker does not really expect that the aspiration level will be satisfied with certainty. In this respect, the role of aspiration levels in the routine model is different from that in the satisficing processes described by Simon, where it is assumed that it can be immediately seen whether an alternative satisfices the aspiration level or not. The situation of the decision maker in the routine model is different. He cannot be certain about what he may achieve by an action. Nevertheless, the construction of the expected feasible set and the subsequent choice of an action is a reasonable method of guiding the decision process by qualitative expectations.

The idea that actions are assumed to shift a realization of a goal variable by at most one step presupposes a reasonable fit between the size of these steps and the quantitative features of the actions. Presumably, such a fit could be established by a dynamic learning process which, however, is not modelled by aspiration adaptation theory. It is assumed that in this respect a reasonable preadaptation has been reached.

8.4. An Example for the Routine Model

In this section, we shall look at the example of a firm with three goal variables: r profitability (profit as a fraction of capital), m market share (sales as a fraction of total industry sales), e owned capital ratio (owned capital as a fraction of total firm capital).

The aspiration scales are assumed to be:

$$L_r = \{k\% \mid k \geqslant -100;\ \text{integer}\}$$
$$L_m = \{5k\% \mid k = 0, ..., 20\}$$
$$L_e = \{10k\% \mid k = 0, ..., 10\}.$$

Table 2 shows the aspiration adaptation scheme. In this aspiration adaptation scheme, the urgency order depends on some critical values of the goal variables, 6% for r, 70% for m, and 30% for e in the case of $m \leqslant 70\%$ as well as 40% for e in the case of $m > 70\%$. Below its critical value, the goal variable is more urgent than above it. The retreat variable always is the least urgent variable. This is a special feature of the example. In general, the retreat variable does not have to be the least urgent variable. Fig. 7 shows a graphical representation of the aspiration adaptation scheme.

The influence scheme is shown in Table 3. In the influence scheme, cost reduction has a negative influence on owned capital because it requires additional investment. The same is true for a broadening of the product line. The other entries in the influence schemes have a straightforward interpretation.

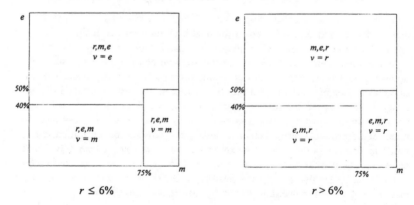

FIG. 7. Graphical representation of the aspiration adaptation scheme. Note: The regions include left and lower borders.

TABLE 2

Aspiration Adaptation Scheme

	Aspiration level			Urgency order	Retreat variable
1.	$r \leqslant 6\%$	$m \leqslant 70\%$	$e \leqslant 30\%$	r, e, m	m
2.	$r \leqslant 6\%$	$m \leqslant 70\%$	$e > 30\%$	r, m, e	e
3.	$r \leqslant 6\%$	$m > 70\%$	$e \leqslant 40\%$	r, e, m	m
4.	$r \leqslant 6\%$	$m > 70\%$	$e > 40\%$	r, m, e	e
5.	$r > 6\%$	$m \leqslant 70\%$	$e \leqslant 30\%$	e, m, r	r
6.	$r > 6\%$	$m \leqslant 70\%$	$e > 30\%$	m, e, r	r
7.	$r > 6\%$	$m > 70\%$	$e \leqslant 40\%$	e, m, r	r
8.	$r > 6\%$	$m > 70\%$	$e > 40\%$	m, e, r	r

We now shall look at a hypothetical course of events over several periods in this example. For the sake of simplicity, we assume that in the first period considered here the directional expectations have been confirmed such that at the beginning of this period no correction of the influence scheme is necessary. Table 4 shows how the expected feasible aspiration level is constructed on the basis of the influence scheme and the realization g.

Table 5 gives a list of the expected feasible aspiration levels together with the actions by which they are reachable.

Figure 8 shows the expected feasible aspiration levels for the actions $A_1, ..., A_m$ and the process of aspiration adaptation. The initial aspiration level (6%, 20%, 30%) is not in the expected feasible set. The retreat variable for this aspiration level is m. The new aspiration level (6%, 15%, 30%) is not connected to an action but it is in the expected feasible set. From there aspiration adaptation proceeds in the most urgent direction r. The final aspiration level is (7%, 15%, 30%). This aspiration level can be reached by only one action, namely A_6. Therefore, A_6 is taken.

We now assume that as a result of taking action A_6 the realization at the end of the period is (6.5%, 16%, 27%). The previous realization was $g^- = (6.8\%, 17\%, 24\%)$. A correction of the influence scheme becomes necessary at the beginning of the second period considered here. Contrary to the last influence scheme, r has been decreased after taking the action A_6. Therefore, in the sixth row in the first column

TABLE 3

Influence Scheme

Actions		r	m	e
A_1	No change of plan	0	0	0
A_2	Price decrease	−	+	0
A_3	Price increase	+	−	0
A_4	Cost reduction	+	0	−
A_5	Broadening of the product line	−	+	−
A_6	Narrowing of the product line	+	−	+
A_7	More favorable credit conditions for customers	−	+	0
A_8	Less favorable credit conditions for customers	+	−	0

TABLE 4

Construction of the Expected Feasible Set

Influence scheme r m e			Expected feasible aspiration level (r, m, e)
A_1	0	0	0	(6%, 15%, 20%)
A_2	−	+	0	(6%, 20%, 20%)
A_3	+	−	0	(7%, 15%, 20%)
A_4	+	0	−	(7%, 15%, 20%)
A_5	−	+	−	(6%, 20%, 20%)
A_6	+	−	+	(7%, 15%, 30%)
A_7	−	+	0	(6%, 20%, 20%)
A_8	+	−	0	(7%, 15%, 20%)

Initial aspiration level	$a^- = (6\%, 20\%, 30\%)$
Realization	$g = (6.8\%, 17\%, 24\%)$

TABLE 5

Expected Feasible Aspiration Levels

(r, m, e)	Reachable by
(6%, 15%, 20%)	A_1
(6%, 20%, 20%)	A_2, A_5, A_7
(7%, 15%, 20%)	A_3, A_4, A_8
(7%, 15%, 30%)	A_6

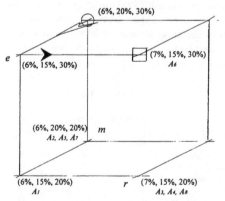

➤ most urgent variable ▷ retreat variable

○ starting point □ final aspiration level

FIG. 8. Process of aspiration adaptation.

in the influence scheme, plus is replaced by minus. The other directional expectations connected to A_6 have been confirmed.

It is an easy exercise to construct the new expected feasible set and to follow the path of aspiration adaptation. The new final aspiration level is (6%, 15%, 30%). Again, action A_6 is chosen.

9. THE PLANNING MODEL

In the planning model it is assumed that the decision maker has access to a calculation rule which for every plan $x = (x_1, ..., x_k)$ permits the determination of an expected combination

$$\varphi(x) = (\varphi_1(x), ..., \varphi_m(x))$$

of values $\varphi_j(x)$ for the goal variables G_j. We think of this calculation rule as a complex algorithm. It is assumed that the function φ is not analytically tractable. For every single plan x, the expected combination $\varphi(x)$ can be computed, but optimization tasks involving φ cannot be attacked directly with the help of necessary conditions on partial derivatives. The planning model is based on the idea that computing $\varphi(x)$ is costly and time consuming such that the calculation can be performed only for a limited number of plans before the decision must be made.

The lack of analytical tractability makes it necessary for the decision maker to form expectations about the outcome of the calculation of further plans. She has to form such expectations in order to determine for which plan x the expected combination $\varphi(x)$ of values for the goal variables should be calculated next. The planning model is based on the idea that this calculation decision is similar to the final decision in the routine model. With the help of an influence scheme, the planner determines a calculation set of aspiration levels which takes the place of the expected feasible set in the routine model.

In the routine model, the construction of the feasible set starts from one combination of goal variables, the realization point. From there, the expectation rule η leads to an expected goal value combination $\eta(A_i, g)$ for every action A_i.

In the planning model, the same expectation rule η is applied not only to one point g but to all goal variable combinations of calculated plans. A new *planning phase* begins after the calculation of a plan, if planning has not yet come to the end. Suppose that at a certain point of the planning procedure the goal variable combinations $g^1, ..., g^K$ have been computed for the plans $x^1, ..., x^K$. Then, for each $i = 1, ..., n$ and each $k = 1, ..., K$, the expected aspiration levels $\eta(A_i, g^k)$ are determined with the help of the influence scheme. The calculation set is the comprehensive hull of all these $\eta(A_i, g^k)$. We could also say that the calculation set is the union of all $R(g^k)$ with $k = 1, ..., K$. Aspiration adaptation to this set is used in order to determine the next plan to be calculated.

We did not yet describe the full structure of a planning phase. A planning phase may also involve a correction of the influence scheme in view of the calculation results of the last calculated plan. The structure of a planning phase is clarified by Fig. 9. The flow chart shown there describes the structure of a period.

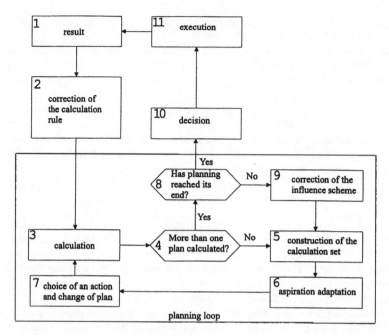

FIG. 9. The planning model.

We now discuss the rectangles and rhomboids.

• *Rectangle* 1. At the end of the last period, the result $g^- = (g_1^-, ..., g_m^-)$ of the plan $x_1^-, ..., x_s^-$ of the last period has been determined.

• *Rectangle* 2. The calculation rule $\varphi(x)$ permits the calculation of a expected goal variable combination g for every plan x. If g^- turned out to be different from $\varphi(x^-)$ then it may be necessary to correct the calculation rule. For this purpose, the decision maker needs a correction rule of the form

$$\varphi = \Phi(\varphi^-, g^-, x^-).$$

Here, φ^- is the calculation rule used in the last period and φ is the new calculation rule revised in the light of g^- and x^-. Clearly, such a correction rule is needed but it is maybe not reasonable to try to specify it without a more detailed view of the environment in which the process takes place. The planning model is not more than a general framework. Since φ is only described as an unspecified complex algorithm, Φ remains unspecified, too.

• *Rectangle* 3. The first plan to be calculated after the correction of the calculation rule is the old plan x^- (the correction does not necessarily achieve $g^- = \varphi(x^-)$). When this rectangle is reached later, the plan selected for calculation at the end of the planning phase is calculated. With rectangle 3, we enter the planning loop indicated in the diagram by the broken line. The process stays there until planning comes to an end.

- *Rhomboid* 4. Here, the question is asked whether more than one plan has been calculated. After the calculation of the first plan, this is not the case. The process moves to rectangle 5.

- *Rectangle* 5. The content of this step already has been discussed above.

- *Rectangle* 6. Starting with the aspiration level a^- taken over from the last period, aspiration adaptation proceeds in the calculation set until a new tentative aspiration level $\bar{a}$ is reached. Whenever we come back to rectangle 5, aspiration adaptation again starts from a^-. The adaptation to $\bar{a}$ remains tentative since the calculation set may change in unforeseen ways in every planning phase.

- *Rectangle* 7. Here, an action is selected according to the same principles as in the routine model. The last calculated plan is changed accordingly. The planning phase ends with the calculation of the new plan in rectangle 3. We then move to rhomboid 8.

- *Rhomboid* 8. Planning may have reached its end because planning time is over or all available planning resources have been spent. We first look at the case that planning has not yet reached its end. In this case, the process moves to rectangle 9.

- *Rectangle* 9. Similar to what is done in the routine model, the influence scheme is corrected in the light of the calculation of the last plan. However, it is possible that more than one row in the influence scheme has to be corrected. It may be possible that the last plan can be obtained by two different sequences of actions, e.g. (A_1, A_2) or (A_2, A_1). If this is the case the calculation results of the last calculated plan have to be compared to those of all earlier plans from which it can be derived by an action. The rows for all these actions, e.g. the rows one and two in the above examples, need to be adjusted as far as directional expectations have not been confirmed on at least one of the paths. After the correction of the influence scheme we come back to rectangle 6.

- *Rectangle* 10. After the planning has come to an end, the decision is made as follows. An *expected feasible set* is formed as a comprehensive hull of all aspiration levels just satisfied by goal variable combinations of calculated plans. In this expected feasible set, aspiration level adaptation proceeds starting from a^-. The adaptation process ends with an aspiration level a. If this aspiration level is just satisfied by only one calculated goal variable combination then the corresponding plan is chosen. If, however, there are several such goal variable combinations one is chosen among those which have the highest calculated value for the most urgent goal. If this criterion fails to narrow down the choice to one of the remaining plans, the plan is chosen arbitrarily, e.g. the one first calculated.

- *Rectangle* 11. Once the plan is executed, then the period result is obtained in rectangle 1 and a new period begins.

In the following, we shall make some comments on features of the planning model. It has already been said that the planning model is only a general framework which leaves the calculation rule and the correction rule for the calculation rule unspecified.

The influence scheme describes expectations about the calculation process. The effects of changing a plan by an action on φ may be different in different regions in the space of plans. The correction of the influence scheme tries to adjust for this. The method by which the expected feasible set is constructed is based on the idea that the calculated plans are sufficiently near to each other to make it not too likely that different influence schemes should be used for different calculated plans. One could try to change the construction of the calculation set in a way which makes it possible to apply different influence schemes to different calculated plans. This would do more justice to the local nature of the experiences which lead to adjustments of the influence scheme. No attempt in this direction is made here because this would make the theory much more complicated without yielding more than a minor improvement of the theory.

The aspiration adaptation within a temporary calculation set always starts with the aspiration level a^- taken over from the last period. One could also consider the possibility that this adaptation starts with the tentative aspiration level reached in the last planning phase. However, it seems to be more adequate not to do this. All adaptations of aspiration levels in the planning loop should be looked upon as tentative. They only serve the purpose to guide the search process for new plans. At the end, the decision is made in rectangle 10 by aspiration adaptation in the expected feasible set starting from a^-. The expected feasible set in the planning model is based on calculated plans only and therefore has another character than the expected feasible set in the routine theory. It is less tentative than the calculation sets of the planning phases. These calculation sets and the aspiration adaptations within them only serve the purpose to guide the process to an expected feasible set which provides favorable conditions for aspiration adaptation starting with a^-. Therefore, it seems to be reasonable to start aspiration adaptation within the calculation sets always with a^-, too.

In the explanation of the diagram it was said that planning comes to an end when planning time is over or planning resources are exhausted. However, it is possible to change the system in such a way that the aspiration adaptation scheme includes goal variables which express a concern for low planning costs. We shall come back to this question after we have described a simpler aspiration adaptation problem in which aspiration levels on search time guide behavior.

10. A SEARCH PROCESS GUIDED BY ASPIRATIONS ON SEARCH TIME

In the following, an example will illustrate the role of aspirations on search costs in a search process guided by aspiration adaptation.

Consider the case of a hypothetical investor who wants to find an opportunity for a long-run fixed interest investment. She already knows one bank which is willing to pay 5% interest. During one week the investor can only receive one offer by a bank. It is always possible to accept one of the offers received up to now. During the first three weeks, the investor feels completely free to search but she would prefer to stop the search then. She can extend the search time up to six weeks, but she would rather like to stop search earlier. The aspiration adaptation scheme of the investor is described by Fig. 10:

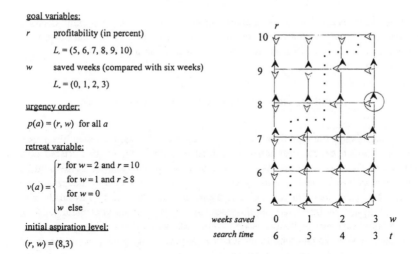

goal variables:

r profitability (in percent)

   $L_r = (5, 6, 7, 8, 9, 10)$

w saved weeks (compared with six weeks)

   $L_w = (0, 1, 2, 3)$

urgency order:

$p(a) = (r, w)$ for all a

retreat variable:

$$v(a) = \begin{cases} r & \text{for } w = 2 \text{ and } r = 10 \\ & \text{for } w = 1 \text{ and } r \geq 8 \\ & \text{for } w = 0 \\ w & \text{else} \end{cases}$$

initial aspiration level:

$(r, w) = (8, 3)$

weeks saved	0	1	2	3	w
search time	6	5	4	3	t

FIG. 10.   Aspiration adaptation scheme of the investor.

In Fig. 10 the dotted line separates the aspiration levels with the retreat variable r on the left side and w on the right side. In the following, r_k will be the interest rate of the offer received in week k. After the first three weeks, the investor can satisfy the aspiration level int $\max(r_1, r_2, r_3)$ and $w = 3$. Here, int x denotes the highest integer not exceeding x. In order to see whether she should continue the search she adapts her initial aspiration level to the feasible set determined in this way. Since the initial aspiration level is at $r = 8$ and $w = 3$, search will not be extended beyond the first three weeks if $\max(r_1, r_2, r_3)$ is at least eight. If this is not the case, downward adaptation is required. The retreat variable at the initial aspiration level is w. Therefore, in this case search would be extended to the fourth week.

It can be seen without difficulty how the search time t depends on the offers $r_1, ..., r_6$:

$$t = 3 \quad \text{for} \quad \max(r_1, r_2, r_3) \geq 8$$

$$t = 4 \quad \text{for} \quad \max(r_1, r_2, r_3) < 8 \quad \text{and} \quad r_4 \geq 8$$

$$t = 5 \quad \text{for} \quad \max(r_1, r_2, r_3, r_4) < 8 \quad \text{and} \quad r_5 \geq 7$$

$$t = 6 \quad \text{for} \quad \max(r_1, r_2, r_3, r_4, r_5) < 7.$$

The example shows how the use of decision resources like weeks of search can be guided by aspiration adaptation. It can be seen that the more decision resources are used, the more difficult it is to satisfy aspirations on other goals.

The use of the aspiration adaptation scheme made by the example is different from that in the routine model and the planning model. Here, no expectations are formed, neither quantitative nor qualitative ones, and the search process is directly guided by aspiration adaptation.

One could easily extend the planning model in a way which permits decision resources as goal variables. In such an extended planning model the number of plans calculated would also be determined by aspiration adaptation.

11. ASPIRATION ADAPTATION AND UNCERTAINTY

If one looks at the way in which firms try to control risks, one often observes a behavior which can be interpreted as guided by aspirations on risk related goal variables. Thus, a firm may have "liquid assets" as a goal variable. This would be the value of assets which can easily be converted to cash without endangering the operation of the firm. The higher liquid assets are, the easier it is to avoid the risk of bankruptcy. In this sense, liquid assets are a risk related goal variable. Risk related goal variables make it possible to limit risks without any reference to subjective or objective probabilities. In most contexts, probability estimates are very hard to form and under such circumstances it is more natural to try to deal with risks by aspirations on risk related goal variables. Sometimes, such aspirations are even fixed as legal or social norms. An example is the norm of k-fold security used in engineering. In order to control the risk that a bridge breaks down, one requires that the construction plans are based on deterministic calculations which indicate that the bridge can withstand forces which are k times as great as those which can be expected maximally in the use of the bridge. Here, k may be a factor like 10, 3, or 2. This factor was once higher than it is now. Technical progress and better methods of calculation have led to a lowering of aspirations on this goal variable.

Where probabilities can be computed they may serve as a basis for the construction of risk related goal variables. Thus, in life insurance it is possible to compute a probability of bankruptcy within a given time, say ten years. Insurance companies form aspiration levels on such bankruptcy probabilities and in some countries are even required to keep such goal variables below a legally prescribed level.

March and Shapira (1988) report empirical investigations about the concepts of risk in the mind of businessmen. Typically, risk seems to be conceived as a maximal loss to be accounted for. Some possible future developments are not considered in the computation of this maximal loss. In some cases these are events which are highly improbable. In others they are maybe not that improbable, but like in atomic war it would not matter which decision was taken if they occurred. This means that the set of all possible future developments is subdivided into two classes, the events to be accounted for and others. Risk is then the greatest possible loss which may occur in an event to be accounted for.

A similar concept of risk is sometimes considered in the context of the security of atomic power plants. Here, one sometimes talks about the "greatest assumable accident." Aspirations are then formed on this variable.

If risk is conceived as the greatest possible loss to be accounted for or the damage incurred by the greatest assumable accident, considerations of probability are not completely ignored. However, only the distinction between highly improbable and other events enters the analysis.

Aspiration levels must be formed in a way which permits the decision maker to decide whether they have been reached or not at least after the consequences of the decision have become clear. Risk related goal variables must conform to this criteria. Therefore, quantitative probabilities can come in only where an objective procedure for their computation is available.

An important example for the use of probabilities as aspiration levels is provided by the practice of hypothesis testing in science. There, the probability of an error of the first kind, i.e. the probability of rejecting the null hypothesis if it is true, can be looked upon as a socially determined aspiration level. It is quite revealing that these levels are usually at prominent numbers like 10%, 5%, 1%, .1%, etc. This clearly points to the conventional nature of significance levels. The significance levels required in empirical research are different in different subject areas. Of course, aspirations on significance levels are not the outcome of purely individual adaptation but rather the result of social processes. The same is true for the number k in the engineering standard of k-fold security.

12. A THEORY OF BOUNDEDLY RATIONAL HOUSEHOLD BEHAVIOR

Karl Otwin Becker (1967) proposed a theory of boundedly rational household behavior which makes use of aspiration adaptation theory. In the following, the basic idea will be described without going too much into detail.

A household (or an individual) is modelled as composed of two parts, a want generator and an approval authority. The want generator is a random mechanism which produces consumption wants, e.g. the desire to buy a pair of shoes or some other object. The approval authority examines consumption wants and either approves or rejects them according to criteria which can be looked upon as aspiration levels. For every class of wants the approval authority has an aspiration on the maximum price (downward directed). Thus, a pair of shoes may not be permitted to cost more than 200 money units.

The approval authority also has another kind of aspiration levels concerning the availability of money for spending. The money available for total expenditures is divided among several funds, e.g. a fund for food, a fund for clothing, etc. The funds are sums of money set aside for classes of specific wants in a time period, e.g. one calendar month. If the want generator produces a consumption want, such as the desire for a specific pair of shoes, the approval authority first checks whether the aspirations on the maximum price are satisfied. If this is the case it is examined whether there is still enough money in the fund for this class of wants. If there is enough money left, the want is approved and the object is bought. If there is not enough money left in the fund it may be possible to transfer some money from another fund to this fund. This, however, is regulated by transfer rules. Such rules may require that the money left in the fund from which the transfer is made is sufficiently abundant relative to the remainder of the time period. It is also possible that the transfers are limited by an absolute amount or by a percentage of the fund from which the transfer is made.

Obviously, Becker had the private household in mind when he developed his theory. However, it is interesting that his picture of household behavior also fits public households quite well, at least in Germany. Universities provide an example. The budget specifies positions for various purposes, e.g. travel to conferences. If somebody applies for travel money, he can only receive support subject to restrictions on price and on the availability of money in the fund. There are also transfer rules which specify up to which limit and under what circumstances money can be transferred from one fund to the other.

Presumably, the similarities between private and public households are not accidental. Historically, public households had their origin in the private households of monarchs and noblemen. It is understandable that a system of expenditure control evolved which reflects rules of good private house keeping.

It would be desirable to develop a more detailed model of the want generator, based on knowledge about the psychology of consumption. Such a model would have to specify the factors which result in the generation of wants. In this way it would be possible to build a behavioral theory of advertising as a direct influence on the want generator. It is often asserted that advertising is capable of creating wants which were not there before.

Another related theory of household behavior has been developed by Schnabl (1979). He presents a complex simulation model based on psychological theory which will not be described here.

13. POSSIBLE MODIFICATIONS SUGGESTED BY EXPERIMENTAL EVIDENCE

A basic structural part of aspiration adaptation theory is the influence scheme. Experimental findings suggest that a deeper theory of qualitative expectation formation is needed. As I have shown in a paper on an oligopoly experiment (Selten, 1967a), subjects make use of mental models which can be described by causal diagrams. A causal diagram is a directed signed graph whose nodes correspond to variables and whose edges symbolize influences from one variable to another. The directions indicate causal influences. The signs plus and minus show whether the corresponding causal influences are positive or negative. A variable X exerts a positive influence on the variable Y if ceteris paribus an increase (decrease) of X causes an increase (decrease) of Y. In the case of a negative influence of X on Y an increase (decrease) of X causes a decrease (increase) of Y.

A causal diagram has instrument variables, intervening variables, and goal variables. The instrument variables correspond to nodes without incoming edges. These are the variables which can be changed by the decision maker. With the help of the instrument variables the decision maker tries to improve the value of the goal variables.

Qualitative expectations are based on causal chains from instrument variables to goal variables. These chains are called main chains. As an example we may look at the following causal diagram in Fig. 11. In this diagram, we find two main chains, one from X over U and V to Y and another from X over W to Y. Each main chain has a sign which describes the character of the influence from the instrument

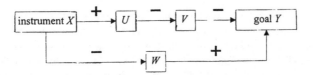

FIG. 11. An example for a causal diagram.

variable to the goal variable via this chain. The sign is positive if the number of minuses is even and negative if the number is odd. In the example, X has a positive influence on Y via the chain over U and V and a negative influence via the chain over W.

A causal diagram is called balanced if all main chains from the same instrument variable to the same goal variable have the same sign. Otherwise, the diagram is imbalanced. Obviously, the causal diagram in our example is imbalanced. An imbalanced diagram does not determine clear qualitative expectations. In our example it cannot be seen whether X has an positive or negative influence on Y. In such situations the decision maker may change his causal beliefs in a way which leads to a balanced diagram. He may, for example, come to the conclusion that the influence from X to W can be neglected since it is relatively unimportant. If the corresponding edge is taken out of the diagram, balance is achieved.

It can be seen immediately how a balanced causal diagram gives rise to an influence scheme for actions which are decreases or increases of single goal variables. This suggests that aspiration adaptation theory could be enriched by modelling qualitative expectations as being derived from causal diagrams.

The aspiration adaptation theory in its original form corrects influence schemes on the basis of the experience made in the last period. The experiments mentioned above (Selten, 1967a) suggest that qualitative expectations are more resistant to change. It takes a considerable amount of experience until subjects come to the conclusion that a hitherto neglected influence should be reintroduced into their mental model and another influence should be neglected in order to achieve balance. It would be desirable to develop a theory about the changes of qualitative causal beliefs in the light of experience. Of course, this can be done adequately only on the background of experimental evidence which still needs to be collected.

The second important structural element of the aspiration adaptation theory is the aspiration adaptation scheme. In the theory in its original form goal variables were thought of as clearly defined quantitative variables; aspirations were described as special values of goal variables and aspiration adaptation was conceived as involving stepwise adjustments on aspiration scales. It now seems to me that this picture is not always adequate.

In experiments on dynamic oligopoly games (Selten, 1967a, 1967b) it was observed that investment decisions were guided by "expansion criteria" which can be interpreted as aspirations on a vaguely defined goal variable "profitability" involving a concern for the control of short-run profit decreases caused by investments. A relatively strict expansion criterion requires that short-run profit is not decreased. A less strict expansion criterion may impose an upper limit on debt. In this way the

214   REINHARD SELTEN

subjects avoid too high interest payments, the main source of short-run profit decreases. Aspiration adaptation involves a transition to another principle expressing concern for profitability rather than a purely quantitative adjustment. The criteria are quantitatively precise, but the required calculations may involve different quantitative variables. In such cases it may depend on the situation, which of the two criteria is less stringent than the other.

In principle it is possible to modify aspiration adaptation theory in this direction. However, it does not seem to be adequate to do this on a purely theoretical basis. More experimental research has to be done.

REFERENCES

Becker, K. O. (1967). *Die wirtschaftlichen Entscheidungen des Haushalts.* Berlin: Duncker & Humblot.

Crössmann, H. J., & Tietz, R. (1983). Market behavior based on aspiration levels. In R. Tietz (Ed.), *Aspiration levels in bargaining and economic decision making, Lecture Notes in Economics and Mathematical Systems,* Vol. 213, pp. 170–185. Berlin/Heidelberg/New York/Tokyo: Springer-Verlag.

March, J. G., & Shapira, Z. (1988). Managerial perspectives on risk and risk-taking. In J. G. March (Ed.), *Decisions and Organizations.* Oxford: Blackwell.

Scholz, R. W. (1980). *Dyadische Verhandlungen.* Königstein/Ts.: Verlag Anton Hain.

Scholz, R. W., Fleischer, A., & Bentrup, A. (1983). Aspiration forming and predictions based on aspiration levels compared between professional and non-professional bargainers. In R. Tietz (Ed.), *Aspiration levels in bargaining and economic decision making, Lecture Notes in Economics and Mathematical Systems,* Vol. 213, pp. 104–121. Berlin/Heidelberg/New York/Tokyo: Springer-Verlag.

Sauermann, H., & Selten, R. (1962). Anspruchsanpassungstheorie der Unternehmung. *Zeitschrift für die gesamte Staatswissenschaft,* **118,** 577–597.

Schnabl, H. (1979). *Verhaltenstheorie und Konsumentscheidung.* Tübingen: J.-C. B. Mohr.

Selten, R. (1967a). Die Strategiemethode zur Erforschung des eingeschränkt rationalen Verhaltens im Rahmen eines Oligopolexperimentes. In H. Sauermann (Ed.), *Beiträge zur experimentellen Wirtschaftsforschung,* pp. 136–168. Tübingen: J. C. B. Mohr.

Selten, R. (1967b). Ein Oligopolexperiment mit Preisvariation und Investition. In H. Sauermann (Ed.), *Beiträge zur experimentellen Wirtschaftsforschung,* Tübingen: J. C. B. Mohr.

Tietz, R. (1975). An Experimental Analysis of Wage Bargaining Behavior. *Zeitschrift für die gesamte Staatswissenschaft,* **131**(1), 44–91.

Tietz, R., & Bartos, O. J. (1983), Balancing of aspiration levels as fairness principle in negotiations, In R. Tietz (Ed.), *Aspiration levels in bargaining and economic decision making, Lecture Notes in Economics and Mathematical Systems,* Vol. 213, pp. 52–66. Berlin/Heidelberg/New York/Tokyo: Springer-Verlag.

Tietz, R., & Weber, H. J. (1972). On the nature of the bargaining process in the Kresko-game. In H. Sauermann (Ed.), *Contributions to experimental economics,* Vol. III, pp. 305–334. Tübingen: J. C. B. Mohr (Paul Siebeck).

Tietz, R., & Weber, H. J. (1978). Decision behavior in multi-variable negotiations. In H. Sauermann (Ed.), *Contributions to experimental economics,* Vol. VII, pp. 60–87. Tübingen: J. C. B. Mohr (Paul Siebeck).

Received: December 31, 1997

[8]

WHY BOUNDED RATIONALITY?
THE MUCH TOO LONG VERSION*

John Conlisk**

Hamlet: 'What a piece of work is a man! how noble in reason! how infinite in faculties!' *Hamlet*, II.2.319.

Puck: 'Lord, what fools these mortals be!' *Midsummer Night's Dream*, III.3.116.

Nearly everyone would see the truth as between Hamlet and Puck. Including Hamlet and Puck. Hamlet is feigning madness, and Puck is just being, well, puckish. Model-writing economists, however, tend not to the middle but to the 'infinite in faculties' extreme. Although the postulate of unbounded rationality has dominated economic modelling for several decades, the dominance seems to be relaxing. Is this encouraging? Why bounded rationality?

In this survey, four reasons are given for incorporating bounded rationality in economic models. First, there is abundant empirical evidence that bounded rationality is important. Second, bounded rationality has proved itself in a wide range of impressive work. Third, the standard justifications for assuming unbounded rationality are unconvincing; their logic cuts both ways. Fourth, deliberation about an economic decision is a costly activity, and good economics requires that we entertain all costs. These four reasons, or categories of reasons, are developed in the following four sections. Most references are to the last 15 years, though many earlier works are also cited.

Given that human cognition is a scarce resource, deliberation about economic decisions is a costly activity. Depending on the magnitude of deliberation cost relative to other costs and benefits in a particular context, bounds on rationality may or may not be

* Fall 1995. Previously unpublished in this form, this is a longer version of the survey published in the *Journal of Economic Literature*, **34**, pp. 669-700 (1996). The shorter version contains about 30 per cent less text and 50 per cent fewer references. Special thanks for helpful suggestions are due to Vincent Crawford, John Pencavel, Garey Ramey, Michael Rothschild, and three extremely helpful referees. Very special thanks for many years of helpful insights are due to Richard Day and Luigi Ermini

** Professor of Economics, University of California, San Diego

Why Bounded Rationality

important. Deliberation cost will be a recurring theme in the next three sections and will be developed on its own in the fourth section. This theme honors the underlying tenet of economics to respect all costs, and it puts rationality specifications in line with other model specifications, as assumptions to be judged context by context rather than once for all.

I.   Spoiling a Good Story: Evidence of Bounds on Rationality

'Should the facts be allowed to spoil a good story?' Michael Lovell (1986, p. 120).

Lovell asked this question about unbounded rationality in forecasting (about rational expectations). We can ask it about unbounded rationality in general. We know there are critical physiological limits on human cognition (see Simon 1990, p. 7), but are the limits important to economics? Do they spoil any of the good story told by the standard theory of optimizing behavior? To be clear, the question is not whether bounds on rationality are always important. They are not; there are many contexts in which the hypothesis of unbounded rationality surely works well. Rather the questions are whether bounds on rationality are often enough important to include in economic analysis and, if so, when.

The evidence sketched in this section will be put in two categories, direct evidence and confounded evidence, though the dividing line is vague. The 'direct' category will concern studies (mostly experimental) which test economic rationality more or less directly by testing the cognitive abilities relevant to economic decisions. The 'confounded' category will concern tests in which rationality hypotheses are entertained jointly with other hypotheses in economic settings.

A.   Direct Evidence — Rationality Tests on Single Individuals

There are many studies in which single individuals are faced with decisions which have objectively correct answers and which test the kinds of reasoning frequently ascribed to agents in economic theory. Do subjects do well in such tests? Often not.

Hundreds of studies of this type have been done, mostly by psychologists but more recently by experimental economists also. There is a mountain of experiments in which people: display intransitivity; misunderstand statistical independence; mistake random data for patterned data and vice versa; fail to appreciate law of large number effects; fail to recognize stochastic dominance; make errors in updating probabilities on the basis of new information; understate the significance of given sample sizes; fail to understand

Why Bounded Rationality

covariation for even the simplest 2X2 contingency tables; make false inferences about causality; ignore relevant information; use irrelevant information (as in sunk cost fallacies); exaggerate the importance of vivid over pallid evidence; exaggerate the importance of fallible predictors; exaggerate the ex ante probability of a random event which has already occurred; display overconfidence in judgment relative to evidence; exaggerate confirming over disconfirming evidence relative to initial beliefs; give answers that are highly sensitive to logically irrelevant changes in questions; do redundant and ambiguous tests to confirm an hypothesis at the expense of decisive tests to disconfirm; make frequent errors in deductive reasoning tasks such as syllogisms; place higher value on an opportunity if an experimenter rigs it to be the 'status quo' opportunity; fail to discount the future consistently; fail to adjust repeated choices to accommodate intertemporal connections; and more.

In such experiments, the mental tasks put to people are typically simple, at least relative to many economic decisions; whereas their responses are frequently way off. The kinds of logical inference that subjects fail to make are much like the kinds of inference that economic models attribute to people. Most important, the reasoning errors are typically systematic rather than simple random errors. Psychologists hypothesize that subjects make systematic errors by using decision 'heuristics,' or rules of thumb, which fail to accommodate the full logic of a decision (as when a person makes systematic forecast errors by using adaptive rather than 'rational' expectations). The systematic errors are often referred to as 'biases,' and the general topic often carries the label 'heuristics and biases.'

The sheer number of experiments reporting biases is so great that a sizable number of books and long survey papers have been written, in part or in whole, just to review the evidence. For books, see Arkes and Hammond (1986), Caverni et. al. (1990), Evans (1989), Hogarth (1980), Kahneman et. al. (1982), and Nisbett and Ross (1980). For survey papers, see Abelson and Levi (1985), Einhorn and Hogarth (1981), Kelley and Michela (1980), Payne et. al. (1992), Pitz and Sachs (1984), Rapoport and Walsten (1972), Slovic et. al. (1977), Slovic et. al. (1988), Tversky and Kahneman (1986), and Williams (1988). Brief reviews of the evidence can be found in texts and readers on cognitive psychology and judgment, such as Anderson (1985), Bazerman (1994), Bourne et. al. (1979), Dodd and White (1980), Osheron (1990), and Sanford (1985). There are also broader works on human fallibility; see, for example, Gilovich (1991), Reason (1990), and Senders and Moray (1991).

Though the vast majority of bias studies are in the psychological and related literatures, a number have begun to appear in economic journals. See, for example, Grether and Plott (1979) and Loomes et. al. (1991) on 'preference reversal' intransitivities, Grether (1980,1992) on Bayes rule tests, Sterman (1989) and Diehl and

Why Bounded Rationality

Sterman (1995) on suboptimal decisions in the face of dynamic complications, and Hernnstein (1991) and Hernnstein and Prelec (1991) on suboptimal dynamic behavior called 'melioration.' Also, see the Camerer survey (1995) and the mini-surveys by Loewenstein and Thaler (1989), Tversky and Thaler (1990), and Kahneman et. al. (1991).

At the same time that psychologists view heuristics as a source of bias, they also view heuristics as critical to problem solving. See, for example, Anderson (1985, p. 205), Groner et. al. (1983), Holyoak (1990, Section 5), Kanal and Kumar (1988), Newell and Simon (1990, Section II), Payne et. al. (1993), Pearl (1984), and Reed (1982, p. 330). At first glance, this seems puzzling. Why not condemn a problem solving approach known to lead to systematic error? The answer is simple. Deliberation cost. For a boundedly rational individual, heuristics often provide an adequate solution cheaply whereas more elaborate approaches would be unduly expensive. As Pitz and Sachs (1984, p. 152) put it, 'a tradeoff exists between cognitive effort and judgmental accuracy.' It is ironic that this economic tradeoff should be better recognized in psychology than in economics. Experimental and various other economists recognize the tradeoff, but the emphasis in economics on unbounded rationality tends to push the tradeoff out of sight.

This summary obviously stresses negative evidence. There are also many experiments in which subjects reason accurately, especially after practice. In principle, we expect that virtually any clear cut reasoning error by a subject can be made to disappear through an experiment which provides adequate incentive and which cleverly enough exposes or punishes the error. Ultimately, we would like to know when and why people get it right or wrong. Psychologists have addressed this question through 'debiasing' tests — that is, tests of whether biases will diminish or disappear when experiments are designed to give subjects stronger incentives, greater initial expertise, better opportunities to learn, and the like. Such design conditions do indeed attenuate biases in the expected ways. However, the attenuation is typically limited, and the broad pattern of results is typically not undercut. The prevailing impression is that biases are not fragile effects which easily disappear, but rather substantial and important behavioral regularities. On debiasing, see the discussions in Battalio et. al. (1990, p. 28), Brehmer (1980), Einhorn and Hogarth (1981, pp. 57-58, 77-80), Fischhoff (1982), Grether (1992), Hogarth (1980, Chapter 5), Nisbett and Ross (1980, pp. 251-254), Payne et. al. (1992, pp. 106, 114-116), Slonim (1994), Slovic et. al. (1977, pp. 14-17), Slovic et. al. (1988, pp. 683-685, 688-689), and Tversky and Kahneman (1986, pp. S274-S278).

As Smith (1989, 1991, 1994) emphasizes, market forces can be potent in attenuating reasoning errors, whereas psychological studies of debiasing do not include market forces. In reviewing a number of economic experiments, including market experiments, Smith and Walker (1993a,b) find that discrepancies between predicted and observed behavior are smaller when experimental payoffs are larger; although discrepancies do not

Why Bounded Rationality

disappear. Regarding the degree of attenuation, Smith and Walker take a deliberation cost view, arguing that decision-makers try 'to achieve a balance between the benefits of better decision making and the effort cost of decision' (1993b, p. 260) and that 'there are both low stake and high stake economic decisions in life' (1993b, p. 249). Experiments by Pingle (1992, 1995) and Wilcox (1993) verify the importance of deliberation cost. See also Day and Pingle (1991, 1996) and Frey and Eichenberger (1994).

There is one other source of (more or less) experimental evidence, vast in quantity and intimately familiar to academic economists. Course exams. We carefully administer mental tests of economic reasoning to many thousands of student subjects; and we provide sizable incentives for getting the right answers (grades, later redeemable for scholarships, higher starting salaries, and other large cash prizes). Though we teach students that agents act as if unboundedly rational, we use gallons of red ink to inform the students that they do not.

In summary, the bias evidence suggests that people are capable of a wide variety of substantial and systematic reasoning errors relevant to economic decisions. Further, the evidence suggests that the magnitude and nature of the errors are themselves systematically related to economic conditions such as deliberation cost, incentives, and experience. In this sense, investigation of bounded rationality is not a departure from economic reasoning, but a needed extension of it.

B. Confounded Evidence — Testing Economic Rationality Jointly with Other Hypotheses

Turn next to tests of predictions based on both unbounded rationality and other hypotheses. If the predictions fail, explanations are confounded. We can't be sure which hypothesis is at fault. What follows are examples, or 'anomalies,' for which a case can be made (i) that conventional economic theory is at odds with the evidence, (ii) that bounded rationality provides a possible reconciliation, and (iii) that economists have not agreed to a better reconciliation. The examples are merely cited, not argued; the citations develop the arguments and give many further references. Thaler is probably the leading anomaly-collector among economists. A number of the citations are to Thaler's anomaly column in the the *Journal of Economic Perspectives,* collected in one place in Thaler (1992).

Consumer behavior

Household consumption data are often at odds with standard life cycle theory. Relative to the theory, people seem to be inefficient in smoothing consumption over the life cycle. Thaler (1990), Carroll and Weil (1994), and Carroll (1994) report that the young and the

Why Bounded Rationality

old consume too little, that consumption is too sensitive to short run income fluctuations, and that consumption is not sensitive enough to expected future changes in income. For example, Shea (1995) finds excess sensitivity to receipt of predictable income increases, using union wage contracts as predictors; and Souleles (1999) finds excess sensitivity to receipt of predictable income tax refunds. In both cases, liquidity constraints fail as an explanation. Aggregate consumption data also display excess sensitivity of consumption to income (Flavin 1981, 1993); and tests of representative agent models of consumption, output, and asset prices are routinely rejected (Singleton 1990). Deaton's (1992) survey of consumption behavior includes a discussion of these anomalies. Attanasio and Weber (1995), however, defend standard theory.

Since wealth is fungible, the components of a person's wealth should not dictate its uses. Yet savings and other behavior are found to be quite sensitive to wealth composition, as if people deny the fungibility of wealth. See Thaler (1990). Along similar lines, consumers appear to prefer spending out of dividends rather than capital gains, thus inducing corporations to pay dividends, even though dividends are taxed at a higher rate than capital gains. See Shefrin and Statman (1984).

In purchasing air conditioners, refrigerators, space heaters, and water heaters, consumers tend to locate at inefficient points on the tradeoffs between initial price and later operating cost (energy cost). In particular, consumers tend to buy appliances with low price and high energy use even though, at plausible discount rates, the initial price saving does not compensate for the later energy dissaving, as if consumers were myopic. See Hausman (1979), Gately (1980), and the discussion in Loewenstein and Thaler (1989, pp. 182-183).

Kunreuther et. al. (1978) report on a large and highly detailed survey of homeowners in flood areas and earthquake areas. The issue is disaster insurance. In the foreword, Kenneth Arrow describes the results as 'certainly disconcerting from the point of view of generally accepted theory' (p. vii). Respondents were often ill-informed about the issues and institutions involved in purchasing insurance, much less the magnitudes needed for a cogent decision. Respondents who could estimate magnitudes often made implausible decisions relative to the magnitudes, purchasing insurance when the ratio of the expected cost to the expected benefit of insurance was very high or not purchasing insurance when the ratio was very low. Both the survey and some associated laboratory experiments by the authors indicate that people tend simply to shrug off low probability risks of catastrophe, regardless of the potential loss or the premium for insurance protection. From a deliberation cost perspective, the cost to a homeowner of learning to make actuarial calculations may be too high; whereas the frequency of catastrophic events is surely too low for learning through passive experience.

Why Bounded Rationality

Rational expectations

Rational expectations can be tested using survey evidence on expectations of inflation and other variables. The data commonly reject the unbiasedness and efficiency predictions of rational expectations. See Cragg and Malkiel (1982), Zarnowitz (1984), Holden et. al. (1985, Chapter 3), Lovell (1986), Frankel and Froot (1987), Pesaran (1987, Part III), De Bondt and Thaler (1990), and Ito (1990). For a study more friendly to rational expectations, see Keane and Runkle (1990).

Rational expectations can be tested jointly with other hypotheses in experiments. The classic probability matching experiments in psychology rejected rational expectations as early as the 1950s; see Winter (1982). Data from recent experimental asset markets rejects rational expectations in favor of adaptive expectations. See, for example, Smith et. al. (1988), Plott and Sunder (1988), Marimon and Sunder (1993), Peterson (1993), and papers surveyed in Sunder (1995). During each experimental period of some of their experiments, Smith et. al. asked subjects to forecast the next period's price. This 'experimental survey' evidence also rejects rational expectation hypotheses in favor of adaptive expectation hypotheses, as does experimental survey evidence in Williams (1987), Bergmann (1988), Beckman (1992), and Hey (1994). Experimenters sometimes emphasize that adaptive subjects move toward rational expectations, 'trying to behave rationally,' as Hey puts it (p. 329). However, adaptive expectations can in principle converge to rational expectations only if the adaptive rules are as rich and flexible as the rational rules, and only if the rational rules are stable enough over time. The evidence suggests that expectations may or may not be rational, depending on experience, difficulty of the forecasting task, and other conditions.

Asset prices

Although we might expect financial markets, with their highly experienced and highly motivated traders, to be the most consistent with optimizing behavior, research on finance seems to generate the most anomalies, perhaps because financial data are the most available. According to the efficient markets hypothesis, arbitrage should force unpredictability out of stock price changes. Yet stock prices display slow mean reversion and other systematic departures from the efficiency hypothesis. See Schachter et. al. (1985), Fama and French (1988), Seyhun (1992), various papers in the Bean et. al. (1991) symposium, Timmermann (1993b), Pesaran and Timmermann (1995), and the De Bondt and Thaler (1995) survey. A simple and striking form of mean reversion is described by De Bondt and Thaler (1985,1987). They find systematic price reversals for stocks which experience large gains or losses over five year periods; the big losers substantially

The Legacy of Herbert Simon I

Why Bounded Rationality

outperform the big winners over the following five years, as if investors had overreacted. Related anomalies have been reported for house prices; see Case and Shiller (1989), Poterba (1991), and references there. Further, security price changes show predictable end-of-week, end-of-month, end-of-year, seasonal, and holiday effects, even though efficient arbitrage would rule them out. Such effects have also been found in experiments. On the significance of anomalies for market-beating portfolios, see Pesaran and Timmermann (1995) and Lo and MacKinlay (1997). On experimental replication of some of these effects, see Thaler (1987a, 1987b), Lakonishok and Smidt (1988), and Sunder (1995).

LeRoy (1989) and Shiller (1989) discuss a large body of evidence that fluctuations in stock prices are too large relative to fluctuations in fundamentals, as if investors overreact. LeRoy (p. 1614) concludes that, 'However attractive (to economists) capital market efficiency is on methodological grounds, it is extraordinarily difficult to formulate nontrivial and falsifiable implications of capital market efficiency that are not in fact falsified.'

Mehra and Prescott (1985) find that equities earn risk premia so large as to defy explanation on risk aversion or other grounds rooted in standard models of efficient markets. Lee et. al (1990, 1991) find that the prices of closed-end mutual funds systematically deviate from the net values of the component securities. New funds tend to sell at a premium and older funds to sell at a discount. Shefrin and Statman (1985), Lakonishok and Smidt (1986), and Ferris et. al. (1988) find that the trading volume on shares that have declined in price is systematically below the volume on shares that have risen in price, even though tax laws favor the sale of declining shares. Shefrin and Statman describe the effect as 'the disposition to sell winners too early and ride losers too long,' which is in part a sunk cost fallacy.

The literature reports 'bubbles' — dramatic price movements which seem to involve deviations from fundamental values, as if logically extraneous beliefs by investors were driving prices. See Camerer (1989b), Stiglitz (1990), and De Long and Shleifer (1991). Smith et. al. (1988) find bubbles in experimental asset markets, even though fundamentals are fully controlled by the experimenters and fully revealed to the subjects.

Various related anomalies are found in foreign exchange rate markets. For example, changes in exchange rates in relation to forward and spot values indicate persistent and sizable departures from the predictions of market efficiency, as if investors suffer from persistent expectational bias. See the surveys by Froot and Thaler (1990), Lewis (1995), and Frankel and Rose (1995). Further, investors seem to display 'home bias;' they forego significant diversification opportunities by an unwillingness to hold assets in other countries. See French and Poterba (1991) and Lewis (1995). Lewis (p. 54) cites work estimating that, 'relative to the US S&P 500 index with a mean of 10% and a standard

Why Bounded Rationality

deviation of 17.3%, portfolios including foreign assets could dominate with means of 13% or more and standard deviations of 16% or less.'

Cutler et. al. (1991, p. 529) suggest four stylized facts as giving an overall pattern to the anomalous price behavior of stocks, bonds, foreign exchange, and some real assets (housing, collectibles, and precious metals): 'First, returns tend to be positively serially correlated at high frequency. Second, they are weakly negatively serially correlated over long horizons. Third, deviations of asset values from proxies for fundamental value have predictive power for returns. Fourth, short term interest rates are negatively correlated with excess returns on other assets.'

Financial management

Patel et. al. (1991) and Zeckhauser et. al. (1991) find that mutual fund buyers act as if they believe that a fund with a superior past performance is a better buy currently, in contradiction to market efficiency. They also find that firms issuing new stock act as if they believe they can identify in advance the times when the price will be higher, again in contradiction to market efficiency. Lakonishok et. al. (1991) find that pension fund managers display puzzling behavior regarding stocks which have performed poorly the preceding quarter. The managers expand holdings of the stocks not currently held but contract holdings of the stocks currently held. The authors hypothesize that fund managers expect the poor performers to bounce back from the preceding quarter, as if mean reversion holds, but that managers want to hide from directors the fact that they held the poor performers the preceding quarter, as if the directors were easily fooled.

Decision experiments

In economic theories of risky decision-making, the agent's objective function is typically defined on the total wealth resulting from choices the agent makes. Thus, changes in wealth resulting from choices are 'integrated' with initial wealth. This 'asset integration' hypothesis contrasts sharply with the Markowitz (1952) hypothesis that utility is defined directly on changes in wealth. The asset integration hypothesis has the status of a rationality postulate in the sense that total wealth, not change in wealth, is what dictates the agent's opportunity set for consumption, where consumption is viewed as the ultimate source of utility. As Machina (1982, Section 2.3) discusses, violations of asset integration can be viewed as violations of the constant tastes assumption. The issue is greatly complicated by the fact that the relevant wealth concept is lifetime wealth, implying that asset integration effects are confounded with intertemporal choice effects. Despite the central role of asset integration in economic theory, there is substantial evidence that

Why Bounded Rationality

asset integration fails under some circumstances. See, for example, Kahneman and Tversky (1979), Camerer (1989a, 1992), Battalio et. al. (1990), and Gertner (1993). Evidence in Thaler and Johnson (1990) suggests that asset integration is neither complete nor absent, but is rather a complicated matter of degree depending on context.

Individuals seem to place higher value on an opportunity if it is associated with the status quo. Samuelson and Zeckhauser (1988) demonstrate the 'status quo bias' using questionnaire evidence for hypothetical choices involving investments, jobs, cars, and social policies. They find that subjects are more likely to select an alternative if its description has been rigged to associate it with the status quo. They also present evidence of status quo bias in choices of medical plans among Harvard employees. Along similar lines, Knetsch (1989, 1992) found that most students first given a fancy mug would then refuse to trade it for a large chocolate bar, whereas most students first given a large chocolate bar would then refuse to trade it for a fancy mug.

Various studies indicate that individuals often display a substantially lower willingness to pay than willingness to accept for a marginal unit of a commodity. Although there is controversy over magnitudes, and although the effect greatly diminishes under practice and market discipline (as in repeated experimental auctions), the body of results is nonetheless hard to reconcile with standard models of economic rationality. Kahneman et. al. (1990), Tversky and Kahneman (1991, p. 1054), and Hartman et. al. (1991) emphasize the magnitude of the anomaly. Coursey et. al. (1987), Shogren et. al. (1994), and Franciosi et. al. (1996) emphasize the mitigating effects of experience and market discipline. Mitchell and Carson (1989, pp. 30-38) discuss the evidence in the context of contingent valuation of public goods.

Experimental auctions and games

Auction experiments provide numerous anomalies. For example, in experimental auctions of an object which has common value to all bidders, but for which the value is uncertain and must therefore be estimated by each bidder, there is a tendency for the winning bid to exceed the value, as if subjects were displaying the winner's curse fallacy (failure to reduce a bid in anticipation of the negative information from other bidders that winning the object would imply). See Roth (1988, Section III), Thaler (1988), and Kagel (1995, Section II). Evidence of a winner's curse is also found in some real auctions. See Thaler (1988), Ashenfelter (1989), and Ashenfelter and Genesove (1992). However, Garvin and Kagel (1994) find that the winner's curse disappears in experiments when subjects gain substantial experience through repeated auctions with the same design settings; and Cox et. al. (1995) find a stronger disappearance effect when subjects are

Why Bounded Rationality

allowed to withdraw from bidding to an alternative activity yielding a positive safe payoff. Thus, the winner's curse, like other anomalies, is conditional on circumstances.

Related experiments suggest overbidding in private-value auctions. See Smith (1989, p. 158) on first price auctions, Kagel et. al. (1987) on second-price auctions, and Kagel (1995, Section I) for a broad survey. For first price auctions, Smith emphasizes that the suggestion of overbidding is only relative to risk neutrality and that the bidding pattern, over wide variation in experimental stakes, can be coherently interpreted as a risk aversion effect. This intepretation, however, strains other dimensions of standard theory. The stakes in the auctions, though varying widely, are still small relative to subjects' base wealth, whereas risk aversion is a second order effect. Thus, substantial risk aversion effects require that we either give up asset integration or give up declining risk aversion. Further, there is the conflict that risk-seeking, risk-neutrality, and risk-aversion are all found, both over losses and over gains (Battalio et. al. 1990, Section 3.2, and references in Conlisk 1993a, p. 259). In second-price auctions, the high bidder wins but pays only the second highest bid. Often bids exceed private values, though such overbidding may be harmful and is never advantageous. Along similar lines, Bennett and Hickman (1993) find that contestants on 'The Price Is Right' television show persistently use suboptimal bidding strategies. Similarly, Metrick (1995) finds strategic suboptimality by contestants on the 'Jeopardy' show.

Many experiments test whether subjects will contribute to public goods or will free ride. See the mini-survey of Dawes and Thaler (1988) and the longer survey of Ledyard (1995). The optimal selfish strategy is free riding, whereas the experiments show substantial contributions. Although most experiments cannot distinguish whether departures from selfish optimality are due to decision error or to altruism, Palfrey and Prisbrey (1996) design an ingenious experiment which allows the distinction. They find substantial decision error and little altruism (for further discussion, see Ledyard 1995, Section IV).

In the large experimental literature on game theory more generally, predictions based on the usual strong rationality postulates are often violated (and often not). See Rapoport et. al. (1976), Roth (1988), Camerer (1990), Camerer et. al. (1993), Bloomfield (1994), Stahl and Wilson (1994), Crawford (1997), and numerous sections in Kagel and Roth (1995).

What are we to make of such empirical anomalies? Some may yield to further optimizing theory. Others, however, seem to achieve anomalous status only because economists push optimizing theory too far. For example, there seems little doubt that consumption-smoothing behavior is observed, that competition is a powerful force in squeezing predictability out of stock price changes, and that game theoretic considerations are common in behavior. However, as theories of these successful ideas

11

Why Bounded Rationality

push to finer and finer margins of optimality, predictions begin to defy the data, as if rationality, a matter of degree, had been pushed too far. Arrow (1986) discusses how much the computational power attributed to agents has increased as economic theory has evolved. Anomalies are not surprising relative to theories which neglect deliberation cost, learning, and other aspects of bounded rationality. Fortunately, the anomalies suggest not just shortcomings of standard optimizing theory but also directions for improved theory. Many of the models surveyed in the next section were motivated by anomalies.

II.   Bounded Rationality in Economic Models: A Sampler

Though a small fraction of the total literature on economic theory, there are many models which allow for bounded rationality. This section is a sampler. The models spread in all directions, making them hard to categorize neatly. The categories used, though each has its own logic, overlap in various ways.

Firms, organizations, and institutions

Coase (1937, 1972, 1992), Chandler (1962, 1977), Cyert and March (1963), March and Simon (1958), Williamson (1975, 1985, 1986), and Marschak and Radner (1972) are classic studies of the nature of firms, organizations, and economic institutions. A central insight is that the existence, size, structure, and workings of organizations are critically shaped by a need to economize on contracting costs, decision costs, and other transaction costs. These costs are traced back in substantial part to agents' limited cognitive abilities. Williamson puts it strongly, 'Economizing on transaction costs essentially reduces to economizing on bounded rationality ...' (1986, p. 110). Following Coase, Williamson hypothesizes that organizations evolve to deal efficiently with transaction costs. Insights from Williamson's viewpoint have had huge impact on the literature of industrial organization (Schmalensee and Willig 1989) and organizational design (Radner 1987, 1992). Although many organizational theorists avoid mention of bounded rationality, preferring imperfect information hypotheses to imperfect rationality hypotheses, some do not. For example, Sah and Stiglitz (1986,1988), Sobel (1992), Koh (1994), and Kennedy (1994) analyze organizational designs which account for the limited abilities of decision-makers. A major emphasis of the organizational tradition is close observation of organizational behavior. A recent example is O'Brien's (1989) study of nominal wage rigidity during the first two years of the Great Depression.

Why Bounded Rationality

X-Inefficiency

An organization can be inefficient because its outputs lie at the wrong point on an efficiency frontier or because its outputs lie inside the efficiency frontier. The latter was dubbed 'X-inefficiency' by Leibenstein (1966), who pioneered in its study. There is now a sizable body of theoretical and empirical work on X-inefficiency, much of it rooted in notions of bounded rationality. See Leibenstein (1987), Leibenstein and Maital (1992, 1994), Frantz (1992), Button and Weyman-Jones (1992, 1993), and references there.

Boundedly rational choice — early models

In standard theory, unboundedly rational agents act as if they had performed exhaustive searches over all possible decisions and had then picked the best. Simon (1955, 1956) hypothesizes that agents instead perform limited searches, accepting the first satisfactory decision. This 'satisficing' theme appears in many forms. A few of the many models inspired by the satisficing idea are Day (1967), March and Simon (1958, Section 3.3), Day and Tinney (1968), Winter (1971), Radner and Rothschild (1975), Herriott et. al. (1985), and Wall (1993). As these models illustrate, satisficing may or may not converge to optimality, depending on circumstance. The satisficing theme is present, in one form or another, in many of the models cited below. The theme is also prominent in cognitive science, where Simon also pioneered (see, for example, Newell and Simon 1972).

A related idea is suboptimization. A decision-maker who finds optimization impossible or unduly costly may instead solve a simpler, approximate optimization problem. For example, a myopic optimization may be substituted for a complex intertemporal optimization. Suboptimization in one period, by leaving out relevant considerations, may call for adjustments the next period. Thus, it is natural to embed suboptimization in a dynamic context which generates feedback. The feedback may include changes in the environment due to decisions of other agents; so the approach is tractable for a population of interacting agents as well as a single agent.

Although suboptimization with feedback can be viewed as having a long history (for example, dynamic Cournot models), Day and colleagues were the first to develop the idea into a broad and coherent approach, which they called 'recursive programming.' Recursive programming has an extensive theory and many empirical applications — to agriculture, coal, steel, petroleum, transportation, regional economics, and economic development. See Day (1963), Day and Kennedy (1970), Day and Singh (1977), Day and Cigno (1978), and references there. Recursive programming models generate a rich variety of dynamic paths, suggesting the complex dynamics of real economies and foreshadowing the recent interest in theories of complex dynamics (see Day 1994).

Why Bounded Rationality

Suboptimization is an implicit ingredient in a wide variety of models, such as hierarchical decision models (Ermini 1987, 1991) and 'case-based decision theory' (Gilboa and Schmeidler 1995).

Markup pricing, adaptive expectations, partial adjustment, imitation, and stochastic choice are examples of more passive decision-making. In the Cross (1973, 1980, 1983) and Himmelweit (1976) models of stochastic choice, an agent chooses at random among a list of possible actions, where the choice probabilities evolve according to the historical performances of the various possibilities. Cross applies the theory to store-choice, lottery decisions, advertising, and other issues. The theory might also be applied to choice among a list of rules of thumb. The approach has precedents in psychological learning theory and is a rough precedent for the economic classifier models discussed below. The theory has also been used as a foundation for evolutionary game theory; see Sarin (1994). Schmalensee's (1975) model of bandit selection, Hey's (1982) model of search heuristics, and McCain's (1991) model of 'groping' are other simple models of passive adaptation.

Biases, heuristics, norms, and other imports from sister disciplines.

As discussed in Section I, psychology and cognitive science have a rich history of discovering, testing, and cataloging biases, and of explaining the biases through rules of thumb, or 'heuristics,' by which people deal with their cognitive limitations. For example, in Tversky's (1972) model of 'elimination by aspects,' an individual chooses among alternatives, not by comparing alternatives in all their aspects at once, but rather by the heuristic of comparing alternatives one randomly chosen aspect at a time, eliminating alternatives along the way. Heuristics are rational in the sense that they appeal to intuition and avoid deliberation cost, but boundedly rational in the sense that they often lead to suboptimal and biased choices. Sociologists and anthropologists also study behavioral rules, often in the form of social norms and conventions. See Elster (1989a,b) on norms in economic behavior. Various models have been inspired by the biases, heuristics, and norms to explain otherwise puzzling economic behavior.

Winter (1982) uses learning heuristics to explain experimental results on 'probability matching' violations of rational expectations. Akerlof and Dickens (1982) use cognitive dissonance (the bias by which people conform their beliefs to what they would like to be true) to model various aspects of worker safety, innovations, advertising, social security, and crime. Rabin (1994) models the individual and social impacts of cognitive dissonance on morally dubious behavior. Akerlof (1991) uses salience (the bias by which people attach undue relative weight to recent or vivid events) to explain why people may procrastinate or show excessive obedience to authorities; and he shows how small effects

Why Bounded Rationality

of this sort may cumulate over time into major behavioral consequences such as inadequate saving, organizational failure, addiction, and crime. Akerlof and Yellen (1987) use biases to sketch microfoundations for traditional Keynesian analysis. Tversky and Kahneman (1991) use loss aversion (the bias by which people are more sensitive to changes perceived as losses than to changes perceived as gains) to explain various behavioral puzzles representable as deformations of an indifference map in the neighborhood of a current consumption point. Benartzi and Thaler (1995) add myopia to loss aversion to propose a resolution of the equity premium puzzle. Arthur (1994a) considers a model in which individuals hold a menu of possible heuristics, shifting among them as experience dictates. Rubinstein (1993), taking inspiration from cognitive science, shows how a monopolist might price discriminate among consumers of unequal cognitive ability, where the consumers use rough partition heuristics. Leibenstein and Maital (1994) use defensive behavior (rationalization of error) in a game theoretic model of X-inefficiency.

Time inconsistency in behavior can be viewed as multiple selves bounding each other's rational choices; the Doer Self wants dessert whereas the Planner Self wants to stick to the diet (terminology from Thaler and Shefrin 1981). Many behavioral rules (for example, don't keep dessert in the house) arise as responses to such conflicts; see Schelling (1984). Negative time preference is a major source of time inconsistency. Loewenstein and Prelec (1991, 1992) use loss aversion to explain time inconsistency flowing from negative time preference; and Kahneman and Thaler (1991) sketch implications for compensation patterns in labor markets. See also Loewenstein (1987)/ Shefrin and Thaler (1988) and Thaler (1990,1994) hypothesize that consumers use simple budgeting rules as devices to discipline temporal consumption behavior. In particular, they hypothesize that consumers allocate their income to different accounts, such as a current spending account, a durable purchase account, and a retirement account, with transfers across accounts not allowed (either by constraint of will or by institutional arrangement). The model helps to explain puzzling anomalies relative to the standard life cycle model.

Some economists argue that inherited emotions and social norms (anger, embarrassment, sensitivity to relative position, loyalty, altruism, manners) can improve economic performance in ways outside the scope of standard economic theory. For example, loyal individuals cooperate better, and a person who involuntary blushes at a lie is better able to win trust. Sen (1977) refers to the selfishly rational agents of economic theory as 'rational fools' since they lack these advantages of emotions and norms. For models of the advantages, see Akerlof (1982, 1983, 1984a) on loyalty and on gift exchanges, Hirshleifer (1987) on emotions as guarantors of threats and promises, Frank (1985a, 1985b, 1987, 1988) and Mui (1995) on emotions and on sensitivity to relative

Why Bounded Rationality

position, Camerer and Thaler (1995) on manners as the resolution of ultimatum anomalies, and Schelling (1978), Samuelson (1993), Bergstrom and Stark (1993), and Simon (1993) on the fitness of altruism. It can be argued that the emotions and norms in question are biologically inherited, since their presence improves evolutionary fitness; or it can be argued that they are culturally inherited through parental training or the like. The dual (biological and cultural) inheritance models of Boyd and Richerson (1985, 1993) contain many insights about inherited transmission of economic behavior. Emotions and norms can be thought of as bounding rationality, not in the cognitive sense, but in the sense that they constrain the behavior which individualistic rationality alone would dictate. Or norms may result from bounded rationality in the cognitive sense. Simon (1993) argues that docility to social norms improves economic fitness by inducing people to augment their limited rationality with the collective wisdom of their social group.

Heiner (1983) introduces the stimulating hypothesis that economic behavior is predictable in large part because it is not optimizing behavior. He hypothesizes that bounded rationality leads people to adopt rules of thumb and that rules of thumb lead to greater regularity and predictability than optimization. Thus, standard economics is subject to an ironic misspecification problem: 'the observed regularities that economics has tried to explain on the basis of optimization would disappear if agents could actually maximize' (Heiner 1983, pp. 586-596). In a series of papers (references in Heiner 1989), Heiner applies the idea to a wide range of economic issues.

Evolutionary economics

This subject might be roughly defined as the study of dynamic theories in which more fit economic behavior gradually prospers at the expense of less fit behavior. Many of the models cited above and below are evolutionary in character. 'Evolution' is not used in a biological sense, although there are helpful parallels between economic dynamics and biological evolution. For insightful discussions, see Winter (1964, 1975), Hirshleifer (1977, 1978), Selten (1991a), Nelson (1994, 1995), and Dosi and Nelson (1994). Evolutionary thought has a long history in economics, is currently experiencing an upswing of interest, and may prove to be the longer run mainstream to which economists return, encompassing optimization models as a part of the broader viewpoint. The subject now has its own journal, the *Journal of Evolutionary Economics,* and a number of recent books are devoted in part or in whole to evolutionary economics, such as Witt (1992), Day and Chen (1993), Hodgson (1993), and England (1994).

Nelson-Winter evolutionary models of technical change

Why Bounded Rationality

Unbounded rationality relates uneasily to models of economic growth. Growth is driven primarily by technical change, whose rate is limited in large part by agents' bounded ability to perceive and exploit opportunities for improving production processes. How can we model technical change without recognizing bounds on the ability to exploit opportunities? Instead, it seems natural to approach growth modelling in the spirit of boundedly rational adaptation. Nelson and Winter do this. Combining adaptive modelling with a variety of growth hypotheses, their contributions over a number of years culminate in *An Evolutionary Theory of Economic Change* (1982). The book contains rich discussions of the issues, a variety of formal models, and many leads for further models. A number of economists have worked with the leads. See, for example, Eliasson (1984, 1991), Iwai (1984), Winter (1984), Silverberg et. al. (1988), Grabowski and Vernon (1987), Conlisk (1989, 1993c), Kwasnicki and Kwasnicka (1992), Lane (1993b), Iosso (1993), Vega-Redondo (1996), and various papers in the *Journal of Evolutionary Economics*. Dwyer's (1994) work on textile plants is an impressive empirical study in the Nelson-Winter spirit. Nonetheless, most growth theorists have ignored the Nelson-Winter lead, even though recognizing inadequate treatment of technical change as their central problem. In a critical comment on the 'new' growth theory, Solow (1994, p. 49) describes its core model, with its constant returns to capital, as merely 'a return to generalized Domar, but with sophisticated bells and whistles.' Raut and Srinivasan (1993) and Conlisk (1989, Appendix 1) make similar criticisms.

Bounded rationality and market outcomes

The effect of bounded rationality on market outcomes is a recurring question. Does bounded rationality make a difference, or are outcomes the same as if all agents optimized? What are the differences and when do they occur? The issues are explored in many models. Some are evolutionary models with full dynamics; others investigate only equilibria.

In a classic early paper, Winter (1971) shows how, under strong conditions, market competition may select for survival only those firms which display 'as if' optimization. However, Witt (1986) addresses the same issue and finds convergence to optimization under some circumstances and not under others. Conlisk (1983) shows how a broad array of firm reaction functions may lead a market to approximate perfect competition; and Gode and Sunder (1993) give examples of double auction markets in which 'zero-intelligence' traders (computers which bid randomly subject only to budget constraints) may achieve near perfect market efficiency. However, Russell and Thaler (1985) show that a small reasoning error by a fraction of the consumers in a market may alter market equilibrium, depending on conditions; and Haltiwanger and Waldman (1985,1991) show

Why Bounded Rationality

how a small proportion of boundedly rational agents in a market may have more than proportionate influence on market equilibrium due to congestion effects (or less than proportionate effect under opposite conditions). Conlisk (1996) relates the severity of fluctuations in a market directly to the deliberation cost of individual firms. Depending on conditions, fluctuations may increase or decrease when deliberation cost increases.

Stimulated by empirical anomalies, a number of authors investigate the effect of boundedly rational traders in asset markets. De Long et. al. (1990, 1991) and Shleifer and Summers (1990) show how boundedly rational traders, by accepting 'too much' risk and thus earning higher returns than unboundedly rational traders, may come to dominate an asset market. Shefrin and Statman (1994) develop a 'behavioral capital asset pricing model' in which some traders display reasoning errors suggested by the bias literature from psychology. The overall model provides a comprehensive and fully structured theory of such issues as price efficiency, return anomalies, option pricing, term structure, volume and volatility, and survival of boundedly rational agents. Timmermann (1995) shows how, in a continually changing environment, learning may itself be the mechanism leading to various anomalies like those observed. Related models are Day and Huang (1990), Cason (1992), Timmermann (1993a), and Campbell and Kyle (1993).

In an old and very simple model, Meade (1964, Chapter V) showed that, as a result of saving and other effects, individuals with superior investment efficiency need not accumulate wealth faster than other individuals. Blume and Easley (1982, 1992) elaborate the logic with modern methods, finding that, in an asset market, 'fit rules need not be rational, and rational rules [need] not be fit' (1992, p. 9).

Kuran (1991) explains how cognitive limitations may influence the evolution of preferences, in which case the whole notion of evolution to optimality becomes problematic. Optimality in relation to biological evolution is discussed in Dupre (1987).

Evolution to rational expectations in markets

Among strong rationality hypotheses, the rational expectations hypothesis is special for at least three reasons. First, rational expectations make a big difference to market outcomes, for example to macroeconomic policy. Second, since departures from rational expectations can be detected without knowing utility functions, rational expectations are easier to test than most implications of unbounded rationality. Third, since an agent's rational expectation depends on knowledge of an entire market or economy, not just on knowledge of the agent's own narrow circumstances, discovery of a rational expectation may involve high deliberation cost.

There has been great interest in whether adaptation might lead agents to rational expectations. The answer depends on exact conditions — on whether the context is

Why Bounded Rationality

simple enough, on whether agents' prior beliefs are compatible with the context, on how agents process new information, and so on. Overall, authors are quite cautious about claiming support for rational expectations on adaptive grounds. For example, see Bray (1982), Blume and Easley (1982), Bray and Savin (1986), Fourgeaud et. al. (1986), Bray and Kreps (1987), Marcet and Sargent (1988, 1989), Woodford (1990), Sargent (1993), DeTemple and Murthy (1994), Kuan and White (1994), Chen and White (1998), and Evans and Honkapohja (1995). In an empirical extension of this work, Timmermann (1994) asks whether stock market investors in the UK could have learned rational expectations from the historical record. Roughly, he makes a case that they could not unless they had good prior information about long run properties of stock price series.

Near rationality, complexity, and market outcome

Akerlof and Yellen (1985a, 1985b) combine two insights to underscore the importance of bounded rationality to market outcomes. First, since objective functions are typically flat at their optima, small departures from unbounded rationality in the sense of lost utility or profit may be associated with large departures in terms of decisions taken; see Cochrane (1989) for a striking example. Second, there may be correlation across individuals in these decision errors, due to common responses to changes in the economy. From these insights, Akerlof and Yellen demonstrate that a fraction of boundedly rational agents in an economy, though suffering utility or profit losses which are only second order small, may cause first order effects on market outcomes. They give various examples; others are in Mankiw (1985), Blanchard and Kiyotaki (1987), Jones and Stock (1987), Naish (1990, 1993), Wang (1993), and Wolinsky (1994). For example, Naish (1993) models an economy in which a fraction of firms use adaptive instead of rational expectations. The firms suffer only tiny profit losses, yet substantially alter macroeconomic outcomes. As Naish emphasizes, a slight deliberation cost in computing rational expectations may outweigh any advantage over adaptive expectations.

Near rationality models suggest that an agent may derive little benefit by upgrading from bounded to unbounded rationality. At the same time, computational complexity models suggest that the deliberation cost of upgrading may be sizable, even astronomical, for routine problems. For example, in many integer programming problems (such as scheduling, capital budgeting, cargo loading, and itinerary problems), computational complexity increases exponentially with problem size; see Garey and Johnson (1979), Papadimitriou and Steiglitz (1982), and Martello and Toth (1990). On the complexity of learning rational expectations, see Board (1994) and references there. A classic example from game theory is chess. As Simon and Schaeffer (1992) note, the optimal strategy in chess is conceptually simple, just as in tic-tac-toe, since both games involve only a finite

Why Bounded Rationality

number of possible sequences of play. However, for chess this number is 'comparable to the number of molecules in the universe' (Simon and Schaeffer 1992, p. 2), making computation of the optimal strategy hopeless. Simon (1990, p. 6) concludes, 'If the game of chess, limited to its 64 squares and six kinds of pieces, is beyond exact computation, then we may expect the same of almost any real-world problem ...'

Self-organizing markets

Consider a population in which some individuals wish to buy and some to sell a certain good, but in which there is no trading center or other institution to organize a market. Suppose buyers and sellers meet pairwise at random, agreeing to trade if their reservation prices allow, otherwise adjusting their reservation prices before the next period. If each new period produces new pairings, there is an expanding web of effects connecting the whole population. It may occur that all reservation prices converge to an equilibrium price, in which case a market is born, even though there is no organizing institution. The market is self-organizing. Lesourne (1992, 1993) and colleagues have developed an enlightening series of models of self-organizing markets. The models deal with such issues as the birth of intermediaries, the emergence of speculators, the formation of opinions, the generation of sunspot equilibria, the founding of unions, changes in the structure of competition, and the effects of critical maverick agents. Albin and Foley (1992) present a model with a similar spirit. Like the population distribution models below, models of self-organizing markets are at the opposite pole from representative agent models. They are rich in interactions among adaptive agents; whereas representative agent models sacrifice virtually all interactions in order to pursue optimization.

In summary of the last four topics, does bounded rationality alter market outcomes? The models answer with a resounding maybe. Depending on circumstances, boundedly rational agents may or may not self-organize into markets. If a market is already organized, boundedly rational agents may have no special effect at all, may affect either the level or variability of price, may have effects that are less or more than proportionate to their numbers, and may have second order effects on themselves but first order effects on the market (or the opposite). With experience, boundedly rational agents may or may not learn more accurate behavioral rules, may do better or worse than unboundedly rational agents in the short run, and may disappear, dominate, or coexist in the long run. Bounded rationality matters, but not in a simple way.

Population distribution models

20

Why Bounded Rationality

In a common type of model, a population of individuals distributes over categories of some sort, making adaptive transitions among the categories as time passes. Transitions are governed by a variety of mechanisms, such as imitation or fitness-sensitive reproduction, with more successful categories gaining population at the expense of less successful categories. (Although evolutionary game models fit this description, they are discussed under separate heading below.) In Farrell (1970), investors distribute over wealth states. In Winter (1971), firms distribute over profitability states. In the older diffusion models surveyed in Bartholomew (1982), and in the newer models of Arthur (1988, 1989) and Ellison and Fudenberg (1993), agents distribute over technological states, informational states, disease states, or the like. In Conlisk (1980), Waldman (1994), and Harrington (1998), individuals distribute over different decision-making rules. In Phelps and Winter (1970), Schmalensee (1978), Smallwood and Conlisk (1979), Granovetter and Soong (1983, 1986), Ellison and Fudenberg (1995), and Kirman (1993), buyers distribute over different sellers (among other interpretations).

Such models are especially useful for investigating direct interactions among individuals, as opposed to indirect interactions through market prices (a distinction stressed in Kirman 1994). Among the interactions considered are imitation, word-of-mouth communication, fads and fashions, bandwagons, threshold effects, herding, increasing returns, lock-ins, and informational cascades. A few themes emerge, but not an encompassing pattern. In a number of the models, one can ask whether the population converges to a well behaved outcome, such as a market equilibrium, a highest quality brand, or a best technology. The typical answer is maybe. Under favorable conditions, there may be convergence to a best outcome. Under less favorable conditions, the population distribution may converge to a unique equilibrium whose closeness to the best outcome can be clearly related to critical parameters. Under still less favorable conditions, there may be multiple stable equilibria for the population distribution, and even the worst outcome may attract the entire population when initial conditions or random events dictate. For example, increasing returns to brand popularity may lead any brand, regardless of quality, to dominate a market (as in Smallwood and Conlisk 1979); or increasing returns to usage may lead a single technology, regardless of objective efficiency, to dominate an industry (as in Arthur 1988, 1989, 1994b). Under other conditions, there may be no equilibria at all; the population distribution may fluctuate forever, either periodically or chaotically. Further, there may be quasi-equilibria in which the model rests for substantial periods of time, only to cascade off to another quasi-equilibrium on the occurrence of a small-probability event.

A recurring theme in these models is that initial conditions and chance events may dictate outcomes. The theme has recently been labelled 'path dependence' and has been used to remind us that 'history matters' in determining 'emergent structures' once we go

Why Bounded Rationality

beyond the unique and globally stable equilibria common in the economic literature. David (1985, 1986) and Arthur (1987, 1988, 1989, 1990, 1994b) emphasize the importance of path dependence. Since simple Markov chains are linear models which allow various types of path dependence, the idea is not new or inherently nonlinear. Nonetheless, many of the population distribution models are nonlinear and more complicated than Markov chains; and many lead to results on stochastic and dynamic processes which are of broader interest. For example, see Bartholomew (1982) on diffusion models, Conlisk (1976, 1982) on interactive Markov chains, Arthur (1987) on generalized urn problems, and Ellison and Fudenburg (1993, 1995) on learning dynamics.

Most of these models view behavior as boundedly rational. In some, however, agents are perfectly rational but imperfectly informed. See Banerjee (1992, 1993), Bhikhchandani et. al. (1992), and Welch (1992) on herding, fads, and informational cascades. The difficulty of distinguishing imperfect rationality from imperfect information is discussed in Section IV.

Games

Game theorists have recently turned to bounded rationality with enthusiasm, either to address experimental results, or to provide a dynamic to select among multiple equilibria, or perhaps simply because game theory, having pushed rationality to the furthest extreme, was ripest for a revision. In one common approach, bounded rationality takes the form of restrictions on available strategies. For example, players may be restricted to strategies that can be implemented by a computer of limited capacity (Rubinstein 1986, 1998, Abreu and Rubinstein 1988, Zemel 1989); players may be restricted to a subset of actions (Sobel 1991, Vega-Redondo 1994); or players may be restricted in the type of inference they display (Stahl 1993). A second approach, sometimes combined with the first, is the adaptive approach.

In a common adaptive, or evolutionary, specification, a given game is played repeatedly, and players modify their strategies in light of experience. The repetitions of play may involve the same pair of opponents, as in Crawford (1974) or Dow (1990). However, the more common approach is a population distribution approach. In a leading case, a large population of players distribute over a set of possible actions for playing a symmetric two-person game. During a period, the players pair at random and play the game. Between periods, the distribution of players adjusts; actions yielding higher average payoffs gain converts at the expense of actions yielding lower average payoffs, sometimes according to the 'replicator dynamic' borrowed from models of biological evolution. For reviews of evolutionary games, see Creedy et al. (1992), Friedman (1998), Marimon and McGrattan (1995); for symposia, see Mailath (1992a), Crawford (1993),

Why Bounded Rationality

Day (1993), and Kalai et. al. (1995); and, for an important recent paper, see Kandori and Rob (1995). Especially interesting are papers which investigate evolutionary rationales for rules of thumb and conventions. Crawford (1991, 1995), Rosenthal (1993a, 1993b), Young (1993a, 1993b), Vega-Redondo (1993), and Broseta (1994) investigate the theory; and Van Huyck et. al. (1994 and references there) report experiments.

As with the population distribution models above, authors ask whether results support traditional equilibria based on strong rationality postulates. Again the answer is maybe, depending on conditions. For example, in a striking early paper, Crawford (1974) showed that, for a two-person game with unique Nash equilibrium in mixed strategies, simple adaptive behavior will lead to endless cycling rather than to the equilibrium; whereas Selten (1991b) and Conlisk (1993b) later showed that, in modified versions of the Crawford model, players detect the cycles and converge to the Nash equilibrium. As another example, Dekel and Scotchmer (1992, p. 392) show that, 'If we interpret replicator dynamics as a learning process, ... non-optimizing behavior can survive'; whereas Cabrales and Sobel (1992) provide sufficient conditions to rule out the Dekel-Scotchmer result. Cabrales (1993) shows how slight variants on the replicator dynamic may alter outcomes.

Dynamics and simulation

Bounded rationality is typically modelled as some form of dynamic adaptation. Using observation and intuition, the model-builders endow agents with adaptive behavioral rules for interacting within some assumed environment, then set the dynamic in motion. Such models include the large macromodels predating the 'rational expectations revolution,' the tatonement price adjustment models now out of fashion, various micro-simulation models (for example, Orcutt et. al. 1986, Bennett and Bergmann 1986, Eliasson 1991, Lane 1993a,b), dynamic versions of computational general equilibrium models (for example, Pereira and Shoven 1988 and Pereira 1993), some parts of the system dynamics literature (see Radzicki and Sterman 1994), and the classifier models discussed under the next heading. Models of this broad sort often yield complex dynamics. Studies which connect economic models to the mathematical field of complex dynamics include Scheinkman (1990), Day (1991, 1994), Medio (1992), and Scheinkman and Woodford (1994). Due to model complexity, simulation is a common part of this broad body of dynamic analysis. Although economists generally have a strong preference for theorems and proofs over simulations, simulation analysts argue that simulation is an important complement to theorem-proving. Simulation models can relax the extreme assumptions often required for theorems; for example, simulations can often handle otherwise intractable institutional realities important to policy models. Further, it is

Why Bounded Rationality

argued, since hypotheses achieve scientific status only through empirical success, it ultimately doesn't matter whether the hypotheses are developed through theorems, simulations, or something else.

Classifier systems

Classifier models of bounded rationality are simulation models in which, roughly speaking, each agent in each period chooses one among a discrete list of actions according to the historical rewards of the actions. Classifier systems originate in the machine learning literature as models of how a machine, starting from a primitive level of ignorance, might by trial and error come to adopt effective decision rules in performing some task. See Holland (1975), Holland and Miller (1991), and Lane (1993b, Section 1). Classifier models have been used in economics, for example, by Marimon et. al. (1990) to study the emergence of a medium of exchange, by Arthur (1991, 1993) to study a multi-arm bandit problem, by Vriend (1995) to study self-organized markets, by Andreoni and Miller (1995) to study auctions, and by Midgley et al. (1995) to study competitive strategies.

Classifier agents engage in primitive trial-and-error learning, as if incapable of active deliberation. Although Arthur (1991, 1993) argues that the 'dial of rationality' in classifier models can be calibrated to match empirically observed behavior, his only example is a multi-arm bandit context, which, by its nature, virtually excludes anything but a trial-and-error approach. Consider a modification of Arthur's context. Suppose that each arm of the bandit stands for an activity involving complex reasoning and that the expected payoff for the arm can be figured out, with no experimentation, through costly deliberation. An unboundedly rational agent (zero deliberation cost) would jump straight to the best arm. A highly naive agent might resort to passive trial-and-error. However, a plausibly rational agent would likely use some combination of deliberation and trial-and-error. It is not clear how to construct a classifier model to handle the deliberation (short of the countless number of iterations needed to build rules of logical deliberation from scratch). That is, human agents facing an economic decision seem typically to start from a much higher cognitive level than the starting position of a classifier model.

Economy of the mind — deliberation technologies and deliberation cost

If rationality is scarce, good decisions are costly. There is a tradeoff between effort devoted to deliberation and effort devoted to other activities, reflecting what Day (1992) calls the 'economy of the mind.' A model of the tradeoff requires some form of 'deliberation technology' by which a decision-maker turns scarce cognitive and other

Why Bounded Rationality

resources into better decisions. These ideas are fairly common in verbal form in the literature; and some models of suboptimization with feedback are close kin to deliberation technologies. As discussed in Section IV below, some standard models (such as human capital models) can be reinterpreted in terms of deliberation cost; and the strong similarity between deliberation cost and information cost suggests that existing models of the former may suggest models of the latter. Despite all this fertile ground, very few explicit models of deliberation cost have appeared. Day and Tinney (1968, Appendix), Marschak and Radner (1972, Sections 9.6-9.7), and Selten (1978) sketch deliberation cost models, but do not develop them.

The first full model of deliberation cost (though not phrased in such terms) seems to be the model of Radner and Rothschild (1975). In their model, a decision-maker, facing several planning activities, does not have enough time to optimize every activity in every period. Thus, the implicit deliberation cost in attending to any one activity is the reduced performance of other activities. See also Radner (1975a) and Rothschild (1975).

Most of the few other models of deliberation cost are more recent. Conlisk (1980, 1993c) and Brock and Hommes (1997) consider models in which different decision rules carry different deliberation costs. Conlisk (1988, 1996), Evans and Ramey (1992, 1995), and De Palma et. al. (1994) consider more detailed specifications in which agents choose the magnitude of a costly deliberation input. Rubinstein (1986), Abreu and Rubinstein (1988), Rosenthal (1993a,b), Goyal and Janssen (1997), Sethi (1995), and Guttman (1996) connect deliberation cost to game contexts. Ermini (1991) relates deliberation cost to hierarchical decision-making. Pingle (1992, 1995), Day and Pingle (1996), and Smith and Walker (1993a,b) demonstrate the importance of deliberation cost in experimental settings. Winston (1989), Day and Pingle (1991), Day (1992), and Warneryd (1994) discuss issues closely related to deliberation cost.

A number of these models show how a deliberation technology can merge standard modeling ingredients (optimization, rational expectations, market equilibrium) with boundedly rational ingredients (costly deliberation, passive learning, rules of thumb). In such models, the 'degree of rationality' of a decision, relative to the decision that would prevail under unbounded rationality, is endogenously determined, along with other model outcomes, by economic forces. The approach seems promising.

III. Yes, But As If: A Dozen Arguments for Unbounded Rationality

The case for investigating bounded rationality has not been convincing to most economists. Arguments for optimizations-only modelling have held powerful sway, shaping the research, the teaching, and the everyday conversations of economists. The

Why Bounded Rationality

arguments are so familiar that a few code words are enough to conjure one up, as in, 'Yes, but you don't understand; no one assumes that people are unboundedly rational, only that they act as if unboundedly rational.' This section works quickly through a dozen prominent arguments for unbounded rationality, giving a brief comment on each. The purpose is partly to review ideas which have made the literature what it is, partly to rebut extreme versions of the arguments, and partly to suggest constructive reinterpretations. A number of the arguments in effect describe conditions under which unbounded rationality seems a sensible assumption. By inspecting the conditions and their opposites, we can turn the arguments toward the more constructive question of when and why bounded rationality is likely to be important. For longer methodological discussions, see Friedman (1953), Koopmans (1957), Latsis (1976), Elster (1979, 1983, 1986), Sen (1977, 1982, 1987), Ermini (1987), Richter (1990), Sugden (1991), Furubotn and Richter (1994), and various papers in the journal *Economics and Philosophy*.

Argument 1. 'As if' rationality. The question is not whether people are unboundedly rational; of course they are not. The question is whether they act approximately as if unboundedly rational; they do. Theory should be tested by its empirical success, not by the realism of its assumptions.

Comment. This is a sketch of Friedman's (1953) hugely influential argument. It is a conditional argument. If people act 'as if' unboundedly rational, we are advised to use that assumption. According to the evidence cited in Section I, however, people sometimes do and sometimes do not act 'as if' unboundedly rational. In the latter case, by the logic of the argument, we should investigate bounded rationality. The admonition to judge assumptions by their empirical success, not their realism, also carries an implicit condition — that it is possible to make the tests. In fact, there are far too many theories in any context to test them all. We can only forecast the likely empirical success of the many candidates and then test the best prospects. It is too big a mouthful to say that an assumption does or does not have a 'good subjective forecast of empirical success,' so we just say 'realistic' or 'unrealistic.' No one has tested whether inflation responds to Elvis sightings, yet we confidently ignore this hypothesis as unrealistic.

Argument 2. Learning. Though people's rationality is bounded, they learn optima through practice, in the end acting as if unboundedly rational. Economists can take a shortcut to the outcome by assuming unbounded rationality from the start.

Comment. Learning extends Argument 1 by suggesting how people come to act 'as if' smarter than they are. However, the learning logic cuts both ways. As Tversky and Kahneman (1986, p. S274) point out, learning does not happen by magic. Learning is promoted by favorable conditions, such as rewards, repeated opportunities for practice, small deliberation cost at each repetition, good feedback, unchanging circumstances, and a simple context. Conversely, learning is hindered or blocked by the opposite conditions.

26

Why Bounded Rationality

That is the message of numerous experiments cited in Section I and numerous models cited in Section II. The learning logic makes us expect that Argument 2 will sometimes apply and sometimes not.

As emphasized by V. Smith (1989, 1991), when the learning logic does apply, markets may be the teachers, guiding individuals to better decisions through economic rewards and punishments meted out in repeated transactions. On the other hand, to the extent that we rely on market forces to support the learning argument, we undercut the case for applying economic theory outside markets.

Economic issues involving long horizons, such as life cycle decisions by individuals and technological evolution by firms, are among the most important in economics, yet are not likely to meet the conditions for effective learning. For example, a young person making a life cycle plan gets no practice and therefore no feedback; the problem is enormously complex; and the environment is likely to change dramatically and unpredictably during the person's lifetime. The person can acquire rough rules of thumb (such as school-first-work-later) by common sense and imitation. But how, with zero practice, can a person jump to the optimum of a personal problem so complex that economists can handle only simple parodies of it?

The famous Friedman and Savage (1948) billiards expert is often used to illustrate the outcome of successful learning. The expert plays optimally, as if a master of the laws of physics, even though he has never studied them. Thaler (1980, p. 57-59) suggests, however, that we also consider nonexpert players. Consider a beginner taking the first shot, in poor light on a badly wrinkled table, with assorted friends and relatives guiding his elbow. Is a young person making life cycle decisions more like the expert player or more like the beginner? Even in the case of the expert, there are serious questions, depending on what we are trying to predict. If we are trying to predict the expert's score (perhaps the analog of predicting income), which depends on the number of shots before a miss, the Friedman-Savage hypothesis is no help since it predicts no misses. Even for the expert, bounds on skill may be the critical issue.

Argument 3. Survivors and tricksters. Agents who do not optimize will not survive.

Comment. The survival argument extends the learning argument; agents who haven't learned aren't around anymore. The argument was originally advanced for firms in classic papers by Alchian (1950) and Friedman (1953), and has been critically evaluated in general terms by many authors, notably Winter (1964, 1975, 1986) and Nelson and Winter (1982). Early on, Koopmans (1957, pp. 140-141) advised formal modeling of the hypothesis; and there are by now the numerous models cited in Section II. The models show Argument 3 to be another highly conditional argument. Nonoptimizing firms survive under some conditions but not under others. Argument 3 has an especially uneasy

Why Bounded Rationality

relation to deliberation cost. In the presence of deliberation cost, the survival logic suggests that a cheap rule of thumb may have higher fitness than a costly optimization.

The survival argument carries lesser force for individuals than for firms. We read in the financial pages that firms fail for lack of profits, but we seldom read in the obituary pages that people die of suboptimization. As consumers, individuals who display wasteful shopping patterns can easily survive at a lower standard of living; and, as workers, individuals who use their talents wastefully can easily survive at a lower wage. Of course, extremely ill-considered actions may lead to death. The argument is again conditional.

There is a more subtle survival argument for individuals. Hirshleifer and Riley (1992), among others, argue that systematic logical error leaves people vulnerable to exploitation. They argue (p. 34), 'If ... people could systematically be fooled, economists would predict that tricksters, confidence men, and assorted rogues ... could win sure-thing income from ... naive individuals.' They give examples of money-pumping devices by which the tricksters would exploit the naive. Pushing Hirshleifer and Riley's argument a bit further than they do, decision theorists often suggest that people cannot survive economically except by overcoming any systematic errors that make them vulnerable to tricksters. Thus, the decision theorists claim, a necessary feature of any good decision theory is that decision rules be non-pumpable by tricksters. For example, Machina (1989, pp. 1623-1624) comments (emphasis in the original):

> Whereas experimental psychologists can be satisfied as long as their models ... perform properly in the laboratory, economists are responsible for the logical implications of their behavioral models when embedded in social settings. ... a naive model of intransitive preferences ... will get eaten alive by a simple 'money pump' argument. ... economists will not, and should not, employ behavioral models that imply economically self-destructive behavior in the presence of other (greedy) economic agents.

This 'nonpumpability criterion,' though widely accepted by theorists, is easily challenged. Suppose that I avoid deliberation by using cheap rules of thumb; and suppose that a number of the rules are in principle pumpable. Will I be eaten alive by tricksters? No such luck for theory. I am indeed barraged by would-be tricksters — at the door, on the phone, through the mail. Yet I am entirely well protected, for two reasons. First, I don't entertain the tricksters' pitches; I have other rules of thumb which tell me to slam the door, hang up the phone, and toss the junk mail. Second, since my behavioral rules are personal, the rare trickster who gets at me doesn't know which pitch to give anyway. So I survive with my pumpable rules intact. The repeated winner's curse experiments discussed above (Section I.B) illustrate the point. The experimenters can be viewed as the tricksters, trying to pump subjects who display winner's curse behavior (overbidding).

Why Bounded Rationality

Some subjects adjust their bidding rules, as the no-pumping criterion would suggest. Others, however, simply withdraw from bidding, in effect slamming the door in the trickster's face with their pumpable rules intact. The nonpumpability argument sometimes applies and sometimes doesn't.

Argument 4. Don't quarrel with success. Economics is built on the postulate of unbounded rationality. Utility-maximization has been a powerful generator of successful hypotheses. It is foolish to quarrel with such success.

Comment. In his well known book *The Economic Approach to Human Behavior* (1976), Becker isn't shy about this argument. He says (p. 14), '... all human behavior can be viewed as involving participants who maximize their utility from a stable set of preferences and accumulate an optimal amount of information ...' To accept the argument, however, we have to grant (a) that the existing success of economics should be credited to optimization hypotheses and (b) that expanded treatments of rationality would not lead to greater success. The models of the preceding section are the rebuttal to (b). Consider (a) in more detail.

Can unbounded rationality really take major credit for the successes of economics? It would seem not. Perhaps the biggest success is the basic textbook analysis of demand and supply; and this analysis depends only on the existence of well behaved demand and supply functions, not on whether demanders and suppliers are optimizing, adaptive, or something else. Becker (1962) himself makes this point through his illustration that well behaved market demand functions can result from random choice by consumers. Similarly, most basic lessons of economic analysis are robust to different treatments of rationality. A striking recent example is the demonstration by Gode and Sunder (1993, 1997) that double auction markets can be virtually as efficient when profit-motivated human agents are replaced by 'zero-intelligence' agents (who bid or ask purely at random, subject only to budget constraints). Market rules, not the intelligence of traders, generate the market efficiency.

But hasn't optimization been a primary stimulus for successful predictions about individual behavior? Consider one of Becker's examples. He discusses a utility-maximizing model of expenditure on medical care due to Grossman (1975). Becker (1976, p. 10) says of this model:

> The economic approach does not merely restate in language familiar to economists different behavior with regard to health, removing all possibility of error by a series of tautologies. The approach implies, for example, that both health and medical care would rise as a person's wage rate rose, that aging would bring declining health although expenditures on medical care would rise, and that more education would induce an increase in health even though expenditures on medical care would fall. None of these or other implications is necessarily true, but all appear to be consistent with the available evidence.

Why Bounded Rationality

The problem here is that, Becker notwithstanding, these implications could easily be changed by rearranging the utility function. For example, consider the predictions about education. We could easily write an alternative utility-maximization model whose restrictions would cause more education, through higher income, to lead people to a more luxuriously unhealthy life style. In the alternative model, more education would induce poorer health and more medical care, the opposite of the predictions given by Becker. In discussing his model, Grossman (1975, p. 148) notes that alternative models are possible and 'can be used to rationalize any observed correlation between two variables.' Thus, did utility maximization generate the predictions listed by Becker, or did it merely package the empirical outcomes? If new evidence overturned the predictions, would we reject utility maximization, or would we merely repaint the utility bullseye around the new empirical arrow?

Goldberger (1989) makes similar points about Becker's work on intergenerational transmission. More generally, Goldberger, Simon (1986, 1989), and Arrow (1986) note that utility maximization has little content without strong auxiliary assumptions on the utility functions and other model ingredients. Since a trained economist can see through the mechanics of a utility maximization, making auxiliary assumptions is often little different from making empirical predictions outright, as, say, a sociologist might. In fact, a skeptic might suggest that economic research typically works backwards from empirical findings to whatever utility-maximization will work. If so, we can reverse the phrases in Argument 4 and say, 'Successful hypotheses are powerful generators of utility-maximizations.' In any case, economists seldom test the predictions of an optimization model against a substantive alternative theory. Instead, the usual procedure is to test a predicted effect against the nonsubstantive null hypothesis that there is no effect at all. This can be likened to arm-wrestling a rag doll; the outcome is revealing only when the rag doll wins.

Argument 5. Sidewalk twenties. A model of unbounded rationality identifies an agent's best opportunity for gain. Since it is implausible for an agent to forego opportunities for gain, unbounded rationality identifies the agent's likely action.

Comment. Forgoing an opportunity for gain, it is claimed, is like seeing a $20 bill on the sidewalk and not picking it up. However, suppose that the $20 is hidden under one of hundreds of rocks beside the walk, and suppose that I must solve a complex logical puzzle to discover which rock. In the face of such deliberation cost, I walk on by. The hidden $20 is then not a true opportunity for gain. More generally, unboundedly rational optima may identify actions which could be discovered by agents only at excessive deliberation cost. Under that condition, unboundedly rational optima may identify false opportunities for gain.

Why Bounded Rationality

In the rational expectations literature, the sidewalk twenties argument appears under the label 'consistent fooling.' It is claimed that an agent with suboptimal expectations would be 'consistently fooled' into foregoing opportunities for gain. However, deliberation cost might make rational expectations cost more than they are worth. Under that condition, their presence rather than their absence would indicate consistent fooling.

Argument 6. Discipline and 'ad hocery'. Without the discipline of optimizing models, economic theory would degenerate into a hodge podge of ad hoc hypotheses which cover every fact but which lack overall cohesion and scientific refutability.

Comment. Discipline comes from good scientific practice, not embrace of a particular approach. Any approach, including the optimization approach, can lead to an undisciplined proliferation of hypotheses to cover all facts. For example, to resolve consumption anomalies within the standard approach, economists have tried to fix life cycle consumption theories by stretching the underlying utility function, by adding constraints, by altering variable definitions, by including more variables, by investigating temporal and cross section aggregation problems, by changing the time series properties of the underlying disturbances, and by adding measurement errors. These may be admirable pursuits; but, as Solow (1989, p. 31) puts it, describing recent macroeconomics more broadly, 'One has the uncomfortable feeling that if you try hard enough — always on subtle and complicated matters — you can find data, functional forms, statistical techniques, lag structures, that will tell you what you want to hear.' That is, there can be an undisciplined proliferation of hypotheses within the optimization approach. Conversely, a bounded rationality hypothesis might in principle produce a parsimonious explanation of a variety of anomalies. For example, as noted in Section II, Shefrin and Statman (1994) use their 'behavioral capital asset pricing model' to address various financial anomalies as a group.

A merit of the deliberation cost idea is that it suggests a discipline for models of bounded rationality. The nature and magnitude of departures from unbounded rationality must be systematically related to the deliberation cost involved.

The phrase 'ad hoc,' in its dictionary meaning as 'specific to the problem at hand,' should not in principle be a pejorative modifier. However, the phrase has come to connote a dismissal, without explanation, of anything but the optimization approach. Perhaps we should call a moratorium on the phrase and provide the explanations.

Argument 7. Trading something for nothing. There is no alternative theory with the power and scope of standard optimization theory. Therefore, there is no reason to start over from scratch with some other approach.

Comment. Even on the premise that bounded rationality meant starting over from scratch, scientific progress in any discipline requires an enthusiasm for finding new paths, or at the very least a tolerance for existing paths that are not yet eight lane freeways.

31

Why Bounded Rationality

More important, the premise is wrong. Models of bounded rationality do not start over from scratch; they build on the same ingredients as models of unbounded rationality, as illustrated by many of the models cited in the preceding section.

Argument 8. Washing out. Departures from unbounded rationality wash out in the aggregate and therefore can be neglected.

Comment. Even if economists had no interest in individual behavior as such, the argument applies only under the right conditions. In a linear model, random departures from unbounded rationality may wash out. In a nonlinear model, however, even white noise errors can influence levels as well as fluctuations of aggregate variables. More important, departures from unbounded rationality are often systematic and correlated across individuals. For example, adaptive expectations at the individual level do not average out to rational expectations at the aggregate level.

Argument 9. Tractability. The unbounded rationality postulate, since it can be formulated through well understood mathematical optimizations, confers tractable analysis and definite outcomes.

Comment. Even if tractability and definiteness were scientific criteria, they are only sometimes promoted by optimization hypotheses. Consider tractability. Optimizations may be arbitrarily complex, whereas boundedly rational behavior can often be represented by relatively simple rules of thumb. Thus, optimization-based models are sometimes more and sometimes less tractable than adaptation-based models. As a spectacular example of the latter, consider macroeconomics. Old fashioned dynamic Keynesian models, with their adaptive expectations and partial adjustment behavioral rules, accommodated multiple categories of agents and a rich variety of other ingredients while retaining tractability. However, recent macrotheory has insisted on rational expectations and intertemporal optimization. Unfortunately, the complexity of the optimizations has forced out so many other ingredients that we end up modeling Robinson Crusoe, pretending he's a $7 trillion economy. Arrow (1986), Blinder (1986), Tobin (1989), Solow (1989), Kirman (1992), and others note the bizarre sacrifices, including markets and exchange, we make to achieve the 'ritual purity' of optimization-only models (Akerlof and Yellen's phrase, 1987, p. 137) in marcroeconomics. As an obsolete macro teacher, I'm reminded of an obsolete saying, 'What a revoltin' development this is!'

Consider definite outcomes. As the argument often goes, suppose we start with utility functions for the various agents in a model. If we consider only optimizing behavior, we have one model. If we consider, say, nine types of adaptive rule for pursuing higher utility, suddenly we have ten models. Aren't we substituting many outcomes for one, thus greatly complicating our theory? There are two main responses. First, if we insist on looking at only one model, there is no clear reason to pick the optimization model; we

Why Bounded Rationality

should select on the basis of evidence or plausibility. Second, the one optimization model may generate multiple equilibria and thus multiple outcomes, whereas all nine adaptive models may converge to the same equilibrium and thus generate a single outcome. This possibility motivates a number of the adaptive models cited in the preceding section.

Argument 10. Logical beauty. The general equilibrium theory of optimizing agents is unmatched in social science for elegance and logical beauty.

Comment. Even if this were a beauty contest, one might argue that adaptation is as beautiful an organizing principle as optimization. In any case, the beauty of optimization-based theory is badly blemished by a problem discussed in detail in Section IV below — an inability to handle deliberation cost.

Argument 11. Definition. Economics is by definition the study of optimizing behavior; bounded rationality is the province of other disciplines.

Comment. According to its most common definition, economics concerns scarcity. Since human reasoning ability is scarce, one could as well argue that economists are by definition required to study bounded rationality. Further, whatever the definition, economists agree that economics should be scientific. If so, every theoretical approach, including the optimization approach, is open to empirical challenge. Regarding the province metaphor, scientific disciplines are in fact clusters of activity, not provinces to be protected by border guards. Whenever theory and evidence suggest a need to settle the sparsely populated areas between clusters, science says welcome. Since most economists would agree in principle, it is surprising how often the 'province of other disciplines' claim is made. Fortunately, we often have reason to doubt that the claims are strongly held. For example, Hirshleifer and Riley (1992), in discussing departures from standard optimizing behavior, argue that 'mental illusions are fruitful activities for psychologists, but ... of relatively little significance for economics.' Yet Hirshleifer is well known for bringing insights from other disciplines into economics (references in the preceding section). As another example, Wilde (1981) asserts that a proper setup for an economic experiment 'requires that individuals have consistent preferences and act so as to maximize their own well-being.' This is a surprising claim since we expect experimentalists to be skeptics to the core, ready to challenge and reject any hypothesis, including optimization. Fortunately, the expectation is realized. The experimental work cited in Section I make it clear that many experimentalists are happy to challenge unbounded rationality.

Argument 12. Appeals to authority. The leaders of modern economic analysis have made the discipline what it is by using the unbounded rationality postulate. What's good enough for them is good enough for us all.

Comment. Friedman (1953), Becker (1976, 1993), Stigler and Becker (1977), Lucas (1986), and others are indeed eminent advocates of the unbounded rationality postulate.

Why Bounded Rationality

However, there are equally eminent skeptics, including Koopmans (1957), Radner and Rothschild (1975), Sen, (1977), Arrow (1982, 1986, 1989), Tobin (1989), Kreps (1990, Chapters 19 and 20), Selten (1990), and Becker (1993). Yes, I have listed Becker on both sides, though somewhat facetiously in the latter case. Always a seeker of nonstandard costs, Becker has recently opened the door a crack for deliberation cost. In his Nobel lecture (1993), Becker says: 'Actions are constrained by income, time, imperfect memory and calculating capacities, and other limited resources ...' (p. 386). 'My work may have sometimes assumed too much rationality ...' (p. 402).

In summary, the standard arguments for the postulate of unbounded rationality are too extreme to be convincing. Put in more flexible form, however, the arguments contain many useful insights about conditions favoring one or another treatment of rationality.

IV. No Free Lunch, Yes Bounded Rationality

'It is evident that the rational thing to do is to be irrational, where deliberation and estimation cost more than they are worth.' Frank Knight (1921, p. 67, footnote).

As a concluding discussion, consider deliberation cost more closely. The starting point is the observation that human cognition is a scarce resource, implying that deliberation about economic decisions is a costly activity. To avoid a free lunch fallacy, we are forced to incorporate deliberation cost (and thus bounded rationality) in economic models.

A.   Economizing Economizing: The Regress Issue

Unbounded rationality is typically formulated as the assumption that a decision-maker optimizes an objective function subject to cost and other constraints. Since it is a routine exercise to include one more cost in an optimization model, a treatment of deliberation cost seems straightforward at first glance. Simply include that extra cost. However, we quickly collide with a perplexing obstacle.

Suppose that we first formulate a decision problem as a conventional optimization based on the assumption of unbounded rationality and thus zero deliberation cost. Suppose we then recognize that deliberation cost is positive; so we fold this further cost into the original problem. The difficulty is that the augmented optimization problem will itself be costly to analyze; and this new deliberation cost will be neglected. We can then formulate a third problem which includes the cost of solving the second, and then a fourth problem, and so on. We quickly find ourselves in an infinite and seemingly intractable

Why Bounded Rationality

regress. In rough notation, let P denote the initial problem, and let $F(.)$ denote the operation of folding deliberation cost into a problem. Then the regress of problems is P, $F(P)$, $F^2(P)$, ...

There are two difficult issues here: (i) what the operator F looks like and (ii) how to deal with the regress. Start with (ii). Few authors mention the regress issue, and most mentions are little more. Consider a few mentions, either of the regress itself or of closely related issues:

It might ... be stimulating, and it is certainly more realistic, to think of consideration or calculation as itself an act on which the person must decide. Though I have not explored the latter possibility carefully, I suspect that any attempt to do so leads to fruitless and endless regression (Leonard Savage, 1954, p. 30).

People often ask: 'Can you do a decision analysis of whether it is worth doing a decision analysis?' I don't know anyone who can give definitive answers ... I suspect one runs into a messy and explosive infinite regression (Howard Raiffa, 1968, p. 266).

... an optimization whose scope covers all considerations including its own costs ... sounds like it may involve the logical difficulties of self-reference (Sidney Winter, 1975, p. 83).

The question of how far to go ... is itself an optimization problem, but a peculiar one in that it can itself not be subjected to analysis ... at least in the last instance. Should one try to analyse the question of how to strike an optimal balance ... , then the same question could be raised in relation to this question, and so on. At some point a decision must be taken on intuitive grounds. (Leif Johansen, 1977, p. 144).

Faced with a choice situation where it is impossible to optimize, or where the computational cost of doing so seems burdensome, the decision maker may look for a satisfactory, rather than an optimal alternative ... In a formal sense, a process of satisficing could always be converted into a process of optimizing. However, this conversion imposes a new ... burden on the chooser: the burden of estimating the expected marginal return of search and the opportunity cost. Solving these estimation problems may be as difficult as making the original choice, or even more difficult (Herbert Simon, 1987, p. 244).

... whenever we apply decision theory, we must make some choices: At the least we must pick the acts, states, and outcomes ... But if we use decision theory to make those choices, we must make yet another set of choices. ... to avoid an infinite regress of decision analyses any application of the theory must be based ultimately on choices that are made without its benefit (Michael Resnik, 1987, p. 11).

... decision problems tend to become more difficult with decision costs taken into account. If one tries to save decision costs by taking them into account, one may easily end up with higher decision costs (Reinhard Selten, 1991a, p. 5).

Why Bounded Rationality

Perhaps the most succinct verbalization of the regress issue is Day and Pingle's phrase 'economizing economizing' (1991, p. 509). If we can economize on economizing, then we can economize on economizing on economizing, and so on.

The regress problem seems to block any effort to maintain optimization as the ultimate logical basis for all behavioral modelling. We cannot formulate an optimization problem which takes full account of its own solution. Wherever we stop in the regress P, $F(P)$, $F^2(P)$,..., there will be a next step. There is no reason to suppose that the sequence converges or, if it does, that the limit corresponds to any problem descriptive of a decision-maker. We seemingly must yield to the idea that some behavioral hypothesis other than optimization, such as learning or adaptation, is needed to escape the regress. In Johansen's words, 'At some point a decision must be taken on intuitive grounds.' In Resnik's words, any application of decision theory 'must be based ultimately on choices that are made without its benefit.' In Simon's words, 'the decision maker may look for a satisfactory, rather than an optimal alternative.' In Knight's words, 'the rational thing to do is to be irrational.'

Beyond the authors quoted, various others have commented on the regress explicitly, among them: Radner (1968, p. 56, and 1975b, p. 254), Marschak and Radner (1972, Sections 9.6-9.7), Elster (1979, pp. 59 and 135, and 1983, pp. 17-18), Gottinger (1982), Heiner (1986, pp. 91-92, 1988, footnote 7), Mongin and Walliser (1988), Conlisk (1988, 1996), H. Smith (1991), Lipman (1991), Pingle (1992, pp. 10-11), Naish (1993, p. 19), and De Palma et. al. (1994, p. 430). This list is surely not exhaustive, especially if the list were to include authors who mention issues closely related to the regress issue. However, a complete list would still be insignificant compared to the vast number of expositions of choice theory which ignore the issue. Further, only three of the works I have found — Mongin and Walliser (1988), H. Smith (1991), and Lipman (1991) — are devoted to a detailed development of the regress issue as such.

Mongin and Walliser are closest to the discussion here. They present a regress of choice problems like P, $F(P)$, $F^2(P)$, ... They argue that a decision-maker is forced to cut off the regress without knowing where best to make the cut. They go on to discuss the regress from our viewpoint as the observer-theorists. In particular, they ask whether the regress P, $F(P)$, $F^2(P)$, ... might converge in some appropriate sense. They give a generally negative answer. Lipman (1991) finds a sense in which a related regress does converge. His regress is A, $D(A)$, $D^2(A)$, ...; where A is a set of possible final decisions, $D(A)$ is a set of possible decision rules for choosing an element of A, $D^2(A)$ is a set of possible decision rules for choosing an element of $D(A)$, and so on. However, Lipman does not offer his analysis as a support for unbounded rationality or for conventional

Why Bounded Rationality

optimization theory. H. Smith (1991) analyzes the regress issue as a philosopher, using the issue to discuss the meaning of 'rationality.'

The regress issue suggests that deliberation cost, though like other costs in reflecting scarcity and implying tradeoffs, has the special feature that it cannot be fully handled within an optimization framework. Although this claim denies optimization the role of ultimate logical foundation for all behavioral modelling, it does not deny optimization an important role.

In formulating models, what should economists do about the regress P, $F(P)$, $F^2(P)$, ...? In fact, economists have ignored all steps beyond the first two. Problem P asks what the perfect decision is. Nearly all economic literature has remained at problem P. Problem $F(P)$ asks in addition how much costly deliberation the decision-maker ought to put into approximating the perfect decision. Only a few models of problem $F(P)$ exist in the literature (cited at the end of Section II). Problem $F^2(P)$ asks in addition how much deliberation to put into deciding how much deliberation to put into approximating a perfect decision. This problem seems overly convoluted, and $F^3(P)$, $F^4(P)$, ... are even more so. Although the regress as a whole is worthwhile to notice, since it helps us to put issues in perspective, neglect of all steps beyond P and $F(P)$ may well be reasonable in most contexts.

B. An Example of P and F(P)

Consider a decision-maker choosing a decision variable X (scalar or vector) to make a payoff function $\Pi(X)$ large. Let $\Pi(X)$ have unique optimizer X^*. Suppose that the decision-maker has enough information in principle to compute the value of $\Pi(X)$ for any X and thus to find X^*. Then $X = X^*$ is the unboundedly rational choice. However, suppose that $\Pi(X)$ is so complex a function that the deliberations in finding $X = X^*$ would be prohibitively costly. Thus, consider a deliberation technology by which the decision-maker 'produces' an approximation X to the perfect decision X^*. Let T be the costly effort devoted to approximating X^*, where C is the cost of one unit of T. Let $X(T)$ be the actual decision resulting from this costly deliberation, and let X_0 be a rule-of-thumb decision that the agent could use for free (zero deliberation). Finally, let u be a random disturbance representing the unpredictability of deliberation (else the agent would know the answer to begin with). A decision technology might then be specified as a function

(1) $$X(T) = G(T, X^*, X_0, u).$$

Why Bounded Rationality

It would be natural to give $G(T, X^*, X_0, u)$ properties such that $X(T)$ moves stochastically from X_0 toward X^* as T increases from 0 to ∞. The formal assumptions might be $G(0, X^*, X_0, u) = X_0$, $(\partial/\partial T)E[G(T, X^*, X_0, u) - X^*]^2 < 0$, and $G(\infty, X^*, X_0, u) = X^*$.

Consider the intuition of (1) under these assumptions. At one extreme, if deliberation is prohibitively costly (C very large), the decision-maker is motivated to do no deliberation ($T = 0$), and (1) yields the pure rule-of-thumb decision $X = X_0$, perhaps a simple adaptive response to experience. At the opposite extreme, if deliberation is free ($C = 0$), the decision-maker is motivated to do infinite deliberation ($T = \infty$), and (1) yields the unboundedly rational choice $X = X^*$. In between, (1) gives a mix among rule-of-thumb behavior, deliberation, and random noise. The mix dictates the decision-maker's 'degree of rationality' for the problem at hand. Algebraically specific deliberation technologies of form (1) are used in Conlisk (1988, 1996) and Evans and Ramey (1992). Conlisk (1996) relates qualitative characteristics of (1) to insights from the cognitive science literature.

The deliberation technology (1) is just one example of how we might heed Simon's (1976) admonition to move from 'substantive' to 'procedural' rationality. To the possible criticism that (1) doesn't look much like human cognition, we might recall that a CES production function doesn't look much like a factory floor. In representing a deliberation technology as in representing a production technology, the object is not faithfulness to cognitive science or to engineering. Rather the object is a simple relationship for representing economic costs and tradeoffs.

In this example, the original problem P is to choose X to make $\Pi(X)$ large. Adding risk neutrality, the augmented problem $F(P)$ may be defined as the problem of choosing the deliberation effort T to make the expected net payoff $E\{\Pi[X(T)]-CT$ large. Summarizing:

> *Original problem P.*   Choose X to make $\Pi(X)$ large.
>
> *Augmented problem F(P).*   Choose T to make $E\{\Pi[X(T)]\}-CT$ large.

C.   Four Rationalities

The problems P and $F(P)$ suggest a rough way of categorizing treatments of rationality in the literature. Most models treat the original decision problem P. Only a few add a deliberation technology and treat the augmented problem $F(P)$. Among models treating P, there are two ways to close the model. Either the decision-maker optimizes, or the

Why Bounded Rationality

decision-maker uses some other behavioral rule, say an adaptive rule. Among models treating $F(P)$, there are the same two ways to close the model. Either the decision-maker optimizes in the sense of finding the optimal deliberation effort to devote to the choice, or the decision-maker follows some adaptive rule. This gives four categories of models.

1. Treat problem P. Optimal closure.
2. Treat problem P. Adaptive closure.
3. Treat problem $F(P)$. Optimal closure.
4. Treat problem $F(P)$. Adaptive closure.

The categories are in decreasing order of size. Category 1 comprises models of unboundedly rational choice, the vast majority of models in the literature. Category 2 includes models of bounded rationality in which adaptive choice rules are specified outright, with no deliberation technology or explicit treatment of deliberation cost. This category includes the vast majority of models of bounded rationality surveyed in Section II. Categories 3 and 4, which require specification of a deliberation technology, contain only the very few models surveyed in the final paragraphs of Section II.

Consider Category 3. It supposes that we have specified a deliberation technology and that the decision-maker chooses the optimal amount of deliberation. In the example, the decision-maker chooses the T, call it T^*, which maximizes $E\{\Pi[X(T)]-CT$. Thirty years ago, Baumol and Quandt (1964, p. 23) dubbed this 'optimal imperfection.' In their words,

> One can easily formulate the appropriate ... marginal conditions for what one may call an optimally imperfect decision, which requires that the marginal cost of ... more refined calculation be equal to its marginal (expected) gross yield.

We might quarrel with the words 'easily formulate,' since Baumol and Quandt did not in fact present a model of optimal imperfection, nor have many authors since. In terms of the $F(P)$ example, the marginal condition referred to by Baumol and Quandt is that the marginal cost of deliberation C equal the expected marginal benefit $\partial E\{\Pi[X(T)]\}/\partial T$. If $F(P)$ is viewed as a stopping problem (when to stop deliberating and take final action), then optimal imperfection means optimal stopping.

However, there is a problem. The phrase 'optimal imperfection,' which might be rephrased 'perfect imperfection' or 'rational irrationality,' sounds paradoxical. And it is. Why would a decision-maker who cannot optimize relative to problem P be able to optimize relative to problem $F(P)$, which will often be more complicated? Yet, if we fold in the cost of deliberating about $F(P)$, we are off again into the regress P, $F(P)$, $F^2(P)$, ... Thus, optimal imperfection raises the regress problem in another guise. Nonetheless, in

Why Bounded Rationality

the literature, the few models which treat problem $F(P)$ often do invoke optimal imperfection.

What is the defense of optimal imperfection? Taking a dynamic view, we might justify optimal imperfection as an equilibrium condition. A model in Category 4 might adapt over time into a model in Category 3, just as, by more familiar adaptive logic, a model in Category 2 might adapt over time into Category 1. However, the conditions for such convergence from Category 4 to Category 3 seem especially delicate. We must suppose that the decision-maker faces a time sequence of original problems $\{P_i\}$ sufficiently complex that deliberation cost remains important, thus leading to a sequence $\{F_i(P_i)\}$ of deliberation cost problems. We must then assume that the optimal deliberation effort is the same for each problem in the sequence $\{F_i(P_i)\}$, so that there is an invariant optimal effort T^* to which the actual efforts $\{T_i\}$ might in principle converge. Finally, we must assume that the decision-maker does manage to converge.

Since these conditions are delicate, a modeler may have to justify optimal imperfection as nothing more profound than a compromise of expedience. Suppose deliberation cost seems important in some context. Category 1 (unbounded rationality) takes no account at all of the deliberation cost; and Category 2 (most models of bounded rationality) takes no explicit account. Thus, the modeler moves on to Category 3, which takes direct and explicit account of deliberation cost and the tradeoffs it implies. Since this is already a big improvement relative to most of the existing literature, the modeler may stop there, not wishing to face the added difficulties of Category 4. This might be a good compromise.

Though optimal imperfection closes a model with an optimization, it is not a retreat to some new form of unbounded rationality. An unboundedly rational decision-maker optimizes every setting; whereas an optimally imperfect one does not. In the example above, an unboundedly rational decision-maker hits both settings $X = X^*$ and $T = T^* = \infty$ (where $T^* = \infty$ because deliberation is free), whereas an optimally imperfect decision-maker hits only $T = T^*$. This difference is large. In the example, an optimally imperfect X turns out to be a mix between the unboundedly rational decision X^* and the rule of thumb decision X_0, subject to a random disturbance. In a particular context, the mix may have substantial consequences for market behavior, policy, or some other issue.

D.   Ex Ante *vs* Ex Post *Posts: Similarities of Deliberation Cost and Information Cost*

If I walk into a lamp post while watching a bird, my family would call it a dumb move. Among economists, however, I can claim that, given the spatial distribution of lamp

Why Bounded Rationality

posts, the expected utility of bird-watching exceeds the expected disutility of a collision. *Ex ante*, the post probably was not there, and it is entirely rational to collide with an ex post post. This example illustrates how rationality issues and information issues can be confounded. An action which is suboptimal after the fact can often be attributed to either imperfect rationality or imperfect information. Am I dumb to walk into a post or merely a rational victim of imperfect information?

Expanding the deliberation cost idea, a natural way for an economist to think about the issue is to view decisions as 'produced' by a decision technology with two inputs: (i) information-gathering and (ii) deliberation about the information gathered. Passages in Arrow (1974, p. 39) and in McCloskey and Klamer (1995) are close to this suggestion; and the suggestion is a natural extension of some of the models cited in the last part of Section II. Given a decision technology, the quality of a decision will depend on the amounts of both inputs. If both inputs are costly, an agent will be motivated to economize on both. The appropriate input mix is person-specific. Sherlock Holmes is more deliberation-intensive than Inspector Lestrade. Since an *ex post* error might have been avoided by either more information or more deliberation, it will typically be impossible to attribute an error to one or the other input. Conventional theory evades the attribution issue through the unbounded rationality postulate. If rationality is unbounded, the deliberation input is effectively infinite; hence any *ex post* error must be attributed to a shortage of information. Little is written on the interaction of imperfect information and imperfect rationality; Heiner (1988) is a rare exception.

A helpful viewpoint is to imagine that all statements relevant to a decision can be partitioned into three sets.

1. Knowledge set. The set of all statements already known to the agent.
2. Further implication set. The set of all statements not known by the agent, but nonetheless implied by statements in the agent's knowledge set.
3. Residual set. The set of all remaining statements.

In this terminology, deliberation is a costly activity for moving statements from Set 2 to Set 1; and information collection is a costly activity for moving statements from either Set 2 or Set 3 to Set 1. For example, most trigonometric identities are in my Set 2. I could move them to Set 1 by mathematical reasoning (deliberation), by looking them up in a book (information collection), or by a mix. Current stock prices are in my Set 3. I could move them to Set 1 only by information collection, not by deliberation. Unbounded rationality is the case when Set 2 is always empty; the decision-maker always knows all inferences of given information. Perfect information might be defined as the case when Set 3 is empty; the decision-maker knows enough to infer everything relevant to the

Why Bounded Rationality

context. Perfect knowledge occurs when Sets 2 and 3 are both empty. Perfect knowledge and perfect information are identical under unbounded rationality but not under bounded rationality.

The similarity of costly deliberation and costly information collection suggests that models of deliberation, as they evolve in economics, will inevitably have a general family resemblance to models of information collection. For example, the illustrative deliberation technology (1) is of the form of some sampling models, with T the analog of a sample size. It is curious that two such similar economic issues, costly deliberation and costly information collection, have been so differently treated in standard economics. Study of information cost, as part of the economics of information, has been considered highly virtuous; at the same time, refusal to study deliberation cost has also been considered highly virtuous. Ironically, it is the similarity of the two issues that allows economists to treat them so differently. Behavior due to imperfect deliberation can be passed off as imperfect information.

For example, Oliver Williamson (1975, 1985, 1986) is a towering figure in industrial organization for his insights about transactions costs. Although he sees these costs as rooted in bounded rationality, formal theories based on his ideas tend to portray the costs as information costs. Kreps (1990, 20.1-20.2) in effect notes this point. Another example is the famous Gang of Four explanation of why we observe cooperation in finitely repeated prisoner's dilemma games even though the familiar unraveling argument of game theory predicts failure to cooperate. Although the observed behavior appears to be boundedly rational, Kreps et. al. (1982) suggest a possible rescue of standard theory by putting the bound on information instead. They assume that, although both players really are unboundedly rational, one player thinks the other might be boundedly rational. This clever (and strained?) informational twist is enough to induce cooperation within the usual rationality assumptions. The Gang of Four approach is in sharp contrast to Selten's (1978) approach to the chain store game, another game in which the unraveling logic produces a counterintuitive prediction. Selten faces the bounded rationality issue directly and sketches a theory of bounded rationality, including a brief discussion of deliberation cost and, implicitly, of the regress issue. See also Selten and Stoecker (1986) and Selten (1991a, especially p. 18) on cooperation, unravelling, and the Gang of Four.

To gain perspective, it is entertaining to imagine an accidentally different history for economic theory. Imagine that modern decision theory began, not with perfect rationality and imperfect information, but with the opposite, imperfect rationality and perfect information. Observed behavior that seemed to be the result of imperfect information was instead passed off by clever economists as the result of bounded rationality. As the idea caught on, strict conventions for proper treatment of bounded rationality developed. Scholars departing from the conventions, or even worse from the perfect information

Why Bounded Rationality

postulate, were chastised as 'ad hoc' and were firmly guided back to proper technique by dissertation supervisors and journal referees. No one claimed that information was literally perfect in real life, merely that agents learned their own situations well enough to act 'as if' perfectly informed; after all, those who didn't would be driven out of business by those who did.

E.   Elephants in the Living Room

Deliberation cost and bounded rationality, like elephants in a living room, are sometimes just too much to ignore. Standard economics is forced to recognize their presence, if not to refer to them by name. Consider two examples, human capital and technical change.

People spend much on human capital, in large part through schooling. Some of the investment is information collection (names and dates); some is skill acquisition (typing); but much is investment in general cognitive development ('learning to think' or even 'learning to think like an economist'). The latter investment must be a response to bounded rationality. Consider a deliberation cost interpretation. Deliberation cost can be specific to a particular decision, as in the $F(P)$ illustration above; or it can be the general cost of all-purpose cognitive training used in many decisions over many years. From this viewpoint, the part of schooling cost which goes into general cognitive development is general deliberation cost, and human capital theory is implicitly concerned with bounded rationality. The assumption that students invest optimally in schooling is just an unusually strong example of optimal imperfection. Explicit recognition of the relation of human capital theory to bounded rationality might bring new insights to the theory.

As a second example, consider technical change. Many technological innovations result from insights that would have been made years earlier if people really did draw all possible inferences from existing information. In this sense, the rate of technical change is largely determined by bounds on rationality and by the resulting delays in exploiting economic opportunities. Yet, according to various models of research and development, decision-makers engage in optimal amounts of search for the unexploited opportunities, as if unboundedly rational. We can view the search cost as (in part) deliberation cost, and we can view the optimal search assumption as an example of optimal imperfection. If the relation of technical change to bounded rationality were openly recognized (as in the evolutionary models cited in Section II), standard models of technical change might be better.

Why Bounded Rationality

V.   Final Words

Why bounded rationality? In four words (one for each section above): evidence, success, methodology, and scarcity. In more words: Psychology and economics provide wide-ranging evidence that bounded rationality is important (Section I). Economists who include bounds on rationality in their models have excellent success in describing economic behavior beyond the coverage of standard theory (Section II). The traditional appeals to economic methodology cut both ways; the conditions of a particular context may favor either bounded or unbounded rationality (Section III). Models of bounded rationality adhere to a fundamental tenet of economics, respect for scarcity. Human cognition, as a scarce resource, should be treated as such (Section IV).

The survey stresses throughout that an appropriate rationality assumption is not something to decide once for all contexts. In principle, we might suppose there is an encompassing single theory which takes various forms of bounded and unbounded rationality as special cases. As with other model ingredients, however, we in practice want to work directly with the most convenient special case which does justice to the context. The evidence and models surveyed suggest that the appropriate special case varies by context, depending on such conditions as deliberation cost, complexity, incentives, experience, and market discipline.

Beyond the four reasons given, there is one more reason for studying bounded rationality. It is simply a fascinating thing to do. We can mix some Puck with our Hamlet.

References

Abelson, R., and A. Levi. 1985. 'Decision Making and Decision Theory.' In G. Lindzey and E. Aronson (editors), *Handbook of Social Psychology: Volume I, Theory and Method*. New York, Random House.

Abreu, D., and A. Rubinstein. 1988. 'The Structure of Nash Equilibrium in Repeated Games with Finite Automata.' *Econometrica* 56, 1259-1281.

Akerlof, G. 1982. 'Labor Contracts as Partial Gift Exchange.' *Quarterly Journal of Economics* 97, 543-569. Reprinted in Akerlof (1984b).

—— 1983. 'Loyalty Filters.' *American Economic Review* 73, 54-63. Reprinted in Akerlof (1984b).

—— 1984a. 'Gift Exchange and Efficiency-Wage Theory: Four Views.' *American Economic Review Papers and Proceedings* 74, 79-83.

—— 1984b. *An Economic Theorist's Book of Tales*. Cambridge, Cambridge University Press.

—— 1991. 'Procrastination and Obedience.' *American Economic Review Papers and Proceedings* 81, 1-19.

Why Bounded Rationality

Akerlof, G., and W. Dickens. 1982. 'The Economic Consequences of Cognitive Dissonance.' *American Economic Review* 72, 307-319. Reprinted in Akerlof (1984b).

Akerlof, G., and J. Yellen. 1985a. 'A Near-Rational Model of the Business Cycle, with Wage and Price Inertia.' *Quarterly Journal of Economics* 100, 823-838.

—— 1985b. 'Can Small Deviations from Rationality Make Significant Differences to Economic Equilibria?' *American Economic Review* 75, 708-720.

—— 1987. 'Rational Models of Irrational Behavior.' *American Economic Review Papers and Proceedings* 77, 137-142.

Albin, P., and D. Foley. 1992. 'Decentralized Dispersed Exchange without an Auctioneer.' *Journal of Economic Behavior and Organization* 18, 27-51.

Alchian, A. 1950. 'Uncertainty, Evolution, and Economic Theory.' *Journal of Political Economy* 58, 211-222.

Anderson, J. 1985. *Cognitive Psychology and Its Implications.* 2nd edition. New York, W. H. Freeman.

Andreoni, J., and J. Miller. 1995. 'Auctions with Aritificial Adaptive Agents.' *Games and Economic Behavior* 10, 39-64.

Arkes, H., and K. Hammond (editors). 1986. *Judgment and Decision Making: An Interdisciplinary Reader.* Cambridge, Cambridge University Press.

Arrow, K. 1974. *The Limits of Organization.* New York, Norton.

—— 1982. 'Risk Perception in Psychology and Economics.' *Economic Inquiry* 20, 1-9.

—— 1986. 'Rationality of Self and Others in an Economic System.' *Journal of Business* 59, S385-S399. Reprinted in Hogarth and Reder (1987).

—— 1989. Untitled chapter in W. Sichel (editor), *The State of Economic Science.* Kalamazoo, Michigan, Upjohn Institute.

Arthur, W. B. 1987. 'Path-Dependent Processes and the Emergence of Macro-Structure.' *European Journal of Operational Research* 30, 294-303.

—— 1988. 'Self-Reinforcing Mechanisms in Economics.' In P. Anderson, K. Arrow, and D. Pines (editors), *The Economy as an Evolving Complex System.* Redwood, California, Addison-Wesley.

—— 1989. 'Competing Technologies, Increasing Returns, and Lock-In by Historical Events.' *Economic Journal* 99, 116-131.

—— 1990. 'Positive Feedbacks in the Economy.' *Scientific American,* February, 92-99.

—— 1991. 'Designing Economic Agents that Act Like Human Agents: A Behavioral Approach to Bounded Rationality.' *American Economic Review Papers and Proceedings* 81, 353-359.

—— 1993. 'On Designing Economic Agents that Behave Like Human Agents.' *Journal of Evolutionary Economics* 3, 1-22.

—— 1994a. 'Inductive Reasoning and Bounded Rationality.' *American Economic Review Papers and Proceedings* 84, 406-411.

—— 1994b. *Increasing Returns and Path-Dependence in the Economy.* Ann Arbor, University of Michigan Press.

Ashenfelter, O. 1989. 'How Auctions Work for Wine and Art.' *Journal of Economic Perspectives* 3, 23-36.

Ashenfelter, O., and D. Genesove. 1992. 'Testing for Price Anomalies in Real-Estate Auctions.' *American Economic Review Papers and Proceedings* 1992, 501-505.

Atkinson, R., R. Herrnstein, G. Lindzey, and R. Luce (editors). 1988. *Stevens' Handbook of Experimental Psychology.* New York, Wiley.

Why Bounded Rationality

Attanasio, O., and G. Weber. 1995. 'Is Consumption Growth Consistent with Intertemporal Optimization? Evidence from the Consumer Expenditure Survey.' *Journal of Political Economy* 103, 1121-57.

Banerjee, A. 1992. 'A Simple Model of Herd Behavior.' *Quarterly Journal of Economics* 107, 797-818.

—— 1993. 'The Economics of Rumours.' *Review of Economic Studies* 60, 309-327.

Bartholomew, D. 1982. *Stochastic Models for Social Processes*. 3rd edition. New York, Wiley.

Battalio, R., J. Kagel, and Komain Jiranyakul. 1990. 'Testing Between Alternative Models of Choice Under Uncertainty: Some Initial Results.' *Journal of Risk and Uncertainty* 3, 25-50.

Baumol, W., and R. Quandt. 1964 'Rules of Thumb and Optimally Imperfect Decisions.' *American Economic Review* 54, 23-46.

Bazerman, M. 1994. *Judgment in Managerial Decision Making*, 3rd edition. New York, Wiley.

Bean, C., M. Dewatripont, and J. Moore (editors). 1991. The Econometrics of Financial Markets. Special issue of *Review of Economic Studies* 58.

Becker, G. 1962. 'Irrational Behavior and Economic Theory.' *Journal of Political Economy* 70, 1-13. Reprinted in Becker (1976).

—— 1976. *The Economic Approach to Human Behavior*. Chicago, University of Chicago Press.

—— 1993. 'Nobel Lecture: The Economic Way of Looking at Behavior.' *Journal of Political Economy* 101, 385-409.

Beckman, S. 1992. 'The Sources of Forecast Errors: Experimental Evidence.' *Journal of Economic Behavior and Organization* 19, 237-244.

Benartzi, S., and R. Thaler. 1993. 'Myopic Loss Aversion and the Equity Premium Puzzle.' *Quarterly Journal of Economics* 110, 73-92.

Bennett, R., and B. Bergmann. 1986. *A Microsimulated Transactions Model of the United States Economy*. Baltimore, Johns Hopkins.

Bennett, R., and K. Hickman. 1993. 'Rationality and the 'Price Is Right'.' *Journal of Economic Behavior and Organization* 21, 99-105.

Bergmann, B. 1988. 'An Experiment in the Formation of Expectations.' *Journal of Economic Behavior and Organization* 9, 137-151.

Bergstrom, T., and O. Stark. 1993. 'How Altruism Can Prevail in an Evolutionary Environment.' *American Economic Review Papers and Proceedings* 83, 149-155.

Bikhchandani, S., D. Hirshleifer, and I. Welch. 1991. 'A Theory of Fads, Fashion, Custom and Cultural Change as Information Cascades.' *Journal of Political Economy* 100, 992-1026.

Blanchard, O., and N. Kiyotaki. 1987. 'Monopolistic Competition and the Effects of Aggregate Demand.' *American Economic Review* 77, 647-66.

Blinder, A. 1986. 'Keynes after Lucas.' *Eastern Economic Journal* 12, 209-216.

Bloomfield, R. 1994. 'Learning a Mixed Strategy Equilibrium in the Laboratory.' *Journal of Economic Behavior and Organization* 25, 411-436.

Blume, L., and D. Easley. 1982. 'Learning to Be Rational.' *Journal of Economic Theory* 26, 340-351.

—— 1992. 'Evolution and Market Behavior.' *Journal of Economic Theory* 58, 9-40.

—— 1993. 'Economic Natural Selection.' *Economics Letters* 42, 281-289.

Board, R. 1994. 'Polynomially Bounded Rationality.' *Journal of Economic Theory* 63, 246-270.

Bourne, L., R. Dominowski, and E. Loftus. 1979. *Cognitive Processes*. Englewood Cliffs, New Jersey, Prentice-Hall.

Boyd, R., and P. Richerson. 1985. *Culture and the Evolutionary Process*. Chicago, University of Chicago Press.

Why Bounded Rationality

—— 1993. 'Rationality, Imitation, and Tradition.' In Day and Chen (1993).

Bray, M. 1982. 'Learning, Estimation and the Stability of Rational Expectations.' *Journal of Economic Theory* 26, 318-339.

Bray, M., and N. Savin. 1986. 'Rational Expectations Equilibria, Learning and Model Specification.' *Econometrica* 54, 1129-1160.

Bray, M., and D. Kreps. 1987. 'Rational Learning and Rational Expectations.' In G. Feiwel (editor), *Arrow and the Ascent of Modern Economic Theory*. New York, New York University Press.

Brehmer, B. 1980. 'In One Word: Not from Experience.' *Acta Psychologica* 45, 223-241. Reprinted in Arkes and Hammond (1986).

Brock, W., and C. Hommes. 1997. 'A Rational Route to Randomness.' *Econometrica* 65, 1059-95.

Broseta, B. 1994. 'Adaptive Learning Processes in Coordination Games.' Ph.D. dissertation, University of California, San Diego.

Button, K., and T. Weyman-Jones. 1992. 'Ownership Structure, Institutional Organization, and Measured X-Efficiency.' *American Economic Review Papers and Proceedings* 82, 439-445.

—— 1993. 'X-Inefficiency and Regulatory Regime Shift in the UK.' *Journal of Evolutionary Economics* 3, 269-284.

Cabrales, A. 1993. Evolutionary Game Dynamics. Ph.D. dissertation, University of California, San Diego.

Cabrales, A., and J. Sobel. 1992. 'On the Limit Points of Discrete Selection Dynamics. ' In Mailath (1992a).

Camerer, C. 1989a. 'An experimental Test of Several Generalized Expected Utility Theories.' *Journal of Risk and Uncertainty* 2, 61-104.

—— 1989b. 'Bubbles and Fads in Asset Prices.' *Journal of Economic Surveys* 3, 3-41.

—— 1990. 'Behavioral Game Theory.' In R. Hogarth (editor), *Insights in Decision Making*. Chicago, University of Chicago Press.

—— 1992. 'Recent Tests of Generalizations of Expected Utility Theory.' In W. Edwards (editor), *Utility: Theories, Measurement, and Application*. Cambridge, Cambridge University Press.

—— 1995. 'Individual Decision Making.' In Kagel and Roth (1995).

Camerer, C., E. Johnson, T. Rymon, and S. Sen. 1993. 'Cognition and Framing in Sequential Bargaining for Gains and Losses.' In K. Binmore, A. Kirman, and P. Tani (editors), *Frontiers of Game Theory*. Cambridge, MIT Press.

Camerer, C., and R. Thaler. 1995. 'Anomalies: Ultimatum, Dictators and Manners.' *Journal of Economic Perspectives* 9, 209-219.

Campbell, Y., and A. Kyle. 1993. 'Smart Money, Noise Trading and Stock Price Behavior.' *Review of Economic Studies* 60, 1-34.

Carroll, C. 1994. 'How Does Future Income Affect Current Consumption?' *Quarterly Journal of Economics* 109, 111-147.

Carroll, C., and D. Weil. 1994. 'Saving and Growth: a Reinterpretation.' *The Carnegie-Rochester Conference Series on Public Policy* 40, 133-92.

Case, K., and R. Shiller. 1989. 'The Efficiency of the Market for Single-Family Homes.' *American Economic Review* 79, 125-137.

Cason, T. 1992. 'Call Market Efficiency with Simple Adaptive Learning.' *Economics Letters* 40, 27-32.

Caverni, J-P., J-M. Fabre, and M. Gonzalez (editors). 1990. *Cognitive Biases*. Amsterdam, New York.

Chandler, A. 1962. *Strategy and Structure*. Cambridge, MIT Press.

Why Bounded Rationality

—— 1977. *The Visible Hand: The Managerial Revolution in American Business*. Cambridge, Harvard University Press.

Chen, X., and H. White. 1998. 'Nonparametric Adaptive Learning with Feedback.' *Journal of Economic Theory* 82, 190-222.

Coase, R. 1937. 'The Nature of the Firm.' *Economica* 4, 386-405. Reprinted in Stigler and Boulding (1952).

—— 1972. 'Industrial Organization: A Proposal for Research.' In V. Fuchs (editor), *Policy Issues and Research Opportunities in Industrial Organization*. New York, National Bureau of Economic Research.

—— 1992. 'The Institutional Structure of Production.' *American Economic Review* 82, 713-719.

Cochrane, J. 1989. 'The Sensitivity of Tests of the Intertemporal Allocation of Consumption to Near-Rational Alternatives.' *American Economic Review* 79, 319-337.

Conlisk, J. 1976. 'Interactive Markov Chains.' *Journal of Mathematical Sociology* 4, 157-185.

—— 1980. 'Costly Optimizers versus Cheap Imitators.' *Journal of Economic Behavior and Organization* 1, 275-293.

—— 1982. 'The law of Supply and Demand as a Law of Markov Chains.' *Journal of Economic Theory* 26, 1-16.

—— 1983. 'Competitive Approximation of a Cournot Market.' *Review of Economic Studies* 50, 597-607.

—— 1988. 'Optimization Cost.' *Journal of Economic Behavior and Organization* 9, 213-228.

—— 1989. 'An Aggregate Model of Technical Change.' *Quarterly Journal of Economics* 104, 787-821.

—— 1993a. 'The Utility of Gambling.' *Journal of Risk and Uncertainty* 6, 255-275.

—— 1993b. 'Adaptive Tactics in Games: Two Solutions to the Crawford Puzzle.' In Day (1993).

—— 1993c. 'Adaptive Firms and Random Innovations in a Model of Cyclical Output Growth.' In Day and Chen (1993).

—— 1996. 'Bounded Rationality and Market Fluctuations.' *Journal of Economic Behavior and Organization* 29, 233-250.

Coursey, D., J. Hovis, and W. Schulze. 1987. 'The Disparity Between Willingness to Accept and Willingness to Pay Measures of Value.' *Quarterly Journal of Economics* 102, 679-690.

Cox, J., H. Dinkin, and V. Smith. 1995. 'Endogenous Entry and Exit in Common Value Auctions.' Manuscript, University of Arizona.

Cragg, J., and B. Malkiel. 1982. *Expectations and the Structure of Share Prices*. Chicago, University of Chicago Press.

Crawford, V. 1974. 'Learning the Optimal Strategy in a Zero-Sum Game.' *Econometrica* 42, 885-891.

—— 1991. 'An Evolutionary Interpretation of Van Huyck, Battalio, and Beil's Experimental Results on Coordination.' *Games and Economic Behavior* 3, 25-59.

—— (editor). 1993. *Adaptive Dynamics. Parts I and II*. Special issues of *Games and Economic Behavior* 5 (July and October issues).

—— 1995. 'Adaptive Dynamics in Coordination Games.' *Econometrica* 63, 103-143.

—— 1997. 'Theory and Experiment in the Analysis of Strategic Behavior.' In D. Kreps and K. Wallis (editors), *Advances in Econometrics: Theory and Applications, Seventh World Congress, Volume I*. Cambridge, Cambridge University Press.

Creedy, J., J. Borland, and J. Eichberger (editors). 1992. *Recent Developments in Game Theory*. Aldershot, England, Edward Elgar.

Why Bounded Rationality

Cross, J. 1973. 'A Stochastic Learning Model of Economic Behavior.' *Quarterly Journal of Economics* 87, 239-266.

—— 1980. 'Learning to Search.' *Journal of Economic Behavior and Organization* 1, 197-221.

—— 1983. *A Theory of Adaptive Economic Behavior*. Cambridge, Cambridge University Press.

Cutler, D., J. Poterba, and L. Summers. 1991. 'Speculative Dynamics.' *Review of Economic Studies* 58, 529-546.

Cyert, R., and J. March. 1963. *A Behavioral Theory of the Firm*. Englewood Cliffs, New Jersey, Prentice-Hall.

David, P. 1985. 'Clio and the Economics of QWERTY.' *American Economic Review Papers and Proceedings* 75, 332-337.

—— 1986. 'Understanding the Economics of QWERTY: The Necessity of History.' In W. Parker (editor), *Economic History and the Modern Economist*. Oxford, Blackwell.

Dawes, R., and R. Thaler. 1988. 'Anomalies: Cooperation.' *Journal of Economic Perspectives* 2, Summer, 187-197.

Day, R. 1963. *Recursive Programming and Production Response*. Amsterdam, North-Holland.

—— 1967. 'Profits, Learning and the Convergence of Satisficing to Marginalism.' *Quarterly Journal of Economics* 81, 302-311.

—— (editor). 1991. Mathematical Dynamics and Economic Process. Special issue of *Journal of Economic Behavior and Organization* 16 (No. 1-2).

—— 1992. 'Bounded Rationality and the Coevolution of Market and State.' In R. Day, G. Eliasson, and C. Wihlborg (editors), *The Markets of Innovation, Ownership and Control*. Amsterdam, North-Holland.

—— (editor). 1993. Adaptive Games. Special issue of *Journal of Economic Behavior and Organization* 22 (No. 1).

—— 1994. *Complex Economic Dynamics*. Cambridge, MIT Press.

Day, R., and P. Chen (editors). 1993. *Nonlinear Dynamics and Evolutionary Economics*. Oxford, Oxford University Press.

Day, R., and A. Cigno. 1978. *Modelling Economic Change: The Recursive Programming Approach*. Amsterdam, North-Holland.

Day, R., and T. Groves (editors). 1975. *Adaptive Economic Models*. New York, Academic Press.

Day, R., and W. Huang. 1990. 'Bulls, Bears and Market Sheep.' *Journal of Economic Behavior and Organization* 14, 299-329.

Day, R., and P. Kennedy. 1970. 'Recursive Decision systems: An Existence Analysis.' *Econometrica* 38, 666-681.

Day, R., and M. Pingle. 1991. 'Economizing Economizing.' In Frantz et. al. (1991).

—— 1996. 'Modes of Economizing Behavior: Experimental Evidence.' *Journal of Economic Behavior and Organization* 29, 191-209.

Day, R., and I. Singh. 1977. *Economic Development as an Adaptive Process*. Cambridge, Cambridge University Press.

Day, R., and E. Tinney. 1968. 'How to Cooperate in Business without Really Trying: A Learning Model of Decentralized Decision Making.' *Journal of Political Economy* 76, 583-600.

Deaton, A. 1992. *Understanding Consumption*. Oxford, Clarendon Press.

De Bondt, W., and R. Thaler. 1985. 'Does the Stock Market Overreact?' *Journal of Finance* 40, 793-808. Reprinted in Thaler (1991).

Why Bounded Rationality

—— 1987. 'Further Evidence on Investor Overreaction and Stock Market Seasonality.' *Journal of Finance* 42, 557-581. Reprinted in Thaler (1991).

—— 1990. 'Do Security Analysts Overreact?' *American Economic Review* 80, 52-57. Reprinted in Thaler (1991).

—— 1995. 'Financial Decision-Making in Markets and Firms.' In. R. Jarrow, V. Maksimovic, and W. Ziemba (editors), *Finance*. Series of Handbooks in Operations Research and Management Science. Amsterdam, Elsevier North Holland.

Dekel, E., and S. Scotchmer. 1992. 'On the Evolution of Optimizing Behavior.' In Mailath (1992a).

De Long, J. B., and A. Shleifer. 1991. 'The Stock Market Bubble of 1929: Evidence from Closed-end Mutual Funds.' *Journal of Economic History* 51, 675-700.

De Long, J. B., A. Shleifer, L. Summers, and R. Waldman. 1990. 'Noise Trader Risk in Financial Markets.' *Journal of Political Economy* 98, 703-738.

—— 1991. 'The Survival of Noise Traders in Financial Markets.' *Journal of Business* 64, 1-19.

De Palma, A., G. Myers, and Y. Papageorgiou. 1994. 'Rational Choice Under an Imperfect Ability to Choose.' *American Economic Review* 84, 419-440.

DeTemple, J., and S. Murthy. 1994. 'Intertemporal Asset Pricing with Heterogeneous Beliefs,' *Journal of Economic Theory* 62, 294-320.

Diehl, E., and J. Sterman. 1995. 'Effects of Feedback Complexity on Dynamic Decision Making.' *Organizational Behavior and Human Decision Processes* 62, 198-215.

Dodd, D., and R. White. 1980. *Cognition: Mental Structures and Processes*. Boston, Allyn and Bacon.

Dosi, G., and R. Nelson. 1994. 'An Introduction to Evolutionary Theories in Economics.' *Journal of Evolutionary Economics* 4, 153-172.

Dow, G. 1990. 'The Organization as an Adaptive Network.' *Journal of Economic Behavior and Organization* 14, 159-185.

Dupre, J. 1987. *The Latest on the Best: Essays on Evolution and Optimality*. Cambridge, MIT Press.

Dwyer, D. 1994. 'Technology Locks, Creative Destruction and Non-Convergence in Productivity Levels.' Manuscript, Columbia University.

Einhorn, H., and R. Hogarth. 1981. 'Behavioral Decision Theory: Processes of Judgment and Choice.' *Annual Review of Psychology* 32, 53-88.

Eliasson, G. 1984. 'Micro Heterogeneity of Firms and the Stability of Indus-trial Growth.' *Journal of Economic Behavior and Organization* 5, 249-274.

—— 1991. 'Modeling the Experimentally Organized Economy: Complex Dynamics in an Empirical Micro-Macro Model of Endogenous Economic Growth.' In Day (1991).

Ellison, G., and D. Fudenberg. 1993. 'Rules of Thumb for Social Learning.' *Journal of Political Economy* 101, 612-643.

—— 1995. 'Word of Mouth Communication and Social Learning.' *Quarterly Journal of Economics* 110, 93-125.

Elster, J. 1979. *Ulysses and the Sirens: Studies in Rationality and Irrationality*. Cambridge, Cambridge University Press.

—— 1983. *Sour Grapes: Studies in the Subversion of Rationality*. Cambridge, Cambridge University Press.

—— (editor). 1986. *Rational Choice*. New York, New York University Press.

—— 1989a. *The Cement of Society*. Cambridge, Cambridge University Press.

—— 1989b. 'Social Norms and Economic Theory.' *Journal of Economic Perspectives* 3, 99-117.

Why Bounded Rationality

England, R. (editor). 1994. *Evolutionary Concepts in Contemporary Economics*. Ann Arbor, University of Michigan Press.

Ermini, L. 1987. Hierarchical Decomposition in Economic Analysis. Ph.D. dissertation. University of California, San Diego.

—— 1991. 'Hierarchical Decomposition in Economic Analysis.' In Frantz et. al. (1991).

Evans, G., and S. Honkapohja. 1995. 'Adaptive Learning and Expectational Stability.' In Kirman and Salmon (1995).

Evans, G., and G. Ramey. 1992. 'Expectation Calculation and Macroeconomic Dynamics.' *American Economic Review* 82, 207-224.

—— 1995. 'Expectation Calculation, Hyperinflation and Currency Collapse.' In H. Dixon and N. Rankin (editors), *The New Macroeconomics of Imperfect Markets and Policy Effectiveness*. Cambridge, Cambridge University Press.

Evans, J. 1989. *Bias in Human Reasoning: Causes and Consequences*. London: Lawrence Erlbaum.

Fama, E., and K. French. 1988. 'Permanent and Temporary Components of Stock Prices.' *Journal of Political Economy* 96, 246-273.

Farrell, M. 1970. 'Some Elementary Selection Processes in Economics.' *Review of Economic Studies* 32, 305-319.

Ferris, S., R. Haugen, and A. Makhija. 1988. 'Predicting Contemporary Volume with Historic Volume at Differential Price Levels: Evidence Supporting the Disposition Effect.' *Journal of Finance* 43, 677-697.

Fishhoff, B. 1982. 'Debiasing.' In Kahneman, Slovic, and Tversky (1982).

Flavin, M. 1981. 'The Adjustment of Consumption to Changing Expectations About Future Income.' *Journal of Political Economy* 89, 974-1009.

—— 1993. 'The Excess Smoothness of Consumption: Identification and Interpretation.' *Review of Economic Studies* 60, 651-666.

Fourgeaud, C., C. Gourieroux, and J. Pradel. 1986. 'Learning Procedure and Convergence to Rationality.' *Econometrica* 54, 845-868.

Franciosi, R., P. Kujal, R. Michelitsch, V. Smith, and G. Deng. 1996. 'Experimental Tests of the Endowment Effect.' *Journal of Economic Behavior and Organization* 30, 213-226.

Frank, R. 1985a. 'The Demand for Unobservable and Other Nonpositional Goods.' *American Economic Review* 75, 101-116.

—— 1985b. *Choosing the Right Pond*. Oxford, Oxford University Press.

—— 1987. 'If Homo Economicus Could Choose His Own Utility Function, Would He Want One with a Conscience?' *American Economic Review* 77, 593-602.

—— 1988. Passions Without Reasons. New York, Norton.

Frankel, J., and K. Froot. 1987. 'Using Survey Data to Test Standard Propositions Regarding Exchange Rate Expectations.' *American Economic Review* 77, 133-153.

Frankel, J., and A. Rose. 1995. 'A Survey of Empirical Research on Nominal Exchange Rates.' In Grossman and Rogoff (1995).

Frantz, R. 1992. 'X-Efficiency and Allocative Efficiency: What Have We Learned?' *American Economic Review Papers and Proceedings* 82, 434-438.

Frantz, R., H. Singh, and J. Gerber (editors). 1991. *Behavioral Decision Making, Handbook of Behavioral Economics, Volume 2B*. Greenwich, JAI Press.

French, K., and J. Poterba. 1991. 'Investor Diversification and International Equity Markets.' *American Economic Review Papers and Proceedings* 81, 222-226.

Why Bounded Rationality

Frey, B., and R. Eichenberger. 1994. 'Economic Incentives Transform Psychological Anomalies.' *Journal of Economic Behavior and Organization* 23, 215-234.

Friedman, D. 1998. 'On Economic Applications of Evolutionary Game Theory.' *Journal of Evolutionary Economics* 8, 15-43.

Friedman, M. 1953. *Essays in Positive Economics*. Chicago, University of Chicago Press.

Friedman, M., and L. Savage. 1948. 'The Utility Analysis of Choices Involving Risk.' *Journal of Political Economy* 56, 279-304. Reprinted in Stigler and Boulding (1952).

Froot, K., and R. Thaler. 1990. 'Anomalies: Foreign Exchange.' *Journal of Economic Perspectives* 4, Summer, 179-192.

Furubotn, E., and R. Richter (editors). 1994. *Symposium on New Institutional Economics. Bounded Rationality and the Analysis of State and Society*. Special issue of *Journal of Institutional and Theoretical Economics* 150, 11-325.

Garey, M., and D. Johnson. 1979. *Computers and Intractability: A Guide to the Theory of NP-Completeness*. San Francisco, Freeman.

Garvin, S., and J. Kagel. 1994. 'Learning in Common Value Auctions: Some Initial Observations.' *Journal of Economic Behavior and Organization* 25, 351-372.

Gately, D. 1980. 'Individual Discount Rates and the Purchase and Utilization of Energy-Using Durables: Comment.' *Bell Journal of Economics* 11, 373-374.

Gertner, R. 1993. 'Game Shows and Economic Behavior: Risk-Taking on 'Card Sharks'.' *Quarterly Journal of Economics* 108, 507-521.

Gilboa, I., and D. Schmeidler. 1995. 'Case-Based Decision Theory.' *Quarterly Journal of Economics* 110, 605-639.

Gilovich, T. 1991. *How We Know What Isn't So: The Fallibility of Human Reason in Everyday Life*. New York, Macmillan.

Gode, D., and S. Sunder. 1993. 'Allocative Efficiency of Markets with Zero-Intelligence Traders: Market as a Partial Substitute for Individual Rationality.' *Journal of Political Economy* 101, 119-137.

—— 1997. 'What Makes Markets Allocationally Efficient?' *Quarterly Journal of Economics* 112, 603-630.

Goldberger, A. 1989. 'Economic and Mechanical Models of Intergenerational Transmission.' *American Economic Review* 79, 504-513

Gottinger, H. 1982. 'Computational Costs and Bounded Rationality.' In W. Stegmuller, W. Balzer, and W. Spohn (editors), *Philosophy of Economics*. Berlin, Springer-Verlag.

Goyal, S., and M. Janssen. 1997. 'Non-Exclusive Conventions and Social Coordination.' *Journal of Economic Theory* 77, 34-57.

Grabowski, H., and J. Vernon. 1987. 'Pioneers, Imitators, and Generics - A Simulation Model of Schumpeterian Competition.' *Quarterly Journal of Economics* 102, 491-526.

Granovetter, M., and R. Soong. 1983. 'Threshold Models of Diffusion and Collective Behavior.' *Journal of Mathematical Sociology* 9, 165-179.

—— 1986. 'Threshold Models of Interpersonal Effects in Consumer Demand.' *Journal of Economic Behavior and Organization* 7, 83-99.

Grether, D. 1980. 'Bayes Rule as a Descriptive Model: The Representativeness Heuristic.' *Quarterly Journal of Economics* 95, 537-557.

—— 1992. 'Testing Bayes Rule and the Representativeness Heuristic: Some Experimental Evidence.' *Journal of Economic Behavior and Organization* 17, 31-57.

Why Bounded Rationality

Grether, D., and C. Plott. 1979. 'Economic Theory of Choice and the Preference Reversal Phenomenon.' *American Economic Review* 69, 623-638.

Groner, R., M. Groner, and W. Bischof (editors). 1983. *Methods of Heuristics.* Hillsdale, New Jersey, Lawrence Erlbaum.

Grossman, G., and K. Rogoff (editors), 1995. *The Handbook of International Economics.* Amsterdam, North Holland.

Grossman, M. 1975. 'The Correlation Between Health and Schooling.' In N. Terleckyj (editor), *Household Production and Consumption.* New York, Columbia University Press.

Guttman, J. 1996. 'Rational Actors, Tit-for-Tat Types, and the Evolution of Cooperation.' *Journal of Economic Behavior and Organization* 29, 27-56.

Haltiwanger, J., and M. Waldman. 1985. Rational Expectations and the Limits of Rationality: An Analysis of Heterogeneity.' *American Economic Review* 75, 326-340.

—— 1989. Limited Rationality and Strategic Complementarity: The Implications for Macroeconomics.' *Quarterly Journal of Economics* 104, 463-483.

—— 1991. 'Responders versus Non-responders: A New Perspective on Heterogeneity.' *Economic Journal* 101, 1085-1102.

Harrington, J. 1998. 'The Social Selection of Flexible and Rigid Agents.' *American Economic Review* 88, 63-82.

Hartman, R., M. Doane, and C-K. Woo. 1991. 'Consumer Rationality and the Status Quo.' *Quarterly Journal of Economics* 106, 141-162.

Hausman, J. 1979. ' Individual Discount Rates and the Purchase and Utilization of Energy-Using Durables.' *Bell Journal of Economics* 10, 33-54.

Heiner, R. 1983. 'The Origin of Predictable Behavior.' *American Economic Review* 73, 560-595.

—— 1986. 'Uncertainty, Signal Detection Experiments, and Modeling Behavior.' In R. Langlois (editor), *Economics as a Process: Essays in the New Institutional Economics.* New York, Cambridge University Press.

—— 1988. 'The Necessity of Imperfect Decisions.' *Journal of Economic Behavior and Organization* 10, 29-55.

—— 1989. 'The Origin of Predictable Dynamic Behavior.' *Journal of Economic Behavior and Organization* 12, 233-258.

Herriott, S., D. Levinthal, and J. March. 1985. 'Learning from Experience in Organizations.' *American Economic Review Papers and Proceedings* 75, 298-302.

Herrnstein, R. 1991. 'Experiments on Stable Suboptimality in Individual Behavior.' *American Economic Review Papers and Proceedings* 81, 360-364.

Herrnstein, R., and D. Prelec. 1991. 'Melioration: A Theory of Distributed Choice.' *Journal of Economic Perspectives* 5, Summer, 137-156.

Hey, J. 1982. 'Search for Rules for Search.' *Journal of Economic Behavior and Organization* 3, 65-82.

—— 1994. 'Expectations Formation: Rational or Adaptive or ...?' *Journal of Economic Behavior and Organization* 25, 329-349.

Himmelweit, S. 1976. 'A Behavioural Model of Learning in Production.' *Review of Economic Studies* 43, 329-46.

Hirshleifer, J. 1977. 'Economics from a Biological Viewpoint.' *Journal of Law and Economics* 20, 1-52.

—— 1978. 'Competition, Cooperation, and Conflict in Economics and Biology.' *American Economic Review* 68, 238-243.

Why Bounded Rationality

—— 1987. 'On the Emotions as Guarantors of Threats and Promises.' In Dupre (1987).

Hirshleifer, J., and J. Riley. 1992. *The Analytics of Uncertainty and Information.* Cambridge, Cambridge University Press.

Hodgson, G. 1993. *Economics and Evolution: Bringing Life Back Into Economics.* Cambridge, Polity Press.

Hogarth, R. 1980. *Judgement and Choice: The Psychology of Decision.* New York, Wiley.

Hogarth, R., and M. Reder (editors). 1987. *Rational Choice: The Contrast Between Economics and Psychology.* Chicago, University of Chicago Press. First appeared as a supplement to the October 1986 issue of the *Journal of Business* 59.

Holden, K., D. Peel, and J. Thompson. 1985. *Expectations: Theory and Evidence.* London, Macmillan.

Holland, J. 1975. *Adaptation in Natural and Artificial Systems.* Ann Arbor, University of Michigan Press.

Holland, J., and J. Miller. 1991. 'Artificial and Adaptive Agents in Economic Theory.' *American Economic Review Papers and Proceedings* 81, 365-370.

Holyoak, K. 1990. 'Problem Solving.' In Osheron and Smith (1990).

Iosso, T. 1993. 'Industry Evolution with a Sequence of Technologies and Heterogeneous Ability: A Model of Creative Destruction.' *Journal of Economic Behavior and Organization* 21, 109-129.

Ito, T. 1990. 'Foreign Exchange Rate Expectations: Micro Survey Data.' *American Economic Review* 80, 434-449.

Iwai, K. 1984. 'Schumpeterian Dynamics II. Technological Progress, Firm Growth, and 'Economic Selection'.' *Journal of Economic Behavior and Organization* 5, 321-351.

Johansen, L. 1977. *Lectures on Macroeconomic Planning. Part 1. General Aspects.* Amsterdam, North-Holland.

Jones, S., and J. Stock. 1987. 'Demand Disturbances and Aggregate Fluctuations: The Implications of Near Rationality.' *Economic Journal* 97, 49-64.

Kagel, J., R. Harstad, and D. Levin. 1987. 'Information Impact and Allocation Rules in Auctions with Affiliated Private Values: A Laboratory Study.' *Econometrica* 55, 1275-1304.

Kagel, J., and A. Roth. 1995. *The Handbook of Experimental Economics.* Princeton, Princeton University Press.

Kagel, J. 1995. 'Auctions: A Survey of Experimental Research.' In Kagel and Roth (1995).

Kahneman, D., J. Knetsch, and R. Thaler. 1990. 'Experimental Tests of the Endowment Effect and the Coase Theorem.' *Journal of Political Economy* 98, 1325-1348.

—— 1991. 'Anomalies: The Endowment Effect, Loss Aversion, and Status Quo Bias.' *Journal of Economic Perspectives* 5, Winter, 193-206.

Kahneman, D., P. Slovic, and A. Tversky (editors). 1982. *Judgment Under Uncertainty: Heuristics and Biases.* Cambridge, Cambridge University Press.

Kahneman, D., and R. Thaler. 1991. 'Economic Analysis and the Psychology of Utility: Applications to Compensation Policy.' *American Economic Review Papers and Proceedings* 81, 341-346.

Kahneman, D., and A. Tversky. 1979. 'Rational Choice and the Framing of Decisions Under Risk.' *Econometrica* 47, 263-291.

Kalai, E., K. Warneryd, and J. Weibull. 1995. *Nobel Symposium.* Special issue of *Games and Economic Behavior* 8 (January issue).

Kandori, M., and R. Rob. 1995. 'Evolution of Equilibria in the Long Run: A General Theory and Applications.' *Journal of Economic Theory* 65, 383-414.

Kanal, L., and V. Kumar. 1988. *Search in Artificial Intelligence.* Berlin, Springer-Verlag.

Why Bounded Rationality

Keane, M., and D. Runkle. 1990. 'Testing the Rationality of Price Forecasts: New Evidence from Panel Data.' *American Economic Review* 80, 714-735.

Kelley, H., and J. Michela. 1980. 'Attribution Theory and Research.' *Annual Review of Psychology* 31, 457-501.

Kennedy, P. 1994. 'Information Processing and Organization Design.' *Journal of Economic Behavior and Organization* 25, 37-51.

Kirman, A. 1992. 'Whom or What Does the Representative Individual Represent?' *Journal of Economic Perspectives* 6, 117-36.

—— 1993. 'Ants, Rationality, and Recruitment.' *Quarterly Journal of Economics* 108, 137-156.

—— 1994. 'Economies with Interacting Agents.' Working paper 94-05-030, Santa Fe Institute Economics Research Program.

Kirman, A., and M. Salmon (editors). 1995. *Learning and Rationality in Economics*. Oxford, Basil Blackwell.

Knetsch, J. 1989. 'The Endowment Effect and Evidence of Nonreversible Indifference Curves.' *American Economic Review* 79, 1277-1284.

—— 1992. 'Preferences and Nonreversibility of Indifference Curves.' *Journal of Economic Behavior and Organization* 17, 131-139.

Knight, F. 1921. *Risk, Uncertainty, and Profit*. Boston, Houghton-Mifflin. Reprinted in 1964 by Augustus M. Kelley, Bookseller. New York, Sentry Press.

Koh, W. 1994. 'Making Decisions in Committees: A Human Fallibility Approach.' *Journal of Economic Behavior and Organization* 23, 195-214.

Koopmans, T. 1957. *Three Essays on the State of Economic Science*. New York, McGraw-Hill.

Kreps, D. 1990. *A Course in Microeconomic Theory*. Princeton, New Jersey, Princeton University Press.

Kreps, D., P. Milgrom, J. Roberts, and R. Wilson. 1982. 'Rational Cooperation in the Finitely Repeated Prisoners' Dilemma.' *Journal of Economic Theory* 27, 245-252.

Kuan, C-M., and H. White. 1994. 'Adaptive Learning with Nonlinear Dynamics Driven by Dependent Processes.' *Econometrica* 62, 1087-1114.

Kunreuther, K., with R. Ginsberg, L. Miller, P. Sagi, P. Slovic, B. Borkan, and N. Katz. 1978. *Disaster Insurance Protection*. New York, Wiley.

Kuran, T. 1991. ' Cognitive Limitations and Preference Evolution.' *Journal of Institutional and Theoretical Economics* 147, 241-273.

Kwasnicki, W., and H. Kwasnicka. 1992. 'Market, Innovation, Competition: An Evolutionary Model of Industrial Dynamics.' *Journal of Economic Behavior and Organization* 19, 343-368.

Lakonishok, J., A. Shleifer, R. Thaler, and R. Vishny. 1991. 'Window Dressing by Pension Fund Managers.' *American Economic Review Papers and Proceedings* 81, 227-231.

Lakonishok, J., and S. Smidt. 1986. 'Capital Gain Taxation and Volume of Trading.' *Journal of Finance* 41, 951-974.

—— and S. Smidt. 1988. 'Are Seasonal Anomalies Real? A Ninety Year Perspective.' *Review of Financial Studies* 1, 403-426.

Lane, D. 1993a. 'Artificial Worlds and Economics, Part I.' *Journal of Evolutionary Economics* 3, 89-107.

—— 1993b. 'Artificial Worlds and Economics, Part II.' *Journal of Evolutionary Economics* 3, 177-197.

Latsis, S. (editor). 1976. *Method and Appraisal in Economics*. Cambridge, Cambridge University Press.

Ledyard, J. 1995. 'Public Goods: A Survey of Experimental Research.' In Kagel and Roth (1995).

Why Bounded Rationality

Lee, C., A. Shleifer, and R. Thaler. 1990. 'Anomalies: Closed-End Mutual Funds.' *Journal of Economic Perspectives* 4, Fall, 153-164.

—— 1991. 'Investor Sentiment and the Closed-End Fund Puzzle.' *Journal of Finance* 46, 75-109.

Leibenstein, H. 1966. 'Allocative Efficiency vs. 'X-Efficiency'.' *American Economic Review* 56, 392-415.

—— 1987. *Inside the Firm: The Inefficiencies of Hierarchy*. Cambridge, Harvard University Press.

Leibenstein, H., and S. Maital. 1992. 'Empirical Estimation and Partitioning of X-Inefficiency: A Data-Envelopment Approach.' *American Economic Review Papers and Proceedings* 82, 428-433.

—— 1994. 'The Organizational Foundations of X-Inefficiency: A Game-Theoretic Interpretation of Argyris' Model of Organizational Learning.' *Journal of Economic Behavior and Organization* 23, 251-268.

LeRoy, S. 1989. 'Efficient Capital Markets and Martingales.' *Journal of Economic Literature* 27, 1583-1621.

Lesourne, J. 1992. *The Economics of Order and Disorder*. Oxford, Clarendon Press.

—— 1993. 'Self-Organization as a Process in Evolution of Economic Systems.' In Day and Chen (1993).

Lewis, K. 1995. 'Puzzles in International Financial Markets.' In Grossman and Rogoff (1995).

Lipman, B. 1991. 'How to Decide How to Decide How to ...: Modeling Limited Rationality.' *Econometrica* 59, 1105-1125.

Lo, A, and A. MacKinlay. 1997. Maximizing Predictability in the Stock and Bond Markets.' *Macroeconomic Dynamics* 1, 102-134.

Loewenstein, G. 1987. 'Anticipation and the Valuation of Delayed Consumption.' *Economic Journal* 97, 666-684.

Loewenstein, G., and D. Prelec. 1991. 'Negative Time Preference.' *American Economic Review Papers and Proceedings* 81, 347-352.

—— 1992. 'Anomalies in Intertemporal Choice: Evidence and an Interpretation.' *Quarterly Journal of Economics* 57, 573-597.

Loewenstein, G., and R. Thaler. 1989. 'Anomalies: Intertemporal Choice.' *Journal of Economic Perspectives* 3, Fall, 181-193.

Loomes, G., C. Starmer, and R. Sugden. 1991. 'Observing Violations of Transitivity by Experimental Methods.' *Econometrica* 59, 425-439.

Lovell, M. 1986. 'Tests of the Rational Expectations Hypothesis.' *American Economic Review* 76, 110-124.

Lucas, R. 1986. 'Adaptive Behavior and Economic Theory.' *Journal of Business* 59, S401-S426. Reprinted in Hogarth and Reder (1987).

Machina, M. 1982. 'Expected Utility' Analysis without the Independence Axiom.' *Econometrica* 50, 277-323.

—— 1989. 'Dynamic Consistency and Non-Expected Utility Models of Choice Under Uncertainty.' *Journal of Economic Literature* 27, 1622-1668.

Mailath, G. (editor). 1992a. *Evolutionary Game Theory*. Special issue of *Journal of Economic Theory* 57 (August issue).

—— 1992b. 'Introduction: Symposium on Evolutionary Game Theory.' In Mailath (1992a).

Mankiw, N. 1985. 'Small Menu Costs and Large Business Cycles: A Macroeconomic Model of Monopoly.' *Quarterly Journal of Economics* 100, 529-537.

Why Bounded Rationality

Marcet, A., and T. Sargent. 1988. 'The Fate of Systems with 'Adaptive Expectations'.' *American Economic Review Papers and Proceedings* 78, 168-172.

—— 1989. 'Convergence of Least Squares Learning in Self Referential Linear Stochastic Models.' *Journal of Economic Theory* 48, 337-368.

March, J., and H. Simon. 1958. *Organizations.* New York, Wiley.

Marimon, R., and E. McGrattan. 1995. 'On Adaptive Learning in Strategic Games.' In Kirman and Salmon (1995).

Marimon, R., E. McGrattan, and T. Sargent. 1990. 'Money as a Medium of Exchange in an Economy with Artificially Intelligent Agents.' *Journal of Economic Dynamics and Control* 14, 329-373.

Marimon, R., and S. Sunder. 1993. 'Indeterminacy of Equilibria in a Hyper-inflationary World: Experimental Evidence.' *Econometrica.* 61, 1073-1107.

Markowitz, H. 1952. 'The Utility of Wealth.' *Journal of Political Economy* 60, 151-158.

Marschak, J., and R. Radner. 1972. *Economic Theory of Teams.* New Haven, Yale University Press.

Martello, S., and P. Toth. 1990. *Knapsack Problems: Algorithms and Computer Implementations.* New York, Wiley.

McCain, R. 1991. 'Groping: Toward a Behavioral Metatheory of Choice.' In Frantz et. al. (1991).

McCloskey, D., and A. Klamer. 1995. 'One Quarter of GDP Is Persuasion.' *American Economic Review Papers and Proceedings* 85, 191-195.

Meade, J. 1964. *Efficiency, Equality and the Ownership of Property.* Cambridge, Harvard University Press.

Medio, A. 1992. *Chaotic Dynamics. Theory and Applications to Economics.* Cambridge, Cambridge University Press.

Mehra, R., and E. Prescott. 1985. 'The Equity Premium: A Puzzle.' *Journal of Monetary Economics* 15, 145-161.

Metrick, A. 1995. 'A Natural Experiment in 'Jeopardy'.' *American Economic Review* 85, 240-253.

Midgley, D. , R. Marks, and L. Cooper. 1995. 'Adaptive Behaviour in an Oligopoly.' In J. Biethahn and V. Nissen (editors), *Evolutionary Algorithms in Management Applications.* Heidelberg, Springer.

Mitchell, R., and R. Carson. 1989. *Using Surveys to Value Public Goods: The Contingent Valuation Method.* Washington, D.C., Resources for the Future.

Mongin, P., and B. Walliser. 1988. 'Infinite Regressions in the Optimizing Theory of Decision.' In B. Munier (editor), *Risk, Decision and Rationality.* Dordrecht, D. Reidel Publishing.

Mui, V.-L. 1995. 'The Economics of Envy.' *Journal of Economic Behavior and Organization* 26, 311-336.

Naish, H. 1990. 'The Near Optimality of Mark-Up Pricing.' *Economic Inquiry* 28, 555-585.

—— 1993. 'The Near Optimality of Adaptive Expectations.' *Journal of Economic Behavior and Organization* 20, 3-22.

Nelson, R. 1994. 'Recent Evolutionary Theorizing about Economic Change.' In N. Smelser and R. Swedberg (editors), *Handbook of Economic Sociology.* Princeton, Princeton University Press.

—— 1995. 'Recent Evolutionary Theorizing about Economic Change.' *Journal of Economic Literature* 33, 48-90.

Nelson, R., and S. Winter. 1982. *An Evolutionary Theory of Economic Change.* Cambridge, Harvard University Press.

Newell, N., and H. Simon. 1972. *Human Problem Solving.* Englewood Cliffs, New Jersey, Prentice-Hall.

Why Bounded Rationality

—— 1990. 'Computer Science as Empirical Inquiry: Symbols and Search.' In J. Garfield (editor), *Foundations of Computer Science: the Essential Readings.* New York, Paragon.

Nisbett, R., and L. Ross. 1980. *Human Inference: Strategies and Shortcomings of Social Judgment.* Englewood Cliffs, New Jersey, Prentice-Hall.

O'Brien, A. 1989. 'A Behavioral Explanation for Nominal Wage Rigidity During the Great Depression.' *Quarterly Journal of Economics* 104, 719-735.

Orcutt, G., J. Merz, and H. Quinke. 1986. *Microanalytic Simulation Models to Support Social and Financial Policy.* Amsterdam, North Holland.

Osheron, D. 1990. 'Judgment.' In Osheron and Smith (1990).

Osheron, D., and E. Smith. 1990. *Thinking: An Invitation to Cognitive Science, Volume 3.* Cambridge, MIT Press.

Palfrey, T., and J. Prisbrey. 1996. 'Altruism, Reputation, and Noise in Linear Public Goods Experiments.' *Journal of Public Economics* 61, 409-27.

Papadimitriou, H., and I. Steiglitz. 1982. *Combinatorial Optimization: Algorithms and Complexity.* Englewood Cliffs, New Jersey, Prentice-Hall.

Patel, J., R. Zeckhauser, and D. Hendricks. 1991. 'The Rationality Struggle: Illustrations from Financial Markets.' *American Economic Review Papers and Proceedings* 81, 232-236.

Payne, J., J. Bettman, and E. Johnson. 1992. 'Behavioral Decision Research: A Constructive Processing Perspective.' *Annual Review of Psychology* 43, 87-131.

—— 1993. *The Adaptive Decision Maker.* Cambridge, Cambridge University Press.

Pearl, J. 1984. *Heuristics: Intelligent Search Strategies for Computer Problem Solving.* Reading, Massachusetts, Addison-Wesley.

Pereira, A. 1993. 'A Dynamic General Equilibrium Analysis of Corporate Tax Integration.' *Journal of Policy Modeling* 15, 63-89.

Pereira, A., and J. Shoven. 1988. 'Survey of Dynamic Computational General Equilibrium Models for Tax Policy Evaluation.' *Journal of Policy Modeling* 10, 401-436.

Pesaran, M. 1987. *The Limits to Rational Expectations.* Oxford, Blackwell.

Pesaran, M., and A. Timmermann. 1995. 'Predictability of Stock Returns: Robustness and Economic Significance.' *Journal of Finance* 50, 1201-1228.

Peterson, S. 1993. 'Forecasting Dynamics and Convergence to Market Fundamentals: Evidence from Experimental Asset Markets.' *Journal of Economic Behavior and Organization* 22, 269-284.

Phelps, E., and S. Winter. 1970. 'Optimal Price Policy Under Atomistic Competition.' In E. Phelps et. al., *Microeconomic Foundations of Employment and Inflation Theory.* New York, Norton.

Pingle, M. 1992. 'Costly Optimization: An Experiment.' *Journal of Economic Behavior and Organization* 17, 3-30.

—— 1995. 'Imitation Versus Rationality: An Experimental Perspective on Decision-Making.' *Journal of Socioeconomics* 24, 281-315.

Pitz, G., and N. Sachs. 1984. 'Judgment and Decision: Theory and Application.' *Annual Review of Psychology* 35, 139-163.

Plott, C., and S. Sunder. 1988. 'Rational Expectations and the Aggregation of Diverse Information in Laboratory Security Markets.' *Econometrica* 56, 1085-1118.

Poterba, J. 1991. 'House Price Dynamics: The Role of Tax Policy.' *Brookings Papers on Economic Activity*, Number 2, 143-183.

Rabin, M. 1994. 'Cognitive Dissonance and Social Change.' *Journal of Economic Behavior and Organization* 23, 177-194.

Why Bounded Rationality

Radner, R. 1968. 'Competitive Equilibrium Under Uncertainty.' *Econometrica* 36, 31-58.

—— 1975a. 'A Behavioral Model of Cost Reduction.' *Bell Journal of Economics and Management Science* 6, 196-215.

—— 1975b. 'Satisficing.' *Journal of Mathematical Economics* 2, 253-262.

—— 1987. 'Decentralization and Incentives.' In T. Groves, R. Radner, and S. Reiter (editors), *Information, Incentives, and Economic Mechanisms*. Minneapolis, University of Minnesota Press.

—— 1992. 'Hierarchy: The Economics of Managing.' *Journal of Economic Literature* 30, 1382-1415.

Radner, R., and M. Rothschild. 1975. 'On the Allocation of Effort.' *Journal of Economic Theory* 10, 358-376.

Radzicki, M., and J. Sterman. 1994. 'Evolutionary Economics and System Dynamics.' In England (1994).

Raiffa, H. 1968. *Decision Analysis: Introductory Lectures on Choices Under Uncertainty*. Reading, Massachusetts, Addison-Wesley.

Rapoport, A., and T. Wallsten. 1972. 'Individual Decision Behavior.' In P. Mussen and M. Rosenzweig (editors), *Annual Review of Psychology*. Palo Alto, California, Annual Reviews.

Rapoport, A., M. Guyer, and D. Gordon. 1976. *The 2X2 Game*. Ann Arbor, University of Michigan Press.

Raut, L., and T. Srinivasan. 1993. 'Theories of Long-Run Growth: Old and New.' In K. Basu, M. Majumdar, and T. Mitra (editors), *Capital, Investment and Development*. Oxford, Blackwell.

Reason, J. 1990. *Human Error*. Cambridge, Cambridge University Press.

Reed, S. 1982. *Cognition: Theory and Applications*. Monterey, California, Brooks/Cole.

Resnik, M. 1987. *Choices: An Introduction to Decision Theory*. Minneapolis, University of Minnesota Press.

Richter, R. (editor). 1990. *Views and Comments on Bounded Rationality as Applied to Modern Institutional Economics*. A collection of short papers in *Journal of Institutional and Theoretical Economics* 146, 648-748.

Rosenthal, R. 1993a. 'Rules of Thumb in Games.' In Day (1993).

—— 1993b. 'Bargaining Rules of Thumb.' In Day (1993).

Roth, A. 1988. 'Laboratory Experimentation in Economics: A Methodological Overview.' *Economic Journal* 98, 974-1031.

Rothschild, M. 1975. 'Further Notes on the Allocation of Effort.' In Day and Groves (1975).

Rubinstein, A. 1986. 'Finite Automata Play the Repeated Prisoner's Dilemma.' *Journal of Economic Theory* 39, 83-96.

—— 1993. 'On Price Recognition and Computational Complexity in a Monopolistic Model.' *Journal of Political Economy* 101, 473-484.

—— 1998. *Modeling Bounded Rationality*. Cambridge, Massachusetts, MIT Press.

Russell, T., and R. Thaler. 1985. 'The Relevance of Quasi Rationality in Competitive Markets.' *American Economic Review* 75, 1071-1082. Reprinted in Thaler (1991).

Sah, R., and J. Stiglitz. 1986. 'The Architecture of Economic Systems: Hierarchies and Polyarchies.' *American Economic Review* 76, 716-727.

—— 1988. 'Committees, Hierarchies and Polyarchies.' *Economic Journal* 98, 451-470.

Samuelson, P. 1993. 'Altruism as a Problem Involving Group versus Individual Selection in Economics and Biology.' *American Economic Review Papers and Proceedings* 83, 143-148.

Samuelson, W., and R. Zeckhauser. 1988. 'Status Quo Bias in Decision Making.' *Journal of Risk and Uncertainty* 1, 7-59.

Why Bounded Rationality

Sanford, A. 1985. *Cognition and Cognitive Psychology*. London, Weidenfeld and Nicolson.

Sargent, T. 1993. *Bounded Rationality in Macroeconomics*. Oxford, Clarendon Press.

Sarin, R. 1994. Stochastic Dynamics in Games: Learning and Evolution. Ph.D. dissertation. University of California, San Diego.

Savage, L. 1954. *The Foundations of Statistics*. New York, Wiley.

Schachter, S., W. Gerin, D. Hood, and P. Andreassen. 1985. *Studies of Dependent and Independent Markets*. A collection of three papers in *Journal of Economic Behavior and Organization* 6, 323-357.

Schelling, T. 1978. 'Altruism, Meanness, and Other Potentially Strategic Behaviors.' *American Economic Review Papers and Proceedings* 68, 229-230.

—— 1984. 'Self-Command in Practice, in Policy, and in a Theory of Rational Choice.' *American Economic Review Papers and Proceedings* 74, 1-11.

Scheinkman, J. 1990. 'Nonlinearities in Economic Analysis.' *Economic Journal* 100, 33-48.

Scheinkman, J., and M. Woodford. 1994. 'Self-Organized Criticality and Economic Fluctuations.' *American Economic Review Papers and Proceedings* 84, 417-421.

Schmalensee, R. 1975. 'Alternative Models of Bandit Selection.' *Journal of Economic Theory* 10, 333-342.

—— 1978. 'A Model of Advertising and Product Quality.' *Journal of Political Economy* 86, 485-503.

Schmalensee, R., and R. Willig (editors). 1989. *Handbook of Industrial Organization, Volume I and Volume 2*. Amsterdam, North-Holland.

Selten, R. 1978. 'The Chain Store Paradox.' *Theory and Decision* 9, 127-159. Reprinted in Selten (1987).

—— 1987. *Models of Strategic Rationality*. Dordrecht, Kluwer.

—— 1990. 'Bounded Rationality.' In Richter (1990).

—— 1991a. 'Evolution, Learning, and Economic Behavior.' *Games and Economic Behavior* 3, 3-24.

—— 1991b. 'Anticipatory Learning in Two-Person Games.' In R. Selten (editor), *Game Equilibrium Models, Volume I: Evolution and Game Dynamics*. Berlin, Springer-Verlag.

Selten, R., and R. Stoecker. 1986. 'End Behavior in Sequences of Finite Prisoner's Dilemma Supergames.' *Journal of Economic Behavior and Organization* 7, 47-70.

Sen, A. 1977. 'Rational Fools: A Critique of the Behavioral Foundations of Economic Theory.' *Philosophy and Public Affairs* 4, 317-344. Reprinted in Sen (1982).

—— 1982. *Choice, Welfare and Measurement*. Cambridge, MIT Press.

—— 1987. 'Rational Behavior.' Entry in J. Eatwell, M. Milgate, and P. Newman (editors), *The New Palgrave: A Dictionary of Economics*. London, Macmillan.

Senders, J., and N. Moray. 1991. *Human Error: Cause, Prediction, and Reduction*. Hillsdale, New Jersey, Lawrence Erlbaum.

Sethi, Rajiv. 1995. 'The Evolutionary Dynamics of Financial Practices.' *Metroeconomica* 46, 246-277.

Seyhun, H. 1992. 'Why Does Aggregate Insider Trading Predict Future Stock Returns?' *Quarterly Journal of Economics* 107, 1303-1331.

Shea, J. 1995. 'Union Contracts and the Life-Cycle/Permanent-Income Hypothesis.' *American Economic Review* 85, 186-200.

Shefrin, H., and M. Statman. 1984. 'Explaining Investor Preference for Cash Dividends.' *Journal of Financial Economics* 13, 253-282.

—— 1985. 'The Disposition to Sell Winners Too Early and Ride Losers Too Long: Theory and Evidence.' *Journal of Finance* 40, 777-792.

Why Bounded Rationality

—— 1994. 'Behavioral Capital Asset Pricing Theory.' *Journal of Financial and Quantitative Analysis* 29, 323-349.

Shefrin, H., and R. Thaler. 1988. 'The Behavioral Life-Cycle Hypothesis.' *Economic Inquiry* 26, 609-643.

Shiller, R. 1989. *Market Volatility*. Cambridge, MIT Press.

Shleifer, A., and L. Summers. 1990. 'The Noise Trader Approach to Finance.' In Stiglitz (1990).

Shogren, J., S. Shin, D. Hayes, and J. Kliebenstein. 1994. 'Resolving Differences in Willingness to Pay and Willingness to Accept.' *American Economic Review* 84, 255-270.

Sichel, W. (editor). 1989. *The State of Economic Science*. Kalamazoo, Michigan, Upjohn Institute.

Silverberg, G., G. Dosi, and L. Orsenigo. 1988. 'Innovation, Diversity and Diffusion: A Self-Organization Model.' *Economic Journal* 98, 1032-1054.

Simon, H. 1955. 'A Behavioral Model of Rational Choice.' *Quarterly Journal of Economics* 69, 99-118. Reprinted in Simon (1982).

—— 1956. 'Rational Choice and the Structure of the Environment.' *Psychological Review* 63, 129-138. Reprinted in Simon (1982).

—— 1976. 'From Substantive to Procedural Rationality.' In S. Latsis (editor), *Method and Appraisal in Economics*. Cambridge, England, Cambridge University Press. Reprinted in Simon (1982).

—— 1982. *Models of Bounded Rationality* (two volumes). Cambridge, MIT Press.

—— 1986. 'Rationality in Psychology and Economics.' *Journal of Business* 59, S209-S224. Reprinted in Hogarth and Reder (1987).

—— 1987. 'Satisficing.' Entry in J. Eatwell, M. Milgate, and P. Newman (editors), *The New Palgrave: A Dictionary of Economics*. London, Macmillan.

—— 1989. Chapter 6 (untitled) of Sichel (1989).

—— 1990. 'Invariants of Human Behavior.' *Annual Reviews of Psychology* 41, 1-19.

—— 1993. 'Altruism and Economics.' *American Economic Review Papers and Proceedings* 83, 156-161.

Simon, H., and J. Schaeffer. 1992. 'The Game of Chess.' In R. Aumann and S. Hart (editors), *Handbook of Game Theory*. Amsterdam, Elsevier.

Singleton, K. 1990. 'Specification and Estimation of Intertemporal Asset Pricing Models.' In B. Friedman and F. Hahn (editors), *Handbook of Monetary Economics, Volume I*. Amsterdam, Elsevier.

Slonim, R. 1994. 'Learning in a Search-for-the-Best-Alternative Experiment.' *Journal of Economic Behavior and Organization* 25, 141-165.

Slovic, P., B. Fischhoff, and S. Lichtenstein. 1977. 'Behavioral Decision Theory.' *Annual Reviews of Psychology* 28, 1-39.

Slovic, P., S. Lichtenstein, and B. Fischhoff. 1988. 'Decision Making.' In Atkinson et. al. (1988).

Smallwood, D., and J. Conlisk. 1979. 'Product Quality in Markets Where Consumers Are Imperfectly Informed.' *Quarterly Journal of Economics* 93, 1-23.

Smith, H. 1991. 'Deciding How to Decide: Is There a Regress Problem?' In M. Bacharach and S. Hurley (editors), *Foundations of Decision Theory*. London, Basil Blackwell.

Smith, V. 1989. 'Theory, Experiment and Economics.' *Journal of Economic Perspectives*. 3, Winter, 151-169.

—— 1991. 'Rational Choices: The Contrast Between Economics and Psychology.' *Journal of Political Economy* 90, 877-897.

—— 1994. 'Economics in the Laboratory.' *Journal of Economic Perspectives* 8, 113-131.

Why Bounded Rationality

Smith, V., G. Suchanek, and A. Williams. 1988. 'Bubbles, Crashes, and Endogenous Expectations in Experimental Spot Asset Markets.' *Econometrica* 56, 1119-1151.

Smith, V., and J. Walker. 1993a. 'Monetary Rewards and Decision Cost in Experimental Economics.' *Economic Inquiry* 31, 237-244.

—— 1993b. 'Rewards, Experience and Decision Costs in First Price Auctions.' *Economic Inquiry* 31, 245-261.

Sobel, J. 1991. 'It's Not What You Know, It's Whom You Know.' In R. Selten (editor), *Game Equilibrium Models II: Methods, Morals, and Markets*. Berlin, Springer-Verlag.

—— 1992. 'How to Count to One Thousand.' *Economic Journal* 102, 1-8.

Solow, R. 1989. Untitled chapter in W. Sichel (editor), *The State of Economic Science*. Kalamazoo, Michigan, Upjohn Institute.

—— 1994. 'Perspectives on Growth Theory.' *The Journal of Economic Perspectives* 8, Winter, 45-54.

Souleles, N. 1999. 'The Response of Household Consumption to Income Tax Refunds.' *American Economic Review* 89, 947-958.

Stahl, D. 1993. 'Evolution of $Smart_n$ Players.' *Games and Economic Behavior* 5, 604-617.

Stahl, D., and P. Wilson. 1994. 'Exerimental Evidence on Players' Models of Other Players.' *Journal of Economic Behavior and Organization* 25, 309-327.

Sterman, J. 1989. 'Misperceptions of Feedback in Dynamic Decision Making.' *Organizational Behavior and Human Decision Processes* 43, 301-335.

Stigler, G., and K. Boulding (editors). 1952. *Readings in Price Theory*. Chicago, Irwin.

Stigler, G., and G. Becker. 1977. 'De Gustibus Non Est Disputandum.' *American Economic Review* 67, 76-90.

Stiglitz, J. (editor). 1990. Symposium on Bubbles. In *Journal of Economic Perspectives* 4, Spring.

Sugden, R. 1991. 'Rational Choice: A Survey of Contributions from Economics and Philosophy.' *Economic Journal* 101, 751-785.

Sunder, S. 1995. 'Experimental Asset Markets: A Survey.' In Kagel and Roth (1995).

Thaler, R. 1980. 'Toward a Positive Theory of Consumer Choice.' *Journal of Economic Behavior and Organization* 1, 39-60.

—— 1987a. 'Anomalies: The January Effect.' *Journal of Economic Perspectives* 1, Summer, 197-201.

—— 1987b. 'Anomalies: Weekend, Holiday, Turn of the Month, and Intraday Effects.' *Journal of Economic Perspectives* 1, Fall, 169-177.

—— 1988. 'Anomalies: The Winner's Curse.' *Journal of Economic Perspectives* 2, Winter, 191-202.

—— 1990. 'Anomalies: Saving, Fungibility, and Mental Accounts.' *Journal of Economic Perspectives* 4, Winter, 193-205.

—— 1991. *Quasi Rational Economics*. New York, Russell Sage.

—— 1992. *The Winner's Curse. Paradoxes and Anomalies of Economic Life*. New York, Free Press. Also available in 1994 paperback from Princeton University Press.

—— 1994. 'Psychology and Savings Policies.' *American Economic Review Papers and Proceedings* 84, 186-192.

Thaler, R., and E. Johnson. 1990. 'Gambling with the House Money and Trying to Break Even: The Effects of Prior Outcomes on Risky Choice.' *Management Science* 36, 643-660. Reprinted in Thaler (1991).

Thaler, R., and H. Shefrin. 1981. 'An Economic Theory of Self-Control.' *Journal of Political Economy* 89, 392-406.

Why Bounded Rationality

Timmermann, A. 1993a. 'How Learning in Financial Markets Generates Excess Volatility and Predictability in Stock Prices.' *Quarterly Journal of Economics* 108, 1135-1145.

—— 1993b. 'Learning, Specification Search and Market Efficiency. With an Application to the Danish Stock Market.' *Scandanavian Journal of Economics* 95, 157-173.

—— 1994. 'Can Agents Learn to Form Rational Expectations? Some Results on Convergence and Stability of Learning in the UK Stock Market.' *Economic Journal* 104, 777-797.

—— 1995. 'Volatility Clustering and Mean Reversion of Stock Returns in an Asset Pricing Model wth Incomplete Learning.' Discussion paper 95-23. University of California, San Diego.

Tobin, J. 1989. Untitled chapter in W. Sichel (editor), *The State of Economic Science*. Kalamazoo, Michigan, Upjohn Institute.

Tversky, A. 1972. 'Elimination by Aspects: A Theory of Choice.' *Psychological Review* 79, 281-299.

Tversky, A., and D. Kahneman. 1986. 'Rational Choice and the Framing of Decisions.' *Journal of Business* 59, S251-S278. Reprinted in Hogarth and Reder (1987).

Tversky, A., and D. Kahneman. 1991. 'Loss Aversion in Riskless Choice: A Reference-Dependent Model,' *Quarterly Journal of Economics* 106, 1039-1062.

Tversky, A., and R. Thaler. 1990. 'Anomalies: Preference Reversals.' *Journal of Economic Perspectives* 4, Spring, 201-211.

Van Huyck, J., J. Cook, and R. Battalio. 1994. 'Selection Dynamics, Asymptotic Stability, and Adaptive Behavior.' *Journal of Political Economy* 102, 975-1005.

Vega-Redondo, F. 1993. 'Competition and Culture in an Evolutionary Process of Equilibrium Selection: A Simple Example.' *Games and Economic Behavior* 5, 618-631.

—— 1994. 'Bayesian Boundedly Rational Agents Play the Finitely Repeated Prisoner's Dilemma.' *Theory and Decision* 36, 187-206.

—— 1996. 'Technological Change and Market Structure: An Evolutionary Approach.' *International Journal of Industrial Organization* 14, 203-206.

Vriend, N. 1995. 'Self-Organization of Markets: An Example of a Computational Approach.' *Computational Economics* 8, 205-231.

Waldman, M. 1994. 'Systematic Errors and the Theory of Natural Selection.' *American Economic Review* 84, 482-497.

Wall, K. 1993. 'A Model of Decision Making Under Bounded Rationality.' *Journal of Economic Behavior and Organization* 20, 331-352.

Wang, Y. 1993. 'Near-Rational Behaviour and Financial Market Fluctuations.' *Economic Journal* 103, 1462-1478.

Warneryd, K. 1994. 'Transaction Cost, Institutions, and Evolution.' *Journal of Economic Behavior and Organization* 25, 219-239.

Welch, I. 1992. 'Sequential Sales, Learning and Cascades.' *Journal of Finance* 47, 695-732.

Wilcox, N. 1993. 'Lottery Choice: Incentives, Complexity and Decision Time.' *Economic Journal* 103, 1397-1417.

Wilde, L. 1981. 'Laboratory Experiments in Economics.' In J. Pitt (editor), *Philosophy in Economics*. Dordrecht, Reidel.

Williams, A. 1987. 'The Formation of Price Forecasts in Experimental Markets.' *Journal of Money, Credit, and Banking* 19, 1-18.

Williams, B. 1988. 'Reinforcement, Choice, and Response Strength.' In Atkinson et. al. (1988).

Williamson, O. 1975. *Markets and Hierarchies: Analysis and Antitrust Implications*. New York, Free Press.

Why Bounded Rationality

—— 1985. *The Economic Institutions of Capitalism: Firms, Markets, Relational Contracting.* New York, Free Press.

—— 1986. *Economic Organization: Firms, Markets and Policy Control.* Brighton, Wheatsheaf.

Winston, G. 1989. 'Imperfectly Rational Choice: Rationality as the Result of a Costly Activity.' *Journal of Economic Behavior and Organization* 12, 67-86.

Winter, S. 1964. 'Economic 'Natural Selection' and the Theory of the Firm.' *Yale Economic Essays* 4, 225-272.

—— 1971. 'Satisficing, Selection, and the Innovating Remnant.' *Quarterly Journal of Economics* 85, 237-261.

—— 1975. 'Optimization and Evolution in the Theory of the Firm.' In Day and Groves (1975).

—— 1982. 'Binary Choice and the Supply of Memory.' *Journal of Economic Behavior and Organization* 3, 277-321.

—— 1984. 'Schumpeterian Competition in Alternative Technological Regimes.' *Journal of Economic Behavior and Organization* 5, 287-320.

—— 1986. 'Comments on Arrow and Lucas.' *Journal of Business* 59, S427-S434. Reprinted in Hogarth and Reder (1987).

Witt, U. 1986. 'Firms' Market Behavior Under Imperfect Information and Economic Natural Selection.' *Journal of Economic Behavior and Organization* 7, 265-290.

—— 1992. *Evolutionary Economics.* Aldershot, Edward Elgar.

Wolinsky, A. 1994. 'Small Deviations from Maximizing Behavior in a Simple Dynamic Model.' *Quarterly Journal of Economics* 109, 443-464.

Woodford, M. 1990. 'Learning to Believe in Sunspots.' *Econometrica* 58, 277-307.

Young, H. P. 1993a. 'The Evolution of Conventions.' *Econometrica* 61, 57-84.

—— 1993b. 'An Evolutionary Model of Bargaining.' *Journal of Economic Theory* 59, 145-168.

Zarnowitz, V. 1984. 'Business Cycle Analysis and Expectational Survey Data.' In K. Oppenlander (editor), *Leading Indicators and Business Cycle Surveys.* Munich, Gower.

Zeckhauser, R., J. Patel and D. Hendricks. 1991. 'Nonrational Actors and Financial Market Behavior.' *Theory and Decision* 31, 257-287.

Zemel, E. 1989. 'Small Talk and Cooperation: A Note on Bounded Rationality.' *Journal of Economic Theory* 49, 1-9.

Part III
Bounded Rationality (2): In Neoclassical Economics

Journal of Economic Methodology 2:2, 281–286 1995

Alchian and 'the Alchian thesis'

Neil M. Kay

Abstract Armen Alchian's article 'Uncertainty, evolution and economic theory' is widely acknowledged as a classic contribution to economics. Its prominence is due in part to Milton Friedman citing it as an influence on his thesis that processes of natural selection produce profit-maximising firms, and this in turn has been widely labelled 'The Alchian–Friedman Argument' or 'The Alchian thesis' in the economic literature.

In fact, 'The Alchian thesis' – that natural selection produces profit-maximising firms – is one to which Alchian did not subscribe. It was instead a doctrine which he carefully and clearly rejected. This paper provides a necessary corrective to the widespread misrepresentation of Alchian's views. It is suggested that the major reason for the misrepresentation is that Friedman's interpretation of Alchian views have been accepted at face value without proper attention being given to what Alchian actually said.

Keywords: Alchian, evolution, selection, Friedman, maximisation, survival.

INTRODUCTION

Armen Alchian's article 'Uncertainty, evolution and economic theory' has been widely recognised, both as a classic contribution in its own right, and as a major influence on Friedman's 1953 work 'The methodology of positive economics' (reprinted and referred to here as Friedman 1984). Friedman's work has been described as the most influential work on economic methodology of this century (Hausman 1984: 41) and has been instrumental in representing and publicising Alchian's views to a wider public than even a classic article might expect; as Blaug (1992: 90) points out, Friedman's piece is 'the one essay on methodological questions that virtually every modern economist has read at some stage in his or her career'. In acknowledgement of Alchian's prior contribution (and consistent with Friedman's thesis), Simon (1963: 230) talks of 'the Alchian survival argument' that 'only profit-maximisers survive', while Samuelson (1963: 231) argues that 'the Alchian doctrine of survival adds something to the maximisation hypothesis'. Blaug (1992: 101) identifies 'the Alchian thesis' that competition represents a Darwinian process which produces the result that consumers maximise utility and firms maximise profits. Hodgson

ISSN 1350–178X

(1988: 76–7) describes 'the Alchian–Friedman argument' that firms tend to maximise because these are the firms that are more likely to survive.

The 'Alchian thesis' that natural selection produces profit-maximising firms is now well established and has been the subject of much critical debate. However, much of this debate is one step removed from Alchian's article, since Friedman's subsequent work (1953) ostensibly developed Alchian's original arguments, and has in turn become the major focus for subsequent debate on whether or not profit-maximising is ensured by Darwinian processes of natural selection. The widespread labelling of such arguments as the 'Alchian' or 'Alchian–Friedman' thesis acknowledges Alchian's work in apparently first introducing these ideas.

It is therefore of interest that 'the Alchian thesis' does not represent Alchian's views as outlined in his 1950 article. Not only did Alchian not propound 'the Alchian thesis', he took great care to argue that the conditions under which profit-maximising behaviour would be possible were unlikely to obtain except in special and unusual circumstances. We shall first of all examine what Alchian actually said concerning the possibility of profit-maximising behaviour in his 1950 article, before suggesting a tentative explanation for the widespread misinterpretation of his ideas.

ALCHIAN AND THE POSSIBILITY OF PROFIT-MAXIMISING

There are three possible routes to profit-maximising that are covered by Alchian's paper. Firstly, firms may adopt profit-maximising behaviour of their own accord; secondly, processes of natural selection may automatically filter out profit-maximising survivors from non-profit-maximising failures; thirdly, over time surviving firms may have to approximate profit-maximising behaviour if they are to continue to survive. The second route represents Simon's characterisation (above) of 'the Alchian thesis', while the third route best fits Friedman's version of the thesis:

> Let the apparent immediate determinant of business behaviour be anything at all – habitual reaction, random chance or whatnot. Whenever this determinant happens to lead to behaviour consistent with rational and informed maximisation of returns, the business will prosper and acquire resources with which to expand; whenever it does not, the business will tend to lose resources and can be kept in existence only by the addition of resources from outside. The process of 'natural selection' thus helps to validate the hypothesis [of profit-maximisation behaviour].
>
> (Friedman 1984: 223)

We shall consider Alchian's treatment of the three possible routes to profit-maximisation, taking each in turn. As far as the first possibility of firms pursuing profit-maximising behaviour of their own accord is concerned,

Alchian makes his position quite clear in the second sentence of his article:

> This approach dispenses with 'profit-maximisation'.
>
> (1950: 211)

The reason for this is the existence of uncertainty:

> Where foresight is uncertain, 'profit-maximisation' is *meaningless* as a guide to specifiable action.
>
> (1950: 211, italics in original)

Interestingly in view of Friedman's argument that the realism of assumptions are irrelevant to the status of a theory, Alchian argues that his approach has the benefit of removing the 'unrealistic postulates' of perfect foresight (p. 211). Uncertainty is taken to be the more 'realistic' general state of affairs and there is therefore no room for the first route to profit-maximisation in Alchian's view of the world.

As far as the second route to profit-maximising behaviour is concerned, Alchian is also very clear. While natural selection does select winners from losers, success is measured in making *any* profit, not necessarily maximum profit:

> Realized positive profits, not *maximum* profits, are the mark of success and viability. It does not matter through what process of reasoning or motivation such success was achieved. The fact of its accomplishment is sufficient. This is the criterion by which the economic system selects survivors: those who realize *positive profits* are the survivors; those who suffer losses disappear.
>
> The pertinent requirement – positive profit through relative efficiency – is weaker than 'maximized profits', with which, unfortunately, it has been confused. Positive profits accrue to those that are better than their actual competitors, even if the participants are ignorant, intelligent, skilful, etc. The crucial element is one's aggregate position relative to actual competitors, not some hypothetically perfect competitors. As in a race, the award goes to the relatively fastest, even if all the competitors loaf. Even in a world of stupid men there would still be profits. Also, the greater the uncertainties of the world, the greater is the possibility that profits would go to venturesome and lucky rather than to logical, careful, fact-gathering individuals.
>
> (Alchian (1950: 213)

Alchian is at pains to emphasise that he is focusing on only one particular objective of economic activity, realised positive profits:

> There are no implications of 'profit maximisation', and this difference is important. Although [profit-maximisation] is a far more extreme objective when definable, only [realised positive profits] is the sine qua non of survival and success. To argue that, with perfect competition, the two

would come to the same thing is to conceal an important difference by means of a very implausible assumption. The pursuit of profits and not some hypothetical and undefinable perfect situation, is the relevant objective whose *fulfilment* is rewarded with survival.

(Alchian 1950: 217–18)

Clearly, profit-maximising is neither a necessary nor indeed an expected consequence of survival in Alchian's view. This leaves only the third alternative route to profit-maximising; could actual survivors converge on profit-maximisation by a process of learning through trial and error, rather in the manner of Friedman's expert billiard player who 'just figures it out'? (1984: 223).

Alchian also casts severe doubt on this possibility:

(Trial and error) has been used with 'profit-maximisation' wherein, by trial and ensuing success or failure, more appropriate actions are selected in a process presumed to converge to a limit of 'profit-maximisation' equilibrium. Unfortunately, at least two conditions are necessary for convergence via a trial and error process, even if one admits an equilibrium situation as an admissible limit. First, a trial must be classifiable as a success or failure. The positions achieved must be comparable with results of other potential actions. . . . The second condition . . . for the convergence via trial and error is the continual rising towards some *optimum optimorum* without intervening descents. Whether decisions and actions in economic life satisfy these two conditions cannot be proved or disproved here, but the available evidence seems overwhelmingly unfavorable.

(Alchian 1950: 219)

Alchian goes further and explains why convergence on profit-maximising solutions is not likely to be a frequently observed outcome:

The above convergence conditions do not apply to a changing environment, for there can be no observable comparison of the result of an action with another. Comparability of resulting situations is destroyed by the changing environment. As a consequence, the measure of goodness of actions in anything except a tolerable–intolerable sense is lost, and the possibility of an individual's converging to the optimum activity via a trial-and-error process disappears. Trial and error becomes survival or death.

(Alchian 1950: 219)

Alchian argues that for economists to analyse situations involving environmental change in conditions of uncertainty it is sufficient that 'those who have their fixed internal conditions closer to the new, but unknown, optimum position now have a greater probability of survival and growth. They will grow relative to other firms and become the prevailing type, since survival conditions may push the observed characteristics of the set of survivors toward the unknowable optimum' (p. 216). While Alchian argues that the dominant firms will be very different if the new environmental conditions persist for a long time, he does not suggest that these new firms will achieve the optimum position. Consistent with Darwinism, his approach deals with comparatives rather than superlatives. He does recognise that optimising behaviour may be a special case of his more general statement (p. 221), but it is clear from his discussion that he does not believe it to be a typical or even frequently observed case.

Thus, Alchian did not believe the third possible route to profit-maximisation to be a credible scenario under normal circumstances. It should be equally clear that what has been termed 'the Alchian thesis' – that natural selection produces profit-maximising firms – is one to which Alchian did not subscribe: indeed it was a doctrine which he carefully and thoughtfully rejected. This raises the subsidiary question as to why his name was attached to these arguments in the first place.

FRIEDMAN AND THE ALCHIAN THESIS

When Friedman introduced his famous (or notorious) example of leaves positioning themselves as if to maximise the amount of sunlight they receive (1984, p. 221–2), he noted in passing (p. 241) 'this example and some of the subsequent discussion, though independent in origin, is similar to and in much the same spirit as an example and the approach in an important paper by Armen A. Alchian' (Alchian's 1950 paper).

In fact, Friedman's example and Alchian's corresponding example are quite different in both content and spirit. Friedman argues that:

> I suggest the hypothesis that the leaves are positioned as if each leaf deliberately sought to maximize the amount of sunlight it receives, given the position of its neighbors, as if it knew the physical laws determining the amount of sunlight that would be received in various positions and could move rapidly or instantaneously from any one position to any other desired and unoccupied position.
>
> (1984: 221)

By way of contrast, the only possible corresponding biological analogy in Alchian's piece concerns itself with relative fitness and differential possibilities for survival and development – consistent with Alchian's argument in his paper, but antithetical to the supposed 'Alchian–Friedman argument':

> Plants 'grow' to the sunny side of buildings not because they 'want to' in awareness of the fact that optimum or better conditions prevail there, but rather because the leaves that happen to have more sunlight grow faster and their feeding systems grow stronger
>
> (Alchian 1950: 214)

Contrary to Friedman's claims, a careful reading of Alchian's arguments confirms there is nothing in this example that could be said to be in the same spirit as Friedman's example. Friedman's leaves position themselves to maximise sunlight. Alchian's plants grow towards sunnier positions because sunnier positions are *relatively* favourable to growth – not because of awareness of 'optimum or better' conditions there. There is nothing about 'as if' maximising in this example, or indeed in any other part of Alchian's general argument. Again, it is about comparative efficiency and relative fitness, not optimising; 'success (survival) accompanies relative superiority' (Alchian 1950: 213).

While this must be speculative, the simplest possible explanation as to why the supposed Alchian 'thesis', 'doctrine' or 'argument' has been mistakenly attributed to Alchian is that subsequent writers have accepted at face value Friedman's claim that Alchian's earlier arguments were similar in spirit to his own approach. Friedman's analysis was, however, quite different in content and spirit from Alchian's work, and it has to be said that Alchian's piece reflects more accurately what patterns of behaviour might reasonably be expected to be associated with natural selection processes in economic environments. The points made here not only provide a necessary corrective as far as Alchian's contribution is concerned, they also help demonstrate that arguments made in Friedman's 1953 article actually did not have the prior intellectual support that he claimed.

University of Strathclyde

REFERENCES

Alchian, Armen A. (1950) 'Uncertainty, evolution and economic theory', *Journal of Political Economy* 57: 211–21.

Blaug, Mark (1992) *The Methodology of Economics: or How Economists Explain*, 2nd edition, Cambridge: Cambridge University Press.

Friedman, Milton (1953) 'The methodology of positive economics', in M. Friedman *Essays in Positive Economics*, Chicago: University of Chicago Press, pp. 3–43. Reprinted as Friedman (1984) in Hausman (1984), pp. 210–44.

Hausman, Daniel M. (1984) *The Philosophy of Economics: an Anthology*, Cambridge: Cambridge University Press.

Hodgson, Geoffrey M. (1988) *Economics and Institutions*, Cambridge: Polity Press.

Samuelson, Paul A. (1963) 'Problems of methodology – discussion', *American Economic Review: Papers and Proceedings* 53: 229–31.

Simon, Herbert A. (1963) 'Problems of methodology – discussion', *American Economic Review: Papers and Proceedings* 53: 231–46.

[10]

Information processing and bounded rationality: a survey

BARTON L. LIPMAN   Queen's University

Abstract. This paper surveys recent attempts to formulate a plausible and tractable model of bounded rationality. I focus in particular on models that view bounded rationality as stemming from limited information processing. I discuss partitional models (such as computability, automata, perceptrons, and optimal networks), non-partitional models, and axiomatic approaches.

Transformation de l'information et rationalité limitée: une revue de la littérature. Ce mémoire examine certaines tentatives récentes pour formuler un modèle plausible et utilisable de la rationalité limitée. L'auteur s'attache en particulier aux modèles qui présentent la rationalité limitée comme un phénomène émanant de la limitation dans la capacité à transformer l'information. L'auteur discute les modèles qu'on appelle 'partitionnels' (computabilité, automates, perceptrons, réseaux optimaux), les modèles 'non partitionnels' ainsi que les approches axiomatiques.

I. INTRODUCTION

In response to criticisms of the assumption of perfect rationality (see, e.g., Simon 1955, 1976; Selten 1978; Binmore 1987, 1988), much attention has turned to finding a tractable and plausible model of *bounded rationality*. Herbert Simon, the originator of the phrase, defines bounded rationality as 'rational choice that takes into account the cognitive limitations of the decision-maker – limitations of both knowledge and computational capacity' (Simon 1987). A useful way to view bounded rationality is to think of an agent as an information processor. 'Inputs' (information) flow to the agent, he processes them in some fashion, and 'output' (decisions) come out. Bounded rationality refers to choice that is imperfect in the sense that the

I thank Debra Holt, Bentley MacLeod, Laura Robinson, and Timothy Van Zandt for comments and suggestions. Financial support from the Social Sciences and Humanities Research Council of Canada is gratefully acknowledged. Of course, any errors or omissions are my own responsibility.

output is often not the 'correct' one but is sensible in that it can be understood as an attempt by the agent to do reasonably well. Put differently, the procedure used is a reasonable compromise between accuracy of the output and the difficulties involved in processing.

Despite the fact that many economists view bounded rationality as a more realistic and more appropriate assumption than perfect rationality at least for many situations, there are very few papers that explore the implications of bounded rationality. The reason for this is very simple: there is no clear agreement on how one models this phenomenon. Instead, the focus of the literature has been on exploring various modelling approaches. In this survey, I shall review some of the approaches that have been suggested in recent years. I should warn the reader that, given the state of the literature, this survey will be quite unlike the others in this volume. While I shall mention some theorems, the focus will be on ideas and approaches, not on results or established facts.

The various approaches I discuss have one theme in common: all treat bounded rationality as limited information processing. However, they vary greatly in the way these limitations are modelled. After presenting an overview model in section II, I turn in section III to *partitional* models of information processing. The common feature of these is that information processing can be summarized in terms of a partition of the set of 'external states' or 'inputs' and how actions are conditioned on this partition. As I explain, these models can be seen as describing an agent who is fully aware of how he is processing his information.

A large number of apparently quite different models fit into this framework. First, I discuss the most basic kind of constraint on behaviour, namely that it be *computable*. Surprisingly, this requirement can have important implications in economic models (Spear 1989; Anderlini 1991; Anderlini and Felli 1992.). Next, I turn to some models that assume some form of cost function for partitions. I primarily discuss the automata literature (Rubinstein 1986; Abreu and Rubinstein 1988; Kalai and Stanford 1988), but I also briefly discuss a few related models. Finally, I discuss models where the costs of paritions are, at least to some extent, derived from a more detailed model of the way the partition is constructed. In this context, I discuss threshold models (Rubinstein 1992; Cho and Matsui 1992a, 1992b) and optimal processing networks (Mount and Reiter 1990; Radner and Van Zandt 1992).

In section IV, I discuss *non-partitional* models – that is, models in which information processing does not generate a partition (Bacharach 1985; Geanakoplos 1989, 1992). This approach seems to have the advantage of greater generality in that partitions are special cases of non-partitional structures. On the other hand, because these models seem to rely on a lack of self-awareness, it may be more difficult to endogenize information processing in this framework. While most of the models in section III derive the nature of information processing from some primitives at least to some extent, so far there has been very little analogous work with non-partitional structures.

In section V, I discuss three recent papers that can be thought of as attempts to provide an axiomatic derivation of certain forms of information processing. In

44   Barton L. Lipman

particular, I discuss Morris's (1992b) work on non-partitional information structures, Lipman's (1992b) derivation of impossible possible worlds, and Gilboa and Schmeidler's (1992b) notion of case-based reasoning. Some concluding remarks are offered in section VI.

Remark 1
My focus on information processing and the computation of decisions leads me to omit many topics related to bounded rationality more broadly defined. In this remark, I shall briefly comment on a few of the most serious omissions. First, I have left out the literature on intransitive indifference (see Suppes, et al. 1989 for a survey or Sileo 1992 for an interesting recent paper), despite the fact that this seems to make a very nice model of imperfect perceptual ability. Second, I have omitted the work on non-additive probabilities (see Gilboa and Schmeidler 1992a for a particularly intriguing introduction to the subject), even though many (such as Shafer 1976; Binmore 1991; and Walley 1991) have described this and related approaches as more realistic models of humans. Third, I have omitted a variety of work on relaxations of expected utility, even though some of these papers seem to be motivated by bounded rationality considerations (particularly Rubinstein 1988; Segal 1990). Fourth, I have not included any discussion of the 'decision-theoretic' approach to game theory (Bernheim 1984; Pearce 1984; Aumann 1987; Aumann and Brandenburger 1991), despite its focus on the effects of knowledge regarding the rationality of others. Fifth, I discuss only analytic models, not simulation-based techniques like genetic algorithms (Holland 1975; Marimon, McGrattan, and Sargent 1990; Holland and Miller 1991; Sargent 1993). Finally, I only briefly mention a few applications of the theory. This is not to suggest that applications are unimportant – on the contrary, I argue in the conclusion that they are crucial. To date, however, there have not been very many applications of these models to specific problems in economics and game theory.

II. OVERVIEW

Each of the models I discuss can be roughly described in the following way. The agent observes some external events, which I shall often refer to as *inputs*. The way the agent processes these inputs determines his 'state of mind' or his view of the problem at hand. This, in turn, determines his behaviour.

More formally, let Ω denote the set of *external states*. For simplicity, I assume Ω is finite. For some of the models discussed below, one must allow for infinite state sets, but I avoid a general discussion of this case to avoid extraneous mathematical complications. Let Θ be the set of inputs and let $\xi: \Omega \longrightarrow \Theta$ tell which input the agent observes as a function of the external state. I shall refer to ξ as the *input function*. That is, in state ω, the agent will observe input $\xi(\omega)$. Note that this implies that the 'true' information content of the input θ is that ω is one of the states generating this input – that is, the true state ω is some element of $\xi^{-1}(\theta)$. However, the agent may not process the input sufficiently to recognize this implication.

Let A be the set of *actions* the agent can choose among. So that the choice problem is non-trivial, I shall always assume that A has at least two elements. The agent has a utility function $u: A \times \Omega \rightarrow \mathbf{R}$, which describes how the state affects the value of the different actions available to the agent. The agent also has a prior probability distribution, q, on Ω.[1]

The agent's information processing tells how the input θ determines his *beliefs* about the external state. Letting Δ denote the set of probability distributions on Ω, then, we have a *belief function* $\beta: \Theta \rightarrow \Delta$. Given the beliefs that result from his information processing, the agent chooses that action he perceives to be optimal. So we have an *action function* $\alpha: \Delta \rightarrow A$. I discuss, below, the sense in which this function is optimal. Note that we can combine the input, belief, and action functions to determine the agent's action as a function of the external state. This gives us a function $f: \Omega \rightarrow A$, defined by $f(\omega) = \alpha(\beta(\xi(\omega)))$. I shall call f the agent's *behaviour rule*.

One may want the belief function to satisfy some kinds of consistency conditions. The main difference between the partitional and non-partitional models is precisely the level of internal consistency of the belief function β that is assumed. For this reason, I make no consistency assumptions at all for the time being.

To understand the belief function as a statement about information processing, consider two extreme cases. First, suppose there is a single belief $\delta \in \Delta$ which the agent holds no matter what input he sees – that is, $\delta = \beta(\theta)$ for all θ. In this case, the agent does not process his information at all, since the information has no effect on him. Intuitively, we would expect that $\delta = q$, the prior distribution, in this case. I emphasize that I shall treat this kind of consistency with the prior as an additional assumption. Alternatively, if he processes his information fully, then he will recognize every implication of his information. That is, he will have a different belief for each different input. So $\theta \neq \theta'$ will imply $\beta(\theta) \neq \beta(\theta')$. Again, we would intuitively expect $\beta(\theta)$ to put probability 1 on the set $\xi^{-1}(\theta)$ or perhaps even to be computed from the prior via Bayes's Rule by conditioning on this event. Again, this consistency is an additional assumption.

Throughout, I shall assume that given his beliefs, the agent's action choice is that action that maximizes expected utility. There are two ways to define optimality more precisely. First, given a belief $\delta \in \Delta$, we can calculate the action that maximizes

$$\sum_{\omega \in \Omega} u(a, \omega)\delta(\omega).$$

Let $\alpha(\delta)$ denote an a which solves this maximization. Carrying out this procedure for each δ gives us an action function α. We can construct a behaviour rule by letting $f(\omega)$ equal the action $\alpha(\delta)$ where δ is the belief that the input $\xi(\omega)$ leads to. That is, for each ω such that $\beta(\xi(\omega)) = \delta$, let $f(\omega) = \alpha(\delta)$. I shall say that this behaviour rule is *interim optimal*.

---

1 One could consider models that do not assume expected utility. In particular, the axiomatic approaches discussed in section V relax this assumption.

46   Barton L. Lipman

Note that this calculation will have the property that if $\beta(\xi(\omega)) = \beta(\xi(\omega'))$, then $f(\omega) = f(\omega')$. That is, if agent has the same beliefs in two external states, then his behaviour is the same in these two states. This implication is sometimes described by saying that f is *measurable with respect to* $\beta(\xi)$. Intuitively, it simply says that the agent doesn't use more information about ω than what he actually processes.

This suggests another approach to calculating the optimal behaviour rule. Suppose we simply compute the behaviour function f that maximizes

$$\sum_{\omega \in \Omega} u(f(\omega), \omega)q(\omega),$$

subject to the constraint that f be measureable with respect to $\beta(\xi)$. Such a behaviour function will be called *ex ante optimal*. Intuitively, an ex ante optimal rule describes an optimal plan for the agent to follow, while an interim optimal rule describes how the agent will behave upon reaching any given situation.

The relationship between these two approaches will depend on how consistent the belief function is with the prior distribution. Loosely, if the belief function is 'consistent enough,' then these approaches are equivalent. When they are not, interim optimality would seem to be the more appropriate criterion.

In some of the models I discuss below, β is also partly endogenous and is chosen optimally. To describe this, suppose f is an interim[2] optimal behaviour rule and let

$$V(\beta) = \sum_{\omega \in \Omega} u(f(\omega), \omega)q(\omega).$$

Thus V gives the ex ante expected pay-off associated with processing information according to the function β. (Recall that β affects f by imposing a constraint on the set of available f's via the measurability requirement.) Then we can model the determination of β by supposing that the agent chooses it to maximize $V(\beta) - c(\beta)$, where c gives the expected information processing costs. Typically, the agent is constrained to choose β from some set $\mathcal{B}$ of feasible belief functions.

Remark 2
People are often troubled by the assumption that the agent chooses his information processing optimally. Certainly, it seems odd to model bounded rationality by assuming a particular form of optimal choice! Even worse, the problem of finding the optimal way to process information seems like a more complex problem than simply choosing the optimal action, given some ω in the first place. There are at least two replies to this criticism. First, it seems more reasonable to believe that the knowledge agents acquire and retain is general knowledge rather than specific knowledge. In other words, they know how to solve problems, even if they do not know the solution to every problem. By analogy, ther is a sense in which deriving

---

2 One could carry out similar analysis using ex ante optimal behaviour rules, but again, interim optimal rules seem to be the more natural focus.

the quadratic formula is harder then finding the roots to a given quadratic equation. However, ex ante, one does not know which quadratic equation one will need to solve. Hence one finds it more useful to know the quadratic formula than to try learning the roots of various quadratic equations! The choice of β and f models the agent's choice of how to solve problems, and, by this argument, it seems more reasonable to believe that this choice is made well than that the choice given any particular ω is made well. An alternative response is that if we are uncomfortable with the assumption that the agent chooses β and f optimally, we must be saying that we have not completely specified the model. That is, our model must be viewed as a model of the world *as the agent perceives it*. If the model is truly a complete description of the agent's perception, then how can he fail to choose what he perceives to be best for him? (This is basically the arguement given in Lipman 1991.) A different form of this view will be discussed briefly in section v.

III. PARTITIONAL MODELS

In this section, I turn to models in which information processing can be summarized by a *partition* Π of Ω. A partition Π of a set, say Z, is a collection of subsets of Z with the property that every $z \in Z$ is in exactly one of these subsets. The elements of the partition Π are often referred to as *events*. A partition Π is said to be *finer* than a partition Π' if for every event $\pi' \in \Pi'$, there are events $\pi_1, \ldots, \pi_k \in \Pi$ such that $\cup_i \pi_i = \pi'$. This is also described by saying that Π' is *coarser* than Π. Intuitively, if Π is finer than Π', then learning which event of Π contains a given z conveys more information than only learning which event of Π' contains z.

Partitions are intimately related to *equivalence relations*. An equivalence relation, say R, on a set Z is a binary relation that is reflexive (that is, zRz always holds), symmetric (zRz' implies $z'Rz$), and transitive (zRz' and $z'Rz''$ implies zRz''). The simplest example of an equivalence relation is the standard notion of 'equal to,' or $=$. A familiar example to economists is the usual indifference relation. Given any equivalence relation, we can partition Z into *equivalence classes* as follows. For any given $z \in Z$, let

$$R(z) = \{z' \in Z | zRz'\}.$$

Thus $R(z)$ is the set of points equivalent under R to z. These sets are called the equivalence classes of R. It is not hard to show that for any z and z', either $R(z) = R(z')$ or else $R(z) \cap R(z') = \emptyset$. Furthermore, since $z \in R(z)$, every point in Z is contained in an $R(z)$ set for some z. Hence the equivalence classes of R form a partition of Z, called the partition *induced* by R. Similarly, given any partition Π, we can define an equivalence relation induced by the partition by saying that z and z' are equivalent if they are contained in the same event in Π.

To return to information processing, recall that we have represented the effect of the agent's processing of information by a function $\beta: \Theta \longrightarrow \Delta$, where $\beta(\theta)$ is the agent's beliefs given input θ. Clearly, we can define an equivalence relation

48   Barton L. Lipman

over Ω by saying that two states ω and ω' are equivalent if $\beta(\xi(\omega)) = \beta(\xi(\omega'))$ – that is, if they lead to the same beliefs. Let Π denote the partition induced by this equivalence relation. I let $\pi(\omega)$ denote that event of Π continuing ω.

The key to the partitional models is that beliefs are assumed to be internally consistent in the sense that if the agent's beliefs are δ only in certain external states, then δ must put all probability only on those states. That is, the support of the probability distribution δ (the set of ω with strictly positive probability) is equal to the set of ω for which $\beta(\xi(\omega)) = \delta$. In all of the partitional models below (and all the ones I know of), a stronger assumption is made – namely, that δ is assumed to be calculated from the prior q via Bayes's Rule. More specifically, given the partition Π,

$$\beta(\xi(\omega))(\omega') = \begin{cases} 0, & \text{if } \omega' \notin \pi(\omega); \\ q(\omega') / \sum_{w \in \pi(\omega)} q(w), & \text{otherwise.} \end{cases}$$

In this sense, the partition can be used to summarize the agent's information processing without explicit reference to the underlying belief function.

The partition Π is easily interpreted in terms of information processing. If Π has only one event (which would have to be the entire set Ω), then the agent is not processing his input at all – he effectively ignores it. This corresponds to the case where $\beta(\theta) = q$ for every θ. By contrast, a partition that has a different event for each different θ involves complete processing in the sense that the agent processes the input so thoroughly that he recognizes every possible distinction between inputs. Here $\pi(\omega) = \xi^{-1}(\theta(\omega))$ – that is, the set of states he would consider possible in state ω would be exactly those in which he receives the same input he receives in ω. More generally, the finer is his partition, the more processing of his information he is carrying out.

Because Π summarizes information processing, we can write $V(\Pi)$ instead of $V(\beta)$. Recall that β was only implicit in our earlier expression for V in any case, so we would simply replace our constraint that f be measurable with respect to $\beta(\xi)$ with a constraint that it be measurable with respect to Π. Also, if we assume that the cost of a given information processing function β depends only on the partition β generates, then we can work with $c(\Pi)$ instead of $c(\beta)$.

The rest of this section is divided in three parts. The first part focuses on computability as a constraint on the processing of information. The second part focuses on models that make certain assumptions about partition cost functions. The main body of research along these lines has been the automata literature, but I also very briefly discuss a variety of other applications of this idea. Finally, the third part discusses two models that analyse the construction of the partitions in more detail.

1. Computability

The most basic requirement we could place on information processing is to restrict the agent to using a *computable* or *recursive* behaviour rule. There are several equivalent ways to define this set of functions. Lossely speaking, it is the set of functions f for which an algorithm exists such that for each input ω, the alogrithm eventually (that is, in finitely many steps) produces output $f(\omega)$. This requirement is restrictive only when Ω is infinite – any function with a finite domain is computable. Typically, one assumes that Ω is countable.

It is easy to show that there are only countably many computable functions. To see this intuitively, imagine you are writing a computer program. There are only finitely many different commands you can use at any given line of the program. Furthermore, the program must be of finite length. Hence there are countably many different programs you could write. Therefore, there are at most countably many functions you can compute. On the other hand, if Ω is infinite, the set of all functions from Ω to A is uncountable. In this sense, 'most' functions are not computable.

For a more intuitive sense of why some functions are not computable, consider the so-called *Halting problem*. We say that a computer program *halts* on a given input if it eventually ceases computation and gives an answer. The Halting problem is the problem of determining whether a given computer program eventually halts on a given input. Obviously, if a given program does halt on a given input, we can learn this fact simply by running the program. If it does not halt, however, it is not obvious that we can determine this fact. Certainly, if we can recognize an infinite loop in the program, we can determine that it will not halt. But clearly there is no simple procedure for finding such a loop. In fact, one can show that the Halting problem is *undecidable* – there is no computable function that can determine whether any given program halts on any given input.

Of course, it is difficult to imagine a real agent using a function that is not computable, and so it seems only reasonable to restrict agents to using only behaviour rules f that are computable. Typically, the literature would assume that the agent uses the optimal computable f. These models are partitional because any computable f can be broken into a computable partitioning of Ω and a computable function from the partition to A.[3]

A number of authors have shown some very surprising consequences of requiring agents to use computable functions. For example, Anderlini (1991) shows that in common interest games with communication, a restriction to computable strategies and, loosely speaking, computably trembling-hand perfect equilibria implies cooperation, even in a one-shot game. Unfortunately, to explain this and other papers in detail would require a lengthy digression on the mathematics of computable functions. I encourage the interested reader to consult Cutland (1980) for an especially readable introduction to the subject and Anderlini (1991), Spear (1989), or Anderlini and Felli (1992) for some of the more interesting applications.

2. Exogenous cost functions

a. Automata

In response to a suggestion by Aumann (1981), Neyman (1985) and Rubinstein

---

3 See Anderlini and Felli (1992) for a demonstration of essentially this point.

50   Barton L. Lipman

(1986) initiated the study of repeated games in which players were restricted to using *finite state automata* (more precisely, Moore machines) to implement their strategies. Both papers treated limitations on rationality as limitations on the number of states of the automata, Neyman by imposing constraints on the number of states, Rubinstein by assuming that states are costly. These papers led to a large body of research, much of which is summarized in Kalai (1991).[4]

An automaton is a stylized description of a simple computing device, which has been studied in the computer science literature since the mid-1950s. (See Hopcroft and Ullman 1979 for an introduction to the subject.) Briefly, an automaton consists of a set of *internal states*, one of which is designated the *initial state*; a *transition function*, which specifies how the automata changes states in response to the opponents' actions; and an *output function*, which gives an action as a function of the state. (I shall give some examples below.) Rather than focus on automata themselves, I shall follow an equivalent approach first noted by Kalai and Stanford (1988), which makes clear how automata fit into the framework above.

Suppose we have an infinitely repeated game. Let H denote the set of possible histories of play. More precisely, a history is a possible finite sequence of actions for each of the players in the game. A strategy in the game is a function σ which specifies an action as a function of the history of the game. After any history, say h, the remaining game is still an infinitely repeated game. Hence a strategy for the overall game, σ, in effect, specifies a continuation strategy for the game which follows the history h. This is what Kalai and Stanford call the *induced strategy* $\sigma|h$. More precisely, $\sigma|h$ is the strategy that, on a history h', specifies the action that σ would prescribe on the history h followed by h'. We can then say that two histories, h and h', are equivalent under σ if they lead to the same induced strategy – that is, if $\sigma|h = \sigma|h'$. It is easy to show that this is an equivalence relation so that it generates a partition of H which will be denoted by $\mathcal{H}(\sigma)$. Clearly, if we know which event of this partition a history lies in, we know enough about the history to determine the strategy it induces. Kalai and Stanford show that the number of internal states of the smallest automata which plays a given strategy is equal to the number of sets in this partition.

To understand this notion more intuitively, it is useful to consider a few examples. Suppose we are analysing a repeated Prisoners' Dilemma game. The actions are 'cooperate' and 'defect.' The strategy 'always cooperate' has exactly one induced strategy: namely, itself. On any history at all, the continuation strategy is identical to the original strategy. Hence the partition has just one event equal to the set of all histories. The automaton this corresponds to has just one state, an output function that specifies cooperation in this one state, and a trivial transition function that stipulates remaining in this one state in response to any action by the opponent.

A slightly more complex example is 'tit-for-tat.' This strategy begins by cooperating and, on every subsequent history, does whatever the opponent did on

---

4 Some relevant papers written since Kalai's survey are Neme and Quintas (1992), Piccione (1992), and Piccione and Rubinstein (1993).

the previous play. This strategy has two induced strategies. On the 'empty history' – that is, at the beginning of the game – or on any history where the opponent cooperated in the previous period, the induced strategy is tit-for-tat. On any history where the opponent defected in the previous period, it is the variant of tit-for-tat that begins by defecting and then does whatever the opponent did on the previous move. Hence the partition has two events: those histories where the opponent co-operated on the last move and those histories where the opponent defected on the last move. The automaton this corresponds to has two states, one that specifies cooperation as its output and one that specifies defection. The transition function specifies moving to the cooperative state in response to cooperation and the de-fecting state in response to defection.

For a last example, consider a k-period trigger strategy. This strategy cooperates until the opponent defects. At this point, it enters a 'punishment mode,' defecting for the next k periods regardless of what the opponent does. Any choices by the opponent are ignored during this period. After the k defections, the strategy returns to cooperation until the next defection by the opponent. It is not hard to see that this strategy has $k + 1$ induced strategies. On the empty history, histories where the opponent has never defected, or any history where the punishment is complete, the induced strategy is the k-period trigger strategy. Then there are k-induced strategies corresponding to the k periods of punishment. In any one of them, there is a certain number of periods in which the player intends to defect and moves by the opponent are ignored. Since the number of remaining periods like this differs over the punishment cycle, each such induced strategy is different. Hence the partition this strategy induces has $k + 1$ events. Again, the corresponding automaton has $k + 1$ states, one with cooperation as its output and the others with defection. The transition function specifies staying in the cooperative state in response to cooperation. In response to defection while in the cooperative state, it moves to the first of the k punishment states. From there, it moves through the k punishment states in sequence in response to any output, finally moving back to the cooperative state.

To relate this to the previous framework, the set of histories plays the role of the set of external states and the set of inputs, so $H = \Omega$ and $\xi(\omega) = \omega$. (Of course, in this case, the probability distribution over H is determined endogenously by the strategy choices of the players in the game.) The set of 'actions,' A, is the set of strategies for the infinitely repeated game. Hence any strategy σ can be described as a function f from $\mathcal{H}(\sigma)$ into A where $f(h) = \sigma|h$. Thus we can divide the choice of a strategy σ into the choice of a partition of the set of histories, Π, and a function from Π to the set of strategies.[5] The cost function c in most of the literature is a function only of the number of events of the partition and is an increasing function of this. Lipman and Srivastava (1990) and Banks and Sundaram (1990) analyse the implications of alternative cost functions.

5 It is important to note that not every partition of H can be generated by some strategy. For example, there is no strategy that induces the partition that puts every history except a single one-period history into one event and this single history into another. Similarly, not every function from such a partition to A will form a legitimate strategy.

52   Barton L. Lipman

b. Related models
Rosenthal (1991a, 1991b) suggests that agents adopt simple rules of thumb which
are approximately optimal for a wide variety of circumstances, even though they
may never be exactly optimal. (This idea has a long history in economics. See,
e.g., Baumol and Quandt 1964.) To model this, he assumes that there is a set of
possible games, Γ, that the agent might play. The input the agent receives is simply
the game to be played, so $\Omega = \Gamma$ and $\xi(\omega) = \omega$. For simplicity, suppose that there
is the same set of feasible strategies in each of these games. This set of stretegies
will be the set of actions A. A rule of thumb is a function $r : \Gamma \longrightarrow A$ specifying
what action to use in which game. Rosenthal assumes that there are costs to these
rules, where the costs increase with the number of different actions which might
be used. Putting it differently, say that two games, G and G', are equivalent given
r if $r(G) = r(G')$. Let Π be the partition this equivalence relation induces. Now
we see that the agent's choice of r corresponds directly to a choice of a partition
Π and a behaviour rule f measurable with respect to Π. Resenthal's cost function
is simply an increasing function of the number of events of the partition.

Dow (1991) considers a model of search with limited memory. Here the input
is a pair of prices, one observed in the first period and one in the second, where
the agent knows he will not be able to remember the first one exactly. An action
is a choice of which price to purchase the good at. Dow's formulation of limited
memory is that the agent has a partition of the set of possible prices and, in the
second period, remembers only which event of the partition the first-period price
fell into. Hence he works directly with a partition Π. He also assumes that costs
are proportional to the number of events of the partition.

A last example of this type of model treats computation as equivalent to costly information acquisition. It has often been suggested (see, e.g., Conlisk 1988; Lipman
1991) that computation is the extraction of information from facts one already
knows and hence is analogous to acquisition of information. This is modelled by
treating computation as simply a choice of a partition Π, such that the agent must
choose f to be measurable with respect to Π. The techniques in these models are
quite standard, but the interpretation is different. That is, this view of computation leads to a model that is quite familiar but suggests including 'information
acquisition' in contexts where, under the usual interpretation, it would be thought
inappropriate. In this literature, it is much less common to assume that the cost of
a partition is simply an increasing function of the number of events in the partition.
Lipman (1992a) applies this approach to the study of the endogenous choice of an
incomplete contract.

3. Modelling the construction of the partition

a. Threshold models
In this class of models, there are no costs associated with information processing,
so $c(\Pi) = 0$ for all $\Pi \in \mathcal{P}$. Also, the external state is observed directly, so $\Omega = \Theta$
and $\xi(\omega) = \omega$. However, the processing of information is constrained to take a

particular form. Rather than the set of feasible partitions being described directly, it is described indirectly by requiring that the partition be constructed according to the following two-step procedure. First, the agent 'translates' ω into a real number using what I shall call a *processing function* μ. Second, the agent observes whether or not $\mu(\omega)$ is above a certain 'threshold.' The important point is that the agent is able to divide Ω into only two sets – those for which $\mu(\omega)$ is above the threshold and those for which it is not.

The threshold form may seem arbitrary at first glance. On the other hand, it does provide a simple way of restricting the construction of partitions. Intuitively, the agent is only able to determine which of two 'positions' ω gives greater support to. Naturally, one may be interested in generalizing the idea to multiple thresholds or some other intermediate level of information processing.

One example of the use of threshold models in economics is Rubinstein's (1992) application of Minsky and Papert's (1988) perceptrons.[6] Here, it is assumed that $\Omega \subseteq R^k$ for some $k \geq 2$. The processing is constrain in the following way. The agent has some number of functions, ϕ, called *perceptrons*, each of which analyses the input ω. A perceptron of order n only conditions on n components of the vector ω – that is, it is completely independent of what appears in the other $k - n$ components. Then the processing function is $\mu(\omega) = \Sigma_i \phi_i(\omega)$ where the ϕ_is are the agent's perceptrons. Notice that the agent's sophistication can be restricted either by restricting the number or order of his perceptrons. This approach is intended to model the idea that the agent combines only 'small' pieces of information about the input in a simple fashion.[7]

To get a sense of how these restrictions affect the set of feasible partitions, consider the following example drawn from the Rubinstein paper. Suppose there are four states in Ω: (b, b), (b, d), (d, b), and (d, d), where b and d are real numbers, $b \neq d$. Obviously, all perceptrons are of either order 1 or order 2. Because the conditioning has to have a threshold form, no feasible partition has more than two events. However, it is easy to see that it is possible to generate any such partition with a single perception of order 2.

Suppose, though, that one is restricted to order-1 perceptrons. Clearly, there is no need to have more than two perceptrons, since there is no need to condition twice on the same component. Let ϕ_1 and ϕ_2 be two order-1 perceptions, where ϕ_i conditions only on the ith component of ω. To get a sense of some of the possible partitions, let $\phi_1(b) = 1$, $\phi_1(d) = 2$, $\phi_2(b) = -2$, and $\phi_2(d) = -4$. Then $\mu((b, d)) = -3$, $\mu((d, d)) = -2$, $\mu((b, b)) = -1$, and $\mu((d, b)) = 0$. Clearly, by choosing the threshold appropriately, one can obtain a partition with (b, d) by itself and the other three in a single event (with a threshold of -2.5), a partition with (b, d) and (d, d) in one event and the other two states in the other (threshold of -1.5), or a partition with (d, b) in one event and the other three in the other (threshold of -0.5). More generally, it is easy to see that with an appropriate choice of ϕ_1 and

---

6 The only other examples I am aware of are Cho and Matsui (1992a, 1992b).

7 Minsky and Papert (1988) discuss a variety of other ways to require perceptrons to depend only on limited amounts of information about the input.

54   Barton L. Lipman

ϕ_2, one can obtain any two-event partition where one event is a singleton. (To do so, simply make ϕ_i on the ith component of this singleton very negative and make ϕ_i equal zero otherwise.) As to two-event partitions where each event contains two states, we showed above how to obtain $\{\{(b,d),(d,d)\}, \{(b,b),(d,b)\}\}$. It is not hard to find perceptrons that generate the partition $\{\{(b,d),(b,b)\}, \{(d,d),(d,b)\}\}$.

This leaves only the partition $\{\{(b,d),(d,b)\}, \{(b,b)(d,d)\}\}$. This partition *cannot* be generated with order-1 perceptrons. To see this, suppose that it is generated by with perceptrons ϕ_1 and ϕ_2 and threshold α. Then we must have[8]

$$\phi_1(b) + \phi_2(d) > \alpha$$

$$\phi_1(d) + \phi_2(b) > \alpha$$

and

$$\phi_1(b) + \phi_2(b) < \alpha$$

$$\phi_1(d) + \phi_2(d) < \alpha$$

Clearly, though, these two pairs of inequalities are contradictory. Summing the first two yields the opposite inequality obtained from summing the second two.

b. Processing networks

As with the threshold models, the work on processing networks provides a more detailed analysis of how information is processed. Because I understand it better (or, at least, believe I do!), I shall focus on the approach taken by Radner (1989) and further pursued in Van Zandt (1990) and Radner and Van Zandt (1992).[9] The interested reader should also consult the related work of Mount and Reiter (1990).

In these models, information flows into a network of *processors*. Each processor has an 'in-box,' a register where it keeps a running total, and the ability to send its total to certain, pre-specified processors. In each period, a processor can remove an item from its in-box, add it to the current register,[10] and send the value of the register to another processor. If it sends the value of its register to another processor, this information goes into the receiving processor's in-box, and the sending processor's register is set to zero. Also in each period, information from outside the network flows into the in-boxes of certain prespecified processors. The choice variables in a network are: (1) the number of processors, (2) which processors receive how much incoming information, (3) when processors send their register to other processors, and (4) which processors they send the information to.

To understand the model, consider the following example drawn from Radner (1992). Suppose that information comes in to the network only in the first period and that it consists of a vector of forty numbers. The goal of the network is to

---

8 Of course, reversing all four inequalities also generates this partition, but this possibility leads to the same contradiction.

9 A very clear introduction to this work is contained in Radner (1992).

10 Addition can be replaced by any associative operation.

compute the sum of these forty numbers. In other words, the set of states equals the set of inputs, $\xi(\omega) = \omega$, and $\Omega = \mathbf{R}^{40}$. The partition we wish to generate is the one induced by the equivalence relation, which treats vectors as equivalent if their components add to the same number. We wish to generate this partition at the lowest possible cost where the cost is increasing in both the number of processors required and the number of periods it takes to compute the sum.

One network that generates this partition is the following. Each of eight processors receives five of the incoming numbers. Over the course of the first five periods, the processors add the five numbers together. At the end of period 5, the eight processors send the totals to four additional processors, each of which receives information from two processors. In periods 6 and 7, these processors add the incoming numbers together. At the end of period 7, they forward the totals to two other processors, each of which receives information from two processors. They total their incoming numbers in periods 8 and 9, forwarding the totals to a single processor at the end of period 9. Finally, in periods 10 and 11, the last processor computes the overall sum. This network requires fifteen processors and takes eleven periods to compute the sum.

Clearly, though, there is much redundancy in this network, since the 'higher-up' processors are idle while they are waiting for the lower processors to add. In fact, the forty numbers can be summed by a network with only eight processors in eight periods. To do this, each of the eight processors receives five numbers. As above, the processors spend periods 1 through 5 adding their numbers. At this point, four of the processors send their totals to the other four, each processor receiving one number. This is added to the processor's previous total in period 6. At the end of this period, two of the four processors send their totals to the other two. These numbers are added to previous totals in period 7, after which one processor sends its total to the other. Finally, the overall total is computed in period 8. Radner (1989) shows that this network is efficient in the sense that one cannot generate this partition with both fewer processors and less delay.

Since there is a trade-off betwen processors and periods, this is not necessarily the minimum cost network. For example, the sum could also be computed by a network with one less processor in one more period. Depending on the relative cost of processors versus delay, either (or neither) network could be optimal.

More generally, it may be optimal to choose a network that provides only a coarser partition. The partition described above is the finest partition that a network of processors can generate. Once the costs of processors and delay are specified,[11] one can derive a cost function for any feasible partition. Then, given a probability distribution over Ω, a set of actions A, and a pay-off function u, one can compute the optimal partition, the optimal network for generating it, and the optimal behaviour

---

11 In the general framework described at the beginning of this section, the costs of the partition are given by some function $c(\Pi)$, completely independently of the 'benefits' of the partition, $V(\Pi)$. When delay matters, it may be more natural to model costs through the use of a discount factor. In this appraoch, benefits and costs cannot be separated quite so simply, but the basic principle is unchanged.

56   Barton L. Lipman

rule measurable with respect to that partition. When new information arrives in
every period as in Van Zandt (1990) or Radner and Van Zandt (1992), the problem
is vastly more complex, but the idea is the same.

I should emphasize that Radner primarily discusses these networks as models
of firms, rather than of individual agents.[12] In this context, the structure of optimal
networks itself is of great interest.

IV. NON-PARTITIONAL MODELS

The partitional models maintain a long tradition of treating information as a partition (see Blackwell 1951; Aumann 1976; etc.). Intuitively, if the agent understands
his information processing, we should be able to describe his processing as a partition. Recall that the key assumption underlying these models is that if the agent's
beliefs are δ exactly when the true external state is in the set $W \subseteq \Omega$, then the
support of δ should be W. That is, the agent should be able to say to himself, 'My
beliefs are δ. But I know I'd have these beliefs if and only if $\omega \in W$. So I shouldn't
be putting any probability on any states outside W.'

Implicit in this view, however, is the condition that the agent will fully process
his information. If he does not do so, he may not have his information in the form
of a partition. Bacharach (1985) was the first author in the economics literature to
point out this possibility. As he noted, there is a very large, very old literature in
philosophy on *modal logic* which addresses this subject. (See Hughes and Cresswell
1968 or Chellas 1990 for an introduction.) Geanakoplos (1989) was the first to
define and analyse a decision theory for non-partitional information.

In section III, we assumed that the belief function β could be written as based
on Bayesian updating from a partition Π of Ω. In the non-partitional models, we
generalize this notion and assume that the belief function can be written as based
on Bayesian updating from what Geanakoplos (1989) calls a *possibility correspon-
dence*. This is a function $P: \Omega \longrightarrow 2^\Omega$, where 2^Ω is the power set of Ω – that is,
the set of all subsets of Ω. Intuitively, $P(\omega)$ is the set of ω' that the agent thinks
are possible after processing input ω. Here P is *not* a choice variable. Instead,
it is assumed to satisfy certain properties, some of which I discuss below. With
partitional models, $\beta(\xi(\omega))$ is generated by updating the prior using Bayes's Rule
to concentrate it on the event in Π that contains ω. With non-partitional models,
$\beta(\xi(\omega))$ is generated by updating the prior via Bayes's Rule to concentrate it on
$P(\omega)$.[13] That is,

$$\beta(\xi(\omega))(\omega') = \begin{cases} 0, & \text{if } \omega' \notin P(\omega); \\ q(\omega')/ \sum_{w \in P(\omega)} q(w), & \text{otherwise.} \end{cases}$$

12 See Turnbull (1992) for a related approach to modelling firms as networks of 'processing machines.'
13 One could take a more general approach, allowing any probability distribution with P as its
  support. See Morris (1992a) or Morris and Shin (1992).

To understand the difference between this approach and the partitional models, it is important to recognize that there is still one aspect of non-partitional models that is quite partitional – and unavoidably so. In both partitional and non-partitional models, we can partition Ω by treating as equivalent inputs that lead to the same beliefs. In the partitional models, the agent's beliefs are internally consistent in the sense that they are based on this same partition. Non-partitional models drop this consistency. In other words, in the partitional models, the agent understands how he is responding to inputs and his beliefs reflect this. In non-partitional models, he has only an imperfect understanding of his own information processing.

Some properties of the possibility correspondence that might be assumed are the following. The first assumption, often called *non-delusion*, is that $\omega \in P(\omega)$. In other words, in state ω, the agent does not mistakenly believe that the state could not possibly be ω. For obvious reasons, this assumption is almost always imposed.

A second property is what Geanakoplos calls *knowing that you know* and is also called *positive introspection*. It says that $\omega' \in P(\omega)$ implies $P(\omega') \subseteq P(\omega)$. To understand this property intuitively and to see why it gets its name, suppose it does not hold. Suppose ω is the true state and suppose that $\omega' \in P(\omega)$ but $P(\omega') \not\subseteq P(\omega)$. For simplicity, let $P = P(\omega)$ and let φ denote the statement that the true state is in P. Since ω is the true state, the set of states the agent considers possible is P. Hence the agent knows that φ is true in the sense that it is true in every situation he considers possible. However, in one of the states he thinks of as possible, namely ω', he would not know that the state is in P, since $P(\omega') \not\subseteq P$. Hence he considers a state possible in which he does not know that φ is true. In this sense, he is not sure that he knows that φ is true. That is, he knows that φ is true but does not know that he knows this fact.

The final property is called *knowing that you don't know, or negative introspection*. It says that if $\omega' \in P(\omega)$, then $P(\omega) \subseteq P(\omega')$. To understand this property intuitively, suppose it does not hold. Again, suppose ω is the true state and that $\omega' \in P(\omega)$. Let $P' = P(\omega')$ and let φ denote the statement that the state is in P'. Suppose $P(\omega) \not\subseteq P'$. Then the agent does not know whether φ is true, since some of the states he considers possible are not in P'. However, in one of the states he considers possible, namely ω', he would know that the true state is in P' and hence would know that φ is true. Hence he does not know that φ is true, but he considers it possible that he does know that φ is true. In this sense, he does not know that φ is true.

It is easy to see that if all three properties hold, then the $P(\omega)$ sets form a partition of Ω. Hence partitional information is a special case. As noted earlier, non-partitional models allow the possibility that the agent does not understand his own information processing, and the properties above should be interpreted in this light. Negative introspection is generally seen as a less realistic assumption than positive introspection. As Geanokoplos (1989) notes, it is the fact that people don't typically notice non-occurrence that enabled Sherlock Holmes to surprise Dr Watson by pointing out the importance of the dog that *didn't* bark in the night.

Because beliefs are not generated from a partition, the consistency of beliefs with the prior needed to guarantee that interim and ex ante rules are equivalent

58   Barton L. Lipman

breaks down. That is, the agent's view of his actions ex ante and after receiving his information may be quite different. To see this point clearly, consider the following example, drawn from Geanakoplos (1992). Let $\Omega = \{\omega_1, \omega_2, \omega_3\}$ and assume that the agent's prior, q, has $q(\omega_1) = q(\omega_3) = 2/7$ and $q(\omega_2) = 3/7$. Let $A = \{a_1, a_2\}$ and let u be given by the following table:

	ω_1	ω_2	ω_3
a_1	-1	1	-1
a_2	0	0	0

Let $P(\omega_1) = \{\omega_1, \omega_2\}$, $P(\omega_2) = \{\omega_2\}$, and $P(\omega_3) = \{\omega_2, \omega_3\}$. (This possibility correspondence satisfies non-delusion and positive introspection, but does not satisfy negative introspection.) Note that given either $P(\omega_1)$ or $P(\omega_3)$, the updated probability on state ω_2 is 3/5. Hence a_1 is optimal, given either possibility set. Obviously, a_1 is optimal when the possibility set is $P(\omega_2)$. Hence the optimal f would appear to be $f(\omega) = a_1$ for all ω. However, notice that the ex ante expected pay-off to this f is $-1/7$, while the ex ante expected pay-off to always choosing a_2 is 0.

There are two odd aspects to this example. First, the agent's optimal plan of action ex ante and his chosen behaviour in response to information differ. This kind of behaviour is referred to as *dynamic inconsistency*.[14] Second, it is particularly striking that this conflict is so severe that, ex ante, the agent would prefer not to get information at all! Geanakoplos (1989) gives necessary and sufficient conditions for this problem to not arise.[15] However, he does not resolve the dynamic inconsistency problem.

There have been a few applications of non-partitional information structures. Geanakoplos (1989, 1992), Samet (1990), and Rubinstein and Wolinsky (1990) consider under what conditions certain standard results with partitional information go through with non-partitional structures (particularly, Aumann's 1976 theorem on agreeing to disagree and Milgrom and Stokey's 1982 no-trade theorem). Also, Brandenburger, Dekel, and Geanakoplos (1992) analyse correlated equilibria with these information structures, generalizing the approach of Aumann (1987). Finally, Morris (1992a) provides a non-partitional generalization of Blackwell's (1951) theorem on comparing the value of information partitions.

Aside from Morris's (1992a) work comparing the value of information structures, there has been very little work on deriving optimal non-partitional information processing.[16] An example due to Robinson (1992) suggests that, in fact, agents who

---

14 The dynamic inconsistency problem often arises outside the context of standard expected utility. In fact, there are a variety of results that show that dynamic consistency essentially requires expected utility. See, for example, Epstein and Le Breton (1993) or Machina (1989).

15 See Morris and Shin (1992) for a generalization and interpretation of this result.

16 Shin (1993) does derive non-partitional information processing, but not using any optimality considerations. He shows that if one interprets knowledge as provability in propositional logic, then the implied possibility correspondence is non-partitional in general.

can choose between partitional and non-partitional information will often prefer the latter. To see the intuition, simply note that much of what an agent learns will be irrelevant. If it costs anything to remember what is irrelevant, the agent will prefer to forget. To be more concrete, Robinson's example has the following structure. Suppose there are two states, ω_1 and ω_2, and two actions, a_1 and a_2. Suppose that a_i is optimal in state ω_i, $i = 1, 2$. Suppose that the agent's prior has the property that in the absence of any information, he will choose action a_1. Clearly, then, the information partition $\{\{\omega_1\}, \{\omega_2\}\}$ is no more useful to the agent than the non-partitional possibility correspondence $P(\omega_1) = \Omega$ and $P(\omega_2) = \{\omega_2\}$. Assuming that it is even slightly more costly for the agent to process input ω_1 enough to recognize it perfectly, he will always prefer the non-partitional structure to the partitional one. Note also that there would seem to be no conflict at all between the agent's ex ante plans and his actual response to information in this example. In general, though, the dynamic consistency problem is likely to complicate greatly the analysis of optimal non-partitional information processing.

There is one conceptual problem that may pose a serious obstacle to endogenizing the amount of information processing in a non-partitional model. Recall that these models are based on the assumption that the agent only imperfectly understands his information processing. But if the agent chooses the properties of his information processing, how can he not understand how he processes? In at least some contexts, this problem does not seem to arise. Certainly, in Robinson's example, there seems to be no difficulty with interpreting $P(\omega_1) = \Omega$ as saying that the agent processes the information ω_1 correctly (i.e., recognizes that the state is ω_1), but then forgets this information. It hardly seems odd to suppose that the agent correctly anticipates the possibility that he will forget some fact..

V. AXIOMATIC APPROACHES TO INFORMATION PROCESSING

So far, I have not addressed the question of how any of the approaches above might be derived axiomatically. In the absence of an axiomatic treatment, we lack a systematic way to evaluate the assumptions being made in the different approaches. With an axiomatic derivation, we can, in principle, answer the question 'what does it mean to assume that an agent behaves this way?' In this section, I describe three recent papers that analyse information processing from an axiomatic perspective.

Remark 3

A different advantage of an axiomatic approach is that it seems to avoid the criticism discussed in remark 2 that bounded rationality is being modelled by assuming rationality. Roughly, the axiomatic approach begins with a description of the agent and then translates this into a model of information processing. Clearly, it then makes no sense to ask whether the agent can carry out this information processing accurately. If the processing is simply a representation of what the agent is doing, the question boils down to asking whether an agent is able to do whatever it is that he does!

60   Barton L. Lipman

The three papers discussed in this section have one fundamental similarity. Traditionally, axiomatic decision theory takes a single preference relation and derives some kind of utility representation for it. Along the way, a notion of conditional preferences – that is, preferences conditional on information – are derived, generally based on assumptions about information processing. All three papers reverse this process: they begin with a set of conditional preferences, one for each piece of information the agent might receive.[17] Then a representation is derived that includes a representation of information processing.

1. Non-partitional information
Morris (1992b) provides an axiomatic approach to non-partional information structures. The idea is to identify what states the agent considers possible by looking at his preferences over state-contingent choices. Loosely speaking, if he does not care what he gets in state ω, then it is as if he knew that the true state is not ω.

More formally, following Savage (1954), let X be a set of *consequences*. A consequence is intended to be a complete description of the pay-off–relevant results of a given choice. An *act* is a function from Ω to X. In other words, an act or action is defined in terms of the relationship between external states and consequences it induces. The set of actions A for this model is the set of all possible acts. If $a \in A$, then, $a(\omega)$ is the consequence that action a yields in state ω. For each $\omega \in \Omega$, the agent has a preference ordering $\succ_\omega$ over A. The interpretation of this is that $\succ_\omega$ is the way the agent ranks the acts, given whatever information the agent derives from processing the input ω.

Savage defines a $\succ_\omega$-*null state* as a state ω' such that for every pair of acts a_1 and a_2 with $a_1(\omega'') = a_2(\omega'')$ for all $\omega'' \neq \omega'$, we have $a_1 \sim_\omega a_2$. ($\sim_\omega$ is the indifference relation associated with $\succ_\omega$.) That is, ω' is $\succ_\omega$-null if the agent does not care what happens to him in that state – only the consequences for other states matter. Morris then defines a possibility correspondence by letting $P(\omega)$ denote the set of ω' such that ω' is not $\succ_\omega$-null.

With this framework, Morris relates conditions on preferences to the conditions on the possibility correspondence discussed in section IV. For example, Morris defines a property he calls *static coherence*. To understand this property, suppose that the agent is able to choose one act from a finite set $D \subseteq A$. For each input ω, we could ask which act in D is optimal, given the preferences $\succ_\omega$. Intuitively, this would tell us how the agent will choose in response to information. Let a_ω^D denote the agent's optimal choice in response to input ω. Define a new act $\tilde{a}^D$ by setting $\tilde{a}^D(\omega) = a_\omega^D(\omega)$. Intuitively, this is the act that the agent is effectively choosing by the way he responds to information. Oversimplifying slightly, the agent's preferences are said to satisfy static coherence if for every D and every ω, the agent weakly prefers $\tilde{a}^D$ to every act in D. Morris shows that static coherence (together with another condition) implies positive introspection and a weakening of non-delusion.

---

17 Myerson (1991, chap. 1) also follows this approach, but his purpose is quite different.

He also discusses some other ways to define the possibility correspondence from preferences and relationships among these approaches. Finally, he discusses changes in the agent's information by considering preferences indexed by time as well as by ω. He uses this approach to address the dynamic consistency issue. Morris does not provide axioms generating the particular decision theory proposed by Geanakoplos (1989) or the weaker version proposed by Morris (1992a).

2. Impossible possible worlds

In Lipman (1992b), I treat inputs differently. Instead of supposing that ξ tells which input the agent receives as a function of the state, I assume that it gives a set of possible inputs. That is, $\xi: \Omega \longrightarrow 2^\Theta$ where $\xi(\omega)$ is the set of inputs that are 'true' at ω. For any input θ, let $\Omega(\theta)$ denote the set of ω such that $\theta \in \xi(\omega)$. In other words, $\Omega(\theta) = \xi^{-1}(\theta)$. For simplicity, suppose that $\Omega(\theta) \neq \emptyset$ for all $\theta \in \Theta$. If $\Omega(\theta) = \Omega(\theta')$ – that is, if θ and θ' contain the same information about Ω – then I shall say that θ and θ' are *logically equivalent*. Like Morris, I assume that there is a set of consequences X and let A denote the set of acts. For each $\theta \in \Theta$, there is a preference ordering $\succ_\theta$ over A that gives the agent's preferences in response to input θ.

The representation I derive is what I call an *extended expected utility representation*. The 'expected utility' part refers to the fact that I derive a utility function over consequences and a probability distribution over states such that one act is preferred to another iff it yields higher expected utility. The 'extended' part refers to the fact that I do this not with the state set Ω but with an enlarged state set Ω^*. The way the state set is enlarged is itself a part of the representation. The 'states' in Ω^* that are not in Ω are referred to as *impossible possible worlds*. They are impossible in the sense that only the original states are really possible; however, they are possible in the sense that the agent does not recognize that they are impossible.

In particular, this kind of representation allows the possibility that θ and θ' are logically equivalent, and yet $\succ_\theta \neq \succ_{\theta'}$ – in words, the agent does not recognize logical equivalence. Normally, we treat two logically equivalent pieces of information as equivalent to the agent, even though this is clearly not consistent with reality. Generally, we learn something when we are shown that two mathematical statements are equivalent, so we ourselves do not immediately recognize logical equivalence!

Roughly, the way the impossible possible worlds are constructed is the following. Say that θ and θ' are *preference equivalent* if $\succ_\theta = \succ_{\theta'}$ and are *strongly equivalent* if they are both logically equivalent and preference equivalent. When θ and θ' are strongly equivalent, I require either both or neither to be true in each of the new states. That is, I maintain their logical equivalence in the new states. If they are logically equivalent but not preference equivalent, then I must add in new states in which one input is true and the other is false. The trick is to add these new states in such a way as to maintain the right relationships.

The impossible possible worlds can be thought of as a representation of the 'logic' in the agent's mind. To see the idea, let $\Omega^*(\theta)$ denote the set of $\omega \in \Omega^*$

62   Barton L. Lipman

such that θ is true. Then when $\Omega^*(\theta) \subseteq \Omega^*(\theta')$, the agent effectively infers that θ' is true when he learns that θ is true. That is, he deduces θ' from θ. Thus, for example, an agent who satisfies $\Omega^*(\theta) \subseteq \Omega^*(\theta')$ whenever $\Omega(\theta) \subseteq \Omega(\theta')$ carries out all appropriate logical deductions. In a similar manner, one can define a variety of notions regarding what kind of deductions the agent carries out. Since the impossible possible worlds are derived from the agent's preferences, this means that the agent's logic is derived from his preferences.

To understand the realtionship to Morris's work, consider the following simple example. Suppose there are three states, ω_1, ω_2, and ω_3. Consider the possibility correspondence $P(\omega_1) = P(\omega_2) = \{\omega_1, \omega_2\}$ and $P(\omega_3) = \{\omega_2, \omega_3\}$. This non-partitional information structure would be derived by Morris if ω_3 is the only $\succ_{\omega_1}$-null state and the only $\succ_{\omega_2}$-null state, while ω_1 is the only $\succ_{\omega_3}$-null state. In my model, this situation is represented differently. Let θ be an input that is true only in states ω_1 and ω_2 and let θ' be an input that is true only in state ω_3. To model the agent above, I would introduce a new state, say ω^*, which is identical to ω_2 except that θ^1 is true there. Then when the agent receives input θ, he infers that the true state is in $\{\omega_1, \omega_2\}$. When he receives the input θ', he infers that the true state is in $\{\omega^*, \omega_3\}$. More generally, the non-partitional structure is replaced by a partitional structure, where some of the worlds are impossible possible worlds that 'mimic' certain of the normal states.

3. Case-based reasoning

Gilboa and Schmeidler (1992b) provide a completely different approach to axiomatically deriving a form of information processing. They derive what they refer to as *case-based reasoning*, named after an approach used in artificial intelligence. Loosely speaking, the idea in artificial intelligence, as put forth by Riesbeck and Schank (1989), is that people reason by analogy to past experience. They remember 'similar' situations in the past and assume that what worked in a similar situation is likely to work again.

More formally, a *case* is a tuple (p, a, r) where p is a *problem* (an element of some set P), a is an action (an element of A), and r is a *result* (a real number). Let C denote the set of possible cases. A *memory* is a finite set of cases, each of which involves a different problem. In the terminology used here, one can think of the memory together with the current problem as serving the role of the input and the external state, where the external state is observed directly ($\xi(\omega) = \omega$). For this reason, I shall use ω to denote a particular specification of the memory and the current problem.

As in Morris (1992b) and Lipman (1992b), the key is to analyse how preferences vary with the input. Oversimplifying a bit, for each input ω, there is a preference relation $\succ_\omega$ over A. They give some axioms on the preferences such that they can be represented in the following manner. There is a function $\psi: P \times P \rightarrow [0, 1]$, where $\psi(p, p')$ is interpreted as describing the similarity between problems p and p'. Given an input ω that specifies current problem p, the agent prefers action a_1 to action a_2 iff

$$\sum_{p'} \psi(p, p')a_1(p') > \sum_{p'} \psi(p, p')a_2(p'),$$

where the sum is taken over problems p' in the memory. The function $a_i(p')$ is the result of choosing action a_i in problem p' according to the memory if in fact this is the action that was chosen. Otherwise, $a_i(p') = 0$. Intuitively, then, the agent evaluates each action by looking through his memory to times when the action in question was used and computing a weighted sum of the results obtained where the weights are the similarity of the current problem to these past problems.

To get a sense of how this representation works, consider the following simple example. Suppose that $P = \{1, 2, \ldots\}$ and $A = \{a_1, a_2, \ldots, a_n\}$. Suppose that $\psi(p, p') = 1$ for all p and p' – that is, all problems are equally similar to one another. When the agent faces the first problem, his memory is the empty set, since he has not faced any problems in the past. Gilboa and Schmeidler treat the sum over an empty set as equal to 0. Hence we have

$$\sum_{p'} \psi(1, p')a_i(p') = 0$$

for all i, so the agent is indifferent between all actions. For simplicity, suppose that, when indifferent, he adopts the tie-breaking rule of choosing the lowest-numbered action. So he would choose a_1. If the pay-off to a_1 is strictly positive, then when the agent faces problem 2, he will choose a_1, since

$$\sum_{p'} \psi(2, p')a_i(p') = \psi(1, 2)a_1(1) = a_1(1) > 0,$$

while the 'expected pay-off' to any other action is zero. He will continue choosing a_1 until the pay-off accumulated so far falls belows zero. Note that it is the *cumulative* pay-off, not the *average* pay-off that is relevant with this representation.

Once the accumulated pay-off to a_1 falls below zero, the agent switches to action a_2, continuing with it as long as its accumulated pay-off exceeds zero, and so on. Once he has chosen every action at least once, then in each period he will choose whatever action has the highest cumulative pay-off to date.

Though I include this paper in the section on axiomatic approaches, Gilboa and Schmeidler seem to downplay the axioms. They appear to view the axioms they use as more of a technical device and to be more interested in exploring this particular representation. Certainly, this form of information processing is quite different from others in the literature. Also, as Gilboa and Schmeidler note and as the example suggests, it has the distinct advantage of having a natural dynamic component. That is, the behaviour of the agent over time is inherently a crucial part of the model. For this reason, it may have especially interesting applications in dynamic models.

Recently, Matsui (1994) has shown that case-based reasoning can be represented by expected utility and vice versa. That is, given a case-based reasoner, we can find a state set, probability distribution, etc., such that the behaviour generated by

64   Barton L. Lipman

expected utility maximization in this model would be equivalent to the behaviour of our case-based reasoner. Furthermore, an expected utility maximizer could be represented as a case-based reasoner.

VI. CONCLUDING REMARKS

It seems almost pointless to conclude by suggesting areas for future research – there is so much left to be done that almost everything is a possibility for future research! Nevertheless, I will comment briefly on some directions that seem especially promising.

First, I shall not even attempt to claim to be unbiased when I say that axiomatic approaches seem to be a very important direction to pursue. As argued above, it is only with an axiomatic approach that we can understand our assumptions on the way the agent processes information.

On the other hand, the axiomatic approach is unlikely to find new ideas on how to model information processing. It certainly seems much more plausible that this approach is useful only after interesting models are found and then as a way of gaining understanding about the models. I believe that the development and exploration of other approaches to modelling the costs or constraints on information processing are still very important. The most promising direction for developing other models would seem to be following the lead of the threshold models and network models in considering more details of how information is processed. Certainly, it is unlikely that a general specification of a set of feasible partitions and a cost function on partitions will lead to concrete results. While these two specific formulations may not prove to be the most useful in the end, the general idea of filling in details this way seems very promising. Perhaps some blending of non-partitional approaches with this kind of more detailed look at information processing will be fruitful.

Finally, I believe it is very important to try applying these models to real economic problems. So far, there has been only a small amount of work in this direction. I believe that we shall really understand these models only when we see what they say in the context of real economic problems, rather than in simple and artificial examples.

REFERENCES

Abreu, D., and A. Rubinstein (1988) 'The structure of Nash equilibrium in repeated games with finite automata.' *Econometrica* 56, 1259–82
Anderlini, L. 'Communication, computability, and common interest games.' Working Paper, St John's College, Cambridge
Anderlini, L., and L. Felli (1992) 'Incomplete written contracts.' Working paper, London School of Economics
Aumann, R. (1976) 'Agreeing to disagree.' *Annals of Statistics* 4, 1236–9
— (1981) 'Survey of repeated games.' In *Essays in Game Theory and Mathematical Economics in Honor of Oskar Morganstern* (Zurich: Bibliographisches Institut)

— (1987) 'Correlated equilibrium as an expression of Bayesian rationality.' *Econometrica*, 55, 1–18

Aumann, R., and A. Brandenburger (1991) 'Epistemic conditions for Nash equilibrium.' Working paper, Harvard Business School

Bacharach, M. (1985) 'Some extensions to a claim of Aumann in an axiomatic model of knowledge.' *Journal of Economic Theory* 37, 167–90

Banks, J., and R. Sundaram (1990) 'Repeated games, finite automata, and complexity.' *Games and Economic Behaviour* 2, 97–117

Baumol, W., and R. Quandt (1964) 'Rules of thumb and optimally imperfect decisions.' *American Economic Review* 54, 23–46

Bernheim, B. (1984) 'Rationalizable strategic behaviour.' *Econometrica* 52, 1007–28

Binmore, K. (1987; 1988) 'Modeling rational players: parts I and II.' *Economics and Philosophy* 3; 4

— (1991) 'DeBayesing Game Theory.' Working paper, University of Michigan

Blackwell, D. (1951) 'The comparison of experiments.' In *Proceedings, Second Berkeley Symposium on Mathematical Statistics and Probability* (University of California Press)

Brandenburger, A., E. Dekel, and J. Geanakoplos (1982) 'Correlated equilibrium with generalized information structures.' *Games and Economic Behavior* 4, 182–201

Chellás, B. (1980) *Modal Logic: An Introduction* (Cambridge: Cambridge University Press)

Cho, L.-K., and A. Matsui (1992a) 'Induction and bounded rationality in repeated games.' Working paper, University of Pennsylvania

— (1992b) 'Learning and the Ramsey policy.' Working paper, University of Pennsylvania

Conlisk, J. (1988) 'Optimization cost.' *Journal of Economic Behavior and Organization* 9, 213–28

Cutland, N. (1980) *Computability: An Introduction to Recursive Function Theory* (Cambridge: Cambridge University Press)

Dow, J. (1991) 'Search decisions with limited memory.' *Review of Economic Studies* 58 (January), 1–14

Epstein, L., and M. Le Breton (1993) 'Dynamically consistent beliefs must be Bayesian.' *Journal of Economic Theory* 61 (October), 1–22

Geanakoplos, J. (1989) 'Game theory without partitions, and applications to speculation and consensus.' Working paper, Yale University

— (1992) 'Common knowledge.' In *Theoretical Aspects of Reasoning about Knowledge: Proceedings of the Fourth Conference*, ed. Y. Moses (San Mateo: Morgan Kaufmann)

Gilboa, I., and D. Schmeidler (1992a) 'Additive representations of non-additive measures and the choquet integral.' Working paper, Northwestern University

— (1992b) 'Case-based decision theory.' Working paper, Northwestern University

Holland, J. (1975) *Adaptation in Natural and Artificial Systems* (Ann Arbor: University of Michigan Press)

Holland, J., and J. Miller (1991) 'Artificial adaptive agents in economic theory.' *American Economic Review Papers and Proceedings* 81, 365–70

Hopcroft, J., and J. Ullman (1979) *Introduction to Automata Theory, Languages, and Computation* Reading, MA: Addison-Wesley)

Hughes, G.E., and M.J. Cresswell (1968) *An Introduction to Modal Logic* (London: Methuen)

Kalai, E. (1991) 'Artificial decisions and strategic complexity in repeated games.' In *Essays in Game Theory* (New York: Academic Press)

Kalai, E., and W. Stanford (1988) 'Finite rationality and interpersonal complexity in repeated games.' *Econometrica* 56, 397–410

Lipman, B. (1991) 'How to decide how to decide how to ...: modeling limited rationality.' *Econometrica* 59, 1105–25

66   Barton L. Lipman

— (1992a) 'Limited rationality and endogenously incomplete contracts.' Working paper, Queen's University
— (1992b) 'Decision theory with impossible possible worlds.' Working paper, preliminary draft, Queen's University
Lipman, B., and S. Srivastava (1990) 'Informational requirements and strategic complexity in repeated games.' *Games and Economic Behavior* 2, 273–90
Machina, M. (1989) 'Dynamic consistency and non-expected utility models of choice under uncertainty.' *Journal of Economic Literature* 27, 1622–68
Marimon, R., E. McGrattan, and T. Sargent (1990) 'Money as a medium of exchange in an economy with artificially intelligent agents.' *Journal of Economic Dynamics and Control* 14, 329–73
Matsui, A. (1994) 'Expected utility and case-based reasoning.' Working paper, University of Pennsylvania
Milgrom, P., and N. Stokey (1982) 'Information, trade, and common knowledge.' *Journal of Economic Theory* 26, 17–27
Minsky, M., and S. Papert (1988) *Perceptrons* (Cambridge, MA: MIT Press)
Morris, S. (1992) 'Revising knowledge: a decision theoretic approach.' Working paper, University of Pennsylvania
Morris, S., and H. Shin (1992) 'Noisy Bayes updating and the value of information.' Working paper, University of Pennsylvania
Mount, K., and S. Reiter (1990) 'A model of computing with human agents.' Working paper, Northwestern University
Myerson, R. (1991) *Game Theory: Analysis of Conflict* (Cambridge, MA: Harvard University Press)
Neme, A., and L. Quintas (1992) 'Equilibrium of repeated games with cost of implementation.' *Journal of Economic Theory* 58 (October), 105–9
Neyman, A. (1985) 'Bounded rationality justifies cooperation in the finitely repeated prisoners' dilemma game.' *Economic Letters* 19, 227–9
Pearce, D. (1984) 'Rationalizable strategic behavior and the problem of perfection.' *Econometrica* 52, 1029–50
Piccione, M. (1992) 'Finite automata equilibria with discounting.' *Journal of Economic Theory* 56 (February), 180–93
Piccione, M., and A. Rubinstein (1993) 'Finite automata play a repeated extensive game.' *Journal of Economic Theory* 61 (October), 160–8
Radner, R. (1989) 'The Organization of Decentralized Information Processing.' Working paper, AT&T Bell Laboratories
— (1992) 'Hierarchy: the economics of managing.' *Journal of Economic Literature* 30, 1382–1415
Radner, R., and T. Van Zandt (1992) 'Information processing and returns to scale.' *Annales d'Economie et de Statistique* 25/26, 265–98
Riesbeck, C., and R. Schank (1989) *Inside Case-Based Reasoning* (Hillsdale: Lawrence Erlbaum Associates)
Robinson, L. (1992) 'The rationality of non-rational information.' Working paper, Columbia University
Rosenthal, R. (1991a) 'Rules of thumb in games.' Working paper, Boston University
— (1991b) 'Bargaining rules of thumb.' Working paper, Boston University
Rubinstein, A. (1986) 'Finite automata play the repeated prisoners' dilemma.' *Journal of Economic Theory* 39, 83–96
— (1988) 'Similarity and decision-making under risk (is there a utility theory resolution to the Allais Paradox?).' *Journal of Economic Theory* 46 (October), 145–53
— (1992) 'On price recognition and computational complexity in a monopolistic model.' Working paper, University of Tel Aviv

Rubinstein, A., and A. Wolinsky (1990) 'On the logic of "agreeing to disagree" type results.' *Journal of Economic Theory* 51 (June), 184–93

Samet, D. (1990) 'Ignoring ignorance and agreeing to disagree.' *Journal of Economic Theory* 52 (October), 190–207

Sargent, T. (1993) *Bounded Rationality in Macroeconomics* (Oxford: Claredon Press)

Savage, L.J. (1954) *The Foundations of Statistics* (New York: Wiley)

Segal, U. (1990) 'Two-stage lotteries without the reduction axiom.' *Econometrica* 58, 349–77

Selten, R. (1978) 'The chain-store paradox.' *Theory and Decision* 9,

Shafer, G. (1976) *A Mathematical Theory of Evidence* (Princeton: Princeton University Press)

Shin, H. (1993) 'Logical structure of common knowledge.' *Journal of Economic Theory* 60 (June), 1–13

Sileo, P. (1992) 'Intransitivity of indifference, strong monotonicity, and the endowment effect.' Working paper, Carnegie Mellon University

Simon, H. (1955) 'A behavioral model of rational choice.' *Quarterly Journal of Economics* 69, 99–118

— (1976) 'From substantive to procedural rationality.' In *Method and Appraisal in Economics*, ed. S.J. Latsis (Cambridge: Cambridge University Press)

— (1987) 'Bounded rationality.' In *The New Palgrave*, ed. J. Eatwell, M. Milgate, and P. Newman (New York: W.W. Norton)

Spear, S. (1989) 'Learning rational expectations under computability constraints.' *Econometrica* 57, 889–910

Suppes, P., D. Krantz, R.D. Luce, and A. Tversky (1989) *Foundations of Measurement*, Vol. II (San Diego: Academic Press)

Turnbull, S. (1992) 'The firm as a team of automata.' Working paper, Ohio State University

Van Zandt, T. (1990) 'Efficient parallel addition.' Working paper, AT&T Bell Laboratories

Walley, P. (1991) *Statistical Reasoning with Imprecise Probabilities* (London: Chapman and Hall)

[11]

GAMES AND ECONOMIC BEHAVIOR **21**, 2–14 (1997)
ARTICLE NO. GA970585

Rationality and Bounded Rationality*

Robert J. Aumann

The Hebrew University of Jerusalem

Received May 7, 1997

INTRODUCTION

Economists have long expressed dissatisfaction with the complex models of strict rationality that are so pervasive in economic theory. There are several objections to such models. First, casual empiricism or even just simple introspection leads to the conclusion that even in quite simple decision problems, most economic agents are not in fact maximizers, in the sense that they do not scan the choice set and consciously pick a maximal element from it. Second, such maximizations are often quite difficult, and even if they wanted to, most people (including economists and even computer scientists) would be unable to carry them out in practice. Third, polls and laboratory experiments indicate that people often fail to conform to some of the basic assumptions of rational decision theory. Fourth, laboratory experiments indicate that the conclusions of rational analysis (as distinguished from the assumptions) sometimes fail to conform to "reality." And finally, the conclusions of rational analysis sometimes seem unreasonable even on the basis of simple introspection.

* This is an updated version of the Nancy L. Schwartz Memorial Lecture presented by the author at the J. L. Kellogg Graduate School of Management of Northwestern University in May 1986.

Research for this lecture was supported by the National Science Foundation under Grant IRI-8814953. Subsequent to the Schwartz lecture, versions of this lecture were presented at a workshop on bounded rationality at the Institute for Mathematical Studies in the Social Sciences (Economics), Stanford University, July 1989; at the Fourth Conference on Theoretical Aspects of Reasoning about Knowledge, Monterey, March 1992; and at the NATO Advanced Study Institute on Game Theoretic Approaches to Cooperation, Stony Brook, July 1994.

2

From my point of view, the last two of the above objections are more compelling than the first three. In science, it is more important that the conclusions be right than that the assumptions sound reasonable. The assumption of a gravitational force seems totally unreasonable on the face of it, yet leads to correct conclusions. "By their fruits ye shall know them" (Matthew 7, 16).

In the following, though, we shall not hew strictly to this line; we shall examine various models that, between them, address all the above issues.

To my knowledge, this area was first extensively investigated by Herbert Simon (1955, 1972). Much of Simon's work was conceptual rather than formal. For many years after this initial work, it was recognized that the area was of great importance, but the lack of a formal approach impeded its progress. Particular components of Simon's ideas, such as satisficing, were formalized by several workers, but never led to an extensive theory, and indeed did not appear to have significant implications that went beyond the formulations themselves.

There is no unified theory of bounded rationality, and probably never will be. Here we examine several different but related approaches to the problem. We will not survey the area, but discuss some of the underlying ideas. For clarity, we may sometimes stake out a position in a fashion that is more one-sided and extreme than we really feel; we have the highest respect and admiration for all the scientists whose work we cite, and beg them not to take offense.

From the point of view of the volume of research, the field has "took off" in the eighties. An important factor in making this possible was the development of computer science, complexity theory, and so on, areas of inquiry that created an intellectual climate conducive to the development of the theory of bounded rationality. A significant catalyst was the experimental work of Robert Axelrod (1984) in the late seventies and early eighties, in which experts were asked to prepare computer programs for playing the repeated prisoner's dilemma. The idea of a computer program for playing repeated games presaged some of the central ideas of the later work; and the winner of Axelrod's tournament—*tit for tat*—was, because of its simplicity, nicely illustrative of the bounded rationality idea. Also, repeated games became the context of much of the subsequent work.

The remainder of this lecture is divided into five parts. First we discuss the evolutionary approach to optimization—and specifically to game theory—and some of its implications for the idea of bounded rationality, such as the development of truly dynamic theories of games, and the idea of "rule rationality" (as opposed to "act rationality"). Next comes the area of "trembles," including equilibrium refinements, "crazy" perturbations, fail-

4 ROBERT AUMANN

ure of common knowledge of rationality, the limiting average payoff in infinitely repeated games as an expression of bounded rationality, ε-equilibria, and related topics. Part 3 deals with players who are modeled as computers (finite state automata, Turing machines), which has now become perhaps the most active area in the field. In Part 4 we discuss the work on the foundations of decision theory that deals with various paradoxes (such as Allais, 1953, and Ellsberg, 1961), and with results of laboratory experiments, by relaxing various of the postulates and so coming up with a weaker theory. Part 5 is devoted to an open problem.

Most of this lecture is set in the framework of noncooperative game theory, because most of the work has been in that framework. Game theory is indeed particularly appropriate for discussing fundamental ideas in this area, because it is relatively free from special institutional features. The basic ideas are probably applicable to economic contexts that are not game-theoretic (if there are any).

1. EVOLUTION

a. Nash Equilibria as Population Equilibria

One of the simplest, yet most fundamental ideas in bounded rationality —indeed, in game theory as a whole—is that no rationality at all is required to arrive at a Nash equilibrium; insects and even flowers can and do arrive at Nash equilibria, perhaps more reliably than human beings. The Nash equilibria of a strategic (normal) form game correspond precisely to population equilibria of populations that interact in accordance with the rules—and payoffs—of the game.

A version of this idea—the evolutionarily stable. strategy—was first developed by John Maynard Smith (1982) in the early seventies, and applied by him to many biological contexts (most of them animal conflicts within a species). But the idea applies also to Nash equilibria—not only to interaction within a species, but also to interactions between different species. It is worthwhile to give a more precise statement of this correspondence.

Consider, then, two populations—let us first think of them as different species—whose members interact in some way. It might be predator and prey, or cleaner and host fish, or bees and flowers, or whatever. Each interaction between an individual of population A and one of population B results in an increment (or decrement) in the fitness of each; recall that the fitness of an individual is defined as the expected number of its offspring (I use "its" on purpose, since, strictly speaking, reproduction must be asexual for this to work). This increment is the payoff to each of the individuals for the encounter in question. The payoff is determined by the genetic endowment of each of the interacting individuals (more or less aggressive or watchful or keen-sighted or cooperative, etc.). Thus one may write a bimatrix in which the rows and columns represent the various possible genetic endowments of the two respective species (or rather those different genetic endowments that are relevant to the kind of interaction being examined), and the entries represent the single encounter payoffs that we just described. If one views this bimatrix as a game, then the Nash equilibria of this game correspond precisely to population equilibria; that is, under asexual reproduction, the proportions of the various genetic endowments within each population remain constant from generation to generation if and only if these proportions constitute a Nash equilibrium.

This is subject to the following qualification: in each generation, there must be at least a very small proportion of each kind of genetic endowment; that is, each row and column must be represented by at least some individuals. This minimal presence, whose biological interpretation is that it represents possible mutations, is to be thought of as infinitesimal; specifically, an encounter between two such mutants (in the two populations) is considered impossible.

A similar story can be told for games with more than two players, and for evolutionary processes other than biological ones; e.g., economic evolution, like the development of the QWERTY typewriter keyboard, studied by the economic historian Paul David (1986). It also applies to learning processes that are perhaps not strictly analogous to asexual reproduction. And though it does not apply to sexual reproduction, still one may hope that, roughly speaking, similar ideas may apply.

One may ask, who are the "players" in this "game?" The answer is that the two "players" are the two populations (i.e., the two species). The individuals are definitely *not* the "players"; if anything, each individual corresponds to the pure strategy representing its genetic endowment (note that there is no sense in which an individual can "choose" its own genetic endowment). More accurately, though, the pure strategies represent kinds of genetic endowment, and not individuals. Individuals indeed play no explicit role in the mathematical model; they are swallowed up in the proportions of the various pure strategies.

Some biologists object to this interpretation, because they see it as implying group or species selection rather than individual selection. The player is not the species, they argue; the individual "acts for its own good," not the good of the group, or of the population, or of the species. Some

6   ROBERT AUMANN

even argue that it is the gene (or rather the allele) that "acts for its own good," not the individual. The point, though, is that *nothing* in this model really "acts for its own good"; nobody "chooses" anything. It is the process as a whole that selects the traits. The most we can do is ask what it is that corresponds to the player in the mathematical model, and this is undoubtedly the population.

A question that at first seems puzzling is what happens in the case of interactions within a species, like animal conflicts for females, etc. Who are the players in this game? If the players are the populations, then this must be a one-person game, since there is only one population. But that doesn't look right, either, and it certainly doesn't correspond to the biological models of animal conflicts.

The answer is that it is a two-person symmetric game, in which both players correspond to the same population. In this case we look not for just any Nash equilibria, but for symmetric ones only.

b. Evolutionary Dynamics

The question of developing a "truly" dynamic theory of games has long intrigued game theorists and economic theorists. (If I am not mistaken, it is one of the conceptual problems listed by Kuhn and Tucker (1953) in the introduction to Volume II of "Contributions to the Theory of Games"—perhaps the last one in that remarkably prophetic list to be successfully solved.) The difficulty is that ordinary rational players have foresight, so they can contemplate all of time from the beginning of play. Thus the situation can be seen as a one-shot game, each play of which is actually a long sequence of "stage games," and then one has lost the dynamic character of the situation.

The evolutionary approach outlined above "solves" this conceptual difficulty by eliminating the foresight. Since the process is mechanical, there is indeed no foresight; no strategies for playing the repeated game are available to the "players."

And indeed, a fascinating dynamic theory does emerge. Contributions to this theory have been made by Young (1993), Foster and Young (1990), and Kandori *et al.* (1993). A book on the subject has been written by Hofbauer and Sigmund (1988) and there is an excellent chapter on evolutionary dynamics in the book by van Damme (1987) on refinements of the Nash equilibrium. Many others have also contributed to the subject.

It turns out that Nash equilibria are often unstable, and one gets various kinds of cycling effects. Sometimes the cycles are "around" the equilibrium, like in "matching pennies," but at other times one gets more complicated behavior. For example, the game

	0		5		4
0		4		5	
	4		0		5
5		0		4	
	5		4		0
4		5		0	

has $((1/3, 1/3, 1/3), (1/3, 1/3, 1/3))$ as its only Nash equilibrium; the evolutionary dynamic does not cycle "around" this point, but rather confines itself (more or less) to the strategy pairs in which the payoff is 4 or 5. This suggests a possible connection with correlated equilibria; this possibility has recently been investigated by Foster and Vohra (1997).

Thus evolutionary dynamics emerges as a form of rationality that is bounded, in that foresight is eliminated.

c. "Rule Rationality" vs "Act Rationality"

In a famous experiment conducted by Güth *et al.* (1982) and later repeated, with important variations, by Binmore *et al.* (1985), two players were asked to divide a considerable sum of money (ranging as high as DM 100). The procedure was that P1 made an offer, which could be either accepted or rejected by P2; if it was rejected, nobody got anything. The players did not know each other and never saw each other; communication was a one-time affair via computer.

"Rational" play would predict a 99–1 split, or 95–5 at the outside. Yet in by far the most trials, the offered split was between 50–50 and 65–35. This is surprising enough in itself. But even more surprising is that in most (all?) cases in which P2 was offered less than 30 percent, he actually *refused*. Thus, he *preferred* to walk away from as much as DM 25 or 30. How can this be reconciled with ordinary notions of utility maximization, not to speak of game theory?

It is tempting to answer that a player who is offered 5% or 10% is "insulted." Therefore, his utilities change; he gets positive probability from "punishing" the other player.

That's all right as far as it goes, but it doesn't go very far; it doesn't explain very much. The "insult" is treated as exogenous. But obviously the "insult" arose from the situation. Shouldn't we treat the "insult" itself endogenously, somehow explain *it* game-theoretically?

I think that a better way of explaining the phenomenon is as follows: Ordinary people do not behave in a consciously rational way in their

8 ·   ROBERT AUMANN

day-to-day activities. Rather, they evolve "rules of thumb" that work in general, by an evolutionary process like that discussed above (Section 1*a*), or a learning process with similar properties. Such "rules of thumb" are like genes (or rather, alleles). If they work well, they are fruitful and multiply; if they work poorly, they become rare and eventually extinct.

One such rule of thumb is "Don't be a sucker; don't let people walk all over you." In general, the rule works well, so it becomes widely adopted. As it happens, the rule doesn't apply to Güth's game, because in that particular situation, a player who refuses DM 30 does not build up his reputation by the refusal (because of the built-in anonymity). But the rule has not been consciously chosen, and will not be consciously abandoned.

So we see that the evolutionary paradigm yields a third form of bounded rationality: rather than consciously maximizing in each decision situation, players use rules of thumb that work well "on the whole."

2. PERTURBATIONS OF RATIONALITY

a. Equilibrium Refinements

Equilibrium refinements—Selten (1975), Myerson (1978), Kreps and Wilson (1982), Kalai and Samet (1984), Kohlberg and Mertens (1986), Basu and Weibull (1991), van Damme (1984), Reny (1992), Cho and Kreps (1989), and many others—don't really sound like bounded rationality. They sound more like super-rationality, since they go beyond the basic utility maximization that is inherent in Nash equilibrium. In addition to the Nash equilibrium, which demands rationality on the equilibrium path, they demand rationality also off the equilibrium path. Yet all are based in one way or another on "trembles"—small departures from rationality.

The paradox is resolved by noting that in game situations, one player's irrationality requires another's super-rationality. *You* must be super-rational in order to deal with *my* irrationalities. Since this applies to all players, taking account of possible irrationalities leads to a kind of super-rationality for all. To be super-rational, one must leave the equilibrium path. Thus, a more refined concept of rationality cannot feed on itself only; it can only be defined in the context of irrationality.

b. Crazy Perturbations

An idea related to the trembling hand is the theory of irrational or "crazy" types, as propounded first by the "gang of four" (Kreps, Milgrom, Roberts, and Wilson, 1982), and then taken up by Fudenberg and Maskin (1986), Aumann and Sorin (1989), Fudenberg and Levine (1989), and no doubt others. In this work there is some kind of repeated or other dynamic game setup; it is assumed that with high probability the players are "rational" in the sense of being utility maximizers, but that with a small probability, one or both play some one strategy, or one of a specified set of strategies, that are "crazy"—that is, have no a priori relationship to rationality. An interesting aspect of this work, which differentiates it from the "refinement" literature and makes it particularly relevant to the theory of bounded rationality, is that it is usually the crazy type, or a crazy type, that wins out—takes over the game, so to speak. Thus, in the original work of the gang of four on the prisoner's dilemma, there is only one crazy type, who always plays tit-for-tat no matter what the other player does, and it turns out that the rational type must imitate the crazy type—he must also play tit-for-tat, or something quite close to it. Also, the "crazy" types, while irrational in the sense that they do not maximize utility, are usually by no means random or arbitrary (as they are in refinement theory). For example, we have already noted that tit-for-tat is computationally a very simple object, far from random. In the work of Aumann and Sorin, the crazy types are identified with bounded recall strategies; and in the work of Fudenberg and Levine, the crazy types form a denumerable set, suggesting that they might be generated in some systematic manner, e.g., by Turing machines. There must be method to the madness; this is associated with computational simplicity, which is another one of the underlying ideas of bounded rationality.

c. Epsilon-Equilibria

Rather than playing irrationally with a small probability (as in Sections 2a and 2b), one may deviate slightly from rationality by playing so as almost, but not quite to, maximize utility; i.e., by playing to obtain a payoff that is within ε of the optimum payoff. This idea was introduced by Radner (1980) in the context of repeated games, in particular of the repeated prisoners' dilemma; he showed that in a long but finitely repeated prisoner's dilemma, there are ε-equilibria with small ε in which the players "cooperate" until close to the end (though, as is well-known, all exact equilibria lead to a constant stream of "defections").

d. Infinitely Repeated Games with Limit-of-the-Average Payoff

There is an interesting connection between ε-equilibria in finitely repeated games and infinitely repeated games with limit of the average payoff ("undiscounted"). The limit of the average payoff has been criticized as not representing any economic reality; many workers prefer to use either the finitely repeated game or limits of payoffs in discounted games

10 ROBERT AUMANN

with small discounts. Radner *et al.* (1986), Forges *et al.* (1986), and perhaps others, have demonstrated that the results of these two kinds of analysis can indeed be quite different.

Actually, though, the infinitely repeated undiscounted game is in some ways a simpler and more natural object than the discounted or finite game. In calculating equilibria of a finite or discounted game, one must usually specify the number n of repetitions or the discount rate δ; the equilibria themselves depend crucially on these parameters. But one may want to think of such a game simply as "long," without specifying *how* long. Equilibria in the undiscounted game may be thought of as "rules of thumb," which tell a player how to play in a "long repetition," independently of how long the repetition is. Whereas limits of finite or discounted equilibrium payoffs tell the players approximately how much *payoff* to expect in a long repetition, analysis of the undiscounted game tells him approximately how to *play*. See Aumann and Maschler (1995), pp. 131–134.

Thus, the undiscounted game is a framework for formulating the idea of a duration-independent strategy in a repeated game. Indeed, it may be shown that an equilibrium in the undiscounted game is an approximate equilibrium simultaneously in all the n-stage truncations, the approximation getting better and better as n grows. Formally, a strategy profile ("tuple") is an equilibrium in the undiscounted game if and only if, for some sequence of ε_n tending to zero, each of its n-stage truncations is an ε_n-equilibrium (in the sense of Radner described above) in the n-stage truncation of the game.

e. Failure of Common Knowledge of Rationality

In their paper on the repeated prisoners' dilemma, the Gang of Four pointed out that the effect they were demonstrating holds not only when one of the players believes that with some small probability, the other is a tit-for-tat automaton, but also if one of them only believes (with small probability) that the other believes this about him (with small probability). More generally, it can be shown that many of the perturbation effects we have been discussing do not require an actual departure from rationality on the part of the players, but only a lack of common knowledge of rationality (Aumann, 1992).

3. AUTOMATA, COMPUTERS, AND TURING MACHINES

We come now to what is probably the mainstream of the newer work in bounded rationality, namely, the theoretical work that has been done since the mid-eighties on automata and Turing machines playing repeated games. The work was pioneered by A. Neyman (1985) and A. Rubinstein

(1986), working independently and in very different directions. Subsequently, the theme was taken up by Ben-Porath (1993), Kalai and Stanford (1988), Zemel (1989), Abreu and Rubinstein (1988), Ben-Porath and Peleg (1987), Lehrer (1988), Papadimitriou (1992), Stearns (1989), and many others, each of whom made significant new contributions to the subject in various different directions. Different branches of this work have been started by Lewis (1985) and Binmore (1987, 1988), who have also had their following. We do not even touch on the more recent work in this area, which has been very active lately.

It is impossible to do justice to all this work in a reasonable amount of time, and we content ourselves with brief descriptions of some of the major strands. In one strand, pioneered by Neyman, the players of a repeated game are limited to using mixtures of pure strategies, each of which can be programmed on a finite automaton with an exogenously fixed number of states. This is reminiscent of the work of Axelrod, who required the entrants in his experiment to write the strategies in a Fortran program not exceeding a stated limit in length. In another strand, pioneered by Rubinstein, the size of the automaton is endogenous; computer capacity is considered costly, and any capacity that is not actually used in equilibrium play is discarded. The two approaches lead to very different results. The reason is that Rubinstein's approach precludes the use of "punishment" or "trigger" strategies, which swing into action only when a player departs from equilibrium, and whose sole function is precisely to prevent such departures. In the evolutionary interpretation of repeated games, Rubinstein's approach may be more appropriate when the stages of the repeated game represent successive generations, whereas Neyman's may be more appropriate when each generation plays the entire repeated game (which would lead to the evolution of traits having to do with reputation, like "Don't be a sucker").

The complexity of computing an optimal strategy in a repeated game, or even just a best response to a given strategy, has been the subject of works by several authors, including Gilboa (1988), Ben-Porath (1990), and Papadimitriou (1992). Related work has been done by Lewis (1992), though in the framework of recursive function theory (which is related to infinite Turing machines) rather than complexity theory (which has to do with finite computing devices). Roughly speaking, the results are qualitatively similar: finding maxima is hard. Needless to say, in the evolutionary approach to games, nobody has to find the maxima; they are picked out by evolution. Thus, the results of complexity theory again underscore the importance of the evolutionary approach.

Binmore (1987, 1988) and his followers have modeled games as pairs (or n-tuples) of Turing machines in which each machine carries in it some kind of idea of what the other "player" (machine) might look like.

12 ROBERT AUMANN

Other important strands include work by computer scientists who have made the connection between distributed computing and games ("computers as players," rather than "players as computers"). For a survey, see Linial (1994).

4. RELAXATION OF RATIONALITY POSTULATES

A not uncommon activity of decision, game, and economic theorists since the fifties has been to call attention to the strength of various postulates of rationality, and to investigate the consequences of relaxing them. Many workers in the field—including the writer of these lines—have at one time or another done this kind of thing. People have constructed theories of choice without transitivity, without completeness, violating the sure-thing principle, and so on. Even general equilibrium theorists have engaged in this activity, which may be considered a form of limited rationality (on the part of the agents in the model). This kind of work is most interesting when it leads to outcomes that are qualitatively different —not just weaker—from those obtained with the stronger assumptions, but I don't recall many such cases. It can also be very interesting and worthwhile when one gets roughly similar results with significantly weaker assumptions.

5. AN OPEN PROBLEM

We content ourselves with one open problem, which is perhaps the most challenging conceptual problem in the area today: to develop a meaningful formal definition of rationality in a situation in which calculation and analysis themselves are costly and/or limited. In the models we have discussed up to now, the problem has always been well defined, in the sense that an absolute maximum is chosen from among the set of feasible alternatives, no matter how complex a process that maximization may be. The alternatives themselves involve bounded rationality, but the process of choosing them does not.

Here, too, an evolutionary approach may eventually turn out to be the key to a general solution.

REFERENCES

Abreu, D., and Rubinstein, A. (1988). "The Structure of Nash Equilibrium in Repeated Games with Finite Automata," *Econometrica* **56**, 1259–1281.

Allais, M. (1953). "Le Comportement de l'Homme Rationnel devant le Risque: Critiques des Postulats et Axioms de l'Ecole Americaine," *Econometrica* **21**, 503–546.

Aumann, R. J. (1992). "Irrationality in Game Theory," in *Economic Analysis of Markets and Games, Essays in Honor of Frank Hahn* (P. Dasgupta, D. Gale, O. Hart, and E. Maskin, Eds.), pp. 214–227. Cambridge/London: MIT Press.

Aumann, R. J., and Maschler, M. (1995). *Repeated Games with Incomplete Information.* Cambridge/London: MIT Press.

Aumann, R. J., and Sorin, S. (1989). "Cooperation and Bounded Recall," *Games Econ. Behav.* **1,** 5–39.

Axelrod, R. (1984). *The Evolution of Cooperation.* New York: Basic Books.

Basu, K., and Weibull, J. W. (1991). "Strategy Subsets Closed under Rational Behavior," *Econ. Lett.* **36,** 141–146.

Ben-Porath, E. (1990). "The Complexity of Computing Best Response Automata in Repeated Games with Mixed Strategies," *Games Econ. Behav.* **2,** 2–12.

Ben-Porath, E. (1993). "Repeated Games with Finite Automata," *J. Econ. Theory* **59,** 17–32.

Ben-Porath, E. and Peleg, B. (1987). "On the Folk Theorem and Finite Automata," Center for Research in Mathematical Economics and Game Theory, Hebrew University, *Res. Mem.* **77.**

Binmore, K. G. (1987). "Modelling Rational Players, I," *Econ. and Philos.* **3,** 179–214.

Binmore, K. G. (1988). "Modelling Rational Players, II," *Econ. and Philos.* **4,** 9–55.

Binmore, K., Shaked, A. and Sutton, J. (1985). "Testing Noncooperative Bargaining Theory: A Preliminary Study," *Amer. Econ. Rev.* **75,** 1178–1180.

Cho, I.-K., and Kreps, D. (1987). "Signaling Games and Stable Equilibria," *Quart. J. Econ.* **102,** 179–221.

David, P. A. (1986). "Understanding the Economics of QWERTY: The Necessity of History," in *Economic History and the Modern Economist* (W. N. Parker, Ed.), Chap. 4. New York: Blackwell.

Ellsberg, D. (1961). "Risk, Ambiguity and the Savage Axioms," *Quart. J. Econ.* **75,** 643–669.

Forges, F., Mertens, J.-F. and Neyman, A. (1986). "A Counter Example to the Folk Theorem with Discounting," *Econ. Lett.* **20,** 7.

Foster, D., and Young, H. P. (1990). "Stochastic Evolutionary Game Dynamics," *Theoret. Popul. Biol.* **38,** 219–232.

Foster, D., and Vohra, R. (1997). "Calibrated Learning and Correlated Equilibrium," *Games Econ. Behav.* **21,** 40–55.

Fudenberg, D., and Levine, D. K. (1989). "Reputation and Equilibrium Selection in Games with a Patient Player," *Econometrica* **57,** 759–779.

Fudenberg, D. and Maskin, E. (1986). "The Folk Theorem in Repeated Games with Discounting and Incomplete Information," *Econometrica* **54,** 533–554.

Gilboa, I. (1988). "The Complexity of Computing Best Response Automatan in Repeated Games," *J. Econ. Theory* **45,** 342–352.

Güth, W., Schmittberger, R. and Schwarze, B. (1982). "An Experimental Analysis of Ultimatum Bargaining," *J. Econ. Behav. Organization* **3,** 367–388.

Hofbauer, J. and Sigmund, K. (1988). *Theory of Evolution and Dynamical Systems*, Cambridge: Cambridge University Press.

Kalai, E. and Samet, D. (1984). "Persistent Equilibria," *Int. J. Game Theory* **13,** 129–144.

Kalai, E., and Stanford, W. (1988). "Finite Rationality and Interpersonal Complexity in Repeated Games," *Econometrica* **56,** 397–410.

Kandori, M., Mailath, G. and Rob, R. (1993). "Learning, Mutation, and Long Run Equilibria in Games," *Econometrica* **61,** 29–56.

14   ROBERT AUMANN

Kohlberg, E., and Mertens, J.-F. (1986). "On the Strategic Stability of Equilibria," *Econometrica* **54**, 1003–37.

Kreps, D., and Wilson, R. (1982). "Sequential Equilibria," *Econometrica* **50**, 863–894.

Kreps, D., Milgrom, P., Roberts, J., and Wilson, R. (1982). "Rational Cooperation in the Finitely Repeated Prisoners' Dilemma," *J. Econ. Theory* **27**, 245–252.

Kuhn, H. W., and Tucker, A. W. (Eds.) (1953). *Contributions to the Theory of Games, Vol. II*, Annals of Mathematics Studies, Vol. 28. Princeton: Princeton University Press.

Lehrer, E. (1988). "Repeated Games with Stationary Bounded Recall Strategies," *J. Econ. Theory* **46**, 130–144.

Lewis, A. (1985). "On Effectively Computable Realizations of Choice Functions," *Math. Social Sci.* **10**, 43–80.

Lewis, A. (1992). "Some Aspects of Effectively Constructive Mathematics that are Relevant to the Foundations of Neoclassical Mathematical Economics and the Theory of Games," *Math. Social Sci.* **24**, 209–236.

Linial, N. (1994). "Game Theoretic Aspects of Computing," in *Handbook of Game Theory with Economic Applications*, Vol. 2, (R. J. Aumann and S. Hart, Eds.), Chap. 38. Amsterdam: North-Holland.

Maynard Smith, J. (1982). *Evolution and the Theory of Games*. Cambridge: Cambridge University Press.

Myerson, R. B. (1978). "Refinements of the Nash Equilibrium Concept," *Int. J. Game Theory* **7**, 73–80.

Neyman, A. (1985). "Bounded Complexity Justifies Cooperation in the Finitely Repeated Prisoners' Dilemma," *Econ. Lett.* **19**, 227–229.

Papadimitriou, C. H. (1992). "On Players with a Bounded Number of States," *Games Econ. Behav.* **4**, 122–131.

Radner, R. (1980). "Collusive Behavior in Noncooperative Epsilon-Equilibria of Oligopolies with Long but Finite Lives," *J. Econ. Theory*, **22**, 136–154.

Radner, R., Myerson, R., and Maskin, E. (1986). "An Example of a Repeated Partnership Game with Discounting and with Uniformly Inefficient Equilibria," *Rev. Econ. Studies* **53**, 59–69.

Reny, P. J. (1992). "Backwards Induction, Normal Form Perfection and Explicable Equilibria," *Econometrica* **60**, 627–649.

Rubinstein, A. (1986). "Finite Automata Play the Repeated Prisoners' Dilemma," *J. Econ. Theory* **39**, 83–96.

Selten, R. (1975). "Reexamination of the Perfectness Concept for Equilibrium Points in Extensive Games," *Int. J. Game Theory* **4**, 25–55.

Simon, H. (1955). "A Behavioral Model of Rational Choice," *Quart. J. Econ.* **64**, 99–118.

Simon, H. (1972). "Theories of Bounded Rationality," in *Decision and Organization* (C. McGuire and R. Radner, Eds.). Amsterdam: North Holland.

Stearns, R. E. (1989). "Memory-Bounded Game Playing Computing Devices," Tech. Rep. 547, IMSSS, Stanford University.

van Damme, E. (1984). "A Relation between Perfect Equilibria in Extensive Form Games and Proper Equilibria in Normal Form Games," *Int. J. Game Theory* **13**, 1–13.

van Damme, E. (1987). *Stability and Perfection of Nash Equilibria*. Berlin: Springer-Verlag.

Young, H. P. (1993). "The Evolution of Conventions," *Econometrica* **61**, 57–84.

Zemel, E. (1989). "Small Talk and Cooperation: A Note on Bounded Rationality," *J. Econ. Theory* **49**, 1–9.

Cambridge Journal of Economics 1997, 21, 323–338

Sargent versus Simon: bounded rationality unbound

Esther-Mirjam Sent*

Sargent called his latest venture *Bounded Rationality in Macroeconomics* and tried to make connections with Simon's programme of bounded rationality and artificial intelligence. The irony is that rational expectations theory, born from the same mother—Carnegie–Mellon University—as bounded rationality, after trying to kill her big sister, then apparently came around to embracing her in the person of Sargent. But was Simon's interpretation of bounded rationality the same as Sargent's? Did Simon and Sargent mean the same by artificial intelligence? Not quite. The different interests of Sargent and Simon resulted in vastly different interpretations of bounded rationality and artificial intelligence.

1. Introduction

Reading the title of this paper you may wonder what Mr Rationality—Sargent—and Mr Bounded Rationality—Simon—could possibly have in common. However, rational expectations theory was born at the same time and in the same nest as bounded rationality: namely, in the 1960s at the Graduate School of Industrial Administration (GSIA) at Carnegie–Mellon University.[1] Keynesians (Holt, an electrical engineer turned economist, and Modigliani), the prophet of bounded rationality (Simon), the father of rational expectations (Muth, who started his career at Carnegie as a graduate student), and the populisers of rational expectations (Lucas, Sargent, and Rapping) were all at Carnegie–Mellon University at some point during the 1960s. Simon (1991) noted that '[i]t is not without irony that bounded rationality and rational expectations, . . . though entirely antithetical to each other, were engendered in and flourished in the same small business school at almost the same time' (p. 250; also see Simon, 1979, p. 486).

Initially, the atmosphere among these adversaries was congenial. For example, Holt, Modigliani, Muth, and Simon (1960) collaborated on a 'Planning and Control of Industrial Operations' project that consisted of developing and applying mathematical techniques to business decision-making. Simon (1991) recalled that the 'four-man team . . . worked closely and amicably together for several years on a joint research

---

Manuscript received 12 June 1995; final version received 28 January 1996.

*University of Notre Dame. I am very grateful to Kenneth Arrow, Orazio Attanasio, Mary Ann Dimand, John Dupré, Timothy Lenoir, Philip Mirowski, Herbert Simon, Matt Weagle, and two anonymous referees for helpful comments on an earlier version.

[1] I should note that Carnegie–Mellon University came into being in 1967, after the merger of the Carnegie Institute of Technology and the Mellon Institute. Our narrative shifts from the Carnegie Institute of Technology to Carnegie–Mellon University.

project' (p. 250). They described dynamic programming methods and showed how these may be applied to managerial decisions in the operation of a factory-warehouse system. Simon (1991) noted that the team had to make strong assumptions to get the project off the ground and attributed these to satisficing: 'By making strong approximating assumptions about costs, we were able to solve an exact maximization problem with little computation. That is to say, we satisficed by finding the optimal policy for a gross approximation to the real world' (p. 167; also see Simon, 1982A, p. 113).

Modigliani left Carnegie in 1960 for MIT and recalled the cordial ambience. According to Modigliani, '[t]he main figure was Herbert Simon, who is no longer in the department of economics (he is now with the psychology department). He was pushing ideas of his own that were against some of the things in which economists believed. But the interaction was always friendly' (Klamer, 1983, p. 119). Muth left in 1964 and did not have much of a direct impact on his colleagues. Modigliani said: 'Muth was there, too, but he is hard to classify. Of all our students he is no doubt the one that has had the deepest impact on the newer generation, as the father of rational expectations' (Klamer, 1983, p. 120; see Muth, 1960, 1961). Rapping came to Carnegie in 1962 and said: 'Muth was at Carnegie–Mellon until '64. His idea was discussed throughout the '60s, but we did not see its possibilities then' (Klamer, 1983, p. 225).

The atmosphere slowly started to turn sour during the 1960s. Simon began to feel more and more alienated and was dismayed by the fact that the newly recruited faculty had little taste or talent for empirical research that did not start (and sometimes end) with formal model-building. 'Over time, a coalition of neoclassical economists and operations research specialists came to dominate the GSIA senior policy committee, making decisions that produced a growing imbalance in the composition of the faculty,' Simon (1991) wrote. 'Although I had never thought I lacked sympathy with mathematical approaches to the social sciences, I soon found myself frequently in a minority position when I took stands against what I regarded as excessive formalism and shallow mathematical pyrotechnics. The situation became worse as a strict neoclassical orthodoxy began to gain ascendancy among the economists' (p. 249; also see Simon, 1991, p. 250). And by 'the 1970s, the war was open and declared' (pp. 270–71). Lucas joined the gang in 1963 and said: '[Simon] used to give us a hard time. He likes to take on the devil's advocate role' (Klamer, 1983, p. 48). Rapping worked closely with Lucas while he was at Carnegie–Mellon, but mentioned: 'For 11 years Herb Simon was the dominant figure in my life. He is a genius' (Klamer, 1983, p. 222). In response to the comment that Simon's ideas were not reflected in the papers that he co-authored with Lucas, Rapping replied: 'Oh no, the Lucas–Rapping work is in the Chicago tradition. The Carnegie influence had not yet taken root in me' (Klamer, 1983, p. 223; see Lucas and Rapping, 1969A, 1969B).

These escalating conflicts eventually caused Simon to leave the GSIA for the psychology department at Carnegie. Simon (1991) wrote: 'Amid these controversies, I slowly retreated from GSIA . . . Eventually, around 1970, I moved my office to the Psychology Department' (p. 251). Simon (1991) pointed to Muth as the one guilty for driving him away: 'It began, oddly enough, with Jack Muth' (p. 251; also see Simon, 1991, p. 167). After having been a valuable member of the Holt–Modigliani–Muth–Simon team when he was a graduate student, 'Jack published in *Econometrica* in 1961 a novel suggestion for handling uncertainty in economics . . . To economists his idea is known today as "rational expectations"' (Simon, 1991, pp. 249–50; see Muth, 1961). Ironically, Muth got his inspiration for rational expectations from the four-man

Sargent versus Simon: bounded rationality unbound   325

research project mentioned before. According to Simon (1979), 'Muth imaginatively saw in this special case a paradigm for rational behaviour under uncertainty. What to some of us in the Holt–Modigliani–Muth–Simon research team was an approximating, satisficing simplification, served for him as a major line of defence for perfect rationality' (p. 486). Simon (1991) argued that '[t]he theory of rational expectations offered a direct challenge to theories of bounded rationality' (p. 250). Moreover, 'Jack Muth, in his announcement of rational expectations in 1961, explicitly labelled his theory a reply to my doctrine of bounded rationality' (pp. 270–71). Simon (1991) wrote: 'Jack's proposal was at first not much noticed by the economics profession, but a decade later it caught the attention of a new young assistant professor at GSIA, Robert Lucas, who had just completed his doctorate at the University in Chicago. Beginning in 1971, Lucas and Tom Sargent, who was also with us for a short time, brought the theory of rational expectations into national and international prominence' (p. 250).

Not only was there a split between Simon and the neoclassical economists at Carnegie, but there was also antagonism within the neoclassical faction. Lucas recalled: 'Tom was at Carnegie for a while. That was his first job when he got out of Harvard. I didn't know him too well then. I'll tell you what happened in those days—it's ridiculous in retrospect. There was a kind of Chicago faction and a non-Chicago faction at Carnegie. Mike Lovell . . . was the non-Chicago leader . . . When Tom came, I associated him with the anti-Chicago group. I thought he didn't show interest in me. We didn't talk very much during the two years he was there' (Klamer, 1983, p. 33).[1] Sargent remembered: 'I first met Lucas at Carnegie–Mellon, but I was way behind him . . . I didn't talk to Lucas very much that year . . . I remember when Lucas and Rapping were writing their paper. I used to talk to Leonard about it, not Bob' (Klamer, 1983, pp. 60–1). Ironically, it was Mike Lovell who interested Sargent in rational expectations: 'I may mention that the one who put me onto rational expectations wasn't Bob Lucas; it was Mike Lovell . . . [Mike] put me onto the Muth article' (Klamer, 1983, p. 61). Since Sargent was at Carnegie from 1968 until 1969, he did not overlap with Muth. He said: 'I don't really know [Muth]. I have met him two times. I've heard him give papers' (Klamer, 1983, p. 63).

Jumping ahead in time, the irony of the relationship between rational expectations and bounded rationality goes on when rational expectations theory, born from the same mother as bounded rationality, after trying to kill her big sister, then tried to come around to embracing her in the person of Sargent. Sargent (1993) called his latest venture *Bounded Rationality in Macroeconomics* and tried to make connections to Simon's programme of bounded rationality and artificial intelligence (pp. 21–2). But was Simon's bounded rationality programme motivated by the same concerns as Sargent's? And did Simon and Sargent mean the same by artificial intelligence? Not quite.

I shall argue that the different interests of Sargent and Simon resulted in vastly different interpretations of bounded rationality and artificial intelligence.[2] Sargent was interested in the conceptual integrity of theory and method. In the late 1970s and early 1980s, the theory he adopted was neoclassical theory and the method consisted of

---

[1] Rapping corroborates this story (Klamer, 1983, p. 225): 'Tom Sargent was at Carnegie–Mellon when Lucas and I were writing [our] paper. He came from Harvard and stayed for a year . . . He did not pay much attention to what Bob and I were doing. He did not talk with Lucas much . . . He must have been aware of the factions at Carnegie at that time. He was considered part of the Harvard group. The Chicago people tended to have reservations about liberals, and the Harvard people were liberals.'

[2] Interests are not meant to carry an ominous meaning here, but simply to reflect the lack of universal standards for science.

vector autoregressions. Hence, when he embraced bounded rationality, he tried to use it to strengthen neoclassical economics. When he adopted artificial intelligence, it implied a focus on adaptive computing and parallel processing. Simon, on the other hand, was interested in the formal foundations of rationality, in finding out how people made decisions. Hence, when he embraced bounded rationality, he tried to use it to reject the basic assumptions of neoclassical economics. When he adopted artificial intelligence, it implied a focus on symbol processing and serial computing.

Since Sargent and Simon disagreed from the beginning over what makes for good research in economics, they did not provide a common interpretation of ideas like bounded rationality and artificial intelligence. Embracing this complexity rather than shying away from it helps us get a deeper understanding and richer reading of their ideas. Consequently, I shall identify the stories Sargent and Simon told about bounded rationality and artificial intelligence in the light of their attitudes towards the standards to be used. The next section will take us through Sargent's side of the bounded rationality and artificial intelligence narrative. The third will give Simon's perspective.

2. Mr Rationality and adaptive computing

Interviews and publications evidence Sargent's *interest in conceptual integrity of theory and method*. He said: 'I tried to figure out the relationship between time-series and economic models. At the time I started the links weren't formal' (Klamer, 1983, p. 60). 'This question about the relationship between theories and time-series has guided my studies. I try to learn both about theories and time-series econometrics with a purpose. I get particularly excited when I see possibilities of merging the two' (Klamer, 1983, p. 64). Sargent (1987A) wrote: '[O]ne of the main substantive economic motivations of my own studies has been to understand the connections between economic theories and econometric tests of those theories' (p. xix).

Eventually, Sargent sought to find conceptual integrity by combining the theory of bounded rationality with the method of artificial intelligence. This may come as somewhat of a surprise, because Sargent was well known as one of the main characters in the rational expectations revolution. However, in many ways rational expectations turned out to be a dead end for Sargent. I shall restrict my attention to a few difficulties that appeared during the late 1970s and early 1980s in his work on rational expectations (for the complete story, see Sent, forthcoming). On the econometric side of the conceptual integrity coin, he went with the flow and focused his attention on restricting *vector autoregressions*. Sargent (1981) justified this by an appeal to economic data: 'Since time series of economic data usually have the properties of high own-serial correlation and various patterns of cross-serial correlation, it seems that there is potential for [specifications] . . . that roughly reproduce the serial correlation and cross-serial correlation in a given collection of time series measuring market outcomes' (p. 215; also see Hansen and Sargent, 1980, 1991B).

As far as economic theory was concerned, Sargent jumped on Lucas's *general equilibrium theory* bandwagon, after spending a year as a visiting professor at the University of Chicago and taking two courses from Lucas (see Klamer, 1983, p. 62; Sargent, 1980, p. 107). According to Sargent, 'Lucas pointed out that agents' decision rules . . . are predicted by [general equilibrium] economic theory to vary systematically with changes in the stochastic process facing agents' (Hansen and Sargent, 1980, p. 91). This observation led Sargent (1981) to explore the implications 'of a single principle from economic theory. This principle is that people's observed behaviour will change when their constraints change' (p. 214). He restricted 'things so that the dynamic economic theory is of the equilibrium variety, with optimizing agents and cleared markets' (p. 214; also see Klamer, 1983, p. 68). I should note that Sargent used the Lucas–Chicago approach to general equilibrium theory rather than the Arrow–Debreu–McKenzie version.

To satisfy his interest in linking vector autoregressions and general equilibrium theory, Sargent availed himself of the concept of *rational expectations*, for '[r]ational expectations modelling promised to tighten the link between theory and estimation, because the objects produced by the theorizing are exactly the objects in which econometrics is cast' (Hansen and Sargent, 1991B, p. 3). Besides, 'Lucas and Prescott [had done] much to clarify the nature of rational expectations as an equilibrium concept, and also pointed the way to connecting the theory with observations' (Sargent, 1987C, p. 76; also see Sargent 1987C, p. 77). Rational expectations modelling resulted in vector autoregressions: 'This is an attractive assumption because the solutions of such problems are known to imply that the chosen variables . . . can exhibit serial correlation and cross-serial correlation' (Sargent, 1981, p. 215).

According to this interpretation, expectations were rational when they depended, in the proper way, on the same things that economic theory said actually determined that variable. A collection of agents was solving the same optimum problems by using the relevant economic theory and the solution of each agent was consistent with the solution of other agents. Econometric methods could then be used to estimate the vector autoregressions that resulted from this economic model. In this rendition of rational expectations, agents did not make any systematic errors because they were little economists and econometricians. According to Sargent (1993), '[t]he idea of rational expectations is . . . said to embody the idea that economists and the agents they are modelling should be placed on an equal footing: the agents in the model should be able to forecast and profit-maximize and utility-maximize as well as the economist—or should we say econometrician—who constructed the model' (p. 21; also see Sargent, 1987C, p. 76, 1987A, p. 440). Or: 'The concept of a rational expectations competitive equilibrium . . . has the attractive property that . . . [the agents] in the model forecast . . . as well as the economist who is modelling them' (Sargent, 1987A, p. 411).

Sargent really wanted everyone to be alike and had previously thought that one of the attractive properties of the concept of rational expectations was that there was symmetry among agents, economists, and econometricians. The trouble for Sargent was that he ended up with *asymmetry* between agents and econometricians when his decisions were further elaborated. It turned out that when implemented numerically or econometrically, rational expectations models imputed more knowledge to the agents within the model (who used the equilibrium probability distributions in evaluating their Euler equations) than was possessed by an econometrician, who faced estimation and inference problems that the agents in the model had somehow solved. The reason is that agents' decision rules are exact (non-stochastic) functions of the information they possess, while the econometrician must resort to some device to convert the exact equations delivered by economic theory into inexact (stochastic) equations susceptible to econometric analysis (see Sargent, 1993, p. 21; Hansen and Sargent, 1980, p. 93). Because, '[d]espite its explicit recognition of uncertainty in modelling behaviour, [rational expectations] theory actually generates behavioral equations without residuals. As with most macroeconomic theory then, we must tack on residuals to obtain empirically usable models and the theory is silent about the nature of the residuals' (Sargent and Sims, 1977, p. 54). Recalling that rational expectations economists and econometricians challenged adaptive expectations ones for fitting models that forecast better than agents, we now observe a reversal of the contested asymmetry. While the agents somehow knew what was going on, Sargent (1987A) was learning about it: '[M]y own process of learning the subject has continually mixed technical tools and economic models' (p. xix). Also: 'My published work is just a record of my learning . . . It's been a painful and slow process. My work is like a journey, a journey of discovery' (Klamer, 1983, p. 74).

Another dead end was that the *convenience* to be found in engineering metaphors drove Sargent's further elaborations of the adoption of vector autoregressions, general equilibrium theory, and rational expectations and ended up as the mother of all rationality in his contributions: 'This paper describes methods for conveniently formu- lating and estimating dynamic linear econometric models under the hypothesis of rational expectations. An econometrically convenient formula for the cross-equation restrictions is derived' (Hansen and Sargent, 1980, p. 91; also see Hansen and Sargent, 1981A, pp. 127, 151, 1981B, p. 255, 1982, pp. 269, 294, 1990, pp. 2–3, 1991D, p. 46, 1991H, p. 3; Lucas and Sargent, 1979, p. 13; Sargent, 1987A, p. 226, 1987B, p. 1). This convenience led him from covariance, stationary, linearly indeterministic processes to Wold's decomposition theorem to moving average representations to autoregressive representations to Wiener–Kolmogorov linear least squares prediction to state-space representations to Kalman filtering to innovations representations (see Sent, 1996). This convenience was the very opposite of an atemporal law-governed rationality. While alluding to the rationality of agents and optimality of outcomes, Sargent was driven to reduce everything to the weak expedient of convenience to justify his own work. Is this not the same as Simon's 'satisficing'? And how come agents get to escape these difficulties?

These dead ends eventually caused Sargent to try to restore symmetry among agents, economists, and econometricians by incorporating learning.[1] Sargent (1993) made a 'call to retreat from . . . rational expectations . . . by expelling rational agents from our model environments' (p. 3) and 'to create theories with behavioral foundations by eliminating the asymmetry that rational expectations builds in between the agents in the model and the econometrician who is estimating it' (pp. 21–2; also see Sargent, 1993, p. 23). However, he tried to reinforce rational expectations by focusing on convergence to this equilibrium: 'One reason for studying the [learning] problem is that the notion of a rational expectations equilibrium would be a more attractive one if there were plausible and undemanding learning schemes which would drive the system towards a rational expectations equilibrium' (Marcet and Sargent, 1992, p. 140; also see Marcet and Sargent, 1988, p. 168, 1989A, p. 360, 1989B, p. 1306, 1989C, p. 120, 1992, p. 140; Sargent, 1993, p. 133).

He also tried to use learning with adaptive expectations to deal with some of the

---

[1] I should note that Boland (1986) has argued that the problem with the rational expectations hypothesis is not that it lacks a theory of learning, but that it relies on a false theory of learning. For the rational expectations hypothesis to work, facts must not only speak for themselves but they must say the same thing to every individual. However, without a reliable inductive logic there is no reason to suspect that this will be the case. Similarly, Richardson (1959, 1960) has noted the impossibility of forming rational expecta- tions in a world of interdependent decisions. He emphasised the necessity of people believing different things if some kinds of economic incoherence are to be avoided. Since there is no room in this paper to elaborate on these issues, the reader is referred to Loasby (1989) for an evaluation.

Sargent versus Simon: bounded rationality unbound   **329**

problems associated with rational expectations. While '[r]ational expectations models sometimes have too many equilibria' (Sargent, 1993, p. 25) 'the adaptive system selects an [equilibrium] path' (Sargent, 1993, p. 134; also see Marcet and Sargent, 1992, p. 140, 1988, p. 168, 1989C). While 'there are particular areas in which the outcomes that [rational expectations] predicts are sharp but very difficult to reconcile with observations' (Sargent, 1993, p. 25), 'incorporating adaptive expectations would serve, at least temporarily, to modify or take the edge off very sharp predictions that arise in some rational expectations models' (Sargent, 1993, p. 134). Furthermore, including learning would deal with some discrepancies in rational expectations, because '[d]espite the fact that they are inconsistent with rational expectations, . . . regime change experiments have been a principal use of rational expectations models in macroeconomics' (Sargent, 1993, p. 27). Finally, incorporating learning could assist in the computation of equilibria, for 'either the least-squares learning scheme or the ordinary differential equation associated with it can suggest effective algorithms for computing a rational expectations equilibrium for applied work' (Marcet and Sargent, 1992, p. 161; also see Sargent, 1993, pp. 106, 152; Marcet and Sargent, 1988, p. 171, 1989B, p. 1320).

Once he moved to restore symmetry among agents, economists, and econometricians by incorporating learning, Sargent had to figure out what version of the learning assumption he wanted to use. Unfortunately, Marcet and Sargent's adaptive expectations approach resulted in a very limited interpretation of learning by the agents. They still had to be quite smart. Instead, Sargent sought an answer in *bounded rationality* in the form of *artificial intelligence*. Sargent (1993) appealed to the ideas of a 'number of economists [who] are answering this question by combing the recent literature on artificial intelligence as a source of methods and insights . . . Some of these methods embody sensible versions of at least aspects of what we might mean by "behave like a scientist"' (pp. 23–4). Sargent (1993) thought he could restore symmetry 'by expelling rational agents . . . and replacing them with "artificially intelligent" agents who behave like econometricians. These "econometricians" theorize, estimate, and adapt in attempting to learn about probability distributions which, under rational expectations, they already know' (p. 3). How did he come up with this move? Sargent (1993) became an enthusiast for the artificial intelligence approach to learning after attending a workshop for economists and physicists at the Santa Fe Institute: 'My interest in studying economies with 'artificially intelligent' agents was spurred by attending a meeting . . . at the Santa Fe Institute in September 1987' (p. vi). Moreover, he left his subgroup on webs with some suggestions about how to deal with some of the classical problems in economics, in particular in the two-nation overlapping generations model, by replacing agents that have perfect foresight with adaptive, rule-based agents who learn.

Out of the several approaches to artificial intelligence, such as symbol processing in digital computers, adaptive computing systems, and expert systems, Sargent chose classifier systems and genetic algorithms, after learning about them from John Holland at Santa Fe: 'Our agents are artificially intelligent and are modelled as using classifier systems to make decisions' (Marimon, McGrattan, and Sargent, 1990, p. 329; also see Marimon, McGrattan, and Sargent, 1990, pp. 329–30). He saw the 'literature on genetic algorithms [as] a good source of ideas on how to proceed' (Marcet and Sargent, 1992, p. 162). John Holland had suggested applying classifiers to economics by finding an established model that 'should be easily extendible in several dimensions so that even more realistic situations can be studied. In [Holland's] opinion, the two-nation overlapping generations model (see the discussion in [Hansen and] Sargent) goes a long way toward meeting these criteria' (Holland, 1988, p. 123; see Hansen and Sargent, 1981A). This model could be modified by using classifier systems and compared with the standard equilibrium solutions that required agents with perfect one-step foresight.

Classifier systems were part of what could be called the adaptive computing approach to artificial intelligence, along with neural networks and connectionist systems (see Anderson, Arrow, and Pines, 1988; Holland and Miller, 1991; Lane, 1993A, 1993B; Marimon, McGrattan, and Sargent, 1990, p. 330; Waldrop, 1992). They were parallel, message-passing, rule-based systems, that modelled their environments by activating appropriate clusters of rules. They were able to model complicated, changing environments, to interpret the internal states of agents in the theory so that the agents seemed progressively to 'model' their world, to make agents able to build up behavioural repertoires that included chains of actions initiated long before the agent obtains the reward, and to make agents able to develop the capacity to plan future actions on the basis of their expectations of what the consequences of those actions will be. Classifier systems had two particularly desirable efficiency properties. First, they did not impose heavy memory requirements on the system. Second, much of the information processing could be carried out in parallel. Very convenient, indeed.

How could these classifier systems be applied to economics? Instead of assuming that agents were perfectly rational, they could be modelled with classifier systems and learn from experience like real economic agents. Instead of modelling the economy as a Lucas–Chicago general equilibrium, societies of classifier systems could organise a set of interacting economic agents into an economy. Reluctant to give up ideas like representative agents or completed arbitrage and to renounce Lucas–Chicago general equilibrium analysis, Sargent did not go all the way with Santa Fe. Rather than using classifier systems to think about populations, he saw them as models of the neurons of an individual's brain (see Sargent, 1993, p. 76). Rather than relinquishing the notion of an equilibrium, he focused on convergence to equilibrium (see Sargent, 1993, p. 153; Marimon, McGrattan, and Sargent, 1990, p. 372).

This is where Simon enters the story. In an interview in 1982, Sargent responded to Simon's criticism of the rationality assumption in neoclassical economics in the following way: 'People who take that criticism seriously end up . . . doing more difficult rational expectations. It remains to be seen whether Simon's criticism is constructive or useful in the sense that I defined earlier, namely that someone builds on it . . . The general principle here is that the less information and the harder the choice problem of agents, the more learning you load in, the more difficult is the problem to analyze and to solve. The art is in keeping a model that captures some elements of these things, but is still tractable' (Klamer, 1983, p. 79).

However, after having encountered numerous dead ends in the attempt to serve his interest in conceptual integrity of theory and method through the use of general equilibrium theory, vector autoregressions, and rational expectations, Sargent published *Bounded Rationality in Macroeconomics* in 1993 and tried to make connections to Simon's programme of bounded rationality and artificial intelligence: 'Herbert Simon and other advocates of "bounded rationality" propose to create theories with behavioral foundations by eliminating the asymmetry that rational expectations builds in between the agents in the model and the econometrician who is estimating it' (pp. 21–2). At about the same time, Simon (1991) lamented: 'My economist friends have long since given up on me, consigning me to psychology or some other distant wasteland' (p. 385). So what is going on? Did Simon's economist friends, represented by Sargent, come back to embrace his work? Was Simon's bounded rationality programme really concerned about asymmetry in neoclassical economics and econometrics? And did Simon and Sargent mean the same by artificial intelligence? Certainly not.

3. Mr Bounded Rationality and symbol processing

Dismayed by the developments at the GSIA at Carnegie–Mellon University during the 1960s, Simon took refuge in the psychology department. Simon (1991) claimed that the disputes that had started at the GSIA 'undoubtedly contributed to the gradual escalation of my conflict with the profession' (p. 271). The disputes were about the assumption of rational agents. Simon's interpretation of bounded rationality was different from Sargent's, since it was shaped by different interests. Simon (1991) wrote in his autobiography: 'Actually, to say that I retreated from the Graduate School of Industrial Administration in only partly correct; I was also drawn to the Psychology Department and the burgeoning new activity around the computer by the shift in my own research interests' (p. 251). 'The Psychology Department provided the platform for launching the cognitive revolution in psychology. A sequence of organizations, culminating in the Computer Science Department, provided the corresponding platform for artificial intelligence' (p. 252). Starting off in political science and then moving through several disciplinary domains, such as management theory, economics, artificial intelligence, and cognitive science, Simon's (1957A) whole academic career has been focused on one problem: a search for 'a science of man' based on 'his dual nature as a social and a rational animal' (p. vii). Simon was interested in *finding out how people made decisions* and was driven by the conviction that neoclassical economists were not all that serious about describing the formal foundations of rationality, whereas he was.

Contrary to Sargent, Simon (1991) embraced 'a logical positivism' that he has 'never relinquished' (p. 44; also see Simon, 1975, p. 45). This has been the source of much criticism of Simon's (1991) work: 'It is true that I am still accused of "positivism" as though that were some kind of felony, or at least a venial sin' (p. 270; also see Simon, 1991, p. 85). It also caused Simon (1991) to criticise the rational expectations programme of Muth: 'Jack published in *Econometrica* in 1961 a novel suggestion for handling uncertainty in economics. He clearly deserves a Nobel for it, even thought I do not think it describes the real world correctly. Sometimes an idea that is not literally correct can have great scientific importance' (pp. 249–50; also see Simon, 1981, p. 47). But Simon was after ideas that were literally correct. For example, Simon (1975) criticised organisational theory for 'superficiality, oversimplification, lack of realism' (p. 38). He even tried to recruit rational expectations economists in his logical positivist camp. Simon (1992) claimed that the 'faith in a priori theory, uncontaminated by empirical observations, has been weakened—even among "rational expectationists". More and more economists are beginning to look for the facts they need in actual observation of business decision-making and in laboratory experiments on economic markets and organizations' (p. 7).

While Sargent's work is hard to capture because he kept changing his interpretation of rational expectations to the point of trying to argue that it was closely linked to bounded rationality, Simon's research is hard to summarise because he has done so much work in so many different disciplines. However, the concepts he developed originally in management science carried over to his research in economics, artificial

332   E.-M. Sent

intelligence, and cognitive science. Simon's positivist conviction that an understanding of rationality should be practical caused him to link management science to decision-making, decision-making to problem-solving, and problem-solving to artificial intelligence and economics. For Simon, both artificial intelligence and economics were about describing how people selected a satisfactory option from a set of alternatives.

Simon's search for how people actually made decisions started from the conviction that there were external, social constraints and internal, cognitive limitations to decision-making.[1] This led him to focus on the process rather than the outcome of decision-making. According to Simon (1975), when we are 'concerned with the limits of rationality', we need to focus on 'the manner in which organization affects these limits for the person making a decision' (p. 241). Awareness of these constraints, for Simon (1966), caused people to use heuristics and satisfice: 'Satisficing heuristics are widely applicable and widely applied in problem domains where the number of possible solutions is far too great to permit exhaustive search and where an efficient maximizing algorithm is not available' (p. 281). Loosely articulated heuristics, or rules of thumb, Simon argued, governed the process of gathering information and choosing alternatives. According to Simon, these heuristics were employed generally because they had been proved successful in the past. Furthermore, they implied that the decision-maker was searching merely for an adequate solution. In Simon's (1992) view, '[t]he selectivity of the search, hence its feasibility, is obtained by applying rules of thumb, or heuristics, to determine what paths should be traced and what ones can be ignored. The search halts when a satisfactory solution has been found, almost always long before all alternatives have been examined' (p. 4; also see Simon, 1960, pp. 21–34, 1976, p. 431, 1978A, p. 455, 1978B, p. 462, 1981, pp. 34–6, 56). That is, people satisficed, they accepted the first solution that was satisfactory according to a set of minimal criteria. 'Most human decision-making,' Simon claimed, 'whether individual or organizational, is concerned with the discovery and selection of satisfactory alternatives; only in exceptional cases is it concerned with the discovery and selection of optimal alternatives' (March and Simon, 1958, pp. 140–1; also see Simon, 1955, pp. 252–3, 1956, p. 261, 1957A, pp. 204–5, 1976, pp. 433, 435, 1978A, pp. 444, 453, 455, 1979, pp. 476, 479, 483–4, 489–90, 1981, pp. 36–7). The minimal criteria to be used were laid down in goals that could be divided into independent sub-goals (sub-tasks). For Simon, '[a]ction is goal-oriented and adaptive' (March and Simon, 1958, p. 169). This, then, allowed a problem to be broken down into sub-problems and, for Simon (1975), implied 'a hierarchy of decisions—each step downward in the hierarchy consisting in an implementation of the goals set forth in the step immediately above' (p. 5; also see March and Simon, 1958, pp. 151–4; Simon, 1981, pp. 51–2).

Now that we have a general taste of the flavour of Simon's work on *bounded rationality*, we may wonder how he saw it in relation to rational expectations. Given his interest in finding out how people made decisions, Simon saw rational expectations and bounded rationality as being opposed to each other. He believed that the neoclassical orthodoxy gave too little attention to institutional constraints on economic behaviour and cognitive constraints on individual decisions. According to Simon (1987B), '[t]he term "bounded rationality" is used to designate rational choice that takes into account the cognitive limitations of the decision-maker—limitations of both knowledge and computational capacity' (p. 266). And, for Simon (1991), '[t]he theory of rational

[1] This analysis draws partly on Keizer (1995) and Walton (1995A, 1995B).

expectations offered a direct challenge to theories of bounded rationality, for it assumed a rationality in economic actors beyond any limits that had previously been considered even in neoclassical theory' (p. 250). Simon (1987A) argued that the 'term "bounded rationality" has been proposed to denote the whole range of limitations on human knowledge and human computation that prevent economic actors in the real world from behaving in ways that approximate the predictions of classical and neoclassical theory: including the absence of a complete and consistent utility function for ordering all possible choices, inability to generate more than a small fraction of the potentially relevant alternatives, and inability to foresee the consequences of choosing the alternatives' (p. 222).

Did the two opposing poles of Simon's bounded rationality and Sargent's rational expectations meet again in Sargent's latest venture? Not really, for instead of using bounded rationality like Sargent to try to strengthen the concept of rational expectations, Simon pointed out in his theory of bounded rationality why the basic assumptions of neoclassical economics did not always work in practice. Simon (1975) foresaw difficulties along three steps of the way to a decision: '(1) the listing of all the alternative strategies; (2) the determination of all the consequences that follow upon each of these strategies; (3) the comparative evaluation of these sets of consequences' (p. 67). According to Simon (1975), 'the subject, in order to perform with perfect rationality in this scheme, would have to have a complete description of the consequences following each alternative strategy and would have to compare these consequences. He would have to know in every single respect how the world would be changed by his behaving one way instead of another, and he would have to follow the consequences of behavior through unlimited stretches of time, unlimited reaches of space, and unlimited sets of values' (p. 69). Hence, Simon's bounded rationality differed in three important respects from Sargent's rational expectations.

First, instead of assuming a fixed set of alternatives, among which the decision-maker chose, Simon's theory of bounded rationality postulated a process for generating alternatives. Appealing to studies in modern cognitive psychology on the processes that human subjects used to choose among given alternatives and to find possible courses of action, Simon argued that under most circumstances it was not reasonable to talk about finding 'all the alternatives'. The generation and evaluation of alternatives was a lengthy and costly process, and one where, in real-world situations, even minimal completeness could seldom be guaranteed. Second, Simon detected another weakness associated with the basic assumptions of neoclassical economics in the fact that individuals had difficulty coming up with original solutions to problems. Cognitive limits—lack of knowledge and limits of ability to forecast the future—played a central role in the evaluation of alternatives. These cognitive limits were not simply limits on specific information. They were almost always also limits on the adequacy of scientific theories that could be used to predict the relevant phenomena. Such observations led Simon to speculate that the mind mostly functions by applying approximate or cookbook solutions to problems. Finally, instead of assuming the maximisation of a utility function, Simon's bounded rationality theory postulated a satisficing strategy. It sought to identify, in theory and in actual behaviour, procedures for choosing that were computationally simpler, and argued that individuals picked the first choice that met a pre-set acceptance criterion. Simon (1978B) concluded that 'neoclassical theory, even with the help of "rational expectations" (more accurately described as "consistent expectations"), is far from adequate to the needs of policy' (p. 471; also see Simon, 1976, pp. 437–8, 1978A, pp. 445, 453, 1979, pp. 485–6, 1981, pp. 29, 47, 178, 1982A, pp. 3, 405).

All right, so Sargent did not quite come around to embracing Simon's interpretation of bounded rationality. But what about Simon's analysis of *artificial intelligence*? Again, Simon's interest in finding out how people made decisions shaped an interpretation of artificial intelligence that was vastly different from Sargent's allusions to parallel processing and adaptive computing. The concepts Simon developed in bounded rationality served as a springboard for his interpretation of artificial intelligence. Simon's bounded rationality programme, though contrary to rational expectations theory, offered an open window into the workings of the human mind. The same ideas of 'heuristic' or 'rule-bound' search, 'satisficing' behaviour, and 'goal, sub-goal' strategy that shaped Simon's theory of bounded rationality also became key concepts in his problem-space approach to reproducing human-style reasoning (see, e.g., Kadane and Simon, 1975; Newell and Simon, 1958; Simon, 1966, pp. 276–81, 1967A, 1972, 1981, pp. 138–44, 155–7, 196–200).

Simon's bounded rationality programme embodied ideas for programming a computer how to think. An understanding of the 'real' processes at work behind human decision-making allowed Simon to build computers that replicated these processes and to serve his interest in finding out how people made decisions. The notions of heuristics and sub-problems suggested that machines could be programmed to solve problems without specifying the solution for every problem in detail and that tasks could be divided into independent, hierarchically ordered sub-tasks. They allowed the development of simple problem-solving procedures for computers. 'In solving problems,' Simon (1960) wrote, 'human thinking is governed by programs that organize myriads of simple information processes—or symbolic manipulating processes if you like—into orderly, complex sequences that are responsive to and adaptive to the task environment and the clues that are extracted from that environment as sequences unfold' (p. 81).

To serve his interests, Simon developed a so-called physical symbol system hypothesis. According to this presupposition, the necessary and sufficient condition for a system to be capable of thinking—doing those things that, if they were done by a human being, we would call thinking—was that it be able to perform symbolic processes. The two main processes predominating this theory of thinking were problem-solving by heuristic search and problem-solving by recognition. This involved: (1) putting symbols in; (2) putting symbols out; (3) storing symbols and relational structures of symbols; (4) constructing, modifying, and erasing such symbol structures; (5) comparing two symbol structures; and (6) following one course of action or another, depending on the outcome of such a comparison. The result was a step-by-step mental search through a vast 'problem space' of possibilities, with each step guided by a heuristic rule of thumb: 'If this is the situation, then that step is worth taking.' If the hypothesis was true, several consequences followed. First, computers, appropriately programmed, then were capable of thinking. Second, the human brain, since it was capable of thinking, was (at least) a physical symbol system.

Simon's interests, therefore, shaped an interpretation of artificial intelligence that was distinctly different from that of Sargent. Rather than focusing on neuronal structures as Sargent had done, Simon analysed the architecture of the mind at the symbolic level without a theory of how these symbolic processes were implemented by neuronal structures. Simon (1993) wanted 'to characterize most of the higher-level and complex cognitive phenomena at the symbol level, rather than attempting to describe it all solely in neurological terms' (p. 644). Rather than analysing the brain as a predominantly parallel device like Sargent, Simon settled on a serial system. Simon (1993) dismissed the conclusion that the brain was predominantly a parallel device, and that for this reason a serial computer could not simulate a brain process, by arguing that this conclusion did not take into account the fact that the details of neuronal implementation were largely independent of the theory of the mind's symbol structures and symbol processes: 'Even extensive parallel processing at the neural level would not imply parallelism at the symbolic level' (p. 644).

Hence, Simon tried to satisfy his interest in finding out how people actually made decisions by constructing a theory of the architecture of the mind and the characteristics of that architecture at the symbolic level, even in the absence of any but a very incomplete and primitive theory of how these symbolic processes were implemented by neuronal structures. Because '[t]hose efforts that undertake to introduce "neurons" possessing relatively realistic biological properties have been limited largely to simple, low-level structures containing few neurons, hence cannot yet be linked in any clear way to models or phenomena at the symbolic level. On the other hand the "neurons" of connectionist models are more numerous, but they have few of the properties of real neurons, and provide a foundation for only very abstract models of thought processes. Moreover, it has not yet been demonstrated that they can account for any wide range of complex cognitive performances in the domains of problem solving, use of language, or reasoning' (Simon, 1993, p. 645). Simon (1993) concluded that 'it is improbable that [connectionist nets or neural networks] will supersede models of the more traditional serial kind as explanations of behaviour at the symbolic level' (pp. 645–6).

4. Conclusion

Motivated by achieving what he would regard as conceptual integrity of theory and method, Sargent initially focused on vector autoregressions, general equilibrium theory, and rational expectations in the late 1970s. Asymmetry between agents and econometricians followed as one of the dead ends, since, while econometricians were learning, agents were supposed to know what was going on. Furthermore, while convenience drove him in his own work, the agents were supposed to be rational and the outcome was considered to be optimal. Sargent sought to restore conceptual integrity of theory and method by adopting artificial intelligence and bounded rationality.

Sargent tried to link his interpretations of bounded rationality and artificial intelligence with those of Simon. This link turned out to be rather weak. Since Sargent wanted to restore symmetry by incorporating learning, he embraced neoclassical theory and parallel adaptive computing systems. At the same time, Simon's interest in human decision-making and the foundations of rationality made him move to the serial symbol processing approach. As a result, he dismissed neoclassical theory and parallel systems. Instead, his interests revealed the structural similarities of his serial symbol processing programme and the 'bounded' alternative to neoclassical choice theory. Searching, rule-bound decisions, goal-oriented behaviour—most of the basic ideas of Simon's bounded rationality theory—were carried over to his interpretation of artificial intelligence.

The point is that important arguments in economics are so rarely joined because the disagreements stem from root-and-branch differences of interests. Ideas do not hinge on a set of contested facts about the world. At issue is what individual economists

336   E.-M. Sent

consider to be good research. Different interests shape different interpretations of ideas like bounded rationality and artificial intelligence. Acknowledging this complexity will help us acquire a fascinating perspective on the history of economic thought.

Bibliography

Anderson, P. W., Arrow, K. J. and Pines, D. (eds). 1988. *The Economy as an Evolving Complex System*, Santa Fe Institute Studies in the Sciences of Complexity, vol. 5, Redwood City, Addison-Wesley

Boland, L. A. 1986. *Methodology for a New Microeconomics*, Boston, Allen & Unwin

Crevier, D. 1993. *AI: The Tumultuous History of The Search for Artificial Intelligence*, New York, Basic Books

Egedi, M., Marris, R., Simon, H. A. and Viale, R. (eds). 1992. *Economics, Bounded Rationality and the Cognitive Revolution*, Brookfield, Vermont, Edward Elgar

Hansen, L. P. and Sargent, T. J. 1980. Formulating and estimating dynamic linear expectations models, *Journal of Economic Dynamics and Control*, vol. 2, no. 1, 7–46. Reprinted in Lucas, R. E. and Sargent, T. J. (eds) (1981), pp. 91–125, *Rational Expectations and Econometric Practice*, Minneapolis, University of Minnesota Press

Hansen, L. P. and Sargent, T. J. 1981A. Linear rational expectations models for dynamically interrelated variables, pp. 127–56 in Lucas, R. E., and Sargent, T. J. (eds), *Rational Expectations and Econometric Practice*, Minneapolis, University of Minnesota Press

Hansen, L. P. and Sargent, T. J. 1981B. A note on Wiener–Kolmogorov prediction formulas for rational expectations models, *Economics Letters*, vol. 8, no. 3, 255–60

Hansen, L. P. and Sargent, T. J. 1982. Instrumental variables procedures for estimating linear rational expectations models, *Journal of Monetary Economics*, vol. 9, no. 3, 263–96

Hansen, L. P. and Sargent, T. J. 1983A. Aggregation over time and the inverse optimal predictor problem for adaptive expectations in continuous time, *International Economic Review*, vol. 24, no. 1, 1–20

Hansen, L. P. and Sargent, T. J. 1983B. The dimensionality of the aliasing problem in models with rational spectral densities, *Econometrica*, vol. 51, no. 2, 377–87

Hansen, L. P. and Sargent, T. J. 1990. Recursive linear models of dynamic economies, *National Bureau of Economic Research Working Paper*, no. 3479

Hansen, L. P. and Sargent, T. J. (eds). 1991A. *Rational Expectations Econometrics*, Boulder, Westview Press

Hansen, L. P. and Sargent, T. J. 1991B. Introduction, pp. 1–12 in Hansen and Sargent (1991A)

Hansen, L. P. and Sargent, T. J. 1991C. Lecture notes on least squares prediction theory, pp. 13–44 in Hansen and Sargent (1991A)

Hansen, L. P. and Sargent, T. J. 1991D. Exact linear expectations models: specification and estimation, pp. 45–76 in Hansen and Sargent (1991A)

Hansen, L. P. and Sargent, T. J. 1991E. Two difficulties in interpreting vector autoregressions, pp. 77–120 in Hansen and Sargent (1991A)

Hansen, L. P. and Sargent, T. J. 1991F. Prediction formulas for continuous time linear rational expectations models, pp. 209–18 in Hansen and Sargent (1991A)

Hansen, L. P. and Sargent, T. J. 1991G. Identification of continuous time rational expectations models from discrete time data, pp. 219–36 in Hansen and Sargent (1991A)

Hansen, L. P. and Sargent, T. J. 1991H. 'Recursive Linear Models of Dynamic Economies', unpublished manuscript

Hansen, L. P. and Sargent, T. J. 1993. Seasonality and approximation errors in rational expectations models, *Journal of Econometrics*, vol. 55, no. 1–2, 21–55

Holland, J. H. 1988. The global economy as an adaptive process, pp. 117–24 in Anderson, Arrow and Pines (1988), 117–24

Holland, J. H. and Miller, J. H. 1991. Artificial adaptive agents in economic theory, *American Economic Review*, vol. 81, no. 2, 365–70

Holt, C. C., Modigliani, F., Muth, J. F. and Simon, H. A. 1960. *Planning Production, Inventories, and Work Force*, Englewood Cliffs, Prentice-Hall

Hoover, K. D. 1988. *The New Classical Macroeconomics*, New York, Basil Blackwell

Kadane, J. B. and Simon, H. A. 1975. Optimal problem-solving search: all-or-none solutions, *Artificial Intelligence*, vol. 6, 235–47. Reprinted in Simon (1982A), 248–60

Keizer, A. B. 1995. 'Herbert A. Simon's Organizational Theories and their Influence', unpublished working paper

Klamer, A. 1983. *Conversations with Economists*, Savage MD, Rowman and Littlefield

Lane, D. A. 1993A. Artificial worlds and economics, part I, *Journal of Evolutionary Economics*, vol. 3, no. 2, 89–107

Lane, D. A. 1993B. Artificial worlds and economics, part II, *Journal of Evolutionary Economics*, vol. 3, no. 3, 177–97

Loasby, B. J. 1989. *The Mind and the Method of the Economist*, Aldershot, Edward Elgar

Lucas, R. E. and Rapping, L. A. 1969A. Real wages, employment, and inflation, *Journal of Political Economy*, vol. 77, no. 5, 721–54

Lucas, R. E. and Rapping, L. A. 1969B. Price expectations and the Phillips curve, *American Economic Review*, vol. 59, no. 3, 342–50

Lucas, R. E. and Sargent, T. J. 1979. After Keynesian macroeconomics, *Federal Reserve Bank of Minneapolis Quarterly Review*, vol. 3, 1–16. Reprinted in Lucas, R. E. and Sargent, T. J. (eds) (1981), pp. 295–320, *Rational Expectations and Econometric Practice*, Minneapolis, University of Minnesota Press,

Marcet, A. and Sargent, T. J. 1986. 'Convergence of Least Squares Learning Mechanisms in Self-referential Linear Stochastic Models', Hoover Institution Working Papers in Economics E-86–33

Marcet, A. and Sargent, T. J. 1988. The fate of systems with 'adaptive' expectations, *American Economic Review*, vol. 78, no. 2, 168–72

Marcet, A. and Sargent, T. J. 1989A. Convergence of least squares learning mechanisms in self-referential linear stochastic models, *Journal of Economic Theory*, vol. 48, no. 2, 337–68

Marcet, A. and Sargent, T. J. 1989B. Convergence of least squares learning in environments with hidden state variables and private information, *Journal of Political Economy*, vol. 97, no. 6, 1306–22

Marcet, A. and Sargent, T. J. 1989C. Least squares learning and the dynamics of hyperinflation, pp. 119–37, in Barnett, W., Geweke, J. and Shell, K. (eds), *Economic Complexity: Chaos, Sunspots, and Nonlinearity*, Cambridge, Cambridge University Press

Marcet, A. and Sargent, T. J. 1992. The convergence of vector autoregressions to rational expectations equilibrium, pp. 139–64 in Vercelli, A. and Dimitri, N. (eds), *Macroeconomics: a strategic survey*, Oxford, Oxford University Press

March, J. G. and Simon, H. A. 1958. *Organizations*, New York, John Wiley

Marimon, R., McGrattan, E. and Sargent, T. J. 1989. Money as a medium of exchange in an economy with artificially intelligent agents, *Hoover Institution Working Papers in Economics E-89–28*

Marimon, R., McGrattan, E. and Sargent, T. J. 1990. Money as a medium of exchange in an economy with artificially intelligent agents, *Journal of Economic Dynamics and Control*, vol. 14, no. 2, 329–74

Mirowski, P. E. 1996. Do you know the way to Santa Fe? pp. 13–140 in Pressman, S. (ed.), *Interactions in Political Economy*, London, Routledge

Muth, J. F. 1960. Optimal properties of exponentially weighted forecasts, *Journal of the American Statistical Association*, vol. 55, no. 290, 299–306

Muth, J. F. 1961. Rational expectations and the theory of price movements, *Econometrica*, vol. 29, no. 3, 315–35

Newell, A. and Simon, H. A. 1958. Heuristic problem solving: the next advance in operations research, *Operations Research*, vol. 6, 1–10. Reprinted in Simon (1982A)

Pool, R. 1989. Strange bedfellows, *Science*, vol. 245, 700–3

Richardson, G. B. 1959. Equilibrium, expectations and information, *Economic Journal*, vol. 69, no. 274, 223–37

Richardson, G. B. 1990. *Information and Investment*, Oxford, Clarendon Press

Sargent, T. J. 1980. 'Tobin's q' and the rate of investment in general equilibrium, pp. 107–54 in Brunner, K. and Meltzer, A. H. (eds), *Carnegie-Rochester Conference Series on Public Policy*, vol. 12, Amsterdam, North-Holland

Sargent, T. J. 1981. Interpreting economic time series, *Journal of Political Economy*, vol. 89, no. 2, 213–48

Sargent, T. J. 1986. *Rational Expectations and Inflation*, New York, Harper and Row

338   E.-M. Sent

Sargent, T. J. 1987A. *Macroeconomic Theory*, 2nd edn, Boston, Academic Press

Sargent, T. J. 1987B. *Dynamic Macroeconomic Theory*, Cambridge, Harvard University Press

Sargent, T. J. 1987C. Rational expectations, pp. 76–85, in Eatwell, J., Milgate, M. and Newman, P. (eds), *The New Palgrave*, London, Macmillan

Sargent, T. J. 1991. Equilibrium with signal extraction from endogenous variables, *Journal of Economic Dynamics and Control*, vol. 15, no. 2, 245–74

Sargent, T. J. 1993. *Bounded Rationality in Macroeconomics*, Oxford, Oxford University Press

Sargent, T. J. and Sims, C. A. 1977. Business cycle modelling without pretending to have too much a priori theory, in Sims, C. A. (ed.), *New Methods in Business Cycle Research: Proceedings From a Conference*, Federal Reserve Bank of Minneapolis, 45–109

Sent, E.-M. 1996. Convenience: the mother of all rationality in Sargent, *Journal of Post Keynesian Economics*, vol. 19, no. 1, 3–34

Sent, E.-M. 1997. *Resisting Sargent*, Cambridge, Cambridge University Press, forthcoming

Simon, H. A. 1955. A behavioral model of rational choice, *Quarterly Journal of Economics*, vol. 69. Reprinted in Simon (1957A), 241–60

Simon, H. A. 1956. Rational choice and the structure of the environment, *Psychological Review*, vol. 63. Reprinted in Simon (1957A), 261–73

Simon, H. A. 1957A. *Models of Man*, New York, John Wiley & Sons

Simon, H. A. 1957B. *Administrative Behaviour*, 2nd edn, New York, Macmillan

Simon, H. A. 1960. *The New Science of Management Decision*, New York, Harper & Row

Simon, H. A. 1966. Thinking by computers, in Colodny, R. G. (ed.), *Mind and Cosmos: Essays in Contemporary Science and Philosophy*, Pittsburgh, University of Pittsburgh Press. Reprinted in Simon (1977), 268–85

Simon, H. A. 1967A. The logic of heuristic decision making, pp. 1–20 in Rescher, N. (ed.), *The Logic of Decision and Action*, Pittsburgh, University of Pittsburgh Press. Reprinted in Simon (1977), 154–75

Simon, H. A. 1967B. Reply to Professor Binkley's comments, pp. 32–3 in Rescher, N. (ed.), *The Logic of Decision and Action*, Pittsburgh, University of Pittsburgh Press,

Simon, H. A. 1972. The theory of problem solving, *Information Processing*, vol. 71, 261–77. Reprinted in Simon (1977), 214–44

Simon, H. A. 1975. *Administrative Behavior*, 3rd edn, New York, Free Press

Simon, H. A. 1976. From substantive to procedural rationality, pp. 129–48 in Latsis, S. J. (ed.), *Method and Appraisal in Economics*, Cambridge, Cambridge University Press. Reprinted in Simon (1982B), 424–43

Simon, H. A. 1977. *Models of Discovery*, Dordrecht, D. Reidel Publishing Company

Simon, H. A. 1978A. Rationality as process and as product of thought, *American Economic Review*, vol. 68, no. 2, 1–16. Reprinted in Simon (1982B), 444–59

Simon, H. A. 1978B. On how to decide what to do, *The Bell Journal of Economics*, vol. 9, no. 2, 494–507. Reprinted in Simon (1982A), 460–73

Simon, H. A. 1979. Rational decision making in business organizations, *American Economic Review*, vol. 69, no. 4, 493–513. Reprinted in Simon (1982A)

Simon, H. A. 1981. *The Sciences of the Artificial*, 2nd edn, Cambridge, MIT Press

Simon, H. A. 1982A. *Models of Bounded Rationality, Vol. 1*, Cambridge, MIT Press

Simon, H. A. 1982B. *Models of Bounded Rationality, Vol. 2*, Cambridge, MIT Press

Simon, H. A. 1987A. Behavioural economics, pp. 221–5, in Eatwell, J., Milgate, M. and Newman, P. (eds), *The New Palgrave*, London, Macmillan

Simon, H. A. 1987B. Bounded rationality, pp. 266–8 in Eatwell, J., Milgate, M. and Newman, P. (eds), *The New Palgrave*, London, Macmillan

Simon, H. A. 1991. *Models of My Life*, New York, Basic Books

Simon, H. A. 1992. Introductory comment, pp. 3–7 in Egedi, Marris, Simon, and Viale (1992)

Simon, H. A. 1993. The human mind: the symbolic level, *Proceedings of the American Philosophical Society*, vol. 137, no. 4, 638–47

Waldrop, M. M. 1992. *Complexity: The Emerging Science at The Edge of Order and Chaos*, New York, Simon and Schuster

Walton, D. 1995A. 'From the Invisible Hand to the Artificial Mind: Herbert Simon and the Economic Construction of Intelligence', mimeo

Walton, D. 1995B. 'When an Economist is Not Just an Economist: From Management to Cybernetics and Back Again', unpublished working paper

Part IV
Bounded Rationality (3): Behavioural Approaches

[13]

Task Complexity and Contingent Processing in Brand Choice

DENIS A. LUSSIER
RICHARD W. OLSHAVSKY*

Further evidence is presented that brand choice strategy is contingent upon task complexity. When three brands were presented, subjects used a compensatory strategy. When more than three brands were presented, subjects first eliminated unacceptable alternatives using a noncompensatory strategy and then evaluated the remaining alternatives using a compensatory process.

The evidence to support the theory that brand choice strategy is influenced in a significant way by the character of the external task environment in which choice occurs is increasing. Several studies using "process tracing" methodologies (Bettman and Kakkar 1977; Jacoby, Szybillo, and Busato-Schach 1977; Payne 1976; Russo and Dosher 1975; Scammon 1977; van Raaij 1976) have found that the strategy by which subjects acquire information is influenced by the number of brands presented, the amount of information presented for each brand, and the format of the information. For instance, Bettman and Kakkar (1977) found that the way the search process was organized, by brand or by attribute, was strongly influenced by the format of the information. And Payne (1976) found that the number of alternatives had a profound influence on choice strategy. When his subjects were presented with only two alternatives from which to choose, they used a form of compensatory strategy—additive or additive difference. In contrast, when his subjects were presented with a more complex task, 6 or 12 alternatives, they used a noncompensatory strategy—conjunctive or elimination-by-aspects.

The finding that brand choice strategy is contingent upon certain aspects of the external task environment has direct implications for both public policy and marketing management. This finding is also significant from a theoretical perspective, because it provides further evidence for the information processing theory advanced by Newell and Simon (1972). Newell and Si-

mon's hypothesis that decision makers will resort to choice strategies that reduce cognitive strain as the complexity of the choice task increases has been supported by these experiments.

Only one of these mentioned studies has directly studied the choice process, however. The information monitoring technique (Bettman and Kakkar 1977; Jacoby et al. 1977) and the eye movement measurement technique (Russo and Dosher 1975; van Raaij 1976) permit direct observation of only the information acquisition strategy; conclusions about choice strategy must be inferred from these search data (Bettman 1976). Only Payne's (1976) study used a methodology that permitted direct observation of the choice strategy.[1] While Payne used the information monitoring technique, he also had his subjects "think aloud" as they made their choice. From these direct, although admittedly incomplete, observations of the choice process, Payne was able to determine directly the type of choice strategies used in each of his experimental conditions. In view of the significance of Payne's results for furthering our understanding of consumer decision making, and given the critical evaluations of the reliability and validity of the protocol analysis technique (Bettman 1974; Bettman and Zins 1977; Wright 1974), further tests of the impact of the external task environment on choice strategy, using a direct measurement technique, are desirable.

In this article we report the results of another empirical study that used protocol analysis to obtain direct measures of choice strategy, under various combinations of number of alternative brands and number of attributes per alternative. Although there are some im-

---

*Denis A. Lussier is Associate Professor of Marketing, Ecole des Hautes Études Commerciales, University of Montreal, 5255 Rue Decelles, Montreal, Quebec, Canada. Richard W. Olshavsky is Associate Professor of Marketing, Graduate School of Business, Indiana University, Bloomington, IN 47401.

[1]See Russo and Dosher (1975) and Russo and Rosen (1975) for after-the-fact "prompted" measures.

154

portant differences in the procedure and the product category used, this study may be viewed as a replication of Payne's study.[2]

Most of the current literature on brand choice focuses on the predictive ability of the different types of models tested. For most authors the only criterion of success is the relative proportion of choices correctly predicted by each model. Our purpose is quite different. To arrive at a typology of brand choice strategies, and to observe how selected variables of the task environment may influence the adoption of a particular strategy, we are less concerned with the predictive ability of current models and more concerned with the identification, from direct observation, of the main processes involved in brand choice.

METHOD

Subjects and Product

Twenty-seven MBA students were recruited on a voluntary basis and a cash incentive was offered. Students were used because very cooperative subjects were needed, considering the particular nature of both the experiment and the product selected. A small sample was used, again because of the nature of protocol data; Payne (1976) analyzed the protocols from only six subjects and Bettman (1970), in an earlier study, used only two.

Portable manual typewriters were selected for study. Several requirements guided this selection. First, to facilitate the development of uniform task perception and goals across subjects, it was desirable to avoid emotionally involved or socially visible products. A pretest led us to believe that typewriters were judged on the basis of cost, manufacturer's reputation, features, and performance. It was also desirable to have a product for which a large number of brands or models and a large number of attributes were usually offered in the marketplace. Most of the product characteristics can be evaluated objectively and the information can be presented in a very "factual" manner.

This product has a high degree of relevance to students. In a pretest, it was found that approximately 70 percent of the students use a typewriter. In our sample, 14 used a typewriter at least once a week and 13 used one at least once a month. Twenty of these subjects owned a typewriter, and seven borrowed a typewriter on a frequent basis. Of the 20 subjects who owned a typewriter, eight bought it themselves, and the remaining 12 received it as a gift. All of those who bought their own typewriter, purchased it new.

Design and Materials

A 3 × 3 fixed effect factorial design was used for this experiment. Three subjects were randomly assigned to

each cell for a total of 27 subjects. Three, 6, and 12 brands, and 5, 10, and 15 product attributes were used. Judging from past research, three brands and five attributes were approximately what consumers really considered.

As the relative attractiveness of the brands may change when the set is enlarged or when more information is provided, an attempt was made to keep this factor constant. An independent sample of 22 students was used to obtain importance ratings and preferences on 26 typewriter characteristics. The mean ratings and standard deviations were used to identify product attributes for which there was a high level of agreement on attribute importance; 15 were retained and used to describe the brands of typewriters.

These 15 attributes were used in the 15-attribute treatment (Hi). A subset of ten was selected for the ten-attribute treatment (Med). Of these, five were retained for the five-attribute treatment (Lo). In the formation of these subsets, an attempt was made to satisfy two requirements simultaneously: (1) each set had to include an equal proportion of more important and less important attributes; (2) a basic set of five attributes was formed by selecting attributes for which the students showed a fairly high level of agreement. This set had to be used for all the treatments, and larger sets were formed by adding the other attributes to this basic subset. It was impossible to meet these conditions perfectly, but they served as guidelines for the formation of the three sets of characteristics.

The brand profiles were constructed in the following manner. A basic set of three brands was constructed first. These three brand profiles were used in all the experimental treatments. Three other brand profiles were added to the initial set to form the set of brands used for the six-brand treatment, and six additional profiles were created for the 12-brand treatment.

The initial three-brand set was created in the following manner. Two brands representing the extreme points on the spectrum of quality and price were created. Then a third brand representing the middle point of the spectrum was created. These three brands were created by first assigning values for the five basic attributes. Then values were assigned for each brand for the secondary and tertiary attributes. The purpose was to control the relative attractiveness of each brand as attributes were added (relative attractiveness was not tested empirically, however).

The next three brands were created in the same manner, as intermediate points on the spectrum of brands established with the first three brands. Finally, Brands 7–12 were created by modifying slightly the profile of each of the first six brands.

Each brand profile was described on a 5- × 7-inch index card. A table format was avoided for these descriptions; the brands were described in a short text. The information concerning product characteristics, such as price or presence of specific features, was given in a factual manner.

---

[2]We were unaware of Payne's study at the time this study was performed. In fact, our study had been completed before Payne's study appeared (Lussier and Olshavsky 1974).

An evaluation of the performance was also included in the description; for example, a rating for "appearance of typed copy" was provided. All the information on product performance was presented as ratings on a ten-point scale. The subjects were told that these ratings had been obtained from a sample of students who had tried each machine.

Procedure

The instructions read to the participants clearly specified the task. The main points were the following:

1. The subject was told that s/he had decided to acquire a new portable manual typewriter for personal use.

2. S/he was asked to choose one machine from the set of machines offered, to proceed as s/he normally would, and to "think aloud."

3. S/he was also told that the brand descriptions were those of real, but unidentified, brands likely to be found in a store, and that the brands were similar to each other in all other respects.

4. Because, in a normal shopping situation, a customer does not necessarily consider all the brands and product characteristics, the instructions invited the subject to behave normally and to consider only those items of information that seemed relevant.

5. Finally, the typewriter characteristics used in the brand descriptions were defined and explained.

After these instructions were read, the brand descriptions were placed on a table in front of the subject and the experiment started. To parallel the format encountered in actual retail outlets, subjects were not permitted to manipulate the cards. As the subject proceeded with a choice, thinking aloud, the experimenter did not interfere. When periods of silence occurred the experimenter reminded the subject to think aloud. All responses were tape recorded for later analysis.

The Warm-Up Exercises

To allow the subjects to get used to the experimental procedure, two warm-up tasks were used—calculation of the unit prices for five typical grocery shopping problems and selection of a ball-point pen.

Qualifications

Because our purpose was to identify the basic choice strategy used and to assess the impact of the task environment on choice strategy, our main concern was the internal validity of the experimental design, and that was obtained at the expense of external validity. Obviously any attempt to generalize the findings from such a study must be made with extreme caution. Even if we are inclined to believe that typewriters are representative of a broad class of products, such as small home

appliances, our results cannot necessarily be extrapolated to all product classes.

Also our group of subjects is hardly representative of the average consumer. The MBA student is more educated and more sophisticated than the average consumer. As s/he has received extensive training in learning, memorizing, and solving complex problems, it may be presumed that s/he can more easily handle complex choice situations.

A more serious problem is the artificiality of the experimental situation and of the data collection method. Consumers placed in an artificial, forced choice situation do not necessarily behave like consumers in a real store environment. Our subjects were motivated to participate in the experiment, but were not necessarily interested in purchasing a typewriter. Presentation of description cards instead of real machines was likely to increase the subject's awareness of certain attributes that would have been otherwise neglected.

Finally, we must underline the special character of our data collection method. Even if several warm-up exercises were performed by each subject before the main experiment, we may suspect that protocol recording produced a strong measurement effect. Asking the subjects to think aloud while choosing a brand probably forced them to be more thorough, systematic, articulate, and rational than they would have been otherwise. However, protocol recording is still the only known approach to expose, however incompletely, what is going on cognitively when one is choosing a brand. The shortcomings of this methodology are in our opinion largely compensated by the richness of the data.

Coding Procedure

Each subject's protocol was first transcribed and then subjected to a step-by-step examination to identify the choice strategy used.[3] To summarize the information contained in the protocols, a descriptive language was developed, largely inspired from existing computer languages, such as Fortran and Basic. With this language, the verbal statements found in the protocols were translated into a series of statements that resemble a computer program.[4]

Obviously, such a translation implied that the verbal

---

[3]See Payne, Braunstein, and Carroll (1978) and Newell and Simon (1972) for a more detailed description of procedures for gathering and analyzing protocols.

[4]Newell and Simon (1972) suggested the Backus Normal Form, a standard notation used to describe the grammar of processing languages. They also developed the Problem Behavior Graph to describe the information processing strategies used by their subjects. We attempted to use this technique, but the differences between the types of problem solving tasks they study (crytoarithmetic, chess, logic theorem proofs) and our brand choice task were so large that it was nearly impossible to apply this technique meaningfully. The Problem Behavior Graph was abandoned, and after experimenting with a few other commonly used techniques, such as discrimination net and flow chart, we decided to develop a technique of our own.

TASK COMPLEXITY AND CONTINGENT PROCESSING   157

EXHIBIT 1

CHOICE PROGRAM OF SUBJECT 20

INPUT BR2		Step 1:	In this phase, we find a mixed process: Subject 20 uses both compensatory comparisons and conjunctive tests. The first two brands are compared and platen length is established as a discrimination criterion. Freedom from paper shift and character size are also used as discrimination criteria. In this first phase, all except two brands (1 and 4) are rejected.
INPUT BR4			
COMPEVAL (BR2:BR4)			
INPUT BR6	Reject BR6 (PL6)		
INPUT BR5	Reject BR5 (PL5)		
INPUT BR1			
COMPEVAL (BR1:BR4)	Preference for BR1		
INPUT BR11	Reject BR11 (PL11)		
INPUT BR10	Reject BR10 (FPS10)		
INPUT BR9	Reject BR9 (PL9)		
INPUT BR8	Reject BR8 (PL8)		
INPUT BR12	Reject BR12 (CS12)		
INPUT BR7	Reject BR7 (CS7)		
REVIEW: COMPEVAL		Step 2:	The two retained brands are reviewed and compared (compensatory).
(BR1:BR4)	Select BR1		

Coding symbols

Operator	Entity
INPUT—Input operation	BRi—Brand *i*
COMP—Basic comparison operation	Pi—Price of brand *i*
HCOMP—Higher order comparison	Gi—Warranty period of brand *i*
COMPEVAL—Compensatory comparison (trade-off model)	Ti—Presence of a tabulator on machine *i*
CORREL—Correlation between two attributes (relationship)	CSi—Character size on machine *i*
ORDER—Rank-order of brands on a particular attribute	SKi—Number of keys on keyboard (standard keyboard: 44 keys)
RANGE—Establish range of a particular attribute	CKi—Number of changeable keys
	PLi—Platen length
	PRi—Key for platen release on machine *i*
	CRi—Number of keys for carriage release (one or two)
	JAMi—Key to clear jams
	ATCi—Rating for appearance of typed copy
	FPSi—Rating for freedom from paper shift
	NOLi—Rating for noise level
	ETTi—Rating for ease of typing a top corner
	ETNi—Rating for ease of insertion of material
	RATi—Performance ratings for brand *i*

comments had to be interpreted by the analyst.[5] To avoid subjective biases and to ensure homogeneous encoding, a set of rules was developed. The first was that all memory-related operations were to be omitted from our code. Even though we may presume that whenever a piece of information about a brand was read by a subject, it was stored in short-term memory and possibly transferred to long-term memory for later use, these processes are always implicit and it was impossible to detect them in the protocol. The second rule concerned certain comparison processes. In many cases, we observed a subject comparing the attribute value of a particular brand to a desired level for this attribute. Sometimes, the resulting knowledge-state was an explicit reject decision about the brand, but in many other cases the outcome was a more or less favor-

able evaluation of the brand. The real problem with this operator was that it was seldom explicitly mentioned by the subjects, hence we were unable to develop a clear set of rules for their interpretation, and decided to classify the operator as one of several choice rules (i.e., conjunctive, lexicographic, etc.).

The third rule pertained to attribute importance weights. There was clear evidence in some of the protocols that such weights were being used by subjects, particularly in the compensatory evaluation phase, but in most cases we could not clearly observe how they were used. Therefore, it was decided to omit them. Although these rules resulted in some sacrifice of detail, they greatly facilitated the identification of the overall strategy and of the differences in strategies across experimental conditions.

Finally, whenever a descriptive model is developed to represent a phenomenon, the model builder must decide on the level of aggregation of the model. S/he may decide to represent the phenomenon in minute detail or, on the other hand, s/he may choose to be more global and aggregate many processes into a few high

---

[5]Only one of the authors transcribed and coded the protocols and tabulated the quantitative measures from the "detailed choice process." There was nearly complete agreement, however, between both authors on the classification of subjects by type of choice strategy (see Table 1) and by type of search strategy.

158   THE JOURNAL OF CONSUMER RESEARCH

EXHIBIT 2

DETAILED CHOICE PROGRAM OF SUBJECT 20

INPUT P2			
INPUT CS2			
INPUT SK2			
INPUT PL2			
INPUT ATC2			
INPUT FPS2			
INPUT P4	COMP (P4:P2)		
INPUT PL4	COMP (PL4:PL2)		
INPUT ATC4	COMP (ATC4:ATC2)		
INPUT FPS4	COMP (FPS4:FPS2)		
INPUT CS4	COMP (CS4:CS2)		
INPUT NOL4	COMP (NOL4:NOL2)		
		COMPEVAL (BR4:BR2)	
INPUT PL6			Reject BR6
INPUT PL5			Reject BR5
INPUT T1	COMP (T1:T4)		
INPUT CS1	COMP (CS1:CS4)		
INPUT ATC1	COMP (ATC1:ATC4)		
INPUT FPS1	COMP (FPS1:FPS4)		
		COMPEVAL (BR1:BR4)	
INPUT PL11			Reject BR11
INPUT PL10			
INPUT FPS10			Reject BR10
INPUT PL9			Reject BR9
INPUT PL8			Reject BR8
INPUT ATC12			
INPUT FPS12			
INPUT CS12			Reject BR12
INPUT CS7			Reject BR7
	COMP (PL1:PL4)		
	COMP (ATC1:ATC4)		
	COMP (FPS1:FPS4)		
	COMP (SK1:SK4)		
	COMP (CS1:CS4)		
	COMP (P1:P4)		
		COMPEVAL (BR1:Br4)	Select BR1

order processes (e.g., INPUT Brand i → EVALUATE Brand i → SELECT Brand i). In the latter case, the representation is so superficial and the loss of information so great that it does not allow understanding of the choice processes involved or of potential differences among subjects. At the other extreme, the analyst may be lost in so many details that the model may fail to give any clear indication about the choice processes involved. For the purpose of this study, two levels of aggregation appeared useful.

To identify the choice strategies used by the subjects and to relate them to the different models in the literature, a more aggregated model revealing the principal processes (e.g., lexicographic, pairwise comparisons of brands) seemed useful. For that purpose, it did not seem useful to describe the way in which a compensa-

tory evaluation of two brands is carried out. On the other hand, it was necessary to show the order in which the brands were considered, evaluated, and compared; the model also had to allow the analyst to make a clear distinction between a noncompensatory and a compensatory comparison of different brands, and between a single stage and a multi-stage comparison. To be useful, the descriptive model needed to account for all the major evaluative operations and their resulting knowledge-states. It had to be sufficient to explain how the brands were accepted or rejected to arrive at a final choice. This first type of model, called in this study "choice programs," was used to describe the choice strategies.

Because our purpose was also to investigate the effects of selected aspects of the external task environ-

EXHIBIT 3

COMPLETE PROTOCOL FOR SUBJECT 20 (CONDITION: 12 BRANDS, 10 ATTRIBUTES)

- #2, $45 . . . pica . . . that's the large character . . . I would omit automatically elite typewriter because the print is too small.
- . . . I can't move these, right?
- (E) No.
- 43 keys . . . a 10-inch platen . . . also I need the large carriage because I type a lot of letters and envelopes . . . it's difficult with a small roller . . . or platen.
- . . . appearance . . . appearance is not important at all.
- Freedom from paper shift, paper shift is very important because I do a lot of erasing, because I make a lot of mistakes.
- . . . (E) Appearance is not the appearance of the machine . . . it's the appearance of the typed copy.
- Oh! that's right . . . the appearance of the typed copy, then appearance is very important.
- #4 . . . also the price is not very important unless it is very expensive.
- . . . this one has a 12-inch roller, the typed copy was excellent . . . the paper shift was average I guess and there's a pica type.
- So #4 is pica type, 12 inches . . . and the noise level is not as . . . the noise level doesn't make any difference.
- Let's see, that seems to be the best so far.
- #6, again a small platen.
- #5, small platen.

- #1 . . . I see it has a tabulator, pica . . . excellent appearance rating . . . rating for shift.
- Let's see, this seems to be better than #4 . . . #1 is better than #4.
- I don't need a tabulator . . . let's see price . . . but it suffers (#4) on appearance of typed copy, paper shift, and noise.
- #11, a 10-inch platen is no good.
- #10, a 12-inch, but freedom from paper shift was rated only 2, that's out.
- #9 is out, a 10-inch platen.
- #8, out, a 10-inch platen.
- #12 . . . appearance of typed copy was 9 and freedom from paper shift 7 . . .
- But it has elite type.
- #7 . . . small type (out).
- So it is between #4 and #1.
- It's definitely #1 without a doubt.
- (E) What for?
- Because a 12-inch roller and the excellent rating of the typed copy and freedom from paper shift.
- Noise is not important to me . . . I don't care about the extra key it has . . . 44 standard keys . . . and it has pica type . . .
- And the price is insignificant because it's about the same.

ment on the processing and usage of the available information, a second series of models was required, more detailed than the choice programs. These models, called "detailed choice programs," had to account for all the usages of operators and all the basic entities upon which they were applied. In fact, this second type of model represents the lowest level of aggregation we could achieve. Many higher-order operators (such as HCOMP, CORREL, and COMPEVAL) could not be described in more detail, because these details do not appear in the protocols; however, a particular effort was made to build models that could allow us to follow every transition of the subject's search path in the brand *x* attributes matrix. This second series of models was used to compare the amount and the intensity of the processing performed in different experimental situations. Exhibits 1 and 2 provide an example of each of the two types of models for Subject 20; the corresponding protocol is shown in Exhibit 3.

RESULTS

As this portion of our results focuses on choice strategies, the analysis was performed with the more aggregated models, the "choice programs." An examination of the major structural elements highlighted by the programs led to two levels of analysis:

- First, from the comparative analysis, two main types of model emerged. For one group of subjects, we could distinctly identify a two-step strategy. In a first step, using noncompensatory evaluation rules, they eliminated some brands, while in a second step, they proceeded with a compensatory comparison of the remaining brands (dynamic trade-off). The other group of subjects showed no evidence of such a round of eliminations. As shown in Table 1, the choice strategy used, one-step or two-step, is contingent upon the number of alternative brands available.

- Second, we could observe different input strategies. Different search paths in the brand *x* attribute matrix were used by the subjects. While most of the subjects proceeded by brands, some subjects used mixed strategies or proceeded by attributes.

Obviously, these two levels are not independent: the input process or the evaluative strategy cannot be considered separately from the overall strategy used by the subject. Nevertheless, in our analysis they will be treated separately.

160

THE JOURNAL OF CONSUMER RESEARCH

FIGURE A

STEP ONE OF THE TWO-STEP ELIMINATION MODEL:
NONCOMPENSATORY ELIMINATION PHASE

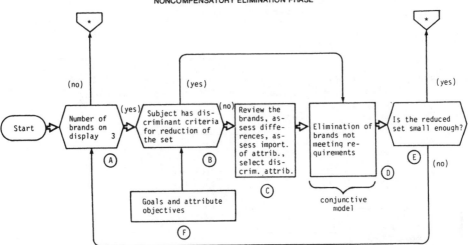

TABLE 1

STRATEGY TYPES BY NUMBER OF ALTERNATIVES
AND ATTRIBUTES PER ALTERNATIVE

| | Number of attributes per alternative | | | | | | | |
| | 5 | | 10 | | 15 | | Total | |
Number of alternatives	One-step	Two-step	One-step	Two-step	One-step	Two-step	One-step	Two-step
3	2	1	3	0	3	0	8	1
6	1	2	0	3	1	2	2	7
12	0	3	0	3	0	3	0	9
Total	3	6	3	6	4	5	10	17

The Two-Step Elimination Model

A comparison of the choice programs of the 27 subjects revealed that no two subjects proceeded in exactly the same way. However, similarities were found for the major aspects of the strategies, and two broad classes of models comprising all individual cases were finally identified. Furthermore, these two classes of models, labelled the one-step compensatory model and the two-step elimination model, appear to be two separate cases of the two-step strategy (Figures A and B).[6] Table 2 summarizes the frequency of occurrence of each type

of rule used and the number of alternatives remaining after the first step, by condition by subject.

As indicated in Figures A and B, the number of brands on display was a major determinant of choice strategy. Subjects who were offered a large number of brands (Box A) used the two-step approach. Using a noncompensatory model, they rapidly eliminated certain brands, and then they used a form of compensatory evaluation process to choose one of the remaining brands. Subjects who were offered a smaller set of brands skipped the elimination phase and immediately started with the compensatory process. The exact number of brands required to trigger the elimination phase varied by subjects, but generally the subjects who were offered more than three brands used such a process.

The elimination phase (Box D) is very similar to the conjunctive model proposed in other studies (Coombs 1964; Einhorn 1970; Simon 1957).[7] Each alternative brand was evaluated on several criteria. If it did not satisfy all the desired criteria above some minimum cut-off level, it was rejected. Several attributes were typically involved, but a brand was usually rejected because it did not satisfy one or two attributes (three at most). In only three cases did the protocol suggest that the alternatives were systematically evaluated on the basis of a single attribute, which is suggestive of a

---

[6]A simplified choice program for each subject in each condition is available from the authors.

[7]According to the conjunctive model, a multidimensional alternative $x = (x_1, x_2, \ldots, x_n)$ is judged acceptable only if $x_i > y_i$ for all i, where $y = (y_1, y_2, \ldots, y_n)$ is the standard.

FIGURE B

STEP TWO OF THE TWO-STEP ELIMINATION MODEL:
COMPENSATORY EVALUATION PHASE

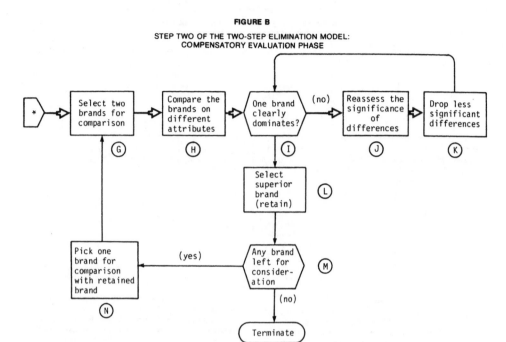

TABLE 2

FREQUENCY OF OCCURRENCE OF CONJUNCTIVE AND COMPENSATORY RULES, AND NUMBER
OF ALTERNATIVES REMAINING, BY CONDITION BY SUBJECT

| | Number of attributes per alternative | | | | | | | | | | | |
| | 5 | | | | 10 | | | | 15 | | | |
Number of alternatives	Subject	Conjunctive rule	Alternatives remaining	Compensatory rule	Subject	Conjunctive rule	Alternatives remaining	Compensatory rule	Subject	Conjunctive rule	Alternatives remaining	Compensatory rule
3	9	1	2	1	8	0	3	2	7	0	3	2
	18	0	3	2	17	0	3	3	16	0	3	2
	27	0	3	2	26	0	3	2	25	0	3	2
6	6	4	2	1	5	5	3	2	4	0	6	5
	15	1	5	4	14	3	3	2	13	4	2	1
	24	0	6	5	23	4	2	1	22	4	2	1
12	3	9	3	3	2	7	5	4	1	10	2	1
	12	8	4	3	11	8	4	3	10	11	1	11
	21	9	3	2	20	10	2	1	19	10	2	1

162   THE JOURNAL OF CONSUMER RESEARCH

lexicographic or elimination-by-aspects model (Tversky 1972). When this latter strategy occurred, it seemed to be part of a familiarization process during which the subjects established their criteria for elimination (Boxes B and C).

In fact, most of the subjects made a fairly complete review of the brands before rejecting any of them. This review (Box C) was usually a straightforward reading of the information cards—occasionally some comments were made about the range or the importance of certain attributes, and the relationships between different attributes were assessed. The subjects usually reduced the number of brands to three or four, which suggests that three or four brands is about the largest set of brands they could examine with a compensatory comparative approach.

Compared to the apparent complexity of the protocols, this part of the model may seem to be a simplistic description of the elimination phase. However, it appears to contain all of the essential elements. The complex and apparently erratic behavior observed in the protocols mainly results from the fact that the discrimination process itself (Box D) was preceded by a familiarization phase (Box C), during which the subject reacted mainly to visual cues to review rapidly the mass of information and develop a general perception of the product offering. Furthermore, some of the input operations had to be repeated because of memory limitations.

In the second phase, a systematic pairwise comparison of the brands was performed to arrive at a final choice. This process was compensatory in the sense that when both brands involved in a particular comparison had some positive and negative attributes, trade-offs were made among attributes to identify which brand was superior. This concept is not new, as it is the central hypothesis of the well known expectancy-value (E-V) theory. However, the structure of this process as revealed by our protocols is quite different from the structure proposed in E-V models. Traditionally, compensatory processes are associated with a weighted summation model. Even if they did not fully reveal the structure of compensatory evaluation processes, the protocols gave us sufficient indication to formulate different hypotheses about the structure of this process. We are led to believe that it is an algorithm based on successive assessments of the differences between the two brands, very similar to the additive difference model proposed by Tversky (Tversky 1969; see also Russo and Rosen 1975), as described in Figure B.

This sequential model of compensatory evaluation seems more realistic than the E-V model, since it involves very simple operations. The basic comparison operation identified in the problem-space is the only required operator and, because the information is processed sequentially, it requires very little from memory. Such a process seems more compatible with the fact that the human brain is a serial processor exhibiting limited capacity with respect to short-term memory. It is a compensatory process, because trade-offs are made between attributes to resolve conflicting situations. However, it is not a perfectly compensatory process like the one generally assumed in the E-V theory. Even if both the absolute value of the difference observed between two brands and the importance of the attribute involved determine the significance of this difference, the process appears to be nonlinear, since, for certain attributes, there is a threshold level below which the differences are ignored. Furthermore, it is a stepwise process involving several independent judgments. Therefore, we suspect that the evaluation criteria vary during the process.

Considering these facts, one could argue that this is not a compensatory evaluation process, if such a process is defined strictly in terms of a mathematical model. However, we think that our model is an adequate description of the way in which consumers make trade-offs in evaluation judgments.

The other dimension of the task environment, the number of attributes, does not seem to influence the basic character of the choice strategy. Subjects who were provided with more attributes about each brand reacted in the same way as those who received less. However, a look at their detailed choice program reveals that if they used a simplifying strategy it was another type of simplification. Most of the subjects used a differential weighting process to compare the brands. This allowed them to drop several attributes from the process. Generally, we found that compensatory comparisons involved a limited number of attributes (up to five attributes). Even when more attributes were available, the subjects did not really use them to compare brands, at least in the comparative part of the process.[8]

The Input Strategy

As previously described, several researchers interpreted the search strategy used by subjects as they proceeded through an information matrix as indirect evidence for the type of choice process being used. From the "choice programs" we could also classify subjects by the type of search strategy used, by brand, by attribute, or by some combination of these two search strategies.

We found 13 subjects who processed the information almost exclusively by brand. Nine other subjects also proceeded mainly by brand. This second group of subjects differs from the first group in that they processed one or two attributes before switching to a by-brand process. Examination of the choice programs of these

---

[8]This conclusion is based on a qualitative observation of the protocols. The quantitative analysis presented later does not support this conclusion, as these data include all references to product attributes, including those occurring during the elimination phase.

subjects reveals that the process-by-attributes approach was used at the beginning of the program to evaluate the range of a particular attribute or to check the correlation between two features. For 22 of our 27 subjects, the search path in the information matrix is systematically by brands. Three subjects used a mixed approach. Their protocols reveal that they largely reacted to cues. This erratic input process was largely confined to the first part of the protocols; the subjects were getting familiar with the brands and establishing their decision criteria. Later on, when the criteria were set, they generally returned to a systematic by-brand process. Only two subjects, both in a three-alternative condition, processed fully by attributes.

Though most of the subjects largely processed by brand, differences were observed, and we finally classified the subjects into four groups—those who processed by brand (13); those who first reviewed one or two attributes and then switched to a process by-brand approach (9); those who mixed by-brand and by-attribute processing (3); and those who processed by attribute (2).

There is a progression in these four groups with respect to the amount of processing performed by attributes, and we used these groups to evaluate the effects of the task environment on the input process. The resulting comparison showed that none of the experimental variables seemed to affect the nature of the input process. Over all brand and attribute treatments, input by brand dominates the process.

The experimental procedure probably accounts for this result. Each brand was described on a 5- × 7-inch card, and the cards were placed on a table; as the subjects could not manipulate the cards, it was easier for them to proceed by brands. However, the fact that processing by brand also appears in the three-brand condition indicates that it may be a natural way to proceed. (In the three-brand condition, there were only three cards on display; because the information on each card was presented in the same way and same order, and because the cards were side-by-side in front of the subject, it would have been easy to process by attributes.)

The finding that nearly all subjects searched by brand is not necessarily inconsistent with the finding that several subjects used a one-step, compensatory strategy. For if these subjects stored in memory the value of the relevant attributes of the standard, this would have precluded the need for overt search by attribute across brands. Alternatively, the incompleteness of the protocols and the particular coding procedures adopted here may account for this apparent inconsistency.

Effect of Alternatives and Attributes Per Alternative: Quantitative Indices

In order to compare choice strategies in a more quantitative way, we developed indices measuring the

TABLE 3

RATIO OF TOTAL NUMBER OF DIFFERENT ATTRIBUTES
REFERENCED TO TOTAL INFORMATION AVAILABLE,
BY NUMBER OF ALTERNATIVES AND ATTRIBUTES
PER ALTERNATIVE

Number of alternatives	Number of attributes per alternative		
	5	10	15
3	1.00	0.93	0.82
6	0.73	0.52	0.71
12	0.48	0.41	0.50

amount of processing performed by the subjects and the extent to which they could have concentrated their processing on a subset of the available information. The "detailed choice program" representation of our subjects' protocols was used to develop these indices, which indicate the number of times and the order in which certain operations or information were used by the subjects.

Each time a subject mentioned a particular attribute for a given brand, it was counted as a reference. We then computed the ratio of the total number of references to the total amount of information available in each condition (number of brands × number of attributes). An analysis of variance showed that as the number of alternative brands increased, there was a significant decrease in the ratio ($F = 16.6, p < 0.01$), but there was no significant effect due to the number of attributes presented per brand. From this, we may infer that as the number of alternatives increased, proportionately less information was used. Payne (1976) found that the proportion of information searched decreased with both the number of alternatives and the number of attributes per alternative. The difference in our results might be due to procedural differences; Payne's analysis was based only on measures of search processes, whereas our data represent combined search and evaluation processes.

Next we counted the number of different information units referenced, to eliminate the effects of multiple references to the same type of attribute for each alternative. We then constructed a ratio of the number of different information units referenced to the total amount of information available in each condition. An analysis of variance of these data (Table 3) indicates that only the number of brands had a significant effect ($F = 25.1, p < 0.01$). As the number of brands increased, the proportion of different information used to that which was available decreased.

The third quantitative measure of information processing activity was the ratio of the number of references made to each product attribute to the number of different attributes referenced. This index measures the intensity of processing over the attributes used by the subject. We expected that with the increase in the number of different information units referenced over increasing values of alternatives and attributes, the intensity of usage of this information would decrease. Analysis of variance of these data revealed that the apparent decrease in this index as number of brands increased was not quite significant at the 0.05 level, and the effect of number of attributes was not significant.

DISCUSSION

These results provide additional support for the recent conclusion that brand choice strategy is contingent upon the character of external task environment. We found that the number of alternative brands had a major influence on the type of strategy used. When the number of alternatives was small (three), subjects evaluated alternatives using a compensatory strategy; when the number of alternatives was increased (to six and 12), subjects used a more complex, two-stage strategy. In the first stage, a noncompensatory (conjunctive) strategy was used to eliminate unacceptable alternatives. In the second stage, a compensatory strategy was used to evaluate the remaining alternatives (usually three or four).

Our results are nearly identical with those reported by Payne (1976). However, we found little evidence for an elimination-by-aspects strategy, and we found strong evidence of a multi-staged or phased strategy for those conditions with a larger number of alternatives. Payne mentions the possibility of a phased strategy, and cites one subject as providing clear evidence of such a strategy. In 16 of 18 conditions where the number of alternatives was greater than three, we found clear evidence for a phased strategy. Other researchers have also presented evidence for a phased strategy (Einhorn 1971; Park 1978; Wright and Barbour 1977). The difference observed between our results and Payne's may be due to the information format; Payne used a display board and we used separate cards for each brand, which could not be manipulated.

We interpret our results within Newell and Simon's (1972) information processing theory. Given the existence of certain types of information processing constraints (e.g., serial processor, limited rate of processing, and limited memory capacity), our subjects selected strategies that permitted them to achieve their goal of selecting the best brand (or a satisfactory brand) within each particular task environment. When too many brands were presented, a noncompensatory screening strategy allowed for the rapid reduction to a more manageable size. The pairwise compensatory strategy allowed remaining alternatives to be evaluated on several attributes in a way that greatly reduced the number of operations and the load on memory. The differential weighting of attributes reduced the total number of attributes actually considered.

In view of the qualifications described earlier, it is difficult to generalize these results. Yet we already know that in real life situations consumers usually con-

sider a limited set of brands (i.e., the evoked set). However, we do not know how they determine which brands will be considered. For choice situations where products and brands are very familiar, we may presume that factors such as knowledge, beliefs, and attitudes (from prior experience, promotion, etc.) greatly influence this selection process. This study suggests, at least for unfamiliar brands, that alternatives are evaluated in a noncompensatory fashion and are eliminated if only one or very few desired attributes are below the cut-off value. More research is needed to test the results in actual situations and to understand what factors determine which attributes are discriminant.

The next phase in the analysis of decision behavior within Newell and Simon's information processing theory is the development of a computer program to simulate the behavior observed in each of our experimental conditions. The model presented here may be seen as a step in that direction. The different choice strategies identified here and in other studies can be viewed as subroutines that are called upon, separately or in combination, in response to certain aspects of the external task environment. Before such a comprehensive model of contingent processing can be formulated and tested (at both the process and outcome levels), more information is required about certain crucial processes. At the present time, protocol analysis represents the only available technique for identifying these processes. Additional details about these processes might be obtainable through the design of further studies that require decisions for a more complete set of alternatives or that require subjects to rank all available alternatives instead of simply selecting one (e.g., Olshavsky and Acito 1979). Another approach that might provide the needed detail is to couple other process-tracing methodologies with the protocol analysis technique (Payne 1976; Russo and Rosen 1975; Russo 1978).

[Received June 1978. Revised April 1979.]

REFERENCES

Bettman, James R. (1970), "Information Processing Models of Consumer Behavior," *Journal of Marketing Research*, 7, 370–6.

——— (1974), "Decision Net Models of Buyer Information Processing and Choice: Findings, Problems, and Prospects," in *Buyer/Consumer Information Processing*, eds. G. David Hughes and Michael L. Ray, Chapel Hill: University of North Carolina Press, pp. 59–74.

——— (1976), "Data Collection and Analysis Approaches for Studying Consumer Information Processing," in *Advances in Consumer Research, Vol. 4*, ed. William D. Perreault, Jr., Chicago: Association for Consumer Research, pp. 342–8.

———, and Kakkar, Pradeep (1977), "Effects of Information Presentation Format on Consumer Information Acquisition Strategy," *Journal of Consumer Research*, 3, 233–40.

————, and Michael A. Zins (1977), "Constructive Processes in Consumer Choice," *Journal of Consumer Research*, 4, 75–85.

Coombs, C. H. (1964), *A Theory of Data*, New York: John Wiley & Sons, Inc.

Einhorn, Hillel J. (1971), "Use of Nonlinear, Noncompensatory Models as a Function of Task and Amount of Information," *Organizational Behavior and Human Performance*, 6, 1–27.

———— (1970), "The Use of Nonlinear, Noncompensatory Models in Decision Making," *Psychological Bulletin*, 73, 211–30.

Jacoby, Jacob, Szybillo, George J., and Busato-Schach, Jacqueline (1977), "Information Acquisition Behavior in Brand Choice Situations," *Journal of Consumer Research*, 3, 209–16.

Lussier, Denis A., and Olshavsky, Richard W. (1974), "An Information Processing Approach to Brand Choice Behavior," paper presented at the Operations Research Society of America/The Institute of Management Sciences Joint National Meeting, San Juan, Puerto Rico.

Newell, Allen, and Simon, Herbert A. (1972), *Human Problem Solving*, Englewood Cliffs, NJ: Prentice-Hall, Inc.

Olshavsky, Richard W., and Acito, Frank (1979), "Conjoint Analysis and Protocol Analysis—A Simultaneous Approach," working paper, Graduate School of Business, Indiana University.

Park, C. Whan (1978), "A Seven-Point Scale and a Decision Maker's Simplifying Choice Strategy: An Operationalized Satisficing-Plus Model," *Organizational Behavior and Human Performance*, 22, 252–71.

Payne, John W. (1976), "Task Complexity and Contingent Processing in Decision Making: An Information Search and Protocol Analysis," *Organizational Behavior and Human Performance*, 16, 366–87.

————, Braunstein, Myron L., and Carroll, John S. (1978), "Exploring Predecisional Behavior: An Alternative Approach to Decision Research," *Organizational Behavior and Human Performance*, 22, 17–44.

van Raaij, W. Fred (1976), "Direct Monitoring of Consumer Information Processing by Eye Movement Recorder," Tilburg Papers on Consumer Evaluation Processes, No. 12, Tilburg University, The Netherlands.

Russo, J. Edward (1978), "Eye Fixations Can Save the World: A Critical Comparison Between Eye Fixations and Other Information Processing Methodologies," in *Advances in Consumer Behavior Vol. 5*, ed. H. Keith Hunt, Chicago: Association for Consumer Research, pp. 561–70.

————, and Dosher, Barbara A. (1975), "Dimensional Evaluation: A Heuristic for Binary Choice," unpublished working paper, Department of Psychology, University of California, San Diego.

————, and Rosen, Larry D. (1975), "An Eye Fixation Analysis of Multi-Alternative Choice," *Memory and Cognition*, 3, 267–76.

Scammon, Debra L. (1977), "Information Load and Consumers," *Journal of Consumer Research*, 4, 148–55.

Simon, Herbert A. (1957), *Models of Man*, New York: John Wiley & Sons, Inc.

Tversky, Amos (1969), "Intransitivity of Preferences," *Psychological Review*, 76, 31–48.

———— (1972), "Elimination by Aspects: A Theory of Choice," *Psychological Review*, 79, 281–99.

Wright, Peter L. (1974), "Research Orientations for Analyzing Consumer Judgment Processes," in *Advances in Consumer Research, Vol. 1*, eds. Scott Ward and Peter L. Wright, Chicago: Association for Consumer Research, pp. 268–79.

————, and Barbour, Frederic (1977), "Phased Decision Strategies: Sequels to Initial Screening," in *Management Science*, (Special Issue) *Studies in Management Sciences, Multiple Criteria Decision-Making, Vol. 6*, eds. M. K. Starr and M. Zeleny, New York: North-Holland, pp. 91–110.

[14]

Psychological Review
1996, Vol. 103, No. 4, 650–669

Reasoning the Fast and Frugal Way: Models of Bounded Rationality

Gerd Gigerenzer and Daniel G. Goldstein
Max Planck Institute for Psychological Research and University of Chicago

Humans and animals make inferences about the world under limited time and knowledge. In contrast, many models of rational inference treat the mind as a Laplacean Demon, equipped with unlimited time, knowledge, and computational might. Following H. Simon's notion of satisficing, the authors have proposed a family of algorithms based on a simple psychological mechanism: one-reason decision making. These fast and frugal algorithms violate fundamental tenets of classical rationality: They neither look up nor integrate all information. By computer simulation, the authors held a competition between the satisficing "Take The Best" algorithm and various "rational" inference procedures (e.g., multiple regression). The Take The Best algorithm matched or outperformed all competitors in inferential speed and accuracy. This result is an existence proof that cognitive mechanisms capable of successful performance in the real world do not need to satisfy the classical norms of rational inference.

Organisms make inductive inferences. Darwin (1872/1965) observed that people use facial cues, such as eyes that waver and lids that hang low, to infer a person's guilt. Male toads, roaming through swamps at night, use the pitch of a rival's croak to infer its size when deciding whether to fight (Krebs & Davies, 1987). Stock brokers must make fast decisions about which of several stocks to trade or invest when only limited information is available. The list goes on. Inductive inferences are typically based on uncertain cues: The eyes can deceive, and so can a tiny toad with a deep croak in the darkness.

How does an organism make inferences about unknown aspects of the environment? There are three directions in which to look for an answer. From Pierre Laplace to George Boole to Jean Piaget, many scholars have defended the now classical view that the laws of human inference are the laws of probability and statistics (and to a lesser degree logic, which does not deal as easily with uncertainty). Indeed, the Enlightenment probabilists derived the laws of probability from what they believed to be the laws of human reasoning (Daston, 1988). Following this time-honored tradition, much contemporary research in psychology, behavioral ecology, and economics assumes standard

Gerd Gigerenzer and Daniel G. Goldstein, Center for Adaptive Behavior and Cognition, Max Planck Institute for Psychological Research, Munich, Germany, and Department of Psychology, University of Chicago.

This research was funded by National Science Foundation Grant SBR-9320797/GG.

We are deeply grateful to the many people who have contributed to this article, including Hal Arkes, Leda Cosmides, Jean Czerlinski, Lorraine Daston, Ken Hammond, Reid Hastie, Wolfgang Hell, Ralph Hertwig, Ulrich Hoffrage, Albert Madansky, Laura Martignon, Geoffrey Miller, Silvia Papai, John Payne, Terry Regier, Werner Schubö, Peter Sedlmeier, Herbert Simon, Stephen Stigler, Gerhard Strube, Zeno Swijtink, John Tooby, William Wimsatt, and Werner Wittmann.

Correspondence concerning this article should be addressed to Gerd Gigerenzer or Daniel G. Goldstein, Center for Adaptive Behavior and Cognition, Max Planck Institute for Psychological Research, Leopoldstrasse 24, 80802 Munich, Germany. Electronic mail may be sent via Internet to giger@mpipf-muenchen.mpg.de.

statistical tools to be the normative and descriptive models of inference and decision making. Multiple regression, for instance, is both the economist's universal tool (McCloskey, 1985) and a model of inductive inference in multiple-cue learning (Hammond, 1990) and clinical judgment (B. Brehmer, 1994); Bayes's theorem is a model of how animals infer the presence of predators or prey (Stephens & Krebs, 1986) as well as of human reasoning and memory (Anderson, 1990). This Enlightenment view that probability theory and human reasoning are two sides of the same coin crumbled in the early nineteenth century but has remained strong in psychology and economics.

In the past 25 years, this stronghold came under attack by proponents of the heuristics and biases program, who concluded that human inference is systematically biased and error prone, suggesting that the laws of inference are quick-and-dirty heuristics and not the laws of probability (Kahneman, Slovic, & Tversky, 1982). This second perspective appears diametrically opposed to the classical rationality of the Enlightenment, but this appearance is misleading. It has retained the normative kernel of the classical view. For example, a discrepancy between the dictates of classical rationality and actual reasoning is what defines a *reasoning error* in this program. Both views accept the laws of probability and statistics as normative, but they disagree about whether humans can stand up to these norms.

Many experiments have been conducted to test the validity of these two views, identifying a host of conditions under which the human mind appears more rational or irrational. But most of this work has dealt with simple situations, such as Bayesian inference with binary hypotheses, one single piece of binary data, and all the necessary information conveniently laid out for the participant (Gigerenzer & Hoffrage, 1995). In many real-world situations, however, there are multiple pieces of information, which are not independent, but redundant. Here, Bayes's theorem and other "rational" algorithms quickly become mathematically complex and computationally intractable, at least for ordinary human minds. These situations make neither of the two views look promising. If one would apply the classical view to such complex real-world environments, this would suggest that the mind is a supercalculator like a Laplacean Demon (Wimsatt, 1976)—carrying around the collected works of Kolmogoroff, Fisher, or Neyman—and simply needs a memory jog, like the slave in Plato's *Meno*. On the other hand, the heuristics-and-biases view of human irrationality would lead us to believe that humans are hopelessly lost in the face of real-world complexity, given their supposed inability to reason according to the canon of classical rationality, even in simple laboratory experiments.

There is a third way to look at inference, focusing on the psychological and ecological rather than on logic and probability theory. This view questions classical rationality as a universal norm and thereby questions the very definition of "good" reasoning on which both the Enlightenment and the heuristics-and-biases views were built. Herbert Simon, possibly the best-known proponent of this third view, proposed looking for models of *bounded rationality* instead of classical rationality. Simon (1956, 1982) argued that information-processing systems typically need to *satisfice* rather than optimize. *Satisficing*, a blend of *sufficing* and *satisfying*, is a word of Scottish origin, which Simon uses to characterize algorithms that successfully deal with conditions of limited time, knowledge, or computational capacities. His concept of satisficing postulates, for instance, that an organism would choose the first object (a mate, perhaps) that satisfies its aspiration level—instead of the intractable sequence of taking the time to survey all possible alternatives, estimating probabilities and utilities for the possible outcomes associated with each alternative, calculating expected utilities, and choosing the alternative that scores highest.

Let us stress that Simon's notion of bounded rationality has two sides, one cognitive and one ecological. As early as in *Administrative Behavior* (1945), he emphasized the cognitive limitations of real minds as opposed to the omniscient Laplacean Demons of classical rationality. As early as in his *Psychological Review* article titled "Rational Choice and the Structure of the Environment" (1956), Simon emphasized that minds are adapted to real-world environments. The two go in tandem: "Human rational behavior is shaped by a scissors whose two blades are the structure of task environments and the computational capabilities of the actor" (Simon, 1990, p. 7). For the most part, however, theories of human inference have focused exclusively on the cognitive side, equating the notion of bounded rationality with the statement that humans are limited information processors, period. In a Procrustean-bed fashion, *bounded rationality* became almost synonymous with *heuristics and biases*, thus paradoxically reassuring classical rationality as the normative standard for both biases and bounded rationality (for a discussion of this confusion see Lopes, 1992). Simon's insight that the minds of living systems should be understood relative to the environment in which they evolved, rather than to the tenets of classical rationality, has had little impact so far in research on human inference. Simple psychological algorithms that were observed in human inference, reasoning, or decision making were often discredited without a fair trial, because they looked so stupid by the norms of classical rationality. For instance, when Keeney and Raiffa (1993) discussed the lexicographic ordering procedure they had observed in practice—a procedure related to the class of satisficing algorithms we propose in this article—they concluded that this procedure "is naively simple" and "will rarely pass a test of

'reasonableness'" (p. 78). They did not report such a test. We shall.

Initially, the concept of bounded rationality was only vaguely defined, often as that which is not classical economics, and one could "fit a lot of things into it by foresight and hindsight," as Simon (1992, p. 18) himself put it. We wish to do more than oppose the Laplacean Demon view. We strive to come up with something positive that could replace this unrealistic view of mind. What are these simple, intelligent algorithms capable of making near-optimal inferences? How fast and how accurate are they? In this article, we propose a class of models that exhibit bounded rationality in both of Simon's senses. These satisficing algorithms operate with simple psychological principles that satisfy the constraints of limited time, knowledge, and computational might, rather than those of classical rationality. At the same time, they are designed to be fast and frugal without a significant loss of inferential accuracy, because the algorithms can exploit the structure of environments.

The article is organized as follows. We begin by describing the task the cognitive algorithms are designed to address, the basic algorithm itself, and the real-world environment on which the performance of the algorithm will be tested. Next, we report on a competition in which a satisficing algorithm competes with "rational" algorithms in making inferences about a real-world environment. The "rational" algorithms start with an advantage: They use more time, information, and computational might to make inferences. Finally, we study variants of the satisficing algorithm that make faster inferences and get by with even less knowledge.

The Task

We deal with inferential tasks in which a choice must be made between two alternatives on a quantitative dimension. Consider the following example:

Which city has a larger population? (a) Hamburg (b) Cologne.

Two-alternative-choice tasks occur in various contexts in which inferences need to be made with limited time and knowledge, such as in decision making and risk assessment during driving (e.g., exit the highway now or stay on); treatment-allocation decisions (e.g., who to treat first in the emergency room: the 80-year-old heart attack victim or the 16-year-old car accident victim); and financial decisions (e.g., whether to buy or sell in the trading pit). Inference concerning population demographics, such as city populations of the past, present, and future (e.g., Brown & Siegler, 1993), is of importance to people working in urban planning, industrial development, and marketing. Population demographics, which is better understood than, say, the stock market, will serve us later as a "drosophila" environment that allows us to analyze the behavior of satisficing algorithms.

We study two-alternative-choice tasks in situations where a person has to make an inference based solely on knowledge retrieved from memory. We refer to this as *inference from memory*, as opposed to *inference from givens*. Inference from memory involves search in declarative knowledge and has been investigated in studies of, inter alia, confidence in general knowledge (e.g., Juslin, 1994; Sniezek & Buckley, 1993); the

GIGERENZER AND GOLDSTEIN

effect of repetition on belief (e.g., Hertwig, Gigerenzer, & Hoffrage, in press); hindsight bias (e.g., Fischhoff, 1977); quantitative estimates of area and population of nations (Brown & Siegler, 1993); and autobiographic memory of time (Huttenlocher, Hedges, & Prohaska, 1988). Studies of inference from givens, on the other hand, involve making inferences from information presented by an experimenter (e.g., Hammond, Hursch, & Todd, 1964). In the tradition of Ebbinghaus's nonsense syllables, attempts are often made here to prevent individual knowledge from impacting on the results by using problems about hypothetical referents instead of actual ones. For instance, in celebrated judgment and decision-making tasks, such as the "cab" problem and the "Linda" problem, all the relevant information is provided by the experimenter, and individual knowledge about cabs and hit-and-run accidents, or feminist bank tellers, is considered of no relevance (Gigerenzer & Murray, 1987). As a consequence, limited knowledge or individual differences in knowledge play a small role in inference from givens. In contrast, the satisficing algorithms proposed in this article perform inference from memory, they use limited knowledge as input, and as we will show, they can actually profit from a lack of knowledge.

Assume that a person does not know or cannot deduce the answer to the Hamburg–Cologne question but needs to make an inductive inference from related real-world knowledge. How is this inference derived? How can we predict choice (Hamburg or Cologne) from a person's state of knowledge?

Theory

The cognitive algorithms we propose are realizations of a framework for modeling inferences from memory, the theory of *probabilistic mental models* (PMM theory; see Gigerenzer, 1993; Gigerenzer, Hoffrage, & Kleinbölting, 1991). The theory of probabilistic mental models assumes that inferences about unknown states of the world are based on probability cues (Brunswik, 1955). The theory relates three visions: (a) Inductive inference needs to be studied with respect to natural environments, as emphasized by Brunswik and Simon; (b) inductive inference is carried out by satisficing algorithms, as emphasized by Simon; and (c) inductive inferences are based on frequencies of events in a reference class, as proposed by Reichenbach and other frequentist statisticians. The theory of probabilistic mental models accounts for choice and confidence, but only choice is addressed in this article.

The major thrust of the theory is that it replaces the canon of classical rationality with simple, plausible psychological mechanisms of inference—mechanisms that a mind can actually carry out under limited time and knowledge and that could have possibly arisen through evolution. Most traditional models of inference, from linear multiple regression models to Bayesian models to neural networks, try to find some optimal integration of all information available: Every bit of information is taken into account, weighted, and combined in a computationally expensive way. The family of algorithms in PMM theory does not implement this classical ideal. Search in memory for relevant information is reduced to a minimum, and there is no integration (but rather a substitution) of pieces of information. These satisficing algorithms dispense with the fiction of the omniscient Laplacean Demon, who has all the time and knowledge

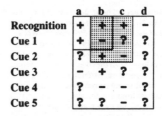

	a	b	c	d
Recognition	+	+	+	−
Cue 1	+	−	?	?
Cue 2	?	+	?	?
Cue 3	−	+	?	?
Cue 4	?	−	−	?
Cue 5	?	?	−	?

Figure 1. Illustration of bounded search through limited knowledge. Objects *a*, *b*, and *c* are recognized; object *d* is not. Cue values are positive (+) or negative (−); missing knowledge is shown by question marks. Cues are ordered according to their validities. To infer whether *a* > *b*, the Take The Best algorithm looks up only the cue values in the shaded space; to infer whether *b* > *c*, search is bounded to the dotted space. The other cue values are not looked up.

to search for all relevant information, to compute the weights and covariances, and then to integrate all this information into an inference.

Limited Knowledge

A PMM is an inductive device that uses limited knowledge to make fast inferences. Different from mental models of syllogisms and deductive inference (Johnson-Laird, 1983), which focus on the logical task of truth preservation and where knowledge is irrelevant (except for the meaning of connectives and other logical terms), PMMs perform intelligent guesses about unknown features of the world, based on uncertain indicators. To make an inference about which of two objects, *a* or *b*, has a higher value, knowledge about a reference class *R* is searched, with *a*, *b* ∈ *R*. In our example, knowledge about the reference class "cities in Germany" could be searched. The knowledge consists of probability cues C_i ($i = 1, \ldots, n$), and the cue values a_i and b_i of the objects for the *i*th cue. For instance, when making inferences about populations of German cities, the fact that a city has a professional soccer team in the major league (*Bundesliga*) may come to a person's mind as a potential cue. That is, when considering pairs of German cities, if one city has a soccer team in the major league and the other does not, then the city with the team is likely, but not certain, to have the larger population.

Limited knowledge means that the matrix of objects by cues has missing entries (i.e., objects, cues, or cue values may be unknown). Figure 1 models the limited knowledge of a person. She has heard of three German cities, *a*, *b*, and *c*, but not of *d* (represented by three positive and one negative recognition values). She knows some facts (cue values) about these cities with respect to five binary cues. For a binary cue, there are two cue values, positive (e.g., the city has a soccer team) or negative (it does not). *Positive* refers to a cue value that signals a higher value on the target variable (e.g., having a soccer team is correlated with high population). Unknown cue values are shown by a question mark. Because she has never heard of *d*, all cue values for object *d* are, by definition, unknown.

People rarely know all information on which an inference

could be based, that is, knowledge is limited. We model limited knowledge in two respects: A person can have (a) incomplete knowledge of the objects in the reference class (e.g., she recognizes only some of the cities), (b) limited knowledge of the cue values (facts about cities), or (c) both. For instance, a person who does not know all of the cities with soccer teams may know some cities with positive cue values (e.g., Munich and Hamburg certainly have teams), many with negative cue values (e.g., Heidelberg and Potsdam certainly do not have teams), and several cities for which cue values will not be known.

The Take The Best Algorithm

The first satisficing algorithm presented is called the *Take The Best* algorithm, because its policy is "take the best, ignore the rest." It is the basic algorithm in the PMM framework. Variants that work faster or with less knowledge are described later. We explain the steps of the Take The Best algorithm for binary cues (the algorithm can be easily generalized to many valued cues), using Figure 1 for illustration.

The Take The Best algorithm assumes a subjective rank order of cues according to their validities (as in Figure 1). We call the highest ranking cue (that discriminates between the two alternatives) the best cue. The algorithm is shown in the form of a flow diagram in Figure 2.

Step 1: Recognition Principle

The recognition principle is invoked when the mere recognition of an object is a predictor of the target variable (e.g., population). The recognition principle states the following: If only one of the two objects is recognized, then choose the recognized object. If neither of the two objects is recognized, then choose randomly between them. If both of the objects are recognized, then proceed to Step 2.

Example: If a person in the knowledge state shown in Figure

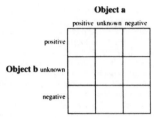

Figure 3. Discrimination rule. A cue discriminates between two alternatives if one has a positive cue value and the other does not. The four discriminating cases are shaded.

1 is asked to infer which of city *a* and city *d* has more inhabitants, the inference will be city *a*, because the person has never heard of city *d* before.

Step 2: Search for Cue Values

For the two objects, retrieve the cue values of the highest ranking cue from memory.

Step 3: Discrimination Rule

Decide whether the cue discriminates. The cue is said to discriminate between two objects if one has a positive cue value and the other does not. The four shaded knowledge states in Figure 3 are those in which a cue discriminates.

Step 4: Cue-Substitution Principle

If the cue discriminates, then stop searching for cue values. If the cue does not discriminate, go back to Step 2 and continue with the next cue until a cue that discriminates is found.

Step 5: Maximizing Rule for Choice

Choose the object with the positive cue value. If no cue discriminates, then choose randomly.

Examples: Suppose the task is judging which of city *a* or *b* is larger (Figure 1). Both cities are recognized (Step 1), and search for the best cue results with a positive and a negative cue value for Cue 1 (Step 2). The cue discriminates (Step 3), and search is terminated (Step 4). The person makes the inference that city *a* is larger (Step 5).

Suppose now the task is judging which of city *b* or *c* is larger. Both cities are recognized (Step 1), and search for the cue values cue results in negative cue value on object *b* for Cue 1, but the corresponding cue value for object *c* is unknown (Step 2). The cue does not discriminate (Step 3), so search is continued (Step 4). Search for the next cue results with positive and a negative cue values for Cue 2 (Step 2). This cue discriminates (Step 3), and search is terminated (Step 4). The person makes the inference that city *b* is larger (Step 5).

The features of this algorithm are (a) search extends through only a portion of the total knowledge in memory (as shown by the shaded and dotted parts of Figure 1) and is stopped imme-

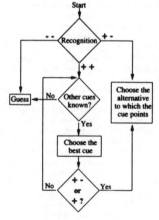

Figure 2. Flow diagram of the Take The Best algorithm.

diately when the first discriminating cue is found, (b) the algorithm does not attempt to integrate information but uses cue substitution instead, and (c) the total amount of information processed is contingent on each task (pair of objects) and varies in a predictable way among individuals with different knowledge. This fast and computationally simple algorithm is a model of bounded rationality rather than of classical rationality. There is a close parallel with Simon's concept of "satisficing": The Take The Best algorithm stops search after the first discriminating cue is found, just as Simon's satisficing algorithm stops search after the first option that meets an aspiration level.

The algorithm is hardly a standard statistical tool for inductive inference: It does not use all available information, it is noncompensatory and nonlinear, and variants of it can violate transitivity. Thus, it differs from standard linear tools for inference such as multiple regression, as well as from nonlinear neural networks that are compensatory in nature. The Take The Best algorithm is noncompensatory because only the best discriminating cue determines the inference or decision; no combination of other cue values can override this decision. In this way, the algorithm does not conform to the classical economic view of human behavior (e.g., Becker, 1976), where, under the assumption that all aspects can be reduced to one dimension (e.g., money), there exists always a trade-off between commodities or pieces of information. That is, the algorithm violates the Archimedian axiom, which implies that for any multidimensional object $a(a_1, a_2, \ldots, a_n)$ preferred to $b(b_1, b_2, \ldots, b_n)$, where a_1 dominates b_1, this preference can be reversed by taking multiples of any one or a combination of $b_2, b_3, \ldots, b_n$. As we discuss, variants of this algorithm also violate transitivity, one of the cornerstones of classical rationality (McClennen, 1990).

Empirical Evidence

Despite their flagrant violation of the traditional standards of rationality, the Take The Best algorithm and other models from the framework of PMM theory have been successful in integrating various striking phenomena in inference from memory and predicting novel phenomena, such as the confidence-frequency effect (Gigerenzer et al., 1991) and the less-is-more effect (Goldstein, 1994; Goldstein & Gigerenzer, 1996). The theory of probabilistic mental models seems to be the only existing process theory of the overconfidence bias that successfully predicts conditions under which overestimation occurs, disappears, and inverts to underestimation (Gigerenzer, 1993; Gigerenzer et al., 1991; Juslin, 1993, 1994; Juslin, Winman, & Persson, 1995; but see Griffin & Tversky, 1992). Similarly, the theory predicts when the hard–easy effect occurs, disappears, and inverts—predictions that have been experimentally confirmed by Hoffrage (1994) and by Juslin (1993). The Take The Best algorithm explains also why the popular confirmation-bias explanation of the overconfidence bias (Koriat, Lichtenstein, & Fischhoff, 1980) is not supported by experimental data (Gigerenzer et al., 1991, pp. 521–522).

Unlike earlier accounts of these striking phenomena in confidence and choice, the algorithms in the PMM framework allow for predictions of choice based on each individual's knowledge. Goldstein and Gigerenzer (1996) showed that the recognition principle predicted individual participants' choices in about 90% to 100% of all cases, even when participants were

taught information that suggested doing otherwise (negative cue values for the recognized objects). Among the evidence for the empirical validity of the Take-The-Best algorithm are the tests of a bold prediction, the less-is-more effect, which postulates conditions under which people with little knowledge make better inferences than those who know more. This surprising prediction has been experimentally confirmed. For instance, U.S. students make slightly more correct inferences about German city populations (about which they know little) than about U.S. cities, and vice versa for German students (Gigerenzer, 1993; Goldstein 1994; Goldstein & Gigerenzer, 1995; Hoffrage, 1994). The theory of probabilistic mental models has been applied to other situations in which inferences have to be made under limited time and knowledge, such as rumor-based stock market trading (DiFonzo, 1994). A general review of the theory and its evidence is presented in McClelland and Bolger (1994).

The reader familiar with the original algorithm presented in Gigerenzer et al. (1991) will have noticed that we simplified the discrimination rule.[1] In the present version, search is already terminated if one object has a positive cue value and the other does not, whereas in the earlier version, search was terminated only when one object had a positive value and the other a negative one (cf. Figure 3 in Gigerenzer et al. with Figure 3 in this article). This change follows empirical evidence that participants tend to use this faster, simpler discrimination rule (Hoffrage, 1994).

This article does not attempt to provide further empirical evidence. For the moment, we assume that the model is descriptively valid and investigate how accurate this satisficing algorithm is in drawing inferences about unknown aspects of a real-world environment. Can an algorithm based on simple psychological principles that violate the norms of classical rationality make a fair number of accurate inferences?

The Environment

We tested the performance of the Take The Best algorithm on how accurately it made inferences about a real-world environment. The environment was the set of all cities in Germany with more than 100,000 inhabitants (83 cities after German reunification), with population as the target variable. The model of the environment consisted of 9 binary ecological cues and the actual 9×83 cue values. The full model of the environment is shown in the Appendix.

Each cue has an associated validity, which is indicative of its predictive power. The *ecological validity* of a cue is the relative frequency with which the cue correctly predicts the target, defined with respect to the reference class (e.g., all German cities with more than 100,000 inhabitants). For instance, if one checks all pairs in which one city has a soccer team but the other city does not, one finds that in 87% of these cases, the city with the team also has the higher population. This value is the ecological validity of the soccer team cue. The validity v_i of the ith cue is

$$v_i = p[t(a) > t(b) | a_i \text{ is positive and } b_i \text{ is negative}],$$

---

[1] Also, we now use the term *discrimination rule* instead of *activation rule.*

Table 1

Cues, Ecological Validities, and Discrimination Rates

Cue	Ecological validity	Discrimination rate
National capital (Is the city the national capital?)	1.00	.02
Exposition site (Was the city once an exposition site?)	.91	.25
Soccer team (Does the city have a team in the major league?)	.87	.30
Intercity train (Is the city on the Intercity line?)	.78	.38
State capital (Is the city a state capital?)	.77	.30
License plate (Is the abbreviation only one letter long?)	.75	.34
University (Is the city home to a university?)	.71	.51
Industrial belt (Is the city in the industrial belt?)	.56	.30
East Germany (Was the city formerly in East Germany?)	.51	.27

where $t(a)$ and $t(b)$ are the values of objects a and b on the target variable t and p is a probability measured as a relative frequency in R.

The ecological validity of the nine cues ranged over the whole spectrum: from .51 (only slightly better than chance) to 1.0 (certainty), as shown in Table 1. A cue with a high ecological validity, however, is not often useful if its discrimination rate is small.

Table 1 shows also the *discrimination rates* for each cue. The discrimination rate of a cue is the relative frequency with which the cue discriminates between any two objects from the reference class. The discrimination rate is a function of the distribution of the cue values and the number N of objects in the reference class. Let the relative frequencies of the positive and negative cue values be x and y, respectively. Then the discrimination rate d_i of the ith cue is

$$d_i = \frac{2x_i y_i}{1 - \frac{1}{N}},$$

as an elementary calculation shows. Thus, if N is very large, the discrimination rate is approximately $2x_i y_i$.[2] The larger the ecological validity of a cue, the better the inference. The larger the discrimination rate, the more often a cue can be used to make an inference. In the present environment, ecological validities and discrimination rates are negatively correlated. The redundancy of cues in the environment, as measured by pairwise correlations between cues, ranges between $-.25$ and $.54$, with an average absolute value of .19.[3]

The Competition

The question of how well a satisficing algorithm performs in a real-world environment has rarely been posed in research on inductive inference. The present simulations seem to be the first to test how well simple satisficing algorithms do compared with standard integration algorithms, which require more knowl-

edge, time, and computational power. This question is important for Simon's postulated link between the cognitive and the ecological: If the simple psychological principles in satisficing algorithms are tuned to ecological structures, these algorithms should not fail outright. We propose a competition between various inferential algorithms. The contest will go to the algorithm that scores the highest proportion of correct inferences in the shortest time.

Simulating Limited Knowledge

We simulated people with varying degrees of knowledge about cities in Germany. Limited knowledge can take two forms. One is limited recognition of objects in the reference class. The other is limited knowledge about the cue values of recognized objects. To model limited recognition knowledge, we simulated people who recognized between 0 and 83 German cities. To model limited knowledge of cue values, we simulated 6 basic classes of people, who knew 0%, 10%, 20%, 50%, 75%, or 100% of the cue values associated with the objects they recognized. Combining the two sources of limited knowledge resulted in 6 × 84 types of people, each having different degrees and kinds of limited knowledge. Within each type of people, we created 500 simulated individuals, who differed randomly from one another in the particular objects and cue values they knew. All objects and cue values known were determined randomly within the appropriate constraints, that is, a certain number of objects known, a certain total percentage of cue values known, and the validity of the recognition principle (as explained in the following paragraph).

The simulation needed to be realistic in the sense that the simulated people could invoke the recognition principle. Therefore, the sets of cities the simulated people knew had to be carefully chosen so that the recognized cities were larger than the unrecognized ones a certain percentage of the time. We performed a survey to get an empirical estimate of the actual co-

---

[2] For instance, if $N = 2$ and one cue value is positive and the other negative ($x_i = y_i = .5$), $d_i = 1.0$. If N increases, with x_i and y_i held constant, then d_i decreases and converges to $2x_i y_i$.

[3] There are various other measures of redundancy besides pairwise correlation. The important point is that whatever measure of redundancy one uses, the resultant value does not have the same meaning for all algorithms. For instance, what counts for the Take The Best algorithm is what proportion of correct inferences the second cue adds to the first in the cases where the first cue does not discriminate, how much the third cue adds to the first two in the cases where they do not discriminate, and so on. If a cue discriminates, search is terminated, and the degree of redundancy in the cues that were not included in the search is irrelevant. Integration algorithms, in contrast, integrate all information and, thus, always work with the total redundancy in the environment (or knowledge base). For instance, when deciding among objects a, b, c, and d in Figure 1, the cue values of Cues 3, 4, and 5 do not matter from the point of view of the Take The Best algorithm (because search is terminated before reaching Cue 3). However, the values of Cues 3, 4, and 5 affect the redundancy of the ecological system, from the point of view of all integration algorithms. The lesson is that the degree of redundancy in an environment depends on the kind of algorithm that operates on the environment. One needs to be cautious in interpreting measures of redundancy without reference to an algorithm.

variation between recognition of cities and city populations. Let us define the *validity* α of the recognition principle to be the probability, in a reference class, that one object has a greater value on the target variable than another, in the cases where the one object is recognized and the other is not:

$$\alpha = p[t(a) > t(b)\,|\,a_r \text{ is positive and } b_r \text{ is negative}],$$

where $t(a)$ and $t(b)$ are the values of objects a and b on the target variable t, a_r and b_r are the recognition values of a and b, and p is a probability measured as a relative frequency in R.

In a pilot study of 26 undergraduates at the University of Chicago, we found that the cities they recognized (within the 83 largest in Germany) were larger than the cities they did not recognize in about 80% of all possible comparisons. We incorporated this value into our simulations by choosing sets of cities (for each knowledge state, i.e., for each number of cities recognized) where the known cities were larger than the unknown cities in about 80% of all cases. Thus, the cities known by the simulated individuals had the same relationship between recognition and population as did those of the human individuals. Let us first look at the performance of the Take The Best algorithm.

Testing the Take The Best Algorithm

We tested how well individuals using the Take The Best algorithm did at answering real-world questions such as, Which city has more inhabitants: (a) Heidelberg or (b) Bonn? Each of the 500 simulated individuals in each of the 6 × 84 types was tested on the exhaustive set of 3,403 city pairs, resulting in a total of 500 × 6 × 84 × 3,403 tests, that is, about 858 million.

The curves in Figure 4 show the average proportion of correct inferences for each proportion of objects and cue values known. The x axis represents the number of cities recognized, and the y axis shows the proportion of correct inferences that the Take The Best algorithm drew. Each of the 6 × 84 points that make up the six curves is an average proportion of correct inferences taken from 500 simulated individuals, who each made 3,403 inferences.

When the proportion of cities recognized was zero, the proportion of correct inferences was at chance level (.5). When up to half of all cities were recognized, performance increased at all levels of knowledge about cue values. The maximum percentage of correct inferences was around 77%. The striking result was that this maximum was not achieved when individuals knew all cue values of all cities, but rather when they knew less. This result shows the ability of the algorithm to exploit limited knowledge, that is, to do best when not everything is known. Thus, the Take The Best algorithm produces the *less-is-more* effect. At any level of limited knowledge of cue values, learning more German cities will eventually cause a decrease in proportion correct. Take, for instance, the curve where 75% of the cue values were known and the point where the simulated participants recognized about 60 German cities. If these individuals learned about the remaining German cities, their proportion correct would decrease. The rationale behind the less-is-more effect is the recognition principle, and it can be understood best from the curve that reflects 0% of total cue values known. Here, all decisions are made on the basis of the recognition principle,

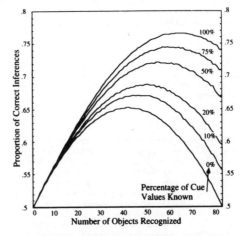

Figure 4. Correct inferences about the population of German cities (two-alternative-choice tasks) by the Take The Best algorithm. Inferences are based on actual information about the 83 largest cities and nine cues for population (see the Appendix). Limited knowledge of the simulated individuals is varied across two dimensions: (a) the number of cities recognized (x axis) and (b) the percentage of cue values known (the six curves).

or by guessing. On this curve, the recognition principle comes into play most when half of the cities are known, so it takes on an inverted-U shape. When half the cities are known, the recognition principle can be activated most often, that is, for roughly 50% of the questions. Because we set the recognition validity in advance, 80% of these inferences will be correct. In the remaining half of the questions, when recognition cannot be used (either both cities are recognized or both cities are unrecognized), then the organism is forced to guess and only 50% of the guesses will be correct. Using the 80% effective recognition validity half of the time and guessing the other half of the time, the organism scores 65% correct, which is the peak of the bottom curve. The mode of this curve moves to the right with increasing knowledge about cue values. Note that even when a person knows everything, all cue values of all cities, there are states of limited knowledge in which the person would make more accurate inferences. We are not going to discuss the conditions of this counterintuitive effect and the supporting experimental evidence here (see Goldstein & Gigerenzer, 1996). Our focus is on how much better integration algorithms can do in making inferences.

Integration Algorithms

We asked several colleagues in the fields of statistics and economics to devise decision algorithms that would do better than the Take The Best algorithm. The five integration algorithms we simulated and pitted against the Take The Best algorithm in a competition were among those suggested by our colleagues.

These competitors include "proper" and "improper" linear models (Dawes, 1979; Lovie & Lovie, 1986). These algorithms, in contrast to the Take The Best algorithm, embody two classical principles of rational inference: (a) complete search—they use all available information (cue values)—and (b) complete integration—they combine all these pieces of information into a single value. In short, we refer in this article to algorithms that satisfy these principles as "rational" (in quotation marks) algorithms.

Contestant 1: Tallying

Let us start with a simple integration algorithm: tallying of positive evidence (Goldstein, 1994). In this algorithm, the number of positive cue values for each object is tallied across all cues ($i = 1, \ldots, n$), and the object with the largest number of positive cue values is chosen. Integration algorithms are not based (at least explicitly) on the recognition principle. For this reason, and to make the integration algorithms as strong as possible, we allow all the integration algorithms to make use of recognition information (the positive and negative recognition values, see Figure 1). Integration algorithms treat recognition as a cue, like the nine ecological cues in Table 1. That is, in the competition, the number of cues (n) is thus equal to 10 (because recognition is included). The decision criterion for tallying is the following:

$$\text{If } \sum_{i=1}^{n} a_i > \sum_{i=1}^{n} b_i \text{, then choose city } a.$$

$$\text{If } \sum_{i=1}^{n} a_i < \sum_{i=1}^{n} b_i \text{, then choose city } b.$$

$$\text{If } \sum_{i=1}^{n} a_i = \sum_{i=1}^{n} b_i \text{, then guess.}$$

The assignments of a_i and b_i are the following:

$$a_i, b_i = \begin{cases} 1 \text{ if the } i\text{th cue value is positive} \\ 0 \text{ if the } i\text{th cue value is negative} \\ 0 \text{ if the } i\text{th cue value is unknown.} \end{cases}$$

Let us compare cities a and b, from Figure 1. By tallying the positive cue values, a would score 2 points and b would score 3. Thus, tallying would choose b to be the larger, in opposition to the Take The Best algorithm, which would infer that a is larger. Variants of tallying, such as the frequency-of-good-features heuristic, have been discussed in the decision literature (Alba & Marmorstein, 1987; Payne, Bettman, & Johnson, 1993).

Contestant 2: Weighted Tallying

Tallying treats all cues alike, independent of cue validity. Weighted tallying of positive evidence is identical with tallying, except that it weights each cue according to its ecological validity, v_i. The ecological validities of the cues appear in Table 1. We set the validity of the recognition cue to .8, which is the empirical average determined by the pilot study. The decision rule is as follows:

$$\text{If } \sum_{i=1}^{n} a_i v_i > \sum_{i=1}^{n} b_i v_i \text{, then choose city } a.$$

$$\text{If } \sum_{i=1}^{n} a_i v_i < \sum_{i=1}^{n} b_i v_i \text{, then choose city } b.$$

$$\text{If } \sum_{i=1}^{n} a_i v_i = \sum_{i=1}^{n} b_i v_i \text{, then guess.}$$

Note that weighted tallying needs more information than either tallying or the Take The Best algorithm, namely, quantitative information about ecological validities. In the simulation, we provided the real ecological validities to give this algorithm a good chance.

Calling again on the comparison of objects a and b from Figure 1, let us assume that the validities would be .8 for recognition and .9, .8, .7, .6, .51 for Cues 1 through 5. Weighted tallying would thus assign 1.7 points to a and 2.3 points to b. Thus, weighted tallying would also choose b to be the larger.

Both tallying algorithms treat negative information and missing information identically. That is, they consider only positive evidence. The following algorithms distinguish between negative and missing information and integrate both positive and negative information.

Contestant 3: Unit-Weight Linear Model

The unit-weight linear model is a special case of the equal-weight linear model (Huber, 1989) and has been advocated as a good approximation of weighted linear models (Dawes, 1979; Einhorn & Hogarth, 1975). The decision criterion for unit-weight integration is the same as for tallying, only the assignment of a_i and b_i differs:

$$a_i, b_i = \begin{cases} 1 \text{ if the } i\text{th cue value is positive} \\ -1 \text{ if the } i\text{th cue value is negative} \\ 0 \text{ if the } i\text{th cue value is unknown.} \end{cases}$$

Comparing objects a and b from Figure 1 would involve assigning 1.0 points to a and 1.0 points to b and, thus, choosing randomly. This simple linear model corresponds to Model 2 in Einhorn and Hogarth (1975, p. 177) with the weight parameter set equal to 1.

Contestant 4: Weighted Linear Model

This model is like the unit-weight linear model except that the values of a_i and b_i are multiplied by their respective ecological validities. The decision criterion is the same as with weighted tallying. The weighted linear model (or some variant of it) is often viewed as an optimal rule for preferential choice, under the idealization of independent dimensions or cues (e.g., Keeney & Raiffa, 1993; Payne et al., 1993). Comparing objects a and b from Figure 1 would involve assigning 1.0 points to a and 0.8 points to b and, thus, choosing a to be the larger.

Contestant 5: Multiple Regression

The weighted linear model reflects the different validities of the cues, but not the dependencies between cues. Multiple regression creates weights that reflect the covariances between predictors or cues and is commonly seen as an "optimal" way to integrate various pieces of information into an estimate (e.g., Brunswik, 1955; Hammond, 1966). Neural networks use the delta rule determine their "optimal" weights by the same principles as multiple regression does (Stone, 1986). The delta rule carries out the equivalent of a multiple linear regression from the input patterns to the targets.

The weights for the multiple regression could simply be calculated from the full information about the nine ecological cues, as given in the Appendix. To make multiple regression an even stronger competitor, we also provided information about which cities the simulated individuals recognized. Thus, the multiple regression used nine ecological cues and the recognition cue to generate its weights. Because the weights for the recognition cue depend on which cities are recognized, we calculated $6 \times 500 \times 84$ sets of weights: one for each simulated individual. Unlike any of the other algorithms, regression had access to the actual city populations (even for those cities not recognized by the hypothetical person) in the calculation of the weights.[4] During the quiz, each simulated person used the set of weights provided to it by multiple regression to estimate the populations of the cities in the comparison.

There was a missing-values problem in computing these $6 \times 84 \times 500$ sets of regression coefficients, because most simulated individuals did not know certain cue values, for instance, the cue values of the cities they did not recognize. We strengthened the performance of multiple regression by substituting unknown cue values with the average of the cue values the person knew for the given cue.[5] This was done both in creating the weights and in using these weights to estimate populations. Unlike traditional procedures where weights are estimated from one half of the data, and inferences based on these weights are made for the other half, the regression algorithm had access to all the information in the Appendix (except, of course, the unknown cue values)—more information than was given to any of the competitors. In the competition, multiple regression and, to a lesser degree, the weighted linear model approximate the ideal of the Laplacean Demon.

Results

Speed

The Take The Best algorithm is designed to enable quick decision making. Compared with the integration algorithms, how much faster does it draw inferences, measured by the amount of information searched in memory? For instance, in Figure 1, the Take The Best algorithm would look up four cue values (including the recognition cue values) to infer that a is larger than b. None of the integration algorithms use limited search; thus, they always look up all cue values.

Figure 5 shows the amount of cue values retrieved from memory by the Take The Best algorithm for various levels of limited knowledge. The Take The Best algorithm reduces search in memory considerably. Depending on the knowledge state, this algorithm needed to search for between 2 (the number of recognition values) and 20 (the maximum possible cue values: Each city has nine cue values and one recognition value). For instance, when a person recognized half of the cities and knew 50% of their cue values, then, on average, only about

4 cue values (that is, one fifth of all possible) are searched for. The average across all simulated participants was 5.9, which was less than a third of all available cue values.

Accuracy

Given that it searches only for a limited amount of information, how accurate is the Take The Best algorithm, compared with the integration algorithms? We ran the competition for all states of limited knowledge shown in Figure 4. We first report the results of the competition in the case where each algorithm achieved its best performance: When 100% of the cue values were known. Figure 6 shows the results of the simulations, carried out in the same way as those in Figure 4.

To our surprise, the Take The Best algorithm drew as many correct inferences as any of the other algorithms, and more than some. The curves for Take The Best, multiple regression, weighted tallying, and tallying are so similar that there are only slight differences among them. Weighted tallying performed about as well as tallying, and the unit-weight linear model performed about as well as the weighted linear model—demonstrating that the previous finding that weights may be chosen in a fairly arbitrary manner, as long as they have the correct sign (Dawes, 1979), is generalizable to tallying. The two integration algorithms that make use of both positive and negative information, unit-weight and weighted linear models, made considerably fewer correct inferences. By looking at the lower-left and upper-right corners of Figure 6, one can see that all competitors do equally well with a complete lack of knowledge or with complete knowledge. They differ when knowledge is limited. Note that some algorithms can make more correct inferences when they do not have complete knowledge: a demonstration of the less-is-more effect mentioned earlier.

What was the result of the competition across all levels of limited knowledge? Table 2 shows the result for each level of limited knowledge of cue values, averaged across all levels of recognition knowledge. (Table 2 reports also the performance of two variants of the Take The Best algorithm, which we discuss later: the Minimalist and the Take The Last algorithm.) The values in the 100% column of Table 2 are the values in Figure 6 averaged across all levels of recognition. The Take The Best algorithm made as many correct inferences as one of the competitors (weighted tallying) and more than the others. Because it was also the fastest, we judged the competition goes to the Take The Best algorithm as the highest performing, overall.

To our knowledge, this is the first time that it has been demonstrated that a satisficing algorithm, that is, the Take The Best algorithm, can draw as many correct inferences about a real-

---

[4] We cannot claim that these integration algorithms are the best ones, nor can we know a priori which small variations will succeed in our bumpy real-world environment. An example: During the proof stage of this article we learned that regressing on the ranks of the cities does slightly better than regressing on the city populations. The key issue is what are the structures of environments in which particular algorithms and variants thrive.

[5] If no single cue value was known for a given cue, the missing values were substituted by .5. This value was chosen because it is the midpoint of 0 and 1, which are the values used to stand for negative and positive cue values, respectively.

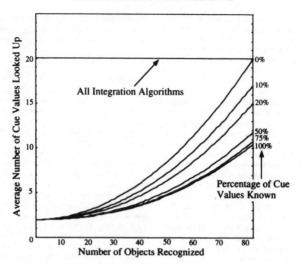

Figure 5. Amount of cue values looked up by the Take The Best algorithm and by the competing integration algorithms (see text), depending on the number of objects known (0–83) and the percentage of cue values known.

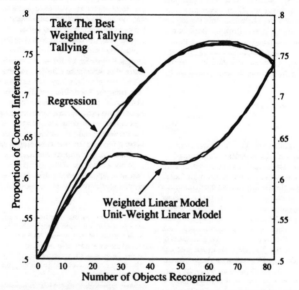

Figure 6. Results of the competition. The curve for the Take The Best algorithm is identical with the 100% curve in Figure 4. The results for proportion correct have been smoothed by a running median smoother, to lessen visual noise between the lines.

Table 2
*Results of the Competition: Average Proportion
of Correct Inferences*

	Percentage of cue values known					
Algorithm	10	20	50	75	100	Average
Take The Best	.621	.635	.663	.678	.691	.658
Weighted tallying	.621	.635	.663	.679	.693	.658
Regression	.625	.635	.657	.674	.694	.657
Tallying	.620	.633	.659	.676	.691	.656
Weighted linear model	.623	.627	.623	.619	.625	.623
Unit-weight linear model	.621	.622	.621	.620	.622	.621
Minimalist	.619	.631	.650	.661	.674	.647
Take The Last	.619	.630	.646	.658	.675	.645

Note. Values are rounded; averages are computed from the unrounded values. Bottom two algorithms are variants of the Take The Best algorithm.

world environment as integration algorithms, across all states of limited knowledge. The dictates of classical rationality would have led one to expect the integration algorithms to do substantially better than the satisficing algorithm.

Two results of the simulation can be derived analytically. First and most obvious is that if knowledge about objects is zero, then all algorithms perform at a chance level. Second, and less obvious, is that if all objects and cue values are known, then tallying produces as many correct inferences as the unit-weight linear model. This is because, under complete knowledge, the score under the tallying algorithm is an increasing linear function of the score arrived at in the unit-weight linear model.[6] The equivalence between tallying and unit-weight linear models under complete knowledge is an important result. It is known that unit-weight linear models can sometimes perform about as well as proper linear models (i.e., models with weights that are chosen in an optimal way, such as in multiple regression; see Dawes, 1979). The equivalence implies that under complete knowledge, merely counting pieces of positive evidence can work as well as proper linear models. This result clarifies one condition under which searching only for positive evidence, a strategy that has sometimes been labeled *confirmation bias* or *positive test strategy*, can be a reasonable and efficient inferential strategy (Klayman & Ha, 1987; Tweney & Walker, 1990).

Why do the unit-weight and weighted linear models perform markedly worse under limited knowledge of objects? The reason is the simple and bold recognition principle. Algorithms that do not exploit the recognition principle in environments where recognition is strongly correlated with the target variable pay the price of a considerable number of wrong inferences. The unit-weight and weighted linear models use recognition information and integrate it with all other information but do not follow the recognition principle, that is, they sometimes choose unrecognized cities over recognized ones. Why is this? In the environment, there are more negative cue values than positive ones (see the Appendix), and most cities have more negative cue values than positive ones. From this it follows that when a recognized object is compared with an unrecognized object, the (weighted) sum of cue values of the recognized object will often be smaller than that of the unrecognized object (which is −1 for

the unit-weight model and −.8 for the weighted linear model). Here the unit-weight and weighted linear models often make the inference that the unrecognized object is the larger one, due to the overwhelming negative evidence for the recognized object. Such inferences contradict the recognition principle. Tallying algorithms, in contrast, have the recognition principle built in implicitly. Because tallying algorithms ignore negative information, the tally for an unrecognized object is always 0 and, thus, is always smaller than the tally for a recognized object, which is at least 1 (for tallying, or .8 for weighted tallying, due to the positive value on the recognition cue). Thus, tallying algorithms always arrive at the inference that a recognized object is larger than an unrecognized one.

Note that this explanation of the different performances puts the full weight on a psychological principle (the recognition principle) explicit in the Take The Best algorithm, as opposed to the statistical issue of how to find optimal weights in a linear function. To test this explanation, we reran the simulations for the unit-weight and weighted linear models under the same conditions but replacing the recognition cue with the recognition principle. The simulation showed that the recognition principle accounts for all the difference.

Can Satisficing Algorithms Get by With Even Less Time and Knowledge?

The Take The Best algorithm produced a surprisingly high proportion of correct inferences, compared with more computationally expensive integration algorithms. Making correct inferences despite limited knowledge is an important adaptive feature of an algorithm, but being right is not the only thing that counts. In many situations, time is limited, and acting fast can be as important as being correct. For instance, if you are driving on an unfamiliar highway and you have to decide in an instant what to do when the road forks, your problem is not necessarily making the best choice, but simply making a quick choice. Pressure to be quick is also characteristic for certain types of verbal interactions, such as press conferences, in which a fast answer indicates competence, or commercial interactions, such as having telephone service installed, where the customer has to decide in a few minutes which of a dozen calling features to purchase. These situations entail the dual constraints of limited knowledge and limited time. The Take The Best algorithm is already faster than any of the integration algorithms, because it performs only a limited search and does not need to compute weighted sums of cue values. Can it be made even faster? It can, if search is guided by the recency of cues in memory rather than by cue validity.

The Take The Last Algorithm

The Take The Last algorithm first tries the cue that discriminated the last time. If this cue does not discriminate, the algo-

---

[6] The proof for this is as follows. The tallying score t for a given object is the number n^+ of positive cue values, as defined above. The score u for the unit weight linear model is $n^+ - n^-$, where n^- is the number of negative cue values. Under complete knowledge, $n = n^+ + n^-$, where n is the number of cues. Thus, $t = n^+$, and $u = n^+ - n^-$. Because $n^- = n - n^+$, by substitution into the formula for u, we find that $u = n^+ - (n - n^+) = 2t - n$.

rithm then tries the cue that discriminated the time before last, and so on. The algorithm differs from the Take The Best algorithm in Step 2, which is now reformulated as Step 2':

Step 2': Search for the Cue Values of the Most Recent Cue

For the two objects, retrieve the cue values of the cue used most recently. If it is the first judgment and there is no discrimination record available, retrieve the cue values of a randomly chosen cue.

Thus, in Step 4, the algorithm goes back to Step 2'. Variants of this search principle have been studied as the "Einstellung effect" in the water jar experiments (Luchins & Luchins, 1994), where the solution strategy of the most recently solved problem is tried first on the subsequent problem. This effect has also been noted in physicians' generation of diagnoses for clinical cases (Weber, Böckenholt, Hilton, & Wallace, 1993).

This algorithm does not need a rank order of cues according to their validities; all that needs to be known is the direction in which a cue points. Knowledge about the rank order of cue validities is replaced by a memory of which cues were last used. Note that such a record can be built up independently of any knowledge about the structure of an environment and neither needs, nor uses, any feedback about whether inferences are right or wrong.

The Minimalist Algorithm

Can reasonably accurate inferences be achieved with even less knowledge? What we call the *Minimalist* algorithm needs neither information about the rank ordering of cue validities nor the discrimination history of the cues. In its ignorance, the algorithm picks cues in a random order. The algorithm differs from the Take The Best algorithm in Step 2, which is now reformulated as Step 2":

Step 2": Random Search

For the two objects, retrieve the cue values of a randomly chosen cue.

The Minimalist algorithm does not necessarily speed up search, but it tries to get by with even less knowledge than any other algorithm.

Results

Speed

How fast are the fast algorithms? The simulations showed that for each of the two variant algorithms, the relationship between amount of knowledge and the number of cue values looked up had the same form as for the Take The Best algorithm (Figure 5). That is, unlike the integration algorithms, the curves are concave and the number of cues searched for is maximal when knowledge of cue values is lowest. The average number of cue values looked up was lowest for the Take The Last algorithm (5.29) followed by the Minimalist algorithm (5.64) and the Take The Best algorithm (5.91). As knowledge becomes more and more limited (on both dimensions: recognition and cue values known), the difference in speed becomes

smaller and smaller. The reason why the Minimalist algorithm looks up fewer cue values than the Take The Best algorithm is that cue validities and cue discrimination rates are negatively correlated (Table 1); therefore, randomly chosen cues tend to have larger discrimination rates than cues chosen by cue validity.

Accuracy

What is the price to be paid for speeding up search or reducing the knowledge of cue orderings and discrimination histories to nothing? We tested the performance of the two algorithms on the same environment as all other algorithms. Figure 7 shows the proportion of correct inferences that the Minimalist algorithm achieved. For comparison, the performance of the Take The Best algorithm with 100% of cue values known is indicated by a dotted line. Note that the Minimalist algorithm performed surprisingly well. The maximum difference appeared when knowledge was complete and all cities were recognized. In these circumstances, the Minimalist algorithm did about 4 percentage points worse than the Take The Best algorithm. On average, the proportion of correct inferences was only 1.1 percentage points less than the best algorithms in the competition (Table 2).

The performance of the Take The Last algorithm is similar to Figure 7, and the average number of correct inferences is shown in Table 2. The Take The Last algorithm was faster but scored slightly less than the Minimalist algorithm. The Take The Last algorithm has an interesting ability, which fooled us in an earlier series of tests, where we used a systematic (as opposed to a random) method for presenting the test pairs, starting with the largest city and pairing it with all others, and so on. An integration algorithm such as multiple regression cannot "find out" that it is being tested in this systematic way, and its inferences are accordingly independent of the sequence of presentation. However, the Take The Last algorithm found out and won this first round of the competition, outperforming the other competitors by some 10 percentage points. How did it exploit systematic testing? Recall that it tries, first, the cue that discriminated the last time. If this cue does not discriminate, it proceeds with the cue that discriminated the time before, and so on. In doing so, when testing is systematic in the way described, it tends to find, for each city that is being paired with all smaller ones, the group of cues for which the larger city has a positive value. Trying these cues first increases the chances of finding a discriminating cue that points in the right direction (toward the larger city). We learned our lesson and reran the whole competition with randomly ordered of pairs of cities.

Discussion

The competition showed a surprising result: The Take The Best algorithm drew as many correct inferences about unknown features of a real-world environment as any of the integration algorithms, and more than some of them. Two further simplifications of the algorithm—the Take The Last algorithm (replacing knowledge about the rank orders of cue validities by a memory of the discrimination history of cues) and the Minimalist algorithm (dispensing with both) showed a compara-

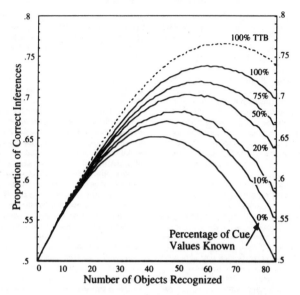

Figure 7. Performance of the Minimalist algorithm. For comparison, the performance of the Take The Best algorithm (TTB) is shown as a dotted line, for the case in which 100% of cue values are known.

tively small loss in correct inferences, and only when knowledge about cue values was high.

To the best of our knowledge, this is the first inference competition between satisficing and "rational" algorithms in a real-world environment. The result is of importance for encouraging research that focuses on the power of simple psychological mechanisms, that is, on the design and testing of satisficing algorithms. The result is also of importance as an existence proof that cognitive algorithms capable of successful performance in a real-world environment do not need to satisfy the classical norms of rational inference. The classical norms may be sufficient but are not necessary for good inference in real environments.

Cognitive Algorithms That Satisfice

In this section, we discuss the fundamental psychological mechanism postulated by the PMM family of algorithms: one-reason decision making. We discuss how this mechanism exploits the structure of environments in making fast inferences that differ from those arising from standard models of rational reasoning.

One-Reason Decision Making

What we call *one-reason decision making* is a specific form of satisficing. The inference, or decision, is based on a single, good reason. There is no compensation between cues. One-reason decision making is probably the most challenging feature of the PMM family of algorithms. As we mentioned before, it is a design feature of an algorithm that is not present in those models that depict human inference as an optimal integration of all information available (implying that all information has been looked up in the first place), including linear multiple regression and nonlinear neural networks. One-reason decision making is based exclusively on one reason (i.e., cue), but this reason may be different from decision to decision. This allows for highly context-sensitive modeling of choice. One-reason decision making is not compensatory. Compensation is, after all, the cornerstone of classical rationality, assuming that all commodities can be compared and everything has its price. Compensation assumes commensurability. However, human minds do not trade everything, some things are supposed to be without a price (Elster, 1979). For instance, if a person must choose between two actions that might help him or her get out of deep financial trouble, and one involves killing someone, then no amount of money or other benefits might compensate for the prospect of bloody hands. He or she takes the action that does not involve killing a person, whatever other differences exist between the two options. More generally, hierarchies of ethical and moral values are often noncompensatory: True friendship, military honors, and doctorates are supposed to be without a price.

Noncompensatory inference algorithms—such as lexicographic, conjunctive, and disjunctive rules—have been discussed in the literature, and some empirical evidence has been reported (e.g., Einhorn, 1970; Fishburn, 1988). The closest relative to the PMM family of satisficing algorithms is the lexicographic rule. The largest evidence for lexicographic processes seems to come from studies on decision under risk (for a recent summary, see Lopes, 1995). However, despite empirical evidence, noncompensatory lexicographic algorithms have often been dismissed at face value because they violate the tenets of classical rationality (Keeney & Raiffa, 1993; Lovie & Lovie, 1986). The PMM family is both more general and more specific than the lexicographic rule. It is more general because only the Take The Best algorithm uses a lexicographic procedure in which cues are ordered according to their validity, whereas the variant algorithms do not. It is more specific, because several other psychological principles are integrated with the lexicographic rule in the Take The Best algorithm, such as the recognition principle and the rules for confidence judgment (which are not dealt with in this article; see Gigerenzer et al., 1991).

Serious models that comprise noncompensatory inferences are hard to find. One of the few examples is in Breiman, Friedman, Olshen, and Stone (1993), who reported a simple, noncompensatory algorithm with only 3 binary, ordered cues, which classified heart attack patients into high- and low-risk groups and was more accurate than standard statistical classification methods that used up to 19 variables. The practical relevance of this noncompensatory classification algorithm is obvious: In the emergency room, the physician can quickly obtain the measures on one, two, or three variables and does not need to perform any computations because there is no integration. This group of statisticians constructed satisficing algorithms that approach the task of classification (and estimation) much like the Take The Best algorithm handles two-alternative choice. Relevance theory (Sperber, Cara, & Girotto, 1995) postulates that people generate consequences from rules according to accessibility and stop this process when expectations of relevance are met. Although relevance theory has not been as formalized, we see its stopping rule as parallel to that of the Take The Best algorithm. Finally, optimality theory (Legendre, Raymond, & Smolensky, 1993; Prince & Smolensky, 1991) proposes that hierarchical noncompensation explains how the grammar of a language determines which structural description of an input best satisfies well-formedness constraints. Optimality theory (which is actually a satisficing theory) applies the same inferential principles as PMM theory to phonology and morphology.

Recognition Principle

The recognition principle is a version of one-reason decision making that exploits a lack of knowledge. The very fact that one does not know is used to make accurate inferences. The recognition principle is an intuitively plausible principle that seems not to have been used until now in models of bounded rationality. However, it has long been used to good advantage by humans and other animals. For instance, advertisement techniques as recently used by Benetton put all effort into making sure that every customer recognizes the brand name, with no effort made to inform about the product itself. The idea behind this is that recognition is a strong force in customers' choices. One of our dear (and well-read) colleagues, after seeing a draft of this article, explained to us how he makes inferences about which books are worth acquiring. If he finds a book about a

great topic but does not recognize the name of the author, he makes the inference that it is probably not worth buying. If, after an inspection of the references, he does not recognize most of the names, he concludes the book is not even worth reading. The recognition principle is also known as one of the rules that guide food preferences in animals. For instance, rats choose the food that they recognize having eaten before (or having smelled on the breath of fellow rats) and avoid novel foods (Gallistel, Brown, Carey, Gelman, & Keil, 1991).

The empirical validity of the recognition principle for inferences about unknown city populations, as used in the present simulations, can be directly tested in several ways. First, participants are presented pairs of cities, among them critical pairs in which one city is recognized and the other unrecognized, and their task is to infer which one has more inhabitants. The recognition principle predicts the recognized city. In our empirical tests, participants followed the recognition principle in roughly 90% to 100% of all cases (Goldstein, 1994; Goldstein & Gigerenzer, 1996). Second, participants are taught a cue, its ecological validity, and the cue values for some of the objects (such as whether a city has a soccer team or not). Subsequently, they are tested on critical pairs of cities, one recognized and one unrecognized, where the recognized city has a negative cue value (which indicates lower population). The second test is a harder test for the recognition principle than the first one and can be made even harder by using more cues with negative cue values for the recognized object, and by other means. Tests of the second kind have been performed, and participants still followed the recognition principle more than 90% of the time, providing evidence for its empirical validity (Goldstein, 1994; Goldstein & Gigerenzer, 1996).

The recognition principle is a useful heuristic in domains where recognition is a predictor of a target variable, such as whether a food contains a toxic substance. In cases where recognition does not predict the target, the PMM algorithms can still perform the inference, but without the recognition principle (i.e., Step 1 is canceled).

Limited Search

Both one-reason decision making and the recognition principle realize limited search by defining stopping points. Integration algorithms, in contrast, do not provide any model of stopping points and implicitly assume exhaustive search (although they may provide rules for tossing out some of the variables in a lengthy regression equation). Stopping rules are crucial for modeling inference under limited time, as in Simon's examples of satisficing, where search among alternatives terminates when a certain aspiration level is met.

Nonlinearity

Linearity is a mathematically convenient tool that has dominated the theory of rational choice since its inception in the mid-seventeenth century (Gigerenzer et al., 1989). The assumption is that the various components of an alternative add up independently to its overall estimate or utility. In contrast, nonlinear inference does not operate by computing linear sums of (weighted) cue values. Nonlinear inference has many varieties, including simple principles such as in the conjunctive and disjunctive algorithms (Einhorn, 1970) and highly complex ones such as in nonlinear multiple regression and neural networks. The Take The Best algorithm and its variants belong to the family of simple nonlinear models. One advantage of simple nonlinear models is transparency; every step in the PMM algorithms can be followed through, unlike fully connected neural networks with numerous hidden units and other free parameters.

Our competition revealed that the unit-weight and weighted versions of the linear models lead to about equal performance, consistent with the finding that the choice of weights, provided the sign is correct, does often not matter much (Dawes, 1979). In real-world domains, such as in the prediction of sudden infant death from a linear combination of eight variables (Carpenter, Gardner, McWeeny & Emery, 1977), the weights can be varied across a broad range without decreasing predictive accuracy: a phenomenon known as the "flat maximum effect" (Lovie & Lovie, 1986; von Winterfeldt & Edwards, 1982). The competition in addition, showed that the flat maximum effect extends to tallying, with unit-weight and weighted tallying performing about equally well. The performance of the Take The Best algorithm showed that the flat maximum can extend beyond linear models: Inferences based solely on the best cue can be as accurate as any weighted or unit-weight linear combination of all cues.

Most research in psychology and economics has preferred linear models for description, prediction, and prescription (Edwards, 1954, 1962; Lopes, 1994; von Winterfeldt & Edwards, 1982). Historically, linear models such as analysis of variance and multiple regression originated as tools for data analysis in psychological laboratories and were subsequently projected by means of the "tools-to-theories heuristic" into theories of mind (Gigerenzer, 1991). The sufficiently good fit of linear models in many judgment studies has been interpreted that humans in fact might combine cues in a linear fashion. However, whether this can be taken to mean that humans actually use linear models is controversial (Hammond & Summers, 1965; Hammond & Wascoe, 1980). For instance, within a certain range, data generated from the (nonlinear) law of falling bodies can be fitted well by a linear regression. For the data in the Appendix, a multiple linear regression resulted in $R^2 = .87$, which means that a linear combination of the cues can predict the target variable quite well. But the simpler, nonlinear, Take The Best algorithm could match this performance. Thus, good fit of a linear model does not rule out simpler models of inference.

Shepard (1967) reviewed the empirical evidence for the claim that humans integrate information by linear models. He distinguished between the perceptual transformation of raw sensory inputs into conceptual objects and properties and the subsequent inference based on conceptual knowledge. He concluded that the perceptual analysis integrates the responses of the vast number of receptive elements into concepts and properties by complex nonlinear rules but once this is done, "there is little evidence that they can in turn be juggled and recombined with anything like this facility" (Shepard, 1967, p. 263). Although we can take account of a host of different factors, and although we can remember and report doing so, "it is seldom more than one or two that we consider at any one time" (Shepard, 1967, p. 267). In Shepard's view, there is little evi-

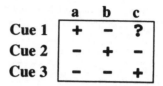

Figure 8. Limited knowledge and a stricter discrimination rule can produce intransitive inferences.

dence for integration, linear or otherwise, in what we term *inferences from memory*—even without constraints of limited time and knowledge. A further kind of evidence does not support linear integration as a model of memory-based inference. People often have great difficulties in handling correlations between cues (e.g., Armelius & Armelius, 1974), whereas integration models such as multiple regression need to handle intercorrelations. To summarize, for memory-based inference, there seems to be little empirical evidence for the view of the mind as a Laplacean Demon equipped with the computational powers to perform multiple regressions. But this need not be taken as bad news. The beauty of the nonlinear satisficing algorithms is that they can match the Demon's performance with less searching, less knowledge, and less computational might.

Intransitivity

Transitivity is a cornerstone of classical rationality. It is one of the few tenets that the Anglo-American school of Ramsey and Savage shares with the competing Franco-European school of Allais (Fishburn, 1991). If we prefer *a* to *b* and *b* to *c*, then we should also prefer *a* to *c*. The linear algorithms in our competition always produce transitive inferences (except for ties, where the algorithm randomly guessed), and city populations are, in fact, transitive. The PMM family of algorithms includes algorithms that do not violate transitivity (such as the Take The Best algorithm), and others that do (e.g., the Minimalist algorithm). The Minimalist algorithm randomly selects a cue on which to base the inference, therefore intransitivities can result. Table 2 shows that in spite of these intransitivities, overall performance of the algorithm is only about 1 percentage point lower than that of the best transitive algorithms and a few percentage points better than some transitive algorithms.

An organism that used the Take The Best algorithm with a stricter discrimination rule (actually, the original version found in Gigerenzer et al., 1991) could also be forced into making intransitive inferences. The stricter discrimination rule is that search is only terminated when one positive and one negative cue value (but not one positive and one unknown cue value) are encountered. Figure 8 illustrates a state of knowledge in which this stricter discrimination rule gives the result that *a* dominates *b*, *b* dominates *c*, and *c* dominates *a*.[7]

---

[7] Note that missing knowledge is necessary for intransitivities to occur. If all cue values are known, no intransitive inferences can possibly result. The algorithm with the stricter discrimination rule allows precise predictions about the occurrence of intransitivities over the course of knowledge acquisition. For instance, imagine a person whose knowledge is described by Figure 8, except that she does not know the value of Cue 2 for object *c*. This person would make no intransitive judgments

Biological systems, for instance, can exhibit systematic intransitivities based on incommensurability between two systems on one dimension (Gilpin, 1975; Lewontin, 1968). Imagine three species: a, b, and c. Species a inhabits both water and land; species b inhabits both water and air. Therefore, the two only compete in water, where species a defeats species b. Species c inhabits land and air, so it only competes with b in the air, where it is defeated by b. Finally, when a and c meet, it is only on land, and here, c is in its element and defeats a. A linear model that estimates some value for the combative strength of each species independently of the species with which it is competing would fail to capture this nontransitive cycle.

Inferences Without Estimation

Einhorn and Hogarth (1975) noted that in the unit-weight model "there is essentially no estimation involved in its use" (p. 177), except for the sign of the unit weight. A similar result holds for the algorithms reported here. The Take The Best algorithm does not need to estimate regression weights, it only needs to estimate a rank ordering of ecological validities. The Take The Last and the Minimalist algorithms involve essentially no estimation (except for the sign of the cues). The fact that there is no estimation problem has an important consequence: An organism can use as many cues as it has experienced, without being concerned about whether the size of the sample experienced is sufficiently large to generate reliable estimates of weights.

Cue Redundancy and Performance

Einhorn and Hogarth (1975) suggested that unit-weight models can be expected to perform approximately as well as proper linear models when (a) R^2 from the regression model is in the moderate or low range (around .5 or smaller) and (b) predictors (cues) are correlated. Are these two criteria necessary, sufficient, or both to explain the performance of the Take The Best algorithm? The Take The Best algorithm and its variants certainly can exploit cue redundancy: If cues are highly correlated, one cue can do the job.

We have already seen that in the present environment, $R^2 = .87$, which is in the high rather than the moderate or low range. As mentioned earlier, the pairwise correlations between the nine ecological cues ranged between $-.25$ and $.54$, with an absolute average value of $.19$. Thus, despite a high R^2 and only moderate-to-small correlation between cues, the satisficing algorithms performed quite successfully. Their excellent performance in the competition can be explained only partially by cue redundancy, because the cues were only moderately correlated. High cue redundancy, thus, does seem sufficient but is not necessary for the successful performance of the satisficing algorithms.

A New Perspective on the Lens Model

Ecological theorists such as Brunswik (1955) emphasized that the cognitive system is designed to find many pathways to the world, substituting missing cues by whatever cues happen to be available. Brunswik labeled this ability *vicarious functioning*, in which he saw the most fundamental principle of a science of perception and cognition. His proposal to model this adaptive process by linear multiple regression has inspired a long tradition of neo-Brunswikian research (B. Brehmer, 1994; Hammond, 1990), although the empirical evidence for mental multiple regression is still controversial (e.g., A. Brehmer & B. Brehmer, 1988). However, vicarious functioning need not be equated with linear regression. The PMM family of algorithms provides an alternative, nonadditive model of vicarious functioning, in which cue substitution operates without integration. This gives a new perspective of Brunswik's lens model. In a one-reason decision making lens, the first discriminating cue that passes through inhibits any other rays passing through and determines judgment. Noncompensatory vicarious functioning is consistent with some of Brunswik's original examples, such as the substitution of behaviors in Hull's habit–family hierarchy, and the alternative manifestation of symptoms according to the psychoanalytic writings of Frenkel-Brunswik (see Gigerenzer & Murray, 1987, chap. 3).

It has been reported sometimes that teachers, physicians, and other professionals claim that they use seven or so criteria to make judgments (e.g., when grading papers or making a differential diagnosis) but that experimental tests showed that they in fact often used only one criterion (Shepard, 1967). At first glance, this seems to indicate that those professionals make outrageous claims. But it need not be. If experts' vicarious functioning works according to the PMM algorithms, then they are correct in saying that they use many predictors, but the decision is made by only one at any time.

What Counts as Good Reasoning?

Much of the research on reasoning in the last decades has assumed that sound reasoning can be reduced to principles of internal consistency, such as additivity of probabilities, conformity to truth-table logic, and transitivity. For instance, research on the Wason selection task, the "Linda" problem, and the "cab" problem has evaluated reasoning almost exclusively by some measure of internal consistency (Gigerenzer, 1995, 1996a). Cognitive algorithms, however, need to meet more important constraints than internal consistency: (a) They need to be psychologically plausible, (b) they need to be fast, and (c) they need to make accurate inferences in real-world environments. In real time and real environments, the possibility that an algorithm (e.g., the Minimalist algorithm) can make intransitive inferences does not mean that it will make them all the time or that this feature of the algorithm will significantly hurt its accuracy. What we have not addressed in this article are constraints on human reasoning that emerge from the fact that *Homo sapiens* is a social animal (Gigerenzer, 1996b). For instance, some choices (e.g., who to treat first in an emergency

---

comparing objects a, b, and c. If she were to learn that object c had a negative cue value for Cue 2, she would produce an intransitive judgment. If she learned one piece more, namely, the value of Cue 1 for object c, then she would no longer produce an intransitive judgment. The prediction is that transitive judgments should turn into intransitive ones and back, during learning. Thus, intransitivities do not simply depend on the amount of limited knowledge but also on what knowledge is missing.

room) need to be justified (Tetlock, 1992). Going with the single best reason, the strategy of the Take The Best algorithm, has an immediate appeal for justification and can be more convincing and certainly easier to communicate than some complicated weighting of cues.

Further Research

Among the questions that need to be addressed in future research are the following. First, how can we generalize the present satisficing algorithm from two-alternative-choice tasks to other inferential tasks, such as classification and estimation? The reported success of the classification and regression tree models (Breiman et al., 1993), which use a form of one-reason decision making, is an encouraging sign that what we have shown here for two-alternative-choice tasks might be generalizable. Second, what is the structure of real-world environments that allows simple algorithms to perform so well? We need to develop a conceptual language that can capture important aspects of the structure of environments that simple cognitive algorithms can exploit. The traditional proposal for understanding the structure of environments in terms of ecological validities defined as linear correlations (Brunswik, 1955) may not be adequate, as the power of the nonlinear satisficing algorithms suggests.

Can Reasoning Be Rational and Psychological?

At the beginning of this article, we pointed out the common opposition between the rational and the psychological, which emerged in the nineteenth century after the breakdown of the classical interpretation of probability (Gigerenzer et al., 1989). Since then, rational inference is commonly reduced to logic and probability theory, and psychological explanations are called on when things go wrong. This division of labor is, in a nutshell, the basis on which much of the current research on judgment under uncertainty is built. As one economist from the Massachusetts Institute of Technology put it, "either reasoning is rational or it's psychological" (Gigerenzer, 1994). Can not reasoning be both rational and psychological?

We believe that after 40 years of toying with the notion of bounded rationality, it is time to overcome the opposition between the rational and the psychological and to reunite the two. The PMM family of cognitive algorithms provides precise models that attempt to do so. They differ from the Enlightenment's unified view of the rational and psychological, in that they focus on simple psychological mechanisms that operate under constraints of limited time and knowledge and are supported by empirical evidence. The single most important result in this article is that simple psychological mechanisms can yield about as many (or more) correct inferences in less time than standard statistical linear models that embody classical properties of rational inference. The demonstration that a fast and frugal satisficing algorithm won the competition defeats the widespread view that only "rational" algorithms can be accurate. Models of inference do not have to forsake accuracy for simplicity. The mind can have it both ways.

References

Alba, J. W., & Marmorstein, H. (1987). The effects of frequency knowledge on consumer decision making. *Journal of Consumer Research, 14*, 14–26.

Anderson, J. R. (1990). *The adaptive character of thought.* Hillsdale, NJ: Erlbaum.

Armelius, B., & Armelius, K. (1974). The use of redundancy in multiple-cue judgments: Data from a suppressor-variable task. *American Journal of Psychology, 87*, 385–392.

Becker, G. (1976). *The economic approach to human behavior.* Chicago: University of Chicago Press.

Brehmer, A., & Brehmer, B. (1988). What have we learned about human judgment from thirty years of policy capturing? In B. Brehmer & C. R. B. Joyce (Eds.), *Human judgment: The SJT view* (pp. 75–114). Amsterdam: North-Holland.

Brehmer, B. (1994). The psychology of linear judgment models. *Acta Psychologica, 87*, 137–154.

Breiman, L., Friedman, J. H., Olshen, R. A., & Stone, C. J. (1993). *Classification and regression trees.* New York: Chapman & Hall.

Brown, N. R., & Siegler, R. S. (1993). Metrics and mappings: A framework for understanding real-world quantitative estimation. *Psychological Review, 100*, 511–534.

Brunswik, E. (1955). Representative design and probabilistic theory in a functional psychology. *Psychological Review, 62*, 193–217.

Carpenter, R. G., Gardner, A., McWeeny, P. M., & Emery, J. L. (1977). Multistage scoring system for identifying infants at risk of unexpected death. *Archives of Disease in Childhood, 53*, 606–612.

Darwin, C. (1965). *The expressions of the emotions in man and animal.* Chicago: University of Chicago Press. (Original work published 1872)

Daston, L. (1988). *Classical probability in the Enlightenment.* Princeton, NJ: Princeton University Press.

Dawes, R. M. (1979). The robust beauty of improper linear models. *American Psychologist, 34*, 571–582.

DiFonzo, N. (1994). *Piggybacked syllogisms for investor behavior: Probabilistic mental modeling in rumor-based stock market trading.* Unpublished doctoral dissertation, Temple University, Philadelphia.

Edwards, W. (1954). The theory of decision making. *Psychological Bulletin, 51*, 380–417.

Edwards, W. (1962). Dynamic decision theory and probabilistic information processing. *Human Factors, 4*, 59–73.

Einhorn, H. J. (1970). The use of nonlinear, noncompensatory models in decision-making. *Psychological Bulletin, 73*, 221–230.

Einhorn, H. J., & Hogarth, R. M. (1975). Unit weighting schemes for decision making. *Organizational Behavior and Human Performance, 13*, 171–192.

Elster, J. (1979). *Ulysses and the sirens: Studies in rationality and irrationality.* Cambridge, England: Cambridge University Press.

Fischer Welt Almanach [Fischer World Almanac]. (1993). Frankfurt, Germany: Fischer.

Fischhoff, B. (1977). Perceived informativeness of facts. *Journal of Experimental Psychology: Human Perception and Performance, 3*, 349–358.

Fishburn, P. C. (1988). *Nonlinear preference and utility theory.* Baltimore: Johns Hopkins University Press.

Fishburn, P. C. (1991). Nontransitive preferences in decision theory. *Journal of Risk and Uncertainty, 4*, 113–134.

Gallistel, C. R., Brown, A. L., Carey, S., Gelman, R., & Keil, F. C. (1991). Lessons from animal learning for the study of cognitive development. In S. Carey & R. Gelman (Eds.), *The epigenesis of mind: Essays on biology and cognition* (pp. 3–36). Hillsdale, NJ: Erlbaum.

Gigerenzer, G. (1991). From tools to theories: A heuristic of discovery in cognitive psychology. *Psychological Review, 98*, 254–267.

Gigerenzer, G. (1993). The bounded rationality of probabilistic mental models. In K. I. Manktelow & D. E. Over (Eds.), *Rationality: Psychological and philosophical perspectives* (pp. 284–313). London: Routledge.

Gigerenzer, G. (1994). Why the distinction between single-event probabilities and frequencies is relevant for psychology (and vice versa).

In G. Wright & P. Ayton (Eds.), *Subjective probability* (pp. 129–161). New York: Wiley.

Gigerenzer, G. (1995). The taming of content: Some thoughts about domains and modules. *Thinking and Reasoning, 1,* 324–333.

Gigerenzer, G. (1996a). On narrow norms and vague heuristics. A reply to Kahneman and Tversky (1996). *Psychological Review, 103,* 592–596.

Gigerenzer, G. (1996b). Rationality: Why social context matters. In P. Baltes & U. M. Staudinger (Eds.), *Interactive minds: Life-span perspectives on the social foundation of cognition* (pp. 319–346). Cambridge, England: Cambridge University Press.

Gigerenzer, G., & Hoffrage, U. (1995). How to improve Bayesian reasoning without instruction: Frequency formats. *Psychological Review, 102,* 684–704.

Gigerenzer, G., Hoffrage, U., & Kleinbölting, H. (1991). Probabilistic mental models: A Brunswikian theory of confidence. *Psychological Review, 98,* 506–528.

Gigerenzer, G., & Murray, D. J. (1987). *Cognition as intuitive statistics.* Hillsdale, NJ: Erlbaum.

Gigerenzer, G., Swijtink, Z., Porter, T., Daston, L., Beatty, J., & Krüger, L. (1989). *The empire of chance: How probability changed science and everyday life.* Cambridge, England: Cambridge University Press.

Gilpin, M. E. (1975). Limit cycles in competition communities. *The American Naturalist, 109,* 51–60.

Goldstein, D. G. (1994). *The less-is-more effect in inference.* Unpublished master's thesis, University of Chicago.

Goldstein, D. G., & Gigerenzer, G. (1996). *Reasoning by recognition alone: How to exploit a lack of knowledge.* Unpublished manuscript.

Griffin, D., & Tversky, A. (1992). The weighing of evidence and the determinants of confidence. *Cognitive Psychology, 24,* 411–435.

Hammond, K. R. (1966). *The psychology of Egon Brunswik.* New York: Holt, Rinehart & Winston.

Hammond, K. R. (1990). Functionalism and illusionism: Can integration be usefully achieved? In R. M. Hogarth (Ed.), *Insights in decision making* (pp. 227–261). Chicago: University of Chicago Press.

Hammond, K. R., Hursch, C. J., & Todd, F. J. (1964). Analyzing the components of clinical inference. *Psychological Review, 71,* 438–456.

Hammond, K. R., & Summers, D. A. (1965). Cognitive dependence on linear and nonlinear cues. *Psychological Review, 72,* 215–244.

Hammond, K. R., & Wascoe, N. E. (Eds.). (1980). *Realizations of Brunswik's representative design: New directions for methodology of social and behavioral science.* San Francisco: Jossey-Bass.

Hertwig, R., Gigerenzer, G., & Hoffrage, U. (in press). The reiteration effect in hindsight bias. *Psychological Review.*

Hoffrage, U. (1994). *Zur Angemessenheit subjektiver Sicherheits-Urteile: Eine Exploration der Theorie der probabilistischen mentalen Modelle* [On the validity of confidence judgments: A study of the theory of probabilistic mental models]. Unpublished doctoral dissertation, Universität Salzburg, Salzburg, Austria.

Huber, O. (1989). Information-processing operators in decision making. In H. Montgomery & O. Svenson (Eds.), *Process and structure in human decision making* (pp. 3–21). New York: Wiley.

Huttenlocher, J., Hedges, L., & Prohaska, V. (1988). Hierarchical organization in ordered domains: Estimating the dates of events. *Psychological Review, 95,* 471–484.

Johnson-Laird, P. N. (1983). *Mental models.* Cambridge, MA: Harvard University Press.

Juslin, P. (1993). An explanation of the hard–easy effect in studies of realism of confidence in one's general knowledge. *European Journal of Cognitive Psychology, 5,* 55–71.

Juslin, P. (1994). The overconfidence phenomenon as a consequence of informal experimenter-guided selection of almanac items. *Organizational Behavior and Human Decision Processes, 57,* 226–246.

Juslin, P., Winman, A., & Persson, T. (1995). Can overconfidence be used as an indicator of reconstructive rather than retrieval processes? *Cognition, 54,* 99–130.

Kahneman, D., Slovic, P., & Tversky. A. (Eds.). (1982). *Judgment under uncertainty: Heuristics and biases.* Cambridge, England: Cambridge University Press.

Keeney, R. L., & Raiffa, H. (1993). *Decisions with multiple objectives.* Cambridge, England: Cambridge University Press.

Klayman, J., & Ha, Y. (1987). Confirmation, disconfirmation, and information in hypothesis testing. *Psychological Review, 94,* 211–228.

Koriat, A., Lichtenstein, S., & Fischhoff, B. (1980). Reasons for confidence. *Journal of Experimental Psychology: Human Learning and Memory, 6,* 107–118.

Krebs, J. R., & Davies, N. B. (1987). *An introduction to behavioral ecology* (2nd ed.). Oxford: Blackwell.

Legendre, G., Raymond, W., & Smolensky, P. (1993). Analytic typology of case marking and grammatical voice. *Proceedings of the Berkeley Linguistics Society, 19,* 464–478.

Lewontin, R. C. (1968). Evolution of complex genetic systems. In M. Gerstenhaber (Ed.), *Some mathematical questions in biology.* Providence, RI: American Mathematical Society.

Lopes, L. L. (1992). Three misleading assumptions in the customary rhetoric of the bias literature. *Theory and Psychology, 2,* 231–236.

Lopes, L. L. (1994). Psychology and economics: Perspectives on risk, cooperation, and the marketplace. *Annual Review of Psychology, 45,* 197–227.

Lopes, L. L. (1995). Algebra and process in the modeling of risky choice. In J. R. Busemeyer, R. Hastie, and D. Medin (Eds.), *Decision making from the perspective of cognitive psychology* (pp. 177–220). New York: Academic Press.

Lovie, A. D., & Lovie, P. (1986). The flat maximum effect and linear scoring models for prediction. *Journal of Forecasting, 5,* 159–168.

Luchins, A. S., & Luchins, E. H. (1994). The water jar experiments and Einstellung effects: I. Early history and surveys of textbook citations. *Gestalt Theory, 16,* 101–121.

McClelland, A. G. R., & Bolger, F. (1994). The calibration of subjective probabilities: Theories and models 1980–1994. In G. Wright & P. Ayton (Eds.), *Subjective probability* (pp. 453–482). Chichester, England: Wiley.

McClennen, E. F. (1990). *Rationality and dynamic choice.* Cambridge, England: Cambridge University Press.

McCloskey, D. N. (1985). *The rhetoric of economics.* Madison: University of Wisconsin Press.

Payne, J. W., Bettman, J. R., & Johnson, E. J. (1993). *The adaptive decision maker.* Cambridge, England: Cambridge University Press.

Prince, A., & Smolensky, P. (1991). *Notes on connectionism and harmony theory in linguistics* (Tech. Rep. No. CU-CS-533-91). Boulder: University of Colorado, Department of Computer Science.

Shepard, R. N. (1967). On subjectively optimum selections among multi-attribute alternatives. In W. Edwards & A. Tversky (Eds.), *Decision making* (pp. 257–283). Baltimore: Penguin Books.

Simon, H. A. (1945). *Administrative behavior: A study of decision-making processes in administrative organization.* New York: Free Press.

Simon, H. A. (1956). Rational choice and the structure of the environment. *Psychological Review, 63,* 129–138.

Simon, H. A. (1982). *Models of bounded rationality.* Cambridge, MA: MIT Press.

Simon, H. A. (1990). Invariants of human behavior. *Annual Review of Psychology, 41,* 1–19.

Simon, H. A. (1992). *Economics, bounded rationality, and the cognitive revolution.* Aldershot Hants, England: Elgar.

Sniezek, J. A., & Buckley, T. (1993). Becoming more or less uncertain. In N. J. Castellan (Ed.), *Individual and group decision making* (pp. 87–108). Hillsdale, NJ: Erlbaum.

Sperber, D., Cara, F., & Girotto, V. (1995). Relevance theory explains the selection task. *Cognition, 57,* 31–95.

Stephens, D. W., & Krebs, J. R. (1986). *Foraging theory.* Princeton, NJ: Princeton University Press.

Stone, G. O. (1986). An analysis of the delta rule and the learning of statistical associations. In D. Rumelhart, J. McClelland, & the PDP Research Group (Eds.), *Parallel distributed processing: Explorations in the microstructure of cognition* (pp. 444–459). Cambridge, MA: MIT Press.

Tetlock, P. E. (1992). The impact of accountability on judgment and choice: Toward a social contingency model. In M. Zanna (Ed.), *Advances in experimental social psychology* (Vol. 25, pp. 331–376). New York: Academic Press.

Tweney, R. D., & Walker, B. J. (1990). Science education and the cognitive psychology of science. In B. F. Jones & L. Idol (Eds.), *Dimensions of thinking and cognitive instruction* (pp. 291–310). Hillsdale, NJ: Erlbaum.

von Winterfeldt, D., & Edwards, W. (1982). Costs and payoffs in perceptual research. *Psychological Bulletin, 91,* 609–622.

Weber, U., Böckenholt, U., Hilton, D. J., & Wallace, B. (1993). Determinants of diagnostic hypothesis generation: Effects of information, base rates, and experience. *Journal of Experimental Psychology: Learning, Memory, and Cognition, 19,* 1151–1164.

Wimsatt, W. C. (1976). Reductionism, levels of organization, and the mind–body problem. In G. G. Globus, G. Maxwell, & I. Savodnik (Eds.), *Consciousness and the brain: A scientific and philosophical inquiry* (pp. 199–267). New York: Plenum.

Appendix

The Environment

City	Population	Soccer team	State capital	Former East Germany	Industrial belt	Licence plate	Intercity trainline	Exposition site	National capital	University
Berlin	3,433,695	−	+	−	−	+	+	+	+	+
Hamburg	1,652,363	+	+	−	−	−	+	+	−	+
Munich	1,229,026	+	+	−	−	+	+	+	−	+
Cologne	953,551	+	−	−	−	+	+	+	−	+
Frankfurt	644,865	+	−	−	−	+	+	+	−	+
Essen	626,973	−	−	−	+	+	+	+	−	+
Dortmund	599,055	+	−	−	+	−	+	+	−	+
Stuttgart	579,988	+	+	−	−	+	+	+	−	+
Düsseldorf	575,794	−	+	−	−	+	+	+	−	+
Bremen	551,219	+	+	−	−	−	+	−	−	+
Duisburg	535,447	−	−	−	+	−	+	−	−	+
Hannover	513,010	−	+	−	−	+	+	+	−	+
Leipzig	511,079	−	−	+	−	+	+	+	−	+
Nuremberg	493,692	+	--	−	−	+	+	+	−	+
Dresden	490,571	+	−•	+	−	−	+	−	−	+
Bochum	396,486	+	−	−	+	−	+	−	−	+
Wuppertal	383,660	−	−	−	+	+	+	−	−	+
Bielefeld	319,037	−	−	−	−	−	+	−	−	+
Mannheim	310,411	−	−	−	−	−	+	−	−	+
Halle	310,234	−	−	+	−	−	+	−	−	−
Chemnitz	294,244	−	−	+	−	+	−	−	−	−
Gelsenkirchen	293,714	+	−	−	+	−	+	−	−	−
Bonn	292,234	−	−	−	−	−	+	−	−	+
Magdeburg	278,807	−	+	+	−	−	+	−	−	−
Karlsruhe	275,061	+	−	−	−	−	+	−	−	−
Wiesbaden	260,301	−	+	−	−	−	+	−	−	−
Münster	259,438	−	−	−	−	−	+	−	−	+
Mönchengladbach	259,436	+	−	−	−	−	−	−	−	−
Braunschweig	258,833	−	−	−	−	−	+	−	−	+
Augsburg	256,877	−	−	−	+	−	+	−	−	+
Rostock	248,088	−	−	+	−	−	+	−	−	−
Kiel	245,567	−	+	−	−	−	+	−	−	+
Krefeld	244,020	−•	−	−	−	−	−	−	−	−
Aachen	241,961	−	−	−	−	−	+	−	−	+
Oberhausen	223,840	−	−	−	+	−	+	−	−	−
Lübeck	214,758	−	−	−	−	−	+	−	−	−
Hagen	214,449	−	−	−	+	−	+	−	−	−
Erfurt	208,989	−	+	+	−	−	+	−	−	−
Kassel	194,268	−	−	−	−	−	+	−	−	+
Saarbrücken	191,694	+	+	−	−	−	+	+	−	+

City	Population	Soccer team	State capital	Former East Germany	Industrial belt	Licence plate	Intercity trainline	Exposition site	National capital	University
Freiburg	191,029	−	−	−	− .ᵗ	−	+	−	−	+
Hamm	179,639	−	−	−	+	−	+	−	−	−
Mainz	179,486	−	+	−	−	−	+	−	−	+
Herne	178,132	−	−	−	+	−	−	−	−	−
Mülheim	177,681	−	−	−	+	−	−	−	−	−
Solingen	165,401	−	−	−	−	−	+	−	−	−
Osnabrück	163,168	−	−	−	−	−	+	−	−	+
Ludwigshafen	162,173	−	−	−	−	−	+	−	−	−
Leverkusen	160,919	+	−	−	−	−	−	−	−	−
Neuss	147,019	−	−	−	−	−	−	−	−	−
Oldenburg	143,131	−	−	−	−	−	+	−	−	+
Potsdam	139,794	−	+	+	−	+	+	−	−	−
Darmstadt	138,920	−	−	−	−	−	+	−	−	+
Heidelberg	136,796	−	−	−	−	−	+	−	−	+
Bremerhaven	130,446	−	−	−	−	−	+	−	−	−
Gera	129,037	−	−	+	−	+	+	−	−	−
Wolfsburg	128,510	−	−	−	−	−	−	−	−	−
Würzburg	127,777	−	−	−	−	−	+	−	−	+
Schwerin	127,447	−	+	+	−	−	+	−	−	−
Cottbus	125,891	−	−	+	−	−	−	−	−	−
Recklinghausen	125,060	−	−	−	+	−	+	−	−	−
Remscheid	123,155	−	−	−	−	−	−	−	−	−
Göttingen	121,831	−	−	−	−	−	+	−	−	+
Regensburg	121,691	−	−	−	−	+	+	−	−	+
Paderborn	120,680	−	−	−	−	−	−	−	−	+
Bottrop	118,936	−	−	−	+	−	−	−	−	−
Heilbronn	115,843	−	−	−	−	−	−	−	−	−
Offenbach	114,992	−	−	−	−	−	−	−	+	−
Zwickau	114,636	−	−	+	−	+	−	−	−	−
Salzgitter	114,355	−	−	−	−	−	−	−	−	−
Pforzheim	112,944	−	−	−	−	−	+	−	−	−
Ulm	110,529	−	−	−	−	−	+	−	−	+
Siegen	109,174	−	−	−	−	−	−	−	−	+
Koblenz	108,733	−	−	−	−	−	+	−	−	+
Jena	105,518	−	−	+	−	+	+	−	−	+
Ingolstadt	105,489	−	−	−	−	−	+	−	−	−
Witten	105,403	−	−	−	+	−	−	−	−	+
Hildesheim	105,291	−	−	−	−	−	+	−	−	+
Moers	104,595	−	−	−	+	−	−	−	−	−
Bergisch Gladbach	104,037	−	−	−	−	−	−	−	−	−
Reutlingen	103,687	−	−	−	−	−	−	−	−	−
Fürth	103,362	−	−	−	−	−	+	−	−	−
Erlangen	102,440	−	−	−	−	−	+	−	−	+

Note. City populations were taken from *Fischer Welt Almanach* (1993).
* The two starred minus values are, in reality, plus values. Because of transcription errors, we ran all simulations with these two minus values. These do not affect the rank order of cue validities, should not have any noticeable effect on the results, and are irrelevant for our theoretical argument.

Received May 20, 1995
Revision received December 4, 1995
Accepted December 8, 1995 ∎

[15]

The Cost Of Thinking

STEVEN M. SHUGAN*

A theory and methodology are developed for explicitly considering the cost of comparing diverse choice alternatives. The theory allows (1) explicit analytical measures of the cost of using various simplified decision strategies, and (2) predictions regarding the distribution of mistakes a consumer is likely to make when reducing decision-making effort.

To the vast majority of mankind nothing is more agreeable than to escape the need for mental exertion. . . . To most people nothing is more troublesome than the effort of thinking (James Bryce, The American Commonwealth 1888).

The finite or quantal choice problem[1] frequently occurs in consumer research (Bettman 1971; Blattberg and Sen 1976; Einhorn 1970; Fishbein and Ajzen 1972; Luce 1959; Marschak and Radner 1972; McFadden 1970; Tversky 1972; Tversky and Kahneman 1979). A consumer or decision maker faces a choice conflict in which the individual must select a choice from some set of alternatives (products, brands or generally choice objects). The consumer, after choosing one of the alternatives or products, derives satisfaction from the product represented by the product's utility (Farquhar 1977; Green and Wind 1973; Herstein and Milnor 1953) or affect (Fishbein and Ajzen 1972). Naturally, many theorists began by assuming individuals would choose their most preferred (optimal) product, thereby maximizing their utility. However, this approach ignored measurement errors and lacked insight for situations in which new alternatives are offered or old alternatives deleted.

Attempts to incorporate nonoptimal alternatives focused on probabilistic predictions of choice. For example, Luce's axiom (Luce 1959) or Clarke's rule (Clarke 1957) and its extensions (Morgan 1974) propose a mechanism where the probability of any product being chosen is a function not only of product preference, but also of the utilities of the nonoptimal prod-

ucts. Marketers began using information from the entire set of products to estimate choice probabilities. McFadden (1970) used statistical estimation implying Luce's assumption (for product addition and deletion) to determine underlying consumer preferences from choice data. Later, Hauser (1976) showed this probabilistic approach to be consistent with deterministic axioms of preference.

Unfortunately, the influence of nonoptimal alternatives is somewhat arbitrary. The actual consumer choice mechanism is not considered. Therefore, it is not difficult to construct choice situations that are inconsistent with Luce's axiom (Becker, DeGroot, and Marschak 1963; Debreu 1960; Tversky and Russo 1969).

One problem with Luce's axiom is its lack of consideration of product differences and similarities. In marketing terms, Luce's axiom implies that when a new brand is introduced, it derives its market share proportionally from all other brands regardless of substitutability. This deficiency was remedied by viewing preferences for characteristics as fundamental (Fishbein and Ajzen 1972; Keeney and Raiffa 1976; Lancaster 1966) rather than preferences for products. Tversky (1972) brilliantly combined the notion of characteristics (albeit binary) with a Luce-type mechanism.

The theory was now sufficiently rich to address problems of new products, deletion of products, and changing preferences for existing products. However, empirical examinations (Bass 1974; Bass, Pessemier, and Lehmann 1972; Hayes 1964; Payne 1976) showed that behavior was far more complex. When faced with a choice conflict, consumer perceptions were formed

* Steven M. Shugan is Assistant Professor of Marketing, Graduate School of Business, University of Chicago, Chicago, IL 60637. Parts of this research were conducted at the University of Rochester. The author wishes to thank Donald Lehmann, Dov Pekelman, Subrata Sen, John Hauser, and the anonymous reviewers for their many helpful comments.

[1] The quantal choice, or "all-or-nothing response," refers to problems where responses can be expressed as "occurring" or "not occurring," e.g., whether an insect is dead or living. Problems such as "how much will he buy?" are not quantal choice problems. A large literature exists on statistical techniques for dealing with quantal response data.

© JOURNAL OF CONSUMER RESEARCH • Vol. 7 • September 1980

100   THE JOURNAL OF CONSUMER RESEARCH

by acquiring information on each product and then processing that information to arrive at an expected utility. Preference only partially influences choice by determining benefits. However, the determination has costs—rife information, numerous alternatives, time pressure, the consumer's limited information processing capabilities, and the general effort exerted to solve the problem. Generally, the net utility of finding the best product from one set of products may be different from the net utility of finding it as best from another set of products. That is, there may be a cost associated with the act of making a decision—the "cost of thinking."

The study of decision-making or thinking costs has been well accepted by many researchers (Coombs 1964; Dawes 1964; Simon 1957; Simon and Newell 1971) who have studied specific simplifying rules for processing information that purport to lower decision-making costs (Bettman 1977; Bettman and Kakkar 1977; Einhorn 1971; Slovic, Fischhoff, and Lichtenstein 1970; Wright and Barbour 1977) and their applications to marketing (Lehmann 1977; Russo 1977; Wright 1975). These rules often search for a "satisfactory" alternative rather than an optimal one, and, hence, the process is referred to as "satisficing" (Simon 1957). This experimental research has provided substantial understanding of consumer behavior. However, the costs associated with these rules have yet to be rigorously defined and measured. To adequately understand, model, predict, and possibly influence the consumer choice process, we must build a theoretical foundation for "thinking costs." We must quantify thinking costs, determine a unit of measurement, and explore how that measurement varies across choice conflicts.

This paper develops a theory of choice that explicitly considers the difficulty in comparing diverse alternatives. The objective is to provide a methodology and development for explicitly dealing with "thinking costs" that use both the notions of preferences over characteristics and probabilistic predictions of choice. Specifically, one objective is to define a measurable (i.e., well-defined and calculable) unit of thought, and then use it to quantify and estimate the cost of utility maximization. Another objective is to examine the precise cost of using various simplifying decision rules as compared to a utility maximizing procedure, allowing a theoretical comparison of various simplifying strategies on a cost basis.

Of course, simplifying decision rules may lead to less than optimal alternatives, which could be called mistakes. An important objective of this paper is to examine these mistakes and how a reduction in thinking costs often leads to a reduction in expected benefits. It will be shown that under certain specific conditions Luce's axiom describes these mistakes, and under more general conditions Tversky's mechanism describes them.

BRIEF REVIEW OF CHOICE THEORY

Strategies that intend to save decision-making costs by simplifying the choice process include conjunctive, disjunctive (or maximax), minimax, and lexicographic strategies, all generally referred to as noncompensatory. That is, one characteristic cannot compensate for a deficiency in another. The conjunctive rule states: any product not meeting a minimum cutoff level on any characteristic is eliminated. The Federal Drug Administration uses a conjunctive strategy in issuing standards (e.g., purity, weight, age) that all ethical drugs must meet. Wright (1975) cites a variation of this strategy, i.e., choosing the product that meets any of the cutoffs.

The disjunctive strategy or rule is a maximax strategy. Products are compared on their best characteristic. The product with the highest rating on its best characteristic is chosen. The minimax strategy suggests products should be judged on their weakest characteristic, and the one with the strongest weakest characteristic should be selected. For example, an electric circuit may be chosen on the basis of its weakest component because once that component fails, the circuit fails. Finally, the lexicographic strategy first ranks the characteristics in order of importance and then selects the product rated best on the most important characteristic. If two or more products rate equally, the next most important characteristic is used as a tie breaker. For example, the winner of a chess tournament is the person winning the most games. However, if two or more people tie on this criterion, a measure of the quality of the opponents may be used as a tie breaker. The lexicographic rule proper will not be dealt with in detail, because a generalization of the Tversky mechanism contains the essential lexicographic elements and represents a much richer model of the consumer decision process.

Note that each of the preceding examples of simplifying strategy usage was justified on the outcome it provided rather than the savings of decision-making costs. The strategies, in fact, determined the best product. It is much more difficult to compare the strategies on the ease of their use than on their potential to select the best alternatives. The first step involves experimentation on the relative ease of adopting various simplifying decision rules. However, a theoretical framework is needed to formally compare the potential savings in decision-making costs for the various strategies.

THE CONFUSION INDEX

Development of a "Thinking Cost"

Let us start by considering the cost of a utility-maximizing model. It will then be possible to determine how simplifying decision rules reduce that cost. Suppose a consumer wishes to choose the best (most preferred) product from several products. For the moment, assume this decision is occurring for the first time. If there are M alternative products under consideration, the consumer must make $M-1$ comparisons to determine the most preferred, i.e., eliminate $M-1$ products. For example, to discover Lysol is the best of four household cleaners, the consumer could compare Lysol with the other three, making $M-1$ comparisons. If there were a fixed cost, f, per comparison, the total cost of the decision could be computed by multiplying that cost by $M-1$. Precisely,

$$\text{difficulty of choice} = (M-1)f, \qquad (1)$$

where,

f = the cost of comparing two products, and
M = the number of alternative products considered.

Equation 1 can be written as,

$$\text{general difficulty of a choice} = m\hat{f}, \qquad (2)$$

where,

m = the number of product comparisons, and
$\hat{f}$ = the average difficulty or cost of comparing two products.

Equation 2 provides a method for computing "thinking costs." However, some products may be harder to compare with each other than other pairs of products. Therefore, a method for computing the cost of comparing two products, f, is required.

The Difficulty of Comparing Two Products

Assume the consumer's preferences are determined (directly or as a cue) by the product's characteristics. Then, a consumer who wishes to choose between two products may proceed by comparing the two products on their characteristics. These comparisons may be viewed as aspect (Tversky 1972), or attribute, comparisons. For example, a consumer choosing between two household cleaning products may first compare them on ammonia content. Second, a comparison on drying speed may take place. Next, the products could be compared on the attractiveness of their respective colors. These comparisons could then proceed until all characteristics of the product are exhausted, uniquely defining each product. The two products may be compared on a multitude of characteristics before a choice is made.

Assume that associated with each characteristic comparison is a fixed cost, a unit of comparison effort. The products must be evaluated on the characteristic and their differences assessed. It is then reasonable to assume that the more comparisons necessary to make a choice, the more difficult the choice. If the choice can be made after comparing the products on one char-

acteristic only, the choice is relatively easy. If, however, several hundred characteristic comparisons are required, the choice can be considered relatively difficult. This paper measures the thinking cost associated with a choice by positing that f is monotonically related to the number of characteristic comparisons made. That is, more difficult decisions require more characteristic comparisons.

This representation of the consumer choice process would be void of implications without a methodology to classify choice situations with respect to the number of comparisons necessary to resolve the conflict. Fortunately, this representation can be interpreted as a sampling problem. The consumer can be viewed as sampling product pair differences by characteristic. For example, consider the household cleaning product comparison. The consumer first compares the products on ammonia content. This comparison is basically sampling from the population of product differences. The sample chosen has one observation—difference in ammonia content. Again, the second comparison on drying speed can be viewed as an observation on drying speed difference. The sample now contains a third observation—color attractiveness difference. At each point in the sampling, the consumer can infer the true difference (i.e., the true preference) between the products. Given a positive inferred difference, the former product will be chosen. Given a negative inferred difference, the latter product will be chosen. Finally, given a difference close to zero, the consumer will remain uncertain and continue sampling, comparing the products on yet another characteristic.

The crucial question becomes: How many product difference comparisons need to be made so that the consumer will feel sufficiently confident to make a decision, i.e., choose the product judged superior on characteristics observed thus far? This number determines f, and, hence, the difficulty of the choice. Given some fairly unrestrictive assumptions (DeGroot 1970), sampling theory would dictate the following three factors as influencing the expected number of characteristic comparisons necessary to make the choice. If z_r is the difference in utility between the products on attribute r, the three factors are:

1. The true difference in mean utility (average relative preference) between the two products. This is the expected value of z_r, r probabilistically chosen, denoted $E(z)$.
2. The confidence level at which the decision must be made, denoted α. This value is the probability of not making a mistake.[2]
3. The variability in the characteristic difference between the two products. This is the variance of z_r, r probabilistically chosen, denoted $var(z)$.

---

[2] The α level has a strong relationship to the psychological theory of involvement.

The first factor is inversely related to the difficulty of the choice. If the true difference in utility between the two products is large, holding factors 2 and 3 constant, few characteristic comparisons will be required and the choice is easy. However, if the true difference in utility is small, many comparisons will be required to determine this small difference, hence the choice is more difficult. Hendrick, Mills, and Kiesler (1968) appear to have contradictory experimental results; however, other factors were not kept constant.

The second factor is directly related to the difficulty of the choice. The consumer may infer, at any time, which is the more preferred product and then choose that product. But the consumer would then be choosing a product before all possible characteristics have been compared.. Hence, the consumer risks a mistake. Requiring more confidence implies a lower acceptable risk, which requires more comparisons and, hence, a more difficult decision. For example, in choosing sticks of gum, the consequence of a mistake is relatively unimportant. Here, the consumer may only consider one product characteristic for comparison, perhaps brand name. However, in choosing a house, the consequence of a mistake may be very costly and more comparisons are required.

Note that α is exogenous to the model. The confidence level, α, reflects how this choice interacts with other decisions and the expected difficulty of the decision at hand. The resources allocated, including thinking effort, to any choice will depend on opportunities made available by other choices. Here, α reflects and captures the effect of all outside choices on the choice at hand. Future research using Bayesian analysis may specify a loss function based on some global optimization.

The third and final factor is inversely related to the difficulty of the choice. As the variability in product characteristic differences increases (actually, the differences in utility), holding average relative preference constant, the number of comparisons necessary to make a choice at a given confidence level increases. This increase, in turn, heightens the difficulty of the decision. For example, in comparing the two household cleaning products, a consumer would find the comparison relatively easy if one product uniformly dominated the other product on all characteristics (color, amount of suds, abrasiveness, etc.), that is, zero characteristic difference variability. Conversely, the consumer would find the comparison relatively difficult if the two household cleaners were not only very different on all characteristics, but also superior on an equal number of characteristics.

The preceding discussion can be formalized for preciseness, as follows:

N = number of characteristics (e.g., ammonia content or color attractiveness for household cleaners) that uniquely identify the choice alternatives.

X_{ij} = the level of the ith characteristic for choice alternative j (e.g., the ammonia content for Windex).

$U_i(X_{ij})$ = satisfaction or utility derived from the ith characteristic for alternative j, abbreviated U_{ij}.

U_j = actual satisfaction or utility derived from the selection of alternative j.

Further, for simplicity, assume[3]

$$U_j = \sum_{i=1}^{N} U_{ij}.$$

Suppose a consumer must choose between product j and product k (for example, between Lysol and Windex). The consumer proceeds to compare the products on a series of characteristics. For each characteristic r, the utilities for both products, U_{rj} and U_{rk}, respectively, are observed and the difference, $z_r = U_{rj} - U_{rk}$, is obtained. If n characteristics are examined, the consumer will choose product j if $\sum_{r=1}^{n} z_r > 0$ and product k if $\sum_{r=1}^{n} z_r < 0$. (The case where $\sum_{r=1}^{n} z_r = 0$ will be discussed later.)

The consumer must, then, choose the number of characteristics to observe (that is, n).[4] This n will depend on the willingness of the consumer to make a mistake, which is represented by α. The consumer requires n to be large enough so that the probability of not making a mistake is less than α. Precisely, the consumer requires both:

Condition A: $P(\bar{z}_n > 0 | U_j - U_k < 0) < 1 - \alpha$,

and

Condition B: $P(\bar{z}_n < 0 | U_j - U_k > 0) < 1 - \alpha$,

where $P\ (\cdot | \cdot)$ is a conditional probability function, $\bar{z}_n$ is the sample mean with sample size n, i.e., $(1/n) \sum_{r=1}^{n} z_r$, and α is the confidence level ($0 < \alpha < 1$).

To minimize thinking cost, the consumer will select the minimum number of characteristic comparisons, n^*, so that the confidence level is maintained. Precisely,

n^* = minimum n, so that Conditions A and B hold.

As stated earlier, n^* is a function of $E(z)$, $var(z)$, and α. Now, the variance of z can be interpreted as the perceptual difficulty in comparing the two products, which can be analyzed by breaking the $var(z)$ into its

---

[3] This assumption does not require a linear utility function, only additive separability over characteristics (see Farquhar 1977). Note that the assumption only concerns consumer preferences, and makes no direct assumption about information processing.

[4] Sequential sampling simply requires the use of standard and well-developed dynamic programming (for example, see Blackwell 1965 or Wetherill 1975) with special emphasis on optimal stopping (DeGroot 1970). However, the mathematics would soon become quite tedious and might obscure the insights of the subsequent development.

FIGURE A

POSITIVE COVARIANCE — A SIMPLE CHOICE

$$\left(\text{cov}\left[U_A, U_B\right] = 1.56\right)$$

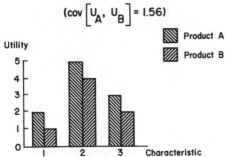

FIGURE B

NEGATIVE COVARIANCE — A DIFFICULT CHOICE

$$\left(\text{cov}\left[U_A, U_B\right] = -.78\right)$$

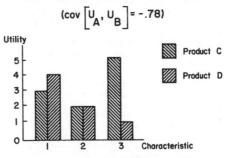

components. Hence,

$$var(z) = var(U_j - U_k),$$
$$= var(U_j) + var(U_k) - 2cov(U_j, U_k),$$

where $cov(U_j, U_k)$ is the covariance between U_j and U_k.

The first term, $var(U_j)$, can be interpreted as the lack of a halo effect (Beckwith and Lehmann 1975; Thorndike, 1920) for product j. For example, if product j has a strong halo effect, i.e., it is perceived similarly on all characteristics, this term will be small. Hence, other factors constant, the larger the halo effect on product j, the easier the choice becomes. The next term, $var(U_k)$, can be analogously interpreted as the lack of a halo effect surrounding product k. Again, the larger the halo, the easier the choice. The final term, $cov(U_j, U_k)$, represents the perceptual similarity of product j and product k.[5] It is inversely related to the cost of thinking. This term will tend to be large if the two products vary similarly, that is, if products j and k are both rated highly on the same attributes.

Consider Figure A. Here, product A and product B are compared on three characteristics. They vary similarly, i.e., A is high on the same characteristics. Product A is superior on all characteristics, the covariance is positive, and the thinking cost is small.

Now consider Figure B, which illustrates two products, C and D. The utility of Product C is the same as Product A, i.e., ten, and the utility of Product D is the same as Product B, i.e., seven. Again, the difference in preference is three units. The respective variances are also identical. However, the covariance is now negative. Product C is superior on only one characteristic. The consumer must trade off the third characteristic with the first and second characteristics. The

result is a more complex and difficult decision. Hence, the covariance term represents the perceptual complexity inherent in the product differences.

Summarizing, the cost of thinking is directly proportional to the perceptual complexity in comparing the products (halo effect and difference effect), and is inversely related to both the difference in preference between the products and the confidence at which the choice must be made. These three factors influence the expected number of comparisons necessary to make a particular choice and, thus, the expected difficulty of comparing two products. These three factors also determine a bound for the number of necessary comparisons and, hence, the potential difficulty; the actual difficulty of comparing the two products will be probabilistic and depend on the characteristic selection. This potential difficulty is a bound on the number of characteristic comparisons necessary to achieve confidence level α. That bound follows for a binary choice and is the sample size sufficient to achieve the desired confidence level, i.e., meet Conditions A and B:

$$f_p = \frac{var[z]}{(1 - \alpha)E[z]^2}, \qquad (3)$$

where f_p = the potential cost of comparing two products. This quantity is an upper bound on f as proven by Theorem 1:

Theorem 1: If f_p comparisons are made then the probability of making a correct choice is at least α.[6]

Equation 3 is an upper bound on the minimum number of comparisons, n^*, and not the actual n. When the exact distribution of z is given, f can be computed directly. However, f_p may vary monotonically with f (i.e., still representing relative difficulty) and, there-

---

[5] However, it does not represent the difficulty in discerning differences as discussed by Thorndike (1920).

[6] Proofs of theorems are given in Appendices, which are available from the author.

fore, f_p provides a method for approximating thinking costs with a closed form expression. The methodology for approaching thinking costs as proposed by this paper is not dependent on using this particular surrogate for f. Three comments in this connection are appropriate.

First, note that f_p defined by Equation 3 can be written in terms of the utilities of product j and product k as follows:

$$f_p = \frac{\sigma_j^2 + \sigma_k^2 - 2\sigma_{jk}}{(1 - \alpha)(\mu_j - \mu_k)^2},$$

where,

$$\mu_j = (1/N) \sum_{r=1}^{N} U_{rj},$$

$$\mu_k = (1/N) \sum_{r=1}^{N} U_{rk},$$

$$\sigma_j^2 = (1/N) \sum_{r=1}^{N} (U_{rj} - \mu_j)^2,$$

$$\sigma_k^2 = (1/N) \sum_{r=1}^{N} (U_{rk} - \mu_k)^2,$$

$$\sigma_{jk} = (1/N) \sum_{r=1}^{N} (U_{rj} - \mu_j)(U_{rk} - \mu_k).$$

Second, f_p is scale invariant. The utilities can be subject to any linear transformation and f_p remains the same. Hence, this f_p is consistent with the use of utility functions unique to a linear transformation, as derived from most axiom systems (Herstein and Milnor 1953; Keeney and Raiffa 1976). Further, the utilities can be measured with standard techniques, such as conjoint analysis (Green and Rao 1971; Green and Srinivasan 1977; Luce and Tukey 1964) or its extensions (Hauser and Shugan 1980).

Third, f_p is either infinite or undefined as the difference in utilities approaches zero while the actual f will approach the total number of characteristics. This means that when two products have exactly the same utility, it is impossible to determine which product is superior.[7]

Comparing Multiple Products

If M products are considered, Equation 1 gives the cost of thinking. Letting f_i be the comparison cost for the ith comparison, Equation 1 can be rewritten as follows:

$$c = \sum_{i=1}^{M-1} f_i = (M-1)\bar{f}, \qquad (4)$$

where,

c = the cost or effort needed to make the choice,

$\bar{f}$ = the average binary comparison cost.

[7] Perhaps the cost of comparisons can no longer be viewed as fixed when many comparisons must occur. In that case, the cost must be marginally increasing or α must be decreased.

In general, the distribution of z_r is unknown. In this case, the average comparison cost, $\bar{f}$, can be replaced by the average potential cost, $\bar{f}_p$. Note, the exact order in which the products are compared may affect both $\bar{f}$ and $\bar{f}_p$. Many ordering criteria are possible.[8] In this paper, the criterion chosen will be the minimum f_p over all nonerrored[9] orders. Hence, assume that nonoptimal products are optimally eliminated. Finally, define c_p as the potential difficulty or "thinking cost" termed the confusion index, formulated as follows:

$$c_p = (M - 1)\bar{f}_p^*, \qquad (5)$$

where,

$\bar{f}_p^*$ = the average cost per comparison given the optimal comparison order,

M = the number of alternatives ($M-1$ is the number of comparisons).

A Numerical Example

Consider a choice involving three household cleaners differing on four characteristics. Table 1 indicates a consumer's utility associated with each product by characteristic. These utility values can be obtained, for example, from part worths in conjoint analysis (Tversky 1967) or by multiplying importance by belief in a linear compensatory model. Theorem 1 can be used to determine the difficulty of each binary comparison (for example, let $\alpha = 0.5$).

The cost of deciding between Windex and Lysol can be computed as follows:

$\mu_{Windex} = 3.75 \quad \sigma^2_{Windex} = 14.19 \quad \sigma_{Windex,Lysol} = 10.44$

$\mu_{Lysol} = 4.75 \quad \sigma^2_{Lysol} = 8.19$

and

$$c_p = \frac{[14.19 + 8.19 - 2(10.44)]}{(1 - 0.5)(3.75 - 4.75)^2} = 3.0.$$

It follows that the cost between Windex and Ajax is:

$$c_p = 54.0,$$

and the cost between Lysol and Ajax is:

$$c_p = 2.0.$$

[8] The expected cost rather than lowest cost is a usual and intuitively appealing measure. However, there are at least two reasons for using lowest cost. (1) Consider a lab psychologist who desires to measure the difficulty of a maze. That psychologist could use the number of necessary turns, for inches traveled, assuming the best possible path is taken, or the psychologist could use the number of necessary turns given a random path. The random path may be a poor measure because some sequences would obviously be eliminated by very simple learning. (2) The mean (expected value) may be a poor measure when f_p is used. This drawback comes from f_p being a potential rather than mean cost. Hence, some values of f_p will drastically overstate f.

[9] These orders assume binary choices are correctly resolved.

COST OF THINKING

TABLE 1

UTILITIES BY CHARACTERISTIC BY HOUSEHOLD CLEANER

| Product | Characteristic | | | | |
	Drying speed	Color attractiveness	Polishing	Scent	Total
Windex	0	2	10	3	15
Lysol	1	4	9	5	19
Ajax	1	3	5	4	13

TABLE 2

UTILITIES BY CHARACTERISTIC

| Product | Characteristic | | | | |
	1	2	3	4	Total
A	1	11	2	5	19
B	5	6	3	7	21
C	8	9	3	3	23
D	4	2	5	4	15
E	1	2	7	6	16

Binary Comparisons. Previously, c_p was argued to have the same monotonic properties as c. Thus, if the actual cost, c, were computed for each product comparison, the respective costs would be 1.7, 3.2, and 0.8, rather than 3.0, 54.0, and 2.0, yielding the same rank order.

The rank order depicts the relative difficulty of the respective binary choices. It becomes clear that choosing between Lysol and Ajax is relatively easy (c_p = 2.0). Lysol is, after all, superior on virtually every characteristic. However, choosing between Windex and Ajax is relatively difficult (c_p = 54.0). The inferior product for this consumer, Ajax, is superior on 3 of 4 attributes, requiring numerous tradeoffs to identify Windex as superior.

Windex versus Lysol versus Ajax. The lowest comparison cost would be achieved by first comparing Lysol and Ajax, eliminating Ajax and then comparing Lysol and Windex, eliminating Windex. The total comparison cost would then be 5.0. This sequential elimination can be pictured as a tournament, with the binary choices representing matches. The minimum f_p can be thought of as the "lowest cost tournament," namely:

- choose between Lysol and Ajax,
- eliminate Ajax as inferior,
- choose between Lysol and Windex,
- select Lysol as superior.

FIGURE C

EXAMPLE OF LOWEST COST TOURNAMENT

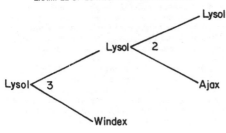

The tournament is illustrated in Figure C. Lysol is first matched against Ajax and found superior, with an associated cost of 2.0. Lysol is then compared to Windex and is found superior with an associated cost of 3.0. The total "thinking cost" of choosing Lysol from these three household cleaners is 2.0 + 3.0 = 5.0.

There are many possible tournaments. The one actually used will depend on numerous factors, such as the expected cost of the tournament, as previously discussed. Again, note that the tournament represents only the expected or potential difficulty of the decision. The actual cost is random and will depend on the luck or skill with which the products are compared.

IMPLICATIONS FOR CHOICE BEHAVIOR

Optimality of Simplified Rules of Behavior

Tversky (1972), Coombs (1964), and Dawes (1964) have proposed simplifying decision rules that disregard information in an attempt to simplify the choice process. Wright (1975) offers a taxonomy of strategies and emphasizes the implication of these strategies to marketing research. Bettman (1971) and others (Payne 1976) have investigated the choice structure from an information processing viewpoint. Einhorn (1970) showed the mathematical relationship of several simplifying rules to linear compensatory models (as limiting cases). However, he emphasizes that "future research should concern the conditions, whether within the individual or in the task" under which these rules should apply. The confusion index previously developed provides a measure of the cost of these simplifying strategies.

A Conjunctive Rule. The conjunctive rule first assigns a minimal acceptable level to each characteristic. For example, if ammonia content is a characteristic of household cleaners, a minimal acceptable level may be 15 percent ammonia. Tversky (1972) extends this concept to define an aspect. Here, if the cleaner has 15 percent or more ammonia content, it is said to have ammonia. Essentially a step-function type of utility is assumed. However, each aspect could represent a level of the characteristic.

TABLE 3

UTILITIES FOR A CONJUNCTIVE STRATEGY

Product	Characteristic[a]				Total
	1	2	3	4	
A	−M	11	−M	5	16 − 2M
B	5	6	3	7	21
C	8	9	3	3	23
D	4	−M	5	4	13 − M
E	−M	−M	7	6	13 − 2M

[a] M approaches infinity.

TABLE 4

UTILITIES FOR A DISJUNCTIVE STRATEGY

Product	Characteristic				Total
	1	2	3	4	
A	0	11	0	0	11
B	0	0	0	7	7
C	0	9	0	0	9
D	0	0	5	0	5
E	0	0	7	0	7

To determine when a conjunctive strategy is less costly than a compensatory model, the confusion index must be computed. Consider the choice between five products (A through E), on four characteristics evaluated, as shown in Table 2. To measure the difficulty of this decision, compute c_p for the lowest cost tournament for which matches are correctly resolved. These matches, and associated costs, are as follows (the superior product labeled with an asterisk):

Comparison	c_p
B* vs. D	4.7
B vs. E*	13.7
A vs. C*	27
B vs. C*	66.

The total cost of using a compensatory model is, therefore, 111.4.

Next, the conjunctive strategy cost can be evaluated. To operationalize the conjunctive strategy, a minimal acceptable level of 3.0 will be assigned to each characteristic. If a characteristic does not meet the assigned level, the consumer utility for that characteristic will be given a very large negative value, called −M. Then, when a difference comparison occurs on that characteristic, the product not meeting the reasonable level is essentially eliminated.

Table 3 illustrates how Table 2 is transformed by a conjunctive strategy. Costs were computed by letting M approach infinity. The total cost of the conjunctive strategy is 76.0. Hence, the conjunctive strategy for this particular choice conflict not only involves less cost, but yields the same outcome (Product C) as the compensatory strategy. Also, the lowest cost tournament structure for the conjunctive strategy is, by coincidence, the same as the compensatory strategy.

An interesting feature of the conjunctive model is that its extreme case would be very costly. In this case, each and every characteristic must be observed to ensure each meets its predetermined minimum level. Therefore, the conjunctive rule was slightly redefined. When comparing two products' characteristics using a conjunctive strategy, the product meeting the fewest levels was eliminated. Then, in a sequential framework

characteristic differences are observed until either one product does not meet the reasonable level or until the consumer is confident both meet all levels, in which case the product with the larger inferred utility is chosen. Therefore, the conjunctive rule implies a product must meet the minimum level on a reasonable number of characteristics. Theorem 2 indicates the cost of using a conjunctive rule.

Theorem 2: The "thinking cost" of eliminating a product (compared to any satisfactory product) with a conjunctive rule is given by:

$$C_{conjunctive} = \frac{(1/k)(N-1)}{(1-\alpha)},$$

where,

k = the number of characteristics on which the product misses the standard level for that characteristic,
N = the total number of characteristics, and
α = the confidence level for the decision.

When the number of characteristics, N, becomes large, the "cost of thinking" associated with the conjunctive rule increases. Wright (1975) has found this result supported experimentally. Now, as the number of characteristics not meeting the minimum level (i.e., k) increases, the "cost of thinking" decreases. For when the product has numerous characteristics at levels below the minimum, it takes few characteristics comparisons to reject the product as inferior. (Because the potential difficulty is being computed, all characteristics are used when computing C even though the consumer will not necessarily observe all characteristics.)

A Disjunctive Rule (Maximax). A disjunctive rule employs a comparison of each product on its best characteristic. For example, if Product A excels on Characteristic 2 and Product B excels on Characteristic 4, then only these two characteristics are used to dictate the choice.

Using a disjunctive strategy, Table 2 is transformed into Table 4. Only the product's best characteristic is used, and all other characteristics are set to zero. Evaluating the lowest cost tournament for the disjunctive strategy yields a total cost of 178.0. Thus, the adoption of a disjunctive rule not only leads to a larger "thinking cost" than either a compensatory strategy or a conjunctive strategy,[10] but also leads, in this case, to the selection of a less than optimal product (i.e., Product A). Theorem 3 indicates the cost of using a disjunctive strategy.

Theorem 3: For the disjunctive strategy, the "thinking cost" involved in comparing a product with the null alternative is given by:

$$C_{Disjunctive} = \frac{(N-1)}{(1-\alpha)},$$

where,

N = total number of characteristics, and
α = the confidence level.

C is a function of N because the consumer must find the best characteristic. This expression reveals the conjunctive strategy always to have less or equal cost than the disjunctive strategy for comparing a product against the null alternative (product elimination).

It also can be shown, using the confusion index, that a decision is easier using disjunctive strategy for comparing two products with the same best characteristic, than when each is best on a different characteristic.

This analysis assumes the consumer knows the best characteristic when it is found. This assumption should be revised in future research to include only the maximum of the sample as the "best known characteristic."

The Maximin Rule. Maximin strategy compares the products on their weakest characteristic. The strategy dictates the selection of the product with the highest value on its weakest characteristic.

Table 5 reflects Table 2 transformed for a Maximin strategy. The total cost of a Maximin strategy for this set of products is 160.0. For this example, the strategy is, therefore, more costly to implement than either the conjunctive or compensatory strategies, and is less costly than the disjunctive strategy. However, the Maximin strategy does determine the optimal product for this example. Note again that the Maximin strategy is redefined along the same lines as the disjunctive strategy. Theorem 4 indicates the relative cost of the Maximin strategy.

Theorem 4: For the Maximin strategy, the "thinking cost" involved in comparing a product against the null alternative is given by:

$$C_{Maximin} = \frac{(N-1)}{(1-\alpha)}.$$

---

[10] Table 4 is the "already processed data," whereas "*c*" reflects the "processing cost." The consumer may not even see all of Table 4 before making a decision. Consider Table 4 as an information board where a consumer sequentially uncovers a datum. Clearly, 75 percent of the time the consumer would have the frustrating experience of finding a "0." To the consumer, guessing which is the best product could be difficult.

TABLE 5

UTILITIES FOR MAXIMIN STRATEGY

Product	Characteristic				Total
	1	2	3	4	
A	1	0	0	0	1
B	0	0	3	0	3
C	0	0	0	3	3
D	0	2	0	0	2
E	1	0	0	0	2

Also, when using a Maximin strategy, the cost of comparing two products is smaller if they have the same worst characteristic rather than different worst characteristics.

Errors and Mistakes

Thus far only costs were considered. However, simplified decision rules reduce expected benefits by allowing mistakes. The previous section assumed that consumers made enough characteristic comparisons so that the chance of error was less than α for each product elimination. It is then possible to state the probability of an error, i.e., not choosing the best product. That probability is one minus the probability of choosing the best product computed by Equation 6.

P(choosing best product)

$$= [1/(\alpha M)][\alpha(1-\alpha)^{M-1} + (1-\alpha) - (1-\alpha)^M], \quad (6)$$

where M = the number of products and α = the confidence level.

Note that for $\alpha = 0.5$, P(choosing best product) is $1/M$.

Until now, some confidence level was set and enough characteristic comparisons were made to achieve that confidence level, the number of necessary comparisons depending on the products. The more comparisons necessary to make the choice, the more costly was the choice. Assume the consumer sets the cost of thinking rather than the confidence level. Here the consumer is assumed to allocate the appropriate thought to the decision to be consistent with an expected utility maximization. For example, let the consumer set the cost of thinking at the lowest possible level, i.e., one. Then, given two products, A and B, Theorem 5 gives the probability the consumer will choose Product A over Product B, denoted $P(A$ over $B)$, and takes the form of Luce's axiom (with ordinary utility functions substituted for Luce's scale values) when (1) consumers minimize thinking costs, (2) the utility functions take just two values (e.g., 0 or 1), and (3) the products have no characteristics in common.

Theorem 5: If the individual seeks to minimize thinking costs, the utility functions are defined over aspects

108

(e.g., 0 or 1), and $U_A \neq U_B$, then:

$$P(A \text{ over } B) = \frac{U_A}{U_A + U_B},$$

if and only if the products possess no common aspects, that is, $U_{rA} \neq 0$ if $U_{rB} = 0$.

The requirement that utility functions take just two values avoids the scaling problems inherent in the theorem, i.e., U_j must be more than ordinal. Hence, Theorem 5 reveals sufficient conditions for using Luce's axiom with ordinary utility functions. Unfortunately, if the products possess common characteristics and their utility functions are not identical, then Luce's axiom fails. Theorem 6 shows the form of $P(A \text{ over } B)$ given common characteristics.

Theorem 6: If the consumer minimizes thinking costs and characteristic utilities only take values 0 or 1, then:

$$P(A \text{ over } B) = \frac{\sum_{r\in R} U_{rA}}{\sum_{r\in R} U_{rA} + \sum_{r\in R} U_{rB}},$$

where,

$R = \{r \mid U_{rA} + U_{rB} = 1\}$.

The summation is over characteristics the products do not have in common. This equation is a special case of Tversky's elimination by aspects mechanism (Tversky 1972). Hence, Tversky's mechanism is much more powerful than Luce's axiom, and takes account of product similarities as well as their relative utilities.

Finally, Condition 2 is relaxed and characteristics will be allowed to have any positive finite utility. In addition, assume the probability of the consumer selecting a particular characteristic for comparing the products is proportional to the discriminatory power (the difference in utilities between the two products) of that characteristic. In this case, the probability of the consumer choosing A is described by a generalization of Tversky's mechanism to include characteristics. Precisely,

$$P[A \text{ over } B] = \frac{\sum_{r\in R'} |U_{iA} - U_{iB}|}{\sum_{r\in R''} |U_{iA} - U_{iB}|}, \qquad (7)$$

where,

$R' = \{r \mid U_{rA} > U_{rB}\}$

$R'' = \{r \mid U_{rA} = U_{rB}\}$ for all i.

The upper summation is over all characteristics for which Product A dominates Product B. The lower summation is over all characteristics for which the products are not equally rated.[11]

---

[11] Theorems 5 and 6 and Equation 7 naturally generalize to three or more products only when the process is conducted as a single stage. For example, when a third product, C, is introduced at utility U_C, then $P(A \text{ over } B \text{ and } C)$ is $U_A/(U_A + U_B + U_C)$ in Theorem 5 only when processing occurs simultaneously rather than sequentially.

Choosing Among Unlimited Numbers of Products

Recalling Equation 2, the expected cost of making a decision was $m\hat{f}$. However, in general, the number of product comparisons may be less than the total number of products. For example, even if there are 30 products, one product could be found superior to five others after four comparisons. The consumer may now stop and feel satisfied (confident) with the decision. In this case, not only is f a random variable, but so is m.

Now if m and f are independent, then we could use Equation 3 to obtain a potential difficulty measure when the number of product comparisons is variable. However, determining the optimal number of products has been well studied in the decision analysis literature (Blackwell 1965; Wald 1947) and in psychology (Pollay 1970), and used to formulate a theory of information and search (Nelson 1970; Stigler 1961; Wilde 1977). Therefore, the problem of determining m independent of f will not be addressed here. If the average or expected number of products m, denoted $\bar{m}$, could be determined, the expected decision difficulty would be $\bar{m}\hat{f}$. Then, $\bar{m}$ would decrease the decision difficulty when the consumer felt future product comparisons would lead to no further improvements, which is consistent with experimental results (Hendrick, Mills, and Kiesler 1968; Kiesler 1966).

Often, m and f are not independent. Then, as the choice process proceeds, the average comparison cost changes. One would expect comparison costs to increase as set size decreases, because $E(z)$ decreases. Hence, the relative costs of different simplifying rules change as the choice proceeds, as has been found experimentally by Payne (1976) and Wright and Barbour (1977).

APPLICATIONS AND IMPLICATIONS

Being able to quantify decision-making costs and the likelihood of mistakes, given reduced decision-making effort, has numerous implications, as the following three examples indicate.

Product Characteristics in an Advertisement

The determination of how many product characteristics should be included in an ad has been more of an art than a science (Kotler 1978). The methodology previously discussed allows the potential for ascertaining how many product characteristics should be included in an ad. For example, suppose consumers sample ads rather than read them in their entirety. Equation 3 implies that when advertised brands are in product categories with high characteristic variability, the ad should mention as many of the brand's favorable characteristics as possible. When the characteristic variability is low, the company should stress only the brand's best characteristics. Similarly, Equation 3 states that high-priced (relative to total income) products requiring large confidence levels should include more characteristics than products with smaller consumer confidence levels, keeping variability constant. Finally, if future research could measure the confidence level (α) at which consumers approach particular product category decisions, the best number of characteristics to advertise to maximize purchase probabilities could be determined.

Information Presentation

In some situations decisions should be made easier, in others more difficult (Russo 1977). For example, in arranging a data base, control panel, or a mail-order catalog, decisions should be made easy. Hence, items should be grouped to minimize average characteristic utility differences (other factors held constant). Also, in some situations changing the difficulty of the decision could change the respective choice probabilities. For example, school cafeterias may want to influence children's meal selections.

New Product Sales Forecasting

New products are generally thought to compete most with "similar" products. These "similar" products are thought to attract people desiring the same characteristics as the new product. However, this phenomenon may require some time. In the short-run when test marketing occurs and ultimate product success is predicted, the consumer may still be gathering information about the new product. Therefore, the purchase probabilities may reflect thinking costs leading to partial product evaluation. The new brand may, in the short-run, receive its market share from competitive products that are easy to compare to the new brand rather than from competitive products for which the effort of comparison is greater, even though long-run shares may be quite different.

Testable Hypotheses

Numerous studies show brand identification can cause a uniformity of perception across attributes (Allison and Uhl 1964). This effect manifests itself by creating strong halo effects about brands (Beckwith and Lehmann 1975). This empirical finding indicates that brand name identification will decrease *var(z)*. By Equation 3, f_p would be decreased, and by Equation 4 the "cost of thinking" is decreased. That is, less information need be sought to maintain the same confidence, α. This implication has had some experimental verification (Jacoby, Szybillo, and Busato-Schach 1977). However, Theorem 1 defines precise implications that could be empirically tested. For example,

f_p could be computed and compared against "stated difficulty," "time spent," and other empirical measures.

The cost of thinking can be reduced by (1) memory, (2) summary statistics, and (3) probabilistic sampling. Thinking costs will be large when the confidence α is large (e.g., for large ticket items relative to total income) and when the characteristic utility variability is large (e.g., products that serve very different markets). In these cases, the consumer may try to reduce costs through memory.

The cost of future decision making can be reduced by remembering large characteristic differences. Just as attribute variability allows greater differentiation (van Raaij 1977), remembering some z_r can reduce c_p. Further, poor memory may encourage adoption of simplifying decision rules. The cost of decision making can also be reduced by gathering summary statistics. Hence, large thinking costs with common tastes, i.e., same $U(\cdot)$, will lead to awards given to best products, certifications, and branding. Finally, if key attributes, those with large variability, are known the consumer can selectively sample characteristics, engaging in probabilistic sampling. Thus, large thinking costs will lead to activities for finding key discriminatory attributes. For example, a consumer buying a boat for the first time may first seek a book about "what to look for in a boat," rather than information on particular boats. Experience may be defined by knowing which attributes have high variability.

LIMITATIONS

In attempting to model and abstract consumer behavior, some restrictive assumptions are often required. This paper provides no exception. Fortunately, quantification has made these assumptions less obscure. For example, the use of single stage sampling rather than sequential sampling was an obvious limitation of the current development. Another limitation is the assumption of a fixed cost per comparison. Although this is a handy assumption, it is clear that this cost should increase as comparisons are made. If "thought" is a limited resource, its use should meet with increasing marginal opportunity costs. This limitation is related to the necessity of requiring α to be determined outside the model.

A third limitation is the static nature of the model. Clearly, the real problem of interest would be the dynamic model. Current research in that area has led to some interesting theories (Lehmann 1977). Although current research on memory (Johnson and Russo 1978) is consistent with this paper, dynamic extensions would require the inclusion of memory and learning. In the dynamic case, it may no longer be appropriate to assume an arbitrary consumer randomly selects characteristics, but instead it may be more appropriate to assume an a priori vector of probabilities. In fact, the behavior of this probability vector over time might hold the key to the most powerful applications of the development. Also, the evaluation costs of the characteristics may change in the dynamic case because of consumer memory.

SUMMARY AND CONCLUSION

A way was provided to explicitly model and measure the cost of thinking. A fundamental unit of thought was defined, which measures the potential difficulty of a decision by examining the characteristic utilities of the alternatives.

With this framework for exploring thinking, a confusion index was derived as a measurable bound on the expected number of necessary units of thinking required to make a choice. It was then possible to determine the relative costs of specific simplifying decision rules as a function of the alternatives. Formulas for computing costs of various decision rules were then derived.

On an individual level, adoption of simplifying choice strategies can leave a consumer vulnerable to manipulation. Choice conflicts can be changed (for example, by the inclusion of nonoptimal and therefore irrelevant products) to lead the consumer to select an inferior product. Hence, by manipulating the choice setting, some degree of control can be exercised over the consumer.

Einhorn and Hogarth (1978) note this effect may occur over an extended period of time. Lack of a proper feedback of information keeps the consumer from learning of the mistakes. Thus, mistakes recur and the best product is never found. Choice rules can, then, have implications for advertising copy decisions, in-store display design, strategies for launching new products, and pricing decisions.[12]

[Received March 1978. Revised February 1980.]

REFERENCES

Allison, Ralph I., and Uhl, Kenneth P. (1964), "Influence of Beer Brand Identification on Taste Perception," *Journal of Marketing Research*, 1, 36–9.
Bass, Frank M. (1974), "The Theory of Stochastic Preference and Brand Switching," *Journal of Marketing Research*, 11, 1–20.
——, Pessemier, Edgar A., and Lehmann, Donald R. (1972), "An Experimental Study of Relationships Between Attitudes, Brand Preference, and Choice," *Behavioral Science*, 17, 532–41.
Becker, Gordon M., DeGroot, Morris H., and Marshak, Jacob (1963), "Probabilities of Choice Among Very

Similar Objects: An Experiment to Decide Between Two Models," *Behavioral Science*, 8, 306–11.
Beckwith, Neil E., and Lehmann, Donald R. (1975), "The Importance of Halo Effects in Multiattribute Attitude Models," *Journal of Marketing Research*, 12, 265–75.
Bettman, James R. (1971), "The Structure of Consumer Choice Processes," *Journal of Marketing Research*, 8, 465–71.
—— (1977), "Data Collection and Analysis Approaches for Studying Consumer Information Processing," in *Advances in Consumer Research Vol. 4*, ed. William D, Perreault Jr., Atlanta, Association for Consumer Research, pp. 342–48.
——, and Kakkar, Pradeep (1977), "Effects of Information Presentation Format on Consumer Information Acquisition Strategies," *Journal of Consumer Research*, 3, 233–40.
Blackwell, David (1965), "Discounted Dynamic Programming," *Annals Mathematical Statistics*, 36, 226–35.
Blattberg, Robert C., and Sen, Subrata K. (1976), "Market Segments and Stochastic Brand Choice Models," *Journal of Marketing Research*, 13, 34–45.
Clarke, F. (1957), "Constant-ratio Rule for Confusion Matrices in Speech Communication," *Journal of the Acoustical Society of America*, 30, 715–20.
Coombs, Clyde H. (1964), *A Theory of Date*, New York: John Wiley & Sons, Inc.
Dawes, Robyn M. (1964), "Social Selection Based on Multidimensional Criteria," *Journal of Abnormal and Social Psychology*, 68, 104–9.
Debreu, Gerard (1960), "Review of Individual Choice Behavior by R. Luce," *American Economics Review*, 50, 186–8.
DeGroot, Morris H. (1970), *Optimal Statistical Decisions*, New York: McGraw-Hill Book Co.
Einhorn, Hillel (1970), "The Use of Nonlinear Noncompensatory Models in Decision Making," *Psychological Bulletin*, 4, 221–30.
—— (1971), "Use of Nonlinear, Noncompensatory Models as a Function of Task and Amount of Information," *Organizational Behavior and Human Performance*, 6, 1–27.
——, and Hogarth, Robin M. (1978), "Confidence in Judgment: Persistence of the Illusion of Validity," *Psychological Review*, 85, 395–416.
Farquhar, Peter (1977), "A Survey of Multiattribute Utility Theory and Applications," in *TIMS Studies in the Management Sciences, Vol. 6*, eds. Martin K. Starr and Milan Zeleny, Amsterdam: North Holland Publishing Co., pp. 59–89.
Fishbein, Martin, and Azjen, Icek (1972), "Attributes and Opinions," *Annual Review of Psychology*, 23, 487–544.
Green, Paul E., and Rao, Vithala (1971), "Conjoint Measurement for Quantifying Judgmental Data," *Journal of Marketing Research*, 8, 355–63.
——, and Srinivasan, Venkataraman (1977), "Conjoint Analysis in Consumer Behavior: Status and Outlook," *Journal of Consumer Research*, 5, 103–23.
——, and Wind, Yoram (1973), *Multiattribute Decisions in Marketing*. Hinsdale, IL: The Dryden Press.
Hauser, John R. (1976), "Consumer Preference Axioms: Behavioral Postulates for Describing and Predicting Stochastic Choice," *Management Science*, 13, 9404–16.
——, and Shugan, Steven M. (1980), "Intensity Measures

---

[12] A relevant yet unanswered question is the effect of simplifying rules on an aggregate market. Perhaps, if consumers continually made mistakes, someone would have the incentive to inform them of their mistakes. Whether a firm could manipulate the behavior of one individual without interference from other individuals remains an unknown.

of Consumer Extended Conjoint Analysis with Intensity Preference," *Operations Research*, 28, 278–320.

Hayes, John R. (1964), "Human Data Processing Limits in Decision Making," *Information System Science and Engineering, Proceedings from Information Processing* New York: McGraw-Hill Book Co.

Hendrick, Clyde, Mills, Judson, and Kiesler, Charles A. (1968), "Decision Time as a Function of the Number and Complexity of Equally Attractive Alternatives," *Journal of Personality and Social Psychology*, 8, 313–8.

Herstein, I. N., and Milnor, John (1953), "An Axiomatic Approach to Measurable Utility," *Econometrika*, 21, 291–7.

Jacoby, Jacob, Szybillo, George J., and Busato-Schach, Jacquelline (1977), "Information Acquisition Behavior in Brand Choice Situations," *Journal of Consumer Research*, 3, 209–16.

Johnson, Eric, and Russo, Edward J. (1978), "What Is Remembered After a Purchase Decision," unpublished working paper, University of Chicago.

Keeney, Ralph L., and Raiffa, Howard (1976), *Decisions with Multiple Objectives*, New York: John Wiley & Sons, Inc.

Kiesler, Charles A. (1966), "Conflict and Number of Choice Alternatives," *Psychological Reports*, 18, 603–10.

Kotler, Philip (1978), *Marketing Management*, Englewood Cliffs NJ,: Prentice-Hall, Inc.

Lancaster, Kelvin (1966), "A New Approach to Consumer Theory," *Journal of Political Economy*, 74, 132–57.

Lehmann, Donald R. (1977), "Consumer Rule Following and Rule Switching Behavior: Theory and Implications," unpublished working paper, Columbia University.

Luce, R. Duncan (1959), *Individual Choice Behavior*, New York: John Wiley & Sons, Inc.

———, and Tukey, John W. (1964), "Simultaneous Conjoint Measurement: A New Type of Fundamental Measurement," *Journal of Mathematical Psychology*, 1, 1–27.

Marschak, Jacob, and Radner, Roy (1972), *Economic Theory of Teams*, New Haven: Yale University Press.

McFadden, Daniel (1970), "Conditional Logit Analysis of Qualitative Choice Behavior," in *Frontiers in Econometrics*, ed. Paul Zarembk, New York: Academic Press, Inc., pp. 105–42.

Morgan, Byron J.T. (1974), "On Luce's Choice Axiom," *Journal of Mathematical Psychology*, 11, 107–23.

Nelson, Phillip (1970), "Information and Consumer Behavior," *Journal of Political Economy*, 78, 311–29.

Payne, John W. (1976), "Task Complexity and Contingent Processing in Decision Making," *Organizational Behavior and Human Performance*, 16, 366–87.

Pollay, Richard W. (1970), "A Model of Decision Times in Difficult Decision Situations," *Psychological Review*, 77, 274–81.

van Raaij, W. Fred (1977), "Consumer Information Processing for Different Information Structures and Formats," in *Advances in Consumers Research, Vol. 4*, ed. William D. Perreault, Jr., Atlanta: Association for Consumer Research, pp. 176–84.

Russo, Edward J. (1977), "The Value of Unit Price Information," *Journal of Marketing Research*, 14, 193–201.

Simon, Herbert H. (1957), *Models of Man*, New York: John Wiley & Sons, Inc.

———, and Newell, Allen (1971), "Human Problem Solving: The State of the Theory in 1970," *American Psychologist*, 26, 145–59.

Slovic, Paul, Fischhoff, Bauch, and Lichtenstein, Sarah (1970), "Behavioral Decision Theory," *Annual Review of Psychology*, 28, 1–39.

Stigler, George J. (1961), "The Economics of Information," *Journal of Political Economy*, 3, 213–25.

Thorndike, Edward L. (1920), "A Consistent Error in Psychological Ratings," *Journal of Applied Psychology*, 4, 25–9.

Tversky, Amos (1972), "Elimination by Aspects: A Theory of Choice," *Psychological Review*, 79, 281–99.

——— (1967), "The General Theory of Polynomial Conjoint Measurement," *Journal of Mathematical Psychology*, 4, 1–20.

———, and Kahneman, Daniel (1979), "Prospect Theory: An Analysis of Decision under Risk," *Econometrika* 47, 263–91.

———, and Russo, Edward J. (1969), "Similarity and Substitutability in Binary Choices," *Journal of Mathematical Psychology*, 6, 1–12.

Wald, Abraham (1947), *Sequential Analysis*, New York: John Wiley & Sons, Inc.

Wetherill, G. B. (1975), *Sequential Methods in Statistics*, London: Chapman and Hall.

Wilde, Louis L. (1977), "Satisfactory Search and the Optimal Use of Information," unpublished working paper, California Institute of Technology.

Wright, Peter (1975), "Consumer Choice Strategies: Simplifying vs. Optimizing," *Journal of Marketing Research*, 12, 60–7.

———, and Barbour, Frederic (1977), "Phased Decision Strategies: Sequels to an Initial Screening," in *Studies in the Management Sciences, Vol. 6*, eds. Martin K. Starr and Milan Zeleny, Amsterdam: North Holland Publishing Co. pp. 91–110.

[16]

Journal of Economic Behavior & Organization
Vol. 38 (1999) 135–144

ELSEVIER

JOURNAL OF
Economic Behavior
& Organization

Emotional arousal as a source of bounded rationality

Bruce E. Kaufman

Department of Economics, Georgia State University, Atlanta, GA 30303, USA

Received 21 February 1997; received in revised form 16 September 1998; accepted 28 September 1998

Abstract

This paper proposes an alternative psychological explanation for bounded rationality. According to Herbert Simon, bounded rationality arises from human cognitive limitations. Following the suggestion of institutional economist John R. Commons, I argue that extremes in emotional arousal also contribute to bounded rationality. This idea is formalized and developed using the Yerkes–Dodson law from psychology. Examples from the popular press and the academic literatures of law, management and economics are presented to illustrate the impact of this type of bounded rationality on human behavior. © 1999 Elsevier Science B.V. All rights reserved.

Keywords: Bounded rationality; Satisficing; Emotional arousal

JEL classification: D00; L21

1. Introduction

The concept of bounded rationality, as developed by Simon and others (Simon, 1987a; Conlisk, 1996), is based on human cognitive constraints, such as limited computational ability and selective memory and perception. In this paper I suggest an additional source of bounded rationality that arises from insufficient or excessive emotional arousal.

Institutional economist, Commons (1934, p. 874) asserted that human behavior is goal oriented and purposive but also heavily influenced by 'stupidity, ignorance, and passion.' Simon (1982, p. 449) acknowledges that in developing the concept of bounded rationality he drew inspiration from Commons' earlier work. Simon, however, locates the source of bounded rationality in the limited processing capability of the human brain ('stupidity') and lack of knowledge of alternatives in the choice set ('ignorance'), but largely ignores the role of 'passion.' This is an important omission, for the literature of psychology suggests that human passions (now called emotional or 'affective' states) can impart

136   *B.E. Kaufman/J. of Economic Behavior & Org. 38 (1999) 135–144*

numerous biases and irrationalities into human decision making (Janis, 1989; Oatley, 1992).

I develop Commons' insight using the Yerkes–Dodson law from psychology. It provides an intuitively appealing explanation for numerous instances of (apparently) non-optimal behavior that cannot be easily explained on the basis of cognitive limitations alone. Illustrative examples are presented from the contemporary press and the research literatures of law, management, and economics.

2. Emotional arousal

Emotions are among the most complex and powerful psychological phenomena. Emotions are subjective mental 'feelings' such as love, hate, anxiety, boredom, fear, sympathy and lust. A variety of theories of emotion exist in the psychological literature, but a popular one (Lazarus, 1991) holds that they are largely cognitive in origin, grow out of some internal or external change that affects a goal of the human agent, vary in intensity in direct proportion to the importance of the goal and the degree to which the internal or external change affects the goal, and take particular forms (e.g., love, hate, anger) depending on the agent's appraisal of the origin, cause, and personal consequences of the internal or external change. Thus, the emotion 'anger' is triggered when the human agent perceives that an event or action threatens a desired goal, in some way demeans or slights personal sense of self-esteem, and is caused by a person (possibly the self) who is judged attributable for the action or event and is thus blameworthy. The experience of this emotion then arouses or energizes the person to action.

The emotions are largely absent from economics' discourse, given the emphasis in the discipline on rational choice (but see Etzioni, 1988; Frank, 1988; Elster, 1998), and even in psychology have remained on the periphery of research until relatively recently (Lewis and Haviland, 1993). This neglect in the modern social and behavioral sciences stands in sharp contrast to the prominent role given to emotions in human affairs by authors and playwrights from the time of the Greeks to the present. Two themes in this literature (and in pre-1960s psychology literature) stand out. The first is that emotions are in many ways the antithesis of reason and rationality, the second is that emotions reflect the lower, more primitive, and often darker side of the human psyche and unless controlled and repressed have the potential to cause great harm and suffering (Hirschman, 1977; Holmes, 1995).

The contemporary view of emotions in psychology is somewhat different. First, while the behaviors caused by emotional states can be irrational, the emotional process itself is largely explicable in rational, scientific terms (Frijda, 1986; de Sousa, 1987). Second, emotions are a central part of the psychological process of motivation (i.e., the process that activates and guides human behavior toward particular ends) as they heighten the saliency of certain desires, wants, and outcomes and thus energize people to pursue them. Third, people adapt and adjust to environmental change by developing 'coping strategies.' Emotions play a key role in such strategies because they signal the human agent that an important goal needs attention (e.g., as when sudden fear alerts a person to jump out of the way of an oncoming car). Finally, the current view is that optimal human performance

B.E. Kaufman / J. of Economic Behavior & Org. 38 (1999) 135–144   137

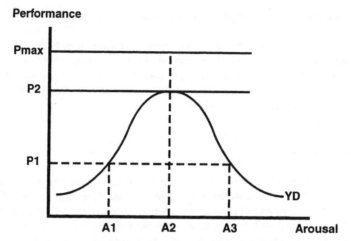

Fig. 1. The relationship between arousal and performance.

requires an intermediate level of emotional intensity – too little emotional intensity and performance suffers from insufficient physical and mental arousal, while too much emotional intensity causes the person to be so aroused that thinking and physical self-control become disorganized (Buck, 1988; Yates, 1990).

It is this last implication that forms the basis of the Yerkes–Dodson law. This law states that the relationship between arousal and performance resembles an inverted U or bellshaped curve, such as the curve YD pictured in Fig. 1 (Petri, 1986). An associated hypothesis is that the optimal level of arousal is lower the more complex the task. The performance measure on the vertical axis can be any type of mental or physical task, while the variable on the horizontal axis can be the general level of arousal (both mental and physiological) or the intensity level of a specific emotion, such as fear or anxiety (Glanzmann, 1985). Although controversy continues among psychologists over the correct specification, domain and theoretical explanation of the law (see Anderson, 1990; Teigen, 1994), the inverse curvilinear relationship between stimulus and task performance first reported by Yerkes and Dodson (1908) from experiments with rats has by now been documented in a sufficiently large number of studies with human beings that the relationship is one of the few in psychology to be called a 'law' (giving it roughly equal status to the 'law of demand' in economics).

Within economics itself, the only economist I am aware of that has introduced the Yerkes–Dodson law into economic theory is Leibenstein (1987). He does not, however, relate it to Simon's concept of bounded rationality, nor does he correctly specify the law in his model of decision making. In particular, Leibenstein makes performance a function of stress or pressure, but stress and pressure can be high at either low or high levels of arousal (Thayer, 1989). As an example, an acutely depressed person may be practically inert (low arousal level) but suffer from severe stress due to frustrated goal attainment and perceived personal inefficacy to resolve the problem.

138   B.E. Kaufman / J. of Economic Behavior & Org. 38 (1999) 135–144

The particular aspect of human performance focused on here is decision making and, in particular, the degree to which decision making leads to the rational behavior depicted in standard neoclassical equilibrium theory. In the typical microeconomic model, the level of rationality is a 'given' in the sense that the quality of decision making remains at the maximum feasible level of the human agent regardless of the nature of the problem to be solved or the potential consequences of the choice decision. In this world, people apply the same level of optimizing, rational choice to decisions involving the personal gain or loss of US\$ 1 or US\$ 10 million or to a decision as simple as which TV program to watch or as complex as deciding yes or no to a proposal for marriage.

Abundant empirical evidence suggests, however, that this conception of human rationality is highly inaccurate (Elster, 1989; Janis, 1989, 1992; Thaler, 1991). A well-researched example is test taking. Psychologists have conducted numerous laboratory experiments in which the arousal level of subjects is manipulated to determine the differential effect of emotional intensity on examination performance. Not unexpectedly, the findings resemble the inverted U shape predicted by the Yerkes–Dodson law (Field et al., 1985; Ashcraft and Faust, 1994). At low levels of arousal (e.g., characterized by boredom), test scores are relatively low. As emotional intensity increases, so do the subjects' test scores until an optimum point is reached. Beyond this point, however, additional emotional arousal (e.g., characterized by substantial anxiety) becomes counterproductive to performance and test scores decline. The same results have been found for a variety of other tasks, such as manual assembly of machine components and mathematical problem solving, and in field settings as well as in the laboratory (Idzikowski and Baddeley, 1983).

Psychologists have identified a number of factors potentially responsible for the arousal/performance relationship (Eysenck, 1982; Thayer, 1989; Eysenck and Calvo, 1992; Forgas, 1995). Very low levels of arousal (such as A1 in Fig. 1), for example, are exemplified by people experiencing depression, melancholy, or boredom. These emotional states are inimical to quality decision making (illustrated by point P1) because little energy is devoted to information gathering and problem solving, attention is focused on other matters than the task at hand, memory is blocked by obsessive thoughts or used to ruminate on non-task considerations, stress is induced by the imbalance between desired and actual stimulation, and autonomic activity (e.g., heart rate, muscle tone) is at a low level (see Davies et al., 1983; Baker and Channon, 1995).

An increase in emotional intensity, such as a shift from depression toward anger or from boredom toward excitement, reduces or alleviates these barriers to optimal decision making, at least up to a point. Additional emotional intensity, for example, causes the person to increase the effort level devoted to information gathering and problem solving (Kahneman, 1973). Other responses include increased autonomic activity (an acceleration of heart rate, a tensing of muscles), a tighter mental focus on the problem at hand, and improved recall from short-term memory (Revelle and Loftus, 1990). These factors increase decision making quality (variously measured, such as amount of profit or error rate in problem solving) until the arousal level A2 is reached where decision making performance reaches its highest level P2. Up to this point emotions play a constructive role in human behavior by helping the agent to develop an effective coping strategy for dealing with change.

B.E. Kaufman / J. of Economic Behavior & Org. 38 (1999) 135–144   139

Further increases in emotional intensity, however, cause a deterioration in the quality of decision making, represented by the downward sloping right hand portion of the YD curve. In effect, the marginal product of arousal becomes negative. At the arousal level of A3, for example, emotional intensity is so great that decision making quality falls back to the level P1, the same poor quality of decision making associated with a state of low arousal. In this situation behavior is less than fully rational because emotions either make preferences no longer well ordered or disrupt the agent's ability to determine optimal outcomes. Some psychologists (e.g., Eysenck, 1982) attribute the decline in performance that occurs with arousal levels beyond A2 to reductions in effort devoted to decision making. A variety of other factors also appear to be involved. Evidence indicates, for example, that high levels of emotional intensity block access to short-term memory, disorganize logical or inferential thought processes, cause loss of control of body parts and functions (e.g., trembling hands, nausea or headaches), block out rational considerations of benefit and cost, and promote acts of aggression and violence (Levitt, 1980; Idzikowski and Baddeley, 1983; Lane, 1991; Lazarus, 1991; Oatley, 1992). In situations of very high emotional intensity, such as infatuated love affairs, theater fires, and wartime battles, decision making loses much of its logical, reasoned character and behavior becomes dominated by impulse, obsession, and instinctive physical reactions (suggested by popular expressions, such as 'driven mad by desire' and 'paralyzed with fear'). Emotional intensity past A2 thus becomes maladaptive with regard to coping with change.

Bounded rationality can be decomposed into two parts, one part arising from cognitive limitations (cognitive BR) and the other from extremes in emotional arousal (emotional BR). In Fig. 1 the horizontal line at Pmax represents the decision making outcome if the human agent possesses 'full' rationality, where full rationality corresponds to neoclassical optimization with perfect cognitive abilities and ideal emotional conditions. Since emotional BR is by definition zero at A2, the gap between the horizontal lines at Pmax and P2 measures the inefficiency in decision making due solely to cognitive BR. For any given individual, the gap Pmax–P2 is larger the more restricted is the agent's cognitive capacity or the more complex the decision making problem.

The amount of emotional BR is then the distance between the horizontal line at P2 and the YD curve at any given arousal level. At arousal level A1, for example, emotional BR is P2 − P1 amount. People who are better able to exercise self-control over their emotions, due either to innate ability or experience gained through training, such as pilots acquire by practicing crash landings on a flight simulator, will have a YD curve which lies closer to the P2 line and will thus suffer less impairment to their decision making at low or high emotional arousal. Note that from this perspective rationality is, in part, a form of learned behavior. However, unless a person is a completely emotionless being, such as Mr. Spock on the *Star Trek* television show, emotional BR is not only an inevitable feature of the human behavior but is likely to be the norm or 'default' state. Although seemingly an extreme position, it was the predominant view of human existence until recent years (Hirschman, 1977; Holmes, 1995). Finally, an increase in the complexity of the decision making problem shifts the peak of the YD curve to the left and may increase or decrease emotional BR. For example, asking a stressed-out person at A3

140   *B.E. Kaufman/J. of Economic Behavior & Org. 38 (1999) 135–144*

to solve a yet more complicated problem will result in a further decline in decision making quality.

3. Implications for satisficing

Simon (1987b, 243) describes the concept of satisficing in these terms, "A decision maker who chooses the best available alternative according to some criterion is said to optimize; one who chooses an alternative that meets or exceeds specified criteria, but that is not guaranteed to be either unique or in any sense the best, is said to satisfice." He goes on to say that satisficing is a direct outcome of cognitive BR (p. 244), "Faced with a choice situation where it is impossible to optimize, or where the computational cost of doing so seems burdensome, the decision maker may look for a satisfactory, rather than an optimal alternative." This is one way of conceptualizing satisficing behavior; the arousal theory provides a complementary explanation.

Kaufman (1990) argues that satisficing can be treated as a phenomenon of human motivation, rather than cognition. In particular, he notes that human beings have a variety of needs that they seek to satisfy and that many needs exhibit the property of 'homeostasis'– i.e., the drive for goal attainment ceases once the need is fulfilled. As Day (1975) notes, homeostasis can be represented in economic theory by assuming that certain needs or wants are subject to satiation, and Day and Robinson (1973) observe that maximization of a preference function when one or more wants or needs are subject to satiation leads to satisficing behavior in the sense that the economic agent chooses a level of the good in question less than the maximum achievable. Kaufman (1990) further suggests that not only are certain wants and needs subject to satiation, but that people also often rank them in terms of priority. Incorporating Maslow's hierarchy of needs theory of motivation into the managerial utility function, for example, he argues that once the firm's profit level exceeds the survival level the need for additional profit is satiated and managers forego additional profit (i.e., they satisfice) and pursue other objectives, such as a quiet life. Analytically, lexicographic preference relations give rise to this form of behavior (Georgescu-Roegen, 1954; Encarnacion, 1964; Day, 1996).

The concept of homeostasis is rooted in the same psychological theory of arousal that underlies the Yerkes–Dodson law and the theory of emotional BR. Just as insufficient arousal leads to conditions of emotional BR, so too does it lead to satisficing. That is, once the satiation level for a good is reached, it no longer exerts motivational 'pull,' arousal falls to zero, and the agent satisfices. Note, first, that while in Simon's model satisficing is a direct consequence of cognitive BR, here satisficing is a complement to bounded rationality in that both originate, albeit independently, from the same psychological source – extremes in arousal. Second, this theory of satisficing is more congruent with existing microeconomic theory, since it is compatible with global optimization, rests on principles of satiation and lexicographic preferences that are more readily incorporated in utility theory, and preserves the condition of continuity in preference relations. Third, this concept of satisficing leads to empirical predictions – e.g., managers in firms with above normal profits will tolerate a certain degree of

B.E. Kaufman / J. of Economic Behavior & Org. 38 (1999) 135–144   141

organizational slack or 'X-inefficiency'– that are not easily derived from Simon's concept (Kaufman, 1990).

4. Illustrations

The usefulness of the bounded rationality construct developed here can be illustrated with four examples drawn, respectively, from the contemporary press and the academic literatures of law, management, and economics.

The first example, drawn from a recent cover story in the *New York Times Magazine* ('Flirting with Suicide,' 15 September, 1996), illustrates human behavior that appears to be far more easily explained by an emotional BR theory than either a cognitive BR or neoclassical 'full' rationality theory. According to the article, a growing number of gay American males are abandoning safe sex practices despite a massive public AIDS prevention campaign and the death of tens of thousands of AIDS victims. It can safely be conjectured that a large majority of adult Americans would judge this behavior to be less than fully rational no matter what end is cited as the ultimate goal (even if suicide is the goal there are numerous less painful and less debilitating ways to die). Defenders of the rational choice model may argue that the preferences of the gay men practicing unsafe sex are quite possibly much different from those of the average person and thus what is irrational behavior in the eyes of some people may well be fully rational in the eyes of another. Although logically correct, the gay men interviewed for the article offer an alternative perspective that is more supportive of an emotional BR theory.

For example, the author says (p. 44) of a young man named Mark who admits to numerous unsafe sex acts with multiple partners, "Like all gay men I have spoken to, but unlike any prevention poster, he [Mark] sees his behavior in an emotional context." He then quotes Mark who says, "It's about love, finally, or what you think is love.... I wanted to experience happiness. Is not that what we all want? Someone who's there for you, even if just for a moment?" Some months later Mark is now HIV positive and admits to his bounded rationality in these words (p. 85), "Sometimes I think that if I had got help 3 years ago – emotional help, psychiatric help – I would not be positive now. I would have a clearer head. But really, it was my own fault." In effect, Mark is saying that he engaged in purposive behavior intended to maximize his utility but that emotional arousal caused him to adopt behaviors that were clearly injurious to his well-being – a fact he cognitively knew at the time but which his emotions overrode.

The second example is from the criminal law. The legal code in this country implicitly recognizes that both cognitive and emotional BR can be causal factors in acts of violence. A 'heat of passion' defense, for example, can get a charge of murder reduced to manslaughter if the jury concludes that the defendant's mental state was sufficiently distorted by sudden emotional excess (Dressler, 1987). The exemplar in the case law of this form of emotional BR is when a husband finds his spouse in the act of adultery and murders the lover in a fit or rage. An alternative defense is 'not guilty by reason of insanity' in which counsel argues that the defendant's mental capacity and ability to reason about right and wrong is so impaired by mental illness or retardation that he/she cannot legally be held responsible for the act. An example of this type of cognitive BR is provided by John Hinckley (Caplan, 1984). Hinckley admitted to his psychiatrist that he shot President Reagan with the intent of killing him, yet the jury found that his thought processes were so deranged by mental illness that he was not in command of his logical faculties.

A third example, this time from the field of management, also illustrates emotional BR at work. In a quest for greater efficiency and profit, many American corporations over the last decade have substantially reduced their work forces through downsizings and restructurings. Yet, paradoxically, evidence from both surveys of business executives and quantitative academic research reveals that profitability in many of these companies is lower after the downsizing and restructurings than before (Cappelli et al., 1997). What accounts for this? According to management consultant (Bardwick, 1991), an important part of the answer is that downsizings and restructurings create rampant fear among employees, sometimes approaching a condition of panic. In particular, she says (p. 34) that, "fear smothers productivity" and goes on to note, "The whole quality of decision making suffers. Employees are always looking over their shoulders. Managers are afraid to take risks." She goes on to attribute the decline in quality of decision making to three psychological consequences of excessive emotional arousal: denial (to avoid fear and stress people deny that the situation has changed), time spent in worrying (people become immobilized by anxiety and spend their time engaged in introspective worrying), and inconsistent behavior patterns (excessive fear leads to behaviors that are often extreme and volatile).

Finally, consider the consequences of emotional BR for economic theory and behavior. An interesting question is whether there can be *too much* competition vis-a-vis achievement of maximum human well being and economic efficiency. This is the position taken by Commons (1934) and, although few economists espouse this point of view today, it has recently found support among a group of psychologists (e.g., Kohn, 1992). Commons maintains that additional competition promotes economic efficiency up to a point, but then becomes dysfunctional when the survival demands placed on the human agent by increased competition outweigh their mental and physical ability to cope. The result of this imbalance is a build-up of excessive 'passion' (i.e., appearance of emotional BR), the occurrence of maladaptive and anti-social behaviors, such as increased resort to methods of unfair competition (e.g., opportunism and fraud), overt acts of violence, and erection of barriers to competition (e.g., restrictive practices of trade unions, government legislation to restrict entry), and an overall diminution of the efficiency with which the economic system works.

With respect to economic theory, Commons' position suggests that a measure of imperfect competition in markets may actually promote social welfare to the extent that the efficiency loss from small amounts of traditional forms of market failure (e.g., economies of scale) are more than offset by the gains in efficiency from lessened competitive pressures, reduced conditions of emotional BR, and improved decision making. With respect to economic behavior, Commons' position offers one explanation for why people in the United States, despite having one of the highest standards of living among industrial countries, also report a much lower self-assessed 'satisfaction with life' score vis-a-vis the people in other advanced economies (Easterlin, 1995). Under this

B.E. Kaufman/J. of Economic Behavior & Org. 38 (1999) 135–144   143

interpretation, the more competitive economic system in the United States generates more material goods and services – a 'plus' for life satisfaction – but also a much higher 'negative' in the form of excessive stress and pressure on the human agent. A concomitant phenomenon of excessive stress is socially undesirable forms of behavior, such as increased incidence of violence in the workplace and on the highways.

References

Anderson, K.J., 1990. Arousal and the inverted-u hypothesis: a critique of Neiss's reconceptualizing arousal. Psychological Bulletin 107(1), 96–100.

Ashcraft, H., Faust, M., 1994. Mathematics anxiety and mental arithmetic performance: an exploratory investigation. Cognition and Emotion 8(2), 97–125.

Baker, J., Channon, S., 1995. Reasoning in depression: impairment on a concept discrimination learning task. Cognition and Emotion 9(6), 579–597.

Bardwick, J., 1991. Danger in the Comfort Zone, AMACOM, New York.

Buck, R., 1988. Human Motivation and Emotion, 2nd ed. Wiley, New York.

Caplan, L., 1984. The Insanity Defense and the Trial of John W. Hinckley. David Godine, Boston.

Cappelli, P., et.al. 1997. Change at Work. Oxford University Press, Oxford.

Commons, J.R., 1934. Institutional Economics: Its Place in Political Economy. MacMillan, New York.

Conlisk, J., 1996. Why bounded rationality? Journal of Economic Literature 34, 669–700.

Davies, D.R., Shackleton, V., Prasuraman, R., 1983. Monotony and boredom. In: Hockey, Robert (Ed.), Stress and Fatigue in Human Performance. Wiley, New York, pp. 1–32.

Day, R., 1975. Adaptive processes and economic theory. In: Day, R.H., Groves, T. (Eds.), Adaptive Economic Models. Academic Press, New York, pp. 1–38.

Day, R., 1996. Satisficing multiple preferences in and out of equilibrium. In: Fabella, R., Dios, E. de (Eds.), Choice, Growth and Development: Emerging and Enduring Issues, Essays in Honor of Jose Encarnacion. University of Philippines Press, Quezon City, The Philippines, pp. 1–23.

Day, R., Robinson, S.M., 1973. Economic decisions with L^{**} utility. In: Cochrane, J., Zeleny, M. (Eds.), Multiple Criteria Decision Making. University of South Carolina Press, Columbia, pp. 84–92.

Dressler, J., 1987. Understanding Criminal Law. Matthew Bender, New York.

Easterlin, R., 1995. Will raising the incomes of all increase the happiness of all?. Journal of Economic Behavior and Organization 27(1), 35–47.

Elster, J., 1989. Solomonic Judgements: Studies in the Limitations of Rationality. Cambridge University Press, New York.

Elster, J., 1998. Emotions and economic theory. Journal of Economic Literature 36, 47–74.

Encarnacion, J., 1964. A note on lexicographic preferences. Econometrica 32, 215–217.

Etzioni, A., 1988. The Moral Dimension: Toward a New Economics. The Free Press, New York.

Eysenck, M., 1982. Attention and Arousal: Cognition and Performance. Springer, New York.

Eysenck, M., Calvo, M., 1992. Anxiety and performance: the processing efficiency theory. Cognition and Emotion 6(6), 409–434.

Field, T., McCabe, P., Schneiderman, N., 1985. Stress and Coping. Lawrence Erlbaum Associates, Hillsdale, NJ, USA.

Forgas, J., 1995. Mood and judgement: the affect infusion model (AIM). Psychological Bulletin 117(1), 39–66.

Frank, R., 1988. Passions Within Reason: The Strategic Role of the Emotions. Norton, New York.

Frijda, N., 1986. The Emotions. Cambridge University Press, New York.

Georgescu-Roegen, N., 1954. Choice, expectations and measurability. Quarterly Journal of Economics 64, 503–504.

Glanzmann, P., 1985. Anxiety, stress, and performance. In: Kirkcaldy, Bruce (Ed.), Individual Differences in Movement. MTP Press, Boston, pp. 89–116.

Hirschman, A., 1977. The Passions and the Interests: Political Arguments for Capitalism Before Its Triumph. Princeton University Press, Princeton, NJ.

144 *B.E. Kaufman/J. of Economic Behavior & Org. 38 (1999) 135–144*

Holmes, S., 1995. Passions and Constraints: On the Theory of Liberal Democracy. University of Chicago Press, Chicago.

Idzikowski, C., Baddeley, A., 1983. Fear and dangerous environments. In: Hockey, Robert (Ed.), Stress and Fatigue in Human Performance. Wiley, New York, pp. 123–144.

Janis, I., 1989. Crucial Decisions: Leadership in Policymaking and Crisis Management. The Free Press, New York.

Janis, I., 1992. Causes and consequences of defective policymaking: a new theoretical analysis. In: Heller, Frank (Ed.), Decision-Making and Leadership. Cambridge University Press, New York, pp. 11–45.

Kahneman, D., 1973. Attention and Effort. Prentice-Hall, Englewood Cliffs, NJ.

Kaufman, B.E., 1990. A new theory of satisficing. Journal of Behavioral Economics 19(1), 35–51.

Kohn, A., 1992. No Contest: The Case Against Competition. Houghton-Mifflin, Boston, MA.

Lazarus, R., 1991. Emotion and Adaptation. Oxford University Press, Oxford.

Lane, R., 1991. The Market Experience. Cambridge University Press, New York.

Levitt, E., 1980. The Psychology of Anxiety, 2nd ed. Erlbaum, Hillsdale.

Leibenstein, 1987. Inside the Firm. Harvard University Press, Cambridge, MA.

Lewis, M., Haviland, J. (Eds.), 1993. Handbook of Emotions. Guillford Press, New York.

Oatley, K., 1992. Best Laid Schemes: The Psychology of Emotions. Cambridge University Press, New York.

Petri, H., 1986. Motivation: Theory and Research, 2nd ed. Wadsworth, Belmont, CA.

Revelle, W., Loftus, D., 1990. Individual differences and arousal: Implications for the study of mood and memory. Cognition and Emotion 4(3), 209–237.

Simon, H., 1982. Models of Bounded Rationality, vol. 2. MIT Press, Cambridge, MA.

Simon, H., 1987a. Bounded rationality. In: Eatwell, John, Milgate, M., Newman, P. (Eds.), The New Palgrave: A Dictionary of Economics, vol. 1. MacMillan, New York, pp. 266–268.

Simon, H., 1987b. Satisficing. In: Eatwell, John, Milgate, M., Newman, P. (Eds.), The New Palgrave: A Dictionary of Economics, vol. 4. MacMillan, New York, pp. 243–245.

Sousa, 1987. The Rationality of Emotion. MIT Press, Cambridge, MA.

Teigen, K., 1994. Yerkes–Dodson: a law for all seasons. Theory and Psychology 4(4), 525–547.

Thaler, R., 1991. Quasi-Rational Economics. Sage, New York.

Thayer, R., 1989. The Biopsychology of Mood and Arousal. Oxford University Press, Oxford.

Yates, J.F., 1990. Judgement and Decision Making. Prentice-Hall, Englewood Cliffs, NJ.

Yerkes, R.M., Dodson, J.D., 1908. The relation of strength of stimulus to rapidity of habit-formation. Journal of Comparative Neurology and Psychology 18, 459–482.

[17]

ELSEVIER

Journal of Economic Behavior and Organization
Vol. 29 (1996) 191–209

JOURNAL OF
Economic Behavior
& Organization

Modes of economizing behavior: Experimental evidence

Mark Pingle [a,*], Richard H. Day [b]

[a] *Department of Economics, University of Nevada, Reno NV 89557, USA*
[b] *Department of Economics, University of Southern California, Los Angeles CA 90089-0253, USA*

Received 9 February 1994; revised 17 July 1995

Abstract

In addition to more or less elaborate, explicitly rational procedures, economic choices in reality are frequently made by trial and error, imitation, following an authority, habit, thoughtless impulse, and hunch. Presenting results from a number of experiments that explicitly incorporate decision cost, this paper explores the extent to which these alternative decision making modes can lead to 'optimal' choices.

JEL classification: D00; C91

Keywords: Economizing behavior; Experimental economics

1. Introduction

Economists generally understand – as Frank Knight (1971, p. 67) recognized long ago – that individuals do not ordinarily make elaborate calculations in deciding what to do. Moreover, in most economic situations, people usually consider only a part of the information and relatively few of the alternatives potentially available. Indeed, they do not always consider information or compare alternatives at all. Instead, they act according to economizing 'modes,' a fact emphasized by Alcian (1950) in a classic article and even earlier by Schumpeter

---

* Corresponding author.

192   M. Pingle, R.H. Day / J. of Economic Behavior & Org. 29 (1996) 191–209

(1934) in his discussions of the circular flow. Day (1984) elaborated this point of view, suggesting that economizing choices could be described by one of seven basic alternative modes: procedural optimizing, experimentation, imitation, following an authority, habit, unmotivated search, and hunch.

While an individual may not display full rationality in a procedural sense, a choice made according to one or the other of these modes may nonetheless be optimal or near optimal. This led Simon (1978) to distinguish what he called 'substantive rationality' from 'procedural rationality.' In his language, a choice is *substantively rational* if it is optimal; that is, the best among all feasible choices, regardless of how the choice is made. Conversely, a choice process is *procedurally rational* if it involves making a choice after comparing two or more alternatives, according to an explicit criterion, regardless of whether or not the choice is optimal.

Finding a best choice over a set of alternatives takes time, energy, and perhaps other valuable resources. Even if one were to possess perfect knowledge of one's budget set and preferences, one would be unable to make a choice without expending real resources. For this reason, the exercise of a given mode can be thought of as resulting from an effort to economize on scarce, cognitive, and computational resources, or to put it in terms we used elsewhere, as the result of 'economizing economizing' (Day and Pingle, 1991). See also, Conlisk (1988).

Because the less rational or non-rational modes may save resources, they make possible improved choices from the point of view of substantive rationality. This observation raises the question, 'To what extent can non-rational modes of behavior allow decision makers to get around decision costs so that optimal or near optimal choices can still be made.' This paper summarizes experimental work designed by Pingle (1992), Pingle (1995a) and Pingle (1995b) to answer this question.

In all of these experiments, an economic setting was constructed in which a well defined optimal choice existed and could be calculated, and for which the cost of making a decision could be introduced. By carefully accounting for the cumulative cost of making decisions and by comparing actual outcomes with the potential outcomes, the success of various strategies could be ascertained.

In a variant of an hypothesis going back at least to Knight, Smith (1991) has argued that appropriate institutions can compensate for the cognitive limitations of market participants and has reported a considerable body of experimental evidence to support this contention. The experiments reported here do not address this hypothesis. Rather, our hypothesis is that decision makers actively economize decision costs by using non-procedurally rational modes of choices. *If substantively rational decisions are made in the face of decision costs, then it may be because decision makers are able to overcome decision cost road blocks by adopting modes of decision making behavior which are not procedurally rational.*

In order to compare the performance of the alternative modes in an experimental setting, it is helpful to distinguish the direct costs of decision making in terms

M. Pingle, R.H. Day / J. of Economic Behavior & Org. 29 (1996) 191–209   193

of time and other resources expended in the process and the indirect cost or loss in potential benefit that occurs because of a failure to choose the best action. We call the former *decision cost* and the latter *misuse cost*. The *total cost of choice* is equal to the sum of these two. While a best choice for a given mode is one in which the misuse cost is equal to zero, we reserve the term 'optimal choice' for a choice where the total cost of choice is equal to zero. That is, an optimal choice is one in which a best choice is made without the use of valuable decision making resources. It is optimal because if a non-optimal choice is made, improved choices exist. If one is attained, it cannot be bettered by any method.

The next section briefly summarizes the main features of the seven modes. We next present evidence that decision costs can influence decision making behavior and outcomes. We then summarize the experimental evidence on the effectiveness of the non-procedurally rational modes of behavior. Our results suggest that Alcian's insights are essentially correct. Individuals pursuing their own advantage can improve their performance in a market setting, not only by being procedurally rational, but by explicitly avoiding optimizing calculation and by using instead the less costly modes.

2. The modes of economizing behavior

Finding a best choice over a set of alternatives takes time, energy, and perhaps other valuable resources. Even if one were to possess perfect knowledge of one's budget set and preferences, one would be unable to make a choice without expending real resources. This fact is obvious in mathematical choice problems which, in all but the simplest cases, can only be solved by means of more or less elaborate algorithms.

Obtaining substantive rationality requires that these decision costs be taken into account and, if possible, avoided. To reduce the cost of comparing alternatives, optimizing procedures in practice involve making a best choice, usually according to a proximate criterion, after the comparison among some subset of alternatives rather than among all alternatives. However, it is also possible to economize on decision costs by using modes of behavior that are not procedurally rational at all.

Trial and error search is one example of a decision making mode which economizes on decision cost. Under trial and error, each action is, in effect, an experiment. Its outcome can be compared with the outcomes of previous actions and a direction for further search determined. Given a sufficiently stable environment, a cost of decision making is relatively low, and a sufficiently regular connection between actions and payoffs, improved decisions can emerge.

Imitation involves an attempt to copy or mimic the actions of another decision maker. This may reduce the effort required to think through a choice problem rationally, but it need not be easy, and it may require rational thought in order to carry it out. Nonetheless, in many situations it will be both cheaper and safer than solving one's own problem from scratch. Indeed, for any occupation that requires great skill, following the practice of a master is usually the quickest way to acquire a satisfactory level of competence.

Following an authority is a common mode of behavior and most people invoke it frequently; especially if we include following the advice of a friend or the evaluation of an expert. (Think here of consumer reports or stock market letters.) Although such behavior may require 'asking around,' or even substantial reading and research, it may cost much less than figuring out what to do for oneself. Tradition is another example, where obedience to the pattern of past behavior which has the authority of custom. One should not suppose that this mode is costless. It is sometimes difficult to follow directions. Indeed, the instruction of an authority or expert may constitute a considerable challenge to rational thought and powers of mimicry. But expert advice can often provide a satisfactory selection of alternatives as a basis for action that short circuits the chain of information gathering, data processing, and reasoning that would otherwise be required.

Many, if not most, of our actions, including numerous routine purchases of consumption items and routine exercise of administrative procedures, involve the unconscious repetition of past behavior, that is, *habit*. Behaving according to habit saves any thinking at all. It also makes it possible to do one thing while thinking about another.

Unmotivated search is difficult to rationalize on economic grounds. It seems to be driven by curiosity, thoughtless impulse, a sense of adventure, and so on. Creative scientists and business innovators seem often to be driven by impulses that bear no calculable reward and that subject the pioneer to unimaginable risks. Nonetheless, they provide a source of perturbation in economic evolution that can have powerful long run effects.

Finally, acting according to *hunch* involves something less – and more – than conscious rational thought. In resource allocation situations, it is the capacity to economize effectively without consciously reasoning. It may be distinguished from habit and unmotivated search, however, in that it may require a special intuitive intellectual faculty that can be sharpened by experience.

Of the seven modes, procedural rationality would appear neither to be the most often used nor to be always the most effective. Indeed, the six alternative modes make possible a focus of scarce cognitive resources and an effectual deployment of rational thought to those problems where it is worth the time and effort involved.

From the constructive or behavioral point of view, then, it follows that choice involves a spectrum of alternative procedures ranging from relatively simple, low cost calculations to very complex, extremely costly algorithms, many of which can be pursued for more or fewer iterations. An agent making a choice must not only make the choice, but must often also decide *how to choose* and *how far to proceed* in applying some particular algorithm.

As in any other economic problem, the selection among the alternative modes

M. Pingle. R.H. Day / J. of Economic Behavior & Org. 29 (1996) 191–209   195

must depend on the costs and benefits. But, just as procedural rationality is not a priori the best method of evaluating choices due to its cost, there is no way to select a choice method in a procedurally optimal manner. The application of procedural rationality to the more general problem would require a costly choice among costly methods of choice, a more complex and demanding problem than the original problem, thus leading to the impossible infinite regress originally described by Winter (1975).

3. The impact of decision cost

Our first experiments (Pingle, 1992) were designed to examine how decision makers respond in environments where decision costs are present.

Each of a number of subjects played a series of computer games in which a consumer problem had to be solved involving a tradeoff between a 'consumption good' and 'leisure' when consumption could only occur if 'labor' was expended. A subject was given a time endowment and a set of 'preferences.' The preferences programmed into the computer determined the 'utility' achieved from leisure and consumption. The subject was shown the maximum utility level possible and was told to make choices in an attempt to achieve that maximum level of utility, given the wage level and price of the consumption good.

The subject could compare the utility levels achieved under various alternatives prior to accepting an alternative as a choice. In a 'costly game,' the computer calculated the subject's leisure time by subtracting from the time endowment *both* the 'work time' chosen and the 'decision time' used to compare alternatives. Because it reduced the time available for work and leisure, decision time used to compare alternatives was valuable. The quantity of decision time used represented the decision cost associated with the choice. In a 'costless game,' the subject could use as much decision time as desired without it being subtracted from the time endowment, meaning there was no decision cost.

Did the existence of a decision cost lead decision makers to economize on decision making resources? Unequivocally, the answer is, 'Yes.' When playing costless games, subjects in the experiment used an average of 20 times more decision time and considered nearly 8 times the number of alternatives than they did when playing the costly games.

In addition to decision cost – the direct costs of decision making in terms of time and other resources expended in the process – decision makers also generally incur an indirect misuse cost – the loss in potential benefit that occurs because of a failure to select the best available alternative. The total cost of choice is equal to the sum of the decision cost and the misuse cost. While a 'best choice' is one in which the misuse cost is equal to zero. Recall that we reserve the term 'optimal choice' for a choice where the total cost of choice is equal to zero. That is, an optimal choice is one in which a best choice is made without the use of valuable decision making resources.

196   M. Pingle, R.H. Day / J. of Economic Behavior & Org. 29 (1996) 191–209

Will the existence of a decision cost reduce decision making quality? To examine this question, we can compare the average misuse cost incurred by subjects when playing costly games to that incurred when playing costless games. In the experiments, a misuse cost of x seconds indicates that the utility level actually attained could have been attained with a time endowment x seconds smaller than the actual time endowment, had the subject made a best choice as opposed the choice actually made. When playing costless games, subjects incurred a mean misuse time level equal to just 2.8 percent of the level they incurred when playing costly games. This is strong evidence that decision costs can reduce decision making quality.

The variability in performance of the subjects is also of interest. The standard deviation for misuse time in the costly games was over 30 times what it was in the costless games. A reasonable explanation for this occurrence is as follows. When decision making resources are free, being good at evaluating alternatives does not matter much. By simply using more of the free decision making resources, those less adept at evaluating alternatives can make choices nearly equal in quality to the choices made by those more adept. However, when evaluating alternatives is costly, differences in decision making skill matter: They lead to differences in performance because there is no free decision resource available which can be used to make up for lacking decision making ability. (Note that this implies scope for imitation, which we discuss in more detail below.)

4. Trial and error

When applying trial and error, each action is an experiment. The decision maker compares previous choices, rather than potential alternatives. By comparing the outcomes of previous choices, an element of rationality is maintained. However, by considering only previous choices, as opposed to the entire set of available potential alternatives, decision cost is also saved. As more and more choices are made in a stable and simple enough environment, performance will tend to improve.

By requiring a group of subjects to make a series of identical choices in the presence of decision cost, trial and error decision making can be examined experimentally. In Pingle's experiment, 8 groups of subjects solved the consumer choice problem described in Section 3 (Pingle, 1992). Each subject made a total of 30 choices. The 30 choices consisted of 3 sets of 10 identical choices. Changes in the decision making environment were made at choices 11 and 21 to allow the impact of environmental change on choice to be examined, while the stable environment within a set allowed the impact of environmental stability to be examined.

In making a choice, a subject could choose to use valuable decision time to compared alternatives prior to making a choice. However, knowing that the same

M. Pingle. R.H. Day / J. of Economic Behavior & Org. 29 (1996) 191–209   197

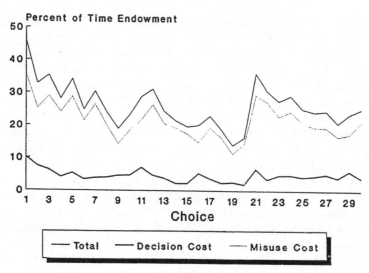

Fig. 1. Cost of choice.

choice was to be made 10 times, the subject could also economize on decision time by adopting a trial and error approach. Of the 1530 choices made by the 51 subjects participating, 1,106 or 72.3 percent were made without comparing any alternatives prior to making a choice.

In spite of this conservation of decision time, subjects found improved choices over each of the 3 sets of 10 identical choices. Fig. 1 displays the mean cost of choice presented as a percentage of the mean time endowment, where the mean is calculated across the 51 subjects in the experiment. The mean is calculated for each of the 30 choices. In game 1 of the first set of games, the mean cost of choice was equal to 46 percent of the mean time endowment, implying 46 percent of the average subject's resources were effectively devoted to decision making as opposed to generating satisfaction. As can be seen in Fig. 1, the cost of choice decreased as subjects repeatedly made the same choice in games 1–10. Most of this improvement was due to improved choices – i.e., a reduction in misuse cost, but some improvement was also due to quicker choices – i.e., a reduction in decision cost. By game 10, the mean cost of choice had decreased to 20 percent of the mean time endowment.

The two changes in the environment, occurring on choices 11 and 21, each led to increases in the cost of choice. However, as can be seen in Fig. 1, subjects were again able to reduce the cost of choice as repeated choices were made within the stable environments of the second and third game sets. The tendency of subjects to avoid comparing alternatives, together with the observed improvements in the quality of choices, is evidence that trial and error was widely used to obtain improved choices over time while economizing on decision time.

198   M. Pingle, R.H. Day / J. of Economic Behavior & Org. 29 (1996) 191–209

5. Imitation

Prior to making a choice, a decision maker may have the opportunity to observe the choices and outcomes of others. This makes imitation possible. By imitating, a decision maker can avoid the decision costs associated with comparing alternatives. At the same time, the choice resulting from the imitation may be of high quality.

Pingle (1995a) designed an experiment to examine how the opportunity to imitate can affect the decision making process when comparing alternatives is costly. Five groups of subjects were formed, with 21 subjects in each group. One group was a control group, where the subjects did not have an opportunity to imitate. Subjects in the other 4 groups had the opportunity to imitate, with the form of imitation varying across the groups.

Each choice involved solving a producer problem, where the stated goal was to maximize profits. The subject, who was able to observe three input prices and the price of the single output produced, selected the input levels for three inputs. The subject was not given the particular form of the production function, nor the maximum level of profit achievable.

To allow the application of procedural rationality, a subject could compare the profitability of alternatives prior to making a choice by entering 'provisional choices' for the three input levels. Upon entering a provisional choice, the computer would calculate and display the associated profit level. By rejecting one provisional choice and entering another, the subject could compare alternative input choices. However, a decision cost was charged for the time used to consider alternatives in this way. While deciding whether or not to accept a provisional choice, the subject could observe the provisional profit level decreasing due the accrual of decision cost.

Each non-control subject played at least 2 sets of 10 games where imitation was possible. The price of an input increased between the first and second set of games, making it more difficult to earn a profit in the second set and changing the optimal input combination.

A third set of games was incorporated in all but one of the experiments in order to model a competitive market, where firms which are able to make profits enter the market and drive down the market price. Operationally, if one subject made a profitable choice in a game, the price received for output by the next subject in the same game was lower, making it more difficult for the next subject to earn a profit and changing the optimal input combination.

Imitation was introduced by allowing subjects to observe the choices and outcomes of those playing the game before them. Of course, the first subject playing the game could not imitate. But, as the play progressed, the number of subjects available for observation increased. In 'experiment 1,' a subject desiring to imitate first had to choose which prior subject to observe, and then the computer would display the choices and outcome of the selected subject. Because subjects

M. Pingle, R.H. Day / J. of Economic Behavior & Org. 29 (1996) 191–209   199

were charged for the time they spent examining previous subjects, this form of imitation was rather costly.

To examine the effect of making imitation less costly, subjects in 'experiment 2' subjects were allowed to examine the outcomes of all of the previous subjects simultaneously prior to selecting the subject whose choices would be observed. This reduces the time necessary to sort through previous subjects. To reduce the cost of imitation still further, subjects in 'experiment 3' were simply presented with the best choice made by the previous subject in the given environment. Finally, to examine the imitation which might occur within a business firm, subjects in 'experiment 4,' prior to playing the games, could learn by actually standing behind the computer and watching (two) subjects play.

There were 42 subjects – in experiments 1 and 2 – who played game 1 without the opportunity to imitate, with game 2 then being played with the opportunity to imitate. In game 1, 78.6 percent of these subjects considered at least two alternatives prior to making a choice, while just 40.5 percent considered two or more alternatives in game 2. Moreover, over the 31 choices made, control group subjects – who did not have the opportunity to imitate – tended to compare alternatives more often than subjects in groups with the opportunity to imitate. In general, this suggests that the availability of imitation reduces the use of procedural rationality.

An exception to this tendency occurred in the third set of games, which turned out to be much more difficult for most subjects in terms of being able to earn positive profit levels. Subjects with the opportunity to imitate did not compare alternatives significantly less often than control group subjects. This indicates that *procedural rationality, in the form of comparing alternatives, may have its primary niche in situations where obtaining improved choices (through any choice method) is particularly difficult.*

The tendency to imitate was greatest when it was first made possible, with the tendency decreasing as the same decision was made repeatedly. Of the 42 subjects mentioned above, 29 or 69.1 percent chose to imitate when the opportunity to imitate was first introduced in game 2. By game 11, the number of subjects choosing to imitate had decreased to 11 or 26.2 percent.

The environmental changes at the beginning of the second and third sets of games also prompted imitation. Between the last game of the first set and the first game of the second set, the percentage of subjects choosing to imitate increased from 26.2 percent to 40.5 percent. Between the last game of the second set and the first game of the third set, the percentage of subjects choosing to imitate increased from 9.5 percent to 42.9 percent.

What tends to extinguish imitative behavior? As repeated choices were made by subjects in a stable environment, the tendency to imitate decreased more rapidly than did the tendency to compare alternatives. In addition, imitative behavior tended to be extinguished more rapidly when the decision cost associated with imitation was lower. This suggests that *imitation may have its primary niche in*

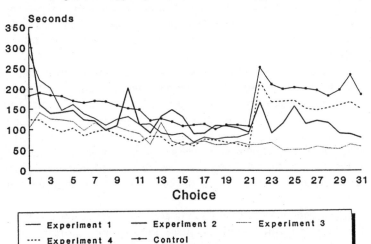

Fig. 2. Cost of choice.

relatively unfamiliar situations, with it falling out of favoring as the gains available through imitation are captured and the decision making environment becomes more familiar.

Fig. 2 presents the mean cost of choice for the choices made in four imitation experiments and the control experiment, where the mean is calculated across the 21 subjects in the particular experimental group. Examining the figure, note that experimental groups where imitation was possible tended to outperform the control group – where imitation was not possible. Second, note that the performance of subjects in experiments 3 and 4 was better than the performance of subject in experiments 1 and 2 over the first two sets of games, an indication how 'low cost' imitation and imitation through an 'apprenticeship' process each enhance the quality of decision making. Finally, note the improvements in the quality of decision making in experiments 1 and 2 as subjects moved from choice 1, where they did not have the opportunity to imitate, to choice 2, where they did have the opportunity to imitate. Using this change in the cost of choice as a measure of the reduction in decision making inefficiency, the introduction of the ability to imitate in game 2 allowed subjects in experiments 1 and 2 to reduce the inefficiency of their decision making from an average of 311 seconds to 192 seconds, or by 38 percent.

In reality, skills are often transmitted from those who are more experienced to those who are less experienced. Sometimes this transmission takes place through formal training. In other instances, skills are transmitted through less formal means; e.g., through imitation. As mentioned above, subjects in experiment 4 had the opportunity to learn how to play the computer games only by watching others

M. Pingle. R.H. Day / J. of Economic Behavior & Org. 29 (1996) 191–209   201

play. No formal training was given. One interesting result from this experiment was that subjects who performed particularly well tended to be followed by subjects who performed particularly poorly. Why?

After the experiment was over, subjects were questioned about their performance. Consistently, those who had performed poorly complained that it was difficult for them to learn how to make good choices because those they were watching made their decisions so quickly. This experimental result points to a practical consideration when it comes to organizing a business, a school, a family, or any other on going organization where the transmission of knowledge is important: Efforts to reduce decision costs can be counter-productive in the long run if they decrease opportunities for the transmission of knowledge through imitation.

The costs and benefits of formal training are widely recognized. However, the costs and benefits of facilitating imitation are probably not so widely recognized. These observations suggest that benefits obtained through formal training might sometimes be obtained less expensively by facilitating imitation.

It is especially important to note that successful behavior governed by *any* mode of economizing can be imitated. Of course, identifying effective behavior itself takes time because it can only be observed through time, so imitation will tend to occur with a lag. But imitation makes possible the diffusion of the benefits of superior action, and benefits of specialization in thinking are gained by one through imitating others who think effectively about something else.

6. Following an authority

Decision makers often make choices where an authority (e.g., an expert, a boss, a parent, a tradition) has prescribed a particular choice. By choosing to follow an authority's prescription, the decision maker avoids decision costs and also avoids any penalties that may be levied for disobedience. In addition, if the prescription is close to optimal, then following the authority might well leave the decision maker better off than if the decision maker were to make the choice using some other method. However, it is possible for a decision maker to incur a large misuse cost, as defined above, by adopting a prescription that is far from optimal.

Here, some results are presented from an experiment (Pingle, 1995b) that was designed to examine how an authority's prescription can affect the decision making process. The experimental framework used was similar to that described above for the imitation experiment. Subjects had to choose the levels of three production inputs with the goal of maximizing profit. As described above, subjects could compare alternatives, but the subjects were charged for the time used to compare alternatives. Rather than having the opportunity to imitate, subjects were shown a prescribed choice and its associated profit level.

Subjects could adopt the prescribed choice, or they could enter a provisional

202   M. Pingle, R.H. Day / J. of Economic Behavior & Org. 29 (1996) 191–209

choice. If the prescribed choice was accepted, then the prescribed choice and the profit level were recorded and a new game was immediately started. On the other hand, if a provisional choice was made, the subject had the option of rejecting or accepting the provisional choice. If the provisional choice was accepted, then the choice and profit level were recorded and a new game was started. If the provisional choice was rejected, then the subject again had the option of accepting the authority's prescription or making another provisional choice. Regardless of whether the subject ended up accepting the authority's prescription or accepting a provisional choice, there was a charge for the decision time used.

In one phase of the experiment, three different groups of subjects each had to make the same choice. For the choice problem given, the optimal choices for the three production inputs were $x_1 = 500$, $x_2 = 119$, and $x_3 = 196$. Each subject played the game 10 times. The groups were distinguished according to the quality of the choice prescribed by the authority.

Group 1 subjects were given the optimal choice as the prescribed choice. They tended to make high quality choices. The actual mean input choices for group 1 subjects were $x_1 = 498$, $x_2 = 118$, and $x_3 = 191$. The mean cost of choice for group 1 subjects was 44.8 seconds, 54 percent of which was decision cost. That is, the use of valuable decision making resources accounted for more than half of the total deviation from optimal decision making, while the remaining deviation was due to the fact that the decision makers did not always make the best choice.

Group 2 subjects were given the choice $x_1 = 30$, $x_2 = 10$, and $x_3 = 20$ as the prescribed choice – a profitable choice, but far from optimal. They tended to make low quality choices. The actual mean input choices for group 2 subjects were $x_1 = 48$, $x_2 = 15$, and $x_3 = 27$. The mean cost of choice was 151.0 seconds, nine percent of which was decision cost. The remaining 91 percent of the cost of choice was misuse cost. Obviously, this group was led far astray by their obedience to authority.

Group 3 subjects were given prescribed choices of intermediate quality. The results were intermediate when compared to those given here for groups 1 and 2. Thus, based upon the results of this of the experiment, the hypothesis that the quality of the prescribed choice does not affect the quality of the decisions actually made can confidently be rejected.

One might expect a group of optimum seeking decision makers to make choices that are randomly distributed around the optimal choice. The experimental results just described indicate that the existence of a prescribed choice can bias actual choices away from the optimal choice in the direction of the prescribed choice. Although group 2 subjects departed from the prescribed choice in the direction of the optimal as repeated choices were made, the actual choice on the 10th repetition ($x_1 = 59$, $x_2 = 18$, and $x_3 = 33$) was still much closer to the prescribed choice than to the optimal choice. The slow progression of this group toward the optimum, combined with the fact subjects in the other two groups also tended to make choices near the prescribed choices, demonstrates that, while an optimal

M. Pingle, R.H. Day / J. of Economic Behavior & Org. 29 (1996) 191–209   203

choice may have a magnetic quality, it may not easily overcome the magnetic quality of a prescribed choice.

In order to examine an authoritarian decision making setting, the impact of punishment for disobedience was studied in a second phase of the experiment. Three groups were formed which differed according to the degree of punishment for disobedience. Each subject in each group solved the same producer choice problem, and each subject in each group was given the same low quality prescribed choice. Group 1 subjects had to pay a 'low fee' for not adopting the authority's prescription; group 2 had to pay a 'high fee;' while group 3 had to pay a 'medium fee.'

Those subjects who faced the higher fees for disobedience tended to submit more often, an observation that is not too surprising. However, what is somewhat surprising is that subjects in the higher fee groups tended to use more time comparing alternatives, even though they may have ultimately adopted the authority's prescription. Also, subjects in higher fee groups, who did not submit to the authority, tended to make choices that were further away from the prescribed choice than did subjects in lower fee groups who did not submit.

What can explain these observations? By comparing alternatives, a subject can learn that the authority's prescription is not the best choice possible. However, for it to be worth deviating from the prescription, subjects facing higher fees for disobedience must find better choices than subjects facing low fees. Finding better choices takes more time, and better choices must be located further away from the prescribed choice. Thus, more severe level of punishment, may (unintentionally) encourage radically deviant behavior, not to mention a waste of decision making resources.

Even when the direct penalty for disobedience is low or nonexistent, the decision maker still faces a potential indirect penalty for disobedience: The choice ultimately made may not be as good as the prescribed choice. Indeed, in the experiment, more than 30 percent of the subjects in the low penalty group were still adopting the authority's poor prescription after facing the same decision 10 times. This is evidence that a *severe direct penalty may not be required to elicit obedience. The indirect cost associated with poor individual decision making may suffice.*

Because decision makers seem to be strongly attracted to prescribed choices, one would expect decision makers to benefit from a prescribed choice which evolves to incorporate learning obtained from experience. To explore this possibility, a third phase of the experiment was conducted with one group of subjects, where the prescribed choice given to a subject in the group was the best choice made by the previous subject in the same environment. Given this design, the first subject had to make choices without a prescription. However, as the number of subjects increased, the experience embodied in the prescribed choice increased.

Fig. 3 shows how four different cost of choice measures evolved as additional subjects participated in the experiment. The curve labelled 'Choice 21' shows the

204   M. Pingle, R.H. Day / J. of Economic Behavior & Org. 29 (1996) 191–209

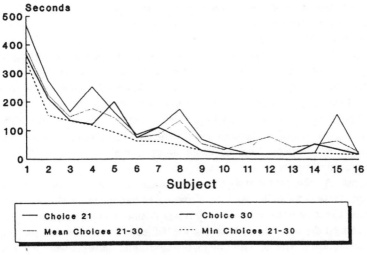

Fig. 3. Cost of choice.

cost of choice for the given subject on choice 21 – the first choice made in the third phase of the experiment. Similarly, the curve labelled 'Choice 30' shows the cost of choice for the given subject on choice 30 – the 10th choice made in the third phase of the experiment. The remaining two curves respectively show the mean and minimum choices by the given subject over choices 21–30. Note that – regardless of which cost of choice measure is used – the prescribed choice did evolve toward the optimum (i.e., the cost of choice decreased toward zero), and the progress made was uneven as additional subjects participated.

Examining the choice 21 curve in more detail, note that the best choice of the first subject, which became the prescribed choice for the second subject, was far from optimal. After this first subject, some subjects were able to find choices better than their prescribed choices, while others could not. By the 10th subject, the prescribed choice was near optimal, where it stayed for the remaining 6 subjects. Of subjects 11–16, all except one made near optimal *first time* choices, illustrating the impact that an evolving prescription can have on decision making efficiency.

Of course, this result was obtained in a stable decision making environment. What if the decision making environment also evolved over time? During the third phase of the experiment, two groups made choices to examine this possibility. In one group, call it group A, the prescribed choice did not change as the environment changed. In the second group, call it group B, the prescribed choice evolved as the environment changed. More precisely, in group B, the prescribed choice received by a subject was the best choice made by the previous subject. The change in the environment was endogenously determined as in the imitation

300   *The Legacy of Herbert Simon I*

M. Pingle. R.H. Day / J. of Economic Behavior & Org. 29 (1996) 191–209   205

experiment described above – when one subject (making a production choice) made a profit in a game, the output price received by the next subject playing the same game would be lower.

In group A, the prescribed choice was set so that the initial subject could earn a sizable, but not maximal, profit by following the authority. By design, as profitable choices by group A subjects drive down the output price, the fixed prescribed choice could eventually become unprofitable. In group B, the prescribed choice was never necessarily profitable, but it could adapt to the changing environment as subjects changed their choices in reaction to price decreases brought on by profitable choices. Each group contained 16 subjects, and each subject played 10 games.

In group A, the first 6 subjects each made at least one profitable choice. However, these profitable choices drove the output price down. Given the production function used, this not only made it more difficult to earn a profit, but it also reduced the optimal input levels. Of subjects 7–16, only one subject found a profitable choice. The actual choices of these latter subjects were not randomly distributed around the optimal choices, but rather were strongly biased in the direction of the prescribed choice. Although profitable choices existed, subjects 7–16 did not find them because they did not search far enough away from the prescribed choice. That is, for these latter subjects, the prescribed choice appeared to be more of a hindrance than a help.

The initial subjects in group B did not make as profitable choices as did the initial subjects in group A. This indicates that the stationary prescription was of high enough quality to be of assistance to the initial subjects in group A. However, as profitable choices led to decreases in the output price, the optimal input choices changed. In group A, this change in the environment was not incorporated in to the prescribed choice, but in group B it was. Thus, while profitable choices virtually ceased after subject 6 in group A, subjects 9, 11, 12, 15 and 16 in group B were each able to find profitable choices. The ability to more consistently earn profits allowed subjects in group B to eventually drive the average output price level below that of group A, an indication of greater decision making efficiency.

7. Unmotivated search, hunch, and habit

In all of the experiments described above, it was usually possible to recognize some sort of strategy or method subjects were using to attack the problem of choice. For example, it was common to see a subject 'take a step in one direction' and examine the outcome comparatively. If the step represented an improvement, then another step was taken in the same direction. Otherwise, a step was taken in the opposite direction, as is typical in trial and error learning.

However, in all of the experiments, there were some subjects who apparently abandoned their 'economizing mode' temporarily in order to make a seemingly arbitrary choice. We do not use the term 'random' to describe these occasions because it is not likely that such deviations are in fact random. Yet, the choices are out of character when compared to the way choices are usually made. In references cited above, Day used the terms 'unmotivated search' and 'hunch' to distinguish among such seemingly arbitrary actions.

It is extremely difficult to identify these types of behavior in the experiments undertaken so far. In many of the experiments, only final choices where recorded, not all alternatives considered. When a radical alternative is considered, it is usually not fruitful and, therefore, tends not to be adopted as a choice. Only successful deviant behaviors are captured in our data.

But, the fact that there were instances of successful deviant behavior is worth noting. When a person is in a new decision making environment, it makes sense to explore. Indeed, there were instances of subjects who made great improvements merely through lucky 'stabs in the dark.' When imitation was possible, or when the improvement could be incorporated into a prescribed choice in the authority experiments, other decision makers were able to benefit from a lucky choice just as much as they would have had the improved choice been found using great skill. This fact implies that, to a certain extent, *a society in pursuit of quality decision making can make up for what it lacks in individual decision making skills by allowing deviant trials and by promoting the inexpensive circulation of information.*

In the experiment where the authority's prescribed choice evolved out of tradition, there were occasional 'mavericks' who significantly deviated from the prescription. Although some found improved choices, most earned *average* profit levels below those earned by subjects who followed the prescription. But arbitrary choice serves a function in the face of decision cost. Although the likelihood of it generating a particularly good choice may not be high, it economizes on decision cost to the extreme. If successful, the decision maker (and all of those able to learn from him) can make an inexpensive jump toward an optimal choice.

Though more work needs to be done, it was apparent in the experiments that habits arise out of a perception that further improvements in decision making are not likely. In cases where the perception is correct, the habits are good habits in that they generate near optimal choices.

Good habits allow valuable decision making resources to be devoted to decisions where those resources will make a difference. Bad habits can be defined as choices which repeat past behavior but which are far from being optimal. In the experiments, we found that the prescribed choices of authorities have the potential of becoming 'addictive' in that many decision makers will gravitate toward prescribed choices even when they are far from being optimal. In general, when bad habits were formed in the experiments, they could be broken by information which would lead decision makers to recognize that the habitual choice was far from optimal.

M. Pingle. R.H. Day / J. of Economic Behavior & Org. 29 (1996) 191–209   207

8. Discussion

Obviously, an optimal choice can be obtained via any choice method which allows the costless consideration of all of the available alternatives. However, in the presence of decision costs, no choice method can guarantee a quality choice. Indeed, seemingly non-rational decision making methods can outperform the explicit comparison of alternatives because they economize on decision costs. The general implication is that decision making in the face of decision costs is an art – the art of getting around the cost of decision making by not being 'too rational,' as Baumol and Quandt (1964) argued. (See Knight, 1971, Conlisk, 1988, and Day and Pingle, 1991 for further discussion of this point.)

Interestingly, this decision making art seems to involve two fundamental economic concepts. One is the law of diminishing returns. As any choice method is continually applied, the incremental benefit declines. As procedural rationality, trial and error, and imitation accomplish their purpose and lead the decision maker to an optimum, they become too expensive to further apply. Habit and authoritarian tradition become dominant. But, as the environment changes, habits and traditions become outdated. This fact, and the fact that unknowns still exist, means that there is room for unmotivated search and hunch to be productive. And, any deviation from optimality again makes procedural rationality, trial and error, and imitation potentially useful. Thus, it appears that those most adept at the art of decision making will not be attached to any particular mode of behavior, but rather will be ready to abandon one mode for another as the perceived need arises.

Specialization and trade is another fundamental economic concept which seems to apply when the goal is good decision making across a whole society. Some have good hunches, some not. Some know best when and when not to search. Some are more adept at applying procedural rationality in particular areas than others. By specializing, or focusing our decision making skills where they are effective, we use our decision making resources where they are most productive. We can then essentially trade for the decision making skills we lack by imitating others or by following some authority or tradition.

The economic settings used for the experiments are far simpler than those usually found in everyday life. For that reason, it might seem remarkable that the seemingly non-rational, economizing modes played such an active role. We are so accustomed to using imitation, habit, and following authority so much of the time that we are scarcely aware of their importance and may grossly underestimate their role in economic life. Moreover, as economists trained in decision theory, we may overestimate the role of procedural rationality and overestimate the irrationality of avoiding that mode.

The economizing principle – as distinct from procedural rationality – resolves this paradox. It may be that near optimal, first time, real world choices are actually made in the face of decision costs, but not because of particularly adept, procedurally rational decision making. Rather, when they occur, they likely arise out of evolutionary processes which generate innovative ways of getting around decision costs, processes which include rationality in the form of a limited comparison of alternatives, but also processes which include maverick entrepreneurs who take stabs in the dark with their successful efforts being imitated by others and recorded in tradition.

There are further implications of our work. If individuals cannot jump to substantively optimal decisions costlessly and if they expend both decision and misuse cost in making economic choices, they may behave out of competitive equilibrium as conventionally defined. If so, special out of equilibrium mechanisms must be instituted to maintain or restore individual feasibility. This is the point of view adopted by Day (1993), who advocates an adaptive evolutionary theory.

Alternatively, the competitive market system may work in such a way as to overcome individual decision and misuse cost so as to bring about general equilibrium and substantially rational economic decision just 'as if' individuals could perceive and behave optimally according to equilibrium prices. That is the view followed by Knight, Friedman, and Lucas, and for which Vernon Smith and others have provided some experimental evidence. Differences in the descriptive and policy implications of these two points of view are substantial. Experiments specially designed to distinguish between them should therefore be undertaken.

9. For further reading

Friedman (1953) and Simon (1987).

References

Alcian, A.A., 1950, Uncertainty, evolution and economic theory, Journal of Political Economy 58, 211–222.

Baumol, W. and R. Quandt, 1964, Rules of thumb and optimally imperfect decisions, American Economic Review 54, 23–46.

Conlisk, J., 1988, Optimization cost, Journal of Economic Behavior and Organization 9, 213–228.

Day, R., 1984, Disequilibrium economic dynamics, Journal of Economic Behavior and Organization 5, 57–76.

Day, R., 1993, Bounded rationality and the coevolution of market and state, Chapter 4, in: R.H. Day, G. Eliasson and C. Wihlborg, eds., The markets of innovation, ownership and control, Amsterdam, North Holland.

Day, R. and M. Pingle, 1991, Economizing economizing, in: R. Franz, H. Singh and J. Gerber, eds., Handbook of Behavioral Economics 2B, Greenwich, Connecticut, JAI Press, 511–524.

Friedman, M., 1953, Essays in Positive Economics, Chicago, University of Chicago Press.

Knight, F., 1971, Risk, uncertainty and profit, Reprint of 1921 edition, Chicago, University of Chicago Press.

Pingle, M., 1992, Costly optimization: An experiment, Journal of Economic Behavior and Organization 17, 3–30.

M. Pingle, R.H. Day / J. of Economic Behavior & Org. 29 (1996) 191–209   209

Pingle, M., 1995a, Imitation versus rationality: An experimental perspective on decision-making, Journal of Socio-Economics 24(2), 281–315.

Pingle, M., 1995b, Submitting to authority: An experimental examination of its effects on decision-making, Forthcoming: Journal of Economic Psychology.

Schumpeter, J.A., 1934, Theory of economic development, (Translated by Redvers Opie), New York, Oxford University Press, 1961 edition.

Simon, H.A., 1978, Rationality as a process and as a product of thought, American Economic Review Papers and Proceedings 68, 1–16.

Simon, H.A., 1987, Rationality in psychology and economics, in: Hogarth. R.M. and M.W. Reder, eds., Rational choice: The contrast between economics and psychology, Chicago, University of Chicago Press.

Smith, V.L., 1991, Rational choice: The contrast between economics and psychology, Journal of Political Economy 99 (4), 877–897.

Winter, S.G., 1975, Optimization and evolution in the theory of the firm, in: R.H. Day and T. Groves, eds., Adaptive economic models, New York, Academic Press, 73–118.

[18]

ENTREPRENEURIAL

INFORMATION SEARCH

ARNOLD C. COOPER
Krannert Graduate School of Management

TIMOTHY B. FOLTA
Krannert Graduate School of Management

CAROLYN WOO
Krannert Graduate School of Management

EXECUTIVE SUMMARY

Information is a key resource for the new venture. Despite the importance of information search practices, little research has examined whether entrepreneurs show a tendency to search for more or less information under particular conditions.

This article considers whether information search might be explained by concepts of bounded rationality. Such theories lead to the counterintuitive expectation that entrepreneurs with less experience or those entering unfamiliar fields would search less because of their more limited understanding of what is needed. In addition, entrepreneurs with higher levels of initial confidence would search less because their "entrepreneurial euphoria" may limit their ability to assess their own needs for additional information.

This study examined the information search practices of 1176 entrepreneurs. It considered six sources of information that were widely used: accountants, friends or relatives, other business owners, bankers, lawyers, and generally available books and manuals. Three measures of search intensity were developed, with the first reflecting the relative importance of all six sources and the remaining two focusing upon the subcategories of professional and personal sources.

It was found that those who had no entrepreneurial experience, on the average, sought more, not less, information. However, as expected, those who ventured into fields which were different and those who had higher levels of initial confidence sought less information. An interaction effect provides insight into these findings and reveals that inexperienced entrepreneurs varied their search depending upon whether they were in familiar or unfamiliar domains. In particular, novice entrepreneurs searched less extensively in unfamiliar domains, a behavior consistent with bounded rationality. By contrast, experienced entrepreneurs did not vary their search pattern. It was also found that entrepreneurs having high levels of confidence sought less information, as expected.

The behavioral tendencies observed here appear to have clear implications for entrepreneurs and their advisors. We might expect that those venturing into fields they do not know would have more

Address correspondence to Krannert Graduate School of Management, Purdue University, West Lafayette, IN 47907-1310.

The authors wish to acknowledge the support and cooperation of the National Federation of Independent Business. An earlier version of this article was presented at the Babson Entrepreneurship Conference, June 1992.

to learn and thus would search more aggressively. However, neither inexperienced nor experienced entrepreneurs acted in this way. In fact, inexperienced entrepreneurs lessened their search as they entered fields they did not know, consistent with the bounded-rationality model. Many prior studies have found that entrepreneurs entering unfamiliar fields are, on the average, less successful (Cooper and Gimeno-Gascon 1992). This certainly raises questions about whether entrepreneurs, both experienced and inexperienced, might benefit from greater emphasis upon gathering and utilizing external information as they enter fields that are new to them. Outside advisors (if the entrepreneur will utilize them) may be helpful in urging and assisting entrepreneurs who enter unfamiliar fields to engage in more extensive information search, even though they may have less developed networks of contacts and less of a feeling for what is needed in such fields. With respect to initial confidence, entrepreneurs and their advisors should recognize that high levels of confidence may lead to lower levels of information search. Recognizing this tendency, they should use care to ensure that entrepreneurial euphoria does not lead to blinders in the search for information.

INTRODUCTION

Much of the process of venture creation involves seeking and interpreting information. In fact, Kirzner suggests that the central role of the entrepreneur is to find and exploit opportunities by taking advantage of economic disequilibria, through knowing or recognizing things that others do not (Kirzner 1973). The process of venture formation might also be viewed as a process of learning, of overcoming the liabilities of newness through information acquisition. Stinchcombe (1990, p. 7) noted that "what is precarious at one time becomes predictable at another time because of new information."

Thus, gathering information for decision-making is a critical activity for the entrepreneur. However, the processes followed by entrepreneurs as they search for information have received only limited attention to date. Gaining insight into any systematic tendencies exhibited by entrepreneurs in gathering information would add to the understanding of entrepreneurial behavior. It would also have implications for advising prospective entrepreneurs.

Theoretical Framework

Processes of information search have been investigated extensively, particularly within the context of established organizations. The amount of information sought and the sources used have been shown to be related to the decision-maker's characteristics and the nature of the problem addressed (Taylor and Dunnette 1974; O'Reilly 1982; Kaish and Gilad 1991; Birley 1985). Some of this work, emphasizing ongoing activity by managers, suggests that feedback processes are operative, with decision-makers seeking more information when performance falls short of objectives (Cyert and March 1963).

Less has been done to examine information search as new ventures are formed. In these contexts, decision-makers are engaged in unstructured activities, with little regular feedback. They must gather information that helps them identify opportunities and then must try to assemble resources and put together a business, all in an iterative process in which they learn about the proposed business and the process of entrepreneurship as they proceed (Stevenson 1989). For some, it is a once-in-a-lifetime activity, in which their previous experience gives them few benchmarks by which to judge whether or not information gathered is adequate. Venture formation is a classic example of "domain-offensive action," involving entry into new fields. Thomas and McDaniels (1990) have noted that the complexity and uncertainty of such moves make them critically dependent upon information.

Actions by entrepreneurs to gather information might be viewed as examples of decision-making under conditions of limited capacity or bounded rationality (Cyert and March 1963). In this framework, the capacity of the human mind for formulating and solving complex problems is viewed as relatively limited. These models emphasize the role of simplifying knowledge structures and cognitive heuristics to reduce complexity. There is no assumption that decision-makers gather and process all relevant information in making decisions. Often, decision-makers work with limited conceptualizations of problems, and the process of information gathering is characterized more by satisfying than by optimizing. In their review article, Lord and Maher (1990) suggested that limited capacity models are most valid in situations where individuals don't know what they are doing, a condition that may apply when individuals are engaged in an act (such as venture formation) for the first time.

The way in which decision-makers conceptualize problems and decide upon what information to seek may reflect the relevant experience that they bring to the situation. Thus, Lord and Maher (1990) noted that experts differed from novices in the way cognitive schema were constructed. The experts' schema were more detailed, more elaborate and meaningful. These schema appeared less superficial than those of the novices who often focused on more literal objects rather than the more subtle dimensions. Experts were also more alert to inconsistencies in the stimuli. All of this suggests that experienced entrepreneurs would attend to more signals and have better appreciation for the value of information being sought than would novices.

In a study of competitive information processing and responses, Smith et al. (1991) suggested that managers with external orientations, that is, orientations toward events outside their organizations, differed from managers with internal orientations. They found that those with external orientations were more likely to gather a richer array of information and to do so with greater speed. On the other hand, an internal orientation was likely to lead to oversimplification and a sense (often premature) that proper conclusions had been drawn. This would be associated with limited channels for search and an early termination of information gathering. In the context of this study, one would expect experienced entrepreneurs, given their prior exposure to customers, competitors, suppliers, regulators, and management professionals, to have more of an external orientation and to possess a greater awareness of external pressures and challenges and to be more aware of information needs.

The theoretical frameworks developed to this point suggest that experience would lead to more elaborate schema and thus more elaborate search; however, one study found the opposite. Involving school superintendents, it found that those with greater experience were less likely to employ elaborate and exhaustive search procedures because they could draw upon routines and responses that have worked well in the past (Carson 1972). However, these managers were operating within the context of well-established organizations. These findings may not apply to the unstructured process of seeking information to start a business.

The theoretical frameworks and empirical studies considered to this point suggest that entrepreneurs with no relevant experience may have simplified models that guide their search. Their limited knowledge may create blinders. As Kaish and Gilad (1991, p. 48) noted, "How can one search for something he doesn't know exists? How will he recognize it when he finds it?" Conversely, those with relevant experience, guided by richer models and greater awareness of what is needed and what is possible, may seek more information than their less experienced counterparts.

Experience relevant to venture formation might be thought of as having two dimensions. One would involve having experience as an entrepreneur—having previously owned and managed a business. Such experience presumably leads to an awareness of what must be done in forming a venture. A second dimension of relevant experience would involve experi-

110   A.C. COOPER ET AL.

ence with the products or services to be offered and markets to be served. This knowledge about a "kind of business" or domain would presumably lead to better understanding of the requirements for success.

The expected relationships between these dimensions of experience and entrepreneurial information search are reflected in the following hypotheses:

> *H1:* Entrepreneurs with no previous entrepreneurial experience will seek less information.

> *H2:* Entrepreneurs operating in less familiar domains will seek less information.

Note that these hypotheses lead to what might be viewed as counterintuitive expectations, namely that entrepreneurs with less relevant experience (and presumably more to learn) would seek less information.

A variant of the bounded rationality model suggests that entrepreneurs may be "blinded" to the need to acquire more information, not because of limited knowledge, but due to overconfidence. Hence, optimism would be a primary cause of non-optimal search behavior. Cooper, Woo, and Dunkelberg (1988) observed that entrepreneurs invariably assigned high probabilities of success to their own ventures, while prescribing noticeably lower odds to other ventures like theirs. These assessments were not systematically related to the nature of their ventures or the backgrounds of the entrepreneurs. Those who appeared poorly pre- pared were just as optimistic as those who were well prepared. The authors suggested that this optimism may limit entrepreneurs' ability to assess objectively their own strengths and weaknesses and the early progress of their firms. This "entrepreneurial euphoria . . . raises serious questions about their ability to diagnose problems, make adjustments, and make objective assessments about whether to continue their heavy personal commitments" (p. 107). It also implies that the entrepreneurs' opinions on the amount of information they need may be biased. Hence, we might expect entrepreneurs with high confidence in their ventures to search less intensely than those with lower confidence levels.[1]

This reasoning is also supported by Guth, Kumaraswamy, and McErlean (1991). In their study, success was thought to be dependent on the degree of congruence between the entrepreneur's cognitive schema and the real environment; however, such schema often reflected an inadequate appreciation of external forces. Yet revisions to an external orientation often did not take place until the entrepreneur experienced failure. Ettlie (1983) also noted that re-examination and the search for information may be triggered by anticipated, rather than actual, deterioration in performance. Both studies illustrated that only when reasons for optimism were challenged (by actual or expected results) did entrepreneurs engage in more active search. Thus, levels of optimism may influence information search, as reflected in the following hypothesis:

> *H3:* Entrepreneurs expressing high degrees of confidence in success of their new ventures will seek less information.

---

[1] Prior research has primarily focused upon how information influences confidence, with additional information having been found to increase the decision-maker's confidence and satisfaction (Oskamp 1965; Chervany and Dickson 1974; O'Reilly 1980). Note that this research considers how confidence influences information search.

RESEARCH METHODOLOGY

Sample

The sample represents a broad cross-section of entrepreneurs, initially surveyed in May 1985. About 13,000 questionnaires were sent to members of the National Federation of Independent Businesses (NFIB) who reported that they had recently become business owners. Responses were obtained from 4814 entrepreneurs. Of these, 2994 were found to have become owners no earlier than 1984. At the time of the survey the average business was 11 months old, so that processes followed in start-up should still be fresh in the entrepreneurs' minds. Tests show the sample to be broadly representative of new businesses in the United States (Cooper et al. 1990). The sample was reduced to exclude those ventures that were not started by the entrepreneur. This was done because we would expect that entrepreneurs who are starting firms would use and value information differently than entrepreneurs who had purchased, inherited, or been promoted to head their ventures. The average firm had less than three employees (counting the founder), so that the skills and knowledge of the entrepreneur were a central resource of the firm. After adjusting for missing values, the total sample consisted of 1176 new ventures.

Dependent Variables

The extent of information utilization was operationalized in this study by responses to the question "When you were planning your business, what sources of information or help were important to you?" Respondents were asked to rate each of a number of possible sources on a four-point scale, ranging from "not used" (1), to "very important" (4). We focus here upon the six sources that were widely used. (At least 60% of respondents reported using each of these sources.) They were: (1) accountant, bookkeeper; (2) friends or relatives; (3) other business owners; (4) bankers; (5) lawyers, attorneys; and (6) generally available books, manuals, etc. A broad measure of information search intensity (INTENSE) was derived by summing the ratings of all six sources. Note that this reflects the number of sources used as well as the relative importance of each. Another approach, and one consistent with much of the empirical research on information search, would be to classify sources into subcategories (O'Reilly 1982; Kaish and Gilad 1991; Birley 1985). Whereas the theoretical frameworks discussed earlier draw no distinctions about categories of sources, studies by O'Reilly and by Kaish and Gilad make it clear that different categories of sources may be utilized to differing degrees, depending upon the circumstances of the decision-makers. Thus, in this exploration of how entrepreneurs search for information, it seems desirable also to consider whether the entrepreneur's relevant entrepreneurial and industry experience bears upon the utilization of different sources.

In response, this study constructed two subcategories of information sources: professional sources (PROFAD) and personal sources (PERS). The categories were developed using factor analysis with varimax rotation (results available from the authors). Two factors were observed with eigenvalues greater than one. One factor, labeled professional sources, was loaded with (1) accountant, bookkeeper; (4) bankers; and (5) lawyers, attorneys. The other factor, labeled personal sources, was loaded with (2) friends or relatives; and (3) other business owners. The dependent variables for professional sources (PROFAD) and personal sources (PERS) were created by summing the ratings of the variables that loaded on the factors. Thus PROFAD ranged from three to 12, whereas PERS ranged from two to eight. Because the books and manuals category did not load cleanly on either factor, it was not included in the two specific source categories. This operationalization of professional sources and personal sources is consistent with Birley's (1985) formulation of "formal" and "informal" sources. In examining the role of network theory in the entrepreneurial process, she classified networks as either formal (banks, accountants, lawyers, Small Business Administration) or informal (family, friends, business contacts).

Independent Variables

Corresponding to the hypotheses stated earlier, four independent variables were examined in the analysis. A binary variable captures the effect of prior ownership experience (ENTR). This variable was created from the following question: "Before going into your present business, what was your highest level of management experience?" Respondents were asked to select one of four levels: (1) no subordinates, supervised no one; (2) supervised workers; (3) supervised one or more managers; or (4) managed or owned own business. Earlier, we hypothesized that prior experience as an entrepreneur would bear directly upon information search. Therefore, those who indicated they had managed or owned their own business were given the value of "1" for the variable ENTR. All others were coded "0."

The analysis also called for an inspection of the effect of entrepreneurs' familiarity with the venture's domain. Respondents to the questionnaire were asked to evaluate the difference between their current ventures and the prior employment context along three dimensions: (1) product or services, (2) customers, and (3) suppliers. In each case, a five-point scale was used ranging from "no difference" (1) to "very different" (5). A continuous measure of domain difference was created by summing these three responses, with a range of three to 15. The reliability coefficient (Cronbach's α) for the construct was 0.87, demonstrating a high degree of internal consistency. Interestingly, the distribution was found to be highly skewed to the extreme points as 20% of the observations summed to "3" ("no difference" on all three questions), 27% summed to "15" ("very different" on all three questions). To capture the effect of the skewness in the model, three categories were created with approximately equal numbers of observations in each. From these categories two binary variables were created, DIFLOW and DIFHI.[2] DIFLOW was coded (1) if the venture was deemed to be not very different, and (0) otherwise. DIFHI is (1) if the venture was very different, and (0) otherwise.

The questionnaire had also posed two questions to calibrate the degree of optimism on the part of the entrepreneurs. These questions were: "What are the odds of your business succeeding?" and "What are the odds of any business like yours succeeding?" Both questions employed a scale of 0 to 10 where "0" represented "no chance of success" and "10" represented "certain chance of success." Optimism might be viewed as the extent to which the entrepreneur viewed his or her chances as substantially better than others for a particular kind of venture. Thus, CONFIDENCE is a continuous variable constructed from the differences in responses to the first and second questions.

Control Variables

Three control variables were used in the research, all of which seem likely to influence entrepreneurs' search behavior. It has been noted that certain organizational realities drive

---

[2] Separate regression models were run with the continuous measure of domain difference and the dummy variables (DIFLOW and DIFHI). Results from these early trials suggested that models incorporating the binary variables more accurately predicted information use.

the tendency to create a denser or richer information environment (Huber and Daft 1988). One of these is the need for *preparation*; the other is the need for decision *legitimation*. In addition, relative resources available to the entrepreneur may influence the amount of information search undertaken. This may be particularly the case for professional sources, where the entrepreneur often incurs costs in seeking information.

The need for preparation and legitimation is likely to increase with the size of a venture and also with outside funding. The degree to which entrepreneurs prepare for decision-making may be strongly related to the size of the venture (Cooper, Woo, and Dunkelberg 1989). O'Reilly, Chatman, and Anderson (1988) suggested that the quantity and quality of information will be related to alternatives considered. Large ventures, because of their greater complexity and larger amount of capital required, are likely to lead to more extensive information use. The amount of initial capital is also a measure of resources available to the entrepreneur. This variable permits us to examine information search patterns while controlling for capital available to the entrepreneur, capital which could be used to support information search. Size was measured by the log of the amount of capital invested at the time of founding (LOGCAP).

The necessity to provide legitimacy may be particularly great when the entrepreneur must justify plans and decisions to others. It has been noted that, in established organizations, this need may cause members to search for more information than is necessary to solve the focal problem. This may, in part, explain the observation that organizational decision-makers acquire "too much" information (O'Reilly and Pondy 1979). It is reasonable to assume that entrepreneurs, as they justify their decisions, are susceptible to the same pressures as managers in larger organizations. In particular, entrepreneurs seeking outside funding are likely to be required to exhaustively research the environment and develop detailed plans. The percentage of funding from sources outside the entrepreneur's family was represented by OUT-FUND.

When there is a founding team, or when partners are involved, the same processes may be at work. Thus, the entrepreneur must justify plans to other partners and this may lead to more extensive information search. Hence, the number of full-time partners in the venture (PARTNERS) was also included as a control variable.

Table 1 presents the variable definitions and the stated hypotheses.

ANALYSIS AND RESULTS

Multiple regression was used to test the previous hypotheses. Table 2 provides the descriptive statistics and the intercorrelation matrix (Pearson) for all variables. Although many of the binary correlations are significant, collinearity does not seem to be a problem.[3]

Table 3 shows the regression results for the three measures of information search (INTENSE, PROFAD, PERS), whereas Table 4 summarizes the extent to which each of the hypotheses was supported. All three models were statistically significant ($p \leqslant .0001$).

To ascertain whether the independent variables significantly contributed to the explanatory power of the models, three reduced models (not shown here), containing only the control variables LOGCAP, PARTNERS, and OUT-FUND, were run against the three dependent

---

[3] This conclusion was reached for three reasons. (1) Though significant, the correlations between independent variables were small. (2) Whereas the highest correlation was found between DIFLOW and DIFHI, stepwise regression revealed that both coefficients and standard errors remain relatively stable. (3) Variance inflation factors (VIFs) indicated no serious multicollinearity problems. In each model, all VIFs were under 1.28. The VIFs are useful in determining which variables may be involved in the multicollinearities. For the ith coefficient, the VIF is defined as $1/(1-R_i^2)$, where R_i^2 is the coefficient of determination of the regression of the ith independent variable on all other independent variables.

114 A.C. COOPER ET AL.

TABLE 1 Description of Variables and Hypothesized Relationships Between Independent Variables and Information Search

Explanatory variables		
Entrepreneur	1 = managed or owned prior business	+
	0 = otherwise	
Difference low	1 = venture similar to prior business	+
	0 = otherwise	
Difference high	1 = venture highly different from prior business	−
	0 = otherwise	
Confidence	(Odds of your business succeeding) minus	−
	(Odds of business like yours succeeding)	
Control variables		
Log capital	Log (capital at start-up)	+
Outside funding	% of funding from outside sources	+
Partners	# of full-time partners	+

TABLE 2 Pearson Correlations, Means, and Standard Deviations for All Variables (n = 1176)

		1	2	3	4	5	6	7	8	9	10
1	Intense	−									
2	Profad	0.786	−								
3	Personal	0.578	0.155	−							
4	Entrepreneur	−0.091	−0.009	−0.138	−						
5	Difference Low	0.039	0.117	−0.019	0.064	−					
6	Difference high	−0.105	−0.129	−0.075	−0.082	−0.456	−				
7	Confidence	−0.037	−0.029	−0.084	0.098	−0.022	−0.039	−			
8	Log capital	0.134	0.248	−0.027	0.123	−0.042	0.055	0.043	−		
9	Outside funding	0.191	0.221	0.097	−0.006	0.025	−0.023	0.046	0.274	−	
10	Partners	0.135	0.188	−0.031	0.018	0.016	−0.047	0.072	0.134	0.144	−
	Mean	17.690	7.603	5.321	0.278	0.331	0.296	2.440	2.995	51.327	0.431
	SD	4.272	2.658	1.704	0.448	0.471	0.457	2.435	1.156	39.457	0.837

Correlations greater than .0569 or less than (−.0569) are significant at $p \leqslant .05$.

variables. Adjusted R^2 values for the models which incorporated only the control variables were 0.0516 (INTENSE as dependent variable), 0.1040 (PROFAD as dependent variable), and 0.0104 (PERS as dependent variable). In comparing the reduced models with the models in columns 1, 2 and 3 of Table 3, F-tests indicated that the inclusion of the independent variables of interest (ENTR, DIFLOW, DIFHI, and CONFIDENT) significantly added to the prediction of all three models ($p \leqslant .001$). Thus we conclude that these independent variables are worthy of further examination in terms of their impact on information use.

Impact of Entrepreneurial Experience on Information Search

After controlling for the effect of size, the presence of partners, and the degree of external funding, entrepreneurial experience (ENTR) was found to be significantly negatively related to both INTENSE ($\beta = -0.1039, p = .0001$) and PERS ($\beta = -0.1307, p = .0001$), indicating that entrepreneurs with no previous entrepreneurial experience sought information more intensely. The coefficient, however, was not significant when ENTR was regressed against use of professional sources. The higher level of search activity appeared to be focused on less formal sources such as family, friends, and other business owners. Thus, less experienced

TABLE 3 Regression Analysis on Two Measures of Information Use (n = 1176; coefficients are standardized)

	Intensity of Search (Intense)		Use of Professional Sources (Profad)		Use of Personal Sources (Pers)	
	(1)		(2)		(3)	
Intercept	**.0000**	[a]	**.0000**	[a]	**.0000**	[a]
	.4399	42.455	.2367	24.263	.1591	35.928
Entrepreneur	**−.1039**	[a]	−.0438		**−.1307**	[a]
	.2712	−3.652	.1645	−1.578	.1105	−4.496
Difference low	−.0126		**.0755**	[c]	**−.0698**	[c]
	.2857	−0.400	.1732	2.462	.1165	−2.169
Difference high	**−.1208**	[a]	**−.1018**	[a]	**−.1155**	[a]
	.2956	−3.824	.1792	−3.305	.1204	−3.577
Confidence	**−.1003**	[a]	**−.0526**	[d]	**−.0822**	[b]
	0.495	−3.552	.0300	−1.911	.0202	−2.848
Log capital	**.1028**	[a]	**.2069**	[a]	−.0359	
	.1097	3.475	.0663	7.181	.0445	−1.188
Outside funding	**.1495**	[a]	**.1423**	[a]	**.1050**	[a]
	.0032	5.098	.0019	4.979	.0013	3.505
Partners	**.1036**	[a]	**.1385**	[a]	**.0248**	
	.1455	3.638	.0882	4.988	.0593	0.851
Model						
F-Value	**15.855**[a]		**25.537**[a]		**8.204**[a]	
R²	0.0868		0.1327		0.0469	
Adj. R²	0.0813		0.1275		0.0412	

[a] Significant at $p < .001$.
[b] Significant at $p < .01$.
[c] Significant at $p < .05$.
[d] Significant at $p < .10$.
Significant coefficients are in bold

founders engaged in significantly greater search with personal sources, but not with professional sources. These findings are directly counter to H1, wherein entrepreneurial experience was expected to lead to greater search.

Impact of Domain Difference on Information Search

A strong and significant effect existed between domain difference and information search. For DIFHI, the relationship was consistently negative and held true for all three measures of search. Entrepreneurs operating in domains greatly different from their previous ventures were less likely to seek information. DIFLOW was found to be positively related to use of professional sources ($\beta = 0.0755$, $p = .014$). This suggests that entrepreneurs operating in similar domains used more professional sources. On the other hand, these entrepreneurs tended to draw less on personal sources ($\beta = -0.0698$, $p = .030$). Whereas this last finding runs counter to the rest, in general, the effects of relatedness of domain tend to support H2.

The question of whether there existed an interaction effect between entrepreneurial experience and differences in domain was also considered. Such an additional test would shed insight on whether experienced and inexperienced entrepreneurs modify their behavior in different ways as they move from similar to different domains. Although not reported in the tables, a separate model incorporating the interaction term was run for each dependent vari-

116   A.C. COOPER ET AL.

Point	ENTR	DIFFER	Mean	Pr > |T| Ho: mean (i) = mean (j)		
				A	B	C
A	No Experience	Similar Domain	18.38			
B	No Experience	Different Domain	17.02	0.0001		
C	Experience	Similar Domain	17.14	0.0001	0.7584	
D	Experience	Different Domain	17.63	0.1557	0.2833	0.395

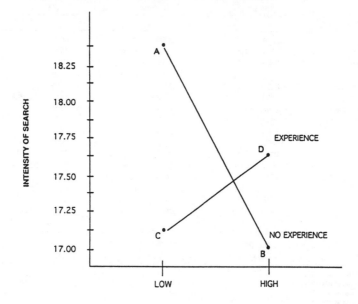

DOMAIN DIFFERENCES

p-values are for *t*-tests on differences between means.

FIGURE 1 Means for interaction between entrepreneurial experience and domain differences on information search (INTS).

able. The interaction was found to significantly add ($p \leqslant .10$) to the models estimating INTENSE and PERS, but did not contribute to the estimation of PROFAD.[4] Therefore, further discussion regarding interaction effects will concentrate on the INTENSE and PERS models.

Interaction terms involving ENTR and DIFLOW were not significant for either model. However, *t*-tests indicated that the interaction terms involving ENTR and DIFHI were significant for INTENSE ($p \leqslant 0.5$) and for PERS ($p \leqslant .10$). This finding suggests that large domain differences trigger different search reactions among experienced and inexperienced entrepreneurs. Figure 1 examines this relationship further with regard to total search intensity (INTENSE). Included with the figure are mean values of search intensity, and *p*-values for the *t*-tests on the differences between the means. Note that search intensity did not change

---

[4]The addition of the interaction terms had little impact on the significance of the main effects (ENTR, DIFHI, and DIFLOW). Because the combination of significant main effects and significant interaction effects makes interpretation more difficult, a more focused analysis will follow.

significantly for experienced entrepreneurs as they moved from similar to different domains ($p = .3950$). However, inexperienced entrepreneurs searched much more intensively for information when they started ventures in fields they knew as compared to when they entered domains which were different ($p = .0001$). Similar patterns of findings existed for PERS, the utilization of personal information sources. Thus, the bounded rationality model applies to inexperienced entrepreneurs in the sense that this group sought more information in fields they knew, but less in domains they did not.

Impact of Confidence on Information Search

The effect of confidence (CONFIDENT) on information search was found to be significant and negatively related to all three measures of search (INTENSE, PROFAD, and PERS).[5] Founders who were more confident sought less information. These results strongly support H3 and the behavioral model.

DISCUSSION

Information is presumably one of the central resources of the new firm. In this study of the processes by which entrepreneurs gather information, we noted that conditions of bounded rationality might well apply. Thus, entrepreneurs with previous entrepreneurial experience and those venturing into fields they knew would engage in a more intensive information search because of their richer schema and their greater awareness of what was needed. In addition, it was hypothesized that more confident entrepreneurs would seek less information.

This study of 1176 new ventures provides mixed support for the hypotheses. Those who had no entrepreneurial experience, on the average, sought more, not less information. However, those who ventured into fields that were very different, on the average, sought less information, supporting the hypothesized relationship. Examination of the interaction between these variables was illuminating. The difference in information search between experienced and inexperienced entrepreneurs primarily occurred when they entered fields they knew; in such conditions the novice entrepreneurs engaged in more intensive search. However, inexperienced entrepreneurs searched less, and at a level equivalent to that of experienced entrepreneurs, when entering fields they did not know well. Experienced entrepreneurs seemed to search with about the same intensity, regardless of whether they knew the field.

In regard to sources, the differences between experienced and inexperienced entrepreneurs were primarily in regard to their utilization of personal sources, not professional sources. It was also in regard to personal sources that the significant interaction effects were observed, with inexperienced founders engaging in more intensive search in fields they knew.

The hypothesized relationship between confidence and search was supported. Those who were more confident searched less intensively.

We can speculate about reasons for these patterns of information search. Experienced entrepreneurs possibly had developed richer schema, but they also were more confident (Table 2). They may have developed more fixed routines, which they did not vary according to whether they knew the field or not. In a sense, they may have become prisoners of their past success. However, the inexperienced entrepreneurs appeared to demonstrate a pattern of search that corresponded to the bounded rational model. Their tendency was to search more intensely (particularly with personal sources) when they knew a field well. However,

---

[5] Significance for PROFAD was at the .10 level.

possibly because of their lower awareness of what was needed, they utilized these sources less as they entered unfamiliar domains. We know that their confidence was somewhat lower and possibly this led to the expectation that there would be lower returns to the effort devoted to search with these less familiar ventures.

The control variables, amount of initial capital, outside investors, and the presence of full-time partners, were all positively and significantly related to search. The primary impact was on utilization of professional sources (and personal sources when there were outside investors). These variables are associated with larger, more complex ventures, in which the entrepreneur must persuade others to make commitments. These may also be more promising ventures, so that additional information may have a greater marginal return. As expected, outside professionals played an important role in these ventures. We should also note that the control variable for initial capital permits us to examine information search patterns while controlling for financial resources available to the entrepreneur. Thus, although experienced entrepreneurs may have accumulated more capital, thereby putting them in a better position to engage in information search, we have controlled for this factor in this multivariate analysis.

It should be acknowledged that the models explain a limited amount of the variance in information utilization by entrepreneurs. Adjusted R^2 values range from 0.0412 for "use of personal sources" to 0.1275 for "use of professional sources." Factors not considered here, such as the decision-making style of the entrepreneur, undoubtedly bear upon patterns of information search and utilization. Nevertheless, there are some systematic relationships, even in this broad cross-sectional study encompassing a wide range of types of start-ups.

There are several limitations of this study that should be noted. The measures of information are relatively broad and are not fine-grained enough to determine the kinds of information obtained from each source and how that may be related to the background of the entrepreneur or the needs of the venture. The costs of searching (in money or effort) are not measured; it may be that some entrepreneurs, because of their reputation or involvement in networks, can search at lower cost than others. (However, it should be noted that the regression analyses control for amount of initial capital. The results reported are not artifacts of the relative resources available to the entrepreneurs.) It should also be noted that the marginal returns from additional information may vary across ventures or entrepreneurs. Higher potential ventures (and more promising entrepreneurs) may realize greater returns to search because the information can be utilized in a more promising venture. (We have no measures of venture potential, but the control for initial capital at least ensures that initial scale is taken into account.) One possible argument would be that more experienced entrepreneurs would realize higher returns to search because they could apply the information gained more effectively. However, this would imply that experienced entrepreneurs should search more, regardless of the degree of domain difference. As noted in Figure 1, this was not the pattern observed. Information search practices are more complicated than this argument would imply and seem to involve an interaction between entrepreneurial experience and domain differences.

Future research could seek to examine these aspects more fully, including the kinds of information gathered, the effort or cost involved, and the potential of the venture. Research might also examine how the decision-making style of the entrepreneur bears upon information search processes (Rowe 1987).

What are the implications of this research for entrepreneurs and their advisors? We see clear evidence of certain behavioral tendencies. We might expect that entrance into unfamiliar domains would be accompanied by a need for more information. Those who venture into fields they do not know presumably have more to learn. However, neither inexperienced nor experienced entrepreneurs act in this way. When inexperienced entrepreneurs enter fields they do not know, they lessen their search, consistent with the bounded-rationality model. This seems surprising in that, as they need to learn more, they search less. This behavioral tendency may compound the liabilities of newness. Experienced entrepreneurs seem to follow patterns of search that do not vary much by whether the domain is familiar or new; their routines appear to be more fixed. One of the most consistent findings in prior research on predictors of new venture performance is that entrepreneurs entering unfamiliar fields tend to be less successful (Cooper and Gimeno-Gascon 1992). This suggests that entrepreneurs, both experienced and inexperienced, might gain from greater emphasis upon gathering and utilizing external information as they enter unfamiliar fields. Such efforts would run counter to the behavioral tendencies suggested by the bounded-rationality model. Outside advisors (if the entrepreneur will utilize them) may be helpful in urging entrepreneurs who enter unfamiliar domains to engage in more extensive information search. Even though the entrepreneurs may lack the elaborate schema that would guide such searches, and even though they may not have existing contacts in such fields, the effort would seem warranted. In regard to the tendency of entrepreneurs who are more confident to seek less outside information, there may or may not be sound reasons for them to act in this way. However, founders and their advisors should be aware of this tendency and should use care to ensure that entrepreneurial euphoria does not lead to blinders in the search for information.

The foregoing comments imply that entrepreneurs venturing into unfamiliar domains would benefit from more extensive information search — that the returns from added search would outweigh the costs. However, future research could seek to examine many aspects of this more fully. The cognitive schema of entrepreneurs operating in familiar and unfamiliar domains could be examined, as could the role of information search in modifying those schema over time.

This study adds to our understanding of the processes by which new ventures are formed. However, information is one of the central resources of the new venture and there is still much to be learned about the ways in which entrepreneurs gather and utilize the information they need.

REFERENCES

Bennis, W., and Nanus, B. 1986. *Leaders: The Strategies for Taking Charge*. New York: Perennial Library.

Birley, S. 1985. The role of networks in the entrepreneurial process. *Journal of Business Venturing* 1:107–117.

Carson, R. 1972. *School Superintendents: Career and Performance*. Columbia, OH: Merrill.

Chervany, N., and Dickson G. 1974. An experimental evaluation of information overload in production environment. *Management Science* 20:1335–1344.

Cooper, A., Dunkelberg, W., Woo, C., and Dennis, W. 1990. *New Business in America: The Firms and Their Owners*. Washington, DC: The National Federation of Independent Business.

Cooper, A., Woo, C., and Dunkelberg, W. 1989. Entrepreneurship and the initial size of firms. *Journal of Business Venturing* 4:317–332.

Cooper, A., Woo, C., and Dunkelberg, W. 1988. Entrepreneurs' perceived chances for success. *Journal of Business Venturing* 3:97–108.

Cooper, A., and Gimeno-Gascon, J. 1992. Entrepreneurs, processes of founding, and new firm performance. In D. Sexton and J. Kasda, eds., *State of the Art of Entrepreneurship Research*. Boston, MA: PWS-Kent Publishing Co.

Ettlie, J.E. 1983. Performance gap theories of innovation. *IEEE Transactions on Engineering Management* 30:39–51.

120 A.C. COOPER ET AL.

Guth, W., Kumaraswamy, A., and McErlean, M. 1991. Cognition, enactment and learning in the entrepreneurial process. *Frontiers in Entrepreneurial Research*. Wellesley, MA: Babson College: 48–49.

Kahneman, D., and Tversky, A. 1979. Prospect theory: an analysis of decision under risk. *Econometrica* 47:263–291.

Kaish, S., and Gilad, B. 1991. Characteristics of opportunities search of entrepreneurs versus executives: sources, interests, general alertness. *Journal of Business Venturing* 6:45–62.

Kirzner, J.M. 1973. *Competition and Entrepreneurship*. Chicago, IL: University of Chicago Press.

Lord, R., and Maher, K. 1990. Alternative information-processing models and their implications for theory, research, and practice. *Academy of Management Review* 15:9–28.

March, J., and Simon, H. 1958. *Organizations*. New York: Wiley.

O'Reilly, C.A. 1980. Individuals and information overload in organizations: is more necessarily better? *Academy of Management Journal* 23:684–696.

O'Reilly, C.A. 1982. Variations in decision makers' use of information sources: the impact of quality and accessibility of information. *Academy of Management Journal* 25:756–771.

O'Reilly, C.A., Chatman, J.A., and Anderson, J.C. 1987. Merging organizational communications and decision making: the acquisition and use of information in organizations. In F. Jablin, L. Putnam, K. Roberts, and L. Porter, eds., *Handbook of Organizational Communication*. Beverly Hills, CA: Sage.

O'Reilly, C.A., and Pondy, L. 1979. Organizational communication. In S. Kerr, ed., *Organizational Behavior*. Columbus, OH: Grid.

Oskamp, S. 1965. Overconfidence in case study judgments. *Journal of Consulting Psychology* 29: 261–265.

Rowe, A.J., and Mason, R.O. 1987. *Managing With Style*. San Francisco, CA: Jossey-Bass: 189–205.

Schwenk, C.R. 1988. The cognitive perspective on strategic decision making. *Journal of Management Studies* 25:41–55.

Shields, M.D. 1983. Effects of information supply and demand on judgment accuracy: evidence from corporate managers. *Accounting Review* 58:284–303.

Smith, K., Grimm, C., Gannon, M., and Chen, M. 1991. Organizational information processing, competitive responses, and performance in the U.S. domestic airline industry. *Academy of Management Journal* 34:60–85.

Stinchcombe, A. 1990. *Information and Organizations*. Berkeley, CA: University of California Press.

[19]

ELSEVIER

A LACK OF INSIGHT:
DO VENTURE CAPITALISTS
REALLY UNDERSTAND
THEIR OWN DECISION
PROCESS?

ANDREW L. ZACHARAKIS
Bentley College

G. DALE MEYER
University of Colorado

EXECUTIVE SUMMARY

What decision criteria do venture capitalists (VCs) use to make their investment decisions? This question has received much attention within entrepreneurship literature (i.e., Wells 1974; Poindexter 1976; Tyebjee and Bruno 1984; MacMillan, Seigel, and Subba Narasimha 1985; MacMillan, Zeman, and Subba Narasimha 1987; Robinson 1987; Timmons et al. 1987; Sandberg, Schweiger, and Hofer 1988; Hall and Hofer 1993; Zacharakis and Meyer 1995) for a number of reasons. First, VC-backed ventures achieve a higher survival rate than non-VC-backed businesses (Kunkel and Hofer 1990; Sandberg 1986; Timmons 1994). Second, a better understanding of the decision process may lead to even better survival rates. Finally, entrepreneurs seeking venture funding benefit if they understand what factors are most important to the VC.

Although past research has greatly contributed to our understanding of the decision, it may be biased and somewhat misleading. The majority of past studies rely on post hoc methodologies (e.g., interviews and surveys) to capture the decision process. Post hoc methods assume that VCs can accurately relate their own decision processes, but studies from cognitive psychology suggest that people, in particular experts, are poor at introspecting. Introspection is subject to rationalization and post hoc recall biases.

Address correspondence to Andrew L. Zacharakis, Management Department, Bentley College, 175 Forest Street, Waltham, MA 02154-4705.

The authors acknowledge the contributions of Roger Smith, Julio DeCastro, Charlene Nicholls-Nixon, Reid Hastie, Gary McClelland, Dale Jasinski, Harry Sapienza, Anne Huff, Robert Keeley and Don Sexton, and two anonymous reviewers for their advice and insight on this research project.

An earlier version of this article was presented at the 1996 Babson College-Kauffman Foundation Entrepreneurship Research Conference.

This research was funded in part by the Center for Entrepreneurial Leadership Inc. and the Ewing Marion Kauffman Foundation. The contents of this publication are solely the responsibility of the authors.

Journal of Business Venturing 13, 57–76
0883-9026/98/$19.00
PII S0883-9026(97)00004-9

58   A.L. ZACHARAKIS AND G.D. MEYER

Using social judgment theory and the associated lens model as a framework, the current study investigates how well VCs introspect about their own decision process and, by extension, whether the past research efforts are biased.

The current research uses policy capturing, a real-time method common in cognitive psychology, to capture the VC's "actual theories in use" versus their "espoused theories" (Hitt and Tyler 1991). Policy capturing requires that VCs make a series of real-time decisions based on various information factors. Regression analysis of each VCs' decision captures how important each of the information factors is to her/his actual decision process. After the VCs make their decisions, they provided a weighting of how they believe they used the information factors. Comparing the captured decision policies to stated decision policies provides a measure of VC insight.

The findings suggest that VCs are not good at introspecting about their own decision process. Even within the confines of a controlled experiment, which greatly reduces the amount of information consid-ered, VCs lacked strong understanding of how they made decisions. Most decision-makers would like to have all relevant information available for their decision. However, as more information becomes available, insight diminishes. Finally, this study finds that VCs are very consistent in their decision process, even though they do not necessarily understand how they make their decisions.

VCs face a plethora of information when making an investment decision (i.e., business plan, outside consultants, due diligence, etc.). It may be difficult for VCs to truly understand their intuitive decision process because of all the noise caused by this information overload. This lack of systematic understand-ing impedes learning. VCs cannot make accurate adjustments to their evaluation process if they do not truly understand it. Therefore, VCs may suffer from a systematic bias that impedes the performance of their investment portfolio. The methodology used in this experiment can be modified and used as a train-ing tool for active VCs. In addition, the consistent nature of VC decision-making (even if they do not have a strong understanding of that process) is favorable to the development of decision aides. Decision aides can minimize the danger of salient information (e.g., the lead entrepreneur is a winner) clouding the VC's judgment.

Past research also needs to be interpreted in a new light. Although VCs undoubtedly use some of the information cited in past studies, the relative importance of that information needs to be reevaluated. VCs may not, for instance, rely most on the background of the entrepreneurial team. In addition, it is likely that the past studies provide more information factors than VCs actually use. People have a tendency to overstate the information they believe they relied upon and to use far less information (typically three to seven factors) to make a decision than they actually think they use. The methodology used in this experiment has the potential to identify the more relevant information factors cited in previous work.

Even though VCs are experts in the new venture funding realm, their decision process has room for improvement. Almost 40% of all backed ventures fail to provide a return to the VC. Considering the billions invested each year, a modest improvement in the failure rate can have a substantial impact on venture portfolio returns. That improvement starts by better understanding the decision process. This study is a step in that direction.   © 1998 Elsevier Science Inc.

INTRODUCTION

New venture survival is tenuous at best, but those backed by venture capitalists (VCs) tend to achieve a higher survival rate than non-VC-backed businesses (Kunkel and Hofer 1990; Sandberg 1986; Timmons 1994). Thus, many researchers have investigated how VCs make their decisions (Wells 1974; Poindexter 1976; Tyebjee and Bruno 1984; MacMillan, Seigel, and Subba Narasimha 1985; MacMillan, Zeman, and Subba Nara-simha 1987; Robinson 1987; Timmons et al. 1987; Sandberg, Schweiger, and Hofer 1988; Hall and Hofer 1993; Zacharakis and Meyer 1995). The underlying justification for these studies is that a better understanding of the VC process may lead to better decisions and thereby more successful ventures. However, the majority of these studies use post hoc methodologies, such as interviews and surveys, which may be subject to post hoc rationalization and recall biases (Barr, Stimpert, and Huff 1992; Sandberg et al. 1988). Such biases likely inhibit how accurately people can introspect about their own thought processes (Fischhoff 1988). Experts who tend to rely on intuition more than non-experts (Simon and Chase 1973) are notoriously poor introspectors (Fischhoff 1988). VCs, experts in new venturing financing, also typically rely on intuition (Khan 1987; MacMillan et al. 1987).

Poor insight can be problematic because VCs—just as executives making important strategic decisions (Stahl and Zimmerer 1984)—need to communicate to other VCs and investors what decision criteria they are using so that the alliance of investors can comfortably commit money. For example, Steier and Greenwood's (1995) case study of a high-tech start-up found that a commitment by one VC led to three others joining the syndicate even though these three had each previously rejected the idea. As such, the funding relationship is a network of co-investors who must communicate effectively with each other and the entrepreneur. A lack of strong self insight hampers the lead VC's ability to effectively communicate.

At the end of Sandberg's (1986) book on new venture performance, he notes "there appears to have been no research that used a decision-making exercise rather than a survey to capture venture capitalists' real criteria and their associated weights" (1986, p. 152). Sandberg (1986) suggests that a policy capturing exercise—similar to one used by Stahl and Zimmerer (1984) to assess merger decisions—might find that VCs are also poor at understanding their own decision process. This study is a first attempt at answering Sandberg's call. The article proceeds as follows: first, the VC decision process is reviewed. Second, the article looks at how biases and heuristics hinder the decision. Next, social judgment theory and the associated lens model are used to provide a theoretical basis for exploring the decision. Then, a series of testable hypotheses is derived from the lens model. The subsequent section explains the policy capturing methodology and the associated experiment. Finally, results of the current study are presented followed by conclusions and implications.

VC DECISION-MAKING

VC firms are "those organizations whose predominant mission is to finance the founding or early growth of new companies that do not yet have access to the public securities market or to institutional lenders" (Gupta and Sapienza 1992, p. 349; Perez 1986; Pratt 1987). As such, Gupta and Sapienza (1992) suggest that VCs add value by:

1. bringing investors and entrepreneurs together in an efficient manner,
2. making better investment decisions than limited partners would make, and
3. providing nonfinancial assistance that in turn enhances survival.

All other things equal, a VC firm's performance is a function of how well it makes the investment decision and how effective its management advice and services are after the investment decision has been made. Therefore, improving the investment decision can improve the VC firm's performance.

VCs assess the probability of success or failure by evaluating information surrounding a venture. To receive funding, new ventures must pass an initial screening (typically a review of the business plan) followed by months of due diligence. A number of researchers have examined what information is critical to the VC's decision (see Table 1). The information appears to fit four categories: (1) entrepreneur/team capabilities, (2) product/service attractiveness, (3) market/competitive conditions, and (4) potential returns if the venture is successful (Wells 1974; Poindexter 1976; Tyebjee and Bruno 1984; MacMillan et al. 1985, 1987; Robinson 1987; Timmons et al. 1987; Hall and Hofer 1993). Although insightful, these studies (except for Hall and Hofer's verbal protocol) likely suffer from introspection biases since they use ex post collection methods.

IMPEDIMENTS TO ACCURATE INTROSPECTION

Decision-makers are not perfectly rational, but are boundedly rational (Cyert and March 1963; Newell and Simon 1972; Simon 1955). It is impossible for decision-makers to fully evaluate all information. Moreover, salient factors within the information typically bias decision-makers (Fiske and Taylor 1991). For instance, the availability bias (Tversky and Kahneman 1974) encourages decision-makers to recall salient information from memory. If a venture under consideration has the same lead entrepreneur as a past successful investment, such available information may bias the VC to overlook other factors that suggest the current venture is likely to fail. For example, VCs may overlook underlying weaknesses in the market if they have lots of faith in the entrepreneur. As such, biases may change the relative importance and use of various information factors between venture proposals.

Biases not only inhibit decision-making, but they also likely impede the VC's ability to accurately report on her/his decision process. Instead of recalling the actual information that was used to make typical decisions, decision-makers likely fixate on one or two past successes (Dawes 1988; Dawes, Faust, and Meehl 1989) and recall information particular to those situations (Fiske and Taylor 1991). Likewise, VCs may fixate on the lead entrepreneur because of that individual's past record of success and because of that person's dynamic personality. As such, VCs often report entrepreneur characteristics as more important to the decision than they actually were (Hall and Hofer 1993). There are numerous other biases that cloud insight and by extension also impede optimal decision-making. Hogarth and Makridakis (1981) provide an excellent review for interested readers.

SOCIAL JUDGMENT THEORY

Social judgment theory (SJT) (Brunswik 1956) from cognitive psychology provides a framework for understanding the VC decision process, as well as a basis for removing post hoc biases. The underlying assumption in SJT is that decision-makers do not have access to "real" information, but instead perceive that information through proximal cues (Strong 1992). These cues quantitatively describe the relationship between an individual's judgment and the information used to make that judgment (Stewart 1988). Hence, SJT captures "theories in use" as opposed to "espoused theories" of action (Hitt and Tyler 1991). Within SJT, the lens model formally represents human judgments.

The lens model basically consists of two systems (cognitive and task) linked together by proximal information cues. The cues (see Figure 1) are the information factors that an individual considers when making a decision (represented by variables x_1 through x_4 that appear in the middle of Figure 1). The right side of the model represents the "cognitive" system. Cues are combined in some manner to make a judgment or

TABLE 1 Information Factors Used in VC Decision

Study	Wells (1974)	Poindexter (1976)	Tyebjee and Bruno (1984)	MacMillan et al. (1985)	MacMillan et al. (1987)	Robinson (1987)	Timmons et al. (1987)	Hall and Hofer (1993)
Method	Personal interviews	Questionnaire	Phone survey and questionnaire	Questionnaire	Questionnaire	Questionnaire	Unstructured interviews	Verbal protocol
Sample size	8	97	46 (Study 1) 41 (Study 2)	100	67	53	47	16
Entrepreneur/team characteristics:								
mgmt skill & experience	X	X	X	X	X	X	X	X
venture team		X	X	X	X	X		X
mgmt stake in firm		X	X					
personal motivation	X					X		
entr personality				X				
Product/service characteristics:								
product attributes	X		X	X	X			
product differentiation			X				X	
proprietary	X			X	X			
growth potential			X					
mkt acceptance				X			X	
prototype				X				
Market characteristics:								
mkt size	X		X	X			X	X
mkt growth	X		X			X	X	
barriers to entry			X				X	
competitive threat				X	X		X	
venture creates new mkt				X				
Financial characteristics:								
cash-out method	X		X					
expected ROR		X	X	X			X	X
expected risk		X						
percentage of equity		X						
investor provisions								
size of investment	X		X	X	X	X		
liquidity								
Other								
references	X					X		
venture development stage		X	X	X				
VC investment criteria								X

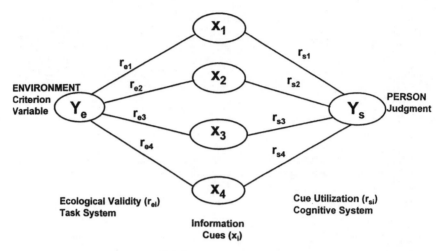

FIGURE 1   Lens model.

decision (Y_s); Y_s captures the expert's judgment policy. In other words, Y_s represents the judge's perception leading to the decision. The correlation of cues to the individual's judgment is represented by r_{si}. The larger the standardized r_{si} (assuming orthogonal cues), the more heavily the decision-maker relies on that cue to make the decision (Stewart 1988).

The "task" system is on the left side of Figure 1. The criterion variable is the actual outcome (Y_e). Each of the cues also correlates (r_{ei}) to the actual outcome. Thus, r_{ei} defines the relationship between the cues and the reality based condition of interest to the decision maker. Just as r_{si} indicates the relative importance of each cue to the decision maker, r_{ei} indicates which cues have the greatest predictive value to the actual outcome. Hammond (1975, p. 73) sums up the lens model as follows:

> Judgment is a cognitive process similar to inductive inference, in which the person draws a conclusion, or an inference, Y_s, about something Y_e, which he cannot see (or otherwise directly perceive). In other words, judgments are made from palpable events and circumstances.

An example may better clarify the use of lens models. The lens model can depict a VC examining a new venture. The VC makes a judgment [(Y_s) invest or not] of the venture's potential [(Y_e) success or failure] based upon a number of information factors [(x_k) e.g., strong team, proprietary protection, etc.]. The VC is not directly observing the venture's ultimate outcome, but instead inferring the venture's potential based upon a number of observable current conditions ($x_1 \ldots x_4$). This brief example illustrates that judges make decisions about potential outcomes that they cannot directly perceive by using a series of information factors (cues) that they can observe. The lens model provides a basis for a series of testable hypotheses.

Information inundates VCs considering new venture proposals. For example, there is information about the entrepreneur (e.g., entrepreneur's industry and start-up experience), the market (e.g., size and growth), and the product/service (e.g., proprietary protection). Not only is there a lot of available information, but much of it is subjective.

For example, VCs often discuss the "chemistry" between themselves and the entrepreneur. The deal often falls through if the chemistry is not right. Such intuitive, or "gut feel" (Khan 1987; MacMillan et al. 1987), decision-making is difficult to quantify or objectively analyze. The added complexity from subjective information further clouds the decision-making process and invites the decision-maker toward more biases. Due to the complexity of the decision and the VCs' intuitive approach, VCs may have a difficult time introspecting about their decision process (Fischhoff 1988). In other words, VCs do not have a comprehensive understanding of how they make the decision.

> *H1:* VCs do not accurately introspect about their decision criteria.

Although decision-makers believe they thoroughly consider all relevant information, most typically rely on only three to seven factors or cues (Stewart 1988). Moreover, people are apt to report using far more information than they actually use (Slovic and Lichtenstein 1971). Thus, as more information becomes available to a particular decision, the VC's ability to introspect about that decision process diminishes.

> *H2:* More information decreases the VC's introspection accuracy about her/his decision process.

Likewise, the type of information available to inform the decision also impacts the VC's ability to accurately introspect. To this point, the hypotheses derive from the cognitive side (right side of Figure 1) of the lens model—factors the VC feels most comfortable using to make the decision. However, information cues on the task side (left side of Figure 1) represent the optimal set of decision cues. These real performance cues best discriminate between eventual outcomes and are statistically derived based on past, actual ventures. Nevertheless, the optimal set of cues may not fit the VC's intuitive understanding of what to consider in the VC decision. The optimal cues may not be in the form or experience with which the VC is familiar or comfortable. Since intuition interferes with introspection, using the optimal cues may increase the VC's understanding of her/his decision process and yield more accurate insight. In other words, the unfamiliarity with the nature of each optimal factor may cause the VC to consciously examine each factor independent of the other factors. As such, VCs who use optimal information cues in a controlled experiment should introspect better than those who use only intuitive cues.

> *H3:* Using optimal information factors increases the VC's introspection accuracy about her/his decision process.

If VCs do not have a clear understanding of their intuitive decision process, an interesting question may be whether they are even consistent in applying that process. In other words, does the inherent complexity, or the many potential biases, or the intuitive nature of most VC decision-making negatively affect the VC's consistency in applying her/his decision process? Although decision-making consistency may vary over time (Brehmer and Brehmer 1988), it is likely that VC decision-making is relatively consistent in the short run. In other words, the VC is likely to judge investments in relatively the same manner from one week to the next. However, if that VC's decisions are compared from one year to the next, consistency might be altered because new criteria are used to judge venture potential. If the decision process is inconsistent in the short run, such inconsistency would impede systematic attempts to understand that process. Moreover, it is important that key decision-makers be able to accurately communicate their decision criteria so that others involved in the decision process can concur and validate that decision (Stahl and Zimmerer 1984). Just as lack of insight deters successful communication, inconsistent decision processes would also hamper communication. If, however, lack of insight does not result in inconsistent decision-making, then the decision process can be studied and hopefully improved. In their study of 42 executives making merger and acquisition decisions, Stahl and Zimmerer (1984) found that the executives are internally consistent ($R^2 = 0.8$), even though they lack insight into their decision process. Likewise, VCs are likely internally consistent.

> *H4:* VCs are consistent in applying their decision policies.

METHODOLOGY

The hypotheses propose that VCs do not have a strong understanding of their decision process. Therefore, the current design captures each VC's actual decision process and then compares it to the VC's stated decision process (how VCs believe they make decisions). The VCs receive several pieces of information about 50 potential investments. The exercise requests that the participants evaluate the ventures as they would during the initial screening stage of an actual decision and judge whether the venture will likely succeed or fail. Regression analysis of the VC's 50 decisions captures the actual decision policy. In addition, the VCs provide a weighting scheme of how they believe they used the information by splitting 100 points among each presented information factor. The VC's weighting scheme can be formulated into a regression equation of the VC's believed or stated decision policy. Comparing the VC's actual decision policy and stated decision policy gives an indication of his/her self insight. The following paragraphs further detail the methodology.

Decision Experiment

The experiment is administered on a notebook PC brought to the VC's office; such convenience likely increases participation. Unlike the majority of past research that uses ex post interviews, the policy capturing methodology elicits the VC's decision policy real time. The experiment does not rely on the VC's conscious efforts to accurately introspect. As such, this methodology eliminates the threat of recall and rationalization biases (Barr et al. 1992; Sandberg et al. 1988). Additionally, policy capturing experiments enable greater control and are conducive to quantitative statistical tests (i.e., regression and ANOVA).

Sample

The sample for this experiment is 53 practicing VCs from two entrepreneurial "hotbeds," (1) the Colorado Front Range (primarily the Denver/Boulder metro area) and (2) the Silicon Valley in California. Two of the 53 participants were removed (one because the PC crashed during the exercise and the other because he did not wish to con-

TABLE 2 VC Demographics

Variable	Description	Range	Mean	SD
VC Firm Demographics:				
Stage of investment	Percentage:			
	Seed	0–100	21.6	21.214
	Start-up	0–100	35.7	21.926
	Early growth	0–60	22.8	15.324
	Expansion	0–60	18.5	17.809
	Decline	0–40	1.5	6.136
Size of VC firm	Dollars under investmant control (in millions)	1–2000	202.9	316.196
Age of firm	Years since founding	1–32	14.0	7.890
Number of associates	FT equivalents actively involved in venture funding decisions	1–35	5.4	5.033
Industry requirements	Percentage of portfolio in high technology versus low technology	0–100	81.4	24.977
Geographic focus	State (1) Regional (2) National (3) International (4) None (5)	1–4	2.4	.753
Average funding per venture	Dollar amount (in thousands)	50–50,000	3304.6	7031.198
Type of VC firm	Independent/private, bank affiliated, corporation affiliated, non-affiliated SBIC	All independent		
Average number of investors per venture	0, 1–3, 4–5, >5	0–>5	2.5	1.525
Individual VC Demographics:				
Age	Measured in years	29–72	46.5	10.366
Gender		50 males 3 females		
Education level	Years of education with a high school graduate = 12; 4 yr college degree = 16, etc., College, Gradute, etc.	14–22	17.8	.977
Education type (number of VCs with degree in field)	Business	44		
	Engineering	23		
	Liberal Arts	17		
	Science	8		
Tenure with firm	Number of years with current firm	1–25	8.7	6.104
Other VC experience	Years	0–19	2.3	4.239
Other relevant experience	Number of years working (including years as VC)	5–49	22.5	10.341

tinue past the first few decisions). Table 2 further delineates the demographics of the sample.

Procedure

The experiment follows a two-step creation process: (1) identify information cues that are valuable to the investment decision and (2) create decision cases for the VC to judge. The number of cases and cues is interrelated (Stewart 1988). The more cases each participant completes, the higher the validity of that person's judgment policy. Unfortunately, too many cases may tire the judge and limit participation. Stewart (1988) suggests that 35 cases is typically sufficient to accurately capture the subject's decision policy. Another rule of thumb is to have a minimum of five cases for every cue that is being tested (Stewart 1991).

66 A.L. ZACHARAKIS AND G.D. MEYER

A policy capturing exercise that uses all the identified information factors from previous research (see Table 1—approximately 25 cues in aggregate form) would be untenable. To achieve an appropriate case-to-cue ratio, the VCs would have to evaluate over 100 cases (5 cases/cue * 25 cues = 125). Evaluating 100 cases would increase the required time to complete the exercise and might tire each participant thereby reducing the experiment's validity. Additionally, such an increased time requirement might discourage VCs from participating in the exercise altogether. Furthermore, several of the identified cues are probably highly correlated with each other. High multicollinearity adversely affects policy capturing methodology (Stewart 1988). Finally, most people, including experts, typically use only three to seven information cues (Stewart 1988), so a smaller set of cues is valid. For the above reasons, the number of cues used in the exercise in a subset of all possible cues.

In order to use a manageable set of cues, cue frequency across studies and reported importance within each study are used as a criterion for a particular cue's inclusion in the experiment. Additionally, cues that are highly correlated with other cues are removed (Lewis, Patton, and Green 1988), retaining the cue that is deemed most important in the literature. A consulting expert VC also verified that the retained cue was more important. Although the list is not exhaustive, it is more probable that the identified cues in this study include unimportant factors rather than exclude important factors, because experts typically identify far more cues than they actually use (Stewart 1988).

Decision cases are created once the pertinent cues have been identified. Cooperative VCs outside the study's sample (primarily VCs based in Chicago and the East Coast) provided actual cases. Robert Keeley provided additional cases based upon one of his previous studies (Roure and Keeley 1990). A stipulation for using the cases was that the entrepreneur, venture, and any associated firms or individuals remain unidentified. Such a provision does not impede this study in any way. Identifying the venture or entrepreneur might bias the participants' decisions. For example, the knowledge that an entrepreneur has achieved substantial success in the past might lead the subjects to view that particular case favorably. Products also are not identified, because many of the actual cases included products identified with unique firms. Moreover, identifying the product might also narrow the available sample size. A VC may be hesitant to make a decision about a biotechnology firm if (s)he specializes in computer disk storage. For the same reasons, financial cues are not included in this experiment. Different VCs use different hurdle rates.

Value ranges given to each cue allow it to be compared across cases (Stewart 1988). Concrete values are used (e.g., market size) for cue values when possible, but purely representative distributions are appropriate for subjective cues (Stewart 1988). A uniform coding system allows consistent coding across the business plans used in building the experiment.

The lead researcher pulled information factors from the business plans. Although there is a potential threat that the information included in the plan is inaccurate (which would carry over into the experiment), Roure and Keeley (1990) find that VCs rarely need to make "intense" corrections. Thus, it is reasonable to assume that the business plans are accurate. To insure interjudge reliability, a colleague also coded all appropriate cues. The lead researcher provided the second coder with the entire list and description of the information factors of interest. He then coded two business plans. Overall interjudge reliability equates to 87.5%. Berelson (1952) reports that interjudge

TABLE 3   MANOVA Results between Actual and Generated Cases

Variable	Cochran's C		Bartlett-Box F
Market familiarity	$p = 0.173$		$p = 0.182$
Leadership ability	$p = 0.813$		$p = 0.817$
Start-up record	$p = 0.154$		$p = 0.152$
Team completeness	$p = 0.854$		$p = 0.857$
Proprietary protection	$p = 0.945$		$p = 0.946$
Product superiority	$p = 0.817$		$p = 0.821$
Time to development	$p = 0.762$		$p = 0.774$
Market size	$p = 0.123$		$p = 0.142$
Market growth	$p = 0.813$		$p = 0.817$
Direct competitors	$p = 0.369$		$p = 0.382$
Competitor strength	$p = 0.274$		$p = 0.287$
Buyer's concentration	$p = 0.499$		$p = 0.509$
Multivariate tests of significance	Pillais	0.731	
	Hotellings	0.731	
	Wilks	0.731	
Multivariate tests of homogeneity	Box's M	0.367	
	Wilks	0.353	

reliability typically ranges from 66 to 95%. As such, the coding is deemed fairly accurate.

A technique to further decrease multicollinearity while maintaining strong external validity is to combine actual and statistically derived cases. A random case generator from Policy PC software package (Stewart 1991) creates a manageable number of statistically derived cases. MANOVA verifies that the statistical cases are from the same population as the actual cases (see Table 3). The independent variables have equal variance between real and generated cases and the multivariate means are equivalent. Furthermore, a consulting expert VC identifies those cases that are not feasible (i.e., combination of cue values that rarely occurs in reality). Unfeasible cases are dropped from the sample of potential candidates.

The final design allows the VCs to use four to eight cues (depending upon the treatment) and judge 50 cases. The independent variables are the decision cues available within each treatment. The dependent variable is the VCs' assessment of how likely the venture is to succeed as measured on a 7- point Likert scale anchored by 1 (highly likely to fail) and 7 (highly likely to succeed). The participants are divided into three groups (see Table 4). Group one uses the information cues associated with a base cognitive model as derived from literature (see Table 4). The cues are from studies (primarily Tyebjee and Bruno 1984; MacMillan et al. 1985, 1987; Robinson 1987; Timmons et al. 1987) that rely on post hoc methods. Thus, these studies basically rely on introspection by the VC as to what are the most important decision factors. Group two uses more cues than either the first or third groups to assess whether more information changes the decision process (see Table 4). Specifically, group 2 cues include the five used by group 1 VCs plus three more commonly cited from the literature. Groups 1 and 2 use cues corresponding to the cognitive side of the lens model (see Figure 1). Group 3 uses the information factors that best distinguish between successful and failed new ventures; these cues correspond to the task side of the lens model (see Figure 1). The current study uses task cues derived by Roure and Keeley (1990). The regression equation for each of the three possible treatments is as follows:

68   A.L. ZACHARAKIS AND G.D. MEYER

TABLE 4   Experiment Treatment Variables

Base Cognitive Cues (Treatment 1)	Additional Cognitive Cues (Treatment 2)	Task Cues (Treatment 3)
1. Market familiarity—average number of years of experience in market/industry for team	Same five cues as base cognitive cues treatment plus:	1. Completeness of team—percentage of key positions which were filled at the time of the first major (over $300,000) outside funding
2. Leadership ability—average number of years of management experience for team	6. Relevant track record–number of past start-up experiences for team	2. Product superiority—how product compares to existing products
3. Proprietary protection—level of protection provided because product/service or process to deliver product/service is unique and difficult to imitate	7. Competitors—number of direct competitors	3. Time to development—number of months from initiation of development to the initial sale as forecast in business plan
4. Market size—market revenues for most current year	8. Competitor strength—five point scale from high strength (large relative market share) to low (numerous small market share competitors)	4. Buyers concentration—measures the number of potential customers in the target market during the first two years of sales
5. Market growth—% over last several years		

Base Cognitive Cues Model

$$Y = a + b_1 \text{ (mktfam)} + b_2 \text{ (lead)} + b_3 \text{ (proprietary)} + b_4 \text{ (mktsize)} + b_5 \text{ (mktgrw)}$$

Additional Cognitive Cues Model

$$Y = a + b_1 \text{ (mktfam)} + b_2 \text{ (lead)} + b_3 \text{ (proprietary)} + b_4 \text{ (mktsize)} + b_5 \text{ (mktgrw)} + b_6 \text{ (start-up)} + b_7 \text{ (competitor)} + b_8 \text{ (strength)}$$

Task Cues Model

$$Y = a + b_1 \text{ (complete)} + b_2 \text{ (product)} + b_3 \text{ (devtime)} + b_4 \text{ (buyer)}$$

RESULTS

The policy capturing experiment provides many interesting insights. In general, VCs have a difficult time introspecting about their decision process. As such, past research needs to be cautiously interpreted. The following paragraphs further explore the results.

All 51 VCs demonstrate statistically significant policy equations at the 0.01 level or better. Adjusted R-squares vary from 0.35 to 0.85 for the VCs' policy equations. Table 5 details how important each information cue is to the VC decision for both her/his actual and stated decision policies. The next section discusses these results further as they relate to each of the hypotheses.

Hypothesis 1, which suggests that VCs do not understand their decision process, receives mixed support (see Table 5—Treatment 1). By visually examining the weights and respective ranks for each cue, it appears that VCs in Treatment 1 have a strong understanding of their decision process. The rank order is generally the same, although two factors (proprietary protection and market growth) are reversed between the actual

TABLE 5   Comparison of Actual Decision Policy with Stated Decision Policy

	Actual Decision Policy			Stated Decision Policy		
Cues	Mean	SD	Rank	Mean	SD	Rank
Cognitive cues (Treatment 1):						
Entr/Team						
Mkt familiar	0.3562	0.1361	1	22.80	6.420	1
Leadership	0.2954	0.1314	3	19.50	6.917	3
Product						
Proprietary	0.3488	0.1460	2	18.95	6.395	4
Market						
Size	0.1556	0.1277	5	17.90	6.711	5
Growth	0.2875	0.1853	4	20.85	7.150	2
Additional cognitive cues (Treatment 2):						
Entr/Team						
Mkt familiar	0.2145	0.1297	5	14.12	5.988	4
Leadership	0.1786	0.1557	7	16.71	6.789	1
Start-ups	0.0897	0.0615	8	8.29	5.181	8
Product						
Proprietary	0.1989	0.1665	6	10.71	5.861	5
Market						
Size	0.2632	0.1504	3	15.29	6.371	3
Growth	0.2221	0.1467	4	15.53	4.976	2
Competitors	0.3133	0.0898	1	9.47	3.676	7
Strength	0.3037	0.1389	2	9.88	4.973	6
Task cues (Treatment 3):						
Entr/Team						
Complete	0.2320	0.1139	2	19.91	15.667	2
Product						
Superior	0.8071	0.0820	1	46.14	18.949	1
Dev time	0.2038	0.1413	3	18.86	10.045	3
Market						
Concentrate	0.1456	0.1264	4	15.07	9.385	4

decision policy and the stated decision policy. However, studying whether the actual decision policy or the stated decision policy explains more variance of the VC's actual decision is a more rigorous test of VC insight (Summers, Taliaferro, and Fletcher, 1970—see Table 6). Within Treatment 1, the actual decision policy explains 13% more of the variance than the stated decision policy. This difference means that the actual decision policy captures the VC's true decision policy better than the VC does. In other words, VC understanding is not perfect. Nonetheless, the strong rank order correlation between the actual and stated decision policies suggests relatively good insight.

Hypothesis 2, which suggests that more information decreases VC understanding, receives support. A comparison of each VC's actual decision policy with her/his stated decision policy (see Table 5—Treatment 2) indicates that understanding may be low. The rank order between the actual and stated decision policies is very different. VCs are relying heavily on number of competitors and competitor strength (actual decision policy), yet they don't believe that to be the case (number of competitors and competitor strength rank as the sixth and seventh most important out of the eight factors presented in the VC's stated decision policy). VCs in Treatment 2 also believe that they are using leadership much more so than they are (ranked as most important in stated decision policy but is actually seventh out of eight in actual decision policy). Perhaps even more

70   A.L. ZACHARAKIS AND G.D. MEYER

TABLE 6   Median Variance Explained of Actual Decision by Actual Decision Policy (ADP) and Stated Decision Policy (SDP)

Cognitive Cues (Treatment 1)			Additional Cognitive Cues (Treatment 2)			Task Cues (Treatment 3)		
Median r^2 for ADP	Median r^2 for SDP	Change in explained variance	Median r^2 for ADP	Median r^2 for SDP	Change in explained variance	Median r^2 for ADP	Median r^2 for SDP	Change in explained variance
0.5937	0.4630	0.1307	0.5869	0.3359	0.2510	0.7107	0.5190	0.1917

striking is that the VCs within Treatment 2 seem to understand their actual decision policy even less than their peers within Treatment 1. In Treatment 2, the VCs' stated decision policy explains 25% less variance than their actual decision policy [versus only a 13% drop in Treatment 1 (see Table 6)]. More information greatly diminishes VC understanding of their actual decision policy.

Hypothesis 3, which suggests that VCs using an optimal set of information factors can better introspect about their decision policy than those using an intuitive set of cues, receives conditional support. Although the rank order between the actual and stated decision policies is identical, the order of magnitude on the most important factor is quite different (see Table 5—Treatment 3). In the stated decision policy, VCs typically rate product superiority 2.3 to 3 times more importantly than the other factors. However, in their actual decision policy, product superiority is 3.5 to 5.5 times more important than the other factors. Within Treatment 3, the decrease in explained variance is 19%, which is also greater than the decrease in Treatment 1 (see Table 6). However, VC understanding is greater than those VCs in Treatment 2 (19% versus 25%). Thus, VCs are more aware of their thought process using optimal cues conditioned upon the number of intuitive cues they use. Since VCs typically rely on far more than the four to eight cues provided in this experiment—whereas optimal models rarely exceed three to seven cues (Stewart 1988)—VCs using optimal cues should have better understanding.

Hypothesis 4, which suggests that VCs are consistent in applying their decision policies even if they do not consciously understand that policy, receives support. Multiple R from the regression analysis of each individual gauges consistency (see Table 7). It appears that VCs across treatments are very consistent in applying their actual decision policies. The very high Multiple R within Treatment 3 is likely a function of the overwhelming reliance on the product superiority cue. A series of repeated cases also tests consistency (see Table 7). VC assessments within +/- 1 of their initial success assessment on the Likert Scale are considered consistent. As Table 7 illustrates, VCs are consistent on approximately four out of five repeated cases on average. These results suggest that VCs are very consistent in applying their actual decision policies.

TABLE 7   VC Consistency of Applying Actual Decision Policy

	Base Cognitive Cues (Treatment 1)	Additional Cognitive Cues (Treatment 2)	Task Cues (Treatment 3)
Multiple R	0.7876	0.7876	0.8639
Portion of unreliable responses on repeated cases	1.1/5	1.3/5	1.1/5

INTERPRETING RESULTS OF POLICY-CAPTURING EXPERIMENTS

Although policy capturing allows real-time, unbiased capture of VC decisions, it does have some limitations. As with any experiment, reductionism is an issue. The subjects participate in a decision situation that does not perfectly mirror the "real-life" decision. Such "paper tests" affect the external validity of many lens model experiments (Brehmer and Brehmer 1988; Strong 1992). Nevertheless, policy-capturing experiments are a valid method for deriving what information decision-makers actually use (Stewart 1993). Although such "paper" experiments have been criticized, Brown (1972) finds that under even the most contrived cases, the decisions reflect actual decisions. Moreover, since the VC decision has a large "paper" component in the real world (i.e., much of the VC's information comes from business plans), correlation between the experimental task and the "real-world" decision should be even higher.

The experiment also forces VCs to make decisions based upon the presented cues. In reality, VCs would (1) have access to a multitude of possible information cues and (2) use interactive due diligence and other methods to clarify and assess reliability of chosen cues. The experiment, for example, gives participants the relative strength of competition on a 5-point scale. This cue is a distillation of several information points within the business plan. Whereas VCs would normally distill and evaluate these elements for themselves, the experiment does it for the VCs. As such, the assigned value for competitor strength (and other subjective cues) possibly differs from the value VCs would assign. Furthermore, the participating VCs are not privy to these other information factors. Thus, they may be less confident in assessing the impact of competition than might otherwise be the case. In an actual evaluation of a business plan, VCs could use other elements to hedge their assessment of competition thereby increasing their confidence in how to interpret competition. For example, a VC might judge competition to be a critical decision criterion because (s)he sees that (1) there are numerous competitors, (2) some of the competitors are very large, (3) the competitors are known to fiercely retaliate against new entrants, etc. The fact that the experiment presents a combined subjective cue impedes such adjustments and may lead to a systematic over/under weighting of subjective cues.[1] Nonetheless, insight is likely greater in this controlled exercise than it is in the information-laden, noise-filled actual decision environment precisely because of all the noise surrounding each criterion.

The experiment also eliminates the interactive due diligence that typifies the decision. A common theme in the follow-up interviews is that VCs like to reserve final judgment until they have a chance to meet with the lead entrepreneur. In essence, meeting with the entrepreneur adds more data points. As such, the real-life decision has far more informational noise than the experiment. As the results suggest, more information impedes insight. In the experiment, the VCs had at most eight cues. It is easy to imagine how hundreds of cues would further confuse understanding.

The fact that VCs had to use the cues given within the experiment and that there was not an opportunity for interactive due diligence somewhat diminishes the study's external validity (as is often the case in controlled experiments). However, considering these results in conjunction with the results gleaned from verbal protocols (Hall and Hofer 1993; Sandberg et al. 1988; Zacharakis and Meyer 1995) add a deep richness to

---

[1] Thanks to a reviewer for highlighting this potential experimental bias.

72 A.L. ZACHARAKIS AND G.D. MEYER

previous survey results. Specifically, verbal protocols provide a sense of (1) how VCs read and assimilate information from a business plan, (2) why they use certain information to make a decision, and (3) how they use that information. Interpreting the results of the current study in light of past verbal protocol studies gives researchers a sense of how VCs pull together information to derive subjective assessments (i.e., competitor strength). Whereas verbal protocols provide a first glimpse at self insight, policy capturing allows a more rigorous and controlled examination of self insight in that the experiment captures the VC's actual and stated policies.

DISCUSSION

This study suggests that VCs do not have a strong grasp on their decision-making process, especially as the decision becomes information laden. Thus, past studies that provide a laundry list of factors may be biased in that they list a multitude of factors that have a relatively small influence on the decision. Slovic and Lichtenstein (1971) assert, for most decisions, that three information cues typically account for 80% of the variance; one cue often explains 40% of the variance. The multitude of available information factors surrounding the actual investment decision likely hinders VC decision-making. Nisbett and Wilson (1977) suggest that poor insight is a function of "ease of access"; people cannot easily access that part of the brain dealing with multiple criteria processing. As such, post hoc studies may not provide as much prescriptive value as they could because they hide the most important factors with others that create noise. Previous ex post studies might mislead not only VCs, but entrepreneurs as well.

Understanding decision criteria are not only important for VCs, but also important for entrepreneurs seeking venture capital. Using criteria identified in previous ex post studies to prepare for the solicitation of venture backing might be a mistake. For example, many of the ex post survey studies (Wells 1974; Poindexter 1976; Tyebjee and Bruno 1984; MacMillan et al. 1985, 1987) would lead entrepreneurs to believe that personal and team characteristics are the most important criteria, but this study coincides with Hall and Hofer (1993) in that the entrepreneur factor does not appear that important. Market characteristics might be better determinants of who gets funding and who does not. Thus, entrepreneurs that spend most of their time and effort presenting the team, while neglecting other factors, may not obtain funding.

Information necessary to the decision is not of equal importance. George Doriot, a pioneer in the VC industry, notes that "a grade-A man with a grade-B idea is better than a grade-B man with a grade-A idea" (as cited in Sandberg 1986). It is evident from this quote that VCs do not view all cues as equally important; they do not receive equal consideration. Notwithstanding the VC's ex post assessment that the entrepreneur is the most important consideration (Wells 1974; Poindexter 1976, Tyebjee and Bruno 1984; MacMillan et al. 1985, 1987), this study derives the actual importance of each presented cue in the VC's decision process. Although the VCs do not have complete freedom in choosing which information cues they wish to use within the experiment, the relative importance of each cue is interesting. Specifically, each VCs' actual decision policy, as represented by a standardized regression equation, indicates how much weight the respective VC places on each information cue.

Table 5 presents the frequency, by experiment treatment, with which each factor is most influential, second most influential, etc., to the VC's decision. Within Treatment 1, proprietary protection is most important, closely followed by entrepreneur/team characteristics (see Table 5). Market factors (market size and market growth) are the least important. Within Treatment 2, market factors (especially competition cues) are the most important with market familiarity and product factors following (see Table 5). Finally, VCs in Treatment 3 exclusively view product superiority as the most important factor. Buyer concentration (a market factor) is least important. In summary, the type of information available influences the VC's decision process. When certain information is available, it causes VCs to shift their attention (i.e., the addition of competitor information in the additional cues treatment causes the focus to shift to market factors from entrepreneur/team factors). In addition, more information seems to shift the importance from the entrepreneur to the market. Such a finding suggests that the entrepreneur is critical when the VC does not have much information about the market. However, if the VC is confident in the market, the entrepreneur is not too important. Such a finding is congruent with those of other real time experiments (Hall and Hofer 1993; Zacharakis and Meyer 1995). Thus, the current results point to biases in post hoc studies that suggest entrepreneur characteristics are typically most critical to the investment decision. It appears that additional policy capturing experiments might provide further identification of the more important information factors. Considering the lack of VC insight, the policy capturing methodology holds much promise for prescriptive advice to VCs (and by extension, to entrepreneurs).

Implications for VCs are numerous. First, VCs may want to re-examine the importance of the entrepreneur. Since the current study and Hall and Hofer's (1993) study suggest that entrepreneur factors are not as important as believed, relying on meetings with the entrepreneur to judge the entrepreneur's capabilities could be dangerous. Trivial factors (i.e., height, appearance, etc.) might bias the VC. The entrepreneur's perceived personality might generate more weight than is appropriate. "I stopped the deal because I did not think we would work well together" or vice versa. Judging entrepreneurs on how well their personality fits with the VC's personality opens a cauldron of potential mistakes. How well can a person get to know an individual in one or even 10 meetings? For example, people place inordinate importance on personal appearance when conducting job interviews (Borman 1991). Likewise, attractive entrepreneurs may be more likely to receive financing. However, the link between appearance and entrepreneurial qualifications is dubious, at best. First impression biases impact hiring decisions, yet do not correlate very strongly with ultimate success (Borman 1991). Thus, it may be wise to screen the potential entrepreneur on her/his paper record. This is not to say that once a venture passes the screening stage that the VC and entrepreneur should not meet. Post-screening meetings enhance venture success by clarifying expectations and jointly evaluating entrepreneur/team capabilities.[2] The VC and entrepreneur can then take remedial action to improve the probability of a successful launch.

Second, VCs face a plethora of information when making an investment decision (i.e., business plan, outside consultants, due diligence, etc.). The noise caused by this information overload may impede insight into the intuitive decision process. This lack of systematic understanding hinders learning. VCs cannot make accurate adjustments to their evaluation process if they do not truly understand it. Therefore, VCs may suffer from a systematic bias that impedes the performance of their investment portfolio. The methodology used in this experiment can be modified and used as a training tool for active VCs. In addition, since VC decision-making is very consistent (even if they do

---

[2] Thanks to a reviewer for suggesting the article clarify between pre- and post-screening meetings.

not have a strong understanding of that process), decision aides can be developed to minimize the danger of salient information (e.g., the lead entrepreneur is a winner) clouding the VC's judgment. Unlike the current study, policy capturing can be customized toward an individual VC or a VC firm; policy capturing can include financial and product factors that were removed from this study. Thus, VC firms can use this methodology to aid individual VCs by helping them understand and improve their decisions.

Third, the study implies that formalizing VC intuition may help them improve their decisions because it allows corrective action. One simple method of formalizing intuition is to use a checklist, or scorecard, of how ventures measure on key criteria. Only 24% of the participating VCs queried in follow-up interviews use some sort of factor checklist. Checklists provide a basis for VCs within the firm to evaluate the lead VCs analysis and, by extension, examine whether certain salient factors are creating a bias. Over time as certain funded ventures succeed and others fail, checklists allow VCs to assess the validity of their decision criteria and make corrections. In fact, several of those VCs that use a checklist did so after they made an investment decision. In other words, the VC made the decision on an intuitive basis and then, after funding the firm, the VC went back and completed the checklist. Such a history of investment decisions allows VCs to learn what works and what does not. It is much more difficult to discern the critical factors if the VC never formalizes the decision process, especially considering post hoc recall and rationalization biases.

Finally, this study demonstrates the strong theoretical basis that SJT and the lens model provide to the VC decision. Although many of the early studies focus on decision criteria, few tie it to a theoretical framework. In fact, Tyebjee and Bruno (1984) acknowledge a lack of theory behind their work. SJT provides that basis not only for the current study, but also for previous studies.

If VCs do not have a strong understanding of their decision process, they cannot systematically work to improve it. Forty percent of VC investments (Ruhnka, Feldman, and Dean 1992) fail to provide a satisfactory return, even though VCs are experts. The value of this study and policy capturing is that it may better identify the important factors for both VCs and entrepreneurs. This study will, hopefully, encourage VCs to step back and reevaluate their decision-making. Moreover, the results of such techniques can be used to build decision aides that can further improve VC decision-making (Zacharakis 1995). Any improvement in understanding (which ultimately leads to improved decision-making) can have a huge economic impact for both the VC community and their funded ventures.

REFERENCES

Barr, P.S., Stimpert, J.L., and Huff, A.S. 1992. Cognitive change, strategic action, and organizational renewal. *Strategic Management Journal* 13:15–36.

Berelson, B. 1952. *Content Analysis in Communications Research.* Glencoe, IL: Free Press.

Borman, W. 1991. Job behavior, performance and effectiveness, in M. Dunnette and L. Hough, eds., *Handbook of Industrial and Organizational Psychology.* Palo Alto, CA: Consulting Psychologist Press, pp. 271–326.

Brehmer, A., and Brehmer, B. 1988. What have we learned about human judgment from thirty years of policy capturing. In B. Brehmer and C. Joyce, eds., *Human Judgment: The SJT View.* North, Holland: Elsevier.

Brown, T.R. 1972. A comparison of judgmental policy equations obtained from human judges under natural and contrived conditions. *Mathematics Bioscience* 15:205–230.

Brunswik, E. 1956. *Perception and the Representative Design of Experiments.* Berkeley, CA: University of California Press.

Cyert, R.M., and March, J.G. 1963. *A Behavioral Theory of the Firm.* Englewood Cliffs, NJ: Prentice Hall.

Dawes, R.M. 1988. *Rational Choice in an Uncertain World.* Fort Worth, TX: Harcourt Brace Jovanovich.

Dawes, R.M., Faust, D., and Meehl, P.E. 1989. Clinical versus actuarial judgment. *Science* 243: 668–1674.

Fischhoff, B. 1988. Judgment and decision-making. In R. Sternberg and E. Smith, eds., *The Psychology of Human Thought.* Cambridge, UK: Cambridge University Press, pp. 155–187.

Fiske, S.T., and Taylor, S.E. 1991. *Social Cognition.* New York: Random House.

Gupta, A.K., and Sapienza, H.J. 1992. Determinants of venture capital firms' preferences regarding the industry diversity and geographic scope of their investments. *Journal of Business Venturing* 7:347–362.

Hall, J., and Hofer, C.W. 1993. Venture capitalists' decision criteria and new venture evaluation. *Journal of Business Venturing* 8(1):25–42.

Hammond, K.R. 1977. Social judgment theory: Application in policy formation. In M. Kaplan and S. Schwartz, eds., *Human Judgments and Decision Processes in Applied Settings.* New York: Academic Press, pp. 1–29.

Hammond, K.R. 1975. Social judgment theory: Its use in the study of psychoactive drugs. In K. Hammond and C. Joyce, eds., *Psychoactive Drugs and Social Judgment: Theory and Research.* New York: Wiley, pp. 69–105.

Hitt, M.A., and Tyler, B.B. 1991. Strategic decision models: Integrating different perspectives. *Strategic Management Journal* 12:327–351.

Hogarth, R.M., and Makridakis, S. 1981. Forecasting and planning: An evolution. *Management Science* 27(2):115–138.

Khan, A.M. 1987. Assessing venture capital investments with noncompensatory behavioral decision models. *Journal of Business Venturing* 2:193–205.

Kunkel, S.W., and Hofer, C.W. 1990. *Why study the determinants of new venture performance: A literature review and rationale.* Presented at Academy of Management meetings, San Francisco.

Lewis, B.L., Patton, J.M., and Green, S.L. 1988. The effects of information choice and information use on analysts' predictions of municipal bond rating changes. *The Accounting Review* 63(2):270–282.

MacMillan, I.C., Zeman, L., and Subba Narasimha, P.N. 1987. Criteria distinguishing unsuccessful ventures in the venture screening process. *Journal of Business Venturing* 2:123–137.

MacMillan, I.C., Seigel, R., and Subba Narasimha, P.N. 1985. Criteria used by venture capitalist to evaluate new venture proposals. *Journal of Business Venturing* 1:119–128.

Newell, A., and Simon, H.A. 1972. Human Problem Solving. Englewood Cliffs, NJ: Prentice-Hall.

Nisbett, R.E., and Wilson, T.D. 1977. Telling more than we can know: Verbal reports on mental processes. *Psychological Review* 84(3):231–259.

Perez, R.C. 1986. *Inside Venture Capital: Past, Present, and Future.* New York: Praeger.

Poindexter, E.A. 1976. *The efficiency of financial markets: The venture capital case.* Unpublished doctoral dissertation. New York: New York University.

Pratt, S.E. 1987. Overview and introduction to the venture capital industry. In S. Pratt and J. Morris, eds., *Pratt's Guide to Venture Capital Sources,* 11th edition. Wellesley, MA: Venture Economics.

Robinson, R.B. 1987. Emerging strategies in the venture capital industry. *Journal of Business Venturing* 2:53–77.

Roure, J.B., and Keeley, R.H. 1990. Predictors of success in new technology-based ventures. *Journal of Business Venturing* 5:201–220.

Ruhnka, J.C., Feldman, H.D., and Dean, T.J. 1992. The "living dead" phenomena in venture capital investments. *Journal of Business Venturing* 7(2):137–155.

Sandberg, W.R. 1986. *New Venture Performance.* Lexington, MA: Lexington.

76   A.L. ZACHARAKIS AND G.D. MEYER

Sandberg, W.R., Schweiger, D.M., and Hofer, C.W. 1988. The use of verbal protocols in determining venture capitalists' decision processes. *Entrepreneurship Theory and Practice* Winter:8–20.

Simon, H.A. 1955. A behavioral model of rational choice. *Quarterly Journal of Economics* 69:99–118.

Simon, H.A., and Chase, W.G. 1973. Skill in chess. *American Scientist* 61(4):394–403.

Slovic, P., and Lichtenstein, S. 1971. Comparison of bayesian and regression approaches to the study of information procession in judgment. *Organizational Behavior and Human Performance* 6:649–744.

Stahl, M.J., and Zimmerer, T.W. 1984. Modeling strategic acquisition policies: A simulation of executives' acquisition decisions. *Academy of Management Journal* 27(2):369–383.

Steier, L., and Greenwood, R. 1995. Venture capitalist relationships in the deal structuring and post-investment stages of new firm creation. *Journal of Management Studies* 32(3):337–357.

Stewart, T.R., 1993. *Notes on the validity of judgment analysis.* Working paper.

Stewart, T.R. 1991. *Policy PC: Judgment Analysis Software Reference Manual.* Albany, NY: Executive Decision Services.

Stewart, T.R. 1988. Judgment analysis: Procedures. In B. Brehmer and C. Joyce, eds., *Human Judgment: The SJT View.* North, Holland: Elsevier.

Strong, K.C. 1992. *A cognitive model of downstructuring strategy.* Unpublished doctoral dissertation. Boulder, CO: University of Colorado.

Summers, D.A., Taliaferro, J.D., and Fletcher, D.J. 1970. Subjective versus objective description of judgment policy. *Psychonomic Science* 18:249–250.

Timmons, J.A. 1994. *New Venture Creation: Entrepreneurship for the 21st Century.* Homewood, IL: Irwin.

Timmons, J.A., Muzyka, D.F., Stevenson, H.H., and Bygrave, W.D. 1987. Opportunity recognition: The core of entrepreneurship. *Frontiers of Entrepreneurship Research* 109–123.

Tversky, A., and Kahneman, D. 1974. Judgment under uncertainty: Heuristics and biases. *Science* 185:1124–1131.

Tyebjee, T.T., and Bruno, A.V. 1984. A model of venture capitalist investment activity. *Management Science* 30(9):1051–1056.

Wells, W.A. 1974. *Venture capital decision-making.* Unpublished doctoral dissertation. Pittsburgh, PA: Carnegie Mellon University.

Zacharakis, A.L., and Meyer, G.D. 1995. The venture capitalist decision: Understanding process versus outcome. *Frontiers of Entrepreneurship Research* 465–478.

Zacharakis, A.L. 1995. *The venture capital investment decision.* Unpublished doctoral dissertation. Boulder, CO: University of Colorado.

[20]

Journal of Economic Behavior and Organization 12 (1989) 159–180. North-Holland

A FAILURE-INDUCEMENT MODEL OF RESEARCH AND DEVELOPMENT EXPENDITURE

Italian Evidence from the Early 1980s

Cristiano ANTONELLI

Politecnico di Milano, 20133 Milano, Italy

Received September 1988, final version received October 1988

Empirical evidence for the Schumpeterian suggestion of a positive relationship between profitability and innovative effort is slim. In fact, the opposite is often suggested. An alternative 'failure-inducement' hypothesis argues that firms make innovative efforts when performance falls below a minimum threshold, resulting in a negative relationship between profitability and R&D expenditures. Data on R&D expenditures in Italian industry in the early 1980s – a period of severe economic crisis – show that both hypotheses are relevant for firms whose profits are well above or well below average, respectively.

1. Profitability and innovative efforts

Empirical research on the relationship between market structure and innovative effort has been clustered primarily around four testable hypotheses: (1) A concentrated market structure is conducive to a faster rate of technological change; (2) Internally generated financial resources are a necessary condition to fund activities directed at generating technological innovation; (3) Large firms are better placed than smaller ones to perform R&D activities and to take advantage of their results; and (4) Diversified firms can reap the benefits of R&D programs better than specialized firms.

The results of years of empirical research on these four main hypotheses give strong support to some of them, but they cast serious doubts on others. The importance of industrial concentration, the degree of firms' diversification and firm size is confirmed, while the effect of liquidity and profitability appears to be unclear.

Within the Schumpeterian approach, liquidity and profitability are expected to enhance the intensity of innovative efforts on the basis of three major factors: (i) Transaction costs in raising external funds to finance R&D activities are especially high because of the reluctance of financial institutions to fund activities characterized by high levels of uncertainty and risk

0167-2681/89/$3.50 © 1989, Elsevier Science Publishers B.V. (North-Holland)

[Grabowski (1968)]; (ii) Exploitation of market power and monopoly rents are likely to be the best way to generate adequate levels of funds for discretionary investments with uncertain rates of return [Scherer (1965)]; (iii) Transient monopolistic profits from innovation are likely to generate strong cumulative incentives to self-finance appropriate levels of R&D activities in order to maintain an innovative lead [Kamien and Schwartz (1978)].

There is substantial empirical evidence regarding the role of profitability and liquidity as determinants of R&D expenditure. It does not appear to be consistent with the traditional Schumpeterian hypotheses. The empirical research has been conducted in a variety of countries at both the firm and sectorial levels, with cross-sections, time series and panels.

Most of the empirical work was conducted in the United States in the 1960s and the early 1970s. Scherer (1965) used data from 448 U.S. corporations to examine the relationships among profits, sales and asset measures in 1955, and R&D expenditures in the same year or patents four years later. His findings were the first to indicate some negative coefficients, and generally low levels of statistical significance in the relationships.

Econometric work by Hamberg (1966) estimated the role of liquidity (profits plus depreciation charges) in explaining R&D intensity (R&D personnel as a percentage of total employment) in 405 firms in 21 U.S. industries for 1960. His results also suggested some negative coefficients and a generally weak relationship. Elliot's (1971) study, based on 53 firms drawn from 16 industries for ten years, provided clear evidence of the significant effects of five different indicators of profitability on R&D intensity. His results, however, also showed a strong negative association in years characterized by slow rates of economic growth. In addition, Branch (1974) found clear evidence for a positive effect of past R&D expenditures on the growth of profits and sales, but only weak support for the hypothesis that 'profit stimulates R&D.'

As far as the United States is concerned, the most convincing evidence is given by Grabowski (1968), who considers typical science-based activities such as the chemical, petroleum and drug industries. He found that liquidity (after-tax profits plus depreciation and depletion charges) had a significant and positive coefficient in a regression of R&D intensity on variables including a measure of the diversification of the firms and an indicator of technological opportunity.

In other countries, quite strong evidence of a negative correlation between profitability, or liquidity, and innovative intensity, has emerged in more recent studies, especially in non-science-based industries and in periods of slow economic growth. In the United Kingdom, Smyth, Samuel, and Tzoannos (1972) provide some evidence of the positive role played by liquidity (undistributed profits plus depreciation) in determining the level of innovative output, measured by the patents granted to 25 firms active in the chemical and machine tool industries. However, their results show that profitability (profits net of tax and interest payments) has no significant effect in all the firms in their chemical, machine tools and electronics industries sample. Bosworth and Westaway (1984) make a much stronger point, by reporting a significant negative coefficient on profitability (gross trading profits plus R&D and advertising expenditures) in a time-series analysis of the determinants of domestic patents granted in the United Kingdom in the period 1950–1975.

In Sweden, Johannisson and Lindstrom (1971) concluded that neither liquid assets (current assets less short term liabilities) nor cash flow (net profits plus depreciation taxes and financial funds) had any significant effects on the determinants of patent applications in Swedish industry. In Italy, Antonelli (1985) analyzed the determinants of R&D expenditures in 16 sectors of Italian manufacturing in the period 1967–1981. His results show that liquidity (sales minus actual cost of goods sold as a ratio of total sales) had a negative sign in three non-science based sectors, while in three science-based ones the variable had a significant and positive coefficient.

In Canada, Howe and McFetridge (1976) study the determinants of R&D expenditures in 81 firms in the electrical, chemical and machinery industries over the period 1967–71. They report a negative coefficient on profits (profits after taxes but before deduction of R&D expenditures) in the machinery industry, although it was only marginally significant and positive coefficients on profits in the chemicals and electrical products industries. The sign for the coefficient on depreciation in the chemical and electrical industries was negative.

Caves, Porter and Spence (1980) found that both net profitability (net profit after taxes divided by total assets) and gross profitability (value added minus payroll and advertising expenditures divided by the value of shipments) had a strong and significant negative role in determining the level of R&D intensity in a cross-sector analysis of Canadian manufacturing industry. Reversing the traditional argument, they comment that 'the negative impact ... could occur because high profits signify the presence of some rent yielding assets which implies the absence of competition and thus the lack of competitive pressure to innovate.' (p. 186)

In conclusion, the results of such an extensive literature appear to be, in a Schumpeterian perspective, somewhat puzzling. Not only is it true, as Kamien and Schwartz (1982) point out, in their review, 'the empirical evidence that either liquidity or profitability are conducive to innovative effort or output appears slim' but evidence of a negative effect of both profitability and liquidity on innovative intensity appears to gain momentum especially in non-science-based industries and in years of slow economic growth such as the post-1974 period. In response to these results it might be claimed that the Schumpeterian literature has been contradicted by empirical evidence counter to one of its central research hypotheses. However, clear indications of a negative causation between profitability and innovative efforts, in fact, received less attention than they deserve [Kamien and Schwartz (1982)].

2. A failure-inducement hypothesis

The empirical evidence gathered seems to suggest that two different and opposite forces underlie the relationship between profitability and R&D efforts. It seems therefore necessary to consider together with the Schumpeterian relationship according to which profits stimulate R&D expenditures, a behavioral hypothesis of failure-inducement of innovative efforts.

In a failure-inducement hypothesis, R&D expenditures can be funded by firms facing declining profits and increasing competition to modify their production mix and market conditions. In such a context it is likely that losses rather than profits influence innovative efforts. In a failure-inducement hypothesis, firms use satisficing criteria such that the search for new technologies is considered only when performance falls below a minimum threshold.

The distinction between failure-induced search for innovation and institutionalized search for innovation made by March–Simon (1958) seems relevant here. 'Modern' firms have in fact institutionalized the search for innovation which is a component of the satisficing level of achievement. According to March–Simon (1958), institutionalized search for innovation implies higher levels of innovative activity with a more stable trend. On the other hand, failure-induced search is characterized by lower levels of current innovative activity, which is more sensitive to failures in achieving targets.

A failure-induced hypothesis thus specifically applies to firms which have not yet institutionalized the search for innovation. Following March and Simon (1958, p. 183), we thus would expect, in firms which have not yet institutionalized the search for technological innovation, 'efforts towards innovation in a company whose share of market, total profits or rate of return on investment had declined... As a corollary to the first point, we would expect data in reports of operating statistics to trigger innovative effort when the data showed performance falling below present standards.'[1]

---

[1]See also Rosenberg (1969) for a similar position: 'It is possible, furthermore, that threats of deterioration or actual deterioration from some previous state are more powerful attention-focusing devices than are vague possibilities for improvement. There may be psychological reasons why a worsening state of affairs, or its prospect, galvanizes those affected into a more positive and decisive response than do potential movements to improved states. The same sort of asymmetry which Duesenberry postulated for consumer units confronted with the need to adjust to a downward revision in their incomes may hold for decision makers who control the allocation of resources for exploring the technological horizon. *Such asymmetrical behavior may possibly be treated more appropriately within a 'satisficing' model of entrepreneurial behavior and response, where alternative technologies are explored only when a firm's profit position falls below some minimum acceptable level.*'

C. Antonelli, A failure-inducement model of research and development expenditure   163

It is important to stress that the failure-inducement hypothesis of R&D expenditures is well differentiated from traditional inducement models of innovation and technical change. The latter aim to explain the *direction* of technical change in terms of the relative price of the factors of production. The former more specifically argues that firms undertake R&D activities as a response to changes in relative prices and to subsequent declines in performance without any strong assumption regarding the factor composition of the new production mix.[2]

Moreover, a failure-inducement hypothesis of R&D expenditures considers the level of profitability as the focusing device, rather than the change in relative prices. Firms in conditions of distress, i.e. with losses or profits below the average, fund R&D activities to acquire information on the technological environment and to appropriate the technological opportunities available to them which best fit the specific features of their production mix, commercial position and existing stock of fixed and human capital. Firms thus invest in R&D activities in order to generate innovations which can minimize the costs of substitution of existing factors of production while permitting improved performance.

In the failure-inducement hypothesis the behavior of firms enjoying high levels of profitability is less well specified. According to Caves, Porter and Spence (1980), one can argue that because they are satisfying certain criteria, firms with above average profitability – presumably enjoying high barriers to entry – are reluctant to innovate. Consequently, not only do losses or below average profits stimulate innovative efforts, but rents depress innovative efforts. Alternatively, following the transaction cost hypothesis, i.e. the failure of financial markets to provide financial resources for uncertain activities such as R&D projects [Grabowski (1968)], one can argue that rents, and consequently high levels of discretionary funds are likely to fund R&D projects.

These models together imply that R&D efforts might follow from both

---

[2]It is worth noting however that the rapid increase of the cost of labor and energy experienced in the Italian economy in the early 1970s can be considered a major determinant in the search of new production techniques in a fairly complementary approach to ours as the theory of localized technical change developed by David (1975) seems to be: 'As soon as one is ready to discard the neoclassical conception of technological progress which insists that innovation and factor-substitution be viewed as logically distinct phenomena, there is no longer any great difficulty in taking an important step toward this proximate objective. Specifically it becomes possible to indicate how the realized factor-saving bias of 'changes in the state of the technical arts' may come under the influence of factor-prices-directly, as well as indirectly through the medium of choice of technique decisions. In regard to the latter, we may for the present purposes eschew less orthodox 'behavioral' approaches to the decision making of firms; the prevailing structure of input prices will therefore continue to be cast in the governing role assigned to them by the traditional theory of the rational, cost-minimizing firm.' [David (1975, pp. 57–58)]. However, it seems important to stress that while David's analysis focuses on the direction of technological change induced by changes in the costs of factors, we are more interested in explaining the level of the activity of search for innovation.

above average profits and below average profits. Firms with average profits, especially if active in non-science-based sectors where R&D is not yet institutionalized, would be less likely to fund innovative efforts because of: (i) the lack of competitive pressure to innovate, and (ii) the failure of financial markets to provide appropriate levels of financial resources for R&D projects.

3. The Italian evidence

3.1. The economic context

In the 1970s Italy faced sharp increases in the relative price of energy and labour. These changes deeply affected the Italian economy, which is highly dependent on oil imports. The performance of Italian firms declined markedly, with major drops in overall profitability and international market shares. In the same period R&D activities grew significantly in real terms, increasing from 0.82 percent of G.N.P. in 1974 to 1.34 percent in 1985 (see table 1). This parallel between the decline in performance and the sharp increase in R&D activities suggests that a failure inducement hypothesis of R&D expenditures may apply in the Italian case.

The failure-inducement hypothesis of R&D expenditures seems to be extremely relevant in an industrial structure such as that of Italy, in which the institutionalization of technological innovation is still lacking and firms rely upon innovations in style and design rather than in science-based technologies. In such a context R&D expenditures clearly have a defensive flavor.[3] In the Italian experience in the early 1980s, it thus seems clear that 'traditional firms', facing adverse changes in their economic environment, invested heavily in R&D activities as part of a long range search. The search was for a new and more productive mix that shed traditional patterns while exploiting existing sunk costs, technological opportunities and strategic interdependence more appropriately. Moreover, the low levels, by international standards, of R&D intensity in Italy, together with the strong sensitivity of Italian R&D expenditures to adverse environmental changes, confirm that the introduction of technological science-based innovations were not yet institutionalized in the Italian economy.[4] Strong structural factors make the failure-inducement hypothesis of R&D activities especially appropriate in analyzing the contingent determinants of R&D expenditures in

---

[3]See Leibenstein (1976, pp. 39–46) for his hypothesis of adversity-driven pressure for change where firms are induced to fund research activities for defensive purposes.

[4]See March and Simon (1958, p. 185). 'It should be possible to distinguish the patterns of innovation of organizations that have institutionalized the innovative process in one way or another from those that have not. For example, we would expect the rate of innovation to be less sensitive to environmental changes in the former rather than in the latter. On the whole, at least under conditions of a relatively stable environment, we would also expect the average rate of innovation to be higher the greater the institutionalization of innovation.'

C. Antonelli, A failure-inducement model of research and development expenditure   165

Table 1

The role of government and public subsidies in the growth of Italian R&D expenditures.

	R&D performed by firms and government (GERD)[a]	R&D performed by firms (BERD)[a]	Percentage BERD/GERD	Public subsidies to BERD[a]	Percentage public subsidies/BERD	Percentage GERD/domestic gross product
1974	916.9	507.2	55.3	26.8	5.3	0.82
1975	1,168.1	650.7	55.7	42.4	6.5	0.93
1976	1,352.6	740.3	54.7	59.9	8.1	0.86
1977	1,684.1	902.3	53.5	99.3	11.0	0.88
1978	1,866.8	1,023.0	54.8	75.5	7.4	0.83
1979	2,288.0	1,335.0	58.3	77.7	5.8	0.85
1980	2,897.0	1,710.5	59.0	158.6	9.3	0.86
1981	4,056.0	2,286.1	56.3	201.2	8.8	1.01
1982	4,916.0	2,790.3	56.8	327.5	11.7	1.08
1983	6,413.0	3,431.0	53.5	644.8	18.8	1.19
1984	8,216.0	3,864.0	47.0	803.7	20.8	1.34

[a]Billions of lire.
Source: ISTAT 1985.

Italy in the early 1980s. At that time Italy, in fact, had features typical of a late industrialized country exposed to a major economic crisis.

According to Fua' (1980), late industrialized countries, i.e. those countries whose industrialization' process took off in the late nineteenth century or in the twentieth century, are characterized by a number of common features. These features include low factor productivity, a strong presence of traditional sectors and the polarization of firms around two types:

– a small number of 'modern' firms with high total factor productivity, high wages, advanced managerial organizational structures which are already active in science-based sectors such as electronics, chemicals and capital goods. Modern firms are the ones which are able to command skilled factors of production, but must operate close to the forefront of technological advance;
– a large number of 'traditional' firms with low total factor productivity and backward technology and management. Traditional firms survive by making extensive use of a low wage workforce, and avoiding fiscal burdens.

The industrial and economic dualism is the result of an historic process of leapfrogging. Countries which started their industrialization process when other countries were already established on international oligopolistic markets, as well ahead in Schumpeterian competition based on innovation and technological advance, had few accumulated tangible and intangible assets. They therefore specialized in activities which were not capital intensive and had low levels of output per worker. However, a few firms in these countries have been able to take advantage of new technological opportunities and thereby reduce the imitation lag, thus closing or reducing the productivity gap with the early industrialized countries. It is a difficult, costly, risky and long-term process to modify the factors of comparative advantage and accumulate scarce intangible assets, and the effort must be tackled on two fronts. Some manufacturers use techniques and production methods similar to those used in the early industrialized countries, while others compete on international markets by adopting a different set of techniques which are less intensive in the use of tangible and intangible assets and employ more low-skilled labour.

Major changes in the international and domestic economic environment have effected the survival of the traditional sector of the Italian economy and have forced many firms to enter the modern sector. The drive to enter the modern sector, especially during the 1970s, was first of all the result of cumulative factors in the labour market. The Italian labour market was formerly composed largely of low paid and poorly skilled manpower with a small fraction of trained workers, mirroring the dualistic structure of industry. The spread of higher salaries from the tiny modern sector to the large traditional sector was very rapid in the 1970s, owing to strong imitation

patterns, a sharp reduction of unemployment rates, high levels of unioniza-
tion and very active union behavior. The pressure of even higher salaries
eroded the economic basis of the traditional sector of the economy,
squeezing profit margins and pushing firms towards more productive uses of
labour, and thus more active R&D strategies.

The entry of new competitors played an important role in altering the
international division of labour, as the traditional competitive advantage in
labor-intensive products was challenged by the growing exports of the newly
industrializing countries. This caused Italian firms to search for technological
and organizational innovations which could help them to reduce production
costs.[5] The search for process innovations, rather than style-intensive
product innovations, led firms to fund R&D activities in science-based
technologies.

Finally, increases in the cost of energy, especially relevant in an oil
dependent country such as Italy, forced firms to look for process innovations
which could compensate for increased total costs relative to international
competitors. Once again, firms, accustomed to applying product-style innovations, had to fund R&D in order to search in science-based technologies.

In conclusion, it seems clear that in the late 1970s and early 1980s Italian
firms were forced into R&D expenditures by increases in the prices of oil
and other inputs, the changing character of the domestic labor market, and
the entry of new competitors on international markets. The position of
Italian firms on the market was changed and rates of profitability fell,
resulting in generally poor economic performance. R&D expenditures was an
important factor which Italian firms used to respond to this adversity. At
that time the large modern firms which were already active in the science-
based sectors and had institutionalized innovative routines continued to fund
R&D projects so as to keep up with the fast pace of technological change.
Consequently, the overall intensity of R&D expenditures in the Italian
economy almost doubled in the period 1974–1984 (see table 1), a rate of
increase in real terms of 16% per annum.

Such a big increase appears also to be due to the active intervention of the
Italian government. In those years the Italian government consistently
increased both its direct participation in R&D and also the subsidies it
granted for R&D carried out by firms, in response to the growing awareness
of the problems faced by Italian industry. This is clearly shown in table 1,
which shows a significant increase in R&D carried out and funded by the
government.

The ratio of gross expenditures on R&D in the business sector (BERD) to
total R&D expenditures (GERD) in 1984 was 47 per cent, compared to an
average of 55 per cent in the 1970s, and international levels of 60 per cent.

---

[5]See Antonelli (1988, pp. 13–32) for an analysis of the adoption of organizational innovations
parallel to the diffusion of new information technologies in Italian industry.

Furthermore, public subsidies to BERD climbed to 21 per cent in 1984 from an average of 10 per cent in the 1970s. One lira out of five spent by the business sector on R&D in Italy was funded by the government. When taking into consideration, the fact that Act 46 subsidies (30 per cent of total public funding in 1984) are given as low interest finance for firms' R&D programs, it is clear that the share of R&D expenditures by firms induced by public intervention increased to at least 40 per cent. It therefore seems clear that R&D was indeed an important factor used by the government to help Italian industry to face its difficulties.

This synthetic account of the major crisis faced during the '70s and early '80s by Italian industry, and the evidence regarding the R&D policy interventions by the Italian government confirm the appropriateness, in the Italian case, of a failure-inducement hypothesis for analysis of the determinants of R&D expenditures. Such a failure-inducement hypothesis seems to be the outcome of both the firms' R&D funding decisions and the government's use of R&D as a policy tool in a period of economic adversity.

The Italian experience of the early 1980s seems to be a case of social learning where many small and medium-sized firms, often belonging to the traditional sectors, discovered, with the substantial help of the interventions of industrial policy, R&D activities as a tool for confronting an adverse contingent environment. Furthermore, they learned to exploit technology-intensive process innovations, rather than style-based product innovations, to change their production mix as well as their market strategies.

4. The data

Data on R&D expenditures at the firm level are not available to the public in Italy; aggregate data published by ISTAT is based on firm's answers to questionnaires, but are covered by the secrecy acts. A broad analysis of the annual reports of some major Italian companies, and the answers to a questionnaire mailed to over two hundred Italian manufacturing firms undertaking some R&D activity, made it possible for the first time to collect information on R&D expenditures in eighty-six Italian firms during the period 1981–1983[6] (see table 2). Total R&D expenditures in these 86 firms represented 72 per cent of Italian industrial BERD in 1982. A sectorial distribution of the firms shows the differences in the coverage of the data collected compared with the ISTAT statistics[7] (see table 2). Data gathered at the firm level seems to correspond with the aggregate statistics.

---

[6]Full data from 1981 to 1983 are available for 83 firms; comparisons with ISTAT data are made on 86 firms for 1982.

[7]Though our attribution to each industry of highly differentiated firms may have been different from the one followed by ISTAT, it can be emphasized that firm level analysis reveals higher R&D expenditures in the mechanical and in the textiles and garment sectors.

C. Antonelli, A failure-inducement model of research and development expenditure   169

Table 2

Sectorial distribution of R&D expenditure (BERD) in the Italian manufacturing industry and sectoral coverage of collected data in 1982.

	R&D lire (000,000)	Percent sector	Employment (000)	Employment percent by sector	Value added percent by sector	R&D (lire) by employees	86 firms lire (000,000)	86 firms total ISTAT percent
Energy	150,770	6.05	202	3.4	7.5	747	24,991	16
Iron and other metals	51,482	2.06	713	12.0	13.1	71	35,293	68
Chemicals	673,060	27.0	297	5.0	6.6	2,265	429,926	63
Metal products	67,317	2.7	415	7.6	7.4	161	7,595	11
Machinery	97,058	3.9	410	6.9	8.1	236	111,512	114
Computers	172,766	6.9	83	1.4	1.7	2,084	170,339	98
Electrical machinery	487,498	19.6	398	6.7	6.2	1,226	375,054	77
Motor vehicles	405,221	16.2	335	5.65	4.6	1,209	293,051	72
Other transportation	288,453	11.6	62	1.05	1.5	4,645	273,213	94
Food-Beverages	21,379	0.8	475	8.0	9.7	44	11,233	52
Textiles-Garments	1,118	0.04	1,432	24.1	16.9	0.8	7,200	636
Furniture	620	0.02	523	8.8	7.2	1.1	–	0
Paper	1,572	0.06	267	4.5	4.8	5.6	4,738	301
Rubber	71,252	2.8	214	3.6	3.6	331	66,717	93.6
Other	1,720	0.7	77	1.3	1.1	22	–	0
Total BERD in manufacturing industry	2,491,624	100	5,941	100	100	419	1,811,075	72

Source: ISTAT 1985 and independently collected data.

Table 3

Share of total R&D expenditure, sales and employment of firms ranked by sales and employment in 1982.

		Rank by sales %			Rank by employment %		
		R&D	Employment	Sales	R&D	Employment	Sales
First	2	3.8	1.4	25.4	11.8	26.7	14.9
	4	13.7	19.1	40.7	15.7	36.9	20.8
	8	17.7	36.6	58.6	34.5	47.5	27.7
	10	25.0	41.6	63.9	38.1	51.1	29.8
	20	48.4	61.1	76.2	56.4	66.0	41.5
	30	64.4	72.3	82.9	65.9	75.6	52.0
	40	69.6	78.7	88.1	76.3	82.9	80.9
	50	82.9	84.9	92.0	82.7	89.1	84.9
	60	87.1	89.8	95.2	87.8	92.9	93.5
	70	91.9	94.8	95.9	95.9	97.2	96.9
	86	100	100	100	100	100	100

Source: Author's calculations, see text.

The data show the strong concentration of R&D expenditures in a small number of firms: 86 firms account for 72 per cent of industrial BERD, but the same 86 firms account for only 12 per cent of total employment and value added. Within the 86 firms, however, the degree of concentration is much lower, as shown by the data in table 3, which ranks the firms by size. In terms of the employment ranking, the first four firms account for 36.9 per cent of total employment and 15.8 per cent of total R&D expenditures; the first eight firms account for 46.5 per cent of employment and 34.4 per cent of R&D expenditures; and the first twenty firms account for 66.0 per cent employment, and 65.4 per cent R&D expenditures. In terms of the sales rankings, the first four firms account for 58.6 per cent of sales, 36.6 per cent of employment and only 17.7 per cent of R&D expenditures; the first twenty firms account for 76.2 per cent of sales, 61.1 per cent of employment and 48.4 per cent of R&D expenditures.

Table 4 provides a picture of the distribution of R&D intensity, as measured by the ratio of R&D expenditures to sales and employment, by firm size. The lowest R&D intensity was registered by firms with more than 30,000 employees, as measured by both R&D expenditures as a percent of sales and R&D expenditures per employee. The distribution of R&D intensity by size of firm indicates that two classes of firms spend relatively more on R&D: small firms with less than 1,000 employees, and medium-sized firms with 20,000 to 29,999 employees.

Table 5 provides a breakdown of percentage nominal increases in R&D expenditures and R&D intensities by firm size from 1981 to 1983. Firms with 10,000 to 19,999 employees lead the increases of R&D intensity with respect

C. Antonelli, A failure-inducement model of research and development expenditure   171

Table 4

Distribution of R&D intensity by size of firms 1981–83.

Size classes in 1981	No. of cases	R&D percent by sales 1981	R&D percent by sales 1982	R&D percent by sales 1983	R&D (lire) by employees 1981	R&D (lire) by employees 1982	R&D (lire) by employees 1983
Less then 1,000	4	7.38	7.12	6.99	8.56	11.53	13.62
Between 1,000 and 1,999	11	3.32	3.58	3.08	2.22	2.64	3.66
Between 2,000 and 2,499	5	3.91	3.29	2.42	3.01	3.86	2.97
Between 2,500 and 4,999	23	3.22	3.33	3.40	2.91	4.08	4.64
Between 5,000 and 9,999	22	3.80	3.58	3.57	2.00	2.32	3.04
Between 10,000 and 19,999	12	3.63	3.83	4.76	2.58	3.19	4.57
Between 20,000 and 29,999	2	6.32	5.93	6.39	2.83	3.78	4.82
Between 30,000 and 49,999	2	1.68	1.79	1.71	0.77	1.01	1.17
More than 50,000	2	1.14	1.17	1.13	0.76	0.94	1.11
Total	83	3.67	3.53	3.72	2.70	3.45	4.23

Source; see table 3.

Table 5

Distribution of percentage increase of R&D expenditure (absolute, per employee and sales) 1981–83 by size of firms.

	Number of cases	R&D sales 1981–83	R&D/Employees 1981–83	R&D absolute 1981–83
Up to 999	4	11.72	56.22	29.66
1,000–1,999	11	36.91	102.10	47.99
2,000–2,499	5	7.22	22.41	20.24
2,500–4,999	23	32.73	70.97	30.74
5,000–9,999	22	21.85	77.73	33.02
10,000–19,999	12	47.60	77.71	29.10
20,000–29,999	2	25.96	69.74	21.89
30,000–49,999	2	17.92	55.51	18.49
More than 50,000	2	1.05	45.68	17.83
Total	83	28.45	73.92	32.02

Source: See table 3.

to employment. Large firms with more than 30,000 employees show very low rates of increase.

5. The econometric test

According to the failure-inducement hypothesis, we argue that in the early 1980s R&D expenditures were one of the main tools Italian firms used to face shrinking rates of profitability caused by growing pressure on international markets and increased labour and energy costs. The test of the failure-inducement hypothesis is conducted within the framework of a number of complementary hypotheses drawn from the literature. The selection of complementary institutional hypotheses on the determinants of R&D expenditures in the Italian business sector stems from an effort to appreciate the distinctive features of the Italian scientific and technological system.

Within this framework, seven main variables have been considered to explain R&D expenditures in the Italian case.

5.1. Profits

High profit levels make available the cash necessary to finance risky and uncertain R&D activities. This is the traditional Schumpeterian argument to support a strong positive effect of profitability on R&D expenditures. In the Italian case, however, the reverse argument seems to apply. Firms facing a short-fall of profitability and a downward trend in their cash generation activities have been forced to expand R&D activities in order to remain and/or gain entry in the modern sector. In this sense, in Italy R&D expenditures appear to have been failure-induced. Furthermore, high technological thresholds may have forced firms belonging to the traditional sector to finance large R&D budgets which do not have high short-term paybacks, and to reduce their profit margins for a long period in order to eventually establish themselves in the modern sector. Finally, and most importantly, the reduction of the marginal costs of resources devoted to R&D activity resulting from public subsidies may have induced higher levels of R&D expenditures than otherwise have been the case given only internal or private external sources. According to such a failure-inducement hypothesis we would expect to find a negative relationship between the level of profitability of Italian firms and the levels of R&D expenditures in the period 1981–83.

Second, a quadratic model of the relationship between the level of profitability and R&D expenditures has been specified in order to test the hypothesis of a differentiated relationship between profitability below or above the average. Such a quadratic model makes it possible to test the hypothesis of a non-linear relation between profitability and R&D expenditures which stems from two distinct forces: the failure-inducement hypothesis which applies to firms with losses or low levels of profitability, and the Shumpeterian hypothesis, which is more pertinent to firms with above average profits.

Such a non-linear specification of the relationship and the underlying hypothesis of a mixed model where both the failure-inducement model and Schumpeterian extraprofit stimulation apply seems especially appropriate to the Italian conditions in the early 1980s. During this period, according to qualitative evidence, innovative efforts were made by large modern firms already active in the science-based sectors, and by a new wave of small and medium-sized traditional firms forced into the new environment by growing losses.

Third, the failure-inducement hypothesis also predicts a negative relationship between the rate of change of profitability and the levels of R&D expenditures.

5.2. Size

The empirical evidence given in tables 3, 4 and 5 suggests that R&D expenditures increases less than proportionally with firm size. However, it seems important to test the role played by size in explaining the levels of Italian R&D expenditures, *together with and under the control* of other institutional factors, such as technological opportunities, membership of financial groups and levels of diversification. In fact, it seems that the true role of size can be valued only when these major features of an industrial structure have been taken into account. The economic and statistical significance of size varies appreciably along with the characteristics of the industrial structures, and econometric tests of the simple relationship between size and R&D expenditures are liable to be seriously biased [see Cohen, Levin and Mowery (1987)].

5.3. Diversification and groups

Relatively high transaction costs for intangible assets, such as knowledge and organizational capital, and technology-intensive inputs and intermediate products on domestic markets characterize late industrialized economies, where the 'modern' sector is still a tiny fraction of the whole manufacturing industry [Williamson (1975)]. So far, firms with high levels of knowledge and organizational capital are induced to capitalize their technological advance by means of administrative coordination of different lines of business. Following the large amount of evidence provided by Grabowski (1968), Scherer (1965) and Caves, Porter and Spence (1980), we expect high levels of diversification and membership to large financial groups to be associated with high levels of R&D expenditures.

5.4. Public subsidies

We argue that R&D expenditures have been perceived by Italian firms as a major tool to modify their current input mix and their ailing comparative advantage. Current comparative advantages were often based on low labor costs. Transition to comparative advantages based on high levels of technical efficiency implies heavy and long term investments in the accumulation of the required levels of knowledge and organizational capital. Public subsidies played a major role in this context, and are thought to have helped firms to fund levels of R&D expenditures beyond those allowed by short-term payback criteria. Consequently, following Howe and McFetridge (1976), Caves, Porter and Spence (1980), Levin and Reiss (1984) and Mansfield and Switzer (1985) we expect that in Italy, too, the levels of public subsidies will have a strong positive role to play in the explanation of R&D expenditures.

5.5. International competition

Exposure to international markets should play a strong positive role in enhancing R&D intensity. Modern Italian firms are, in fact, supposed to be forced by international competitive standards to remain at the forefront of technological advance [Caves, Porter and Spence (1980)], while traditional firms must counter the growing competitive pressure of newly industrializing countries by introducing technology-intensive process innovations which only R&D activities can provide.

5.6. International technological environment

The international rate and direction of technological change and the strategies of major technological leaders such as U.S. firms are expected to

C. Antonelli, A failure-inducement model of research and development expenditure 175

Table 6

Variables of the econometric test.

R&D	= R&D expenditures in 1983 expressed in thousands of lire.
SIZE	= The size of firms in terms of value added in 1981, expressed in millions of lire.
GROUP	= A dummy with value 1 for firms belonging to financial groups and/or active in more than three digits sector, and value 0.01 in the other cases.
SUBSIDIES	= The average level of public subsidies by sector of activity of firms in terms of the ratio of public subsidies to total R&D expenditures realized by firms in 1982.
EXPORT	= Share of international sales on the total as measured by the ratio of export and sales of incorporated affiliates operating abroad to total sales in 1982.
USRD	= The pressure of the international technological environment, expressed by the average ratio of R&D expenditures to sales of U.S. firms active in the same sector (data from Business Week) in 1982.
PROFIT	= The level of profitability expressed by the average price–cost margin (measured as value added minus wages/sales) for the period 1981, 1982, 1983.
D. PROFIT	= 83/81 = The difference in profitability (measured by *PROFIT*) in 1983 with respect to 1981 (calculated as *PROFIT* 1983 – *PROFIT* 1981/*PROFIT* 1981).

play a major role in explaining the R&D intensity of Italian firms [Wilson (1977)]. Such a relationship can be considered to result from the effort of Italian firms to appropriate the advantages offered by the technological environment.

According to the failure-inducement hypothesis outlined and the available data, the following eqs. (1), (2), (3) and (4) have been specified in multiplicative and additive form:

$$\log RD = a - b_1 \log PROFIT + b_2 \log SIZE + b_3 \log GROUP$$
$$+ b_4 \log SUBSIDY + b_5 \log EXPORT + b_6 \log USRD, \qquad (1)$$

$$RD = a - b_1 PROFIT + b_2 SIZE + b_2 GROUP + b_2 SUBSIDY$$
$$+ b_5 EXPORT + b_6 USRD, \qquad (2)$$

$$RD = a - b_1 PROFIT + b_2 (PROFIT)^2 + b_3 SIZE + b_2 GROUP$$
$$b_5 SUBSIDY + b_6 EXPORT + b_7 USRD, \qquad (3)$$

$$\log RD = a - b_1 \log D . PROFIT\ 83/81 + b_2 \log SIZE$$
$$+ b_3 \log GROUP + b_4 \log SUBSIDY + b_5 \log EXPORT$$
$$+ b_6 \log USRD, \qquad (4)$$

where the multiplicative specification of eqs. (1) and (4) is written in natural logarithms, the content of variables is given in table 6 and the signs are the expected ones.

Table 7

Results of the OLS test of eqs. (1), (2), (3), (4).

$\log RD = -0.177 - 0.138 \log PROFIT + 0.339 \log SIZE + 0.135$ (1)
    (1.301) (1.817)   (2.507)   (2.585)

    $\log GROUP + 0.371 \log SUBSIDY + 0.507 \log EXPORT$
           (3.196)   (5.288)

    $+ 0.257 \log USRD$ $R^2 = 0.563$ $F = 16.543$
    (2.925)

$RD = -12,226.069 - 4.363 PROFIT + 0.019 SIZE + 17,115.843$ (2)
   (1.369) (1.734)   (2.308)   (2.265)

   $GROUP + 7.709 SUBSIDY + 4.815 EXPORT + 0.019 USRD$
       (2.725)   (2.791)   (1.594)

$R^2 = 0.452$ $F = 10.456$

   $RD = 630.414 - 17.120 PROFIT + 1.703 (PROFIT)^2 + 0.015 SIZE$ (3)
    (1.101) (2.172)   (1.705)   (1.777)

  $+ 14,682.386 GROUP + 8.267 SUBSIDY + 4.993 EXPORT$
    (1.932)   (2.939)   (2.925)

  $+ 0.018 USRD$ $R^2 = 0.472$ $F = 9.603$
   (1.508)

$\log RD = -0.351 - 0.251 \log D PROFIT\ 83/81 + 0.489 \log SIZE$ (4)
    (0.431) (1.706)   (3.690)

   $+ 0.178 \log GROUP + 0.312 \log SUBSIDY + 0.601 \log$
   (3.038)   (2.239)   (5.310)

    $EXPORT + 0.287 \log USRD$ $R^2 = 0.511$ $F = 12.611$
       (2.870)

t statistics in parentheses.

Cross-section estimates of eqs. (1), (2), (3) and (4) have been performed using the standard OLS procedure. The results are shown in rows 1 and 2 of table 7 for the multiplicative and the additive models, respectively. The result of the test of quadratic specification of the relationship between profitability and R&D expenditures is given in row 3. The estimates from eq. (4), where the differences in profitability are considered, are shown in row 4.

The results from the estimation of eqs. (1), (2), (3) and (4) are consistent with the hypotheses. The coefficients of all the variables are significant and have the expected signs. More than 0.5 of the total variance is explained.

As expected, PROFIT enters eq. (1) with a strong negative parameter, significant at a 93 per cent level of a two-tailed test. This negative sign seems to confirm that most Italian firms carried on R&D activities within the context of a failure-induced model: during the 1970s, and more sharply at the beginning of the 1980s, Italian firms were induced to fund R&D activities (together with major changes in the levels of vertical integration, investment strategy, the size and location of manufacturing plants) in the context of a sharp process of industrial reorganization undertaken to increase the level of profitability, which had dropped to an historic minimum after World War II. The results of eq. (3), moreover, provide a deeper insight. The test of the quadratic specification of the relationship between profitability and R&D expenditures yields well determined estimates with significant coefficients for both the first (significant at 98%) and the second term (significant at 92%), and both estimated coefficients have the correct sign. As expected, the true relationship seems to be represented by a parabolic curve with a minimum in the proximity of the average values of profitability. According to the results from eq. (3), innovative efforts were funded with greater intensity by firms with below average profitability, thus confirming the failure-inducement hypothesis, and by firms with above average profitability, thus confirming the Schumpeterian hypothesis. Firms with average profitability appear to be less R&D intensive. The results from eq. (4) confirm that the decline in the levels of profitability exerted, in the period 1981–1983, a positive and significant effect on the innovative efforts of Italian firms.

As clearly shown by eq. (1), *SIZE* plays a significant role in determining R&D expenditures. As expected (see tables 4 and 5), the value of the coefficient (0.339) confirms that the elasticity of R&D expenditures with respect for firm size, controlling for a number of institutional and technological variables, is significantly smaller than 1; i.e. R&D expenditures increases less than proportionately with the size of firms. Results from eq. (2), moreover, show that for an increase in value added of one billion lire R&D expenditures increased by only 15–20 million lire. It is clear, however, that these results apply only to firms which carry out R&D, and not to all Italian firms. *GROUP* is an important factor in explaining R&D expenditures, and is significant at the 99 per cent level. It may be argued that heavy transaction costs in high tech products force innovative firms to substitute hierarchical coordination for market transaction, in order to extract the maximum quasi rents from the introduction of innovation.

SUBSIDIES, as expected, is a significant factor in explaining R&D expenditures in the Italian case. Important transfer of financial resources from the State to the business sector helps to increase the levels of R&D expenditures of Italian firms. The elasticity of R&D expenditures with respect to direct subsidies estimated in eq. (1) (0.37) is strikingly close to the estimates of Mansfield and Switzer (1985) with respect to indirect (fiscal) subsidies for Canadian companies. This suggests some sort of threshold effect in the elasticity of companies' funding of R&D activity with respect to both direct and indirect public subsidies. *EXPORT* – which has the largest and best determined coefficient in row 1 confirms that the R&D intensity of Italian firms is export-led; i.e. it is stimulated by the levels of exposure of Italian firms to international competition. *USRD* – significant in eq. (1) at the 99 per cent level – is further evidence of the influential role played by the international exposure of Italian firms to the technological opportunities perceived by U.S. firms, and to their technological strategies.

6. Conclusion

A careful examination of the existing literature on the relationship between profitability and innovative efforts reveals that the conventional Schumpeterian hypothesis has slim empirical evidence in its favor. Instead, the evidence suggests a reverse relationship may apply in which losses rather than profits stimulate innovative efforts. This negative relationship has received little analytical attention, and only a few researchers have tried to place it in the appropriate theoretical context. Such an effort has been made in this paper, and a failure-inducement hypothesis of R&D expenditures has been formulated on the basis of the behavioral approach elaborated by March and Simon (1958), and tested using data on the R&D expenditures of Italian manufacturing firms.

The results of the econometric analysis on data from 86 firms, which account for 72% of the total Italian R&D expenditures, confirm that a large part of Italian R&D efforts has been carried out by firms with low levels of profitability, facing an adverse economic environment. The results from the quadratic specification, however, showed that the model fit the data well, and gave clear evidence regarding the positive role of extra profits in stimulating innovative efforts. Empirical evidence from Italy in the early 1980s on the determinants of innovative efforts therefore appear to confirm *both the failure-inducement hypothesis*, which applies to firms facing the need to change their production mix, and the *Schumpeterian hypothesis*, which applies to firms with high profit levels and a consequent abundance of discretionary funds available for uncertain R&D activities.

Other results confirmed that in the Italian case small firms belonging to large groups often have more aggressive technological strategies than large firms specializing in few business lines. The important role of both the international technological environment and the exposure to international competitiveness was confirmed, as was the strong positive role played by public subsidies.[8]

The picture emerging from this empirical evidence is that of an industrial structure which has undertaken an intensive effort to modify its current role in the international division of labor. This effort has been based on reshaping previous comparative advantages in low skilled labour-intensive and scale-

[8]For similar results on the role of government subsidies see also Levy and Terlecky (1983) and Lichtenberg (1984).

intensive industries which were undermined during the 1970s by sharp increases in oil prices, labour costs and the entry of new competitors.[9] R&D expenditures have clearly been one of the factors used by Italian firms to modify asymmetric market conditions and to overcome barriers to entry into international oligopolistic markets in science-based industries. Public subsidies played a major role in helping Italian firms to complete the entry process and to establish themselves inside markets which had entry barriers.

In this context it seems reasonable to argue that in the early 1980s Italy underwent a transition from a contingent model of failure-inducement of R&D expenditures to a model of institutionalized technological innovation wherein the introduction of science-based technological innovations becomes a programmed component of organizational behavior.

[9]Present advantage in some scale-intensive industries is itself the result of explicit strategies performed by a number of large firms in the 1950s and 1960s.

References

Antonelli, Cristiano, 1985, Confronti settoriali di determinanti delle spese in ricerca e sviluppo dell' industria manifatturiera Italiana, L'Industria 6, 379–397.

Antonelli, Cristiano (ed.), 1988, New information technology and industrial change: The Italian case (Kluwer, Boston, MA).

Atkinson, Anthony and Joseph Stiglitz, 1969, A new view of technical change, Economic Journal 79, 573–578.

Biswanger, H., et al., 1978, Induced innovation: Technology institutions and development (John Hopkins University Press, Baltimore, MD).

Bosworth, D. and Westaway, T., 1984, The influence of demand and supply side pressures on the quantity and quality of inventive activity, Applied Economics 16, 131–146.

Branch, Brian, 1974, Research and development activity and profitability: A distributed lag analysis, Journal of Political Economy 82, 999–1011.

Brown, H., 1957, Innovation in the machine tool industry, Quarterly Journal of Economics 71, 406–425.

Caves, Richard E., Michael Porter and Michael Spence, 1980, Competition in the open economy: A model applied to Canada (Harvard University Press, Cambridge, MA).

Cohen, Wesley M., Richard C. Levin and D.C. Mowery, 1987, Firm size and R&D intensity: A re-examination, Journal of Industrial Economics 35, 543–567.

Cremer, Jacques and M. Sirbu, 1978, Une analyse econometrique de l'effort de recherche et development de l'industrie Francaise, Revue Economique 29, 940–957.

Cyert, Richard M. and James G. March, 1963, A behavioral theory of the firm (Prentice-Hall, Englewood Cliffs, NJ).

Dasgupta, Partha, 1988, Patents priority and imitation, Economic Journal 98, 66–80.

David, Paul A., 1975, Technical choice innovation and economic growth (Cambridge University Press, London, England).

Day, Richard and Theodore Groves, 1975, Adaptive economic models (Academic Press, New York, NY).

Elliott, Jan W., 1971, Funds flow vs expectational theories of research and development expenditures in the firm, Southern Economic Journal 37, 409–422.

Fua', G., 1980, Problemi dello sviluppo tardivo (Il Mulino, Bologna).

Grabowski, Henry G., 1968, Determinants of industrial research and development: A study of the chemical drug and petroleum industry, Journal of Political Economy 76, 292–306.

Hamberg, Daniel, 1966, R&D: Essays on the economics of research and development (Random House, New York, NY).

Howe, J.D. and D.G. McFetridge, 1976, The determinants of R&D expenditures, Canadian Journal of Economics 9, 57–71.

ISTAT, 1985, Indagine statistica sulla ricerca scientifica, Supplemento al Bollettino Mensile ISTAT, Roma.

Jewkes, J., D. Sawers and R. Stillerman, 1969, The sources of invention (St. Martin Press, New York, NY).

Johannisson, B. and C. Lindstrom, 1971, Firm size and inventive activity, Swedish Journal of Economics 73, 427–442.

Kamien, M.I. and N.L. Schwartz, 1978, Self financing of an R&D project, American Economic Review 68, 252–261.

Kamien, M.I. and N.L. Schwartz, 1982, Market structure and innovation (Cambridge University Press, Cambridge, MA).

Leibenstein, Harvey, 1976, Beyond economic man (Harvard University Press, Cambridge, MA).

Levin, Richard C. and Peter C. Reiss, 1986, Tests of a Schumpeterian model of R&D and market structure, in: Z. Griliches (ed.), R&D patents and productivity (University of Chicago Press for NBER, Chicago, IL).

Levy, David M. and N.E. Terleckyj, 1983, Effects of government R&D on private R&D investment and productivity: A macroeconomic analysis, Bell Journal of Economics, 14, 551–561.

Lichtenberg, Erik R., 1984, The relationship between federal contract R&D and company R&D, American Economic Review P&P 74, 73–78.

Mansfield, Edwin and Lorne Switzer, 1985, The effect of R&D tax credits and allowances in Canada, Research Policy 14, 97–107.

March, James C. and Herbert A. Simon, 1958, Organizations (John Wiley & Sons, New York, NY).

Mueller, Dennis C., 1967, The firm decision process: An econometric investigation, Quarterly Journal of Economics 81, 58–87.

Needham, D., 1975, Market structure and firms' R&D behavior, Journal of Industrial Economics 23, 241–255.

Nelson, Richard R. and Winter, Sidney G., 1982, An evolutionary theory of economic change (Harvard University Press, Cambridge, MA).

OECD, 1984, Sciences and technology indicators, recent results, OECD, Paris.

Porter, Michael E., 1985, Competitive advantage (The Free Press, New York, NY).

Rosenberg, Nathan, 1969, The direction of technological change: Inducement mechanisms and focusing devices. Economic development and cultural change, later published in N. Rosenberg, 1976, Perspectives on technology (Cambridge University Press, Cambridge, MA).

Scherer, Frederic M., 1965, Firm size market structure opportunity and the output of patented inventions, American Economic Review 55, 1097–1125.

Scherer, Frederic M., 1980, Industrial market structure and economic performance (Rand McNally, Chicago, IL).

Scherer, Frederic M., 1984, Innovation and growth: Schumpeterian perspectives (MIT Press, Cambridge, MA).

Simon, Herbert A., 1979, Rational decision making in business organizations, American Economic Review 69, 493–512.

Simon, Herbert A., 1982, Models of bounded rationality (MIT Press, Cambridge, MA).

Smyth, David J., J.M. Samuels and J. Tzoannos, 1972, Patents profitability liquidity and firm size, Applied Economics 4, 77–86.

Williamson, Oliver E., 1975, Markets and hierarchies (Free Press, New York, NY).

Wilson, Robert W., 1977, The effect of technological environment and product rivalry on R&D effort and licensing of inventions, Review of Economics and Statistics 59, 171–178.

[21]

A Chaotic Model of Innovative Search: Some Answers, Many Questions

Kenneth W. Koput

University of Arizona, 405 McClelland Hall, Tucson, Arizona 85721

Abstract

The dynamics of innovative search are investigated. A formal learning model is explicated to understand (1) how attention is allocated and (2) how attention and ideas are related during an active search. A particular chaotic regime of the model is shown to have dynamics similar to an actual search process. This motivates an agenda for research along three primary directions: refinements to the model, extensions that link the model to actions and decisions, and surroundings required to embed such a model in a larger context. The findings here suggest that chaos can occur in specific organizational processes over particular periods of time. Whether such chaos is beneficial to organizations is unclear.

(*Innovative Search*; *Organizational Learning*; *Chaos*; *Mathematical Models*)

1. Introduction

Since the very beginnings of organization theory, the factors affecting innovation have been considered as among the most important for organizational scholars to understand (March and Simon 1958). Yet, after more than 30 years of study, our knowledge of the innovation process seems shallow (Teece 1987). Old problems remain unsolved (Van de Ven 1986, Dougherty and Heller 1994). This paper attempts to deepen our understanding of just one aspect of organizational innovation: the dynamics of attention during active search. A formal learning model of attention allocation is explicated, which links attention to the identification of important ideas for innovation. In short, this paper addresses two related questions implied by the paradoxes and dilemmas of organizational innovation: (1) How is attention allocated while innovating? and (2) What is the role of attention in shaping the identification of important ideas for innovation?

Innovation is both an outcome and a process.[1] As an outcome, an innovation is "a new idea, which may be a recombination of old ideas, a scheme that challenges the present order, a formula, or a unique approach that is perceived as new" (Van de Ven 1986, p. 591). The process of innovation is the "development and implementation of new ideas by people who over time engage in transactions with others within an institutional context" (Van de Ven 1986, p. 591). These definitions imply that innovation is a perceptual process that unfolds over time and can take many forms. As such, attention should play an important role in the search for and development of innovative ideas.

Attention is also a key variable in organizational learning (March 1988). The learning perspective has been helpful in understanding the central problem of how attention is triggered to *initiate* search (Van de Ven 1986, 1993; March 1988). Models of organizational learning have also been fruitfully applied to investigate adaptive search (Levinthal and March 1981) and specific aspects of the innovation process (Cohen and Levinthal 1990, Lant and Mezias 1990), including the control of an explicitly random search process (Mezias and Glynn 1993).

The dynamics of attention *during* innovation remain poorly understood. Simple trial-and-error models of learning have proven of little use in understanding the dynamics of innovation during times of active search (Garud and Van de Ven 1992, Van de Ven and Polley 1992). Cheng and Van de Ven (1996) have argued that innovation may begin in chaos and end in stable behavior, only the latter being amenable to simple models of learning. However, Van de Ven and his colleagues examined actions (decisions to continue, expand or contract), outcomes (accomplishments or failures) and context events (environmental incidences), but not the search components per se: attention and ideas. Koput (1992) studied the search components for one of the innovative ventures later examined by Cheng and Van de Ven and found them to be chaotic, but offered no formal model. These works motivate the current effort to understand the mechanisms of innovative search and make the potential to exhibit chaos an important criterion in the development of a formal model.

1047-7039/97/0805/0528/$05.00
Copyright © 1997. Institute for Operations Research
and the Management Sciences

2. Notes Toward a Formal Model

Historically, the innovation process has been thought of as divisible into two sequential stages: search and implementation (Zaltman et al. 1973). Campbell's (1960) observation that innovative search is "blind" has achieved a taken-for-granted status (Robert and Weiss 1988). In organizational learning, for example, Mezias and Glynn (1993) have offered a model for what they term innovative search. However, their model really addresses the control of a search process, while the search itself is explicitly random. They explicate: "searches are draws from a uniform distribution" (Mezias and Glynn 1993, p. 96). Such randomness might be obtained by opening the organization's doors to the confusing and turbulent world (March 1981, Levitt and March 1988), or via a technology of "foolish," unorganized behavior (March 1971). Psychological approaches suggest this can be done by recruiting individuals on the basis of traits (Kuhn 1986, Roche 1986), or reputation (Albert 1975, Helson 1988), and institutionalizing mechanisms for training (Isaksen 1988). Social psychological and organizational behavior models focus on increasing the *intrinsic* motivation of key individuals to engage in undirected activities (Amabile 1983, 1988), while maintaining a supportive, unintrusive context (Geis 1986, Kanter 1988).

Becoming innovative by exposing one's organization to confusion, turbulence, or foolishness is, however, an incomplete prescription. As Day (1994, p. 149) reports, "Clearly, ideas or inventions alone are not enough." Once ideas are in hand, the second stage, implementation, must begin. The goal of implementation is to ensure reliable and accountable production as swiftly as possible. While search requires unpredictability, foolishness, and randomness, implementation requires efficiency, reliability and organization. By conventional wisdom, the former are hazardous to the latter and the latter drive out the former. Somehow, therefore, implementation and production must be separated and buffered from search and idea generation (Gronhaug and Reve 1988, Holbek 1988). Two ways of accomplishing this separation have been considered: differentiation in either (a) space or (b) time.

The possibility of differentiating in space emphasizes the need to separate innovative activities from the rest of the firm (Galbraith 1982). Hence, search and implementation are housed in distinct organizational units. For instance, research and development is often made a separate function and housed in a special area, frequently off the production site entirely. Cutting searching subunits away from the rest of the organiza-

tion is intended to free individuals from external constraints: producing search in the form of intrinsically-motivated play. The activities of these units are then "loosely-coupled" (Weick 1982) with the rest of the organization, which is designed to eliminate unpredictability (Blau and Scott 1962).

There are a number of problems in managing innovation under such arrangements. Of present concern are those surrounding the allocation of attention. When looking for an innovative idea—where *exactly* what is wanted cannot be specified ex ante—there is no way of immediately knowing whether ideas discovered in the isolated searching unit will be relevant to the sponsoring organization. That is, many ideas may have a mix of attributes that the sponsoring organization neither needs nor wants, yet others will be valuable. While this unpredictability is an innate aspect of innovation, it nevertheless presents the possibility that the search may provide ideas in ways that frustrate implementation. Of these frustrating aspects, I want to highlight three observations involving the *number* of ideas over time. First, there may be too many ideas to process. Second, there may be too few ideas to warrant serious consideration. Third, ideas may simply come at the wrong times. Somehow, the level of innovative search activity must be linked to the organization's capacity for processing and implementing the outcomes of that activity. To achieve face validity, then, a model of innovative search must include such links.

Previously, the integration of search and implementation has been accomplished by prescribing the use of screening activities. Screening takes place at the point of interface between the searching and implementing units (i.e., between an R & D division and the focal organization). Screening activities have been treated as though they are independent of the prior search activities (March and Simon 1958). It seems likely, though, that tradeoffs exist between our ability to generate search and our ability to screen its results: the greater the search, the more costly it is to screen. When goals are ambiguous, both search and screening are at their most difficult and most needed levels. Unless an organization has unlimited slack resources, the activities cannot safely be treated as uncoupled. If the search for innovative ideas is independent of the subsequent implementation, there is no way of assuring that the level of search generated will be appropriate to either the capacity to screen or the requirements of implementation. If search is uncoupled from the organization, then there is no way of increasing the innovative capacity of organizations without suffering undue costs. Hence, while screening may still be part of a search model, it is not sufficient as the primary link between the flows of attention and ideas.

The possibility of differentiating in time attempts to avoid these downfalls by incorporating search and implementation within the same organizational walls. In these "intrapreneurial" organizations, the same individuals and groups "invent" and implement, just at different times (Guth and Ginsberg 1990, Frost and Egri 1991). First, ideas are found; then, they are "championed" (Day 1994). The process remains sequential, with screening done in between. The organization is "turned off" for the first step, allowing individuals to pursue intrinsically-motivated activities. Once invention occurs, the organization is turned back on. This takes place through the management of reward and control systems, sometimes as subsumed under the rubric of culture (Kanter 1988).

Recent observations of the innovation process in actual organizations blur this sequential model. The stages of search and implementation cannot be so readily separated into independent subsystems. Each part contains elements needed for the other. We do not simply have an invention that needs to be operationalized, but an indeterminate pattern of reinvention, proliferation, reimplementation, discarding and termination (Van de Ven et al. 1989).

Thus, search is a dynamic process that continues throughout the stage of implementation. A continual balance must be struck among rewards and controls to simultaneously produce appropriate amounts of searching, screening, and implementation. Does the complexity of this juggling act make it impossible to plan and design organizations for innovation, as conjectured by Kanter (1988)?

Perhaps not. Despite the incumbent problems just detailed, it has been empirically demonstrated that firms sometime become more innovative (Miles and Cameron 1982), and can be innovative over time (Jelinek and Schoonhoven 1990). To explain this, a model is needed that incorporates the three key insights from the above discussion. (1) That innovation is not a linear, sequential process, but rather one involving complex, orderly feedback structures in which search, screening and implementation are reciprocally embedded. (2) That the amount of attention and number of ideas are important determiners of the feedback levels. And, (3) that the resulting, manifested dynamics must appear erratic and unpredictable.

I begin the work of formally explicating such a model in the next section. Then, I demonstrate that a particular chaotic regime of the model is similar in dynamics

to the search components of an empirical innovation studied by Van de Ven and his colleagues (the Therapeutic Apheresis Program, see Van de Ven et al. 1989, Van de Ven and Polley 1992, Cheng and Van de Ven 1996), as presented in Koput (1992). The purpose of such a comparison is to show sufficient similarity between the model and an actual innovation to support the plausibility of the model's general structure. The model is then used to motivate an agenda for innovation research centered on the link between attention, ideas, decisions, and actions.

3. The Structure of Innovative Search: A Formal Model

As noted, an emerging criterion for a model of innovative search is that it be capable of manifesting chaos. For at least a decade, the notion that creative processes may be chaotic has been fermenting (Prigogine and Stengers 1984). Chaos seems much like randomness, but is meaningfully distinguished by the presence of a simple order underlying very complex and turbulent behavior.[2]

Structurally, feedback is the cornerstone of chaos. As such, chaos requires a dynamic model. That is, the variables at any given time are a function, at least in part, of the same variables at an earlier time. Also, the model must have nonlinear variables. However, the model need not be very complicated. Nonlinearity simply requires that there be at least two not-entirely-compatible underlying forces or sources of demands. Put together, "nonlinear dynamics" means there must be both positive and negative feedback loops. With this type of system, irregular and unpredictable behavior can arise endogenously, that is, without any exogenous, truly random inputs. This occurs when the balance between the positive and negative feedbacks is especially severe.[3]

The elements of the model are displayed graphically in Figure 1 and algebraically in Figure 2. The model is formulated to provide insight into the feedback structures that underlie the level of attention allocated to search and the number of ideas being churned through the search process. Although the content of ideas is often of ultimate interest (such as the attributes of a physical product, characteristics of the manufacturing process, definition of a market, or structure of a relationship), the number of ideas is itself an important variable (Merton 1935, Nelson 1962, Schiffel and Kitti 1978, Suarez-Villa 1990, Staw 1990). Organizations that are experiencing demands for innovation can show good faith in part through allocating attention and

KENNETH W. KOPUT   *Chaotic Model of Innovative Search*

Figure 1   The Structure of Innovative Search

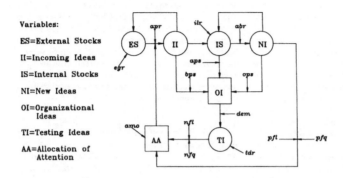

Variables:

ES=External Stocks

II=Incoming Ideas

IS=Internal Stocks

NI=New Ideas

OI=Organizational
Ideas

TI=Testing Ideas

AA=Allocation of
Attention

Parameters:

egr=external growth rate

apr=attention payoff rate

ilr=internal loss rate

abr=associative birth rate

aps=attrition and preselection

bps=borrowing preselection

ops=origination preselection

*dem=discussion and evaluation
at meetings*

tdr=testing death rate

pfl=positive feedback linear

pfq=positive feedback quadratic

nfl=negative feedback linear

nfq=negative feedback quadratic

amo=attention momentum

positing ideas, regardless of content. In a way, the number of ideas, on average, represents the "innovative capacity" of the search process.

The model contains 7 variables and fourteen parameters. For purposes of exposition, they will be described in order of their relative position in a typical account of innovative search. Variables are denoted in upper-case (XX); parameters are denoted in lower-case (yyy). I make the simplifying assumption that the parameters are time-independent. That is, while the variables are time-subscripted, the parameters are not. I invoke this assumption for two inter-related reasons. First, this paper is about the dynamics of attention *during* active search. Changes in the parameters represent second-order learning, which would control whether the search process is active or not. Second, while we know little about the dynamics of active search, much is known about the initiation and control of the innovation process into and out of search. My goal is to take some first steps in understanding the former. I acknowledge the need to connect the two aspects as a direction for research in the discussion section below.

Consider a firm that has just realized innovation is needed. Algorithmic or heuristic routines initiate the Allocation of Attention (AA) to search activities. As Simon (1986) notes:

> [Discovery] involves search through large spaces of possibilities, the search being guided and made efficient by the use of heuristic principles and previously developed theory.

Where are these "large spaces of possibilities"? Those searching might begin by looking within the organization to see what has been done in similar situations before, what "solutions" the organization may already know something about that could be brought to bear on the new problem, and so forth. Ideas and information that are already known to the organization are referred to as Internal Stocks (IS).

But, innovation requires such a "tremendous store of raw information" (Gluck 1986) that any one organization cannot rely solely on its own memory. Organizations also look to see what others are doing, what is known about the problem for which an innovative solution is needed, and what basic research findings might be pertinent. Outside the organization, they will look to sources of ideas and information such as competitors, customers, suppliers, trade associations, universities and others. I refer to these as External Stocks (ES) in the model.

Not all attention is effective. Attention is wasted when much of what is encountered is irrelevant, when the organization does not recognize relevant items, and when individuals spend time in truly foolish pursuits (Feldman and March 1981). Hence, the flow of ideas and information from the external stocks into the organization is controlled by the attention payoff rate (apr). This parameter represents the extent to which attention pays off by bringing innovation-relevant information and ideas into the organization.

The innovation-relevant information and ideas that flow into the organization are referred to here as

KENNETH W. KOPUT   *Chaotic Model of Innovative Search*

Incoming Ideas (II). The amount of incoming ideas at any time is a function of the size of the external stocks available prior to that time, the amount of attention allocated since the last inflow, and the attention payoff rate. A simple function is proposed:

$$II_t = apr \cdot ES_t \cdot AA_t. \tag{1}$$

The role of attention to both inside and outside sources of "old ideas" is enabling: allowing the organization to build its "absorptive capacity" for innovation (Cohen and Levinthal 1990). The internal stock accumulates as incoming ideas arrive from external stocks. However, there is some attrition. Organizational memory is not foolproof (Levitt and March 1988). Pieces of information can be lost. Past ways of doing things can become forgotten as those in the organization try to keep up with new possibilities (March 1991). This attrition is captured in an internal loss rate (ilr). The size of the internal stock at any given time is proposed to be a function of the size at a prior time adjusted for loss, plus the addition of incoming ideas at that time and New Ideas (NI) that arise over the prior period:

$$IS_t = ilr \cdot IS_{t-1} + NI_{t-1} + II_{t-1}. \tag{2}$$

From where do these new ideas come? As an organization builds up its internal stocks, temporal association can lead to the occurrence of new ideas in two ways. First, if the firm has developed the ability to combine, order, or connect this information in a "novel and better" way (March and Simon 1958, Gluck 1986, Gryskiewicz 1988), then ideas may be created willfully. Second, and perhaps more common, new ideas also occur if the organization notices serendipitous "accidents" and surprises in contrast to what "old" ideas suggest should have happened. Simon (1986) says:

> To exploit an accident ... one must observe the phenomenon and understand that something surprising has happened. No one who did not know what a dish of bacteria [for example] was supposed to look like could have noticed the pathology of the dish that was infected by mold nor would have been surprised if it had been called to his or her attention. It is the surprise, the departure from the expected, that creates the fruitful accident; and there are no surprises without expectation, nor expectations without knowledge [of prior ideas].

Both association mechanisms are captured in the parameter representing the associative birth rate (abr) of ideas held in memory. The number of new ideas in any time period is then just the product of the size of the internal stock in the prior period (since new ideas require temporal association, those that are fermenting in current period are not yet available) and the association parameter:

$$NI_t = abr \cdot IS_{t-1}. \tag{3}$$

New ideas are neither transferred to implementation nor otherwise acted on immediately upon their occurrence. Instead, they are mixed back into the internal stocks, subject to further association, until some time at which meetings are held. Meetings occur only at certain intervals, whether regular or irregular. Meanwhile, the internal stocks are subject to attrition and preselection (aps). Some ideas are simply forgotten, while others die as the result of individuals' self censoring. Borrowed ideas and ideas that are new just prior to a meeting are subject only to preselection (bps and ops, respectively).

Organizational Ideas, denoted in the model as OI, are those deemed to be of strategic importance. As such, not only have organizational ideas been discovered (whether generated or borrowed), they have survived all screening mechanisms. It is these ideas that make it to the organization's table, and not just those that occur in the heads of individuals, which shape innovation. Individuals have many ideas that go unnoticed by the organization, some unspoken and others overlooked. Individuals also have ideas that could not be verbalized were it not for dynamic properties of groups (March and Simon 1958). The number of organizational ideas is taken to be a linear function of the quantity of new ideas, the size of the internal stock, and the number of incoming ideas, parameterized, respectively, by ops, aps, and bps:

$$OI_t = ops \cdot NI_t + aps \cdot IS_t + bps \cdot II_t. \tag{4}$$

When meetings occur, the stock of ideas is finally reported. So far, these ideas have been treated as conceptions held in the minds of individuals, ideas that survive discussion and evaluation at Meetings (dem) represent the result of a dynamic organizational process, not an individual event. The discussion and evaluation result in some ideas being selected for testing; other ideas are held for further development. There are those ideas, too, which will be left on the "meeting-room floor", and some that may undergo changes in form or content. Even having made it this far, an idea still suffers some chance of failing during testing or implementation. The testing death rate (tdr) captures the impact of subsequent events on the survival of organizational ideas. Ideas that do not fail during testing accumulate. The number of such ideas,

ORGANIZATION SCIENCE/Vol. 8, No. 5, September–October 1997

referred to in the model as Testing Ideas (TI), is then found by summing the surviving ideas (tdr · TI) up to that point and adding the organizational ideas that come out of that periods' meeting:

$$TI_t = tdr \cdot TI_{t-1} + dem \cdot OI_t. \qquad (5)$$

So far, I have traced the model in one direction, from the initial allocation of attention, taken as given, to search through a fixed external stock, to the selection of ideas for innovation. Ideas have a reciprocal influence back to the allocation of attention in a number of ways. First, positive feedback occurs at two points. For any particular source of "old ideas," one might expect that if the attention allocated is very low, the organization may not have accumulated sufficient information to develop "absorptive capacity" (Cohen and Levinthal 1990). Or, relationships with external gatekeepers may be too poor to gain access to more valuable items. As a result, few new ideas may occur. If so, small increases in attention to some sources are likely to bring disproportionate benefits for innovativeness. This positive feedback from initial increases in attention brings further attention to the associated sources. There is a limit to this effect, as any firm faces some finite capacity to allocate attention to search activities. Yet, as the number of ideas generated begins increasing, positive feedback also grows, signals of legitimacy gain resources and support (Feldman and March 1981), expanding attention capacity. This effect is likewise limited, as external sources of support will themselves face limits to their resources and patience. For now, these effects are distilled into a single quadratic specification, controlled by the parameters pfl and pfq (positive feedback linear and quadratic).

Negative feedback also occurs in multiple ways. When attention is limited, the amount allocated to searching each source becomes interdependent with all the others. At some point, constraints on available attention will provide negative feedback (March 1978). Another provider of negative feedback is the potentially deleterious effect too much attention to absorptive capacity for some sources that allocating too much attention to other sources can have. This negative feedback curtails continued increases to those particular sources. Furthermore, search and implementation are not as independent as often presumed. The more ideas discovered, the more selection and testing required, taking attention away from search. The successful testing of ideas initially increases demand for development, and eventually reduces the need to allocate any attention to search. These effects are captured in a single quadratic

controlled by the parameters nfl and nfq (negative feedback linear and quadratic), which are reverse in sign to pfl and pfq.

The result of these feedback effects is that the allocation of attention to search is a nonlinear function of the number of new ideas and the number of testing ideas. Attention also has a certain momentum (amo); it tends to continue at prior levels (or some proportion thereof) unless otherwise directed by feedback:

$$AA_t = amo \cdot AA_{t-1} + pfl \cdot NI_{t-1} + pfq \cdot NI_{t-1}^2$$
$$+ nfl \cdot TI_{t-1} + nfq \cdot TI_{t-1}^2. \qquad (6)$$

Lastly, the external stocks (ES) are neither totally static nor completely exogenous. Since others may be working on similar problems, or undertaking basic research that may bear on the innovative pursuit, the external stocks are subject to a natural growth rate (egr). Also, once an idea or piece of relevant information has been brought in, it is no longer a proper object of the search (neglecting for the moment those ideas that had been brought in and then were forgotten). The size of the external stock at any time is the size at a prior time increased by natural growth (egr) and decreased by inflows (II):

$$ES_t = egr \cdot ES_{t-1} - II_{t-1}. \qquad (7)$$

Combined, as shown in Figure 2, these equations form a model of innovative search that exhibits a wide range of dynamic behavior. A full exposition of the model's dynamics and implications for innovation would be unwise at this preliminary stage. For now, I wish to demonstrate that a particular chaotic regime of the model closely resembles the dynamics of the empirical search studied by Koput (1992). I do this in the next section using two key dynamic properties: dimension and entropy.

Figure 2   The Formal Model of Innovative Search

Variable	Equation	Number, page ref.
Incoming Ideas (*II*)	$II_t = apr \cdot ES_t \cdot AA_t$	1. p. 532
Internal Stocks (*IS*)	$IS_t = ilr \cdot IS_{t-1} + NI_{t-1} + II_{t-1}$	2. p. 532
New Ideas (*NI*)	$NI_t = abr \cdot IS_{t-1}$	3. p. 532
Organizational Ideas (*OI*)	$OI_t = ops \cdot NI_t + aps \cdot IS_t + bps \cdot II_t$	4. p. 532
Testing Ideas (*TI*)	$TI_t = tdr \cdot TI_{t-1} + dem \cdot OI_t$	5. p. 533
Attention Allocation (*AA*)	$AA_t = amo \cdot AA_{t-1} + pfl \cdot NI_{t-1} + pfq \cdot NI_{t-1}^2$ $+ nfl \cdot TI_{t-1} + nfq \cdot TI_{t-1}^2$	6. p. 533
External Stocks (*ES*)	$ES_t = egr \cdot ES_{t-1} - II_{t-1}$	7. p. 533

4. The Chaotic Dynamics of Search

The simulation of the model used in the comparison was programmed in MATLAB (The Mathworks 1994).[4] To ensure that the results are not the artifact of a particular combination of initial values and parameter settings, a total of 1,000 simulations were run. Each simulation was run for 1,000 time periods, randomly varying parameter settings over the ranges shown in Table 1. This "monte carlo" approach to sensitivity analysis was dictated by the nonlinear nature of the system under study. As with any nonlinear system, small changes in any one parameter may well destroy particularities of the dynamics. But, when a nonobvious offsetting change is made in some other parameter, the dynamics could be reinstated. Hence, sensitivity is best analyzed by randomly varying the parameters in conjunction.

The initial values and ranges from which the parameters were drawn are inductively determined and, as such, are intended to be reasonable. However, the values and settings are neither definitive, nor are they intended to be exclusive as values capable of manifesting chaotic or otherwise important dynamics. They are based on my subjective examination of the transcripts of the MIRP studies analyzed by Cheng and Van de Ven (1996) and Koput (1992), as well as my past experiences working with innovative organizations in the engineering consulting industry The initial size of the external stocks was quite arbitrarily set at 50; the initial allocation of attention, at 0.20, was derived from the MIRP transcript. Other initial values are set to zero to simulate a search process with no history. Of

the 1,000 simulations, approximately 10% (93) exhibited chaos at "equilibrium." The ability of the model to manifest chaos is robust in that no particular combination of, or relationship between, parameters was responsible for inducing chaos: the 93 runs were a diverse sample with regard to parameter settings. I have also obtained similar results with vastly different initial values and parameter settings, as well as with numerous alternative specifications of the model. The remaining simulations exhibited protracted periods of transitory dynamics (including chaos), followed by regimes of stable behavior. Figures 3 and 4 exhibit

Figure 3   Simulated Attention

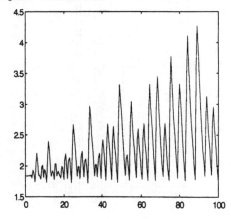

Figure 4   Simulated Ideas

Table 1   Initial Values and Settings for "Monte Carlo" Simulations of the Model

Variable	Initial Value	Parameter	Setting / Range
II	0	apr	[0.025, 0.25]
IS	0	ilr	[0.10, 0.30]
NI	0	abr	[0.20, 0.80]
OI	0	aps	[0.10, 0.30]
TI	0	bps	[0.10, 0.30]
AA	0.20	ops	[0.40, 0.60]
ES	50	dem	1.0
		tdr	[0.15, 0.40]
		pfl	[0.025, 0.25]
		pfq	[−0.005, −0.025]
		nfl	[−0.001, −0.10]
		nfq	[0.0001, 0.001]
		amo	1.0
		egr	[1.001, 1.01]

KENNETH W. KOPUT   *Chaotic Model of Innovative Search*

the relevant values of attention and ideas from one of the chaotic regimes, selected arbitrarily.

Figures 5 and 6 exhibit the raw data analyzed by Koput (1992).[5] Note that there are qualitative similarities to the simulated data. Although the actual data contain an expanding-then-contracting trend, they both exhibit a spiky, nonperiodic pattern. Of course, visual inspection is hardly persuasive. I turn next to a numerical comparison of the empirical and simulated data.

Figure 5   TAP Attention

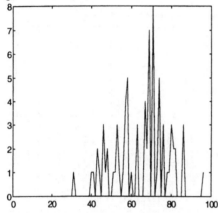

Figure 6   TAP Ideas

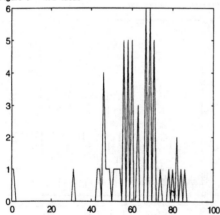

5. Comparison of Dynamics: Model Versus Data

A very brief overview (provided to facilitate interpretation, not to introduce the subject) of the statistical methods used to numerically compare the empirical and simulated data is presented in the Appendix (for a comprehensive and comprehensible introduction to the theory and methods of chaos, see Peitgen et al., 1992). The appended description focuses on two numerical measures that can characterize chaotic dynamics: the correlation dimension and the K2-entropy.[6] Nonlinear, chaotic dynamics can, in general, be characterized by three properties: fractal dimension, disorder (or divergence of nearby trajectories, also known as sensitive dependence), and nonlinear, temporal dependence (Peitgen et al. 1992). The correlation dimension is used to assess whether the data has a fractal microstructure, as illustrated in Table 2. Stable deterministic systems —or random systems with strong, stable autocorrelation—provide zero or integer values. Random systems have infinite values. Chaotic systems are distinguished by positive, noninteger values. The K2-entropy measures disorder. While the Lyapunov exponent can also be used to assess divergence, it has often been misused in empirical studies to indicate randomness when it, in fact, cannot distinguish chaos from randomness. The Lyapunov exponent is not used here, however, simply because Koput (1992) reported not being able to obtain stable and robust estimates for the data of interest.[7] Table 3 shows the ranges of K2-entropy associated with different types of dynamical behavior. For chaos, the value must be positive, but finite. Nonlinear dependence can be evidenced by the BDS statistic. However, Brock et al. (1991) report that the BDS statistic has little power to identify nonlinear dependence in data sets with fewer than 300 points. There-

Table 2   Interpretation of Correlation Dimension

Type of Dynamic Behavior	Correlation Dimension Characteristics	Example	Correlation Dimension
Stable, Fixed Point	Zero	Quadratic Map, $\kappa = 1.8$	0
Stable, Periodic	Nonnegative, Integer	Quadratic Map, $\kappa = 3.2$	0
Chaotic	Positive, Noninteger	Quadratic Map, $\kappa = 3.9$	1.1
Random	Infinite	Uniform(0, 1)	Infinity

KENNETH W. KOPUT *Chaotic Model of Innovative Search*

Table 3   Interpretation of K2-Entropy

Type of Dynamic Behavior	K2-Entropy Characteristics	Example	K2-Entropy
Stable, Fixed Point	Zero	Quadratic Map, $\kappa = 1.8$	0
Stable, Periodic	Zero	Quadratic Map, $\kappa = 3.2$	0
Chaotic	Positive, Finite	Quadratic Map, $\kappa = 3.9$	0.8
Random	Infinite	Uniform(0,1)	Infinity

Table 4   Comparison of Model and Empirical Dynamics

Variable	Embedding Dimension	Correlation Dimension	Linearity Diagnostic	K2-Entropy
Model:				
Attention	4	1.521 (0.007)	0.999	0.696 (0.015)
Ideas	4	1.524 (0.006)	0.999	0.695 (0.020)
Data:				
Attention	4	1.541 (0.041)	0.994	0.742 (0.171)
Ideas	4	1.595 (0.031)	0.994	0.742 (0.109)

Notes: All effects are significant at or beyond the 0.05 level. The empirical results are taken from Koput (1992).

fore, only the first two measures will be used. Keep in mind that the point here is not to conclusively prove that either the modeled or empirical time series is chaotic. Rather, methods from the "chaos theorist's" toolkit are used as diagnostics, to compare otherwise intractable dynamics.

While all chaotic systems have noninteger correlation dimension, positive entropy, and temporal dependence, different chaotic systems will generally have different values for these measures. More to the point, in order for a set of variables to have the same underlying system, they must have the same values for these measures. Hence, we can use these measures in exploring relationships between variables that might otherwise seem unrelated. If two or more variables have similar values for these indicators, the evidence is consistent with their either comprising or having arisen from the same underlying system. In practice, when the measures are estimated from finite data, we must use some judgment in making this evaluation.[8] In any event, the evidence cannot be taken as conclusive, since it is not always the case that different systems will have noticeably different dynamics.

Results

Results are presented in Table 4.[9] The table is read as next described. The first column gives the name of the variable for which estimates were obtained. The first two rows are the search components of attention and ideas from the model presented in Section 3, parameterized as shown in Table 1. Rows 3 and 4 present results from the empirical data described in Koput (1992).[10] All of the variables presented here were found to be chaotic. The second column "Embedding Dimension" gives the dimension, d^*, of abstract space needed to view the dynamics. This measure is related to the minimal number of independent influences that might

explain the time series. We see from the results that perhaps only two or three forces underlie the dynamics. The third column displays the value of the correlation dimension and its standard error, for the embedding dimension listed. The correlation dimension indicates chaos if it is noninteger. All of the entries pass statistical tests for being noninteger. More importantly, they are all roughly the same, suggesting that the model replicates the observed behavior in this key dynamic characteristic. Assuming that the lowest correlation dimension value in Table 4 is underestimated and the highest value overestimated, all of the values in the table become nearly identical. The fourth column, "Linearity," is simply a helpful diagnostic: the closer to 1, the better. All of the values are very close to 1, indicating that the estimates are robust.

The last column of Table 4 gives the K2-entropy and its standard error. The K2-entropy estimates support the conclusion that the dynamics of the search components of attention and ideas are similar in both the simulation and empirical data. While the entropies of the model do not differ significantly from those of the empirical data, they are nonetheless lower. The difference in entropy estimates suggests that the real world is more disorderly than the computer-simulated model.

6. Discussion: Notes Toward an Agenda for Research

The model explicated here provides some new answers to important questions about organizational learning and innovative search. To the question "How is attention allocated during active search?," the model suggests that attention can be allocated endogenously: by feedback loops which balance the need to attend to search, evaluation, testing, and so forth over time. The question "How is attention linked to the identification of important ideas for innovation?" is answered through those same structures. The influence of attention on ideas occurs through the parameters of specifiable mechanisms (such as temporal association, inflow, etc.) The results here suggest that these mechanisms of attention are sufficient to regulate the flow of ideas, in terms of quantities residing at different locations within the feedback systems.

There are also many new questions for organizational research; I posit three. I begin by considering some refinements to the model of search. Then, I speculate on how the search components of attention and ideas might be linked to actions and decisions within an extended learning model. Finally, I broaden the discussion to consider issues of organizational design, albeit in a very limited way. The discussion is neither conclusive nor complete; rather, the comments are merely intended to start a dialogue and suggest research directions that seem most promising.

Refinements: What Adjustments Are Needed in the Chaotic Model of Search?

Although not simple, the model is, nonetheless, a simplified representation of the innovative search process. To begin, a number of feedback mechanisms have been collected into just two quadratic effects. Feedback is critical to the ability of the model to manifest chaos. Research on the correct specification of separable feedback effects is needed before the full dynamics of the model can be analyzed to interpret parameter settings. What makes the balance between positive and negative feedback especially severe? What does severity mean in this context? How does the process move from different regimes of dynamic behavior, such as stability and chaos? These are questions in need of answers before any prescriptions can be drawn from the model.[11] The other mechanisms in the model should also be scrutinized. Effects assumed linear may be better treated as nonlinear, and vice versa.

Certain observations about innovative dynamics have been intentionally left out at this early stage. For instance, attention often increases, or becomes more effective, as deadlines or meetings approach (March and Simon 1958). Not all mechanisms need to be included in the model. The goal of any mathematical model in behavioral research is to help understand qualitative aspects of the behavior under study. Hence, only those mechanisms that significantly influence the qualitative dynamics of the model need to be included. Research is needed to determine which mechanisms are important. This may require simulating the model

by including each, in turn or in combinations guided by behavioral theory, and carefully analyzing the results.

Also, as observed by one of the anonymous reviewers, there is as yet no reason to think that the time index of the model corresponds to any increment of real time, such as weeks or months. Along these lines, it may well be that microloops of the IS → NI → AA structure may operate on a different time clock than the OI → TI → AA link.

Lastly, the specified model focuses on the aggregate aspects of an innovative search process. In particular, the total number of ideas for an organization, in each time period, is modeled; particular ideas or pieces of information are not tracked. A deep understanding of innovative search may require a more micro analysis, in which the unit of analysis is the idea rather than the organization.

Fleshing out and refining the model explicated here should involve both deductive and inductive lines of research, working toward a convergence. Polley and Van de Ven (1995) have already begun work of this type.

Extensions: How Are the Search Components of Attention and Ideas Linked to Implementing Actions and Decisions?

Chaotic systems have unique cross-level properties and a lower intrinsic variance than a random process with the same manifestation (Conrad 1986). What do these mean in behavioral or organizational terms? Does a search process with a structure[12] that can produce chaos provide the diversity of experiences required to "creatively redefine organizational routines" when innovating (Dougherty and Heller 1994) in a more knowable or less risky way than a truly "blind," random search? Chaos has several additional mathematical properties which may lend themselves to speculations about organizational interpretations. I discuss just one property, that relates to the link between attention, ideas, actions and decisions.

Innovation efforts are typically subject to ambiguous demands. Although unknown a priori, once an attractive idea is manifest, the preferences might be revealed. The model explicated here, by linking attention and ideas to screening and evaluation through feedback loops, provides a mechanism for uncovering such preferences. The disappearance of ambiguity is not tied to a change in preference structure, but rather to a narrowing of attention or ideas which allows preferences to become known. This occurs endogenously, not exogenously, through a phenomenon exhibited by many chaotic systems known as *intermittency*.

An intermittency occurs when the range of variation exhibited by the system suddenly and dramatically narrows. For instance, in the TAP development, attention might lock in on a particular criteria, such as blood flow rate. Further, the considered possibilities for flow rate may have varied widely for a while, but suddenly narrowed to within a relatively small range. Consider the way such a qualitative change would be felt by the individuals or organizations in the system. Upon experiencing a sudden narrowing, attributions of consensus are likely. These attributions can substitute for the revelation of preferences, with similar effects: decisions being made and implemented. In this way, the system provides its own *shared* choice opportunities, aiding implementation (Gryskiewicz 1988).

Pursuing this example, imagine what might happen when the range of variation widens out again, as is characteristic. While developing an innovation, there are many aspects, or attributes, of the product and its manufacture that need to be worked out. Each decision, then, might reflect the determination of one such attribute. When the range of variation narrows, consensus is perceived around one of the attributes. When the variation widens again, the discussion centers on the next attribute, and so on (Gryskiewicz 1988).

This type of emergent behavior does not require well-known preferences or even known alternatives. Therefore, actions can even be taken under "adverse" conditions for "rational" calculations (March 1981). Attention is an important variable in such a theory, linking search and decision making.

These conjectures need to be operationalized and tested. An appealing start would be to bridge the work in this paper with that of Cheng and Van de Ven (1996). They have shown that action and outcome events are chaotic during the period of active search for the same innovation process modeled here. They have also presented evidence that actions may transition from chaos into periodicity, as the innovation process moves from active search into implementation or toward termination. How this occurs is a fascinating, unanswered question.

Surroundings: How Is a Chaotic Search Process Embedded in Larger Organizational Structures or Processes?

Many organizational arrangements are plausibly related to the potential of an organization to generate innovation chaotically. The empirical data analyzed here came from a joint, internal venture of three firms. Is this type of arrangement needed to support a chaotic search process? Is the "intrapreneurial" culture of the

principal partner important? Or, is the nature of the decision processes what matters? I say a few words about the last possibility, but stop short of offering any formal hypotheses.

Impressionistic decision processes are characterized by high commitment, close market relations, decisions by hunches, and a strong can-do attitude. Ambiguity is high, since goals are steeped in terms like "meeting market demands," "providing quality," or "being innovative." The ideology focuses attention away from uncertainty, thus building confidence and a sense of personal commitment in members. Rationalistic processes, by contrast, are low in ambiguity, but high in uncertainty and external accountability. Goals are stated in terms of exact profit margins, for example. Decisions are made on the basis of extensive calculations. However, the algorithms used continually confront individuals with the need to provide exact information, which is typically impossible in an innovative venture. This inhibits action (Brunsson 1982, 1985).

Impressionistic decision processes seem to hold more potential for cultivating and integrating with a chaotic search process. Whether chaos is actually beneficial likely depends on how such processes are embedded in information structures. The types of channels, existence of search routines, timing of meetings for sharing information and evaluating ideas, and centralization of decision making are all important in the chaotic model.

Lastly, the scope of this paper was restricted to investigating the dynamics of attention *during* an activated search process. This leaves open the question of whether there are second-order feedback loops that control the parameters of the model, hence determining the qualitative dynamics of the search process: chaotic, stable or shut off entirely. For some of the simulations that exhibit transitory chaos, the chaotic regime eventually "blows up." That is, the values of the variables increase exponentially, due to unchecked growth in the external stocks. Whether this helps to explain the failure of the TAP venture is unclear. One interpretation is that accelerating costs in the race to market (against competing ventures) forced the venture's termination. To capture this, a second-order feedback could be included in the model, such that a value or growth rate of attention or ideas in excess of a certain threshold would induce a parameter shift.

A particularly promising avenue of research would be to connect the present model of search with the control mechanisms in the model of Mezias and Glynn (1993). This would simply involve substituting the chaotic model explicated here for the random draws that Mezias and Glynn equated with search.

7. Conclusion

The model explicated in this paper implies that we cannot so readily split the innovative process into separable, sequential stages, such as those of search, screening and implementation. Instead, each part is inextricably intertwined with the others in both space and time. Chaos may have an underlying organizational order, suggesting that it is possible to design stable processes—retaining certain values, practices, and routines—that may also be able to generate and select new innovative ideas. Carefully structured feedback loops endogenously manage the process and, perhaps, exhibit certain unique dynamic properties that provide opportunities for consensus and choice. Understanding how these work, and whether they are beneficial or harmful for organizations, is a great challenge for organizational research.

But the model, as it stands, is too preliminary to meet this challenge, it is only a first step. The model is in need of refinements, extensions, and surroundings before we can begin the difficult work of mapping it onto specific cases, such as the Therapeutic Apheresis Program, and answering the intriguing question posed by one of the *Organization Science* reviewers: "What would a chaotic model of innovation look like if it were instantiated in an organization?"

Acknowledgments

This research was supported by funds from the Institute of Industrial Relations, University of California, Berkeley and by the College of Business and Public Administration, University of Arizona. Many helped shape this work, among them Andy Van de Ven, Tom Cottrell, Jim Wade, John Sterman, participants of the Social Organization Seminar at the University of Arizona and four anonymous reviewers at *Organization Science*. I am grateful to Douglas Polley and Andy Van de Ven for allowing me to analyze the data they collected on the therapeutic apheresis program. I also thank Sarah M. Kurtzweil for her expert assistance in copyediting this manuscript.

Appendix on Statistical Methods
Correlation Dimension

The correlation dimension will indicate whether the object is built with "fractal" construction, which is unique to chaotic systems. While there exist a number of measures of fractal dimension, the one that has been most successfully used, especially in the case of raw data subject to noise, is the correlation dimension (Grassberger and Procaccia 1983, Ben-Mizrachi et al. 1984, Grassberger 1986). The correlation dimension can be thought of as a measure of the type of construction used in building an object. In our case, the object consists of an abstract reconstruction from an observed time series of behavior. The reconstruction takes place in this way. Consider an n-dimensional system. Typically, we observe only some small subset of the n independent variables. Given observations on just *one* of

the state variables $x(t)$, we can reconstruct the dynamics of the original system by constructing a phase portrait from some set of d time delays of the variable x: $x, x(t), x(t + 1), x(t + 2), \ldots, x[t + (d - 1)]$ (Takens 1984). This *pseudo phase portrait* will have the same dynamical properties, including fractal dimension, as the original system (Glass et al. 1986, Helleman 1980). The value of d needed to view the full object is known as the *embedding dimension*. An algorithm for calculating the correlation dimension and embedding dimension simultaneously, using discrete data, is available (Grassberger and Procaccia 1983, Ben-Mizrachi et al. 1984).

In the discrete case, the correlation integral, $C(r)$, is defined, for a given embedding dimension d, by (Rasband 1990):

$$C_d(r) = \lim_{N \to \infty} \frac{1}{N^2} \sum_{i \neq j} \Theta\left(r - \|\vec{x}_{d,i} - \vec{x}_{d,j}\|\right),$$

where $\vec{x}_{d,i}$ and $\vec{x}_{d,j}$ are vectors of time delays, as defined above, of dimension d equal to the embedding dimension. Also, r is a separation value against which the distance, defined by any norm $\|\cdot\|$ between two points, $\vec{x}_i, \vec{x}_j$, is compared, and $\Theta(\alpha)$ is the Heaviside function $\Theta(\alpha) = 0$, $\alpha \leq 0$; $\Theta(\alpha) = 1$, $\alpha > 0$. For small values of r, $C_d(r)$ behaves as a power of r:

$$C_d(r) \propto r^{\nu_d},$$

where ν_d is the correlation dimension associated with the embedding dimension, d. The overall *correlation dimension*, ν, is the limit as the embedding dimension is increased:

$$\nu = \lim_{d \to \infty} \nu_d.$$

We can understand the estimation in terms of a regression formulation. Taking logs of both sides of the above equation, we get a linear model:

$$\ln C_d(r) = \beta_{d,0} + \nu_d \ln r.$$

From this we can see that ν_d is the slope of a straight-line portion of the log-log plot of $C(r)$ versus r. Where the straight-line portion exists[13], the model can be fit by least-squares regression (Smith 1991). This is done for a range of embedding dimensions, d, until either of two things happens. First, the estimate of ν_d may stabilize at some specific value, ν^*. Stability is obtained if ν_d stops increasing with increasing d at some sufficiently low d, say d^*. This value, ν^*, then becomes the estimate of the correlation dimension, ν. Alternatively, if ν_d continues increasing with increasing d, we dismiss the possibility that the data provides any useful evidence of chaos. When the slope stabilizes, we say that saturation has occurred. Typically, if saturation occurs, it will be above some portion of the graph that exhibits a nonsaturating slope. This nonsaturating portion represents randomness in the system.

The conservative statistical test for chaos is as follows. If saturation does not occur, we reject any possibility of chaos and simply presume the data is random. If saturation occurs, we test that ν^* is noninteger against the hypothesis that it is actually the nearest integer. This can be done using a t-test of the regression coefficient

KENNETH W. KOPUT   *Chaotic Model of Innovative Search*

(Takens 1984). The R^2 of the regression can be used as a diagnostic to ensure that a straight-line portion has been found.

K2-Entropy

In general, entropy is a measure of disorder in a system (Lindgren 1990). The *K2-entropy* is defined, for the discrete-data case, by

$$K_2 = \lim_{d \to \infty} \ln \frac{C_d(r)}{C_{d+1}(r)}.$$

The K2-entropy is calculated for discrete data with the algorithm proposed by Grassberger and Procaccia (1983). In terms of the regression formulation used above, the K2-entropy can be defined as $\beta_{d^*,0} - \beta_{d^*+1,0}$. Hence, the K2-entropy is simply the vertical distance by which the regression lines for successive embedding dimensions are displaced, once saturation has occurred. If saturation does not occur, no estimate can be obtained. When that happens, $\beta_{d,0}$ will be heading toward infinity; randomness will be concluded.

The K2-entropy is a particular entropy definition that is convenient not only computationally, but also conceptually. K2-entropy is closely related to positive Lyapunov exponents, the most widely used and accepted measure of chaos in theoretical analysis (Moon 1987). Direct computation of Lyapunov exponents in short time length data series subject to noise is not robust (Kapitaniak 1988), and the measure has been subject to some misuse as an indicator of chaos in empirical investigations. Algorithms to estimate the K2-entropy appear to be more stable, and its interpretation has been less erroneous. K2-entropy is numerically equivalent to the sum of the first two positive Lyapunov exponents. Where no positive Lyapunov exponents exist, the K2-entropy is zero; hence, if the K2-entropy is positive, then so must be the first Lyapunov exponent (Katok 1980). Since stable systems with a positive Lyapunov exponent must also have, at least, one zero and one negative exponent, chaotic systems must have at least three Lyapunov exponents. Each exponent corresponds to an orthogonal axis in phase space. It follows that chaotic systems must exist in a phase space of minimum dimension equal to three. It also follows that for a three-dimensional attractor, the K2-entropy is identically equal to the first Lyapunov exponent. Since the true dimension of the underlying phase space, n, and the embedding dimension of the reconstructed pseudo phase space, d, are related by the inequality: $d \le 2n + 1$, the equivalence of the K2-entropy and the first Lyapunov exponent extends to observed embedding dimensions of up to $d = 7$.

Endnotes

[1] I thank an anonymous reviewer for calling my attention to this important distinction and for reminding me of the definitions that follow.

[2] Sensitive dependence on initial conditions is an often-cited characteristic of chaos. It is one of the features that makes chaotic systems manifest behavior that seems random. However, sensitive dependence is shared by both chaotic and random systems. Only within the class of deterministic models does sensitive dependence distinguish chaos. For empirical data, chaos is distinguished from randomness by the presence of "periodic-point density." This is indicated by low-dimensional correlation in the structure of otherwise seemingly random data. See the section on statistical methods.

[3] More precisely, when the phase plot of the system contains an hyperbolic point. A full explanation can be found elsewhere. See, e.g., Devaney (1989).

[4] A listing of the program is available from the author.

[5] Koput identified three types of external stocks in the TAP data: those held by parent organizations, industry groups, and government agencies. Attention to industry sources is used in the comparison, as this best corresponds to the use of the attention variable as currently specified in the model. The dynamics of the different types of attention are very similar and could be freely substituted for the comparison without altering any of the conclusions.

[6] Note that classical methods for comparing the distributions of data assumed to be independent draws from some random probability model, such as the Kolmogorv-Smirnov test, are inappropriate for comparing distributions that may be chaotic. Two portions of a single chaotic series could have very different data distributions while still having the same properties when viewed dynamically via the measures used here. Conversely, two different distributions, one random and one chaotic, might appear identical under the Kolmogorv-Smirnov test, but have very different properties when viewed dynamically.

[7] The algorithm for computing Lyapunov exponents from a time series requires the investigator to set, a priori, three parameters to which estimates are highly sensitive. The K2-entropy algorithm requires less exogenous input.

[8] If the R^2s from the regressions described above are close to unity, indicating linearity in the log-log plot of $C(R)$ versus r, then the estimates can be compared with t-tests.

[9] All estimates were obtained in MATLAB (The Mathworks 1994). Both the empirical and simulated results passed Brock's (1986) residual test, as well as Brock and Sayer's (1988) shuffle diagnostic. For the simulated data, a simple first-order autocorrelated process was assumed. See Endnote 11 for details on the empirical data.

[10] These results are excerpted from Koput (1992). Koput ran several autoregressive models, settling on an ARMA(5, 2) specified as:

$$y_t = \beta X + \alpha_1 y_{t-1} + \alpha_2 y_{t-2} + u_t; u_t - \phi_1 u_{t-1} - \cdots \phi_5 u_{t-5}$$

$$= e_t \sim N(0, \sigma^2).$$

The ARMA(5, 2) process removed a nonlinear time trend of the following form. The number of attention events and innovative ideas initially increased with time, as the project got underway. Eventually, a point was reached at which this trend reversed. From then until the termination of the project, attention and idea generation both dropped off somewhat.

[11] As noted by an anonymous reviewer, the resulting prescriptions may not be novel. Even so, developing a formal model helps us understand why certain structures or processes foster innovation and enables us to pinpoint how the process can be controlled.

[12] By structure I mean the mathematically explicable structure of the search process, e.g., feedback loops, etc. I do not mean the structure of an organization, as normally considered.

[13] We expect the straight-line portion to occur at smaller values of r. However, for finite data its existence is not guaranteed.

KENNETH W. KOPUT   *Chaotic Model of Innovative Search*

References

Albert, R. (1975), "Toward a Behavioral Definition of Genius," *American Psychologist*, 30, 140–151.

Amabile, T. (1983), "Social Psychology of Creativity: A Componential Conceptualization," *Journal of Personality and Social Psychology*, 45, 357–377.

____ (1988), "A Model of Creativity and Innovation in Organizations," in B. Staw and L. Cummings, (Eds.), *Research in Organizational Behavior*, Vol. 10, Greenwich, CT: JAI Press, 123–167.

Ben-Mizrachi, A., L. Procaccia and P. Grassberger (1984), "Characterization of Experimental (Noisy) Strange Attractors," *Physical Review A*, 29, 2, 975–977.

Blau, P. and R. Scott (1962), *Formal Organizations*, San Francisco, CA: Chandler.

Brock, W. A. (1986), "Distinguishing Random and Deterministic Systems: Abridged Version," *Journal of Economic Theory*, Vol. 40, 168–195.

____, D. A. Hsieh, and B. LeBaron (1991), *Nonlinear Dynamic, Chaos, and Instability*, Cambridge, MA: MIT Press, Cambridge.

____ and C. L. Sayers (1988), "Is the Business Cycle Characterized by Deterministic Chaos?" *Journal of Monetary Economics*, Vol. 22, 71–90.

Brunsson, N. (1982), "The Irrationality of Action and Action Rationality: Decisions, Ideologies, and Organizational Actions," *Journal of Management Studies*, 19, 29–34.

____ (1985), *The Irrational Organization: Irrationality as a Basis for Organizational Action and Change*, New York: Wiley.

Campbell, D. (1960), "Blind Variation and Selective Retention in Creative Thought as in Other Knowledge Processes," *Psychological Review*, 67, 380–400.

Cheng, Y. T. and A. H. Van de Ven (1996), "Learning the Innovation Journey: Order Out of Chaos?" *Organization Science*, 7, 6, 593–614.

Cohen, W. and D. Levinthal (1990), "Absorptive Capacity: A New Perspective on Learning and Innovation," *Administrative Science Quarterly*, 35, 128–152.

Conrad, M. (1986), "What is the Use of Chaos?" in A. V. Holden (Ed.), *Chaos*, Princeton, NJ: Princeton University Press.

Day, D. L. (1994), "Raising Radicals: Different Processes for Championing Innovative Corporate Ventures," *Organization Science*, 5, 2, 148–172.

Devaney, R. L. (1989), *An Introduction to Chaotic Dynamical Systems*, 2d ed., Reading, MA: Addison-Wesley.

Dougherty, D. and T. Heller (1994), "The Illegitimacy of Successful Product Innovation in Established Firms," *Organization Science*, 5, 2, 200–218.

Feldman, M. S. and J. G. March (1981), "Information in Organizations as Signal and Symbol," *Administrative Science Quarterly*, 26, 171–186.

Frost, P. J. and C. P. Egri (1991), "The Political Process of Innovation," *Research in Organizational Behavior*, 13, 229–235.

Galbraith, J. (1982), "Designing the Innovating Organization," *Organizational Dynamics*, 10, 5–25.

Garud, R. and A. H. Van de Ven (1992), "An Empirical Evaluation of the Internal Corporate Venturing Process," *Strategic Management Journal*, 13, 93–109.

Geis, G. (1986), "Risk Taking, Innovation, and Organizational Environment," in R. Kuhn, (Ed.), *Frontiers in Creative and Innovative Management*, Cambridge, MA: Ballinger, chapter 10.

Glass, L., A. Shrier and J. Belair (1986), "Chaotic cardiac rhythms," in A. V. Holden (Ed.), *Chaos*, Princeton, NJ: Princeton Univ. Press, 257–270.

Gluck, F. (1986), "Big Bang Management," in R. Kuhn, (ed.), *Frontiers in Creative and Innovative Management*, Cambridge, MA: Ballinger, chapter 7.

Grassberger, P. (1986), "Estimating the Fractal Dimensions and Entropies of Strange Attractors," in A. V. Holden (ed.), *Chaos*, Princeton, NJ: Princeton Univ. Press.

____ and I. Procaccia (1983), "Characterization of Strange Attractors," *Physical Review Letters*, 50, 5, 346–348.

Gronhaug, K. and T. Reve (1988), "Entrepreneurship and strategic management: Synergy or antagony?" in K. Gronhaug and G. Kaufmann, (Eds.), *Innovation: A Cross-Disciplinary Perspective*, Oslo, Norway: Norwegian University Press, 331–346.

Gryskiewicz, S. (1988), "Trial by Fire in an Industrial Setting: A Practical Evaluation of Three Creative Problem-solving Techniques," in K. Gronhaug and G. Kaufmann, (Eds.), *Innovation: A Cross-Disciplinary Perspective*, Oslo, Norway: Norwegian University Press, 205–232.

Guth, W. and A. Ginsberg (1990), "Guest Editor's Introduction: Corporate Entrepreneurship," *Strategic Management Journal*, 11, 2, 5–16.

Helleman, R. H. G. (1980), "Self-generated Chaotic Behavior in Nonlinear Systems," in E. Cohen (Ed.), *Fundamental Problems in Statistical Mechanics*, Vol. 5, Amsterdam: Elsevier North-Holland.

Helson, R. (1988), "The Creative Personality," in K. Gronhaug and G. Kaufmann, (Eds.), *Innovation: A Cross-Disciplinary Perspective*, Oslo, Norway: Norwegian University Press, 29–64.

Holbek, J. (1988), "The Innovation Design Dilemma: Some Notes on Its Relevance and Solutions," in K. Gronhaug and G. Kaufmann, (Eds.), *Innovation: A Cross-Disciplinary Perspective*, Oslo, Norway: Norwegian University Press, 253–278.

Isaksen, S. (1988), "Educational Implications of Creativity Research: An Updated Rationale for Creative Learning," in K. Gronhaug and G. Kaufmann, (Eds.), *Innovation: A Cross-Disciplinary Perspective*, Oslo, Norway: Norwegian University Press, 167–204.

Jelinek, M. and C. B. Schoonhoven (1990), *The Innovation Marathon: Lessons from High Technology Firms*, New York: Basil Blackwell.

Kanter, R. (1988), "When a Thousand Flowers Bloom: Structural, Collective, and Social Conditions for Innovation in Organizations," in B. Staw and L. Cummings (Eds.), *Research in Organizational Behavior*, Vol. 10. Greenwich, CT: JAI Press, 169–211.

Kapitaniak, T. (1988), *Chaos in Systems with Noise*, Princeton, NJ: World Scientific.

Katok, A. (1980), "Lyapunov Exponents, Entropy, and Periodic Orbits for Diffeomorphisms," *Publications in Mathematics, IHES*, 51, 137–173.

Koput, K. W. (1992), *Dynamics of Innovative Idea Generation in Organizations: Randomness and Chaos in the Development of a New Medical Device*, Ann Arbor, MI: UMI Press.

KENNETH W. KOPUT *Chaotic Model of Innovative Search*

Kuhn, R. (1986), "Personality and Innovation: How Creative Types Think and Act," in R. Kuhn, (Ed.), *Frontiers in Creative and Innovative Management*, Cambridge, MA: Ballinger, chapter 11.

Lant, T. and S. Mezias (1990), "An Organizational Learning Model of Convergence and Reorientation," *Organization Science*, 3, 1, 47–71.

Levinthal, D. and J. March (1981), "A Model of Adaptive Organizational Search," *Journal of Economic Behavior and Organization*, 2, 307–333.

Levitt, B. and J. G. March (1988), "Organizational Learning," *Annual Review of Sociology*, 14, 319–340.

Lindgren, K. (1990), "Entropy and Correlations in Discrete Dynamical Systems," in J. Casti and A. Karlqvist (Eds.), *Beyond Belief*, Boca Raton, FL: CRC Press, 88–109.

March, J. (1971), "The Technology of Foolishness," *Civilkonomer (Copenhagen)*, 18, 4, 4–12.

____ (1978), "Bounded Rationality, Ambiguity, and the Engineering of Choice," *The Bell Journal of Economics*, 9, 2, 587–608.

____ (1981), "Footnotes to Organizational Change," *Administrative Science Quarterly*, 26, 563–577.

____ and H. Simon (1958), *Organizations*, New York: Wiley.

March, J. G. (1988), *Decisions and Organizations*, New York: Basil Blackwell.

____ (1991), "Exploration and Exploitation in Organizational Learning," *Organization Science*, 2, 1, 70–87.

The Mathworks, Inc. (1994), *MATLAB version 4.2c*, Natick, MA: The Mathworks, Inc.

Merton, R. (1935), "Fluctuations in the Rate of Industrial Invention," *Quarterly Journal of Economics*, 49, 2, 454–502.

Mezias, S. J. and M. A. Glynn (1993), "The Three Faces of Organizational Renewal: Institution, Revolution, and Evolution," *Strategic Management Journal*, 14, 77–101.

Miles, R. H. and K. Cameron (1982), *Coffin Nails and Corporate Strategies*, Englewood Cliffs, NJ: Prentice Hall.

Moon, F. C. (1987), *Chaotic Vibrations*, New York: Wiley.

Nelson, R. (1962), *The Rate and Direction of Inventive Activity*, Princeton, NJ: Princeton University Press.

Nystrom, P., B. Hedberg and W. Starbuck (1976), "Interacting Processes as Organization Designs," in R. Kilmann, L. Pondy and D. Slevin (Eds.), *The Management of Organization Design*, I, New York: Elsevier North-Holland, 209–230.

Peitgen, H-O, H. Jurgens and D. Saupe (1992), *Chaos and Fractals: New Frontiers of Science*, New York: Springer-Verlag.

Polley, D. and A. H. Van de Ven (1995), "Learning by Discovery During Innovation Development," Discussion paper, Strategic Management Research Center, University of Minnesota, Minneapolis.

Prigogine, I. and I. Stengers (1984), *Order Out of Chaos*, New York: Bantam.

Rasband, N. S. (1990), *Chaotic Dynamics of Nonlinear Systems*, New York: Wiley.

Robert, M. and A. Weiss (1988), *The Innovation Formula*, Cambridge, MA: Ballinger.

Roche, G. (1986), "Route to the Top," in R. Kuhn (Ed.), *Frontiers in Creative and Innovative Management*, Cambridge, MA: Ballinger, chapter 8.

Schiffel, D. and C. Kitti (1978), "Rates of Invention: International Patent Comparisons," *Research Policy*, 7, 4, 37–63.

Simon, H. (1986), "What We Know about the Creative Process," in R. Kuhn (ed.), *Frontiers in Creative and Innovative Management*, Cambridge, MA: Ballinger, chapter 1.

Smith, R. (1991), Optimal Estimation of Fractal Dimension, in M. Casdagli and S. Eubank (eds.), *Nonlinear Modeling and Forecasting*, New York: Addison-Wesley.

Staw, B. M. (1990), "An Evolutionary Approach to Creativity and Innovation," in M. West and J. Farr (Eds.), *Innovation and Creativity at Work*, New York: Wiley, 287–308.

Suarez-Villa, L. (1990), "Invention, Inventive Learning, and Innovative Capacity," *Behavioral Science*, 35, 4, 290–310.

Takens, F. (1984), "On the Numerical Determination of the Dimension of an Attractor," in D. A. Rand and J. P. Eckmann (Eds.), *Springer Lecture Notes in Mathematics*, 1125, New York: Springer-Verlag, 99–106.

Teece, D. (Ed.) (1987), *The Competitive Challenge: Strategies for Industrial Innovation and Renewal*, Cambridge, MA: Ballinger.

Van de Ven, A. (1986), "Central Problems in the Management of Innovation," *Management Science*, 32, 590–607.

Van de Ven, A. H., H. L. Angle and M. S. Poole (eds.) (1989), *Research on the Management of Innovation: The Minnesota Studies*, New York: Ballinger.

____ and D. Polley (1992), "Learning While Innovating," *Organization Science*, 3, 1, 92–116.

____ (1993), "Managing the Process of Organizational Innovation," in G. P. Huber and W. Glick (Eds.), *Organizational Change and Redesign: Ideas and Insights for Improving Performance*, New York: Oxford University Press, 269–294.

Weick, K. (1982), "Change in Loosely-coupled Systems," in P. Goodman (Ed.), *Change in Organizations*, San Francisco, CA: Jossey-Bass.

Zaltman, G., R. Duncan and J. Holbek (1973), *Innovations and Organizations*, New York: Wiley.

Accepted by Andrew Van de Ven; received May 31, 1994. This paper has been with the author for three revisions.

[22]

ELSEVIER

Research Policy 24 (1995) 1–12

research
policy

How learning by doing is done: problem identification in novel process equipment *

Eric von Hippel and Marcie J. Tyre

Massachusetts Institute of Technology, Alfred P. Sloan School of Management, 50 Memorial Drive, E52-556, Cambridge, MA 02139, USA

Final version received July 1993

Abstract

The unit cost of producing manufactured goods has been shown to decline significantly as more are produced. It has been argued that 'learning by doing' is at the root of this phenomenon, but the modes of learning actually involved have not been studied in detail. In this paper we attempt to provide a better understanding of the learning behaviors involved in learning by doing via a study of 27 problems that affected two novel process machines in their first years of use in production.

First, 'interference finding,' is described, a form of learning by doing that appears to be central to the discovery of the problems studied. Next, the reasons why the problems identified by templating were not discovered *prior* to field use – before 'doing' – are explored. Two causes are identified: an inability to identify existing problem-related information in the midst of complexity, and the introduction of new problem-related information by users and other problem solvers who learn by doing *after* field introduction of the machine. We find that problems due to information lost in complexity emerge earlier than do problems due to user learning by doing. Tests of reason are used to show why it would be very difficult to eliminate doing from learning by doing. Finally, other implications of the study findings are discussed.

1. Introduction

Beginning with Wright [28] a number of studies have shown that the unit cost of producing manufactured goods tends to decline significantly as more are produced. It has been argued that this effect is the result of the development of increasing skill in production attained by what

---

* We would like to express our gratitude to Anne Carter, Shmuel Ellis, Dietmar Harhoff, Stephan Schrader and Stefan Thomke for their very helpful comments on the ideas embodied in this paper.

Arrow [4] has termed 'learning by doing.' More recently, Rosenberg [20] has shown that similar gains can accrue to the end users of a product as their skill or understanding grows through 'learning by using.' (For example, after a given jet engine has been in use for a decade, the cost of maintenance may have declined to only 30% of the initial level as a result of learning by using [20, p. 131].)

Although the economic significance of learning by doing and using has been made clear, the *process* by which these gains are achieved is still quite unclear [1]. That is, we do not know the micro-level mechanisms by which learning by doing is actually done, nor do we know whether or why doing is essential to such learning. In this paper we explore these matters by means of an empirical study of a particular kind of doing, the identification and diagnosis of problems that affect novel process machines during factory use.

We begin (section 2) by discussing how learning by doing fits into the broader framework of problem solving. Next, we describe our study methods (section 3) and present our empirical findings (section 4). We then consider whether there is a substitute for learning by doing that does not involve doing (section 5). Finally, we discuss the implications of our findings (section 6).

2. Learning by doing as problem solving

Learning by doing is a form of problem solving that involves application of a production process in a use environment. In order to better understand this learning process, a brief digression into the general nature of problem solving will be useful.

Research into problem solving shows it to consist of trial and error, directed by some amount of insight as to the direction in which a solution might lie [6, pp. 43–47]. This finding is supported by empirical studies of problem solving in the specific arena of product and process development [3,15]. Such studies show trial and error (or, more precisely, trial, failure, learning, revision and re-trial) as a prominent feature.

Trial and error procedures guarantee a problem solution only in the instance of 'well-structured' problems, which are defined as those for which one can precisely *specify* a process of trial and error that will lead to a desired solution in a practical amount of time [18,19,21]. For example, a traveling salesman problem can be well structured, because one can precisely specify a generator of alternative solutions and a solution testing procedure that are guaranteed to eventually identify the best solution. However,

> In general, the problems presented to problem solvers by the world are best regarded as ill structured problems. They become well structured problems only in the process of being prepared for the problem solvers. It is not exaggerating much to say that there are no well structured problems, only ill structured problems that have been formalized for problem solvers... [21, p. 186]

Ill-structured problems may involve an unknown 'solution space' (a precisely specifiable domain(s) in which the solution is known to lie). They may also involve unknown or uncertain alternative solution pathways, inexact or unknown connections between means' and ends and/or other difficulties. Ill-structured problems are solved by a process of first generating one or more (typically several) alternative solutions. These may or may not be the best possible solutions, one has no way of knowing. These alternatives are then tested against a whole array of requirements and constraints [15,22, p. 149]. Test outcomes are used to revise and refine the solutions under development, and, generally, progress is made in this way towards an acceptable result.

In sum, learning by doing and learning by using almost always address ill-structured problems. We can therefore anticipate that the problem-solving process associated with such learning will have the general characteristics described for ill-structured problems, plus some more particular attributes associated with doing or using.

3. Study methods

Our empirical study explored learning by doing associated with the use of novel process machines in factory production processes. We elected to focus our study on the early field use of two types of process machine, a solder paste profiler and a component placer. These machines were developed to automate manual procedures previously used to attach surface-mounted integrated circuits to large, complex circuit boards. [1] Both machines were developed by a computer manufacturer for use in its own factories. Although carried out within a single firm, the development of each machine was an independent event. Each

E. von Hippel, M.J. Tyre / Research Policy 24 (1995) 1–12   3

was designed and built by different equipment development groups, and each was first applied in a different factory of the firm by different process engineers and plant-based users.

At the time of the study, both machine types had been installed in several factories. The first solder paste profiler had been placed into service 18 months before data collection began, and the first component placer 2 years before data collection began. As is often the case when novel machines are first introduced to the field, machine users had encountered a number of problems with the machine during this period of early use [11,14,24]. These field problems were the subject of our study of learning by doing.

The sample of field problems used as a study sample consisted of all machine problems that met the following three criteria: They had been observed after the machines had been introduced to the field; they were considered sufficiently serious to merit repair; they had been diagnosed

---

[1] A brief description of solder paste profiling and component placing machines: The board assembly process begins with the application of a tiny dab of 'solder paste', a form of solder which has the consistency of toothpaste at room temperature, to each location on a circuit board where an electrical connection must be made between the board and an attached component. (The spacing between dabs can be as small as 25 thousands of an inch today, and each dab may be as small as the period at the end of this sentence.) Next is inspection (or profiling) of the solder paste, this is where the first machine that we studied (the 'paste profiler') plays its role. The machine scans the board surface with a laser-based vision system and determines whether the location, amount and configuration of each dab of solder paste applied to the board is as specified. If all is correct, the board is then passed on to the next operation, where components are placed on the boards.

The next machine we studied was designed to automate the placement of complex components. It uses a vision system and a robot arm to pick up integrated circuits (which look like small plastic boxes with two or more rows of tiny metal legs protruding from the bottom) and place them on the circuit board at precisely the right locations, with each metal leg of each component resting exactly on one of the dabs of solder paste previously applied to the board. When this step is completed, the board is passed through an oven that heats the solder paste and converts it into liquid solder. When the board cools, the solder hardens into solid metal and the 'placed' components have been permanently soldered onto the board.

as to cause (although not always fixed) at the time of the study. Problems meeting these criteria were identified by contacting both the engineers involved in using each type of machine in the factories where it had been installed, and contacting the engineers involved in designing the novel equipment. We asked each for an exhaustive list of all 'significant' problems observed after factory use of each machine began that had subsequently been diagnosed. (Note that under this procedure factory machine users determine both what constitutes a problem and what constitutes a solution. Thus, a problem can entail a machine failure to perform as designed, *or* significant user dissatisfaction with a machine that is functioning as intended by its designers.) A total of 27 problems were identified by this method, 12 affecting the profiler and 15 affecting the component placer.

Our analysis of patterns in learning by doing was based on a grounded research approach [8]. Data for our analyses were collected through interviews with both the users of each machine (the process engineers at the factories where they were installed) and developers (key people in the process equipment development teams). Most interviewees had been with the projects studied from their inception to the present. Initial interviews were conducted on-site where respondents could refer to contemporary logbooks and could demonstrate the problems they described on the actual equipment. Interviews lasted from three to six hours, including plant tours. Respondents were interviewed both separately and, to the extent possible, together. Follow-up questions were discussed in additional face-to-face meetings, and by telephone and electronic mail.

4. Findings: how learning by doing is done

In the course of our empirical study of learning by doing we explored three matters: (1) the link between factory use of a machine and the discovery of problems with machine functioning; (2) the nature of the problem-related information that was uncovered as a result of machine use; (3) the time at which different types of problems

4   E. von Hippel, M.J. Tyre / Research Policy 24 (1995) 1–12

were discovered. We report on each finding in turn.

4.1. Templating the process of problem discovery

A central form of doing in the factory is the use of process machinery in the course of production. We were interested in determining whether the problems in our sample were *first* discovered in the course of such 'doing', or whether some of these matters had been identified (but not fixed) at an earlier stage. We did this by asking the developers of the machines we studied to separate the sample of field problems we had collected into two categories: (1) problems the developers had first become aware of as a result of field use of the machines; (2) problems that they had known about prior to field introduction, but had not yet fixed due to constraints such as a lack of time. As can be seen in Table 1, 22 (81%) of the problems we studied were first identified in the course of field use. The distribution of our sample with respect to this matter shows no significant difference between the two machines studied ($p < 0.27$, Fisher exact test).

Thus, doing did appear to be closely associated with problem identification in the field. The 22 problems first identified during factory use were invariably first observed by factory personnel, who would report to the machine developers something like: "The machine stops working (or fails

to perform as we want it to) under X conditions: Fix it!" Consider the following example drawn from our sample of cases.

Example: yellow circuit board problem

The component-placing machine uses a small vision system incorporating a TV camera to locate specific metalized patterns on the surface of each circuit board being processed. To function, the system must be able to 'see' these metalized patterns clearly against the background color of the board surface itself.

The vision system developed by the machine development group functioned properly in the lab when tested with sample boards from the user plant. However, when it was introduced into the factory, users found that it sometimes failed, and called this to the attention of the machine developers. The development engineers came to the field to investigate, and found that the failures were occurring when boards that were light yellow in color were being processed.

The fact that boards being processed *were* sometimes light yellow was a surprise to lab personnel. While factory personnel knew that the boards they processed varied in color, they had not volunteered the information to the lab because they did not know that the designers would be interested. Early in the machine development process, factory personnel had simply provided samples of boards used in the factory to the lab.

Table 1
When were problems affecting the machines first recognized?

	No. of problems affecting		
	profiler	placer	total
(1) *After* machine was installed in field, as a result of use	9	13	22
– *Example*: After the component placing machine was installed in the field, users noticed that it was unable to pick up parts that had 'tilted' heat sinks on top. This problem was a surprise to developers. They had not known that such parts existed, and had not designed the machine to handle them.			
(2) *Before* machine was first installed in field	3	2	5
– *Example*: Specifications called for machine to handle all boards to be processed without needing extra setup. Developers couldn't find a way to do this during the development time frame; users and developers agreed that this problem would be resolved after machine introduction.			
Total	12	15	27

E. von Hippel, M.J. Tyre / Research Policy 24 (1995) 1–12   5

And, as it happened, these samples were green in color. On the basis of the samples, developers had then (implicitly) assumed that all boards processed in the field were green. It had not occurred to them to ask users, "How much variation in board color do you generally experience?" Thus, they had designed the vision system to work successfully with boards that were green.

The yellow board problem illustrates recognition of an unanticipated problem as a consequence of doing, operating a machine in its actual use environment. But *how* does field use aid in problem discovery? The question is especially interesting because, given the additional complexity of using equipment in an actual factory environment rather than in a lab, one might expect that the difficulty of problem discovery would increase, not decrease with field introduction. In examining the process of problem discovery, we found a form of learning we call 'templating', a variant of trial and error problem solving, was present in all 22 of our cases of problem discovery through field use.

Templating can be described as a form of pattern recognition. A pattern is essentially a set of features or characteristics that describes an object (or event, or stimulus). This bundle of features then may be used as a standard against which one may compare new objects. Thus, one may wish to focus on the *similarities* between patterns in a process called pattern matching. (Systems designed to recognize objects with known characteristics ranging from handwriting to military targets often use algorithms based on pattern matching.) Or, one may wish to use subtractive pattern matching to highlight the *differences* between two or more patterns. For example, astronomers may compare two star maps of the same area of sky taken at two different times in order to 'subtract' everything that is the same and highlight only what is changing, rapidly moving comets for example.

Templating is a form of pattern matching which is sensitive to the interferences among objects (such as a process machine and a plant environment) that may have very different features or functions. Alexander [2, p. 19] describes the

essence of templating when he discusses a means for characterizing the fit between form and context:

> It is common practice in engineering, if we wish to make a metal face perfectly smooth and level, to fit it against the surface of a standard steel block, which is level within finer limits than those we are aiming at, by inking the surface of this standard block and rubbing our metal face against the inked surface. If our metal face is not quite level, ink marks appear on it at those points which are higher than the rest. We grind away these high spots, and try to fit it against the block again. The face is level when it fits the block perfectly, so that there are no high spots which stand out any more.

The process of templating we observed in our sample of process machine problems is a more complex version of the process just described. Here, two very different and highly complex patterns, the new machine and the plant context, are brought in close juxtaposition during field use: 'doing.' As a result, previously unsuspected and often subtle interferences are discovered because they evoke an obvious symptom, poor machine performance. Thus, in the case of the yellow board problem described earlier, an obvious symptom (machine failure) led developers to discover that they had not properly adapted the machine to the color of circuit boards being processed in the plant.

In problem identification by doing, therefore, we find that the unique contribution of 'doing' to problem discovery in the field environment is precisely the *precipitation* of obvious symptoms. These are then traced via diagnosis [26] to previously unrecognized interferences between machine and use environment.

4.2. Information availability and unanticipated problems

We next focused on the 22 problems that were discovered as a result of field use, and attempted to understand *why* they had not been anticipated earlier. Since the causes of all of the problems in

6   *E. von Hippel, M.J. Tyre / Research Policy 24 (1995) 1–12*

our sample had been diagnosed, we were able to approach this task knowing both the initial symptom and the 'cause' of each problem. (Problems can be understood and solved at many levels. For example, if machine operators find they must make frequent machine adjustments and find this troublesome, one level of solution would involve making the adjustment process easier. A solution at a deeper level would involve reducing or eliminating the need for adjustment. In our analyses we focused on the level of diagnosis and solution actually selected and implemented by the problem solvers studied.) We drew on the diagnosis of each problem to identify the information that would have allowed engineers to resolve each prior to field use, if only that information had been incorporated into the machine as originally designed.

We found (Table 2) that the information associated with a problem fell into two major classes with respect to its potential availability to machine developers during the design process. In 15 cases, the information existed in the use environment prior to and during the period that the machines were being designed, and so was potentially available to the machine developers for use in problem avoidance. In the remaining seven cases, the information that proved problematic was only introduced into the use environment

after the machine had been designed and installed in the field.

To give the reader a better feeling for this distinction, and for the nature of the variability in information availability that we found, we will illustrate each of the four categories in Table 2 by means of a brief case example.

In cases tabulated under 1(a) in Table 2, the information needed to understand or predict problems did exist in the intended use environment during the development of the machine. Indeed, in each of the instances in this category, interviewees told us that the information could easily have been provided to the lab, had the developers thought to ask and/or had users thought to volunteer it. But, the relevance of the information was overlooked until it was made clear by templating during use of the machine in the field. The yellow circuit board case example presented earlier illustrates this category of problem.

In cases coded under 1(b) in Table 2, the information needed to understand or predict problems was actually present in the machine design [2] lab but, again, its relevance was not seen until made clear by field failure. This was often understandable: 'having all the information' did not mean that it was easy to predict the often subtle chain of cause and effect that eventually

Table 2
At the time the machine was designed, what was the availability of the information which could have been used to avoid an unanticipated field problem?

Availability of problem-related information	No. of problems affecting		
	profiler	placer	total
(1) Problem-related information *existed* in use environment when machine was designed, but:			
(a) was not known to machine designers	2	3	5
(b) was known but not used by designers	5	5	10
(2) Problem-related information was created *after* machine was introduced to field by problem solvers outside of the design lab who were:			
(a) users working directly with machine	1	4	5
(b) problem solvers working on other aspects of the production process	1	1	2
Total	9	13	22

E. von Hippel, M.J. Tyre / Research Policy 24 (1995) 1–12   7

resulted in an unanticipated field problem. Consider the following example.

Example: component slippage problem

Just before the component placing machine places components on a board, little dabs of solder-containing paste are applied to the board, one at each spot where an electrical connection is to be made between a component leg (a wire protruding from the base of the component) and the board. The machine designers knew about this, but chose to use adhesive tape instead of solder in their laboratory simulation of the use environment. (Use of solder would have required setting up the lab to comply with rules regarding the handling of hazardous materials, a costly matter.)

When the component placer was installed in the field, users noticed that components unexpectedly slipped sideways to an unacceptable degree when the robot arm was pressing them onto the board. Investigation showed that the mound-shaped dabs of solder paste were firm enough to push the component sideways if the legs touched down on their sides instead of directly on their tops. This effect did not occur in the lab because the lab had not used solder in its tests.

In the second category of Table 2, the information that might have allowed designers to anticipate and forestall a field problem was introduced to the use environment *after* field introduction of the machine by problem solvers who

were not machine developers. In most instances (category 2a) these problem solvers were machine users who, in the course of their field experience with the machine, decided that they wanted something different from the originally specified performance. In many of these cases users experimented with changes to the use environment and/or to the machine itself [27] in order to develop their suggested improvements. Consider the following example.

Example: location adjustment problem

Each time a new board design was processed by the component placing machine, operators had to tell the machine where to put each of the components to be placed on the new board. They did this by entering the X and Y coordinates of each part location in the machine's computer memory. In case these coordinates required later adjustment, operators and machine designers both assumed that the operators would re-enter new X and Y coordinates.

After the machine was installed in the plant, users discovered that they had to adjust X and Y coordinates very frequently. They also found that it was very cumbersome to do this by re-entering new coordinates. Instead, they learned to make the needed adjustments via an obscure 'move it over by X amount' command that was buried several layers down in a software menu on the machine's control panel. The problem that users then brought to the attention of machine designers was: The 'move it over by X amount command' is very hard to reach and use. Make a more convenient one!

In two instances (category 2b), the problem solvers who created field problems after the machine was introduced were not machine users, they were individuals working on other aspects of the printed circuit board production process. Consider the following example.

Example: solder mask problem

Some months after the solder paste profiling machine was introduced to the field, engineers working on the printed circuit board production process decided to slightly reduce the thickness

---

[2] Three of the cases coded under 1b deserve special mention. In these, unanticipated field problems were caused by the premature failure of machine parts due to design error (for example, an inappropriately small bearing was designed into the machine, and quickly failed). It seems to us reasonable to classify these under 'information known by lab but not used' because the problems could have been anticipated and avoided prior to field use by using only information available to the lab and, for example, subjecting the machine to longer life tests in the lab. (The intended field operating life of the machine was known to the lab.) *If* the attributes of the use situation causing the failure had *not* been known to the lab in cases of premature parts failure (e.g. "We didn't know that you were going to process such heavy parts"), we would have coded the cases under category 1a in Table 2.

8   E. von Hippel, M.J. Tyre / Research Policy 24 (1995) 1–12

of the plastic film (called a solder mask) which served as the topmost coating of the printed circuit boards being processed. This was done to solve a problem unrelated to the profiler, the engineers wanted to improve the uniformity with which solder flux was being applied to the board. However, as an unanticipated side effect, the profiling machine's measurements suddenly became unreliable.

When engineers responsible for the profiling machine investigated the sudden rash of failures, they eventually found that the thinner solder mask was the cause. The profiler was designed to identify the top surface of the board to be measured by reflecting a laser beam from that surface. Introduction of the thinner solder mask resulted in greater amounts of laser light passing *through* the film and reflecting off layers of metal located inside the circuit board. As a consequence, the machine sometimes judged these lower layers to represent the surface of the solder mask film, which in turn led to incorrect measurements.

In sum, then, we see from Table 2 that some information associated with field problems existed at the time the machine was developed, while in other cases the information was created after the introduction of the machine, usually as a result of user learning associated with using the machine in the field.

4.3. Time sequence in problems identified by learning by doing

Next, we explored whether there was a difference in the timing of problem discovery when information pre-exists problem introduction, versus when information was created as a result of users' experience with the machine. It seemed reasonable that users would discover problems caused by pre-existing conditions sooner than they would develop new needs or encounter new conditions of use. As Table 3 shows, we do see a significant tendency in this direction. Problems due to pre-existing conditions were generally identified more quickly (within one month of machine introduction) than were those created by user learning or other changes in field conditions (Fisher exact test $P < 0.02$).

The pattern that we show in Table 3 cannot be taken as an iron rule. After all, desirable improvements might sometimes be perceived very quickly, and/or the symptom of an existing interference between a machine and a use environment might not occur immediately when the machine (or product or service) is introduced. With respect to the latter, consider that the machine and/or the environment might not be configured in a way that would cause a problem associated with a pre-existing field condition to be immediately expressed. (For example, if a problem was associated with the 'annual report' section of a software package, the user might not see a related symptom until that section of the package was activated.) Also, the symptom of a problem may not be manifested immediately, as in the case of premature wear failures in a machine. (We had three such cases in our problem sample, and two of these took many months to emerge.) None the less, it is interesting to see that the pattern shown in Table 3 emerges so clearly in this study sample.

Table 3
How soon after machine was introduced to the field was the problem symptom noticed?

Availability of problem-related information	No. of months after machine installed that problem symptom first noticed				
	≤ 1	1–2	> 2	n.a.	total
(1) Problem-related information *existed* in use environment when machine was designed	11	1	3	0	15
(2) Problem-related information was created *after* machine was introduced to field by problem solvers outside of the design lab [a]	0	2	2	1	5 [a]

[a] The sample in Table 3 is the same as in Table 2 except that the two cases in Table 2's category 2b are excluded from category 2 in Table 3. The reason: In these cases, the creation of problem-related information was independent of the machine under study. (Inclusion of these cases would have strengthened rather than weakened the statistical finding reported here.)

E. von Hippel, M.J. Tyre / Research Policy 24 (1995) 1–12   9

5. Does learning require doing?

We have seen that problems are discovered in the course of doing as a result of templating. In order to understand the need for 'doing' in this process, we next apply tests of reason to explore whether it would be possible to obtain the same learning without actually using process machines in their intended field environments. Rosenberg [20, p. 122] and Habermeier [10, pp. 276–278] have argued that doing or using is required because the possible interactions between products and their use environments are sometimes too complex to be predicted. In what follows, we offer support for this idea and develop it further. We distinguish between situations in which problem-related information is available at the start of a machine (or product or service) design project, and situations in which the problem-related information is only introduced after the machine is in use.

5.1. Learning without doing in stable use environments

As noted above, in many cases the information needed to predict field problems exists during the design process. Even in these cases, however, engineers who wish to predict all potential field problems face a difficult task, for two reasons. First, the use environment and the machine that will interact with it contain a myriad of highly specific attributes that could potentially interact to cause field problems. Second, which items among these will actually be associated with problems are *contingent* on the solution path taken by the engineer designing the product. We can illustrate both of these matters via the yellow circuit board problem described earlier.

With respect to the first point, note that the property of the board at issue in the yellow board case was problematic in a very narrow and specific way. That is, the problem with the board was not that it had 'physical properties,' nor that it had a color. The problem was precisely that the boards were yellow, and a particular shade of yellow at that. Since a circuit board, indeed, most components, have many attributes in addition to

color (shape, size, weight, chemical composition, resonant frequency, dielectric constant, flexibility, and so on) it is likely that problem solvers seeking to avoid all field failures would have to analyze a very large (perhaps unfeasibly large) number of potentially problematic items and interactions to achieve this.

With respect to the second point, note that the problem caused by the yellow color of the board was *contingent* on the design solution to the component placing problem selected by the engineer, and this was only done during the development process. That is, the color of printed circuit boards in the user factory became relevant only when engineers, during the course of their development of the component placer, decided to use a vision system in the component-placing machine they were designing, and the fact that the boards were yellow only became relevant when the engineers chose a video camera and lighting that could not distinguish the metalized patterns on the board against a yellow background. Since engineers often change the alternatives they are developing during the course of their development work [3,15], the relevance of any particular item of information to potential field problems can also change frequently during the development process.

Of course, we do not intend to suggest by this litany of difficulties that one cannot anticipate and avoid a field failure when use environments are stable with respect to that problem's cause. It simply says that to do so can be complex and costly. Methods for reducing the likelihood of unanticipated field problems include simulating the use environment in the lab more completely: if the simulation is totally complete and accurate, one can cause all unanticipated failures to occur in the test lab instead of in the field. (This is the approach taken by airlines which seek to train pilots in simulators that are so accurate that simulator time is counted as the equivalent of actual flight time.). Also, one can use various analytical procedures such as 'fault trees' [12] which can help make the search for possible causes of failure more systematic. Further, one can hire very experienced engineers who have prior experience with failure modes on existing

10   *E. von Hippel, M.J. Tyre / Research Policy 24 (1995) 1–12*

products, and so are more likely to anticipate them when designing similar new products. One can also try to incorporate subsystems in one's design which have already been tested under field conditions. Also, one can try to make some of the subtasks in a design project well structured so as to reduce the possibility of unanticipated field failure in these. [3] And, one can lessen the likelihood of failure by making the solution more robust, less dependent on possible variations in the use environment and/or more redundant. (The practice of incorporating safety margins into the design of bridges and buildings is an example of the first approach; the design of fault-tolerant computers an example of the latter.)

Both the costs and the benefits of identifying potential field failure prior to use of a new product differ from project to project. Learning by doing is the default strategy, other approaches are simply attempts to anticipate and prevent problems that will otherwise make themselves known through templating. Thus, one can expect that designers will invest more or less heavily in the fault anticipation strategies just listed depending upon the costs and benefits that they expect. For example, one would expect designers of nuclear power plants to invest a lot in attempting to anticipate and avoid potential field failures, and they do [17].

5.2. Learning without doing in changing use environments

The problems coded in the second category of Table 2 were *created* by changes in machine uses

---

[3] Despite the restrictiveness of the criteria for well-structured problems, designers can often partition an overall design task in such a way as to create some well-structured subproblems. For example, Smith and Eppinger ([23], plus private discussion with the authors) studied a subproblem in the design of automobile brakes that seems to us so tightly constrained as to meet the criteria of a well-structured problem. The goal was that 'the brakes on car model A should not squeal when they are used under test conditions X'. To achieve this goal, it was permissible to manipulate only three well-understood variables, such as the composition of the brake lining material, in precisely specified ways.

or the use environment that occurred after the machine was installed in the field. These changes were carried out by users (category 2a) or others associated with the production process (category 2b) rather than by machine designers.

The possibility that the use environment might change is a very significant matter to the designer who is attempting to anticipate and resolve potential field problems without 'doing.' When, as in the cases discussed just above, the designer is the only problem solver active on a problem, he or she is in the same position as a scientist or engineer asking a question of 'nature.' These problem solvers know that the answer they seek may be complex and hard to puzzle out. But they also know that it is not being changed as they work due to the actions of other problems solvers. For example, engineers building the first supersonic plane did not know all they needed to know about the stresses the airplane would encounter in supersonic flight. But they knew that nature would remain stable as they learned more, and that the correct answer would not change half-way through the project. In contrast, a use environment populated by and/or affected by autonomous problem solvers offers no such assurance. Under such conditions the use environment and thus the nature of the desirable solution that the designer is seeking to provide may well change during or after completion of the design process.

When problems are created by autonomous problem solvers, designers are *very* unlikely to be able to generate the same information by other means, thus avoiding related field failures and requests for improvement. The autonomous problem solvers are both posing hard-to-anticipate problems, and are generating an unpredictable set of proposed alternative solutions. Some of these may well involve changes in the machine (or product or service) provided by a particular manufacturer.

Neither game theorists' models of cooperative games ([5] nor psychologists' models of 'mutual adaptation' [13, p. 248]) offer us much help in predicting the path or the outcomes of this type of multi-party problem solving. Although both developer and user are presumably motivated towards mutual adaptation (or, at least, the ma-

E. von Hippel, M.J. Tyre / Research Policy 24 (1995) 1–12   11

chine developers are motivated to adapt to their user-customers), the problems that machine users are framing and partially solving are, as noted earlier, ill structured. Therefore, as our section 2 discussion of ill-structured problems indicates, the problem solving path that will be taken by user problem solvers cannot be predicted by the designers with certainty.

6. Discussion

The approach we have taken to studying learning by doing involved conducting grounded research on multiple instances of a single type of learning by doing event, the identification of an unanticipated problem in a factory. We identified templating as a learning mechanism associated with this type of event. We also found that problems identified by learning by doing in our sample were associated with (1) information that existed in the use environment but was 'lost in complexity,' and (2) information that was newly introduced to the use environment.

We have observed templating only within a very specific context. None the less, it appears to be quite general, and may therefore be a useful way to describe the process of learning by doing and using [4] in a range of contexts. Templating may also prove to underlie a significant *proportion* of the gains associated with learning by doing. Thus, Mishina [16] analyzed the learning curves associated with the production of the B-17 airplane, and found that learning in production is more closely associated with changes to the production process than with the number of units produced over time. This finding is congruent with a central role for templating in learning by doing, because that mechanism applies specifically to adapting to novelty in the production process.

Our findings allow us to suggest a particular shape for a learning curve that will be induced by the introduction of a *particular* change into a use environment. Recall that we found that most pre-existing interferences between the new machines we studied and the use environment were flagged within one month of the machines' installation, while improvements derived from user machine-related learning followed later. If a significant proportion of the total problems flagged as worth working on were due to the identification and resolution of existing interferences, and if these were diligently diagnosed and solved – and they certainly would be if they caused grossly unacceptable performance – one would then find a relatively high rate of learning by doing immediately after the introduction of the novel element, that would drop to a lower level over time. A study by Tyre and Orlikowski [25] of the rate of adaptation of a particular process machine over time shows such a pattern. We propose that the type of micro-level understanding of learning by doing we have pursued in this paper can contribute to a better understanding of learning curves for entire production processes, since these learning curves are the aggregate of more micro-level changes.

Our discovery that some of the problems in our sample were caused by changes to the use environment introduced *after* introduction of the machine has an additional interesting implication for the innovation process. Stable problems with stable causes can eventually be gotten right, although, as we have seen, probably not without learning by doing. Dealing with this type of problem will involve viewing initial implementation as an extension of the innovation process [14]. For example, one might shift from product and service development methods that assume that one can specify a user need and use environment accurately at the start of a project to methods

---

[4] Rosenberg distinguished larning by doing and learning by using are distinguished by the context in which learning occurs ("...gains that are internal to the production process (doing) and gains that are generated as a result of subsequent use of that product (using)" [20, p. 122]) rather than by attributes of the learning process itself. On the face of it, we see no reason why the learning process will differ between these two contexts, and so suspect that our findings will apply to both.

12 *E. von Hippel, M.J. Tyre / Research Policy 24 (1995) 1–12*

such as rapid prototyping [5] that incorporate trial and error in the use environment into the development process.

But problems caused by changes in the use environment after introduction of the machine, primarily due to user learning by doing, will presumably continue to arise. This suggests that one can never get it right, and that innovation may best be seen as a continuous process, with particular product embodiments simply being arbitrary points along the way.

References

[1] Paul S. Adler and Kim B. Clark, Behind the Learning Curve: A Sketch of the Learning Process, *Management Science* 37 (3) (1991).

[2] Christopher Alexander, *Notes on the Synthesis of Form* (Harvard University Press, Cambridge, MA, 1964).

[3] Thomas J. Allen, Studies of the Problem-Solving Process in Engineering Design, *IEEE Transactions on Engineering Management* EM-13 (2) (1966) 72–83.

[4] Kenneth J. Arrow, The Economic Implications of Learning by Doing, *Review of Economic Studies* 29 (1962) 155–173.

[5] Robert Axelrod, *The Evolution of Cooperation* (Basic Books, New York, NY, 1984).

[6] Jonathan Baron, *Thinking and Deciding* (Cambridge University Press, New York, NY, 1988).

[7] Barry W. Boehm, Terence E. Gray, and Thomas Seewaldt, Prototyping Versus Specifying: A Multiproject Experiment, *IEEE Transactions on Software Engineering* SE-10 (3) (1984) 290–303.

[8] Barney G. Glaser and Anselm L. Strauss, *The Discovery of Grounded Theory: Strategies for Qualitative Research* (Aldine de Gruyter, Hawthorne NY,).

[9] Hassan Gomaa, The Impact of Rapid Prototyping on Specifying User Requirements, *ACM Sigsoft Software Engineering Notes* 8 (2) (1983) 17–28.

[10] K.F. Habermeier, Product Use and Product Improvement, *Research Policy* 19 (1990) 271–283.

[11] Robert L. Hayes and Kim B. Clark, Exploring the Sources of Productivity Differences at the Factory Level, in: K.B. Clark, R.L. Hayes and C. Lorenz (Editors), *The Uneasy Alliance* (HBS Press, Boston, MA, 1985) pp. 425–458.

[12] Ernest J. Henley and Hiromitsu Kumamoto, *Reliability Engineering and Risk Assessment* (Prentice Hall, Englewood Cliffs, NJ, 1981), chs 2, 3 and 7.

[13] Charles A. Lave and James G. March, *An Introduction to Models in the Social Sciences* (Harper and Row, New York, NY, 1975).

[14] Dorothy Leonard-Barton, Implementation as Mutual Adaptation of Technology and Organization, *Research Policy* 17 (1988) 251–265.

[15] David L. Marples, The Decisions of Engineering Design, *IRE Transactions on Engineering Management* (1961) 55–71.

[16] Kazuhiro Mishina, Learning by New Experiences, division of research working paper 92-084, Harvard Business School, Boston, MA, May 1992.

[17] Nuclear Regulatory Commission Report # 75/014, October 1975.

[18] Harry E. Pople, Jr. Heuristic Methods for Imposing Structure on Ill-Structured Problems: The Structuring of Medical Diagnostics, in: Peter Szolovits (Editor), *Artificial Intelligence in Medicine* (Westview Press, Boulder, CO, 1982) ch. 5.

[19] W.R. Reitman, *Cognition and Thought* (Wiley, New York, 1965).

[20] Nathan Rosenberg, *Inside the Black Box: Technology and Economics* (Cambridge University Press, New York, NY, 1982).

[21] H.A. Simon, The Structure of Ill Structured Problems, *Artificial Intelligence* 4 (1973) 181–201.

[22] Herbert A. Simon, *The Sciences of the Artificial*, 2nd edn (MIT Press, Cambridge, MA, 1981).

[23] Robert P. Smith and Steven D. Eppinger Identifying Controlling Features of Engineering Design Iteration, Sloan School of Management Working Paper # 3348-91-MS, December 1991.

[24] Marcie Tyre and Oscar Hauptman, Effectiveness of Organizational Response Mechanisms to Technological Change in the Production Process, *Organization Science* 3 (1992) 301–321.

[25] Marcie J. Tyre and Wanda Orlikowski, Windows of Opportunity: Temporal Patterns of Technological Adaptation, *Organization Science*, forthcoming.

[26] Marcie J. Tyre and Eric von Hippel, Locating Adaptive Learning: The Situated Nature of Adaptive Learning in Organizations, Sloan School of Management working paper #BPS 3568–93, May 1993.

[27] E. von Hippel, *The Sources of Innovation* (Oxford University Press, New York; 1988).

[28] T.P. Wright, Factors Affecting the Cost of Airplanes, *Journal of Aeronautical Science* 3 (February (1936) 122–128.

---

[5] Initially developed for use in software development, rapid prototyping is explicitly designed to shuttle repeatedly between manufacturer and user in order to better determine the 'real need' for a given software package. First, key functions of proposed software products are simulated (prototyped) and provided to users for trial. Users then experiment with these prototypes, and ask manufacturers for improvements based upon what they have learned. This back and forth process continues until users are satisfied. This approach has been found to be better at creating a good fit between need and solution than methods that rely upon the accuracy of an initial statement of need by users [7,9].

[23]

Journal of Management Studies 34:3 May 1997
0022-2380

SEEING ISN'T BELIEVING: UNDERSTANDING DIVERSITY IN THE TIMING OF STRATEGIC RESPONSE*

PAMELA S. BARR

Emory University

ANNE S. HUFF

Cranfield School of Business and University of Colorado

ABSTRACT

There is general consensus in the strategy literature that successful firms alter strategy to address changes in their environments and enact more favourable conditions. Studies of organizational change suggest that this adjustment is not always made in a timely manner. Different beliefs about cause and effect have been established as a plausible explanation for differential responses to environmental change. This exploratory study of six pharmaceutical firms suggests more specifically that multiple concepts associated with environmental changes must be directly linked to organizational performance before new strategies are initiated. The results emphasize the importance of stress as a precursor to strategic response and have implications for the way we conceptualize 'response' when referring to significant changes in strategy.

INTRODUCTION

One fundamental normative prescription is consistent throughout almost all of the strategy literature: firm strategists must continually monitor the environment and make strategic decisions that keep firm strengths aligned with new opportunities and threats in the environment (Andrews, 1987; Ginsberg, 1988; Miles and Snow, 1978; Mintzberg, 1978; Porter, 1980; Quinn, 1980; Hofer and Schendel, 1978). Research has demonstrated that firms changing strategy in response to changes in the environment outperform those that maintain current strategies in the face of new circumstances (Haveman, 1992; Smith and Grimm, 1987). Further, the evidence suggests that firms failing to adjust in a timely fashion may enter a downward spiral from which they do not escape (Cameron et_al., 1988; Hambrick and D'Aveni, 1988).

Despite the obvious benefits of adjusting strategy to meet the changing demands of the environment, a number of recent articles point out that it is often difficult or impossible for firms to change strategy (Miles and Snow, 1978;

Address for reprints: Pamela S. Barr, Goizueta Business School, Emory University, Atlanta, Georgia 30322, USA

Miller and Friesen, 1984; Oster, 1982; Schwenk and Tang, 1989; Tushman and Romanelli, 1985; Zajac and Shortell, 1989). For example, limitations on strategic change have been attributed to established commitments (Monteverde and Teece, 1982; Thompson, 1967), the existence of buffering organizational slack (Chakravarthy, 1982; Cyert and March, 1963), and the development of standard operating procedures (Hannan and Freeman, 1984). It is therefore not surprising to note that firms in profoundly changing environments and/or firms with significantly deteriorating performance vary significantly in the timing of their attempts to alter strategy (Ginsberg and Buchholtz, 1990; Haveman, 1992; Miles and Snow, 1978; Miles, 1982; Smith and Grimm, 1987).

The question that interests us is why some firms are able to overcome the forces of inertia more quickly than others, and we begin with the assumption that the timing of strategic adjustment is significantly affected by top managers' interpretation of the environment's impact on the firm. Researchers have proposed that environmental interpretation affects action through such precursors to action as problem definition (Lyles and Mitroff, 1980; Mintzberg et al., 1976) and strategic issue diagnosis (Dutton and Duncan, 1987; Dutton et al., 1983). Dutton and Duncan specifically suggest that '. . . a major reason organizations respond differently to changes in the environment involves how strategic issues are triggered and interpreted by decision makers' (p. 279). We follow this line of reasoning, and discover that perceived connections between the environment and the firm explain differences in the timing of strategic response.

The paper addresses three issues in sequence. First, it pulls together several theoretic arguments needed to address the timing issue. Second, it reviews the methodological issues that have to be addressed before the details of timing can be explored. It then presents empirical evidence of interpretive distinctions among six pharmaceutical companies that differed by up to five years in their response to new regulatory change.

THE LINK BETWEEN MANAGERIAL INTERPRETATION AND STRATEGIC CHANGE

The effect of interpretation on firm adaptation to changes in the environment has enjoyed increased empirical attention since Weick's (1979) statement that the environment is not an objective 'thing' to be known, but rather the product of interpretation and action. Interpretation has been found to affect the response of hospitals to a doctors' strike (Meyer, 1982), the revision of basic philosophical and theological principles by a religious order (Bartunek, 1984), university reaction to a drop in the number of available 18 year olds (Milliken, 1990), the passage of new patient care regulations by mental hospitals (Scheid-Cook, 1992), and response to crisis in the Finnish banking industry (Myllys, 1994).

These five studies share certain similarities. Each looks at firm response to a significant event in the environment, an event that was expected to affect the strategic behaviour of all firms in the sample. Despite the similarity of the organizations studied, however, the response of each to the external changes varied significantly (with the exception of Bartunek's study of a single organization). Each author concludes that variability in the content or certainty of strategic response could be attributed to variations in interpretation about the environment.

SEEING ISN'T BELIEVING 339

These interesting studies also raise issues that are problematic for relating interpretation and change. First, the studies vary in their explicit recognition of the cognitive processes involved in interpreting new events. Second, each (with the exception of Myllys, 1994) does not *explicitly* address level of analysis issues that are automatically raised when one applies an individual level concept, such as interpretation, to organization level behaviour. Third, they do not adequately account for why some organizations are more quickly impressed by environmental change than others. Further understanding requires that these issues be brought together in the same theoretic account. In the following discussion, we address each of these issues individually and then bring them together in a single model of interpretation and strategic change that we then use to guide our empirical study.

Schematic Frameworks as the Basis for Interpreting the Environment

The processes of noticing and interpreting stimuli have been linked by cognitive scientists to schemas the individual has already formulated (Fiske and Taylor, 1991; Neisser, 1967). 'Schemas' and other related concepts (frames, mental models) identify the simplified and abstracted representations individuals use to make sense of and act within their environments (Gioia and Sims, 1986; Kelly, 1955; Minsky, 1975; Rumelhart, 1980; Walsh, 1995; Weick and Bougon, 1986). A schema is a set of interrelated, largely unquestioned assumptions that highlights certain characteristics of new stimuli and establishes the grounds for categorizing them as similar to or different from those encountered before (Fiske and Taylor, 1991). Nisbett and Ross (1980), for example, found that when questioned, individuals will recall elements of a stimulus that are most salient in their mental models, while ignoring other characteristics that are not central to that general frame. Researchers interested in organizational contexts also suggest that individuals pay greater attention to occurrences that support their existing assumptions (Hedberg et al., 1976) and then act to confirm these beliefs (Kiessler and Sproull, 1982). Stimuli that can't be placed within existing frameworks may generate new schema, but this is a time-consuming and uncertain process. Starbuck and Milliken (1988) note that the belief systems held by managers regarding what is important in the environment are more likely to push information that might indicate the need for new schemata to the background of attention where they are unlikely to be acted upon.

The basic concept of schema has been very useful to researchers concerned with the complex, confusing and ambiguous settings that characterize most organizations (Allison, 1971; March and Simon, 1958). Schematic frameworks have been proposed as critical simplifying and sensemaking mechanisms that allow the individual to make sense of stimuli-rich contexts and act within them (Daft and Weick, 1984; Kiesler and Sproull, 1982). The proposition that managers hold schematic frameworks related to their firms has been empirically illustrated by several authors. Extensive work by Colin Eden and colleagues (e.g. Eden et al., 1979, 1983), for example, uses cognitive mapping techniques to uncover schematic frameworks of several different organizational concepts held by managers at different organizations. Importantly, this work highlights the fact that interpretations or beliefs about the environment are highly subjective and often idiosyncratic. It is these idiosyncrasies, or differences in schematic frameworks that we suggest accounts for much of the diversity in timing of response to significant environmental changes. Before such a proposal can be investigated, however, it is necessary to move this individual-based concept to the level of the organization.

Beyond the Individual: Shared Schematic Frameworks as the Basis for Co-ordinated Activity
Researchers interested in linking firm response to the environment to cognitive processes typically treat 'the firm' as if it were a unitary actor noticing changes in its situation, and thus draw directly upon the kind of cognitive arguments just cited. This practical simplification is problematic, of course, because cognition is an attribute of individuals. One way out of the conundrum is to consider the absolute necessity of *common* schematic frameworks for achieving co-ordinated action. Several interesting lines of inquiry outside of the management field emphasize the necessity of shared belief and interpretation as the basis for social behaviour. These streams of research also suggest how commonalities that support collective activity come about. For example, an interest in the source of scientific discovery led Kuhn (1970) to define scientific communities on the basis of a shared paradigmatic framework. This work emphasizes the importance of shared understanding for defining the most important scientific work to be pursued. Kuhn points to professional training, established procedures, compelling experiments, and formal and informal interaction among scientists as the means of establishing and solidifying common assumptions.

An analogous line of reasoning in political science investigates the development of 'epistemic communities' (Haas, 1992). This work is driven by an interest in understanding how new policies (e.g. monetary reform or environmental protection) are developed by government agencies. Peter Haas suggests that such groups have:

(1) a shared set of normative and principled beliefs, that provide a value-based rationale for the social action of community members;
(2) shared causal beliefs, that are derived from their analysis of practices leading or contributing to a central set of problems in their domain and which then serve as the basis for elucidating the multiple linkages between possible policy actions and desired outcomes;
(3) shared notions of validity – that is, intersubjective, internally defined criteria for weighing and validating knowledge in the domain of their expertise; and
(4) a common policy enterprise – that is, a set of common practices associated with a set of problems to which their professional competence is directed, presumably out of the conviction that human welfare will be enhanced as a consequence. (Haas, 1992, p. 3)

These and other works are convincing testimony for the necessity of shared understanding to accomplish co-ordinated social tasks. The possibility of co-ordination is what leads to social organization in the first place (Barnard, 1938) and there are strong philosophical arguments that extensive commonalities are necessary for *any* kind of social exchange (Gilbert, 1989; Kelly, 1955). The consequence for the organization is that 'organizational cognition cannot be seen as an individualised act, but rather as an "inseparable aspect" (Lave and Wenger, 1991) of the continual, local negotiation and re-negotiation of meanings between actors' (Wood, 1996, p. 1). Thus, organization cognition is a reciprocal concept, in which the individual's interpretation is shaped by the organization and other social contexts, but that cognition is simultaneously creating context (Weick, 1979). There is room for individual differences, but patterns emerge from the whole (Allard Poesi, 1994; Ehlinger, 1994; Fiol, 1994; Stjernberg and Ullstad, 1994).

The underlying assumption of this paper is that organizations, and especially the top management team of organizations, must be 'epistemic communities' of some strength in order to be viable economic units. While individuals continue to have unique beliefs and interpretations, they share many beliefs and understanding with others (Bougon et al., 1977; Hodgkinson and Johnson, 1994). To the extent that beliefs are shared by key actors, the resulting shared schematic frameworks simplify a complex world and provide the basis for co-ordinated activity. Similar structures have been labelled 'shared understanding' (March, 1991), 'cognitive consensuality' (Gioia and Sims, 1986), 'dominant logic' (Prahalad and Bettis, 1986), or shared 'strategic frames' (Huff, 1982) within the organization.

In sum, the cognitive psychology literature suggests that the processes of noticing and interpreting stimuli are directed by cognitive structures called schema. We extend this concept to the organizational level by recognizing the necessity of some level of shared understanding to conduct co-ordinated activity. We term these shared belief systems 'shared schematic frameworks'. In the following section we address the issue of why some firms appear to be more quickly impressed by environmental change by introducing the concepts of stress and inertia.

Stress Opposing Inertia as the Explanation for Timing Differences
Anomalous stimuli that capture attention but cannot easily be interpreted or responded to in terms of past experience are stressful. At the individual level, new life experiences (marriage, job change, divorce, etc.) have long been recognized as stimuli (Holmes and Rahe, 1967) that are likely to call into question the validity or usefulness of past schema. The range of positive and/or negative emotion attached to such events raises their salience and helps trigger new understanding. On the other hand, schematic frameworks are remarkably resilient. Experiments by Ross and his associates (Anderson et al., 1980; Ross et al., 1975), for example, show that people can persist in explanations even when shown that the evidence they relied on to form those explanations is false.

We believe such accounts of individual cognitive processes are consistent with theoretical assessments of stress and inertia at the organization level (Bigelow, 1982; Ginsberg, 1988; Huff et al., 1992; Olivia et al., 1988; Tushman and Romanelli, 1985). Recent work has emphasized the many factors that help maintain organization activity in the face of environmental change. The general argument is that many impediments to change are a result of deliberate attempts to establish relationships and develop structures and routines that institutionalize beneficial ways of acting (Nelson and Winter, 1982; Selznick, 1957). The more successful these past adaptations have been, the less likely significant departure from current ways of acting becomes (Dimaggio and Powell, 1983; Ginsberg and Buchholtz, 1990; Powell and Dimaggio, 1991). In addition to affecting organizational activities, these organizational and institutional forces of inertia are likely to affect the processes of noticing and interpretation (Meyer, 1982; Milliken, 1990). For example, external institutional norms may blind managers to the need to change by emphasizing conformity to a certain set of accepted interpretations, and structural configurations (Hannan and Freeman, 1984) can exacerbate lack of managerial attention by limiting and biasing available information (Starbuck and Milliken, 1988).

In addition to inertial forces developed to maintain status quo, there exist forces for change that serve as organizational corollaries to individual-based concepts of stress. As discussed above, individual stress results from stimuli that cannot easily be addressed with past schema and behaviours. At an organization level, stress follows from stimuli that is interpreted as challenging the appropriateness of current actions and procedures. For example, new circumstances (innovation, government actions, competitive moves, changing leadership, etc.) weaken the 'fit' between an organization and its environment and thus set the stage for calling current structures and routines into question (Andrews, 1987). While stress can arise from direct performance downturns (an indicator that current structures/routines are inappropriate), anticipated circumstances or new achievements by competitors can also be perceived as stressful. These examples of likely stressful events are taken from the strategy literature as examples of stimuli likely to result in a questioning of the appropriateness of current activities, structures and routines. It is important to emphasize, however, that stress is an interpretive construct; any given event or situation may be interpreted in some organizations as stressful, and either overlooked or noticed but not perceived as stressful in others. It is this difference in interpretation that is the focus of attention in our empirical study, and that we propose is at least partially responsible for diversity in the timing of response to environmental change.

In relatively straightforward models, strategic change becomes more and more probable as the stress level (pressure for change) resulting from various stimuli exceeds the current level of inertia (pressure to maintain the status quo) (Huff et al., 1992; Olivia et al., 1988). Of course, both individuals and firms demonstrate the homeostatic capacity to adjust; that is, they are able to mediate stressful events by making changes compatible with existing commitments and schematic frameworks. At this level of inertia, this capacity not only becomes a part of existing procedures, it 'trains' individual managers to be more flexible and adaptive in their interpretations. Adaptive capabilities thus can reduce the impact of many stressful events, but they do not address the firm's vulnerability to events that fall outside of previous experience. Over time, the stress associated with noticed events that cannot be adequately responded to with current activities and procedures exceeds the ability to adjust and significant change is required.

To this point in the paper we have discussed several issues related to taking an interpretation-based view to the timing of strategic change. In the following section, we combine the concepts of shared schematic frameworks and stress and inertia into a single model of strategic change.

A Model of Strategic Change

Figure 1 provides a general model for understanding the timing of strategic change that incorporates work on stress and inertia with ideas of schema-based interpretive processes. Organizations are assumed to have various formal and informal mechanisms in place to scan their environments. These mechanisms are more or less sensitive to bits of information that might be used to reconsider firm wellbeing. Failure to notice potentially anomalous stimuli results in continued routine scanning. Even if an anomaly producing event is given attention, it must be interpreted or given meaning (Daft and Weick, 1984). Any given event is likely to be imbued with many types of meaning. Of particular relevance to the idea of stress/inertia and strategic change is interpretation of the likely impact (if any) of the event on the firm. Such an interpretation may result in one of two basic outcomes. First, the stimuli may collectively be interpreted as not having a significant impact on the firm. In this case current routines/procedures are not questioned and, thus, the event is not considered stressful. The level of organizational stress is not increased and scanning continues, although future events (or input from other scanning mechanisms) may result in a reinterpretation at a later time.

When an event is interpreted as having an impact on the firm, the pressure to make some change in activity will increase. At this point, a second determination

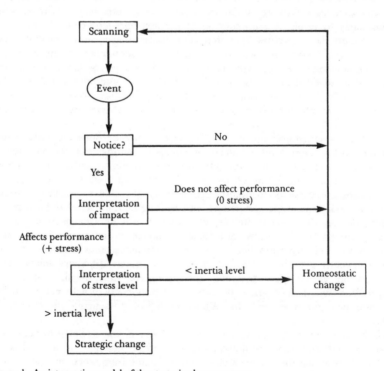

Figure 1. An interpretive model of the strategic change process

must be made: Is the pressure to change (level of stress) greater than the pressure to maintain the status quo (level of inertia)? If stress is less than inertia, it is probable that discomfort will be addressed through homeostatic adjustments in current strategy. However, as stress exceeds inertia, strategic change is more and more likely to occur.

We used this model as an organizing device in designing an empirical study of timing issues. Linking interpretation to action required solving a number of methodological issues, which will be discussed before returning to the model and our analysis.

STUDY DESIGN

To assess the relative capacity of firms as 'epistemic communities' to recognize and respond to stimuli potentially indicating a need for a change, we needed to identify a relatively homogeneous set of firms and isolate a strong, unconfounded change in the competitive arena shared by these firms. Data had to be available from the time period in which the event took place, and similar data had to be available for all companies studied. Further, the firms had to be homogeneous enough to be expected to be similarly affected by the environmental change. In addition to these questions of study definition, we needed to establish methods for separately identifying strategic actions and the shared schematic framework or 'strategic frame' that might be expected to direct these activities.

The challenges of identifying environmental changes with relatively homo-geneous effects are typically solved by looking at key events in the relatively small number of industries dominated by single business firms (Meyer, 1982; Scheid-Cook, 1992; Smith and Grimm, 1987). We followed this tradition by choosing to study the US pharmaceutical industry. A long period of sustained growth and profitability after the Second World War is evidence of a relatively stress free environment. On the other hand, it is a regulated industry and we were particularly drawn to the 1962 amendments to the Food, Drug and Cosmetic Act of 1938 as an interesting example of significant environmental change.

The Exogenous Shock of 1962 Regulatory Change
The 1962 amendments to the Food and Drug Act were preceded by years of government hearings and the introduction of several proposed regulatory changes in both the House and Senate. The powerful Pharmaceutical Manufac-turers Association was able to influence the content of these amendments and many observers felt they might even defeat the congressional proposals being made in the early 1960s. However, the unexpected Thalidomide disaster in Europe and Canada came to light in early 1962 and public concern about birth defects caused by prescription sleeping pills (and by extension negative side-effects of other prescription drugs) added new dimensions to the bill being considered in Congress, considerably strengthening the provisions the drug companies had anticipated, and hastened the bill's approval.

The bill contained many provisions, but its major impact was to add several new phases to the drug approval process. The time the Food and Drug Administration (FDA) had to approve a new drug was doubled, with automatic extensions granted to the FDA if the deadline was not met. The FDA was also given the power to withdraw without notice approval from existing drugs if they were found to be unsafe, lacked 'substantial' evidence of effectiveness (evidence of effectiveness was a new requirement in itself), or contained misstated applications. The 17-year legislated life of a drug patent begins at the time the patent is awarded. To protect prospective new drugs from competition, patents commonly are applied for at the time of discovery and prior to testing. The new, more stringent testing requirements resulting from the amendments thus increased the time and expense associated with introducing a new drug and decreased the time available for profiting from patent protection. In fact, the time elapsing from FDA processing time from submission of a New Drug Application to approval increased from 17 months in 1962 to 44 months by 1969 (Temin, 1980), significantly reducing the effective life of the patent.

Several subsequent trends in the industry have been attributed to these changes in the environment. First, there was a significant decline in the number of new drugs introduced in the United States. Between 1950 and 1961, 564 new chemical entities (NCEs), the basis of the FDA approval and patent protection process, were introduced. In the next eight years only 159 went through the system. While a portion of this decrease is due to a 'knowledge plateau', comparative studies of new drug introductions in the USA and UK suggest the amendments also contributed significantly to the decline in new drug introductions (Grabowski et al., 1978; Wardell, 1971).

Second, US pharmaceutical manufacturers became increasingly active overseas. Foreign sales as a percent of total for all US manufacturers increased steadily during the 1960s (Temin, 1980), and US firms increased their investments in overseas activities. For example, the percentage of NCEs first studied and tested in the USA by US firms decreased from 100 per cent at the time the amendments were enacted, to less than 80 per cent by 1970, and 50 per cent by 1974 (Lasagna and Wardell, 1975).

A third major trend in the industry following enactment of the 1962 amendments was growth through diversification. Most of this activity occurred through acquisitions, both inside and outside the pharmaceutical industry. Of particular significance, US pharmaceutical companies diversified into non-prescription medicines, consumer products such as cosmetics and sundries, and medical equipment and diagnostic aids. Cool (1985) attributes these moves to the pharmaceutical companies' ability to transfer technical knowledge and take advantage of established distribution channels, as well as the hefty profit margins and growth rates available in these markets.

To summarize, the 1962 changes in FDA regulation are seen by analysts as leading to significant changes in the industry, including significant increase in the time and expense associated with bringing a new product to market and a shorter effective patent life. These changes in the environment were reflected in strategic change across the industry, including an increase in overseas expansion and diversification into related businesses. Our questions were: (1) Could we identify significant changes in the *timing* of such responses to the 1962 legislation? (2) Could these changes be explained in terms of the theoretic ideas summarized in figure 1?

Sample Selection

Selection of a homogeneous sample for the study was based on four criteria. First, since the stimulus event was significant change in US regulation, we decided candidate firms had to be US-owned, with over 50 per cent of their business conducted in the USA at the start of the study period. Second, all firms in the sample had to have significant commitment (which we defined as over 50 per cent of US sales) to pharmaceutical manufacturing in 1962. Third, all sample firms were required to have at least ten years of history in the pharmaceutical industry prior to the beginning of the study period, to assure the formation of relatively well-developed schemata, which at the organizational level we call 'strategic frames', prior to the change in legislation. Sample firms were also required to be financially healthy at the time of the regulatory change, to avoid confounding changes in strategic frames due to regulatory change with responses to other performance concerns. Our criterion was that changes in profitability do not differ significantly from the experience of the industry as a whole; it was not necessary to be more specific, since financial performance in the study period was not a discounting factor for any of the firms considered. Finally, sufficient financial and textual data had to be available for analysis.

Due to the extensive coding requirements of the cause mapping methodology described below, which we use to identify the strategic frames of each firm over a minimum of seven years, the sample size had to be restricted to a relatively small number of firms. For that reason, the sample was drawn from Forbes' 1962 list of the top ten US pharmaceutical companies. Of those ten, six manufacturers met the four criteria and thus make up the final study sample. These firms are: Abbott Laboratories (Abbott), Merck and Company (Merck), Parke, Davis and Company (Parke-Davis), Smith Kline and French (SKF), Charles Pfizer (Pfizer), and Schering. Once the sample was identified, the next steps were to identify the points in time in which significant changes in strategic action occurred in each firm during the period of interest and to identify the strategic frames of each firm for each year during the same time period. We then used the outcomes of both processes to categorize firms as fast or slow responders and to link the content of strategic frames to the timing of strategic change.

Points of Change in Strategic Action

Two preliminary analyses were required before the core questions of the study could be addressed. The first involved identifying the timing of strategic change in each sample firm. Following the definition of strategy proposed by Mintzberg and Waters (1982), change in strategy was defined as a significant break in the pattern of resource allocations made by the firm. Four variables associated with industry trends following the 1962 amendments were selected as important indicators of potential strategic change that could be tied to the effects of the amendments: percentage of foreign assets to total assets, research and development (R&D) expenditures as a percentage of sales, selling expense as a percentage of sales, and liquid to total assets.[1] Percentage of foreign assets to total assets was assumed to reflect directly strategic orientation toward geographic expansion. R&D as a percentage of sales was used as an indication of commitment to the development of new ethical pharmaceuticals: an increase in this measure is a likely indicator of increased investment due to the new testing requirements, a more diversified focus might be reflected in a decline in R&D as a percentage of total sales. Selling expense as a percentage of sales is also a measure of product emphasis; the marketing of pharmaceuticals required sales visits to physicians that were typically more expensive than marketing over-the-counter remedies or other consumer products. Lastly, liquid to total assets reflects significant changes in capital expenditure. Historically, pharmaceutical manufacturers had been fiscally conservative, funding capital expansion through internal funds. Shifts in this measure following 1962 are primarily attributed by industry observers to the significant increase in diversification via acquisition.

Data were collected from published financial reports of each firm from the period 1950 to 1970 – 20 years surrounding the change in regulation chosen for study. Breakpoints indicating change in strategy along key dimensions were identified through the use of cluster analysis, a procedure frequently used by strategy researchers to identify strategic change (Hambrick, 1984; Harrigan, 1985; Smith and Grimm, 1987). Firms were analysed individually using Ward's method of cluster analysis. This clustering method was considered the most appropriate of the several that might have been used (SAS Institute Inc., 1990) because it offers a straightforward translation of the idea of patterns in resource allocation. Ward's method clusters data by minimizing variance within clusters and maximizing variance across clusters. The algorithm involved initially separates the four measures for each year; it then joins clusters beginning with those that explain the least variance by existing separately. The procedure continues until all cases are joined in a single cluster. The researcher must decide when the programme begins to join clusters with inappropriately high variance, using the semipartial R^2 of each clustering iteration as an initial indicator of the appropriate clustering solution (number of clusters) (Hartigan, 1976). A review of the output indicated that a semipartial R^2 of greater than .1 represented a significant loss of explained variance in the next iteration of the programme. The final determination of the number of clusters was made much easier because of the easy interpretability of the clusters themselves (Evritt, 1980). No restrictions were placed on the algorithm to force sequential clusters. With one exception, however, when the procedure was terminated the breakpoints between clusters allowed them to be placed in longitudinal sequence, which suggests that the selected variables do capture cohesive strategic decisions made over time.

The one exception involved Parke-Davis. For this company, a significant drop in sales, coinciding with an increase in asset expenditures, led to a significant dip in liquid assets as a percentage of total from 1960 to 1963. This dip caused the clustering algorithm to identify the 1957–59 cluster as being much more similar to the 1964–69 cluster than to the 1960–63 cluster. Analysis of the remaining three variables suggested, however, that it was reasonable to maintain the three breakpoints involved, and thus the ultimate decision was that significant changes in strategy occurred in 1957, 1960 and 1964.

Table I summarizes the breaks identified in the pattern of each firm's strategic decisions, along with the descriptive statistics used to guide our decisions. As shown, the 1962 regulatory change coincided with the third or fourth strategic change made by the sample firms during the 1952–70 study period. Based on the starred dates, we initially identified Merck and Parke-Davis as the fastest

348   PAMELA S. BARR AND ANNE S. HUFF

Table I. Initial categorization of firm responsiveness based on cluster analysis

Firm	1st strategy	2nd strategy	3rd strategy	4th strategy
Merck	1952–57 (.582)[b]	1958–63 (.115)	1964*–70	
Parke-Davis[a]	1952–56 (.413)	1957–59 (.210)	1960–63 (.101)	1964*–69
SKF	1952–56 (.540)	1957–64 (.207)	1965*–70	
Pfizer	1952–56 (.442)	1957–60 (.211)	1961–64 (.121)	1965*–70
Schering	1952–54 (.251)	1955–58 (.373)	1959–65 (.146)	1966*–70
Abbott	1952–56 (.231)	1957–60 (.439)	1961–66 (.129)	1967*–70

Notes:
[a] Parke-Davis was purchased by Warner-Lambert in 1970, and so the last cluster terminates in 1969.
[b] Numbers in brackets are the semi-partial R^2s. This is the loss in explained variance that occurs if the cluster is combined with the cluster to the right.

responders to legislative changes in 1962, with new strategic actions initiated in 1964. SKF and Pfizer, firms that show evidence of significant strategic change in 1965, were identified as midgroup responders. Schering and Abbott, with changes in 1966 and 1967 respectively, were identified as the slowest two firms to respond.

Identifying Strategic Frames
The second stage of preliminary analysis involved identifying the strategic frames used by the top management team of each firm. This task posed its own methodological challenges. Questionnaires can be used to ask about environmental and strategic changes (e.g. Milliken, 1990; Smith and Grimm, 1987), but the very act of asking an individual to reflect on an issue may cause his or her *a priori* interpretations to be re-evaluated, a problem that becomes more acute as the events of interest fall out of active memory (Golden, 1992). Real-time interviews avoid the retrospective nature of questionnaires, but also suffer from intervention effects. In fact, face-to-face contact heightens the distorting human tendency to impress the observer (Eden et al., 1993). Ethnographic approaches to the study of changing interpretations provide a less obtrusive method of study (Bartunek, 1984; Meyer, 1982; Scheid-Cook, 1992), though impression management cannot be discounted. In addition, these studies are even more time-consuming than interviews and rely more heavily on subjective interpretations by the researcher.

We were attracted to studying a stressful event that occurred over thirty years ago because the impact of the focal event and possible confounding effects were easier to identify after the passage of time. None of the four methods just described are very practical in this circumstance, however, and thus we were drawn to a fourth methodological alternative, content analysis of documents written during the period of interest. Documents are a real-time, non-intrusive indicator of the interpretations of top managers that are especially attractive when, as in this case, other data sources (interviews, questionnaires, direct observations, etc.) are not available. The basic assumption is that the subjects that decision makers discuss in communications such as letters to shareholders reflect concerns of importance to the speaker. This assumption dates back to the first recorded use of content analysis, an investigation of the heretical content of new hymns in eighteenth-century Sweden (Woodrum, 1984).

Annual reports are the most obvious documentary data source for longitudinal studies, since they are produced by many companies at the same time of the year and they are readily available. In addition, we believe that annual reports and other public documents are an important forum in which strategic frames are articulated. They both reflect and help create needed commonalities in the interpretation of events. Further, they have been used in past research to assess and explain corporate strategies (Bowman, 1984; Fahey and Narayanan, 1989; Fiol, 1989; Lant et al., 1992), to identify key arenas of competition (Birnbaum-More and Weiss, 1990) and to explore causal reasoning within firms (Bettman and Weitz, 1983; Clapham and Schwenk, 1991).

To expand the data set available from annual reports, we also tried to locate public speeches made by representatives of the study firms in our study period. None of the six firms was able to provide transcripts of speeches from the time period studied.[2] There were, however, a total of 19 speeches from this time period published in the *Wall Street Transcripts*, a publication that provides a full record of many executive speeches to securities analysts and similar audiences. At least two speeches were available for each of the six firms in the sample, with the exception of Schering, for which we found only one.

The exact authorship of both letters to shareholders and speeches is open to question, but when a shared strategic frame is the unit of analysis, ambiguity about authorship of such documents is not particularly problematic. The notion of epistemic community discussed earlier, and increased emphasis on the fact that the leadership of larger organizations is dispersed among many individuals (Hambrick and Mason, 1984), make it plausible to use such documents as an indicator of shared understanding.

Annual reports and speeches to analysts are more problematic because they are persuasive documents and subject to deliberate distortion; but persuasion and distortion accompany all possible data sources. We have noted already that biased recall and impression management can have contaminating effects on data drawn from questionnaires, interviews and participant observations. Even accounting data and financial information can be slanted to present the firm in the best possible light. While we recognize that annual reports and speeches are explicitly persuasive, we echo Giere's (1988) argument that unrealistic theoretic statements in science are constrained by a broad body of 'common observation'. Securities analysts, institutional investors, the business press and the Securities and Exchange Commission all constrain errors of commission and omission. Salancik and Meindl (1984) present evidence that firms are rewarded for being truthful in these circumstances. The bottom line is that we chose to study a set of documents that are not the ideal indicator of shared belief, but no ideal data source exists.

Despite their limitations, these documents provided a very interesting source of data for study. Even before beginning detailed coding, initial analysis of statements made in the documents for Pfizer, Abbott and Parke-Davis provided insights that required a change in the original categorization of faster versus slower responders. (That is, we found we had an error rate of 50 per cent using a method commonly used in strategy research to identify strategic change.) Beginning with the general premise that topics covered in the letters to share-holders and speech transcripts reflect issues of importance to top managers, we looked for statements concerning the legislation and related events (hearings, introductions of earlier versions of the legislation, etc.) in the documents of each firm. Letters and speeches for Pfizer and Abbott during 1959–61 contained several statements concerning senate investigations of the industry and the intro-duction of the Kefauver bill in early 1961.[3] Pfizer letters and speeches following the 1962 change in legislation make no mention of it. Abbott continued to mention the legislation but only as a side issue; statements concerning the potential change in legislation during the 1959–61 time period were much more frequent and substantial than statements made after 1961. In short, the 1965 change in action for Pfizer and 1967 change for Abbott appear not to be directly related to the new legislation that provided the stimulus event for this study. Content analysis indicates that both firms made a *proactive* response to initial legislative moves rather than wait for the actual enactment of the legisla-tion in 1962. This conclusion was corroborated by a systematic study of business press and industry articles about each firm during this same time period. Both companies therefore were recategorized as faster responders.

A review of the content of Parke-Davis documents was even more interesting. The data reveal *no* references to regulatory issues over the entire study period. This company's statements were focused on relative lack of R&D productivity and declining sales of Chloromycetin, their primary product. Complete lack of attention to legislative events, combined with numerous statements made regarding R&D, suggest that their 1964 change in strategy was not strongly motivated by the legislative change that interested us as a stressful event. This firm was therefore excluded from comparative assessment of response to stressful legislation. Of course, Parke-Davis did compete in an environment almost all other observers felt was significantly restricted by new legislation. This environ-ment presumably had an impact on the outcome, if not the formulation, of their strategy. It is well to remember, however, that even 'major' changes in the envir-onment do not have a homogeneous effect on all firms.

Given the cross-check of quantitative measures of change in allocation of strategic resources with qualitative content pertaining to government actions, our final classification is shown in table II. Pfizer and Abbott are identified as fast responders to new regulation with 1961 changes in strategic action anticipating 1962 legislation. Merck, SKF and Schering are classified as slower responders with changes in action occurring in 1964, 1965 and 1966, respectively. Parke-Davis must be analysed separately and is addressed in the discussion section of this paper.

EMPIRICAL EVIDENCE OF THE INTERPRETIVE PRECURSORS TO STRATEGIC CHANGE

Once it was clear that there were significant differences in the timing of response to 1962 regulatory changes among pharmaceutical firms, we wanted to determine if these responses could be explained in terms of the theoretic ideas

Table II. Re-assignment of firms based on content analysis

Response time	Name of firm	Years	Description
Faster response	Pfizer	1957–60	Internal product line expansion. Internal foreign expansion
		1961–64	Diversification via acquisition. Foreign expansion via acquisition
	Abbott	1957–60	Internal product line expansion. Internal foreign expansion
		1961–66	Product line expansion via acquisition. Diversification via acquisition. Continued foreign expansion
Slower response	Merck	1958–63	Internal product line expansion. Limited foreign expansion
		1964–70	Diversification via acquisition. Limited foreign expansion
	SKF	1957–64	Internal product line expansion
		1965–70	Foreign expansion. Diversification via acquisition
	Schering	1959–65	Internal foreign expansion. Internal product line expansion
		1966–70	Product line expansion via acquisition. Diversification via acquisition. Foreign expansion via joint-venture acquisition
Non-response	Parke-Davis		

summarized in figure 1. The figure suggested three points at which the interpretive processes of faster responding firms might be significantly different from slower firms. Faster firms might: (1) more rapidly notice changes in the environment; (2) more quickly interpret changes as significant; or (3) more quickly determine that the stress associated with the new event merited action. Differences at even one of these points might explain differences in the timing of strategic action; alternatively, faster firms might be distinguished from slower firms by multiple indicators of difference. To address these issues we looked more closely at statements made in annual reports and the *Wall Street Transcripts*.

Causal Mapping Methodology
Of the several procedures available to systematically content analyse written documents (Huff, 1990), we chose to focus on causal reasoning under the assumption that firms typically initiate strategic actions based on the shared belief that they will cause desirable changes; many other organization researchers have made the same assumption (e.g. Allard Poesi, 1994; Barr et al., 1992; Bougon et al., 1977; Eden, 1993; Ehlinger, 1994; Jenkins, 1994; Laukkanen, 1994; Markoczy and Goldberg, 1995; Narayanan and Fahey, 1990; Salancik and Meindl, 1984; Shrivastava and Lin, 1984). The method of 'cause mapping' we

Table III. Coding categories

Symbol	Definition
/+/	Positively affects
/−/	Negatively affects
/⊖/	Will not hurt, does not prevent, is not harmful to
/⊕/	Will not help, does not promote, is of no benefit to
/a/	May or may not be related to, affects indeterminably
/m/	Affects in some non-zero way
/0/	Does not matter for, has no affect on, has no relation
/=/	Is an equivalent to, is defined as*
/e/	Is an example of, is one member of*

Note:
*Categories not used by Axelrod.

used was initially developed by Axelrod (1976) and elaborated by Huff et al. (1990). The process is time-consuming, but the resulting maps provide a parsimonious synthesis of a great deal of material.

The procedure requires that all statements of relationship in the document analysed be identified by the coder. The nature of the relationship is placed into one of the nine categories identified in table III. After all relational statements have been identified, the linked concepts are examined. Those judged to be equivalent are given the same code. A cause map is then constructed by connecting coded concepts with arrows and labelling the arrows with the appropriate symbol for the type of relationship. As a simple example; the sentence 'Substantial construction was undertaken in 1961 for the manufacture of new products as well as increased capacity to meet rising demands for established ones', would be coded as follows:

Substantial construction   + [ability to] manufacture new products
undertaken in 1961 (1.a)   (1.b)

Substantial construction   + [ability to] meet rising demand for
undertaken in 1961 (1.a)   established products (1.c)

and then represented in graphical form as shown below:

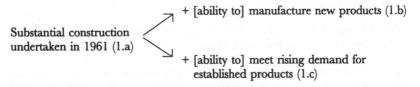

Substantial construction
undertaken in 1961 (1.a)

+ [ability to] manufacture new products (1.b)

+ [ability to] meet rising demand for
established products (1.c)

The coding manual also makes provisions for linkages that are not directly stated, but are implied by context. These coder decisions are distinguished on the map by use of a dotted, rather than a solid arrow. In addition, sometimes the ultimate effect of a chain of reasoning is implied rather than explicit. The coding procedure therefore allows the coder to specify a positive or negative impact on the 'utility' of some actor or entity. All inferences, even linking words such as those in the above example, are indicated by brackets, which signify a departure from the source material.

The documents utilized for coding in this study were the 42 letters to share-holders (LTS) from the annual reports for each firm from 1960 to 1966 (one year prior to the earliest response among the firms and one year after the latest response) and transcripts of the eight speeches recorded in the *Wall Street Transcript* (*WST*) (out of 19) that included references to government legislation. Letters to shareholders averaged two 8.5" × 11" typed pages of text while the *WST*s averaged six 8.5" × 11" typed pages. In total, approximately 132 pages of text were coded. Comparisons of maps from both data sources show consistency in causal assertions for all six firms studied, a consistency in causal reasoning also found by Axelrod (1976) and his associates. Material from the *WST* speeches was therefore added to LTS of the same year.

Document coding was performed by two independent research assistants unaware of the research questions. Each coder was trained separately in the coding process by the first author. Two *WST* speeches from sample firms were coded by both coders to ascertain intercoder reliability. These texts were among the longest and most complicated documents to be coded, consisting of 122 total statements. Based on Robinson's (1957) measure of agreement, which is also used by Axelrod (1976), intercoder agreement on the number of codable asser-tions was 82 per cent. This is a reasonable degree of reliability, though not outstanding; the differences between coders, however, were primarily due to two sentences with particularly subtle causal assertions. Had the coders agreed on these two statements, reliability would have been 89 per cent, well within the range of acceptability. Agreement on which part of the statement contained the causal concept was 98 per cent. Identification of the part of the statement containing the effect was 97 per cent. Agreement as to the sign of the causal relationship was 88 per cent, with most differences involving subtle signs such as 'no effect on' and 'no negative effect on'.

Once training was satisfactorily established, the remaining documents were divided between the coders, who completed all coding independently. In analysing the results we were guided by the three questions drawn from figure 1: (1) Do firms that quickly take action more rapidly identify changes in their environments? (2) Do they more quickly interpret unfamiliar stimuli as important?, and/or (3) do they more rapidly identify stressful consequences of new stimuli?

Finding 1: Faster firms could not be distinguished from other firms in our data set by their attention to legislation change.

The most straightforward link between the interpretation of an event and new strategic action is direct stimulus–response. That is, the most basic hypothesis relevant to our interest in the length of time it takes firms to respond to environ-ment change would be that the strategic frame used by faster responding firms will contain references to a precipitating environmental event prior to slower responding firms. Figure 1 proposes, however, that the simple process of noticing significant changes in the environment is not in and of itself a sufficient trigger for adaptive changes in strategy.

In analysing the maps in the data set, any and all concepts dealing with proposed or actual legislation were identified, regardless of how they were connected to other concepts. Because the faster responders changed in 1961, both the 1960 and 1961 maps for all sample firms were analysed. The maps of both early and late responders make references to the proposed legislation as early as 1960. Only Parke-Davis, as noted above, failed to attend to either the pending legislation or to its enactment.

Finding 2: A necessary condition for strategic actions in our sample is that firms perceive their welfare is directly affected by environmental change.

As indicated in table II, the faster firms (Pfizer and Abbott) actually responded in 1961, prior to the 1962 change in legislation. Therefore, the 1961 cause maps of each firm are examined. These maps show that the proposed change in legislation is directly linked to concepts affecting firm performance and well-being in the faster responding firms. In analysing the maps, strength of association was determined by the type of linkage (a direct, stated association, versus an indirect, implied association), the strength of the linkage code (e.g. $+$ and $-$ versus $\ominus$ and $\oplus$) and the number of linkages between the concepts surrounding the new legislation and concepts about performance and well-being (the greater the number of linkages, the stronger the association).

The 1961 cause map of Pfizer (excerpted in figure 2) can be used to illustrate the type of associations displayed. The bill itself (concept 47e) has a total of nine linkages to Pfizer utility (1b) and Pfizer's growth (2g). In addition to the seven direct linkages to Pfizer utility (47m.1–47m.3; 47n.1–47n.4), the bill is seen as an example of government actions which, in turn, are causing both problems and opportunities for the firm, of which Pfizer is 'aware' (47h and 47j) and is 'preparing for' (47i and 47k). These preparations are seen as having a direct and positive effect on Pfizer's growth (a performance measure). Abbott's maps reflect similar causal associations between the proposed legislation and firm performance. In this company's 1961 map, the proposed legislation is directly linked to firm utility and to R&D, a concept that is in turn linked directly and strongly to measures of firm performance.

The 1961 maps of the three slower responding firms do not exhibit this type of association. The cause map of Schering does not contain any concepts related to the legislation. Merck's map contains concepts related to the senate subcommittee investigation of the pharmaceutical industry that preceded the introduction of the legislation, but not to the legislation itself. While this map does demonstrate an understanding of the implications of the investigation, the implications are all linked to *industry* utility. There is no connection between the investigation and concepts related to firm specific performance. Finally, SKF's map also contains legislation concepts but, like Merck, this understanding is not related to firm-specific performance or well-being.

We then looked at the 1962 maps of the slower responding firms. If significant connections between legislation concepts and measures of firm performance existed as soon as the bill was adopted, the assertion that a distinguishing charac-

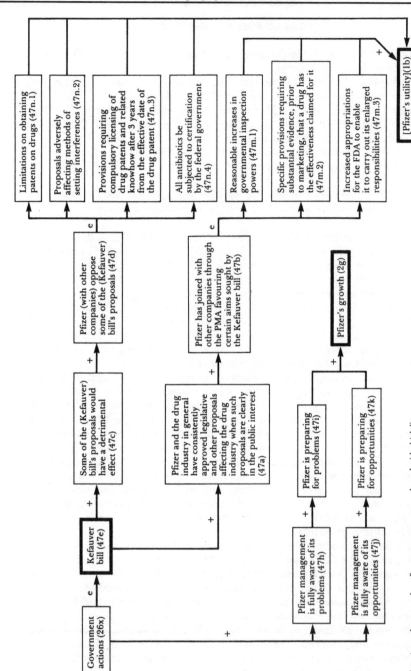

Note: Amendment and performance concepts are boxed with thick lines.

Figure 2. Portion of Pfizer 1961 cause map

teristic of rapidly responding firms is a strategic frame with strong and direct links between the 1962 legislation and measures of firm performance would be undermined. However, once again firms that were slower to respond did not relate aspects of change in their environment to concepts concerning organization performance or well-being, even after the stressful event had taken place. The relevant portion of the 1962 map of SKF (figure 3) illustrates this finding. In this map SKF is 'prepared to speak out against any such legislation' (25o) that it equates with being 'unnecessary or restrictive...' (25q), but these concepts are not connected in any way to firm utility or measures of performance. The event (25k) is also expected to have some effect (m) on the industry (25l) and the cost of doing business (24f.1) yet it is not expected to increase ($\oplus$) alarm over SKF profitability (25n.2) or growth (25n.1). Schering's interpretation of the new amendments is also unrelated to firm performance or utility. In 1961 this firm did not address impending legislation; by 1962 concepts related to the new amendments are seen as having a negative association with industry utility, but they are not interpreted as directly affecting the firm itself.

The 1962 map of Merck differs somewhat from the two just described. In Merck's 1962 map (figure 4), legislation is weakly linked to firm performance or well-being at two points. First, the legislation 'if properly administered' (18a.1) is

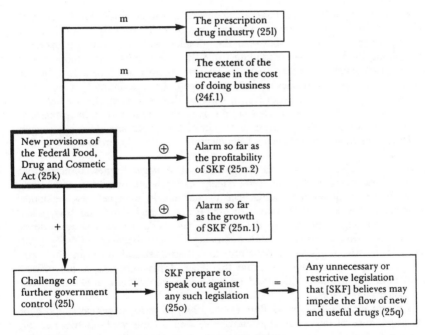

Note: Amendment and performance concepts are boxed with thick lines.

Figure 3. Portion of SKF 1962 cause map

SEEING ISN'T BELIEVING   357

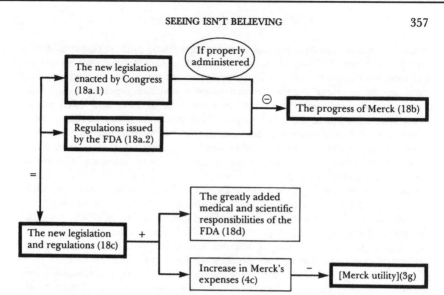

Note: Amendment and performance concepts are boxed with thick lines.

Figure 4. Portion of Merck 1962 cause map

weakly linked by a 'does not have a negative affect on' code (⊖) to 'the progress of Merck' (18b), an implied performance indicator. This weak causal link is a more peripheral connection between the stimulus event and firm performance than found in the rapidly responding firms. It is also weak when compared to the stronger linkages other concepts have to performance measures in the complete map. A second relevant link comes from the expectation that legislation will increase company expenses (4c), a concept that is in turn directly linked to firm utility (3g). However, given that the regulation itself is not interpreted as significantly affecting the progress of the firm, this single link does not suggest that the legislation is interpreted as significantly affecting this measure of performance.

In sum, the maps, taken as an indictor of strategic frames, indicate that attention was being paid to the 1962 change in legislation by all five responding firms. However, slower responding firms do not initially interpret new regulation as affecting *firm* level performance or well-being in any significant way, while firms responding more quickly do interpret those changes as having a direct impact on firm performance and well-being. To use Milliken's (1987, 1990) term, there was no 'state uncertainty' for pharmaceutical firms in the early 1960s. It appears from the data that the slower firms were well aware of new legislation, but did not understand or believe its implications until much later than their competitors.

A recent empirical study by Barr et al. (1992) provides empirical support for the importance of this additional interpretive step. In this study of two railroad companies facing increasing competition, it was found that both companies quickly noticed changes in the transportation industry in the period following World War II. However, only the firm that survived into the 1970s linked changing conditions to a need to change their own strategy. The second firm noticed and discussed changes in the environment, but failed to interpret them as requiring action. This company delayed changing its strategy, suffered financial decline and eventually went bankrupt. Taken together, it appears reasonable to conclude that it is interpretation rather than noticing that plays the most important role in triggering strategic adaptation; noticing appears to be a necessary but not sufficient precursor to change. Firms must not only recognize a new event in the environment, they must understand its connection to their own activities. In fact, our data suggests that even more connections must be made before action is likely.

Finding 3: Firms do not act until they identify multiple effects of environmental change *and* these effects are supported by other indicators of the need for strategic change.

The third focus of attention in this study is the amount of stress created by an external event before strategic change occurs. Two scenarios are suggested by research on the causes of continuing inertia. First it may be that a single perceived consequence of an external event is not sufficient to significantly change performance expectations for the firm. At the individual level it has been argued that actors are not completely open to developing new ideas for action because so much of the individual's identity and activity are based on current understandings (Anderson et al., 1980; Ross et al., 1975). The general consensus is that there must be significant modification in understanding before adjustments in activity are made. Analogous reasoning at the organization level suggests that a change in the environment may have to be interpreted as having *many* significant connections to concepts of firm performance and/or well-being.

Our data support the idea, formalized in figure 1, that attention to multiple direct effects of the environment must precede strategic change. To investigate this idea, the maps from the three years up to and including the year of change in strategic action were examined for each of the five responding firms. The 1962 legislation was considered to have multiple direct effects if there was more than one direct linkage to concepts about firm performance or well-being. All five firms exhibited such linkages. Once again the 1961 map of Pfizer (figure 2) is illustrative. The Kefauver bill (47e) contains proposals that Pfizer opposes (47d) as well as some that Pfizer supports (47b). Leading from these concepts are seven aspects of the bill that are interpreted as having strong direct effects on Pfizer's utility (1b).

The remaining maps provide less dramatic support for the idea that identifying multiple impacts will precede strategic change. Table IV lists each firm and the number of linkages between legislative concepts and firm performance and well-being in each year analysed. As shown, Abbott's change in strategy in 1961 is accompanied by two links between legislation and the firm. SKF and Merck each establishes two links the year before new actions take place. Schering makes two such connections in 1964, but does not change strategy until 1966.

A second scenario about the type of stress that must precede strategic change involves the linkage between a stressful event and other events that are also perceived to have an impact on performance. If one event is perceived to have relatively few direct connections to firm performance, it may have to be seen in

SEEING ISN'T BELIEVING 359

Table IV. Number of linkages between legislative concepts and measures of performance and well-being

	1960	*1961*	*1962*	*1963*	*1964*	*1965*	*1966*
Merck			0	2	0		
SKF				0	2	0	
Pfizer	0	7					
Schering					2	0	0
Abbott	0	2					

association with other events that also impact performance measures before strategic change occurs. In examining this idea, the maps for the three years up to and including the year of change in strategic action were again analysed. *All concepts with a strong, direct link to measures of firm performance or well-being were traced back to their concept of origin and these concepts were examined for connections to the new legislation.*

The overall results of this analysis are that *multiple maps exhibit the presence of more than one triggering event before a change in strategic action.* This is a finding that strongly supports the idea that stress must accumulate before strategic change occurs (Huff et al., 1992). The 1964 map of SKF (figure 5) illustrates the kind of reasoning involved. The map shows three event interpreted by firm management as impacting SKF utility (1g). First, as discussed earlier, the 1962 amendments (25k) affect utility through a decline in new medicines (26i) brought on by increased paperwork (26h.2) and approval times (26k). A second, related event is the withdrawal, by the FDA, of SKF's drug Parnate (28i). This is related to the new regulations by a common relationship to the FDA because all paperwork for drug approval is submitted to the FDA. Also related to the FDA and SKF utility is 'new regulations of the Department of Health, Education, and Welfare' (25o), which increase the administrative problems 'now harassing the FDA and the industry' (29a). In short, as the firm changes its strategy, three different events, all related to FDA activities, are interpreted as having strong negative links to the utility of the firm.

As a summary of the other data supporting this finding, table V lists each sample firm and the related events found in the maps immediately prior to that firm's change in strategic action. All concepts were related through some form of government institution or action. It must be noted that it was not until 1965, one year after the change in strategy we identified through examining the pattern of resource allocation, that Merck's maps indicate concern with any other issues. However, the maps do reveal that those issues are connected to a long-standing concern over 'continuing government intervention' in the industry that may indicate some unstated concern with these other events prior to 1965.

DISCUSSION

The purpose of this study was to use the ideas of strategic frames and stress and inertia to explore the temporal relationship between firm level interpretation of

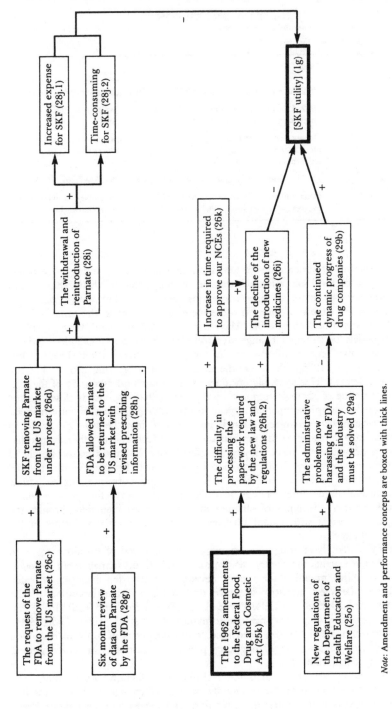

Note: Amendment and performance concepts are boxed with thick lines.

Figure 5. Portion of SKF 1964 cause map

Table V. Related events by firm

Firm	Events
Merck	1962 Amendment, Medicare 1965, 'other far-reaching legislation' 1965
SKF	1962 Amendment, withdrawal of Parnate (major product) by the government 1964, changes in HEW regulations 1964
Pfizer	Delany Food Additives Amendment 1958, Government contracts with foreign firm for tetracycline (a Pfizer patented product) 1960, 1961 proposed amendment (Kefauver bill)
Schering	1962 Amendment, overseas regulatory changes 1964, Medicare, 1965
Abbott	Delany Food Additives Amendment 1958, Proposed change in taxation of overseas earnings 1961, 1961 proposed amendment (Kefauver bill)

an important environmental event and significant changes in strategy. We began by referring to the basic tenet of strategic management that firms should alter their strategies to adapt to new conditions, but noted that there exists wide variation in the timing of such an adjustment across firms in the same industry (Ginsberg and Buchholtz, 1990; Haveman, 1992; Smith and Grimm, 1987). Many models of strategic change and problem formulation include a trigger which sets the process of change in motion (Ginsberg, 1988; Lyles, 1981; Mintzberg et al., 1976). However, the nature of the triggering process has not been well defined. This study significantly expands our understanding of the triggering or timing of strategic response by suggesting that response is closely linked to changes in interpretation that appear in the strategic frames of the organization. How a newly recognized event is incorporated into the strategic frame, in particular how it relates to the performance of the firm and to other events that impact performance, is more closely associated with variations in the timing of strategic response across firms than noticing the event. In other words, the old strategic frames, which are unlikely to hold concepts corresponding to a new environmental event, must change in quite specific ways before new action is initiated. Further, the types of changes in interpretation identified through the maps are consistent with extant theories of stress and inertia as factors in the timing of change.

Several studies have sought to investigate the potential of cognitive maps to both provide insights for theory development and to aid management practice. Use of cognitive mapping for theory development has, for example, revealed correlations between industry structure and managers' understanding of the environment (Calori et al., 1994; Porac et al., 1989; Reger and Huff, 1993) and between cognitive maps and firm performance (Barr et al., 1992; Hall, 1984). Mapping techniques have also been used to aid managers in problem resolution and strategic planning by highlighting previously unstated, or unrecognized, beliefs (e.g. Eden, 1990, 1993).

In this study, we utilize mapping techniques to identify organization level beliefs (strategic frames) and then identify patterns of change in these maps that reflect changes in noticing and interpretation. Our results reveal a temporal relationship between these patterns of change in maps and changes in strategic action, and thus represent an important step forward in our understanding of the link between interpretation and action.

The changes in strategic frames associated with the timing of strategic change identified in this study are directly consistent with stress and inertia theories of change which suggest that inertial forces that build in firms over time work to prevent second order change until they are surpassed by higher levels of stress (Ginsberg, 1988; Huff et al., 1992). The data indicate that stress may follow from either or both of two types of strategic frame characteristics. First, the interpreted strength of the impacts of the event on the firm appears to be moderately important to the timing of response. The maps of all of the five responding firms exhibited multiple links between amendment concepts and firm performance prior to strategic change, suggesting that the event was interpreted as having a very strong impact on the firm. Further, while the maps of faster responding firms did not exhibit stronger links between the event and firm performance than slower responding firms, they did exhibit multiple links prior to the slower firms. This suggests that strength of impact, represented in this study by the number of perceived impacts on the firm, is an important trigger to change.

Another observation related to stress involves the effect of multiple events. The five firms in our sample related the change in legislation to several other events, all of which exhibited direct links to firm performance or well-being prior to changing strategy. The immediate implication of these results is that these multiple linkages reflect increased levels of stress that are likely to surpass existing levels of inertia and trigger change. Because change did not occur until after these links appeared in the maps, it adds to the argument that stress is a necessary component to the triggering of change.

A broader implication of these results is that strategy researchers must look more closely at what we mean by the term 'response'. First, we found a very large discrepancy between quantitative and qualitative indicators of strategic change. Second, more detailed analysis of the maps suggested that strategic actions which might easily be attributed to widely recognized changes in the industry were not necessarily made in response to legislation alone. Rather, change in strategy can be linked to the effects of numerous, related events. For example, early responders undertook a change in strategy prior to actual enactment of the 1962 version of the bill. It was the introduction of an earlier version of the bill that, combined with the perceived impacts of other *prior* government events, increased the pressure for change beyond the level of inertia. Late responders, whose maps indicated no prior concern regarding government actions prior to the change in legislation, did not change strategy until the occurrence of additional governmental actions which were linked, in the maps, to firm performance.

The 'non-response' of Parke-Davis also highlights the importance of related events and trends to organizational response. As noted earlier, the maps of Parke-Davis suggest that their 1964 change in strategy was not strongly motivated by legislative change. Rather, concepts related to performance and well-being during the time were concerned with R&D, a lack of new product development (NPD), and declining sales of their primary product. Parke-Davis' R&D efforts had not resulted in a significant new product since the late 1950s.

SEEING ISN'T BELIEVING   363

Further, 43 per cent of sales in 1960 was from a single product, Chloromycetin, which was due to come off patent in 1966, and was already suffering declines in sales overseas where patent protection was less strictly enforced. Certainly the lack of NPD could have been exacerbated by the change in legislation. However, because the 'event' of a lack of NPD began prior to 1962, the effect from the legislation was, perhaps, made less salient. In fact, the 1964 change in strategy undertaken by this firm, an increase in diversification, is not accompanied by changes in map concepts related to the external environment. This suggests that the change in strategy was less a response to a change in the external environment than it was a response to trends in the internal environment – the continued lack of NPD coupled with the impending loss of patent protection on, and declining sales of, their primary product. While Parke-Davis may not have 'responded' to the change in legislation, it is interesting that its maps are consistent with the theory of interpretation and change suggested by the maps of the other five firms. Before strategic change, three concepts (R&D, NPD and patents) in the maps are strongly and directly linked to Parke-Davis' performance and well-being. Further, concepts related to both R&D and concerns about Chloromycetin can be traced back to lack of NPD; differential issues with a common root.

In general, the results of analysis of the maps from all firms suggest that actions undertaken following a significant event in the environment are not just a response to that event. Rather, strategic change responds to a perceived *trend* in the environment, in this case increased governmental action in the external environment or a lack of NPD in the internal environment, that impacts firm performance. Although beyond the scope of this study, action may also reflect the constellation of external stakeholders who are making their own interpretation of these events. The experience of early responders may also play a role, though this influence is not explicit in the data set we used. These complexities are consistent not only with stress/inertia theories of strategic change, but also with other theories which suggest significant changes in strategy are undertaken in response to shifts in the environment in general, while response to specific events is limited to activities of a more tactical nature (Meyer, 1982).

Several questions are raised by this study that serve as directions for continued research on the link between strategic frames and strategic response. First, why the strategic frames of some firms quickly associated environmental change with performance concepts while others did not is unclear from our analysis. We purposely selected an event for study that was specifically designed to impact the manner in which *all* members of the industry operated. Thus, one would expect a greater consistency across firms in their realization that this event would impact their firm than, perhaps, would be expected in response to less overarching events, such as moves made by competitors (Porac et al., 1989). It may be that some organizations, because of their history, the prior experiences of top management, or the information processing capacity of the top management team (Thompson and McDaniel, 1990) have more complex strategic frames with more linkages to performance issues. This complexity should increase the likelihood that a major event will be conceptually linked to performance and well-being. It may also be that frequent, though minor, changes in strategic behaviour enhance the complexity of strategic frames and make it more likely that new stimuli can be interpreted in terms of strategic action (Hedberg et al., 1976).

A second question raised by the study is related to the type of data we used to construct the maps. Clearly, the firms in our sample differ in the way in which they interpret the new legislation, especially the aspects of the legislation that are highlighted as onerous, or stressful. But it also is interesting to step back, and consider these differences in light of the data sources used. Since the source documents are speeches and annual reports designed to communicate with multiple audiences, diversity in response may also reflect this diversity in audience, or firm stakeholders. In other words, our finding that multiple indicators of pressure on the firm precedes action could be as much an effort to persuade multiple stakeholders of the need for change (or respond to multiple demands for change) as it is an indication of internal sensemaking alone. The observations are beyond the scope of the study, but well worth further investigation. Complicated conditions of sensemaking only add to our interest in the problem of timing, and underscore the potential significance of the patterns we found.

Finally, another interesting sensemaking complication lies in the observation that the slower responding firms may be learning from the faster responding firms. Because only the largest firms in the industry were selected for study, all the firms had the resources to wait and observe the experiences of others prior to forming their own strategies. Such an explanation for timing differences is consistent with the notion of industry recipes and industry influences proposed by Spender (1989) and Huff (1982), but it is not inconsistent with the premise that interpretation impacts the timing of response. It is certainly possible, in fact likely, that the 'borrowed experiences' (Huff, 1982) of faster responding firms might aid managers of the slower firms in forming their own interpretations, though there is no explicit reference to such influences in the data sources we used. Mimetic behaviour is of interest to institution theorists (e.g. DiMaggio and Powell, 1983), but we also need further enquiry into the conditions that encourage some firms to relate environmental change to their welfare without such examples.

CONCLUSION

Establishing the links between interpretation and action is frequently called for (Walsh, 1995) but only recently tackled by research on managerial and organization cognition. Previous research has suggested that the *type* of strategic change made by a firm is linked to managerial interpretation of the environment (Bateman and Zeithaml, 1989; Dutton and Jackson, 1987; Thomas et al., 1993). This study addresses the issue of the *timing* of strategic response to environmental change. Our results suggest that the timing of change involves more than just assigning meaning to a particular event. Consistent with work on individual cognition (Isabella, 1990), the results show that events that are not interpreted as affecting central concepts (performance or well-being) in the firm's strategic frame do not lead to a change in action. Further, change appears to be triggered by interpretations that link a given event to other concurrent or prior events, consistent with stress/inertia theories of change.

Finally, it may appear that our analysis counters suggestions by Weick (1979), Starbuck and Milliken (1988) and others that managers act first and interpret their actions later. However, we suggest the results of this study point to an important middle ground between researchers who are interested in the purposeful, deliberate development of strategy and those who feel that strategy is more often an outcome of action. The changes in interpretation we identify here focus on an important interpretive step before change can take place: the realization that *something* needs to be done. Theories of institutional inertia and evolutionary theories of organization change we summarized provide needed insight into why this interpretive step is not taken without significant pressure to do so. Additional study of strategic frames and their relationship to the content of strategic response may provide a more clear picture of enactment processes, and poses an interesting avenue for future research. What our study suggests is that firms need a map in which they have confidence, before they undertake a major journey (Weick, 1990); they must 'know something' before they act. With this confidence, they then 'see what they do', and develop more detailed knowledge of new terrain in the way that Weick, Starbuck and others have been describing.

NOTES

*Presented at the 1992 Strategic Management Society Meeting, London, 14–17 October. This work draws significantly from the first author's dissertation. Support from the Richard D. Irwin Foundation, and the input of the dissertation committee is gratefully acknowledged.

[1] A fifth variable, R&D emphasis on specific therapeutic categories of drugs, was also identified as a significant strategic variable. However, relevant firm-level information is not publicly available and therefore this dimension of strategy could not be investigated.

[2] All six companies were contacted about the availability of historical documents, but only two have promising repositories. To ensure equal level of documentation for each firm, documents from these two firms were not used in this analysis.

[3] The Kefauver bill referred to in this text is the original bill submitted to committee early in 1961. The two main provisions of this early version were compulsory licensing of new drugs after three years, and the requirement that new drugs be efficacious in use, as well as safe. This bill died in committee in 1962.

REFERENCES

ALLARD POESI, F. (1994). 'From individual causal maps to a collective causal map'. *Second International Workshop on Managerial and Organizational Cognition Proceedings*. Brussels, 26–27 May, 1–25.

ALLISON, G. (1971). *Essence of Decision*. Boston: Little, Brown.

ANDERSON, C., LEPPER, M. and ROSS, L. (1980). 'Perseverance of social theories: the role of explanation in the persistence of discredited information'. *Journal of Personality and Social Psychology*, **39**, 1037–49.

ANDREWS, K. (1987). *The Concept of Corporate Strategy*. Homewood, IL: Irwin.

AXELROD, R. (1976). *Structure of Decision*. Princeton, NJ: Princeton University Press.

366   PAMELA S. BARR AND ANNE S. HUFF

BARNARD, C. (1938). *The Functions of the Executive*. Cambridge, MA: Harvard University Press.

BARR, P., STIMPERT, J. L. and HUFF, A. (1992). 'Cognitive change, strategic action, and organizational renewal'. *Strategic Management Journal*, Summer Special Issue, 15–36.

BARTUNEK, J. (1984). 'Changing interpretive schemes and organizational restructuring: the example of a religious order'. *Administrative Science Quarterly*, **29**, 355–72.

BATEMAN, T. and ZEITHAML, C. (1989). 'The psychological context of strategic decisions: a model and convergent experimental findings'. *Administrative Science Quarterly*, **10**, 59–74.

BETTMAN, J. and WEITZ, B. (1983). 'Attributions in the board room: causal reasoning in corporate annual reports'. *Administrative Science Quarterly*, **28**, 165–83.

BIGELOW, J. (1982). 'A catastrophe model of planned organizational change'. *Behavioral Science*, **27**, 26–42.

BIRNBAUM-MORE, P. H. and WEISS, A. R. (1990). 'Discovering the basis of competition in 12 industries: computerized content analysis of interview data from the US and Europe'. In Huff, A. S. (Ed.), *Mapping Strategic Thought*. Chichester: Wiley, 53–69.

BOUGON, M., WEICK, K. E. and BINKHORST, D. (1977). 'Cognition in organizations: analysis of the Utrecht Jazz Orchestra'. *Administrative Science Quarterly*, **22**, 609–32.

BOWMAN, E. H. (1984). 'Content analysis of annual reports for corporate strategy and risk'. *Interfaces*, **14**, 61–71.

CALORI, R., JOHNSON, G. and SARNIN, P. (1994). 'CEO's cognitive maps and the scope of the organization'. *Strategic Management Journal*, **15**, 437–57.

CAMERON, K., SUTTON, R. and WHETTEN, D. (1988). *Readings in Organizational Decline*. Cambridge, MA: Ballinger.

CHAKRAVARTHY, B. (1982). 'Adaptation: a promising metaphor for strategic management'. *Academy of Management Review*, **7**, 33–44.

CLAPHAM, S. and SCHWENK, C. (1991). 'Self-serving attributions, managerial cognition, and company performance'. *Strategic Management Journal*, **12**, 219–29.

COOL, K. (1985). 'Strategic group formation and strategic group shifts: a longitudinal analysis of the US pharmaceutical industry, 1963–1982'. Unpublished doctoral dissertation, Purdue University, West LaFayette, Indiana.

CYERT, R. and MARCH, J. (1963). *A Behavioral Theory of the Firm*. New Jersey: Prentice-Hall.

DAFT, R. and WEICK, K. (1984). 'Toward a model of organizations as interpretive systems'. *Academy of Management Review*, **9**, 284–95.

DIMAGGIO, P. J. and POWELL, W. W. (1983). 'The iron cage revisited: institutional isomorphism and collective rationality in organizational fields'. *American Sociological Review*, **48**, 147–60.

DUTTON, J. and DUNCAN, R. (1987). 'The creation of momentum for change through the process of strategic issue diagnosis'. *Strategic Management Journal*, **8**, 279–95.

DUTTON, J. and JACKSON, S. (1987). 'Categorizing strategic issues: links to organizational action'. *Academy of Management Review*, **12**, 76–90.

DUTTON, J., FAHEY, L. and NARAYANAN, V. K. (1983). 'Toward understanding strategic issue diagnosis'. *Strategic Management Journal*, **4**, 307–24.

EDEN, C. (1990). 'Working on problems using cognitive mapping'. In Littlechild, S. C. and Shutler, M. (Eds), *Operations Research in Management*. London: Prentice-Hall.

EDEN, C. (1993). 'Strategy development and implementation: cognitive mapping for group support'. In Hendrix, J., Johnson, G. and Newton, J. (Eds), *Strategic Thinking*. Chichester: John Wiley.

EDEN, C., JONES, S. and SIMS, D. (1979). *Thinking in Organizations*. London: Macmillan.

EDEN, C., JONES, S. and SIMS, D. (1983). *Messing about in Problems*. Oxford: Pergamon.

EDEN, C., ACKERMANN, F. and TAIT, A. (1993). 'Comparing cognitive maps: methodological issues'. Paper presented at 1st International Workshop on Managerial and Organizational Cognition, Brussels.

EHLINGER, S. (1994). 'How do centre's and peripheral units' cognitions interact during the strategic planning process?' *Second International Workshop on Managerial and Organizational Cognition Proceedings*, Brussels, 26–27 May, 151–78.

EVRITT, B. (1980). *Cluster Analysis*, 2nd edn. London: Heinemann Educational.

FAHEY, L. and NARAYANAN, V. K. (1989). 'Linking changes in revealed causal maps and environmental change: an empirical study'. *Journal of Management Studies*, **26**, 361–78.

FIOL, M. (1989). 'A semiotic analysis of corporate language: organizational boundaries and joint venturing'. *Administrative Science Quarterly*, **34**, 277–303.

FIOL, C. M. (1994). 'Consensus, diversity, and learning in organizations'. *Organization Science*, **5**, 403–19.

FISKE, S. T. and TAYLOR, S. E. (1991). *Social Cognition*. New York: McGraw-Hill.

GIERE, R. (1988). *Explaining Social Science: A Cognitive Approach*. Chicago: The University of Chicago Press.

GILBERT, M. (1989). *On Social Facts*. Princeton, NJ: Princeton University Press.

GINSBERG, A. (1988). 'Measuring and modelling changes in strategy: theoretical foundations and empirical directions'. *Strategic Management Journal*, **9**, 559–75.

GINSBERG, A. and BUCHHOLTZ, A. (1990). 'Converting to for-profit status: corporate responsiveness to radical change'. *Academy of Management Journal*, **33**, 445–77.

GIOIA, D. and SIMS, H. (1986). 'Social cognition in organizations'. In Sims, H. and Gioia, D. (Eds), *The Thinking Organization*. San Francisco: Jossey-Bass, 1–19.

GOLDEN, B. (1992). 'The past is past – or is it? The use of retrospective accounts as indicators of past strategy'. *Academy of Management Journal*, **35**, 848–57.

GRABOWSKI, H., VERNON, J. and THOMAS, L. (1978). 'Estimating the effects of regulation on innovation: an internal comparative analysis of the pharmaceutical industry'. *Journal of Law and Economics*, April, 133–63.

HAAS, P. M. (1992). 'Introduction: epistemic communities and international policy coordination'. *International Organization*, **46**, 1–35.

HALL, R. (1984). 'The natural logic of management policy making: its implications for the survival of an organization'. *Management Science*, **30**, 905–27.

HAMBRICK, D. (1984). 'Taxonomic approaches to studying strategy: some conceptual and methodological issues'. *Journal of Management*, **10**, 27–42.

HAMBRICK, D. and D'AVENI, R. (1988). 'Large corporate failures as downward spirals'. *Administrative Science Quarterly*, **33**, 1–23.

HAMBRICK, D. and MASON, P. (1984). 'Upper echelons: the organization as a reflection of its top managers'. *Academy of Management Review*, **9**, 193–206.

HANNAN, M. and FREEMAN, J. (1984). 'Structural inertia and organizational change'. *American Sociological Review*, **49**, 149–64.

HARRIGAN, K. (1985). 'An application of clustering for strategic group analysis'. *Strategic Management Journal*, **6**, 55–74.

HARTIGAN, J. A. (1976). *Clustering Algorithms*. New York: John Wiley.

HAVEMAN, H. (1992). 'Between a rock and a hard place: organizational change and performance under conditions of fundamental environmental transformation'. *Administrative Science Quarterly*, **37**, 48–75.

HEDBERG, B., NYSTROM, P. and STARBUCK, W. (1976). 'Camping on seesaws: prescriptions for a self-designing organization'. *Administrative Science Quarterly*, **21**, 41–65.

HODGKINSON, G. P. and JOHNSON, G. (1994). 'Exploring the mental models of competitive strategists'. *Journal of Management Studies*, **31**, 525–49.

HOFER, C. and SCHENDEL, D. (1978). *Strategy Formulation: Analytical Concepts*. St Paul, MN: West Publishing.

HOLMES, T. and RAHE, R. (1967). 'The social readjustment rating scale'. *Journal of Psychosomatic Research*, **11**, 213–18.

HUFF, A. S. (1982). 'Industry influences on strategy reformulation'. *Strategic Management Journal*, **3**, 119–31.

HUFF, A. S. (1990). 'Mapping strategic thought'. In Huff, A. S. (Ed.), *Mapping Strategic Thought*. Chichester: John Wiley, 11–49.

HUFF, A. S., NARAPAREDDY, V. and FLETCHER, K. E. (1990). 'Coding the association of concepts'. In Huff, A. S. (Ed.), *Mapping Strategic Thought*. Chichester: John Wiley, 311–25.

HUFF, J. O., HUFF, A. S. and THOMAS, H. (1992). 'Strategic renewal and the interaction of cumulative stress and inertia'. *Strategic Management Journal*, **13**, 55–75.

ISABELLA, L. (1990). 'Evolving interpretations as a change unfolds: how managers construe key organizational events'. *Academy of Management Journal*, **33**, 7–41.

JENKINS, M. (1994). 'Creating and comparing strategic causal maps'. *Second International Workshop on Managerial and Organizational Cognition Proceedings*, Brussels, 26–27 May, 299–328.

KELLY, G. (1955). *The Psychology of Personal Constructs*, Volumes 1 and 2. New York: Norton.

KIESLER, S. and SPROULL, L. (1982). 'Managerial response to changing environments: perspectives on problem sensing from social cognition'. *Administrative Science Quarterly*, **27**, 548–70.

KUHN, T. (1970). *Structure of Scientific Revolutions*, 2nd edn. Chicago: University of Chicago Press.

LANT, T., MILLIKEN, F. and BATRA, B. (1992). 'The role of managerial learning and interpretation of strategic persistence and reorientation: an empirical exploration'. *Strategic Management Journal*, **13**, 585–608.

LASAGNA, L. and WARDELL, W. (1975). 'The rate of new drug discovery'. In Helms, R. (Ed.), *Drug Development and Marketing*. Washington DC: The American Institute for Public Policy Research.

LAUKKANEN, M. (1994). 'Comparative cause mapping of organizational cognitions'. *Organization Science*, **5**, 322–43.

LAVE, J. and WENGER, E. (1991). *Situated Learning*. Cambridge: Cambridge University Press.

LYLES, M. (1981). 'Formulating strategic problems: empirical analysis and model development'. *Strategic Management Journal*, **2**, 61–75.

LYLES, M. and MITROFF, I. (1980). 'Organizational problem formulation: an empirical study'. *Administrative Science Quarterly*, **25**, 102–19.

MARCH, J. (1991). 'Exploration and exploitation in organizational learning'. *Organization Science*, **2**, 71–87.

MARCH, J. and SIMON, H. (1958). *Organizations*. New York: Wiley.

MARKOCZY, L. and GOLDBERG, J. (1995). 'A method for eliciting and comparing causal maps'. *Journal of Management*, **21**, 305–33.

MEYER, A. (1982). 'Adapting to environmental jolts'. *Administrative Science Quarterly*, **27**, 515–38.

MILES, R. (1982). *Coffin Nails and Corporate Strategy*. New Jersey: Prentice-Hall.

MILES, R. and SNOW, C. (1978). *Organizational Strategy, Structure, and Process*. New York: McGraw-Hill.

MILLER, D. and FRIESEN, P. (1984). *Organizations: A Quantum View*. Englewood Cliffs, NJ: Prentice-Hall.

MILLIKEN, F. (1987). 'Three types of uncertainty about the environment: state, effect, and response uncertainty'. *Academy of Management Review*, **12**, 133–43.

MILLIKEN, F. (1990). 'Perceiving and interpreting environmental change'. *Academy of Management Journal*, **33**, 42–63.

MINSKY, M. (1975). 'A framework for representing knowledge'. In Winston, P. H. (Ed.), *The Psychology of Computer Vision*. New York: McGraw Hill.

MINTZBERG, H. (1978). 'Patterns in strategy formulation'. *Management Science*, **24**, 934–48.
MINTZBERG, H. and WATERS, J. (1982). 'Tracking strategy in an entrepreneurial firm'. *Academy of Management Journal*, **25**, 465–99.
MINTZBERG, H., RAISINGHANI, D. and THEORET, A. (1976). 'The structure of unstructured decision processes'. *Administrative Science Quarterly*, **21**, 246–75.
MONTEVERDE, K. and TEECE, D. (1982). 'Supplier switching costs and vertical integration in the automobile industry'. *Bell Journal of Economics*, 207–13.
MYLLYS, K. (1994). 'Cognitive approach to managerial work – an empirical study of Finnish bank managers in crisis situation'. *Second International Workshop on Managerial and Organizational Cognition Proceedings*. Brussels, 26–27 May, 419–44.
NARAYANAN, V. K. and FAHEY, L. (1990). 'Evolution of revealed causal maps during decline: a case study of admiral'. In Huff, A. S. (Ed.), *Mapping Strategic Thought*. Chichester: John Wiley, 109–33.
NEISSER, U. (1967). *Cognitive Psychology*. Englewood Cliffs, NJ: Prentice-Hall.
NELSON, R. R. and WINTER, S. G. (1982). *An Evolutionary Theory of Economic Change*. Cambridge, MA: Cambridge University Press.
NISBETT, R. and ROSS, L. (1980). *Human Inference*. Englewood Cliffs, NJ: Prentice-Hall.
OLIVIA, T. A., DAY, D. L. and MACMILLAN, I. C. (1988). 'A generic model of competitive dynamics'. *Academy of Management Review*, **13**, 374–89.
OSTER, S. (1982). 'Intraindustry structure and the ease of strategic change'. *Review of Economics and Statistics*, **64**, 376–83.
PORAC, J., THOMAS, H. and BADEN-FULLER, C. (1989). 'Competitive groups as cognitive communities: the case of Scottish knitwear manufacturers'. *Journal of Management Studies*, **26**, 397–416.
PORTER, M. (1980). *Competitive Strategy*. New York: Free Press.
POWELL, W. and DIMAGGIO, P. (1991). *The New Institutionalism in Organization Analysis*. Chicago: University of Chicago Press.
PRAHALAD, K. and BETTIS, R. (1986). 'The dominant logic: a new linkage between diversity and performance'. *Strategic Management Journal*, **7**, 485–501.
QUINN, J. (1980). *Strategies of Change, Logical Incrementalism*. Homewood, IL: Irwin.
REGER, R. and HUFF, A. (1993). 'Strategic groups: a cognitive perspective'. *Strategic Management Journal*, **14**, 103–24.
ROBINSON, W. (1957). 'The statistical measure of agreement'. *American Sociological Review*, **22**, 17–25.
ROSS, L., LEPPER, M. and HUBBARD, M. (1975). 'Perseverance in self-perception and social perception'. *Journal of Personality and Social Psychology*, **32**, 880–92.
RUMELHART, D. (1980). 'Schemata: the building blocks of cognition'. In Spiro, Bruce and Brewer (Eds), *Theoretical Issues in Reading Comprehension*. Hillsdale, NJ: Erlbaum, 33–58.
SALANCIK, G. and MEINDL, J. (1984). 'Corporate attributions as strategic illusions of management control'. *Administrative Science Quarterly*, **29**, 238–54.
SAS INSTITUTE, INC. (1990). *SAS Users Guide: Basics*, Version 6, 4th edn. Chapter 6, 53–101.
SCHEID-COOK, T. (1992). 'Organizational enactments and conformity to environmental prescriptions'. *Human Relations*, **45**, 537–54.
SCHWENK, C. and TANG, M. (1989). 'Economic and psychological explanations for persistance'. *Omega*, **17**, 559–70.
SELZNICK, P. (1957). *Leadership in Administration*. Evanston, IL: Row, Peterson.
SHRIVASTAVA, P. and LIN, G. (1984). 'Alternative approaches to strategic analysis of environments'. Paper presented at the 4th Annual Strategic Management Society Conference, Philadelphia.
SMITH, K. and GRIMM, C. (1987). 'Environmental variation, strategic change, and firm performance: a study of railroad deregulation'. *Strategic Management Journal*, **8**, 363–76.

370 PAMELA S. BARR AND ANNE S. HUFF

SPENDER, J. C. (1989). *Industry Recipes: An Inquiry into the Nature and Sources of Managerial Judgement.* Cambridge, MA: Basil-Blackwood, Inc.

STARBUCK, W. and MILLIKEN, F. (1988). 'Executives perceptual filters: what they notice and how they make sense'. In Hambrick, D. (Ed.), *The Executive Effect: Concepts and Methods for Studying Top Managers.* Greenwich, CT: JAI.

STJERNBERG, T. and ULLSTAD, C. (1994). 'Organization images – organizational diagnosis by transformation of individuals' cognitive maps into shared local theories'. *Second International Workshop on Managerial and Organizational Cognition Proceedings,* Brussels, 26–27 May, 601–22.

TEMIN, P. (1980). *Taking Your Medicine: Drug Regulation in the United States.* Cambridge, MA: Harvard University Press.

THOMAS, J., CLARK, S. and GIOIA, D. (1993). 'Strategic sensemaking and organizational performance: linkages among scanning, interpretation, action, and outcomes'. *Academy of Management Journal,* **36,** 239–70.

THOMPSON, J. (1967). *Organizations in Action.* New York: McGraw-Hill.

THOMPSON, J. and McDANIEL, R. (1990). 'Interpreting strategic issues: effects of strategy and the information-processing structure of top management teams'. *Academy of Management Journal,* **33,** 286–306.

TUSHMAN, M. and ROMANELLI, E. (1985). 'Organizational evolution: a metamorphosis model of convergence and reorientation'. *Research in Organizational Behavior,* **7,** 171–222.

WALSH, J. (1995). 'Managerial and organizational cognition: notes from a trip down memory lane'. *Organization Science,* **6,** 280–321.

WARDELL, W. (1971). 'Introduction of new therapeutic drugs in the US and Great Britain: an international comparison'. *Clinical Pharmacology and Therapeutics,* **14,** 773–90.

WEICK, K. (1979). *The Social Psychology of Organizing.* Reading, MA: Addison-Wesley.

WEICK, K. (1990). 'Cartographic myths in organizations'. In Huff, A. S. (Ed.), *Mapping Strategic Thought.* Chichester: John Wiley, 1–10.

WEICK, K. and BOUGON, M. (1986). 'Organizations as cognitive maps: charting ways to success and failure'. In Gioia, D. and Sims, Henry Jr. (Eds), *The Thinking Organization.* San Francisco: Jossey-Bass.

WOOD, M. (1996). 'Situating cognition: organizations as communities-of-practice'. *4th International Workshop on Managerial and Organizational Cognition Proceedings,* Stockholm, 29–30 August, 1996.

WOODRUM, E. (1984). 'Mainstreaming content analysis in social science – methodological advantages, obstacles, solutions'. *Social Science Research,* **13,** 1–9.

ZAJAC, E. and SHORTELL, S. (1989). 'Changing generic strategies: likelihood, direction, and performance implications'. *Strategic Management Journal,* **10,** 413–30.

Part V
Bounded Rationality (4): Sympathetic Critics

[24]

Herbert Simon's human rationality*

The sixty papers included in the two volumes of Herbert Simon's
Models of Bounded Rationality (1982) constitute, in the author's words,
'a reasonably complete collection of my economic works that have not
been published elsewhere in book form' (1982, 1: p.xviii). In this
chapter I propose to use this collection as a single body of evidence to
illuminate not only Simon's view of economics, but also his view of the
human situation. It is always dangerous to consider a set of pieces
published over a period of more than forty years without reference to
their temporal sequence, but neither in his general nor in his sectional
introductions does Simon suggest that he has discarded any of his earlier
ideas. There are some qualifications and some changes of emphasis,
but not many even of these. In appraising Simon's work, time does not
seem to be important: as we shall see later, that statement bears more
than one interpretation. Whereas Hahn's attitude to equilibrium, which
we examined in Chapter 8, appears to be undergoing a process of
change, Simon's view of processes appears to be in stable equilibrium.
This attempt to summarize and comment on what one might call
Simon's decision premises (to use his own terminology) may help us to
understand not only his own work but also the reaction – or lack of
reaction – to it by economists of various persuasions.

Complexity and pragmatism

Let us start with an article of 1971 which bears a characteristic title:
'Designing organizations for an information-rich world' (1982, 2:
pp.171–85). Here Simon argues forcefully that plentiful information
will not resolve the difficulties which we face in trying to behave reasonably. The abundance of information accentuates the scarcity of our
means of handling it. Although we must attempt to recognize externalities and interdependencies, we must also recognize that:

> . . . the dream of thinking everything out before we act, of making certain
> we have all the facts and know all the consequences, is a sick Hamlet's
> dream. It is the dream of someone with no appreciation of the seamless web

*An earlier version of this chapter was presented at George Mason University,
Virginia, in May 1985

of causation, the limits of human thinking, or the scarcity of human attention. (1982, 2: p.180)

That the complexity of our environment, natural and artificial, extends
far beyond the bounds of our rationality is the central fact with which
Simon has been trying to deal throughout his career. One obvious
consequence is that we must expect to make mistakes, sometimes
serious mistakes.

> The world will always remain the largest laboratory, the largest information
> store. . . . Of course it is costly to learn from experience; but it is also
> costly, and frequently much less reliable, to try through research and analysis
> to anticipate experience. (1982, 2: p.180)

In other words, don't expect too much from any model – and don't
claim too much for it either. Nevertheless, there is no need to worry.

> We must assume, as mankind has always assumed, that a reasonable allo-
> cation of our limited attention and powers of thought will solve the crucial
> problems facing us at least as fast as new ones arise. (1982, 2: p.181)

Before turning to the implications of this assumption, let us briefly
consider the parenthesis, 'as mankind has always assumed'. As an
assertion about human history, this is obviously false; but it tells us a
great deal about Simon. First, it demonstrates that his recognition of
the central fact of bounded rationality is matched with a central belief:
a belief in the capacity of human reason (and perhaps; like Einstein,
in the fairness of God) which is so fundamental that Simon simply
assumes that it must be shared by all reasonable men. That belief sets
unrecognized bounds to his own rationality: and it may serve to remind
us that our own systems of thought almost certainly contain basic
elements which we have just never thought of as open to question.
Second, such an assertion could hardly have been made by someone
who is deeply interested in history: Simon looks back only to draw the
lessons of immediate experience, and then quickly forward to the next
problem. Third, he is a pragmatist, who gives little attention to philosophical issues. As with Oliver Edwards, who (in ˉBoswell's *Life of
Johnson*) had often tried to be a philosopher, cheerfulness is always
breaking in.

   Life is a succession of problems, to be tackled successively. It appears
to embody no grand theories, no opportunities for global optimization.
Nevertheless, the challenge of new problems, and their successful resolution, makes life an intellectual adventure (1982, 2: p.132). I am

142   The mind and method of the economist

reminded of a saying by Charles Suckling (a research chemist who became General Manager, Research and Technology, in ICI) that 'the best things we can leave to our children are unsolved problems'. If this is to be a message of hope, then we must assume that we can solve crucial problems as fast as new ones arise – but preferably not much faster.

Simon's central assumption implies an interest in processes rather than equilibrium, but, since all models are incomplete representations of the phenomena to which they are applied, equilibrium concepts may be used on occasion. It implies a systems view which is, in some respects, almost the opposite of that taken by general equilibrium theorists. First, the overall system is not to be regarded as complete: there are transactions across its boundaries which are not fully modelled. Second, the behaviour of this overall system is explained in terms of the aggregate behaviour of its subsystems, each of which is explained in turn by the aggregate behaviour of its own subsystems; there is no attempt to relate overall system performance directly to its basic elements. Third, the usual problem addressed is the ongoing management of the system in response to extraneous data, rather than the calculation of equilibrium states or equilibrium flows. Finally (and particularly for Simon), the problem of system management often causes interest to be focused not on the 'real world' elements – the usual variables of economic models – but on the organizational arrangements and decision routines by which these variables are handled.

A combination of these last two elements is implied by the title of Simon's essay 'From substantive to procedural rationality' (1982, 2: pp.424–43). Instead of seeking to derive from axioms and data the values which would be ascribed to the relevant variables by an optimal decision, attention is turned to the processes by which reasonable decisions might be made. The complexity of the decision environment places optimality beyond reach, and often beyond definition; what is sought is a feasible procedure for achieving satisfactory results, and ways of checking on experience as a possible guide to doing better.

This concern for effective means of handling complexity sometimes leads Simon to argue that the progress of management science permits increasing centralization of decision-making in partial replacement of the market and that, since this centralization allows us to handle more interactions, it will improve the quality of decisions (1982, 2: pp.61–2). Although he reminds town planners that what happens in a city depends on the behaviour of its citizens, who have no intention of surrendering their freedom of action to those who have been given 'certain very limited powers to modify the design' (1982, 2: p.52), he does not appear to recognize the effects of centralization on the quality of the information supplied; he tends to be absorbed by the technology of information processing and the challenge of the conscious design of institutions. What preserves him from the advocacy of any kind of system of central planning is his continuing conviction that, for all our technical advances, the scale and complexity of the problems cannot be sensibly handled in that way. We need rather to look for means of coupling together partial decision rules – for example, through the price mechanism – or even sometimes to content ourselves with securing 'compatibility requirements', so that one decision procedure will not produce results which actually impede the effectiveness of another (1982, 1: p.191).

Loose coupling of partial systems (which is exemplified in Cyert and March's (1963) analysis of organizational behaviour) implies a set of objectives rather than any kind of single objective function, however complicated. What we do not find in these papers is a recognition of the potential value of incompatible systems: insistence on compatibility may prevent certain kinds of exploration which do not fit in with present ideas or present practices. But Simon does not consciously envisage the intellectual adventure of solving human problems as a competitive discovery procedure – although this is clearly what it is, even in several areas of pure science. Though he favours a competitive economy, he does not explain why. Neither entrepreneurship nor spontaneous organization are significant concepts in Simon's work.

Whether the fundamental cause of the difficulties which we face is to be found in our inadequate ability to cope with complexity or because at least part of the future is unknowable is not an issue which he ever raises. Unlike Shackle, he is not very interested in the philosophical issues. His continuing fascination with chess, computers, and artificial intelligence suggests that he believes the cause to be complexity: although, as we shall see later, he recognizes the indeterminacy of interdependent decisions, he does sometimes give the impression that we do live in a fully defined system, if only we had the wit to understand it. But his understanding of computers and of artificial intelligence do not give him any hope that we shall ever acquire the wit fully to understand complexity; and perhaps his interest is attracted by the belief that there are more usefully solvable problems in complexity than in ignorance. (Neoclassical economists, in his view, too often make their problems soluble by making the solutions useless.) He has no expectation of constructing a comprehensive system, no ideals to match those of many physicists or economists. His business is piecemeal social engineering.

144 The mind and method of the economist

Optimization

In some respects Simon appears very conventional. He is an enthusiast of mathematical analysis and welcomes the increasing mathematization of the social sciences. He is obviously pleased (1982, 2: p.3) at his success at translating into mathematical form the theory of group inter-action proposed by the sociologist G.C. Homans (1982, 2: p.33–42), to which he applies the standard economic method of deriving comparative static equilibria. At the end of an article entitled 'Some economic effects of technical change', after acknowledging the unrealism of the models presented, he offers an argument which we might expect to hear from another author.

> If such models have no other value, they are of use in permitting a precise statement of the Malthusian hypothesis, and an examination of the conditions under which that hypothesis holds. (1982, 1: p.305)

In what ways this examination might be useful he does not say. However, he insists that mathematical social science should be applied mathematics: the language of mathematics should be used to say some-thing about its nominal subject-matter, and not merely about the language itself. Logical coherence is no substitute for empirical validity (1982, 2: p.209). As we observed in Chapter 8, Hahn (1984, p.312) characteristically stresses the converse proposition.

Neoclassical methods are justified, Simon argues (1982, 1: p.xix), if the assumptions which are made are not too far removed from the real world to invalidate the conclusions – a question to be settled by exam-ining the assumptions, not (as with Friedman, 1953) the conclusions – and also if the data required are obtainable and the computations feasible. When he judges that these conditions are met, he has had no hesitation in using neoclassical techniques. Indeed, a study undertaken in the late 1940s of the likely impact of nuclear power on US national income (1982, 1: pp. 325–53) anticipates both the methods and the results of the 'new economic history' – the methods in comparing the projected nuclear economy with an optimally adapted non-nuclear economy, and the results in the conclusion that, in a world full of alternatives, nothing actually matters very much.

More instructive is his attitude to the extensive collaborative work which he undertook on production scheduling and inventory control, in which optimization techniques were freely applied to quadratic cost functions which were acknowledged to be false. He makes no use of Friedman's arguments, to which he strongly objects elsewhere (1982, 2: p.369–71). The use of false assumptions is justified on two grounds:

first, they make the problem manageable, by requiring managers to supply relatively few estimates which need not be very accurate and which can be used in fairly straightforward computations (1982, 2: pp.386–8); second, as is argued in some detail (1982, 1: pp.202–11), each is a reasonably good approximation to the likely truth within the range of variation to which the decision rules are meant to apply.

It is this reasonable, and usable, approximation which, he asserts (1982, 2: p.371), is far more significant for the acceptability of data than the significance which statisticians emphasize. The best-fitting equation is not necessarily the most useful. The limits of acceptability may then be tested by sensitivity analysis, which sometimes assures us of the robustness of our conclusions, and at other times warns us of their vulnerability to estimates which have no sure foundation (1982, 1:p.264).

As Simon (1982, 2: p.486) has observed, this work has had an ironic sequel: one of his collaborators, John Muth, impressed by their success in calculating apparently optimal actions from the expected values of probability distributions, proposed that such expected values, each derived from the relevant economic theory, should be taken as the basis of rational decisions. To Simon, of course, the optimizing procedure which they had devised was itself an example of satisficing, not to be generalized without detailed examination: the optimization of artificially simplified models is not, he reminds us, a good strategy for solving problems in chess (1982, 2: p.414). But, even if we can assume that the world supplies us with probability distributions which allow us to make unbiased forecasts, and that the cost of obtaining the necessary information does not render the acceptance of possible bias optimal, the derivation of rational decisions from rational expectations is straightforward only if the loss function is quadratic (as was assumed for the original study). 'Unbiased estimation can be a component of all sorts of rational and irrational behavior rules' (1982, 2: p.438).

If Simon is sceptical about the merits of rational expectations, aggregate Cobb–Douglas production functions are dismissed with scorn. The apparent evidence in favour of such functions and of their success in predicting labour's share of output is declared to be vitiated by faulty econometric method (1982, 1: pp.444–59): 'these results are a statistical artifact without economic significance' (1982, 1: p.405). 'The data say no more than that the value of product is approximately equal to the wage bill plus the cost of capital services' (1982, 1: p.454); and since the latter explanation is adequate and simpler, it should be preferred (1982, 1: p.458). In making this recommendation, it has to be said that Simon reveals a failure to understand the purpose of Cobb–Douglas

146   The mind and method of the economist

functions, or indeed of production functions as a class: Simon's preferred explanation is very far from adequate for the issues which neoclassical economists deem important. We shall return to this issue at the end of this chapter.

Aggregate production functions are under some suspicion because of the dangers of aggregation. These dangers engendered a spirited and notorious dispute between Cambridge, England and Cambridge, Massachusetts; but the reluctance of the disputants to look beyond the problems of capital aggregation suggests that the dispute was ideological, and not empirical – perhaps the reason why Simon seems never to have referred to it. The plausibility of aggregation and decomposition in the analysis of complex systems is an obvious issue for him to investigate, and it is no surprise to find him giving his paper on that subject in this collection a very high place among 'scientific publications of which I am proud' (1982, 1: p.404). It is no surprise, either, to find that it is a technical inquiry into a practical problem, not a philosophical discussion (1982, 1: pp.411–41). In *The Sciences of the Artificial* (1969), he is less technical, but still emphasizes the practical issues.

The great majority of economists still do not appear to find the issues of aggregation and decomposability of either practical or philosophical importance, even though they are central to the present confusion over what used to be called macroeconomics. Simon's own analysis no doubt helps to buttress his belief in our ability to solve problems at least as fast as they are created; but although he recognizes the practical importance of the varying speeds with which different interactions take effect, nevertheless for one who prefers process to equilibrium as an organizing principle, he seems to have very little sense of the significance of time in human affairs. Compare his writings with those of Marshall, Shackle, or the later Hicks, and one is immediately conscious of a great difference in attitude and style.

Rationality
With the increasing focus on choice, rationality has become almost the distinguishing characteristic of economic analysis; but it is rationality in a sense not recognized in the other social sciences. Simon (1982, 2: p.383) points to the contrast with psychology.

> It is only a slight exaggeration to say that what an economist or statistical theorist regards as a 'rational decision process' is what a psychologist might regard as 'habitual behavior'; while what a psychologist regards as 'rational choice', an economist would refuse to regard as 'rational' at all.

But economists have great difficulty in pursuing rigorously their rational programme – although they are often unaware of the diffi-culties. Neither the objectives nor the limiting conditions within which economic agents optimize can themselves be derived on the rational principles which the economist wishes to use. Boundary conditions must be imposed – and often they are imposed unconsciously. But the analysis of constrained optimization implies a shadow price for each constraint, and the fully rational optimizer would redefine his problem to include the optimization of these constraints. The standard specifi-cation of the economic problem, with resources, technology and prefer-ences all given, is necessarily an exercise in bounded rationality, what-ever its practitioners may think, and the decision – if it is a decision, and not the result of unconsidered habit – to pose the problem in this form cannot be explained by optimization, whatever recourse may be had to search costs and the economics of information. It also excludes some of the most important questions, as economists as different as Marshall and Schumpeter well realized.

The current fascination of many theorists with the concept of games is surely due in part to the delusion that the rules of whatever game is being modelled have the same status that such theorists implicitly (though dubiously) accord to natural laws. But we might remember that the game of rugby football was created by a player of association football who broke the rules; and more-or-less orderly revision of the rules is not uncommon in sport. Some revisions, such as the introduction of the tie-break in lawn tennis, result directly from a redefinition of system boundaries. Shackle has frequently drawn attention to the limi-tations imposed on the applicability of game theory by its exclusion of surprise; these limitations are characteristically underrated because only by placing all surprises out of bounds can theorists preserve the ration-ality of the players. Simon is well aware of the fallibility of human decisions, and of our ability to generate unexpected problems: yet surprise is not a concept which belongs in his pattern of thought.

Even with no surprises, as is well known, rationality may prove an elusive goal. The search for rational solutions to the oligopoly problem can probably continue for as long as anyone thinks it worthwhile. The Cournot model, which has come back into favour in recent years, does possess a quasi-rational equilibrium (reached by an irrational process); but, as Simon (1982, 2: p.216) observes, it does not achieve fully informed rationality since, if one agent were correctly to predict the others' decision rules, then he could do better by changing his own. The unpalatable fact is that it is impossible to define an equilibrium of interdependent optimizing agents unless 'we can assume that not more than one participant is unlimitedly clever in predicting the reactions of

148   The mind and method of the economist

the other participants to his behavior' (1982, 2: p.217). Simon here anticipates Coddington's (1975b) dictum that there can be at most one omniscient being.

The case is actually stronger than Simon realizes. He appears to accept (1982, 2: pp.215–16) that the assumptions of perfect competition, however empirically dubious, do allow every economic agent rationally to treat the actions of every other in the same way that he is supposed to treat the conventional 'givens' of the environment – 'as some kind of responsive or unresponsive mechanism'. But as Richardson (1960) has shown, this is not so: even in perfect competition, the consequences of any one person's action depend on the actions of others. The familiar cobweb theorem, whatever its deficiencies in other respects, suffices to demonstrate that the usual assumptions of perfect competition are not enough to guarantee even the (unconsciously bounded) rationality which is sought.

Determinate solutions are attainable by the axiomatic method only for problems which have been defined by non-rational constraints. Fully rational optimization within limits arbitrarily defined is one response to the unavoidable phenomenon of bounded rationality; as Simon makes clear in many places, this is sometimes a perfectly satisfactory response (and, I would add, often one useful component of a satisfactory response). The other response is to accept limits, not on the definition of the problem, but on the rationality of the procedure used to cope with it. It is the second approach which is characteristic of the study of organizational behaviour (which is to be distinguished sharply from almost everything that economists call industrial organization or the theory of the firm) and of the work of psychologists on human decision-making; and it is in the study of organizations and in psychology that Simon has primarily sought to improve our understanding of the ways in which human beings may solve problems at least as fast as new ones are created.

Institutions

If actions are to be based on reason – not, of course, to be demonstrably optimal in the way that many economists would like – then the knowledge requirements must be reduced. Decomposability of the systems within which decisions are made is a principal means of reducing these requirements, and one particularly important kind of decomposability is that which allows the actions of other people to be tolerably well predicted most of the time by the patterns of behaviour which correspond to their roles. Economies are stabilized by their institutions, in the widest sense of that word: by the recognizable sets of decision premises which are embodied in the roles and conventions of the social (including of course the industrial) system (Simon, 1982, 2: pp.390–1). Although Simon does not go so far, his position is compatible with that of Richardson: the atomistic and anonymous competition beloved of economic theorists imposes information requirements which are impossible to satisfy; although it may, under certain assumptions, be formally compatible with a general equilibrium, it has no means of achieving or maintaining coherence. The perfectly competitive model is not appropriate for an enquiry into the working of a competitive economy.

The contrary idea, that the predominance of programmed behaviour is necessary for the combination of coherence and originative choice, is not without its supporters; among economists, we may point to Schumpeter (1934), and Kirzner (1973), in addition to Simon and Richardson. Schumpeter's theory of development depends on the ability of innovators to base their novel calculations on the routines of the circular flow – when the routines are thrown into confusion by innovation, the innovators find that they have destroyed the conditions of their own success – while Kirzner's entrepreneurs profit from their less alert contemporaries' persistence in error.

Perhaps more significant – yet never mentioned in this collection – is the similar position taken by some of those who have approached the problems of human knowledge more directly, through the philosophy of science. We have seen in Chapter 2 that both Kuhn and Lakatos set bounds to scientific rationality; and Popper, though rejecting the idea that paradigms or research programmes prevent wider thought, nevertheless affirms that the process of scientific enquiry can only be carried out within a framework which, for a time, must be placed beyond question. He even begins *The Logic of Scientific Discovery* (1972, p.13), by observing that scientists have an important advantage over philosophers of science in their ability (almost always) to work within an already defined problem-situation. That rational decision-making is easier in a substantially programmed environment is precisely what Simon argues (1982, 2: p.390).

As Simon points out (1982, 2: p.391), the stability of institutions is therefore a critical issue, although it is one that he deals with somewhat inadequately. He is not, as we have previously noted, much bothered about general problems such as this, although he has, of course, given much attention to the question of stability within formal organizations. Practitioners of institution-free economics are not likely to pay much attention to what they have decided to ignore; but the consequences of their neglect can be dangerous. It is not surprising, for example, that such economists have found it hard to discover any significant costs of inflation – even those who are most insistent that we must follow a monetary policy which will avoid (or cure) it. This failure gives us no reason for confidence in their policy prescriptions, whatever they may be. Leijonhufvud's (1975) anger was thoroughly justified.

Whereas Richardson's inquiry into the possible institutional framework for rational decision focused on relations between firms, Simon's attention has been concentrated on formal and informal organization – following Barnard (1938) in giving attention to the link between the two. (Both these research strategies rely on the decomposability of a multi-level system.) Organizational structures, and the relationships which develop within them, determine roles (1982, 2: p.308), each of which is to be understood (1982, 2: p.345) as '*a social prescription of some, but not all, of the premises that enter into an individual's choice of behaviors*'. The prescription of some of the decision premises assists prediction by others who need a reasonable basis for their own decisions; that not all are prescribed leaves some room for the exercise of reasoning power, and the making, on occasion, of novel choices. In addition to decision premises, organizations store information, and the contents of both stores change with experience (1982, 2: p.441); indeed, 'a technology exists largely in the minds of its labour force' (1982, 2: p.144).

This view of organizations has been effectively developed by Nelson and Winter (1982), who draw attention to the difficulty of defining precisely the content of any individual's knowledge and of any organization's capabilities (or programmes), and explain how institutions drift over time. This drift, as successive events are construed by individuals in terms of their own interpretative frameworks (Kelly, 1963), can help to stabilize institutions through adaptation; it may also undermine them, if the expectations of interdependent groups diverge – and that is not impossible, even if (which is unlikely) they are all exposed to the same set of phenomena.

Nelson and Winter also develop Simon's (1982, 2: p.397) observation that 'the interdependence of organization units is a strong force toward conservatism'; each unit has a strong interest in preserving the stability of its environment in order to facilitate the formation of confident expectations, and that implies a reluctance to disturb established decision programmes among its neighbours. Organizations may be stable because their members fear that they will not prove resilient. There is thus a strong tendency to try to fit innovations into existing systems; and indeed we see that innovations which typically require extensive reconstruction of existing institutions meet with great resistance and are accomplished only slowly, if at all. They may succeed only by circumventing existing structures and developing in new locations or in new industries. Schumpeter's emphasis on the necessarily destructive consequences of creativity can be justified in Simon's terms; so, in a different way, can Marshall's emphasis on the cumulative importance of incremental change, occurring in a large population of freely competing firms, each with its own established customers and competitors, but each with its own slightly idiosyncratic set of decision programmes, which facilitates particular and localized types of beneficial adjustments.

Perception and theory
In considering the role of institutions we should recognize (even though he himself does not) the warning implicit in Simon's insistence that 'the decision-maker's information about his environment is much less than an approximation to the real environment. . . . In actual fact the perceived world is fantastically different from the "real" world' (1982, 2: p.306). Because of the limitations of the human brain, selection and distortion are inevitable both in perception (the acquisition of information) and inference (the processing of the information acquired). Although Simon (1982, 2: p.307) insists that the filtering which takes place is an active process, he does not go on to point out that this process necessarily implies the imposition of a conjectural framework as a means of selection and interpretation. This is mildly surprising, not only because of his substantial interest in psychology, but also because he observes (1982, 2: p.391) that, for any individual decision-maker, 'the "facts" on which he acts obtain their status as facts by a social process of legitimation, and have only a very tenuous and indirect connection with the evidence of his senses'.

He appears to imply that such a social process is necessarily beneficial when he claims (1982, 2: p.399) that the need for stable expectations makes it 'more important, in some circumstances, to have *agreement* on the facts than to be certain that what is agreed upon is really fact. Hence we often find that the procedures for fact finding and for legitimating facts are themselves institutionalized.' The processes of social legitimation of facts are certainly important, and their neglect by economists a source of serious error; but Simon seems to have no sense of the potential fragility of the structures based on such 'pretty, polite techniques'. The stability and resilience of institutions, and of the expectations which they support, remains problematic. Leijonhufvud's (1973) 'corridor hypothesis' still awaits development, even within its original macroeconomic context. But Simon must be given full credit for recognizing that such stability ought to be – though it is not – a central concern of economics.

152   The mind and method of the economist

The significance of institutions is not diminished by the increasing availability of information. Greater information makes more acute the need to economize on attention, and increases the significance for decision-making of the means of economizing. Information-processing systems are of no value unless they are net absorbers of information (1982, 2: p.175). Among the most efficient information-processing systems is science, which exploits the redundancy of facts in a world which appears to obey natural laws by substituting the laws, which are few, for the facts, of which there are very many. 'With each important advance in scientific theory, we can reduce the volume of explicitly stored knowledge without losing any information whatsoever' (1982, 2: p.178). Thus, scientific advance simplifies our problems. 'To become a research chemist should involve less learning today than it did fifty years ago, because physical chemistry and quantum mechanics have provided such powerful tools for organizing facts, and indeed making them derivable from theory' (1982, 2: p.142).

Organizations have theories too, sometimes set out in detailed principles of corporate strategy, sometimes the result of imposing simple structures on their past record. For example, the research director of a chemical business which had lost money trying to develop self-assembly furniture, for which they produced only the bulk filler, not the surface laminates, defined his research strategy thereafter as 'no more bloody flat things' – certainly an efficient information-processing rule! But Simon does not explicitly consider the processes by which organizations acquire and amend their theories; nor do Nelson and Winter, although they do focus on the issue of knowledge within organizations. None of them recognizes that theories (or any other information-processing system) may impose misleading patterns. There can be no way of guaranteeing that an active filtering process will not lead its users astray; and to argue that no-one will persist in error (a proposition which can itself be misleading) is not sufficient reason to pay attention only to those situations in which no errors are made. Simon's own failure to recognize the possibility of faulty decisions arising from misleading theories is particularly striking when we recall that his criticism of conventional economics is precisely that the theoretical filters which it employs are inappropriate for many of its purposes. Unfortunately, his analyses of information processing are not founded on any adequate theory of the growth of knowledge.

Simon versus neoclassical economics
Simon fails to use his own (incomplete) theories of institutional conservatism and data absorption to explain the resistance of the great

majority of economists to his ideas. His own explanation (1982, 2: p.401) is one of the weakest elements in the book: 'Now I learned that behavior was of interest to economists . . . only if it had important implications for matters of policy at the level of the economy, or at least of the industry.' The proposition that the prime concern of economists is economic policy, primarily macro-policy, is an active filter which destroys more information than it absorbs.

Let us apply a little of Simon's analytical apparatus. Economists, like other people, face the problem of information overload, and they recognize the value of science in making 'facts derivable from theory'. What, then, could possibly be better than the well developed structure of microeconomics: 'deductive theory which requires almost no contact with empirical data – once the underlying assumptions are accepted or verified – to establish its propositions' (1982, 2: p.321)? Although Simon (1982, 2: p.476) points out that Occam's razor is double-edged, so that the 'much stronger assumptions . . . about the human cognitive system' which are required for theories of utility or profit maximization than for satisficing might be deemed a disqualification, succinctness is likely to be a far more powerful argument for anyone conscious of the need to absorb information. It is indeed an argument which Simon himself employs to justify the use of such theories when he deems them appropriate.

In moving from models of fully informed optimization to models of bounded rationality, one accepts increasing complexity in the specification of the decision procedure. Moreover, complexity is not the only cost: 'At each step we have (at least potentially) gained realism, but lost certainty' (1982, 2: p.235). Perfect competition 'is an essential condition for unambiguous prediction of behavior from the classical assumptions of economic rationality' (1982, 2: p.339). Although these two observations are intended as criticisms of conventional economics, they may also be used as a defence. The analyst's bounded rationality leads him to use models which generate clear outcomes. The certainty may have been false, but its disappearance is still perceived as a loss.

Moreover, let us remember that 'it may be more important to have agreement on the facts than to be certain that what is agreed upon is really fact'. Agreement on the 'fact' that the established structure of economics is broadly appropriate for economists' purposes is important in that it permits them to work within an agreed framework, and therefore to work (in some sense) more effectively. Economics is a fairly well-ordered intellectual adventure in which problems can be solved as fast as new ones are created, as long as the structure is protected by its interdependencies. The interdependence of economic

154   The mind and method of the economist

theories, mutually reinforced by their derivation from a small set of ideas and assumptions, provide them with an armour which is not easily penetrated. It is this interdependence which protects Cobb–Douglas production functions and allows Occam's razor to be deployed in their defence – and in defence of every other part of the structure in turn.

This application of Simon's own arguments needs to be supplemented by the philosophical argument – which is actually psychological – supplied by Adam Smith (1980) and Shackle (1967), and set out in Chapter 1. A single, apparently well integrated theory is much more comfortable than a set of partial theories which are not readily commensurable; for it not only provides a means of accommodating all phenomena, but leaves no doubts about the relationship between the particular explanations which are employed on different occasions. If we rely on a cluster of theories which clearly do not fit together very well, then the more sensitive we are to the problems of the human condition, the more concerned we are likely to be that such obviously incomplete theories may be inadequate or misleading – and therefore unreliable as a basis for expectations and for decisions. Even if we can quieten our doubts by pretending to more assurance than we feel, nevertheless contemplation of the future brings, in Shackle's (1967, p.288) words, 'the uneasy consciousness of mystery and a threatening unknown'.

It is perhaps the most remarkable feature of Simon's work that it appears to be the product of a man who is prepared to face the unknown without a general theory, but with a faith that, despite the bounds on their rationality, human beings can display enough flexibility and imagination to recognize and to solve their problems fast enough to maintain, and even to improve their situation. If his faith is justified, few people will have done more to help us realize it.

Works referred to by Brian J. Loasby in 'Herbert Simon's Bounded Rationality'

Barnard, C. (1938), *Functions of the Executive*, Cambridge, MA, Harvard University Press.

Coddington, A. (1975), 'Creaking Semaphore and Beyond', *British Journal for the Philosophy of Science*, **26**: 151–63.

Cyert, R.M. and March, J.G. (1963), *A Behavioral Theory of the Firm*, Englewood Cliffs, NJ, Prentice-Hall.

Hahn, F.H. (1984), *Equilibrium and Macroeconomics*, Oxford, Blackwell.

Kelly, G.A. (1963), *A Theory of Personality*, New York, W.W. Norton.

Kirzner, I. (1973), *Competition and Entrepreneurship*, Chicago, IL, University of Chicago Press.

Leijonhufvud, A. (1977), 'Costs and Consequences of Inflation', in Harcourt, G.C. (ed.) *The Microeconomic Foundations of Macroeconomics*, London, Macmillan.

Nelson, R.R. and Winter, S.G., Jr (1982), *An Evolutionary Theory of Economic Change*, Cambridge, MA, Harvard University Press.

Popper, K.R. (1972), *The Logic of Scientific Discovery*, 6th imprint, London, Hutchinson.

Richardson, G.B. (1960), *Information and Investment*, Oxford, Oxford University Press (republished, 1990).

Schumpeter, J.A. (1934), *The Theory of Economic Development*, Cambridge, MA, Harvard University Press.

Shackle, G.L.S. (1967), *The Years of High Theory*, Cambridge, Cambridge University Press.

Simon, H.A. (1969), *The Sciences of the Artificial*, Cambridge, MA, MIT Press.

Simon, H.A. (1982), *Models of Bounded Rationality: Volume I, Economic Analysis and Public Policy; Volume II, Behavioral Economics and Business Organization*, Cambridge, MA, MIT Press.

Smith, A. (1980), 'The Principles Which Lead and Direct Philosophical Inquiries: Illustrated by the History of Astronomy', in Wightman, W.P.D. (ed.) *Essays in Philosophical Subjects* (originally published in 1795), Oxford, Oxford University Press, 33–105.

25

Review of Political Economy, 2.2 (1990), pp 149–67

The unsatisfactoriness of satisficing: from bounded rationality to innovative rationality *

Marina Bianchi *Duke University and University of Rome*

Traditional theory allows for uncertainty in the form of risk or random shocks, without altering the form of the problem of rational choice. Theories of bounded rationality introduce genuine constraints upon the chooser, such as limitations upon the chooser's processing capabilities relative to the complexity of the problem. Three analyses in this newer tradition are examined here (Heiner, Nelson and Winter, and Simon). All three tend to conclude that complexity will engender behaviour governed by rules and routines. This leaves us short of a thoery to account for changes in the routines themselves. The paper shows how a learning procedure must be introduced which renders the process of change endogenous. Rationality in this context must involve search activity which is linked to the recognition of a problem situation and ends up enlarging the set of possible alternative solutions.

I Introduction

The crucial issue for any theory of decision and choice is how to model the impact of uncertainty on behaviour, while allowing to agents' an ability to learn and to adapt. Recent models of choice – those having a common reference to the notion of bounded rationality – try to show how the presence of uncertainty strongly alters individual decision rules. In these models uncertainty arises because the subjective computational abilities of agents are limited and partial when compared with the complexity of a changing environment. Under these circumstances the individual's response consists in restricting the process of choice to simple behavioural rules.

This way of representing choice is contraposed to the standard one, where uncertainty does not seem to really affect choice. In fact, if uncertainty takes the form of unpredictable exogenous shocks, it is modelled by introducing uncorrelated error terms. If uncertainty, on the other hand, is represented as risk, what is required is a more complex kind of behaviour, involving increasing skills of computation and of detecting information. In either case

---

* I would like to thank for their helpful comments Bob Coats, Neil de Marchi, Bob Nau, Ian Steedman, Malcolm Ratherford, Roy Weintraub, the participants in the Duke Economic Thought Workshop, and two anonymous referees. This work has been conducted with support from the Ente per gli Studi Monetari, Bancari e Finanziari Luigi Einaudi.

uncertainty does not alter the way choice is portrayed. The structure of behaviour remains based on the formally unchanged optimization rule (in the second case, even more strengthened).

In the recent alternative ways of representing choice the role, but also the meaning of uncertainty, has clearly changed. The uncertainty does not belong any more to a supposed nature of the environment but to the chooser. In the new framework in fact uncertainty captures the perceived difficulty of processing information, decoding signals, framing problems, decomposing complex systems.

Thus we have in these models a new sense of uncertainty introduced, different from the dual possibility that uncertainty stems from unpredictability or from risk. This is an important contribution, rich in potential implications. Consider the already substantial array of attempts to endogenize uncertainty and formalize the individual and social behavioural rules that emerge from the interaction of environmental complexity and computational insufficiency. Examples here include the new institutional theory, and in particular, analyses of strategic behaviour linked to the emergence of norms and other institutions (Schotter, 1981); evolutionary models applied to economic change and organizations;[1] and some of the psychological literature on heuristic processes (Kahneman *et al.*, 1982).

In this article I select three exemplars of this already vast and increasing literature, the work of Heiner, Nelson and Winter, and Simon. Despite differing standpoints and purposes, the three analyses have in common that uncertainty in the new sense specified above directly engenders rules and routinized behaviour. Rules, habits, routines are the behavioural responses by which the complexity of choice is handled. As already noted, the perspectives opened up by these complementary explanations are important, challenging the old optimization rule with different, uncertainty-driven rules of behaviour. Nonetheless, there is a problem with these explanations. If the perceived uncertainty related to complex environmental change can explain routines, routines for their part cannot explain change. In other words, how routines themselves change, how new rules emerge, remains completely outside these analyses. This kind of change, however, has been explored. It is the Schumpeterian innovative change, which emerges 'from within' and not from an unexplained external motor. What search processes activate and discover is precisely this internal change. In this different perspective therefore uncertainty becomes, positively, the source of innovation and change and not only, negatively, a source of limiting behavioural rules.

All the models we refer to show an internal struggle in trying to cope with this kind of endogenous change. While they emphasize the importance of search activity, the routinized result of searches which they posit directs

---

[1] Examples of evolutionary models are to be found in Day and Eliasson, 1986. Useful analyses from among the burgeoning organizational literature are in Morgan, 1986.

attention to a permanent aspect of behaviour rather than to its change. The solution in fact usually consists of invoking an otherwise unexplained exogenous change as the source of changing routines: just because routines are a self-perpetuating form of behaviour, they can change only exogenously.

By reformulating the sequence of the search process explicitly in terms of learning procedures and problem-solving situations we can begin to see how this endogenous change may be handled. Along these lines many interesting suggestions and examples are to be found in the literature on learning and organizations (see, for example, the holographic approach to organizations and the newer literature on self referential systems as is discussed in Morgan (1986), and Loasby's original contributions to the analysis of decision procedures (1976; 1986)).

I shall return to this later in the paper. First we focus on our three chosen exemplars within the bounded rationality tradition starting with Heiner. His theory of routinized behaviour will then be contrasted with the endogenous innovation approach of Schumpeter. Nelson and Winter may be seen as trying to provide a possible synthesis of routines and innovative change. Their work is examined in Section IV. A comparison with Simon (Section V) shows, however, that a deeper analysis of a search process must be undertaken. Some suggestions toward that end are made in the final section.

II A theory of constrained behaviour

Heiner's thesis is the following. 'Uncertainty' exists because individual competence and perceptual abilities cannot entirely cope with the processes of rightly interpreting information and selecting potential actions (1983: 585). Even when information is complete, therefore, there still remains the problem of correctly responding to it (see for example Heiner, 1988a: 30).[2]

In order to reduce this gap between the agent's competence and the 'difficulty of decision' (what Heiner calls the C-D gap), standard choice theory simply assumes a perfect ability on the part of the agent to respond to the available information. By providing individuals with the most sophisticated learning procedures and probability adjustment processes, the behavioural uncertainty is removed and encapsulated in an innocuous stochastic 'error' term. In this way the theory in fact makes behaviour deterministic and therefore perfectly predictable. Heiner's critique overturns

---

[2] Hodgson correctly stresses that information problems are not simply those connected with its scarcity, as is typically held. More often the problem is that of an overload of information, of an excess of sense data: '. . . rationality is not simply "bounded" in the sense that there is too little information upon which reason can be based, but also that there is too much information to compute or to assess'. (1986: 81, 108–109).

152   *The unsatisfactoriness of satisficing*

this argument (1983: 569–70). Perfect ability to respond to information does not improve predictability of behaviour, rather it seems to reduce it. Examples of decision-making problems, such as the prisoner's dilemma, Rubic's cube, Simon's studies on heuristic processes (and their simulation by digital computer), show that the best performances derive from those strategies that specify more restricted behavioural rules, rather than from those that infinitely amplify the individual's prediction abilities.[3] These examples show in fact that it is not simply from a lack of information, but from an inability to decipher and decode heterogeneous and complex signals that the difficulty of selecting an optimal course of action arises.

The 'simple analytical engine' that Heiner constructs to investigate the problem of the C-D gap (1983: 75) is based on the concept of a 'reliability condition' combined with the principles suggested by psychological studies of detection skills and cognitive tasks.

> The intuition behind this approach is that agents who are not fully competent to always select preferred actions (i.e. who are not able to maximize in the traditional sense) may consequently not be sufficiently reliable to benefit from selecting successively more actions. This will tend to restrict agents to smaller repertoires, with resulting behavioural patterns that are simpler than if all potentially optimal actions could be correctly chosen. In this way, regularities manifested in behaviour are indirectly generated by uncertainty that limits the reliability of selecting potential actions (1973: 72).

In short, increases in uncertainty, i.e., increases in the complexity of the environment or decreases in agents' perceptual abilities, or both, will decrease the range of reliable possible actions. This causes a decrease in the flexibility of behaviour in a direction that is thus quantitatively predictable.

This analytical engine, Heiner argues, may be applied simply and efficaciously to reformulate many traditional economic problems, such as the law of demand; supply behaviour in production theory; or lagged reactions and imperfect responses (Heiner, 1988b); or even restrictive moral rules (Heiner, 1989). The result, he says (1989: 23) is 'to extend existing theory so that optimal decision rules become limiting cases within a larger set of behavioural possibilities'.

The nub of the matter, then, is this. If in the standard theory of choice objective difficulties of decision are simply transferred and solved via a supposed increase in the agent's subjective power of computation, in Heiner the same difficulties are given as the reason for restrictions on behaviour. Moreover, if the uncertainty factors that standard theory places in the stochastic 'error' terms play no role in explaining choice, in Heiner the same

---

[3] In the game of chess, as in Rubic's cube, it is possible in principle 'to exhibit every possible sequence of moves on a gigantic decision tree'. Nonetheless '. . . a detailed consideration of a small number of moves selected by informal judgement is more effective than an attempt to evaluate every possible move'. (Loasby, 1976: 42).

factors are responsible for producing behavioural regularities. Finally, while constrained behavioural rules are for Heiner at the basis of predictable patterns of behaviour, the traditional supposed ability of agents to respond with perfect flexibility to information will, as he sees it, tend to produce systematic deviations from these patterns.

What are the limitations of this ingenious and challenging construction? We anticipate two, postponing a more complete analysis to our examination of the models of bounded rationality with which Heiner shares many analytical assumptions.

We have seen in the standard theory of choice and in Heiner's alternative that the behavioural hypotheses are quite opposed. But, despite this opposition, the framework within which choice is conceived is exactly the same. In both cases in fact actors are seen as simply reacting to given external constraints. These constraints, in the form of environmental complexities or limited computational capabilities, are the real motor of individual choice as well as of its changes. People's behaviour simply responds to different environmental settings (Heiner, 1985: 263), either with the the best or something less than the best adaptation.

Heiner's tacit adoption of the traditional framework of choice prevents him from analysing the active role of search activity and confines his attention only to the negative role of the complexity of decisions. Uncertainty activates only defensive, constrained responses: how to prevent, how to minimize errors by constructing limiting rules, is the only aspect of choice he analyses.

Thus the sense in which choice implies search activity and a learning procedure is absent from Heiner's analysis, even if his mention of some feedback mechanism in choice (1985: 263) may suggest the presence of some kind of learning process (see also Heiner, 1989: 27). But if we try to introduce a learning procedure in Heiner's model we are faced with two possibly paradoxical results.

On the one hand, the introduction of learning may mean the improvement of individual perceptual abilities, an increase in the reliability condition and an increase in the flexibility of behaviour. Through learning therefore, agents in Heiner's own model may reach or approximate the same optimal solution that is otherwise rejected.

On the other hand, Heiner clearly stresses that more flexibility in responding to perturbations in the environment does not facilitate improved performance in choice and does not produce easily recognizable patterns (1983: 562). The result of introducing learning thus may be, either an increasing individual inability to choose, or an increasing rigidity in behaviour.

We may escape these conclusions only by clarifying the role played by learning and the possible changes that learning activates. Solving problems through learning may imply exploring new opportunities and modifying the

154   *The unsatisfactoriness of satisficing*

given set of difficulties. Learning therefore may enlarge the range of possible alternatives rather than restricting them.[4] We will see how search problems may be analysed when we turn to Simon; but the real precursor of the view that behaviour may actively exploit unexplored possibilities and create new frontiers of action is Schumpeter.

III Innovative change

1 Endogenous change

Schumpeter distinguishes between two kinds of change. One is the continuous, imperceptible change that characterizes economic life in its 'circular flow', in its tendency towards an equilibrium. Like the circulation of the blood, the 'circular flow' runs on in channels that are essentially the same year after year, always within the same framework. But there are also changes which involve a change of the framework, of the traditional course itself. They '. . . cannot be understood by means of any analysis of the circular flow, although they are purely economic and although their explanation is obviously among the tasks of pure theory' (Schumpeter, 1934: 61).

This second kind of change on which, for Schumpeter, the evolutionary character of the economic process is dependent, is not due merely to changes in the social and natural environment. Those changes, such as wars and revolutions, or the quasi-automatic increase in population, or the vagaries of the monetary system, often condition industrial change, but they are not its prime movers. The fundamental impulse 'that sets and keeps the capitalistic engine in motion' and 'incessantly revolutionizes' the economic structure, comes from within, not from without (Schumpeter, 1950: 82).

So we have, in Schumpeter:

> 1) a mechanism of economic change conceived not as continuous change in the data of static theory, but as discontinuous, revolutionary, innovative change;
> 2) a mechanism that is endogenous, not exogenous;
> 3) a strong result, namely that the lack of a solution to the problem of change means a lack of understanding of the very mechanism of economic development.

2 The new combinations

This internal source of development consists in the carrying out of new combinations: new goods, new methods of production, new markets, new

---

[4] As an aside, we might note that the literary example Heiner offers of constrained behaviour – Ulysses voluntarily binding himself to prevent the temptation of the sirens (1983: 573) – strangely seems to prove the opposite of his thesis. Ulysses constrains himself in the presence of the known temptation in order to be free to explore the unknown world, to follow 'virtue and knowledge'.

sources of supply, new organization. 'Enterprise' and 'entrepreneurs' are the levers of these newly discovered combinations. They do not exist in the circular flow, where there is neither profit nor loss.

But why is the carrying out of new combinations a special process and the object of a special kind of 'function'? Schumpeter's answer relies on a sharp distinction between the routines which channel the circular flow and the new structures arising from within. This is where entrepreneurship comes in, where true leadership plays a role (1950: 84).

The ability of the entrepreneur to discover and exploit opportunities is based on 'values' and motivations that are the opposite of the traditional, 'utilitarian' ones:

> In one sense, he [the entrepreneur] may be called the most rational and the most egoistical of all. For, as we have seen, conscious rationality enters much more into the carrying out of new plans . . . than into the mere running of an established business, which is largely a matter of routine. And the typical entrepreneur is more self-centred than other types, because he relies less than they do on tradition and connection and because his characteristic task . . . consists precisely in breaking up old, and creating new, traditions (1950: 91–92).

But he is rational in no other sense. In no sense is his motivation of the hedonistic kind. Hedonistically, his conduct would be irrational. He 'does not seem to verify the picture of economic man balancing probable results against disutility of effort and reaching in due course a point of equilibrium beyond which he is not willing to go. Effort, in our case, does not seem to weigh at all in the sense of being felt as a reason to stop' (p. 92). And his motivations – the will to conquer, the impulse to fight, the joy of creating, of getting things done, or simply of exercising one's energy and ingenuity, seeking out difficulties, changing in order to change, delighting in ventures – are most distinctly anti-hedonistic motivations (pp. 93–94) (unless we make wants include any impulse whatsoever, reducing our definition to tautology (p. 92)).

In Schumpeter, then, the endogenous mechanism of change and innovation is tightly linked to the role of the entrepreneur and his ability to exploit unexplored alternatives and create new solutions. He transforms uncertainty due to new opportunities into a source of profits, discovering new ways of producing goods, enlarging and developing the old pattern of production.[5] Through this economic figure, uncertainty is no more a 'noise' in the regular economic flow, or simply the source of new 'regularities', but represents the very spring of economic change. In this sense uncertainty is not just a difficulty impinging on choice, it actually plays a positive role.

---

[5] The additional induced change produced by a new or improved product, or technology, flowing across industry boundaries, is analysed and examplified by Scherer in his flows matrix applied to the USA (1984: 32 ff).

156 *The unsatisfactoriness of satisficing*

In the same way Schumpeter clearly sees how in this searching behaviour the laws of traditional rationality are reversed: they are not simply temporarily suspended or weakened in restricted behavioural rules, but transformed in an active exploration of new solutions which endogenously change the givens.

We may note however thàt despite Schumpeter's insistence on an endogenous mechanism, the way in which innovations really manifest themselves is not explained. They start where the boundaries of routine stop, when former accustomed activities become obsolete, and the will and action of the entrepreneur may exercise their creative powers. But we do not know, nor we are able to reconstruct, this shift of behaviour from routine to innovation. We do not know when this outsider, this newcomer makes his innovative contribution. The conditions of this contribution remain external, temporary, episodic.

Even the internal mechanism of innovation is difficult to reconstruct. It relies on a particular individual function, on a psychological virtue, whose subjectivity makes it difficult to analyse and predict. And in fact when this function loses its importance in the social process – because economic progress tends to become depersonalized and automatized or because innovation itself is reduced to routine – then the process of innovation ceases or is undermined (as Schumpeter shows in his *Capitalism, socialism and democracy*, 1950).

Change, then, starts from within, but only by chance. It is endogenous, but can appear only spontaneously, casually. So, the distinction between endogenous and exogenous change, even if it is drawn, is not clear, and the move from a routinized, conservative situation where no change at all occurs to an innovative one is left unexplored.

Only by linking this innovative process to the more general features of search and learning activities are we likely to be able to reconstruct 'internally', as was Schumpeter's intention, this process of change.

IV An evolutionary theory of change

Nelson and Winter share and develop the Schumpeterian view of economic change as an endogenous breach of equilibrium conditions. Their effort consists in modeling the external conditions that permit, or inhibit, this internal change and consequently in reconstructing the processes that link 'changes in firm decision rules and procedures (including productive techniques) to a changing economic environment' (Nelson and Winter, 1982: 36).

The dynamics of the internal adjustment to the changing external conditions is described as an evolutionary selection process whose 'organizational genetics' (1982: 135) is based on the routinized behaviour of the firms. The selective response and adaptation of the firms consists in fact in constructing, developing and transmitting routines (diachronically, through 'genetic inheritance' and synchronically, through imitation).

Routines are conceived as the targets and components that operate to channel the organizational change; they constitute memory and specific operational knowledge: they may engender truce (1982: 98 ff.). Routines store and facilitate the diffusion of information and help co-ordinate actions. Much of the knowledge that is embedded in rules is tacit, not consciously known nor articulable (1982: 134). Information of this sort does not run in codifiable channels.

Routines thus inform the process of developing and adopting new routines (heuristics, or routines as strategies). In this way innovations, changes of routines, may be incorporated in the pattern of rules and behavioural processes that form the organizational structure of the firm, the opposition between change and sameness being attenuated in a form of 'routinized innovation' (1982: 133).

This process of adapting routines is opposed to the optimal behavioural rule of the standard theory of choice. The formation of routines, in fact, captures the objective difficulty of coping with a complex reality (diversity of firms, nature of time, information costs) as well as with the limited subjective computation capabilities of firms. The rational action rule is contracted from an unbounded maximization to a profit-seeking, satisficing behaviour (1982: 31; see also Nelson and Winter, 1974). Consequently, the range of possible actions is restricted to specific, limited, socially transmitted skills.

The models Nelson and Winter build try to generate empirical correlations between the external conditions (market structure, technological regimes, firm size) and the internal behavioural structure of firms. The results of their simulation models show the responses in technique changes and investment decisions to profit signals activated by exogenous changes (1982: 227; cf. also Nelson, 1986: 149). At the same time the 'search and selection' evolutionary metaphor and the improvability of procedure assumption allow for a diversity and pluralism of responses (1982: 402; Winter, 1986).[6]

---

[6] Consider for example Winter (1986). In the paper it is proposed that Schumpeter's two positions on innovation (1912; 1942) are associated with different technological regimes (the entrepreneurial and the routinized regime). These are obtained by postulating different parameter values concerning the 'quality' of external R&D. In the routinized regime the probability of succesfully tapping this external R&D is much lower (because of the routinized behaviour of the large firms), but the benefits of a successful 'draw' are correspondingly higher (because of the high barriers to entry and the presence of secrecy and patent protection). This implies that the routinized regime has lower prices, higher output and higher R&D expenditures. Moreover, in the entrepreneurial regime adopted innovations associated with new entry outnumber those by established firms, whereas in the routinized regime the numbers of new-entry innovations are very low (because of the incremental innovation process of the routinized regime); for the same reasons the routinized regime generates more innovative policies among firms than does the entrepreneurial regime (Winter, 1986: 221).

The great diversity of technological progress and industrial development is therefore a reflection of the underlying system of knowledge sources that feed the progress (1986: 228).

158   *The unsatisfactoriness of satisficing*

The importance of this empirical exploration is that it offers new factual evidence on the external conditions of inventing (Nelson, 1981), but the structure within which this relationship takes place is similar to the traditional one. In this analysis, in fact, the problem of explaining the mechanism of endogenous change is shifted to the problem of describing routinized adaptation to an exogenous change. Even if this process of adaptation now incorporates a (probabilistic) chance of innovative behaviour, of changing rules, the analysis of the sequence of innovation, of the learning and decisional pattern of the firm, being conditional upon the appearance of an exogenous change, is left unexplored. Better put, the sequence is restricted to the mechanism of profit-seeking responses to the exogenous changes in a way predetermined by the 'genetic' code and via imitation (Nelson and Winter, 1982: 149, 211).

Strangely enough, while understanding change is the central point of this analysis, the result turns out to be an analysis of rules of how to prevent, structure and channel change and novelties. Also, the strong Schumpeterian intuition of enterprises actively searching for new solutions is lost in this world of predictable routines, or, rather, of given probabilities of tapping new routines.

This is not to undervalue the importance and the role of routines. Rules may be regarded as the organizational structure of a search activity, the ordering selective process of a problem-solving activity. But the search process itself is nonroutine. It starts with a break, a crisis, a failure of organized solutions. It activates a process of discovery of tentative new solutions, and it is this process that it is crucial to reconstruct if change is be understood.

Routines do not exhaust the range of a firm's behaviour. They represent only the conservative, economizing aspect of this behaviour, so that the main selective effort can be devoted to problem-solving activity. But it is this decision process that must be reconstructed in order to analyse change.

The strongest effort to address this is Simon's, whose view of computationally bounded rationality is strictly linked to the problem of understanding procedures for reaching rational decisions.

V Bounded rationality

In the analysis of Nelson and Winter and in that of Heiner we have seen that the perceived environmental difficulties involve subjective constraints

---

The theoretical problem with this model is that the learning procedures connected with discoveries and problem-solving activities are absent. Probably, once introduced, many of the data would become endogenous variables and the distinction between the two regimes would be less stringent (see, for example, how 'learning externalities' involved in R&D may affect the technological opportunities, as shown by Von Hungern-Sternberg in his comment of Winter's article – 1986: 239).

on behaviour. This form of constrained behaviour is what Simon has called subjective or bounded rationality. For Simon theories of bounded rationality already exist in traditional economic theory. They can be constructed by modifying the classical assumptions of the theory of choice in a variety of ways: by altering the nature of the constraints (risk and uncertainty can be introduced in the demand and cost functions); by altering the nature of the given conditions (the alternatives may be assumed to be incompletely known); or by altering the nature of the given goals (goals different from the classical goal of maximization may be postulated). Expected utility theory, search theories, monopoly theories are the consequences of these new boundaries added to the classical constraints on choice. These alternative ways of constraining rational behaviour mostly locate the new constraints in the environment, outside the 'skin' of the rational actor (Simon, 1972: 409), in the form of probability distributions of unknown events, limits upon and costs of information. In this way they 'do nothing to alleviate the computational complexities facing the decision maker . . . but simply magnify and multiply them' (Simon, 1979: 504) by requiring an increased effort to control a (still) more complex environment.

The theory of bounded rationality that Simon constructs, by contrast, incorporates the constraints in the very information-processing and computing capabilities of the actor. The hypothesis of bounded rationality in fact claims, as Heiner later reasserted, that human computation skills are too limited compared to the difficulty of the perceived environment – the innumerable variables and information to which the actors might attend (Simon, 1986: 34).[7]

Under conditions of bounded rationality it is the *process* of choice which becomes relevant. Search processes and selecting activities are the new required skills (Simon, 1978a: 2; 1976).

Simon distinguishes two kinds of decision processes: 'programmed' and 'nonprogrammed' decisions. (This distinction, Simon reminds us, is analogous to the distinction between 'habitual' behaviour and 'genuine' decisions made by Katona, or between 'routine' and 'critical' decisions made by Selznik (Simon, 1958: 380). (It is recurrent, we may add, in all the analyses we have referred to.)[8]

Programmed decision making is decision making in the context of a fixed and specified frame of reference, with alternatives given in advance and with

---

[7] Thus, as Simon clearly puts it: 'the domains where a theory of computation, normative or descriptive, is likely to prove useful are the domains that are too complex, too full of uncertainty, too rapidly changing to permit the objectively optimal actions to be discovered and implemented' (1978b: 504).

[8] The corresponding idea that choices are optimal or nearly so in a steady or immutable world, and that choices are not optimal in a world of discontinuous changes, is also widely held (see, for example, Winston, 1982). This distrinction holds only if choices are seen as simply reflecting the external environment.

160 *The unsatisfactoriness of satisficing*

known (or probabilistically known) connections between alternatives and their consequences. The classical theory of the firm is, for Simon, a good example of rational programmed decision making, even if, as he notes, also in such a simple economic model as this a number of simplifying assumptions have to be made in order to bring the problem within the bounds of practical solvability.

In the nonprogrammed decision on the other hand, where the alternatives are not given in advance, and where the means-ends connection is not known, a search process must be activated to discover the new alternatives and in order to explore the consequences of choices.

Nonprogrammed decisions in fact are those characterized: 1) by a search process which is highly unsystematic and nonexhaustive; and 2) by an unsystematic change of 'set', i.e., by a sudden switch from one frame of reference (or set) to another.

Given Simon's dual characterization of choices the crucial question is the following: when do actors shift from a determinate framework of choice to another one? In other words, the problem is to determine when the search process becomes operative, when the new alternatives must be discovered, when the world is perceived as being so complex that a selective activity is required. This also amounts to answering the question of why actors do not remain within the limits of their habitual behaviour. The problem is that of Schumpeter – habits become dragchains; what was formerly a help becomes a hindrance (Schumpeter, 1934: 80, 88).

A first answer Simon gives to his own question follows immediately from the previous analysis. A nonprogrammed decision is required when the external situation presents a genuine novelty. In this situation, characterized, for example, by exogenous shocks, we can imagine that the previous ranking of alternatives changes or becomes obsolete, the consequences of choice become less predictable, the complexity of the variables to control grows. In all these cases search activities must be initiated.

A second answer is related to what Simon calls 'aspiration level'. A search for a new concrete alternative to replace the old one is involved when the result the decision maker expects from a course of action is inferior to his aspiration level. A search for a new programme is initiated by 'the failure of the current one to satisfy aspirations' (Simon, 1958: 397).

Aspirations are expectations of the result of an action that can be reasonably attained (1958: 399). Contrary to the optimization hypothesis aspirations are not formed on the basis of a complete evaluation of all the possible alternatives. 'Indeed their principal usefulness lies in the fact that they remove the necessity for such evaluations until the failures of existing programs indicate the need for innovations' (1958: 399). The innovation process, then, represents the discovery of new programmes that can be regarded as good enough, as satisfactorily compatible with aspirations.

In his first answer Simon simply shifts the problem of when to begin a search onto the emergence of an unexplained exogenous event. Through this second one he achieves the important result of analysing the very steps and sequences of search activity. Starting with the failure of the existing programmes to offer good solutions and a perceived need to discover new ones, the search process stops when a new satisfactory solution is found (Simon, 1979: 503). This result is relevant and new because through it Simon enters into and reconstructs the mechanism of choice, its selective activity, its looking for new alternatives. This mechanism produces change,[9] a theoretical result that Simon shares with Schumpeter and 'his domain of long term dynamics' (search for new products and new marketing strategies – see Simon, 1978b: 505).

But there is a double difficulty in this second answer. The first lies in the concept of aspiration level. Even if it is described as not static, but changing with the environment (1979: 503), this behavioural feature remains difficult to define and to detect. It retains many of the psychological characteristics of the optimality principle it supplants and runs the same risk of being tautologous. Moreover, and more importantly, as long as search activity is involved, it suggests that, once the desired level of satisfaction has been reached, the process of search may be considered concluded until a new exogenous change and a new element of complexity in choice intervenes. Finally, the reference to subjective levels of aspirations does not seem strictly necessary. As we shall see in a moment, once choice is well specified as a process, as a search and selection of new alternatives, through error correction and the finding of tentative solutions, there is no more need to invoke assumptions about psychological motivations, drives and scales of preferences.

A second difficulty lies in the distinction Simon draws between routinized and nonroutinized behaviour (between programmed and nonprogrammed actions). This distinction, which is an assumption that all the analyses we have looked at accept without question, suggests and reinforces the idea that satisficing behaviour – the search process, the innovative solution are activities present only in extraordinary, exceptional circumstances. Why marginalize search in this way? Is ′ it not part of choice under all circumstances?

VI Constrained versus maximized behaviour

At this point it may be helpful to summarize the contrasts we have uncovered.

The theories of constrained behaviour we have analysed utilize a concept of uncertainty whose role and meaning in the process of choice is rather different from the traditional one. While traditionally uncertainty represents

---

[9] As is shown in Newell and Simon, 1972.

162   *The unsatisfactoriness of satisficing*

the 'environmental' unpredictability of choice in the sense both of probabilistic and of stochastic uncertainty, here uncertainty represents the limited ability of the individual to comprehend and act in an unstable environment; it is the indecipherable complexity of all the possible alternatives and consequences of a decision problem; it is the difficulty of rightly selecting potential actions (on which see Rutherford, 1988).

This shift of meaning implies that uncertainty is internal to the choice problem, it is another way of defining the difficulty of choosing. It arises when choice arises, it becomes relevant whenever a decision process is involved. Hence we may properly call this uncertainty endogenous.[10]

From this different representation of uncertainty there results a different view of the process of choosing. In the standard theory, choice proceeds from exogenous, known (or probabilistically known) constraints to the unique optimal solution, through a free, unbounded, maximization process (with the stochastic 'error' term capturing the casual exogenous shocks). By contrast, in this alternative view, choice proceeds from endogenous, complex and not completely known constraints, to a range of suboptimal solutions (satisficing solutions). The process is one of selection and ends in behavioural rules, habits, norms. Errors here begin to play a substantial, not a merely nominal, role.

The effects on behaviour too are different. In the standard theory the presence of environmental uncertainty simply requires agents to display an enhanced computational ability. In the alternative approach, perceived uncertainty goes together with a recognition of limited computational skills and restricted rules of behaviour.

But in the two constructions there are similarities too. Both solutions in fact refer to uncertainty as a negative event (cf, noise, constraints). In both cases action and choice are conceived uniquely as a process of reducing this negative uncertainty (successfully in the traditional theory, partially successfully in the theory of bounded rationality and its counterparts). Thus, even if the process of adaptation to the given conditions of uncertainty is different, the framework within which this process acts seems to be the same. It consists of finding the best solution, or the solution that is good enough, compatible with given conditions. In both cases the solution represents also the end of the search process, of the process of adaptation, until a new perceived event or a change in the aspiration level, any of which may change the starting conditions, activates a new search activity.

In the case of the alternative views we have seen that, the given conditions being different, the search process plays a different and more decisive role. But we cannot escape the impression that this process remains episodic, nonsystematic, conditional upon the appearance of an exogenous shock, and

---

[10] For the difference between Simon and Muth, see Simon, 1979: 505.

is exhausted when the new shock is correctly channelled into the new rules. Not by chance this real search process is nonetheless always contraposed to a world of stability and repetitiveness where, the variables of choice being controllable and known, solutions would be optimal and search superfluous. Again, not by chance some critiques of bounded rationality have stressed substantial similarities between these two different views of choice (see, for example, Hodgson, 1986: 100).[11]

These similarities, however, are often taken too far. Hahn, for example, tends to exploit them in order to reduce bounded rationality to a special case within the traditional framework. Simon's aim, argues Hahn, is to enlarge the range of constraints upon choice, by including the time and effort spent in discovering the set of possible actions, or the trouble of self-scrutiny involved in identifying our own preferences. But after all 'Simon's argument gains what force it has by the existence of the pure theory which he finds wanting' (Hahn, 1985: 15).

Hahn's critique, for its part, has force as long as the choice process is represented as ending up only in routines: for then choice complexity may be translated into additional constraints. Similarly, if the search process is episodic, it may be regarded merely as a response to changed givens.

But the criticism is incorrect as long as satisficing behaviour is reformulated so as to emphasize the active role of search and its innovative character. Satisfactory solutions are inherently unstable, always open to challenge by some new, different or better solution. Satisfactory solutions have internal, 'critical' weaknesses and limitations; they are partial, subject to possible failures. How to discover, how to exploit, how to take advantage of this internal uncertainty in order to offer new solutions constitutes the true scope of search activity.

This carries an implication which has not been fully explored. Search activity does not need an external motor, an exogenous change, to be activated. It relies on the tentative, temporary character of a discovered new solution. It starts from the failure of an old solution to solve the problem for which it was advanced, and it temporarily stops when a new tentative solution is discovered. Hereby change becomes endogenous.

Once so reformulated the search process is not simply added to an already structured theory, but, by implying an endogenous change, changes the conditions of the theory itself. Search itself continuously modifies the givens.

Again, once so reformulated, the psychological framework of satisficing behaviour is no longer necessary and becomes redundant. In fact, a solution works or fails not because it matches, or does not, a psychological aspiration

---

[11] Hodgson, for example, argues that bounded rationality theory, like the traditional theory, retains the same rationalistic structure which proceeds through linear logical deductions from an individual's premises and given knowledge to a set of outcomes (1986: 100).

level, but because it can or cannot cope with the problem to solve which it was advanced. Thus, the ability of a solution to prove itself a good solution is logical, not psychological.[12]

VII From a psychological to a logical theory of choice

There are two points in the bounded rationality analyses we have referred to that are compelling. One is the idea that uncertainty is choice-related. That means that uncertainty does not simply lie outside in the changing environment, but it arises in connection with the selective activity of choice in the form of a perceived difficulty of choosing. Now we can add, and in so doing add precision, that this subjective difficulty does not simply lie inside the psychological or computational inabilities of the individual to cope with the complex environment; rather it arises in the form of a problem situation, unsolved questions, unexplored alternatives. Hence even if the complexity of the environment could be simplified (as in a hypothetical perennially stable environment) and the computational abilities improved (e.g., by the discovery of new computers), still problem-solving situations might arise, signalling the *logically* temporary character of our solutions.

Uncertainty in fact arises as a break, a failure in the previous solutions to the choice problem. We do not know what to do on the basis of the old solutions. This is a signal that a selecting and searching activity must be activated in order to render choice possible. Uncertainty is the specific difficulty of a specific problem situation. In this form it endogenously affects choice.

A second point which it is interesting to stress is that a different process of choice results from this alternative perspective, a process in which not only rules and routines are formed but also active learning is stimulated. For the result of introducing uncertainty in choice is that we must learn from uncertainty, from errors; we must learn how to explore the weaknesses of the present solutions in order to suggest new, unperceived ones.

The idea, originally Schumpeter's, that the process of decision making involves essentially innovative behaviour has undergone recent important developments. Neo-Austrian economists such as Lachmann, and other theorists such as Shackle and Bausor, all share, even if from different standpoints, the view that the choice process necessarily involves creativity. Historical time, the uniqueness of events, the irreversibility of choice are the ingredients that make choice refractory to any optimizing calculation and fundamentally unpredictable.[13] The problem with these explanations of

---

[12] Boland has stressed at length the importance of a logical reconstruction of the choice process. Still his analysis seems to stop at a methodological level rather than reconstructing the steps and results of the process itself.

[13] As Shackle points out (1984: 391), if economic theory 'could tell us what will take place, it would rob us of all claim to be, in the elemental sense, creatively original'. In the

choice in terms of imaginative search is that the positive relevance assigned to creativity is made completely unbounded and lawless, as well as unique and unpredictable. Knowledge is important but cannot be known.

By contrast, when search is represented explicitly in terms of learning, the openness and unending character of learning is retained but within a structure. Learning means the appearance of new possible solutions, but within the boundaries of the specific and concrete problem-solving situation within which it arises.

Interesting developments and suggestions in this direction may be found in Loasby (1976; 1986), as well as in the recent literature on organization which applies learning to the analysis of organizational structures.

Loasby's framework of 'partial ignorance' (1976: 9)[14] is the basis of a choice process which must be logically preceded by a search for possible actions, but a search can start only if a problem is recognized. The analysis of the reference standards or models employed to detect a problem, to direct search, to evaluate choice, to implement and to appraise the result, gives us the criteria, as well as concrete directions in the several phases of this sequential decision process (1976: 96 ff).

The idea that organizations are complex communication systems is one of the basic issues of recent organizational analyses. In this framework, organizations are viewed as systems able to learn and to learn to learn ('double-loop' learning as opposed to the 'single-loop' learning of the more simple cybernetic systems (cf, for example, Argyris, 1982).[15] They are able to detect and correct errors in operating norms and therefore change the rules and the standards that guide their actions. Reframing problems and changing reference standards become recognizable and important inherent elements of the decision process.

These final examples show the natural and unavoidable directions in which the introduction of learning processes into choice forces us. They open up the prospect of a useful shift from the study of bounded rationality to the study of rational innovativeness.

---

irrepetible time's flow learning is powerless: '. . . the learning process is at all times eating its own heart' (1984: 392). Bausor, similarly, says: 'We may have sensory evidence and memory of the past, but only imagination of the future' (1986: 94; 1984).

14 'Uncertainty reduction may be the principal activity of both science and management; but it is uncertainty creation which provides the major opportunities for both' (Loasby, 1976: 103; see also Loasby, 1986: 52–53).

15 As Morgan says (1986: 90) '. . . highly sophisticated single-loop learning may actually serve to keep the organization in the wrong course, since people are unable . . . to challenge underlying assumptions'. This kind of organization '. . . is rarely able to tolerate high levels of uncertainty'. On the problem of the levels of knowledge see also Watzlawick *et al.* (1967: 260).

166   *The unsatisfactoriness of satisficing*

VIII References

Argyris, C. 1982: *Reasoning, learning and action*. San Francisco: Jossey–Bass.

Bausor, R. 1984: Toward a historically dynamic economics: examples and illustrations. *Journal of Post Keynesian Economics* 3, 360–410.

—— 1986: Time and equilibrium. In Mirowski, P., editor, *The reconstruction of economic theory*, Boston: Kluwer–Nijhoff Publishing, 93–136.

Boland, L.A. 1986: *Methodology for a new microeconomics*. London: Allen and Unwin.

Day, R.H. and **Eliasson, G.E.**, editors, 1986: *The dynamics of market economies*. Amsterdam: Elsevier.

Hahn, F. 1985: In praise of economic theory. In Hahn, F., *Money, growth, and stability*, Oxford: Basil Blackwell.

Heiner, R.A. 1983: The origin of predictable behaviour. *American Economic Review* 4, 560–95.

—— 1985: Experimental economics: a comment. *American Economic Review* 1, 260–63.

—— 1986: Uncertainty, signal-detection experiments, and modeling behaviour. In Langlois, R.N., editor, *Economics as a process: essays in the new institutional economics*, Cambridge: Cambridge University Press, 116–59.

—— 1988a: The necessity of imperfect decisions. *Journal of Economic Behaviour and Organization* 10, 29–56.

—— 1988b: The necessity of delaying economic adjustment. *Journal of Economic Behaviour and Organization* 10, 255–86.

—— 1989: Imperfect choices and self-stabilizing rules. *Economics and Philosophy* 5, 19–32.

Hodgson, G.M. 1988: *Economics and institutions*. Philadelphia: University of Pennsylvania Press.

Kahneman, D., Slovic, P. and **Tversky, A.** 1982: *Judgment under uncertainty: heuristics and biases*. Cambridge: Cambridge University Press.

Lachmann, L. 1977: *Capital, expectations, and the market process*. Kansas City: Sheed, Andrews and McMeel.

Loasby, B.J. 1976: *Choice, complexity and ignorance*. Cambridge: Cambridge University Press.

—— 1986: Organization, competition and the growth of knowledge. In Langlois, R.N., editor, *Economics as a process. Essays in the new institutional economics*, Cambridge: Cambridge University Press, 41–58.

Morgan, G. 1986: *Images of organization*. Beverly Hills: Sage Publications.

Nelson, R.R. 1981: Research on productivity growth and differences. *Journal of Economic Literature* 3, 1029–64.

—— 1986: The tension between process stories and equilibrium models:

analyzing the production growth slowdown of the 1970's. In Langlois, R.N., editor, *Economics as a process: essays in the new institutional economics*, Cambridge: Cambridge University Press, 135–52.

Nelson, R.R. and **Winter, S.G.** 1974: Neoclassical vs evolutionary theories of economic growth: critique and prospectus. *Economic Journal* 4, 886–905.

—— 1982: *An evolutionary theory of economic change*. Cambridge, MA: Belknap Press.

Newell, A. and **Simon, H.A.** 1972: *Human problem solving*. Englewood Cliffs, NJ: Prentice Hall.

Rutherford, M. 1988: *Rational expectations in the light of modern psychology*. Mimeograph.

Shackle, G.L.S. 1984: Comment on the papers by Randall Bausor and Malcom Rutherford. *Journal of Post Keynesian Economics* 3, 388–93.

Scherer, F.M. 1984: *Innovation and growth. Schumpeterian perspectives*. Cambridge, MA: MIT Press.

Schotter, A. 1981: *The economic theory of social institutions*. Cambridge: Cambridge University Press.

Schumpeter, J.A. 1934 (1912): *The theory of capitalistic development*. Cambridge: Harvard University Press.

—— 1950 (1942): *Capitalism, socialism, and democracy*. New York: Harper and Brothers.

Simon, H.A. 1958: The role of expectations in an adaptive or behaviouristic Model. In Simon, 1982: 380–400.

—— 1972: Theories of bounded rationality. In Simon, 1982: 408–23.

—— 1976: From substantive to procedural rationality. In Latsis, S.J., editor, *Method and appraisal in economics*, Cambridge: Cambridge University Press, 129–48.

—— 1978a: Rationality as a process and as a product of thought. *American Economic Review* 2, 1–16.

—— 1978b: On how to decide what to do. *The Bell Journal of Economics* 2, 494–507.

—— 1979: Rational decision making in business organizations. *American Economic Review* 4, 493–513.

—— 1982: *Models of bounded rationality*. Cambridge, MA: MIT Press.

—— 1986: On the behavioural and rational foundations of economic dynamics. In Day, R.H. and Eliasson, G., 1986: 21–41.

Watzlawick, P., Bavelas, J.B. and **Jackson, D.D.** 1967: *Pragmatics of human communication*. New York: Norton and Company.

Winter, S.G. 1986: Schumpeterian competition in alternative technological regimes. In Day, R.H. and Eliasson, G., 1986: 199–232.

Winston, G.C. 1982: *The timing of economic activity*. Cambridge: Cambridge University Press.

26

Cambridge Journal of Economics 1997, **21**, 663–684

The ubiquity of habits and rules

Geoffrey M. Hodgson*

Under what circumstances is it necessary or convenient for an agent to rely on habits or rules? This paper focuses on the types of decision situation giving rise to their use. Even optimisation requires the deployment of rules, and for this reason mainstream economics cannot legitimately ignore these questions. The argument is that habits and rules are ubiquitous in human activity. In a new taxonomy, seven types of decision situations are considered, classified according to the type of information problem involved. Neither neoclassical nor behavioural economics can provide a complete account of the bases of habits or rules in these cases.

Economists have typically ignored the procedures and rules that are knowingly or unwittingly employed by agents when deciding and acting in the real world. In a highly influential essay Milton Friedman (1953, p. 22) conveniently side-stepped pleas for more realistic analyses of the way in which business people decide and act. He disregarded empirical evidence of the routine-driven nature of business activity with the famous argument:

Let the apparent immediate determinant of business behaviour be anything at all—habitual reaction, random chance, or whatnot. Whenever this determinant happens to lead to behaviour consistent with rational and informed maximization of returns, the business will prosper and acquire resources with which to expand; whenever it does not, the business will tend to lose resources and can be kept in existence only by the addition of resources from outside.

Thus for decades economists have largely ignored the actual processes governing decision and action, presuming that the mysterious forces of 'natural selection' ensure that 'correct predictions' about human behaviour are likely to come from a much more 'economical' account of human behaviour—that of the agent with fixed preference functions, mechanically programmed to maximise some objective function.

The argument that 'natural selection' necessarily leads to the predominance of profit or utility maximisers has been criticised elsewhere and need not be discussed further here (Winter, 1964; Hodgson, 1994). Remarkably, it has been recently demonstrated using computer simulations—using the technique of genetic programming—that in a complex decision environment artificially intelligent agents are likely to generate and apply simple decision-making rules, because of the insurmountable informational difficulties involved

Manuscript received 6 November 1995; final version received 10 October 1996.

* University of Cambridge. A version of this paper was first presented at the American Economic Association special session on institutions, Washington DC, 6 January 1995. The author is very grateful to Elias Khalil, Nigel Pleasants, Yngve Ramstad, Mattia Rattaggi, Herbert Simon, two anonymous referees and several other people for helpful and critical remarks.

664   G. M. Hodgson

in global, optimising behaviour (Dosi *et al.*, 1993). The conclusion of this analysis is that economists cannot reasonably avoid study and analysis of the processes of formation of representations and behavioural rules, and the problem cannot be avoided on the grounds suggested by Friedman years ago.

The central question here is: in what circumstances are agents required to, or likely to use, habits or rules? It is suggested that the need to rely on habits or rules is quite general, even when facing well-defined optimisation problems. The ubiquity of habits and rules locates optimisation as a special case of a broader class of decision problems. This does not necessarily mean that an alternative 'general theory' of human behaviour is possible or desirable; instead it suggests more clearly that a detailed analysis of the evolution of specific habits and rules—including the pecuniary rationality of a market economy—should be instated at the core of economics and social theory. However, the full discussion of the implications of the argument here must be left to another work.

Section 1 examines in detail the possible circumstances in which habits and rules are advantageous for human decision-making or action. Such habits and rules are advantageous in the sense that they help agents to decide, learn or act. Although much of the argument here is based on previous work by other authors, the proposed taxonomy is novel and seemingly exhaustive of all possibilities. A concise exposition of seven types of decision situation is offered, even at the risk of briefly revisiting some familiar points. Note that the taxonomy does not exclude the possibility that the framework of rational optimisation may be applicable to a significant class of decision situations. Instead, the emphasis is put on the reliance of rational behaviour on habits and rules. Even if the domain of applicability of the rational actor paradigm is significant, it is not universal. It is one of seven types of decision situation which are reliant on habits or rules. Section 2 concludes the essay by extending the argument briefly to institutions and making some observations concerning neoclassical, behavioural and institutional economics and their different treatments of the uses of habits and rules. Some final remarks concern the direction of future research.

1. When are habits or rules conveniently deployed?

Habit is defined by Charles Camic (1986, p. 1044) as 'a more or less self-actuating disposition or tendency to engage in a previously adopted or acquired form of action'. Rules are conditional or unconditional patterns of thought or behaviour which can be adopted either consciously or unconsciously by agents. Generally rules have the form: in circumstances X, do Y. Habits may have a different quality: rule-following may be conscious and deliberative whereas habitual action is characteristically unexamined (Murphy, 1994). Rules do not essentially have a self-actuating or autonomic quality but clearly, by repeated application, a rule can become a habit. Typically it is easier to break a rule than to change a habit, since our awareness of our own habits is often incomplete and they have a self-actuating character because they have become established in subliminal areas of our nervous system. However, habits still have the same general form: in circumstances X, action Y follows. Hence for much of the following discussion it is not necessary to address the important distinction between habits and rules. Both apply to situations that, in essential terms, are actually or potentially repetitive and non-unique. Although the qualitative differences between habits and rules are important, they are not central to the preliminary issues that are addressed in this essay.

Clearly some habits or rules are efficacious and others are not. Some rules—such as when tragedy strikes, sacrifice a favoured animal to placate the gods—may have no scientific foundation. However, the association of ritual sacrifice with subsequent well-being is consistent with a system of belief, and recourse to the rule is thus explicable in those terms. Cultures can foster enduring explanations and justifications of even the most ill-founded of rules. There are also bad habits. Repeated behaviours may become ingrained even if they are disadvantageous. Nevertheless, if bad habits are common this does not undermine the proposition that recourse to habit is often necessary. On the contrary, humans and other animals have evolved the ability to form habits to deal with elaborate and changing circumstances. The evolved capacity for habituation may produce maladaptations and errors but this does not undermine the fact that habits of some kind are indispensable. For these reasons the efficacy or otherwise of particular habits or rules need not concern us here. The argument is more general, in terms of a pervasive requirement to use rules or form habits as part and parcel of the human condition.

Some habits and rules may be advantageous for a society or group but not for specific individuals, like obeying the orders of an army officer and thereby risking death in battle, or the adult placing him/herself in danger to protect or rescue a child. Explanations of the origin and reproduction of habits and social rules that confer dubious individual benefit may be problematic for a conventional utilitarian framework, but are not the topic of discussion in this paper.[1] The concern here is simply to examine the circumstances in which agents are likely to turn to habits and rules.

Furthermore, we need not address the origins of particular habits or rules themselves, although their genesis and replication is a vital additional issue. In many cases it could be argued that we have habits and we follow rules because of our biological nature. Again, this proposition is not central to the investigation in this paper. The important question of the extent to which habits or rules are biologically grounded is side-stepped, to place emphasis on the issue of the kind of *decision or action situation* in which it is advantageous to rely upon habits or rules. Seven instances calling for the employment of habits or rules are considered:

1. *Optimisation*: where the choice set is known and it is possible to employ procedures and decision-rules to find an optimum.
2. *Extensiveness*: where the information may be readily accessible and comprehensible but the search for it requires the application of substantial time and other resources.
3. *Complexity*: where there is a gap between the complexity of the decision environment and the analytical and computational capacity of the agent.
4. *Uncertainty*: where crucial information and probabilities in regard to future events are essentially unobtainable.
5. *Cognition*: the general problem of dealing with and interpreting sense data.
6. *Learning*: the general process of acquiring crucial knowledge about the world.
7. *Communication*: the general need to communicate regularly with others.

Note at the outset that not all the above are mutually exclusive and that situations frequently arise involving aspects of more than one. For example, (5) and (6) are closely related. We shall consider each of the seven elements in turn. Furthermore, it should be noted at the outset that these seven types of decision situation are not merely subjective states of mind experienced by the agent. Each decision situation concerns both the

---

[1] Notable attempts to explain such 'altruistic' or self-sacrificial behaviour include Frank (1988) and the sociobiology of Dawkins (1976) and Wilson (1975).

666   G. M. Hodgson

subjective knowledge and mental capabilities of the agent, on the one hand, and objective characteristics of the decision problem, on the other. This point should become clear in the discussion of the seven types of decision situation below.

1.1 Optimisation

A familiar question of enduring controversy is the extent to which optimising techniques are applicable to decision situations in the real world. Modern neoclassical economics is founded on the assumption that they are.[1] Even if assumptions of perfect information are dropped, it is typically assumed that uncertain or complex decision problems can still be accommodated using probabilistic methods, by assuming that well-defined probability distributions can be attached to key variables. Against this, a number of critics have argued that a significant proportion of decision problems are not amenable to stochastic or other optimisation techniques (Veblen, 1919; Knight, 1921; Keynes, 1936; Hayek, 1948; Simon, 1957; Shackle, 1972). Arguably, optimisation applies to a limited set of static and closed decision contexts. For the purposes of the following discussion, however, the extent to which optimisation can apply to the real world need not be considered at length.

Against the view that the extensive use of habits and rules is incompatible with the picture of rational, optimising 'economic man', Rutherford (1994, pp. 53–4) writes:

> The fact that individuals develop and follow rules does not, in and of itself, indicate that they are not behaving rationally. For example, the usual game theoretic discussion of the emergence of social conventions out of the situation of a repeated game is an attempt to explain a social rule in a way compatible with standard notions of rational maximization. Even more obviously, it is perfectly rational for an individual to comply with an existing social or legal norm if the costs of compliance make adherence to the norm his maximizing choice on each and every occasion.

However, the two examples in this quotation refer to rule-compliance rather than rule-driven behaviour. The 'usual game theoretic discussion' of the emergence of rules purports to explain rule-compliance on the basis of rational choice and utility maximisation. This explanation involves continuously optimising agents who happen to favour a particular rule from the menu of options available to them. This is not the same thing as being driven by a habit or rule where other options are either non-existent or not considered at all.

Much of the game theoretic literature is concerned primarily with the emergence of rules or the basis of rule-compliance. In contrast, the question raised here is the extent to which the very act of optimising behaviour must intrinsically involve rules of decision and action. We are concerned here first and foremost with rule-driven or rule-following behaviour, rather than processes of rule-generation or instances of rule-compliance.

Vanberg (1988, 1993) suggests that rational choice and rule-following behaviour are incompatible. He argues that it is inherently inconsistent to speak of a 'rational choice to follow rules' or a 'rational choice among rules'. To Vanberg, the essence of following a rule is not to deliberate or calculate in every single case but to some extent to be unresponsive to the changing particularities of each choice situation. This is contrasted

---

[1] Neoclassical economics may be conveniently defined as an approach which (1) assumes rational, maximising behaviour by agents with given and stable preference functions, (2) focuses on attained, or movements towards, equilibrium states, and (3) excludes chronic information problems. Although recent developments in economic theory—such as game theory—may push beyond these boundaries, this optimisation paradigm remains dominant in textbook and applied economics.

with the concept of choice, where an individual is deemed free of such '*pre-programmed* behavior'.

However, this argument is not entirely convincing. First, the quality of being unresponsive to changing particularities is not an universal feature of rule-following behaviour. As Vromen (1995, p. 81) argues, a distinction can be made between conditional and unconditional rules. Conditional rules discriminate between different environmental conditions and point to different outcomes in different circumstances. Second, the very idea of rational *calculation*, as elaborated below, must itself depend on computational rules.

What Vanberg ignores is the fact that strict optimisation must necessarily exclude choice. The optimiser of neoclassical economics is essentially a taste-satisfying machine. The outcome is mechanical, determined by given preference functions, relative prices and endowments, and questions of real will or purpose fade away. As Shackle (1972, p. 122) puts it: 'if the world is determinist, then it seems idle to speak of choice'. The observation that strict optimisation is programmed behaviour that essentially denies choice has been made by a number of authors (Buchanan, 1969; Loasby, 1976). If choice means the possibility of acting otherwise then it cannot be predetermined by either preference functions or rules. Vanberg correctly notes the opposition between rule-following and choice but does not see that optimisation also excludes genuinely 'free' choice. Rule-following and optimising behaviours are not necessarily mutually exclusive.

Having cleared that ground we now consider ways in which optimisation may involve the employment of rules. Consider mathematical optimisation problems and their solutions. The procedures of linear programming and differential calculus, for example, all involve methods of optimisation with strict rules. Optimising procedures always involve rules and are rule-governed. These are not essentially the 'rules of the game', but the rules of computation and optimisation itself.

In practice, the human agent cannot be a 'lightning calculator', quickly, effortlessly and inexplicably finding the optimum just as we can readily locate the lowest point of a U-curve in a simple textbook diagram. Even with given and unambiguous information, complex optimisation problems typically involve difficulties not only of specification but of computability (Cutland, 1980). Artificially intelligent systems even in moderately complex environments require 'inherited' framing procedures to structure the incoming information (Cosmides and Tooby, 1994; Pylyshyn, 1987).

Conventional accounts sometimes neglect the universal need for rules of calculation to reach optima. One reason for this is that optimisation is coupled with equilibrium. Statements of equilibrium conditions are not the same thing as the specification of algorithmic or other procedures required to attain equilibria. Yet, often, outcome is confused with process. Another reason for the neglect is the widespread belief that optimisation involves choice and rule-following denies it. On the contrary, as suggested above, optimisation may exclude genuine choice.

Whatever the extent of its application, optimisation must involve rules. This raises the secondary but important question of their origin. Notably, optimisation itself cannot provide a complete explanation of either the origin of rules or the adoption of rule-driven behaviour. As all optimisation involves intrinsic rules, the idea of explaining all rules on the basis of the optimising behaviours of agents involves circular reasoning and is thus misconceived (Field, 1979, 1981, 1984). Hence the question of 'where do the original rules come from?' remains, *and it cannot be answered completely in terms of optimisation itself.* It is necessary to consider additional explanations of their genesis, at least to supplement the optimisation story. In search of this 'first cause' we are forced to consider explanations other than optimisation for the reliance of the individual upon habits and rules. This primary reliance on habits or rules limits the scope of rational optimisation. This itself must always depend on prior habits or rules as props (Hodgson, 1988). Hence rational optimisation can never supply the complete explanation of human behaviour and institutions that some theorists seem to be striving for.[1] There is thus a limit to the 'imperialism' of neoclassical economics. Given that explanation in social science requires more than this powerful idea at its core, it may be surmised that we must rely on more complex, contingent and multifaceted behavioural specifications.[2]

1.2 Extensiveness

Extensiveness here refers to the problem of dealing with large amounts of information, even when it is potentially understandable, accessible and its location is known. We typically face this problem when we search through a library for information on a given topic. A large mass of information is accessible but the library is so vast that an exhaustive search is impossible. Note that the problem being addressed here is not one of complexity, or of interpretation of the information when it is accessed, although these additional features are often present. It is a problem of the 'computational limitations' of the agent only in the narrow sense of dealing with the *amount* of information available. Practical limitations of time and attention are being addressed here.

The problem here is often conventionally put down to the perceived net 'cost' of obtaining further information. Given the expected benefits of the search it does not seem worth using more time and resources in continuing. The 'cost of information' problem is now widely discussed, but recognition of it is not new. One of the earliest accounts is in the writings of the neglected American institutional economist John Maurice Clark (1918, p. 25) who wrote: 'a good hedonist would stop calculating when it seemed likely to involve more trouble than it was worth'. Hence Simon's concept of satisficing behaviour finds its origin in the work of an 'old' institutional economist.

Importantly, there is more to Clark's analysis than this. Because the searcher for the optimum 'could not in the nature of the case tell just when this point has been reached ...no claim to exactness' (*ibid.*) can be made. Thereby the concept of complete optimisation or global rationality is undermined (Winter, 1964, p. 264; Conlisk, 1980). As Pingle (1992, p. 8) writes: 'The paradoxical difficulty facing the consumer when optimizing is costly is that it is not possible to make an optimal choice and know that the choice made is optimal.' Both the costs and the benefits of further search are unknown. Thus, even if we were at the optimum we would not be able to know it and recognise it as such.

It is true that agents may *attempt* to optimise when faced with a problem of extensiveness. If time is regarded as relatively expensive then, typically, the search for further information will be abandoned. But only the expected, not the actual, benefit of further search enters into this calculation. And even if the expectations of costs and benefits were correct, the would-be optimiser could not in principle be aware of this fact.

---

[1] For instance, note Schotter's (1981, p. 5) 'definition of *economics* as *the study of how individual economic agents pursuing their own selfish ends evolve institutions as a means to satisfy them*' (emphasis in original).

[2] Accordingly, neoclassical economics could be regarded as a special and (highly) restricted case of the 'old' institutional economics, which accepted the ubiquity of habits and rules. In contrast to their image as myopic and anti-theoretical data-gatherers, institutionalists have the potential to achieve a higher level of theoretical generality.

Admittedly, the costs of search may be so great and the expectations of benefits so small that it seems clear that further search is not worthwhile. It may thus be suggested that such cases of extensiveness may be treated as conventional optimisation problems. Leaving aside the leap of faith required in forming expectations in such a case, in general it should be evident that many day-to-day problems of extensiveness do not have such a clear excess of costs over perceived benefits.

The problem of information extensiveness is often restated in terms of the net 'cost of obtaining information', in the mistaken belief that this type of problem can always be restated and accommodated in conventional, optimising terms. However, as noted above, the problem of information extensiveness in fact undermines one of the core precepts of orthodox economics: even if agents attempt to optimise they cannot recognise the optimum. Accordingly, the 'cost of information' idea does not in general reduce the problem of extensiveness to one of conventional optimisation with a full information set.

In an essay on the key behaviouralist concept of 'satisficing', Simon discusses the problem of extensiveness without distinguishing it from the issue of complexity. He thus (Simon, 1987B, p. 244) writes of 'searching for a needle in a haystack', where there are 'needles of varying degrees of sharpness' and the objective is to find a sharp needle. Do we search through the entire haystack to find the sharpest needle or find one that is good enough to sew? Frequently we face equivalent problems of extensiveness in our everyday lives. We know the location of all the local supermarkets, but we have not got the time to visit every one and check the prices of all the items we are likely to buy. Even within a single, typical supermarket there are at least 10,000 different products, and we cannot be expected to examine each item and make a fully informed and optimal choice within our budget constraint (Earl, 1983, p. 65). The problem is not one of complexity but of 'information overload'.

Faced with this kind of problem we frequently employ habits or rules. We visit a particular supermarket because it is familiar and we are in the habit of provisioning our needs from its shelves. Or we invoke implicit rules: do not search through all the books in the library, just those by recognised authors, in a definite subject area and published after a specific date.

Nevertheless, unlike the other six factors considered here, extensiveness may not itself be a sufficient basis for habits or rules. While we frequently use habits and rules in such a context, there is no reason for us always to do so. We could rely on mere whim, such as stopping at a particular supermarket simply because we encounter it on another journey. Although rules and habits are inevitably going to be involved even in capricious behaviour, extensiveness is in fact their weakest grounding. This is despite its frequent appearance in discussions of rule-governed behaviour and of the limits to rationality.

1.3 Complexity

The problems of complexity and extensiveness are conceptually quite different, although many real-world information problems have both these properties. Complexity refers to the density of structural linkages and interactions between the parts of an interdependent system, and is not necessarily or primarily a problem of extensiveness or scale. As noted above, the problem of extensiveness may apply to information in regard to which there is little complexity or analytical difficulty. In contrast, consider a situation where all the required information to make an optimal decision is in our hands but because of the complexity of the problem we are unable to analyse it fully and reach an optimal decision.

The problem of complexity also differs from that of cognition, discussed below. The

670   G. M. Hodgson

problem here is not one of the cognition of the sense data but of analysing and using the information that we already possess. Even after the act of cognition, when the sense data are categorised and interpreted, we are not necessarily in a position to use the information that we have acquired.

It is again important to emphasise that there is much more involved than the 'cost' of information here. Some time ago Boulding (1956, p. 84) saw globally rational choice as involving 'a feat of mathematical agility which would take centuries of experience and enormous electronic calculators to perfect.' This recognition of computational limitations has, of course, become a central feature of the behaviouralist research programme of Simon (1957, 1976) and his followers.

Heiner (1983) also addresses the agent's problem of full use of available data. Using empirical support from psychology and elsewhere, Heiner argues that normally there is a gap between the 'competence' of an agent and the 'difficulty' in selecting the preferred alternatives. Such a 'C-D gap' could result from the burden of complex information placed upon the agent in making a decision. Rationality is here 'bounded' because the known information is too complex to compute or assess. As pointed out elsewhere (Heiner, 1983, pp. 563–4; Simon, 1976), some of the best preliminary illustrations of this are the game of chess and puzzles such as Rubic's cube.

There are a very large number of possible initial positions from which to unscramble Rubic's cube. However, the data required in any attempt to work out the quickest way of doing this are readily available by observing the scrambled patterns on the six faces. A 'rational maximiser' with unbounded computational agility could use all this data and find the best way of solving the puzzle. In practice, however, it is too difficult and time-consuming to proceed in this way. Hence cube analysts have developed simple procedures to unscramble the cube (Heiner, 1983, p. 564). These are largely independent of the initial scrambled position and are sub-optimal in that they do not typically unscramble the cube in the minimum number of moves. But from an operational point of view these rules are much more useful than trying to compute and execute the 'optimal' solution.

The chessboard, like Rubic's cube, readily displays all the data required to compute the optimal solution. Chess is thus a game with 'perfect information'. According to game theory, there is always a strategy which will assure one of the players of a win or a tie. Owing to finite speed and memory, however, even fast modern computers are generally unable to analyse all the options available and quickly derive the optimal solution. Consequently, computer programmers have followed and extended the decision procedures of the human chess expert. A skilled human player routinely memorises a large collection of possible patterns of the pieces, together with procedures for exploiting the relations that appear in these patterns. A computer program for playing chess relies less on pattern recognition, and more on an extended search of the move possibilities, according to more rigid decision rules. However, in both cases, players do not 'maximise' by computing the optimal strategy but 'satisfice' by finding one that is 'good enough'.

Rubic's cube and the chess algorithm provide excellent examples of available data that are imperfectly used. Hence a prevailing interpretation of Simon's work can be faulted. Baumol and Quandt (1964), Jensen and Meckling (1976, p. 307n) and others argue that all satisficing behaviour is essentially cost-minimising, once the 'cost of obtaining information' is taken into account. Clearly, cost-minimising behaviour is just the dual of the standard assumption of maximisation. If 'satisficing' was essentially a matter of minimising costs, then it would amount to maximising behaviour of the orthodox type.

However, contrary to this 'cost-minimising' misinterpretation, Simon's concept of bounded rationality refers primarily to the matter of computational capacity and not to additional 'costs'. Once it is recognised that 'bounded rationality' is essentially about limited computational capacity relative to a complex or extensive decision environment, rather than primarily the scarcity or cost of information, then its indissoluble link with the twin concept of satisficing is evident. The term 'satisficing' is employed by Simon precisely to distance his conception from global rationality and maximising behaviour. As Simon himself has always made clear, the twin concepts of bounded rationality and satisficing both involve a direct attack on the concept of global rationality. Indeed, as Dosi and Egidi (1991, p. 151) show, with changing and uncertain environments 'the very notion of "optimality" becomes an ambiguous theoretical notion'. In open and evolving systems the canonical idea of optimisation under constraint is inapplicable because the constraints, if not the objective functions, are moving and changing. In a complex, open and evolving world the very idea of agents with global rationality is not simply empirically unfounded—it is theoretically misconceived.

With limited computational capacity in the face of complexity, attempts to do the calculations implicit in the standard rational choice model would cripple the decision-maker, leaving many vital decisions unattended. We thus fall back on habits and rules of thumb. In mainstream economics there is inadequate recognition of the complexity of the real world and the relatively limited analytic and computational competence of the human brain. Some decision problems may be tractable, but often we encounter those that are not. It is only in a textbook world that we deal typically with a few factors of production and a well-defined space of decision alternatives. In reality, there is a huge variety of heterogeneous resouces, related together in complex ways. Analysis is thwarted by the many-dimensional decision space, the explosive scale of the decision tree and the non-linearity of functional relations. Accordingly, although managers may be able to make use of the methods of operations research to obtain solutions to some optimisation problems, as Teece and Winter argue (1984), most real-world management problems are dynamic, complex and often difficult to structure analytically. They suggest that in these circumstances the neoclassical assumption of transparently rational decision-making in a world of known outcomes or probabilities is of relatively little use.

By wrongly presupposing that all individuals can make optimal decisions in complex environments it is suggested that every individual has an unlimited ability to process complex information, a boundless computational capacity, and the analytical abilities of an advanced mathematician. In fact this assertion is not only problematic, it is also a denial of the principle that resources are generally scarce. Computational capacity and analytical competence are scarce resources too (Pelikan, 1989). We cannot assume unbounded human rationality and universal resource scarcity at the same time.

1.4 Uncertainty

Complexity should not be confused with uncertainty. The latter term appears in mainstream economics texts but with the assumption that agents can attach numerically definite probabilities to events. This is better described as risk and comes within the compass of the optimisation problems discussed above. True uncertainty, in the sense of Knight (1921) or Keynes (1936), applies to situations where the calculation or attribution of a numeric probability is impossible. Arguably, such ignorance makes the attachment even of subjective probabilities implausible. Accordingly, the idea of uncertainty in this radical sense is inconsistent with optimising behaviour. Without a calculus of probability and risk, agents would not be able to locate an optimum.

672   G. M. Hodgson

Subjective probability theorists attempt to tame uncertainty and subsume it under risk, by considering subjective attachments of probability, whether or not such attachments are warranted by the objective situation in the real world. In this way the Bayesian probability calculus is purportedly extended to cover the types of event that are described as uncertain by Keynes and Knight. This attempt cannot be considered in detail here, sufficient to note that there is a significant amount of evidence that agents do not generally make decisions which are consistent with the axioms of this approach (Arrow, 1982; Ellsberg, 1961; Feldman, 1963; Kahneman *et al.*, 1982). The following discussion is defensible insofar as the existence in the real world of a degree of uncertainty in the Keynesian or Knightian sense is accepted.

Consider an example. We are in the possession of a number of shares in a company and their price begins to plunge. We have no clear or reliable information about the reason for the fall. The slide continues relentlessly, so what do we do? Even if we are profoundly uncertain about what is likely to happen, it is reasonable to assume that there is some underlying reason for the share price to fall and to consider selling the shares. Conveniently, as Keynes (1973, p. 114) put it, we often 'fall back on the judgement of the rest of the world which is perhaps better informed.' If others sell it may be reasonable for us to follow, on the assumption that they know something that we do not.

Note that this is not primarily a problem of complexity. We are not in possession of clear information, with the primary difficulty being one of tractability and analysis. Neither is it primarily a problem of extensiveness: a problem of dealing with large amounts of information, even when it is potentially understandable and accessible. Instead there is 'uncertainty—the fact of ignorance and necessity of acting upon opinion rather than knowledge' (Knight, 1921, p. 268). The concept of uncertainty refers primarily to our lack of knowledge of the future. In contrast to complexity and extensiveness, it is not wholly a problem of analysing or accessing *existing* information; it is one of dealing with unpredictable future events.

In such situations it is often reasonable either to follow others or to rely on conventions (Keynes, 1973, pp. 114, 124). The habit of doing what we had done before remains efficacious, despite our uncertainty. Regularities of behaviour and conventions become established, by conforming with the current behaviour of others, or by carrying on with the same routines on the assumption that the world will continue as before.[1]

Thus uncertainty does not banish rigidity and routine. Instead it is a situation in which rule-governed behaviour can be appropriate, as the simulations carried out by Dosi *et al.* (1993) suggest. Of course, uncertainty itself does not give rise to these habits and routines: their origin must come from elsewhere. Yet a situation of uncertainty provides the context in which certain habits and routines may prevail. It is in this manner that Knight (1921, p. 271) argued that the existence of institutional arrangements such as the capitalist firm and the wage system were 'the direct result of the fact of uncertainty'. Nevertheless, it is still necessary to supplement this account with an historical explanation of the origins of particular institutions.

Heiner (1983) sees the origin of 'predictable behavior' in 'uncertainty'. On close inspection, however, Heiner is saying something slightly different from Knight and Keynes. In his paper the term 'uncertainty' is not clearly defined, but related—as in the phrase 'additional uncertainty from a larger *C-D* gap' (p. 562)—to the 'gap between the

---

[1] For discussions of Keynes's idea of the emergence of conventions under uncertainty see Littleboy (1990, especially pp. 28–34, 269–71) and Shackle (1972, pp. 220–8). Shackle also highlights the important article on this theme by Townshend (1937).

agent's competence and the difficulty of the decision problem'. Clearly, this is not the same thing as uncertainty in the sense of Knight and Keynes. What Heiner primarily has in mind is the problem of complexity, as defined here.

Furthermore, Heiner's article is centred misleadingly on 'predictable' rather than habitual or rule-governed behaviour. As argued elsewhere (Hodgson, 1988, pp. 289–90), the complete absence of uncertainty and the lack of any gap between competence and difficulty can also give rise to predictable behaviour. With perfect knowledge the rational maximiser will reach and rest at the attainable and predictable maximum. The fast-calculating genius will find the optimal procedure for unscrambling Rubic's cube on every occasion. Even without complexity and uncertainty, predictable outcomes are possible. Instead of 'the origin of predictable behaviour', the focus in this present paper is the bases of habits and rules.

1.5 Cognition

Modern economics has become more and more concerned with 'information problems'. Typically, however, these problems are specified in an overly narrow fashion, emanating from a deficient conception of information or knowledge, based on an empiricist epistemology. The picture is not rectified simply by assuming that 'information' is scarce, or unequally distributed between individuals, or unattainable without cost. The danger is a misconception of the very nature of knowledge and information.

The idea that unambiguous evidence existing 'out there' is a sufficient basis for direct knowledge and understanding of the world is the central proposition of empiricist epistemology. It assumes that we receive information directly from the outside world without a prior framework of conceptions, rules and theories. Information is treated as atomistic 'facts', knowledge of which is seemingly independent of the conceptual frameworks involved. All sense data are thus directly understood and readily transformed into useful knowledge in the form of certainties or probabilities. Essence is dissolved into appearance: we have direct access to the real world. This view is pervasive but it is untenable.

First it is necessary to distinguish between sense data and information. Sense data consist of the multitude of aural, visual and other signals that reach the brain. We have no other contact with the outside world other than through this sense data. However, they do not come packaged with concepts and meanings. Our knowledge of the world does not spring alive from the sensory data as they reach the brain. To derive information it is necessary that a prior conceptual framework is imposed on the jumble of neurological stimuli, involving implicit or explicit assumptions, categories or theories which cannot themselves be derived from the sense data alone. Often the sense data are open to different interpretations, as some simple and celebrated optical illusions demonstrate. The attribution of meaning is not direct or automatic. Sense data, like the proverbial facts, do not speak for themselves. There has to be a process of cognition, to provide a form that is meaningful and has informational content for the agent.

The attribution of meaning to apparently chaotic mass of data requires the use of acquired concepts, symbols, rules and signs. Perception is an act of categorisation, and in general such categories are learned (Bruner, 1973, p. 12). Through processes of development and education we acquire cognitive habits and perceptual frameworks. These are essential for us to gain knowledge of and act within our environment.

If sense data from experience remain seemingly consistent with the existing cognitive schema they are readily accepted. If they are apparently incongruent, either the information is ignored or the schema is altered to accommodate the incoming information (Whitehead, 1976). Typically, information is interpreted in ways which are consistent with previous conceptions and theories about the world. But because cognitive schema are additional to the sense data themselves, different cognitive frameworks are possible with the same sensory input (Choi, 1994). This gives rise to a persistent problem of ambiguity (March, 1994, p. 9).

All this becomes understandable and relevant once we have abandoned an empiricist epistemology. Because all perception is concept- or theory-bound, the empiricist conception of knowledge is flawed. Even if sense data are available, they cannot be handled or understood without acts of interpretation and cognition. These require conceptual frameworks which are previously inherited or learned but which do not necessarily provide us with a single, reliable view of the truth.

Cognition does not simply involve the sorting and categorisation of data. Because of the confusing disorder of sense data it is often necessary to ignore some bits and highlight others. Cognitive psychology thus provides examples of available data that are imperfectly used, showing that the full use of available data is a rare exception rather than the rule (Spradley, 1972, pp. 9–10). It is typical of human behaviour, even with sophisticated economic agents with the full use of modern information technology, to ignore some of the received sense data. We are required to be selective and treat much of it as 'noise'. Case studies in politics and international relations suggest that decisions are not made on the basis of all the accessible information, but in regard to the subset of information which is meaningful or acceptable in relation to existing cognitions and choices (Axelrod, 1976; Wohlstetter, 1962).

Cognitive processes are built primarily on habit and tacit knowledge (Polanyi, 1967) rather than on conscious and codifiable rules. With higher levels of education involving codifiable knowledge and rules, the priority of the tacit and uncodifiable remains. This applies to the trained scientist as well as to the casual observer (Kuhn, 1970, pp. 191–8).

Cognitive habits are essential to the process of interaction with the outside world. At the same time, however, because cognition means placing a restrictive interpretation on the data, typically by ignoring much of it, cognition inevitably constrains opportunities as well as enabling the actor to understand his or her environment. We are both liberated and incarcerated by our necessary habits of cognition.

1.6 Learning

Strictly, learning is not separable from cognition. It is treated here as a separate category for expository convenience. Even the cognition of an object of a known type involves learning of the existence of that object. The acquisition of our cognitive habits and perceptual frameworks is necessarily a developmental and learning process. Learning can mean the cognition of additional information or the acquisition of new conceptual frames. Typically, it involves both.

The phenomenon of learning has now made its way into mainstream economic theory but there it is based on an untenable and empiricist conception of knowledge. Learning is thus treated as the mere acquisition and accumulation of information, as if it were a transferable substance 'out there'. On the contrary, learning involves the continuous reconstruction and reformation of knowledge, involving a changing relationship between the agent and the external environment. It involves cognitive framing and selection of information. It is a process of problem-formulation and problem-solving, rather than the acquisition and accumulation of given, objective 'bits' of information. This process involves conjecture and error, in which mistakes become opportunities to learn rather than mere random perturbations (Berkson and Wettersten, 1984; Popper, 1972; Rutherford, 1988).

Consider the rational expectations hypothesis. Here it is assumed that agents 'learn' and become aware through experience of the 'true' underlying model of the economy. It is typically presumed that such learning proceeds through observation and some consequent Bayesian updating process of parametric variables. There are several major flaws here. It is mistakenly assumed that the required information is unambiguous and directly amenable to the Bayesian calculus. Information is simply discovered and accumulated, rather than cognitively generated or reformulated (Wible, 1984–85). It is assumed that incorrect perceptions will always be gradually corrected through learning, whereas there is widespread evidence that misperceptions can be lasting or permanent, even when confronted with contrary evidence (Frey, 1992). Evidence from psychology suggests 'that people have neither an intuitive understanding of standard probability concepts nor any innate psychological ability to learn directly through experience to characterize their environments accurately or arrive at optimal problem solutions' (Rutherford, 1988, p. 51).

The internal contradictions in the empiricism implicit in the rational expectations hypothesis become apparent when it is realised that whatever 'learning' takes place, agents are saddled with a given underlying model of the economy, which is usually one involving the quantity theory of money, assumptions of market clearing, and so on (Buiter, 1980; Tobin, 1980). Accordingly, on the one hand it is assumed that agents have boundless powers of 'learning' when it comes to parametric adjustment, but no powers of further enlightenment when it comes to the structural features of the 'true' underlying model. Because these models treat learning as the mere accumulation of information, and knowledge once acquired is presumed to be certain and stable, the problems, conjectures, rules, procedures and concepts involved in the process of learning are ignored. But, as Bianchi (1992) argues, without these issues the concept of learning is empty.

Generally, mainstream economists treat learning as the progressive discovery of pre-existing 'blueprint' information, or Bayesian updating of subjective probability estimates in the light of incoming data (Bray and Kreps, 1987). There are severe problems, however. For instance, as Hey (1981) demonstrates, a process of Bayesian learning in search of an optimum depends upon the assumption of correct prior knowledge. Accordingly, such search models may break down if such an assumption does not apply. Furthermore, as Dosi (1988), Dosi and Egidi (1991), Nelson (1980) and others have argued, the Bayesian approach is a very limited way of conceiving of the role of learning, which in reality is much more than a process of blueprint discovery or statistical correction.

It is not simply the rational expectations hypothesis that is undermined by these arguments. All economic models that suggest that information is transparent and unambiguous or that agents are likely to react in similar ways to the same information can be challenged. For instance, this applies to much work in game theory, as Kreps (1990, p. 111) has noted. The psychological and cultural frameworks through which information is selected and interpreted cannot legitimately be ignored.

Contrary to the empiricist conception of knowledge, much more than the acquisition of facts is involved in learning. Additionally, learning involves cognitive development and the acquisition of practical and intellectual skills. Learning is often prompted by problem situations involving something novel: contrary to our beliefs or expectations. This leads to conjecture and possible error, as we search for alternative solutions and interpretations.

Once a solution is acquired it is nevertheless fallible, provisional and tentative (Berkson and Wettersten, 1984; Gregg, 1974; Laudan, 1977; Popper, 1972).

Typically, successful learning involves the establishment of habits that fix patterns of cognition and behaviour and remove them from full, conscious deliberation. This formation of habits is indispensable for the acquisition of all sorts of practical and intellectual skills. At first, while learning a technique, we must concentrate on every detail of what we are doing. It takes us a great deal of time and effort to learn a new language, or to play a musical instrument, or to type, or to become familiar with a new academic discipline. Eventually, however, intellectual and practical habits emerge. This is the very point at which we regard ourselves as having acquired the skill. When analytical or practical rules are applied without full, conscious reasoning or deliberation then the technique can be said to have been mastered. Again, the concept of tacit knowledge is relevant. Even if codifiable instructions can be helpful, the formation of durable habits and tacit knowledge is unavoidable in these cases.

However, as Koestler (1967, p. 131) points out: 'There are two sides to this tendency towards the progressive mechanization of skills.' On the positive side, mechanical habits help us to deal with complexity and information overload, by removing several aspects of action from conscious deliberation. On the negative side, mechanical habits can remove important actions from the due exercise of deliberation and creative skill. This limitation is likely to be more serious with the more complex activities, and especially in a changing environment. While the very rigidity of habits is necessary to fix learning and fasten skills, such rigidity can often be disabling, particularly when faced with a new and complex problem. Despite this, the adoption of habits and rules is essential to the learning process.

1.7 Communication
Communication need not be verbal. In both the animal and the human worlds there are many cases of communication that do not involve language. Signalling is defined as the non-linguistic communication of intents or outcomes by means of regular and established patterns of behaviour. Frank (1988, p. 97) distinguishes usefully between signalling 'between parties with common goals from those between parties who are potentially in conflict'. An example of the former is the signalling of information from a bridge player to his or her partner by the pattern of card play, according to previously agreed interpretative rules.

Situations of potential conflict often involve the signalling of a precommitment to a given pattern of behaviour or response. Such precommitment problems are discussed extensively in game-theoretic and other approaches to the analysis of rules and institutions. Accordingly, individuals adopt rules such as 'never give in to blackmailers' and governments try to establish rules such as 'never negotiate with terrorists', in order to indicate to potential blackmailers or terrorists that there will be little or no advantage to their actions. Key issues raised here include the credibility of a threat or response and the establishment of reputations by actors (Frank, 1988; Kreps, 1990, ch. 14; Schelling, 1984).

Precommitment can thus be treated as a case of individual optimisation, but clearly this is not necessarily so. Boundedly rational individuals could also see advantages in signalling to others. Indeed, precommitment may be even more important in situations of complexity or uncertainty. In such circumstances it would still be reasonable to attempt to signal regularities of behaviour. Whether it is optimal or otherwise, as Frank (1988, pp. 96, 102-3) elaborates, signalling behaviour can evolve in the natural world even without any design or intention by the organisms involved. With no prior deliberation, humans typically make facial expressions or use 'body language' suggesting, for example, welcome or repugnance, happiness or fear. Just as rational calculation can give rise to signalling, so too can evolution produce such behaviour in unintended or instinctive form.

What are often underestimated in game-theoretic and other formal models involving signalling behaviour are the problems of cognition and interpretation involved in attributing meaning to the signal and the consequent possible mistakes or ambiguities. An action intended to signal one thing can be interpreted differently. Behavioural rules themselves require rules of interpretation. Thus signalling cannot itself provide a complete explanation of the origin of habits or rules. Signalling must involve an interpretative language. Clearly, there are other cases where a communicative language is employed and to these we now turn.

Our education and socialisation in early years help us to develop our innate perceptual equipment and to form a conceptual basis to understand and interact in a complex and changing world. At least for the socialised adult, most concepts and perceptual frames are expressed in terms of a social language. For this reason, cognition, development and learning are social, and thus have cultural specificity. The acquired conceptual framework reflects our culture and the social norms and rules that we inherit (Lloyd, 1972). The acquisition of knowledge about the world is not simply an individual but a social act (McLeod and Chaffee, 1972).

The old idea that language is primarily a representation of the world is fatally flawed. Language cannot be merely a symbolic vehicle for information. As Gödel's theorem suggests (Nagel and Newman, 1959; Hofstadter, 1979), there are limits to all language systems and formal representations of our universe. Language cannot completely and consistently represent the world because language is part of the world and it cannot represent itself. This imposes severe limitations on the representation of the world through any symbolic or linguistic system. A wedge is driven between essence and appearance and again the empiricist conception of knowledge is undermined.

Language involves habits and rules; it is a social institution *par excellence*. It disciplines our behaviour and provides us with a very limited choice of meaningful utterances from the vast array of sounds that could conceivably be vocalised. Yet these very constraints, once likewise adopted by others, enable us to communicate an immense variety of statements and feelings. In part this problem of communication can be treated as a 'coordination game', where an infinite number of possible 'equilibria' exist concerning the signs and utterances to be associated with a given statement. However, that is not the whole story, as the repertoires of meanings, utterances statements must themselves be explained. What is clear is that over thousands of years, a specific and durable language gradually evolves through social interaction. A very narrow set of possible utterances become established as the code, and is subsequently reinforced through regular usage. It is only through the evolution of such habits and linguistic rules that extensive social communication becomes possible.

2. In conclusion: neoclassicism, behaviouralism, institutionalism

Although optimisation problems have not been excluded from the above analysis, it has been argued that the assumption of optimising behaviour by agents cannot itself give a complete explanation of rule-driven, rule-observing or rule-generating behaviour.

678   G. M. Hodgson

Accordingly, neoclassical economic theory must invoke additional explanations of the origin of habits and rules.

But the problems do not end there. The possibility of optimisation is hemmed in by alternative types of decision situation that seem to exclude such behaviour. Extensiveness involves problems of the very identification of the optimum, complexity undermines the idea of effective optimisation, and uncertainty excludes quantifiable assessment. Furthermore, cognition, learning and communication each expose the limits of the empiricist conception of information and knowledge that permeates neoclassical theory.

Note that the empiricist epistemology which is so fundamental to mainstream economics is the other side of the coin of the assumption of rational, optimising behaviour. Empiricism suggests that individuals are capable of learning and revealing the essential features of the world simply through observation and experience: mistakenly asserting the possibility of discovering causal relations simply through empirical evidence, and denying the social character of cognition, enquiry and learning. The assumption of global rationality assumes that the information set is given to the agent, and is not itself subject to critical problems of cognition, calculation, communication and necessarily selective vision. Rational choice between alternatives requires a fixed, bounded and unambiguous choice set, expressed in terms of certainties or computable probabilities. Hence the deployment of an empiricist conception of knowledge: it vastly reduces the nature and scale of all information problems, and helps the rational optimiser to evaluate the 'given' facts and find the optimum according to given, individual preferences. But the empiricist conception of knowledge is untenable. In order to gain knowledge of the world we require prior clues and cognitive frames that are provided in part through social interaction with others.

Simon's (1957, 1976, 1987A,B) twin concepts of 'bounded rationality' and 'satisficing' apply principally to the problems of extensiveness, complexity and uncertainty. In such circumstances, we are obliged to fall back on rules of thumb instead of global optimisation. The limitations of human knowledge and decision-making capacity thus provide a reason for human reliance on habits and rules. Their repeated use in turn gives rise to organisations and institutions: 'It is only because individual human beings are limited in knowledge, foresight, skill, and time that organizations are useful investments for the achievement of human purpose' (Simon, 1957, p. 199).

However, Simon sees the problematic nature of decision-making as emanating solely from the limitations of the given agent. In contrast, in this paper information problems are classified in terms of a *relationship* between a specific type of phenomenon and the actor's epistemic and computational abilities. Especially in the cases of cognition, learning and communication discussed above, it is clear that this simultaneously involves relationships between multiple agents and between agents and the decision environment. It is also recognised here that the cognitive, analytic and computational abilities of agents develop through time. This contrasts with Simon's one-sided emphasis on the limitations of the individual agent.

This point dovetails with an earlier criticism of Langlois (1986, p. 236, 1990) who argues that the work of Simon and his followers puts supreme emphasis on the explanation of the behaviour of the single agent, to the neglect of interactions with other agents. In contrast, the prime goal of social science is not to explain individual behaviour but the intended and unintended outcomes of the interacting behaviours of many agents. Rule following is assumed, but there is no adequate analysis of where rules come from. While it is a major improvement on the neoclassical paradigm, the behaviouralist approach neglects the social character of individual decision-making and also lacks a theory of the origin and adoption of rules and habits themselves.

In any explanation of the origin, adoption and transmission of habits and rules it is important to avoid the functionalist trap. The beneficial consequences of the adoption of a habit or rule do not themselves explain why individuals adopt the habit or rule. Such an explanation commits the functionalist error of seeing the beneficial functions of a phenomenon as themselves causes for its existence. A principal alternative to functionalism is an evolutionary explanation, in which the advantageous character of a habit or rule in a given environment confers a selective advantage on those adopting it (Veblen, 1899, 1919; Hayek, 1982, 1988; Hodgson, 1993B).

Table 1 summarises the results of the foregoing discussion, with respect to both neoclassical and behaviouralist approaches. What of the 'old' institutionalist alternative? This is discussed in more detail elsewhere (Hodgson, 1988; Rutherford, 1994) and we are confined here to the briefest of remarks.

The 'old' institutionalists founded their approach on the pragmatist philosophy of Charles Sanders Peirce and others. Peirce rejected the Cartesian notion of the supremely rational, calculating agent, to replace it by a conception of agency propelled in part by a bundle of habits and routinised behaviours. For Peirce (1934, pp. 255–6) habit does not merely reinforce belief, the 'essence of belief is the establishment of habit'. Accordingly, as Commons (1934, p. 150) put it, Peirce dissolved the antimonies of rationalism and empiricism at a stroke, making 'Habit and Custom, instead of intellect and sensations, the foundation of all science'. As a result, 'old' institutional economists such as Veblen, Commons and Mitchell rejected the continuously calculating, marginally adjusting agent of neoclassical theory to emphasise inertia and habit instead.[1]

This does not necessarily mean that all action is driven by habits and rules. Indeed, as Peirce, Veblen and Commons noted, account has to be taken of novelty and creativity as well. Creativity may itself emerge from the clash or combination of rival languages or rules, or it may be essentially undetermined or 'uncaused'. These questions are not raised because an answer is possible here, but to indicate that the ubiquity of habits and rules should not be taken to mean that such factors are excluded. On the contrary, a theoretical focus on habits and rules should include explanations of their origin, evolution, breakdown and replacement.

When they are shared and reinforced within a society or group, individual habits assume the form of socio-economic institutions. In accord with a wider practice in social science, institutionalists define institutions not in terms of the narrow sense of formal organisations, but in the broad sense of socially habituated behaviour: 'a way of thought or action of some prevalence and permanence, which is embedded in the habits of a group or the customs of a people' (Hamilton, 1932, p. 84). In the work of institutional economists the notion of an institution is linked to cultural values and norms. However, Veblen and other institutionalists rebut the assumption that institutions must necessarily serve human needs. Instead, some institutions are often regarded as 'archaic' or 'ceremonial', alongside those of a more functional character.

This paper has established reasons why habits and rules are efficacious for human decision and action. Institutions are grounded on the common social transmission and replication of such habits and rules. Accordingly, many rules and institutions enable

---

[1] Hayek (1982, Vol. 1, p. 11) writes that: 'Man is as much a rule-following animal as a purpose-seeking one.' On this question, at least, Hayek's theoretical position is close to that of the 'old' institutionalists (Leathers, 1990).

680   G. M. Hodgson

Table 1. *The deployment of habits and rules in neoclassical and behavioural economics*

Type of problem giving rise to use of habit or rule	Is the explanatory basis of habits or rules accommodated by:	
	neoclassical economics, involving models of behaviour with rational optimisation?	behavioural economics, involving models of bounded rationality or satisficing?
1. Optimisation	Completely accommodated, by definition: rules for finding an optimum are readily incorporated, habit, if blind, less so. However, the process of acquisition of these rules is not explained, hence insurmountable difficulties with problems of types 5, 6 and 7 below	Procedures or rules for finding an optimum are readily incorporated, but only within the limits prescribed by 'bounded rationality'. However, the process of acquisition of these rules is not explained, hence difficulties with problems of types 5, 6 and 7 below
2. Extensiveness	Accommodated on the basis of 'cost of obtaining information' explanations but generally without recognition that the agent cannot ever know that he or she is at the optimum in such circumstances	Completely accommodated, giving limited acceptance of 'cost of information' explanations but within a satisficing framework
3. Complexity	Not accommodated. Problems of computation and analysis of given information are generally ignored. The rational agent is a 'lightning calculator'	Completely accommodated. But the recognition of computational and analytic limits implies a rejection of 'cost of information' explanations in such circumstances
4. Uncertainty	Not accommodated. Uncertainty in the strict Knightian or Keynesian sense is rejected by neoclassical theory	Completely accommodated. It is recognised that it is often difficult to attach calculable probabilities to events
5. Cognition	Difficult to accommodate adequately, because cognitive issues undermine the empiricist conception of knowledge upon which rational optimisation theories rest	Generally accommodated, but more in the sense of selection, filtering or analysis of information rather than the interpretation and cognitive framing of sense data
6. Learning	Accommodated only in the limited and unsatisfactory sense of the revelation to the agent of somehow pre-existing information 'out there'	Partially accommodated, but more in the sense of the acquisition and analysis of information rather than an interactive and social process of skill acquisition and cognitive development
7. Communication	The implicit empiricist conception of knowledge involves an interpretation of language merely as a symbolic means of communication of existing information—but not as a means of actually constructing information and meaning	Accommodated only minimally— behavioural economics is concerned primarily with the decisions and actions of a given agent

rather than merely constrain action. Thus it is a major error to regard rules or institutions wholly or principally as impediments or constraints. This point has major implications for economic and social theory, including institutional economics itself, but its further exploration must be the subject of another work.

Where should the analysis go next? In focusing simply on the efficacy and ubiquity of habits and rules many loose ends have been identified. First, for instance, it is necessary to examine the particular origins of those habits and rules. Second, the ways in which new rules and habits are created and displace others have to be addressed. Third, the criteria of efficacy have to be considered, including cases where habits or rules are more useful in some contexts rather than others, or may be advantageous for groups but not for individuals, or vice versa. Fourth, the mechanisms by which habits and rules build up to social routines and institutions have to be analysed, as well as the feedback loop by which institutions help in turn to reinforce particular habits and rules. Unlike the preliminary discussion in this paper, it is likely in further work that the distinguishing features of habits *versus* rules will become more important and it will thus be necessary to differentiate between them.

The degree of generality obtainable in such a theory is open to question. Unlike neo-classical economics, no single and formal theoretical framework may be possible. However, given the ubiquity of habits and rules and the greater number of decision and action contexts that they cover, it may be possible to develop a set of concepts and theoretical approaches that apply to a richer set of contexts and information problems. Nevertheless, such generalities can only take us so far: detailed historical enquiry and particular analysis of specific institutions is likely to prove irreplaceable.

Bibliography

Arrow, K. J. 1982. Risk perception in psychology and economics, *Economic Inquiry*, vol. 20, no. 1, January, 1–9

Axelrod, R. M. (ed.) 1976. *Structure of Decision*, Princeton, NJ, Princeton University Press

Baumol, W. J. and Quandt, R. E. 1964. Rules of thumb and optimally imperfect decisions, *American Economic Review*, vol. 54, no. 2, March, 23–46

Berkson, W. and Wettersten, J. 1984. *Learning from Error*, La Salle, Open Court

Bianchi, M. 1992. Knowledge as expected surprise: a framework for introducing learning in economic choice, *Research in the History of Economic Thought and Methodology*, vol. 10, 43–58

Bray, M. and Kreps, D. M. 1987. Rational learning and rational expectations, pp. 597–625 in Feiwel, G. R. (ed.), *Arrow and the Ascent of Modern Economic Theory*, London, Macmillan

Boulding, K. E. 1956. *The Image: Knowledge in Life and Society*, Ann Arbor, University of Michigan Press

Bruner, J. S. 1973. *Beyond the Information Given*, London, Allen and Unwin

Buchanan, J. M. 1969. Is economics the science of choice?, pp. 47–64 in Streissler, E. (ed.), *Roads to Freedom: Essays in Honour of Friedrich A. von Hayek*, London, Routledge and Kegan Paul

Buiter, W. H. 1980. The macroeconomics of Dr Pangloss: a critical survey of the new classical macroeconomics, *Economic Journal*, vol. 90, no. 1, March, 34–50

Camic, C. 1986. The matter of habit, *American Journal of Sociology*, vol. 91, no. 5, 1039–87

Choi, Y. B. 1994. *Paradigms and Conventions: Uncertainty, Decision Making, and Entrepreneurship*, Ann Arbor, University of Michigan Press

Clark, J. M. 1918. Economics and modern psychology, parts I and II, *Journal of Political Economy*, vol. 26, nos 1–2, January–April, 1–30, 136–66. Reprinted in Clark, J. M. 1967. *Preface to Social Economics*, New York, Augustus Kelley, 92–169

Commons, J. R. 1934. *Institutional Economics—Its Place in Political Economy*, New York, Macmillan. Reprinted with a new introduction by Rutherford, M., New Brunswick, NJ, Transaction, 1990

682   G. M. Hodgson

Conlisk, J. 1980. Costly optimizers versus cheap imitators, *Journal of Economic Behavior and Organization*, vol. 1, no. 3, September, 275–93

Cosmides, L. and Tooby, J. 1994. Beyond intuition and instinct blindness: towards an evolutionary rigorous cognitive science, *Cognition*, vol. 50, nos 1–3, April–June, 41–77

Cutland, N. 1980. *Computability: An Introduction to Recursive Function Theory*, Cambridge, Cambridge University Press

Dawkins, R. 1976. *The Selfish Gene*, Oxford, Oxford University Press

Dosi, G. 1988. The sources, procedures, and microeconomic effects of innovation, *Journal of Economic Literature*, vol. 26, no. 3, September, 1120–71

Dosi, G. and Egidi, M. 1991. Substantive and procedural uncertainty: an exploration of economic behaviours in complex and changing environments, *Journal of Evolutionary Economics*, vol. 1, no. 2, April, 145–68

Dosi, G., Marengo, L., Bassanini, A. and Valente, M. 1993. 'Norms as Emergent Properties of Adaptive Learning', unpublished mimeo

Earl, P. E. 1983. *The Economic Imagination: Towards a Behavioural Analysis of Choice*, Brighton, Wheatsheaf

Ellsberg, D. 1961. Risk, ambiguity, and the Savage axioms, *Quarterly Journal of Economics*, vol. 75, 643–69

Feldman, J. 1963. Simulations of behavior in the binary choice experiment, in Feigenbaum, E. A. and Feldman, J. (eds), *Computers and Thought*, New York, McGraw-Hill, 329–46

Field, A. J. 1979. On the explanation of rules using rational choice models, *Journal of Economic Issues*, vol. 13, no. 1, March, 49–72. Reprinted in Hodgson, 1993C

Field, A. J. 1981. The problem with neoclassical institutional economics: a critique with special reference to the North/Thomas model of pre-1500 Europe, *Explorations in Economic History*, vol. 18, no. 2, April, 174–98

Field, A. J. 1984. Microeconomics, norms and rationality, *Economic Development and Cultural Change*, vol. 32, no. 4, July, 683–711. Reprinted in Hodgson, 1993C

Frank, R. H. 1988. Passions within reason: the strategic role of the emotions, New York, Norton

Frey, B. S. 1992. *Economics as a Science of Human Behavior: Towards a New Social Science Paradigm*, Boston, Kluwer

Friedman, M. 1953. The methodology of positive economics, pp. 3–43 in Friedman, M., *Essays in Positive Economics*, Chicago, University of Chicago Press

Gregg, L. W. (ed.) 1974. *Knowledge and Cognition*, New York, Wiley

Hamilton, W. H. 1932. Institution, pp. 84–9 in Seligman, E. R. A. and Johnson, A. (eds), *Encyclopaedia of the Social Sciences*, Vol. 8. Reprinted in Hodgson, 1993C

Hayek, F. A. 1948. *Individualism and Economic Order*, London and Chicago, George Routledge and University of Chicago Press

Hayek, F. A. 1982. *Law, Legislation and Liberty*, 3 Vols, London, Routledge and Kegan Paul

Hayek, F. A. 1988. *The Fatal Conceit: The Errors of Socialism*, Vol. I in Bartley III, W. W. (ed.), *The Collected Works of Friedrich August Hayek*, London, Routledge

Heiner, R. A. 1983. The origin of predictable behavior, *American Economic Review*, vol. 73, no. 4, December, 560–95. Reprinted in Hodgson, 1993C

Hey, J. D. 1981. Are optimal search rules reasonable? And vice versa? *Journal of Economic Behavior and Organization*, vol. 2, no. 1, March, 47–70

Hodgson, G. M. 1988. *Economics and Institutions: A Manifesto for a Modern Institutional Economics*, Cambridge and Philadelphia, Polity Press and University of Pennsylvania Press

Hodgson, G. M. 1993A. Institutional economics: surveying the 'old' and the 'new', *Metroeconomica*, vol. 44, no. 1, 1–28. Reprinted in Hodgson, 1993C

Hodgson, G. M. 1993B. *Economics and Evolution: Bringing Life Back into Economics*, Cambridge, UK and Ann Arbor, MI, Polity Press and University of Michigan Press

Hodgson, G. M. (ed.) 1993C. *The Economics of Institutions*, Aldershot, Edward Elgar

Hodgson, G. M. 1994. Optimisation and evolution: Winter's critique of Friedman revisited, *Cambridge Journal of Economics*, vol. 18, no. 4, August, 413–30

Hofstadter, D. R. 1979. *Gödel, Escher, Bach: An Eternal Golden Braid*, New York, Basic Books

Jensen, M. C. and Meckling, W. H. 1976. Theory of the firm: managerial behavior, agency costs and ownership structure, *Journal of Financial Economics*, vol. 3, 305–60

Kahneman, D., Slovic, P. and Tversky, A. (eds) 1982. *Judgement Under Uncertainty: Heuristics and Biases*, Cambridge, Cambridge University Press

Keynes, J. M. 1936. *The General Theory of Employment, Interest and Money*, London, Macmillan

Keynes, J. M. 1973. *The General Theory and After: Defence and Development, The Collected Writings of John Maynard Keynes*, Vol. XIV, London, Macmillan

Knight, F. H. 1921. *Risk, Uncertainty and Profit*, New York, Houghton Mifflin

Koestler, A. 1967. *The Ghost in the Machine*, London, Hutchinson

Kreps, D. M. 1990. *A Course in Microeconomic Theory*, London, Harvester Wheatsheaf

Kuhn, T. S. 1970. *The Structure of Scientific Revolutions*, 2nd edn, Chicago, University of Chicago Press

Langlois, R. N. (ed.) 1986. *Economics as a Process: Essays in the New Institutional Economics*, Cambridge, Cambridge University Press

Langlois, R. N. 1990. Bounded rationality and behavioralism: a clarification and critique, *Journal of Institutional and Theoretical Economics*, vol. 146, no. 4, December, 691–95

Laudan, L. 1977. *Progress and its Problems: Towards a Theory of Scientific Growth*, London, Routledge and Kegan Paul

Leathers, C. G. 1990. Veblen and Hayek on instincts and evolution, *Journal of the History of Economic Thought*, vol. 12, no. 2, June, 162–78

Littleboy, B. 1990. *On Interpreting Keynes: A Study in Reconciliation*, London, Routledge

Lloyd, B. B. 1972. *Perception and Cognition: A Cross-Cultural Perspective*, Harmondsworth, Penguin

Loasby, B. J. 1976. *Choice, Complexity and Ignorance: An Enquiry into Economic Theory and the Practice of Decision Making*, Cambridge, Cambridge University Press

March, J. G. 1994. *A Primer on Decision Making: How Decisions Happen*, New York, Free Press

McLeod, J. M. and Chaffee, S. H. 1972. The construction of social reality, pp. 50–99 in Tedeschi, J. T. (ed.), *The Social Influence Processes*, Chicago, Aldine-Atherton

Murphy, J. B. 1994. The kinds of order in society, pp. 536–82 in Mirowski, P. (ed.), *Natural Images in Economic Thought: Markets Read in Tooth and Claw*, Cambridge and New York, Cambridge University Press

Nagel, E. and Newman, J. R. 1959. *Gödel's Proof*, London, Routledge and Kegan Paul

Nelson, R. R. 1980. Production sets, technological knowledge, and R&D: fragile and overworked constructs for analysis of productivity growth? *American Economic Review Papers and Proceedings*, vol. 70, no. 2, May, 62–7

North, D. C. and Thomas, R. P. 1973. *The Rise of the Western World*, London, Cambridge University Press

Peirce, C. S. 1934. *Pragmatism and Pragmaticism*, Vol. V in Hartshorne, C. and Weiss, P. (eds), *Collected Papers of Charles Sanders Peirce*, Cambridge, MA, Harvard University Press

Pelikan, P. 1989. Evolution, economic competence, and corporate control, *Journal of Economic Behavior and Organization*, vol. 12, 279–303

Pingle, M. 1992. Costly optimization: an experiment, *Journal of Economic Behavior and Organization*, vol. 17, no. 1, January, 3–30

Polanyi, M. 1967. *The Tacit Dimension*, London, Routledge and Kegan Paul

Popper, K. R. 1972. *Objective Knowledge: An Evolutionary Approach*, Oxford, Oxford University Press

Pylyshyn, Z. W. (ed.) 1987. *The Robot's Dilemma: The Frame Problem in Artificial Intelligence*, Norwood, NJ, Ablex

Rutherford, M. C. 1988. Learning and decision-making in economics and psychology: a methodological perspective, in Earl, P. E. (ed.), *Psychological Economics: Development, Tensions, Prospects*, Boston, Kluwer, 35–54

Rutherford, M. C. 1994. *Institutions in Economics: The Old and the New Institutionalism*, Cambridge, Cambridge University Press

Schelling, T. C. 1984. *Choice and Consequence*, Cambridge, MA, Harvard University Press

Schotter, A. 1981. *The Economic Theory of Social Institutions*, Cambridge, Cambridge University Press

Shackle, G. L. S. 1972. *Epistemics and Economics: A Critique of Economic Doctrines*, Cambridge, Cambridge University Press

Simon, H. A. 1957. *Models of Man: Social and Rational*, New York, Wiley

Simon, H. A. 1976. From substantive to procedural rationality, in Latsis, S. J. (ed.), *Method and Appraisal in Economics*, Cambridge, Cambridge University Press

Simon, H. A. 1987A. Bounded rationality, pp. 266–8 in Eatwell, J., Milgate, M. and Newman, P. (eds), *The New Palgrave Dictionary of Economics*, Vol. 1, London, Macmillan

684   G. M. Hodgson

Simon, H. A. 1987B. Satisficing, pp. 243–5 in Eatwell, J., Milgate, M. and Newman, P. (eds), *The New Palgrave Dictionary of Economics*, Vol. 4, London, Macmillan

Spradley, J. P. (ed.) 1972. *Culture and Cognition: Rules, Maps, and Plans*, San Francisco, Chandler Publishing

Teece, D. J. and Winter, S. G. 1984. The limits of neoclassical theory in management education, *American Economic Review Papers and Proceedings.*, vol. 74, no. 2, May, 116–21

Tobin, J. 1980. Are new classical models plausible enough to guide policy? *Journal of Money, Credit, and Banking*, vol. 12, 788–99

Townshend, H. 1937. Liquidity-premium and the theory of value, *Economic Journal*, vol. 47, no. 1, March, 157–69

Vanberg, V. J. 1988. Rules and choice in economics and sociology, *Jahrbuch für Neue Politische Ökonomie*, vol. 7, 1–22, Tübingen, Mohr. Reprinted in Hodgson, 1993C and Vanberg, 1994

Vanberg, V. J. 1993. Rational choice vs adaptive rule-following: on the behavioural foundations of the social sciences, *Jahrbuch für Neue Politische Ökonomie*, vol. 12, Tübingen, Mohr. Reprinted in Vanberg, 1994

Vanberg, V. J. 1994. *Rules and Choice in Economics*, London, Routledge

Veblen, T. B. 1899. *The Theory of the Leisure Class: An Economic Study of Institutions*, New York, Macmillan

Veblen, T. B. 1919. *The Place of Science in Modern Civilisation and Other Essays*, New York, Huebsch. Reprinted with a new introduction by Samuels, W. J., New Brunswick, NJ, Transaction, 1990

Vromen, J. J. 1995. *Economic Evolution: An Enquiry into the Foundations of New Institutional Economics*, London, Routledge

Whitehead, J. 1976. *Personality and Learning*, London, Hodder and Stoughton

Wible, J. R. 1984–85. An epistemic critique of rational expectations and the neoclassical macroeconomics research program, *Journal of Post-Keynesian Economics*, vol. 7, no. 2, Winter, 269–81

Williamson, O. E. 1975. *Markets and Hierarchies: Analysis and Anti-Trust Implications: A Study in the Economics of Internal Organization*, New York, Free Press

Williamson, O. E. 1985. *The Economic Institutions of Capitalism: Firms, Markets, Relational Contracting*, London, Macmillan

Wilson, E. O. 1975. *Sociobiology*, Cambridge, MA, Harvard University Press

Winter, Jr, S. G. 1964. Economic 'natural selection' and the theory of the firm, *Yale Economic Essays*, vol. 4, 225–72

Wohlstetter, R. 1962. *Pearl Harbor, Warning and Decision*, Stanford, Stanford University Press

Part VI
Decomposability and Hierarchy

[27]

THE ARCHITECTURE OF COMPLEXITY

HERBERT A. SIMON*

Professor of Administration, Carnegie Institute of Technology

(*Read April 26, 1962*)

A NUMBER of proposals have been advanced in recent years for the development of "general systems theory" which, abstracting from properties peculiar to physical, biological, or social systems, would be applicable to all of them.[1] We might well feel that, while the goal is laudable, systems of such diverse kinds could hardly be expected to have any nontrivial properties in common. Metaphor and analogy can be helpful, or they can be misleading. All depends on whether the similarities the metaphor captures are significant or superficial.

It may not be entirely vain, however, to search for common properties among diverse kinds of complex systems. The ideas that go by the name of cybernetics constitute, if not a theory, at least a point of view that has been proving fruitful over a wide range of applications.[2] It has been useful to look at the behavior of adaptive systems in terms of the concepts of feedback and homeostasis,

and to analyze adaptiveness in terms of the theory of selective information.[3] The ideas of feedback and information provide a frame of reference for viewing a wide range of situations, just as do the ideas of evolution, of relativism, of axiomatic method, and of operationalism.

In this paper I should like to report on some things we have been learning about particular kinds of complex systems encountered in the behavioral sciences. The developments I shall discuss arose in the context of specific phenomena, but the theoretical formulations themselves make little reference to details of structure. Instead they refer primarily to the complexity of the systems under view without specifying the exact content of that complexity. Because of their abstractness, the theories may have relevance—application would be too strong a term—to other kinds of complex systems that are observed in the social, biological, and physical sciences.

In recounting these developments, I shall avoid technical detail, which can generally be found elsewhere. I shall describe each theory in the particular context in which it arose. Then, I shall cite some examples of complex systems, from areas of science other than the initial application, to which the theoretical framework appears relevant. In doing so, I shall make reference to areas of knowledge where I am not expert—perhaps not even literate. I feel quite comfortable in doing so before the members of this society, representing as it does the whole span of the scientific and scholarly endeavor. Collectively you will have little difficulty, I am sure, in distinguishing instances based on idle fancy or sheer ignorance from instances that cast some light on the ways in which complexity exhibits itself wherever it is found in nature. I shall leave to you the final judgment of relevance in your respective fields.

I shall not undertake a formal definition of

---

* The ideas in this paper have been the topic of many conversations with my colleague, Allen Newell. George W. Corner suggested important improvements in biological content as well as editorial form. I am also indebted, for valuable comments on the manuscript, to Richard H. Meier, John R. Platt, and Warren Weaver. Some of the conjectures about the nearly decomposable structure of the nucleus-atom-molecule hierarchy were checked against the available quantitative data by Andrew Schoene and William Wise. My work in this area has been supported by a Ford Foundation grant for research in organizations and a Carnegie Corporation grant for research on cognitive processes. To all of the above, my warm thanks, and the usual absolution.

[1] See especially the yearbooks of the Society for General Systems Research. Prominent among the exponents of general systems theory are L. von Bertalanffy, K. Boulding, R. W. Gerard, and J. G. Miller. For a more skeptical view—perhaps too skeptical in the light of the present discussion—see H. A. Simon and A. Newell, Models: their uses and limitations, *in* L. D. White, ed., *The state of the social sciences*, 66–83, Chicago, Univ. of Chicago Press, 1956.

[2] N. Wiener, *Cybernetics*, New York, John Wiley & Sons, 1948. For an imaginative forerunner, see A. J. Lotka, *Elements of mathematical biology*, New York, Dover Publications, 1951, first published in 1924 as *Elements of physical biology*.

[3] C. Shannon and W. Weaver, *The mathematical theory of communication*, Urbana, Univ. of Illinois Press, 1949; W. R. Ashby, *Design for a brain*, New York, John Wiley & Sons, 1952.

"complex systems."[4] Roughly, by a complex system I mean one made up of a large number of parts that interact in a nonsimple way. In such systems, the whole is more than the sum of the parts, not in an ultimate, metaphysical sense, but in the important pragmatic sense that, given the properties of the parts and the laws of their interaction, it is not a trivial matter to infer the properties of the whole. In the face of complexity, an in-principle reductionist may be at the same time a pragmatic holist.[5]

The four sections that follow discuss four aspects of complexity. The first offers some comments on the frequency with which complexity takes the form of hierarchy—the complex system being composed of subsystems that, in turn, have their own subsystems, and so on. The second section theorizes about the relation between the structure of a complex system and the time required for it to emerge through evolutionary processes: specifically, it argues that hierarchic systems will evolve far more quickly than non-hierarchic systems of comparable size. The third section explores the dynamic properties of hierarchically-organized systems, and shows how they can be decomposed into subsystems in order to analyze their behavior. The fourth section examines the relation between complex systems and their descriptions.

Thus, the central theme that runs through my remarks is that complexity frequently takes the form of hierarchy, and that hierarchic systems have some common properties that are independent of their specific content. Hierarchy, I shall argue, is one of the central structural schemes that the architect of complexity uses.

---

[4] W. Weaver, in: Science and complexity, *American Scientist* **36**: 536, 1948, has distinguished two kinds of complexity, disorganized and organized. We shall be primarily concerned with organized complexity.

[5] See also John R. Platt, Properties of large molecules that go beyond the properties of their chemical sub-groups, *Jour. Theoret. Biol.* **1**: 342–358, 1961. Since the reductionism-holism issue is a major *cause de guerre* between scientists and humanists, perhaps we might even hope that peace could be negotiated between the two cultures along the lines of the compromise just suggested. As I go along, I shall have a little to say about complexity in the arts as well as in the natural sciences. I must emphasize the pragmatism of my holism to distinguish it sharply from the position taken by W. M. Elsasser in *The physical foundation of biology*, New York, Pergamon Press, 1958.

HIERARCHIC SYSTEMS

By a *hierarchic system,* or hierarchy, I mean a system that is composed of interrelated subsystems, each of the latter being, in turn, hierarchic in structure until we reach some lowest level of elementary subsystem. In most systems in nature, it is somewhat arbitrary as to where we leave off the partitioning, and what subsystems we take as elementary. Physics makes much use of the concept of "elementary particle" although particles have a disconcerting tendency not to remain elementary very long. Only a couple of generations ago, the atoms themselves were elementary particles; today, to the nuclear physicist they are complex systems. For certain purposes of astronomy, whole stars, or even galaxies, can be regarded as elementary subsystems. In one kind of biological research, a cell may be treated as an elementary subsystem; in another, a protein molecule; in still another, an amino acid residue.

Just why a scientist has a right to treat as elementary a subsystem that is in fact exceedingly complex is one of the questions we shall take up. For the moment, we shall accept the fact that scientists do this all the time, and that if they are careful scientists they usually get away with it.

Etymologically, the word "hierarchy" has had a narrower meaning than I am giving it here. The term has generally been used to refer to a complex system in which each of the subsystems is subordinated by an authority relation to the system it belongs to. More exactly, in a hierarchic formal organization, each system consists of a "boss" and a set of subordinate subsystems. Each of the subsystems has a "boss" who is the immediate subordinate of the boss of the system. We shall want to consider systems in which the relations among subsystems are more complex than in the formal organizational hierarchy just described. We shall want to include systems in which there is no relation of subordination among subsystems. (In fact, even in human organizations, the formal hierarchy exists only on paper; the real flesh-and-blood organization has many inter-part relations other than the lines of formal authority.) For lack of a better term, I shall use hierarchy in the broader sense introduced in the previous paragraphs, to refer to all complex systems analyzable into successive sets of subsystems, and speak of "formal hierarchy" when I want to refer to the more specialized concept.[6]

---

[6] The mathematical term "partitioning" will not do for what I call here a hierarchy; for the set of subsystems,

SOCIAL SYSTEMS

I have already given an example of one kind of hierarchy that is frequently encountered in the social sciences: a formal organization. Business firms, governments, universities all have a clearly visible parts-within-parts structure. But formal organizations are not the only, or even the most common, kind of social hierarchy. Almost all societies have elementary units called families, which may be grouped into villages or tribes, and these into larger groupings, and so on. If we make a chart of social interactions, of who talks to whom, the clusters of dense interaction in the chart will identify a rather well-defined hierarchic structure. The groupings in this structure may be defined operationally by some measure of frequency of interaction in this sociometric matrix.

BIOLOGICAL AND PHYSICAL SYSTEMS

The hierarchical structure of biological systems is a familiar fact. Taking the cell as the building block, we find cells organized into tissues, tissues into organs, organs into systems. Moving downward from the cell, well-defined subsystems—for example, nucleus, cell membrane, microsomes, mitochondria, and so on—have been identified in animal cells.

The hierarchic structure of many physical systems is equally clear-cut. I have already mentioned the two main series. At the microscopic level we have elementary particles, atoms, molecules, macromolecules. At the macroscopic level we have satellite systems, planetary systems, galaxies. Matter is distributed throughout space in a strikingly non-uniform fashion. The most nearly random distributions we find, gases, are not random distributions of elementary particles but random distributions of complex systems, i.e. molecules.

A considerable range of structural types is subsumed under the term hierarchy as I have defined it. By this definition, a diamond is hierarchic, for it is a crystal structure of carbon atoms that can be further decomposed into protons, neutrons, and electrons. However, it is a very "flat" hierarchy, in which the number of first-order subsystems belonging to the crystal can be indefinitely large. A volume of molecular gas is a flat hierarchy in the same sense. In ordinary usage, we

and the successive subsets in each of these defines the partitioning, independently of any systems of relations among the subsets. By hierarchy I mean the partitioning in conjunction with the relations that hold among its parts.

tend to reserve the word hierarchy for a system that is divided into a *small or moderate number* of subsystems, each of which may be further subdivided. Hence, we do not ordinarily think of or refer to a diamond or a gas as a hierarchic structure. Similarly, a linear polymer is simply a chain, which may be very long, of identical subparts, the monomers. At the molecular level it is a very flat hierarchy.

In discussing formal organizations, the number of subordinates who report directly to a single boss is called his *span of control*. I will speak analogously of the *span* of a system, by which I shall mean the number of subsystems into which it is partitioned. Thus, a hierarchic system is flat at a given level if it has a wide span at that level. A diamond has a wide span at the crystal level, but not at the next level down, the molecular level.

In most of our theory construction in the following sections we shall focus our attention on hierarchies of moderate span, but from time to time I shall comment on the extent to which the theories might or might not be expected to apply to very flat hierarchies.

There is one important difference between the physical and biological hierarchies, on the one hand, and social hierarchies, on the other. Most physical and biological hierarchies are described in spatial terms. We detect the organelles in a cell in the way we detect the raisins in a cake—they are "visibly" differentiated substructures localized spatially in the larger structure. On the other hand, we propose to identify social hierarchies not by observing who lives close to whom but by observing who interacts with whom. These two points of view can be reconciled by defining hierarchy in terms of intensity of interaction, but observing that in most biological and physical systems relatively intense interaction implies relative spatial propinquity. One of the interesting characteristics of nerve cells and telephone wires is that they permit very specific strong interactions at great distances. To the extent that interactions are channeled through specialized communications and transportation systems, spatial propinquity becomes less determinative of structure.

SYMBOLIC SYSTEMS

One very important class of systems has been omitted from my examples thus far: systems of human symbolic production. A book is a hierarchy in the sense in which I am using that term. It is generally divided into chapters, the chapters into sections, the sections into paragraphs, the paragraphs into sentences, the sentences into clauses and phrases, the clauses and phrases into words. We may take the words as our elementary units, or further subdivide them, as the linguist often does, into smaller units. If the book is narrative in character, it may divide into "episodes" instead of sections, but divisions there will be.

The hierarchic structure of music, based on such units as movements, parts, themes, phrases, is well known. The hierarchic structure of products of the pictorial arts is more difficult to characterize, but I shall have something to say about it later.

THE EVOLUTION OF COMPLEX SYSTEMS

Let me introduce the topic of evolution with a parable. There once were two watchmakers, named Hora and Tempus, who manufactured very fine watches. Both of them were highly regarded, and the phones in their workshops rang frequently —new customers were constantly calling them. However, Hora prospered, while Tempus became poorer and poorer and finally lost his shop. What was the reason?

The watches the men made consisted of about 1,000 parts each. Tempus had so constructed his that if he had one partly assembled and had to put it down—to answer the phone say—it immediately fell to pieces and had to be reassembled from the elements. The better the customers liked his watches, the more they phoned him, the more difficult it became for him to find enough uninterrupted time to finish a watch.

The watches that Hora made were no less complex than those of Tempus. But he had designed them so that he could put together subassemblies of about ten elements each. Ten of these subassemblies, again, could be put together into a larger subassembly; and a system of ten of the latter subassemblies constituted the whole watch. Hence, when Hora had to put down a partly assembled watch in order to answer the phone, he lost only a small part of his work, and he assembled his watches in only a fraction of the man-hours it took Tempus.

It is rather easy to make a quantitative analysis of the relative difficulty of the tasks of Tempus and Hora: Suppose the probability that an interruption will occur while a part is being added to an incomplete assembly is p. Then the probability that Tempus can complete a watch he has started without interruption is $(1-p)^{1000}$—a very small number unless p is .001 or less. Each interruption will cost, on the average, the time to as-

semble $1/p$ parts (the expected number assembled before interruption). On the other hand, Hora has to complete one hundred eleven sub-assemblies of ten parts each. The probability that he will not be interrupted while completing any one of these is $(1-p)^{10}$, and each interruption will cost only about the time required to assemble five parts.[7]

Now if p is about .01—that is, there is one chance in a hundred that either watchmaker will be interrupted while adding any one part to an assembly—then a straightforward calculation shows that it will take Tempus, on the average, about four thousand times as long to assemble a watch as Hora.

We arrive at the estimate as follows:

1. Hora must make 111 times as many complete assemblies per watch as Tempus; but,

2. Tempus will lose on the average 20 times as much work for each interrupted assembly as Hora [100 parts, on the average, as against 5]; and,

3. Tempus will complete an assembly only 44 times per million attempts ($.99^{1000} = 44 \times 10^{-6}$), while Hora will complete nine out of ten ($.99^{10} = 9 \times 10^{-1}$). Hence Tempus will have to make 20,000 as many attempts per completed assembly as Hora. $(9 \times 10^{-1})/(44 \times 10^{-6}) = 2 \times 10^4$. Multiplying these three ratios, we get:

$$1/111 \times 100/5 \times .99^{10}/.99^{1000}$$
$$= 1/111 \times 20 \times 20,000 \sim 4,000.$$

[7] The speculations on speed of evolution were first suggested by H. Jacobson's application of information theory to estimating the time required for biological evolution. See his paper, Information, reproduction, and the origin of life, in *American Scientist* **43**: 119–127, January, 1955. From thermodynamic considerations it is possible to estimate the amount of increase in entropy that occurs when a complex system decomposes into its elements. (See, for example, R. B. Setlow and E. C. Pollard, *Molecular biophysics*, 63–65, Reading, Mass., Addison-Wesley Publishing Co., 1962, and references cited there.) But entropy is the logarithm of a probability, hence information, the negative of entropy, can be interpreted as the logarithm of the reciprocal of the probability—the "improbability," so to speak. The essential idea in Jacobson's model is that the expected time required for the system to reach a particular state is inversely proportional to the probability of the state—hence increases exponentially with the amount of information (negentropy) of the state. Following this line of argument, but not introducing the notion of levels and stable subassemblies, Jacobson arrived at estimates of the time required for evolution so large as to make the event rather improbable. Our analysis, carried through in the same way, but with attention to the stable intermediate forms, produces very much smaller estimates.

THE ARCHITECTURE OF COMPLEXITY

BIOLOGICAL EVOLUTION

What lessons can we draw from our parable for biological evolution? Let us interpret a partially completed subassembly of k elementary parts as the coexistence of k parts in a small volume—ignoring their relative orientations. The model assumes that parts are entering the volume at a constant rate, but that there is a constant probability, p, that the part will be dispersed before another is added, unless the assembly reaches a stable state. These assumptions are not particularly realistic. They undoubtedly underestimate the decrease in probability of achieving the assembly with increase in the size of the assembly. Hence the assumptions understate—probably by a large factor—the relative advantage of a hierarchic structure.

Although we cannot, therefore, take the numerical estimate seriously the lesson for biological evolution is quite clear and direct. The time required for the evolution of a complex form from simple elements depends critically on the numbers and distribution of potential intermediate stable forms. In particular, if there exists a hierarchy of potential stable "subassemblies," with about the same span, s, at each level of the hierarchy, then the time required for a subassembly can be expected to be about the same at each level—that is proportional to $1/(1-p)^s$. The time required for the assembly of a system of n elements will be proportional to $\log_s n$, that is, to the number of levels in the system. One would say—with more illustrative than literal intent—that the time required for the evolution of multi-celled organisms from single-celled organisms might be of the same order of magnitude as the time required for the evolution of single-celled organisms from macromolecules. The same argument could be applied to the evolution of proteins from amino acids, of molecules from atoms, of atoms from elementary particles.

A whole host of objections to this oversimplified scheme will occur, I am sure, to every working biologist, chemist, and physicist. Before turning to matters I know more about, I shall mention three of these problems, leaving the rest to the attention of the specialists.

First, in spite of the overtones of the watchmaker parable, the theory assumes no teleological mechanism. The complex forms can arise from the simple ones by purely random processes. (I shall propose another model in a moment that shows this clearly.) Direction is provided to the

scheme by the stability of the complex forms, once these come into existence. But this is nothing more than survival of the fittest—i.e., of the stable.

Second, not all large systems appear hierarchical. For example, most polymers—e.g., nylon—are simply linear chains of large numbers of identical components, the monomers. However, for present purposes we can simply regard such a structure as a hierarchy with a span of one—the limiting case. For a chain of any length represents a state of relative equilibrium.[8]

Third, the evolution of complex systems from simple elements implies nothing, one way or the other, about the change in entropy of the entire system. If the process absorbs free energy, the complex system will have a smaller entropy than the elements; if it releases free energy, the opposite will be true. The former alternative is the one that holds for most biological systems, and the net inflow of free energy has to be supplied from the sun or some other source if the second law of thermodynamics is not to be violated. For the evolutionary process we are describing, the equilibria of the intermediate states need have only local and not global stability, and they may be stable only in the steady state—that is, as long as there is an external source of free energy that may be drawn upon.[9]

Because organisms are not energetically closed systems, there is no way to deduce the direction, much less the rate, of evolution from classical thermodynamic considerations. All estimates indicate that the amount of entropy, measured in physical units, involved in the formation of a one-celled biological organism is trivially small—about -10^{-11} cal/degree.[10] The "improbability" of evolution has nothing to do with this quantity of entropy, which is produced by every bacterial cell every generation. The irrelevance of quantity of

---

[8] There is a well-developed theory of polymer size, based on models of random assembly. See for example P. J. Flory, *Principles of polymer chemistry*, ch. 8, Ithaca, Cornell Univ. Press, 1953. Since *all* subassemblies in the polymerization theory are stable, limitation of molecular growth depends on "poisoning" of terminal groups by impurities or formation of cycles rather than upon disruption of partially-formed chains.

[9] This point has been made many times before, but it cannot be emphasized too strongly. For further discussion, see Setlow and Pollard, *op. cit.*, 49–64; E. Schrodinger, *What is life?* Cambridge Univ. Press, 1945; and H. Linschitz, The information content of a bacterial cell, in H. Questler, ed., *Information theory in biology*, 251–262, Urbana, Univ. of Illinois Press, 1953.

[10] See Linschitz, *op. cit.* This quantity, 10^{-11} cal/degree, corresponds to about 10^{13} bits of information.

information, in this sense, to speed of evolution can also be seen from the fact that exactly as much information is required to "copy" a cell through the reproductive process as to produce the first cell through evolution.

The effect of the existence of stable intermediate forms exercises a powerful effect on the evolution of complex forms that may be likened to the dramatic effect of catalysts upon reaction rates and steady state distribution of reaction products in open systems.[11] In neither case does the entropy change provide us with a guide to system behavior.

PROBLEM SOLVING AS NATURAL SELECTION

Let us turn now to some phenomena that have no obvious connection with biological evolution: human problem-solving processes. Consider, for example, the task of discovering the proof for a difficult theorem. The process can be—and often has been—described as a search through a maze. Starting with the axioms and previously proved theorems, various transformations allowed by the rules of the mathematical systems are attempted, to obtain new expressions. These are modified in turn until, with persistence and good fortune, a sequence or path of transformations is discovered that leads to the goal.

The process usually involves a great deal of trial and error. Various paths are tried; some are abandoned, others are pushed further. Before a solution is found, a great many paths of the maze may be explored. The more difficult and novel the problem, the greater is likely to be the amount of trial and error required to find a solution. At the same time, the trial and error is not completely random or blind; it is, in fact, rather highly selective. The new expressions that are obtained by transforming given ones are examined to see whether they represent progress toward the goal. Indications of progress spur further search in the same direction; lack of progress signals the abandonment of a line of search. Problem solving requires *selective* trial and error.[12]

A little reflection reveals that cues signaling progress play the same role in the problem-solving process that stable intermediate forms play in the biological evolutionary process. In fact, we can take over the watchmaker parable and apply it also to problem solving. In problem solving, a partial result that represents recognizable progress toward the goal plays the role of a stable subassembly.

Suppose that the task is to open a safe whose lock has ten dials, each with one hundred possible settings, numbered from 0 to 99. How long will it take to open the safe by a blind trial-and-error search for the correct setting? Since there are 100^{10} possible settings, we may expect to examine about one-half of these, on the average, before finding the correct one—that is, fifty billion billion settings. Suppose, however, that the safe is defective, so that a click can be heard when any one dial is turned to the correct setting. Now each dial can be adjusted independently, and does not need to be touched again while the others are being set. The total number of settings that has to be tried is only 10×50, or five hundred. The task of opening the safe has been altered, by the cues the clicks provide, from a practically impossible one to a trivial one.[13]

A considerable amount has been learned in the past five years about the nature of the mazes that represent common human problem-solving tasks—proving theorems, solving puzzles, playing chess, making investments, balancing assembly lines, to mention a few. All that we have learned about these mazes points to the same conclusion: that human problem solving, from the most blundering to the most insightful, involves nothing more than varying mixtures of trial and error and selectivity. The selectivity derives from various rules of

---

[11] See H. Kacser, Some physico-chemical aspects of biological organization, Appendix, pp. 191–249 in C. H. Waddington, *The strategy of the genes,* London, George Allen & Unwin, 1957.

[12] See A. Newell, J. C. Shaw, and H. A. Simon, Empirical explorations of the logic theory machine, *Proceedings of the 1957 Western Joint Computer Conference,* February, 1957, New York: Institute of Radio Engineers; Chess-playing programs and the problem of complexity, *IBM Journal of Research and Development* 2: 320–335, October, 1958; and for a similar view of problem solving, W. R. Ashby, Design for an intelligence

amplifier, 215–233 in C. E. Shannon and J. McCarthy, *Automata studies,* Princeton, Princeton Univ. Press, 1956.

[13] The clicking safe example was supplied by D. P. Simon. Ashby, *op. cit.,* 230, has called the selectivity involved in situations of this kind "selection by components." The even greater reduction in time produced by hierarchization in the clicking safe example, as compared with the watchmaker's metaphor, is due to the fact that a random *search* for the correct combination is involved in the former case, while in the latter the parts come together in the right order. It is not clear which of these metaphors provides the better model for biological evolution, but we may be sure that the watchmaker's metaphor gives an exceedingly conservative estimate of savings due to hierarchization. The safe may give an excessively high estimate because it assumes all possible arrangements of the elements to be equally probable.

THE ARCHITECTURE OF COMPLEXITY

thumb, or heuristics, that suggest which paths should be tried first and which leads are promising. We do not need to postulate processes more sophisticated than those involved in organic evolution to explain how enormous problem mazes are cut down to quite reasonable size.[14]

THE SOURCES OF SELECTIVITY

When we examine the sources from which the problem-solving system, or the evolving system, as the case may be, derives its selectivity, we discover that selectivity can always be equated with some kind of feedback of information from the environment.

Let us consider the case of problem solving first. There are two basic kinds of selectivity. One we have already noted: various paths are tried out, the consequences of following them are noted, and this information is used to guide further search. In the same way, in organic evolution, various complexes come into being, at least evanescently, and those that are stable provide new building blocks for further construction. It is this information about stable configurations, and not free energy or negentropy from the sun, that guides the process of evolution and provides the selectivity that is essential to account for its rapidity.

The second source of selectivity in problem solving is previous experience. We see this particularly clearly when the problem to be solved is similar to one that has been solved before. Then, by simply trying again the paths that led to the earlier solution, or their analogues, trial-and-error search is greatly reduced or altogether eliminated.

What corresponds to this latter kind of information in organic evolution? The closest analogue is reproduction. Once we reach the level of self-reproducing systems, a complex system, when it has once been achieved, can be multiplied indefinitely. Reproduction in fact allows the inheritance of acquired characteristics, but at the level of genetic material, of course; i.e., only characteristics acquired by the genes can be inherited. We shall return to the topic of reproduction in the final section of this paper.

ON EMPIRES AND EMPIRE-BUILDING

We have not exhausted the categories of complex systems to which the watchmaker argument can reasonably be applied. Philip assembled his

[14] A. Newell and H. A. Simon, Computer simulation of human thinking, *Science* 134: 2011–2017, December 22, 1961.

Macedonian empire and gave it to his son, to be later combined with the Persian subassembly and others into Alexander's greater system. On Alexander's death, his empire did not crumble to dust, but fragmented into some of the major subsystems that had composed it.

The watchmaker argument implies that if one would be Alexander, one should be born into a world where large stable political systems already exist. Where this condition was not fulfilled, as on the Scythian and Indian frontiers, Alexander found empire building a slippery business. So too, T. E. Lawrence's organizing of the Arabian revolt against the Turks was limited by the character of his largest stable building blocks, the separate, suspicious desert tribes.

The profession of history places a greater value upon the validated particular fact than upon tendentious generalization. I shall not elaborate upon my fancy, therefore, but will leave it to historians to decide whether anything can be learned for the interpretation of history from an abstract theory of hierarchic complex systems.

CONCLUSION: THE EVOLUTIONARY EXPLANATION OF HIERARCHY

We have shown thus far that complex systems will evolve from simple systems much more rapidly if there are stable intermediate forms than if there are not. The resulting complex forms in the former case will be hierarchic. We have only to turn the argument around to explain the observed predominance of hierarchies among the complex systems nature presents to us. Among possible complex forms, hierarchies are the ones that have the time to evolve. The hypothesis that complexity will be hierarchic makes no distinction among very flat hierarchies, like crystals, and tissues, and polymers, and the intermediate forms. Indeed, in the complex systems we encounter in nature, examples of both forms are prominent. A more complete theory than the one we have developed here would presumably have something to say about the determinants of width of span in these systems.

NEARLY DECOMPOSABLE SYSTEMS

In hierarchic systems, we can distinguish between the interactions *among* subsystems, on the one hand, and the interactions *within* subsystems —i.e., among the parts of those subsystems—on the other. The interactions at the different levels may be, and often will be, of different orders of

	A1	A2	A3	B1	B2	C1	C2	C3
A1	—	100	—	2	—	—	—	—
A2	100	—	100	1	1	—	—	—
A3	—	100	—	—	2	—	—	—
B1	2	1	—	—	100	2	1	—
B2	—	1	2	100	—	—	1	2
C1	—	—	—	2	—	—	100	—
C2	—	—	—	1	—	100	—	100
C3	—	—	—	—	2	—	100	—

FIG. 1. A hypothetical nearly-decomposable system. In terms of the heat-exchange example of the text, A1, A2, and A3 may be interpreted as cubicles in one room, B1 and B2 as cubicles in a second room, and C1, C2, and C3 as cubicles in a third. The matrix entries then are the heat diffusion coefficients between cubicles.

A1	B1	C1
A2		C2
A3	B2	C3

magnitude. In a formal organization there will generally be more interaction, on the average, between two employees who are members of the same department than between two employees from different departments. In organic substances, intermolecular forces will generally be weaker than molecular forces, and molecular forces than nuclear forces.

In a rare gas, the intermolecular forces will be negligible compared to those binding the molecules —we can treat the individual particles, for many purposes, as if they were independent of each other. We can describe such a system as *decomposable* into the subsystems comprised of the individual particles. As the gas becomes denser, molecular interactions become more significant. But over some range, we can treat the decomposable case as a limit, and as a first approximation. We can use a theory of perfect gases, for example, to describe approximately the behavior of actual gases if they are not too dense. As a second approximation, we may move to a theory of *nearly decomposable* systems, in which the interactions among the subsystems are weak, but not negligible.

At least some kinds of hierarchic systems can be approximated successfully as nearly decomposable systems. The main theoretical findings from the approach can be summed up in two propositions:

(*a*) in a nearly decomposable system, the short-run behavior of each of the component subsystems is approximately independent of the short-run behavior of the other components; (*b*) in the long run, the behavior of any one of the components depends in only an aggregate way on the behavior of the other components.

Let me provide a very concrete simple example of a nearly decomposable system.[15] Consider a building whose outside walls provide perfect thermal insulation from the environment. We shall take these walls as the boundary of our system. The building is divided into a large number of rooms, the walls between them being good, but not perfect, insulators. The walls between rooms are the boundaries of our major subsystems. Each room is divided by partitions into a number of cubicles, but the partitions are poor insulators. A thermometer hangs in each cubicle. Suppose that at the time of our first observation of the system there is a wide variation in temperature from cubicle to cubicle and from room to room—the various cubicles within the building are in a state of thermal disequilibrium. When we take new temperature readings several hours later, what shall we find? There will be very little variation in temperature among the cubicles within each single room, but there may still be large temperature variations *among* rooms. When we take readings again several days later, we find an almost uniform temperature throughout the building; the temperature differences among rooms have virtually disappeared.

We can describe the process of equilibration formally by setting up the usual equations of heat flow. The equations can be represented by the matrix of their coefficients, r_{ij}, where r_{ij} is the rate at which heat flows from the ith cubicle to the jth cubicle per degree difference in their temperatures. If cubicles i and j do not have a common wall, r_{ij} will be zero. If cubicles i and j have a common wall, and are in the same room, r_{ij} will be large. If cubicles i and j are separated by the wall of a

[15] This discussion of near-decomposability is based upon H. A. Simon and A. Ando, Aggregation of variables in dynamic systems, *Econometrica* 29: 111–138, April, 1961. The example is drawn from the same source, 117–118. The theory has been further developed and applied to a variety of economic and political phenomena by Ando and F. M. Fisher. See F. M. Fisher, On the cost of approximate specification in simultaneous equation estimation, *Econometrica* 29: 139–170, April, 1961, and F. M. Fisher and A. Ando, Two theorems on *Ceteris Paribus* in the analysis of dynamic systems, *American Political Science Review* 61: 103–113, March, 1962.

room, r_{ij} will be nonzero but small. Hence, by grouping all the cubicles together that are in the same room, we can arrange the matrix of coefficients so that all its large elements lie inside a string of square submatrices along the main diagonal. All the elements outside these diagonal squares will be either zero or small (see figure 1). We may take some small number, ϵ, as the upper bound of the extradiagonal elements. We shall call a matrix having these properties a *nearly decomposable matrix*.

Now it has been proved that a dynamic system that can be described by a nearly decomposable matrix has the properties, stated above, of a nearly decomposable system. In our simple example of heat flow this means that in the short run each room will reach an equilibrium temperature (an average of the initial temperatures of its offices) nearly independently of the others; and that each room will remain approximately in a state of equilibrium over the longer period during which an over-all temperature equilibrium is being established throughout the building. After the intra-room short-run equilibria have been reached, a single thermometer in each room will be adequate to describe the dynamic behavior of the entire system—separate thermometers in each cubicle will be superfluous.

NEAR DECOMPOSABILITY OF SOCIAL SYSTEMS

As a glance at figure 1 shows, near decomposability is a rather strong property for a matrix to possess, and the matrices that have this property will describe very special dynamic systems—vanishingly few systems out of all those that are thinkable. How few they will be depends, of course, on how good an approximation we insist upon. If we demand that epsilon be very small, correspondingly few dynamic systems will fit the definition. But we have already seen that in the natural world nearly decomposable systems are far from rare. On the contrary, systems in which each variable is linked with almost equal strength with almost all other parts of the system are far rarer and less typical.

In economic dynamics, the main variables are the prices and quantities of commodities. It is empirically true that the price of any given commodity and the rate at which it is exchanged depend to a significant extent only on the prices and quantities of a few other commodities, together with a few other aggregate magnitudes, like the average price level or some over-all measure of economic activity. The large linkage coefficients are associated, in general, with the main flows of raw materials and semi-finished products within and between industries. An input-output matrix of the economy, giving the magnitudes of these flows, reveals the nearly decomposable structure of the system—with one qualification. There is a consumption subsystem of the economy that is linked strongly to variables in most of the other subsystems. Hence, we have to modify our notions of decomposability slightly to accommodate the special role of the consumption subsystem in our analysis of the dynamic behavior of the economy.

In the dynamics of social systems, where members of a system communicate with and influence other members, near decomposability is generally very prominent. This is most obvious in formal organizations, where the formal authority relation connects each member of the organization with one immediate superior and with a small number of subordinates. Of course many communications in organizations follow other channels than the lines of formal authority. But most of these channels lead from any particular individual to a very limited number of his superiors, subordinates, and associates. Hence, departmental boundaries play very much the same role as the walls in our heat example.

PHYSICO-CHEMICAL SYSTEMS

In the complex systems familiar in biological chemistry, a similar structure is clearly visible. Take the atomic nuclei in such a system as the elementary parts of the system, and construct a matrix of bond strengths between elements. There will be matrix elements of quite different orders of magnitude. The largest will generally correspond to the covalent bonds, the next to the ionic bonds, the third group to hydrogen bonds, still smaller linkages to van der Waals forces.[16] If we select an epsilon just a little smaller than the magnitude of a covalent bond, the system will decompose into subsystems—the constituent molecules. The smaller linkages will correspond to the intermolecular bonds.

It is well known that high-energy, high-fre-

---

[16] For a survey of the several classes of molecular and inter-molecular forces, and their dissociation energies see Setlow and Pollard, *op. cit.*, chapter 6. The energies of typical covalent bonds are of the order of 80–100 k cal/mole, of the hydrogen bonds, 10 k cal/mole. Ionic bonds generally lie between these two levels, the bonds due to van der Waals forces are lower in energy.

quency vibrations are associated with the smaller physical subsystems, low-frequency vibrations with the larger systems into which the subsystems are assembled. For example, the radiation frequencies associated with molecular vibrations are much lower than those associated with the vibrations of the planetary electrons of the atoms; the latter, in turn, are lower than those associated with nuclear processes.[17] Molecular systems are nearly decomposable systems, the short-run dynamics relating to the internal structures of the subsystems; the long-run dynamics to the interactions of these subsystems.

A number of the important approximations employed in physics depend for their validity on the near-decomposability of the systems studied. The theory of the thermodynamics of irreversible processes, for example, requires the assumption of macroscopic disequilibrium but microscopic equilibrium,[18] exactly the situation described in our heat-exchange example. Similarly computations in quantum mechanics are often handled by treating weak interactions as producing perturbations on a system of strong interactions.

SOME OBSERVATIONS ON HIERARCHIC SPAN

To understand why the span of hierarchies is sometimes very broad—as in crystals—sometimes narrow, we need to examine more detail of the interactions. In general, the critical consideration is the extent to which interaction between two (or a few) subsystems excludes interaction of these subsystems with the others. Let us examine first some physical examples.

Consider a gas of identical molecules, each of which can form covalent bonds, in certain ways, with others. Let us suppose that we can associate with each atom a specific number of bonds that it is capable of maintaining simultaneously. (This number is obviously related to the number we usually call its valence.) Now suppose that two atoms join, and that we can also associate with the combination a specific number of external bonds it is capable of maintaining. If this number is the same

[17] Typical wave numbers for vibrations associated with various systems (the wave number is the reciprocal of wave length hence proportional to frequency):
    steel wire under tension—10^{-10} to 10^{-9} cm^{-1}
    molecular rotations—10^0 to 10^2 cm^{-1}
    molecular vibrations—10^2 to 10^3 cm^{-1}
    planetary electrons—10^4 to 10^5 cm^{-1}
    nuclear rotations—10^9 to 10^{10} cm^{-1}
    nuclear surface vibrations—10^{11} to 10^{12} cm^{-1}.
[18] S. R. de Groot, *Thermodynamics of irreversible processes*, 11–12, New York, Interscience Publishers, 1951.

as the number associated with the individual atoms, the bonding process can go on indefinitely—the atoms can form crystals or polymers of indefinite extent. If the number of bonds of which the composite is capable is less than the number associated with each of the parts, then the process of agglomeration must come to a halt.

We need only mention some elementary examples. Ordinary gases show no tendency to agglomerate because the multiple bonding of atoms "uses up" their capacity to interact. While each oxygen atom has a valence of two, the O_2 molecules have a zero valence. Contrariwise, indefinite chains of single-bonded carbon atoms can be built up because a chain of any number of such atoms, each with two side groups, has a valence of exactly two.

Now what happens if we have a system of elements that possess both strong and weak interaction capacities, and whose strong bonds are exhaustible through combination? Subsystems will form, until all the capacity for strong interaction is utilized in their construction. Then these subsystems will be linked by the weaker second-order bonds into larger systems. For example, a water molecule has essentially a valence of zero—all the potential covalent bonds are fully occupied by the interaction of hydrogen and oxygen molecules. But the geometry of the molecule creates an electric dipole that permits weak interaction between the water and salts dissolved in it—whence such phenomena as its electrolytic conductivity.[19]

Similarly, it has been observed that, although electrical forces are much stronger than gravitational forces, the latter are far more important than the former for systems on an astronomical scale. The explanation, of course, is that the electrical forces, being bipolar, are all "used up" in the linkages of the smaller subsystems, and that significant net balances of positive or negative charges are not generally found in regions of macroscopic size.

In social as in physical systems there are generally limits on the simultaneous interaction of large numbers of subsystems. In the social case, these limits are related to the fact that a human being is more nearly a serial than a parallel information-processing system. He can carry on only one conversation at a time, and although this does not limit the size of the audience to which a mass communication can be addressed, it does

[19] See, for example, L. Pauling, *General chemistry*, ch. 15.

VOL. 106, NO. 6, 1962]
THE ARCHITECTURE OF COMPLEXITY 477

limit the number of people simultaneously involved in most other forms of social interaction. Apart from requirements of direct interaction, most roles impose tasks and responsibilities that are time consuming. One cannot, for example, enact the role of "friend" with large numbers of other people.

It is probably true that in social as in physical systems, the higher frequency dynamics are associated with the subsystems, the lower frequency dynamics with the larger systems. It is generally believed, for example, that the relevant planning horizon of executives is longer the higher their location in the organizational hierarchy. It is probably also true that both the average duration of an interaction between executives and the average interval between interactions is greater at higher than at lower levels.

SUMMARY : NEAR DECOMPOSABILITY

We have seen that hierarchies have the property of near-decomposability. Intra-component linkages are generally stronger than intercomponent linkages. This fact has the effect of separating the high-frequency dynamics of a hierarchy—involving the internal structure of the components—from the low frequency dynamics—involving interaction among components. We shall turn next to some important consequences of this separation for the description and comprehension of complex systems.

THE DESCRIPTION OF COMPLEXITY

If you ask a person to draw a complex object— e.g., a human face—he will almost always proceed in a hierarchic fashion.[20] First he will outline the face. Then he will add or insert features: eyes, nose, mouth, ears, hair. If asked to elaborate, he will begin to develop details for each of the features—pupils, eyelids, lashes for the eyes, and so on—until he reaches the limits of his anatomical knowledge. His information about the object is arranged hierarchicly in memory, like a topical outline.

When information is put in outline form, it is easy to include information about the relations among the major parts and information about the internal relations of parts in each of the suboutlines. Detailed information about the relations of subparts belonging to different parts has no place

[20] George A. Miller has collected protocols from subjects who were given the task of drawing faces, and finds that they behave in the manner described here (private communication). See also E. H. Gombrich, *Art and illusion*, 291–296, New York, Pantheon Books, 1960.

in the outline and is likely to be lost. The loss of such information and the preservation mainly of information about hierarchic order is a salient characteristic that distinguishes the drawings of a child or someone untrained in representation from the drawing of a trained artist. (I am speaking of an artist who is striving for representation.)

NEAR DECOMPOSABILITY AND COMPREHENSIBILITY

From our discussion of the dynamic properties of nearly decomposable systems, we have seen that comparatively little information is lost by representing them as hierarchies. Subparts belonging to different parts only interact in an aggregative fashion—the detail of their interaction can be ignored. In studying the interaction of two large molecules, generally we do not need to consider in detail the interactions of nuclei of the atoms belonging to the one molecule with the nuclei of the atoms belonging to the other. In studying the interaction of two nations, we do not need to study in detail the interactions of each citizen of the first with each citizen of the second.

The fact, then, that many complex systems have a nearly decomposable, hierarchic structure is a major facilitating factor enabling us to understand, to describe, and even to "see" such systems and their parts. Or perhaps the proposition should be put the other way round. If there are important systems in the world that are complex without being hierarchic, they may to a considerable extent escape our observation and our understanding. Analysis of their behavior would involve such detailed knowledge and calculation of the interactions of their elementary parts that it would be beyond our capacities of memory or computation.[21]

[21] I believe the fallacy in the central thesis of W. M. Elsasser's *The physical foundation of biology*, mentioned earlier, lies in his ignoring the simplification in description of complex systems that derives from their hierarchic structure. Thus (p. 155) : "If we now apply similar arguments to the coupling of enzymatic reactions with the substratum of protein molecules, we see that over a sufficient period of time, the information corresponding to the structural details of these molecules will be communicated to the dynamics of the cell, to higher levels of organization as it were, and may influence such dynamics. While this reasoning is only qualitative, it lends credence to the assumption that in the living organism, unlike the inorganic crystal, the effects of microscopic structure cannot be simply averaged out; as time goes on this influence will pervade the behavior of the cell 'at all levels.'"
But from our discussion of near-decomposability it would appear that those aspects of microstructure that control the slow developmental aspects of organismic

I shall not try to settle which is chicken and which is egg: whether we are able to understand the world because it is hierarchic, or whether it appears hierarchic because those aspects of it which are not elude our understanding and observation. I have already given some reasons for supposing that the former is at least half the truth—that evolving complexity would tend to be hierarchic—but it may not be the whole truth.

SIMPLE DESCRIPTIONS OF COMPLEX SYSTEMS

One might suppose that the description of a complex system would itself be a complex structure of symbols—and indeed, it may be just that. But there is no conservation law that requires that the description be as cumbersome as the object described. A trivial example will show how a system can be described economically. Suppose the system is a two-dimensional array like this:

$$
\begin{matrix}
A & B & M & N & R & S & H & I \\
C & D & O & P & T & U & J & K \\
M & N & A & B & H & I & R & S \\
O & P & C & D & J & K & T & U \\
R & S & H & I & A & B & M & N \\
T & U & J & K & C & D & O & P \\
H & I & R & S & M & N & A & B \\
J & K & T & U & O & P & C & D
\end{matrix}
$$

Let us call the array $\begin{vmatrix} AB \\ CD \end{vmatrix} a$, the array $\begin{vmatrix} MN \\ OP \end{vmatrix} m$, the array $\begin{vmatrix} RS \\ TU \end{vmatrix} r$, and the array $\begin{vmatrix} HI \\ JK \end{vmatrix} h$. Let us call the array $\begin{vmatrix} am \\ ma \end{vmatrix} w$, and the array $\begin{vmatrix} rh \\ hr \end{vmatrix} x$. Then the entire array is simply $\begin{vmatrix} wx \\ xw \end{vmatrix}$. While the original structure consisted of 64 symbols, it requires only 35 to write down its description:

$$ S = \frac{wx}{xw} $$

$$ w = \frac{am}{ma} \qquad x = \frac{rh}{hr} $$

$$ a = \frac{AB}{CD} \qquad m = \frac{MN}{OP} \qquad r = \frac{RS}{TU} \qquad h = \frac{HI}{JK} $$

We achieve the abbreviation by making use of the redundancy in the original structure. Since

dynamics can be separated out from the aspects that control the more rapid cellular metabolic processes. For this reason we should not despair of unravelling the web of causes. See also J. R. Platt's review of Elsasser's book in *Perspectives in biology and medicine* **2**: 243–245, 1959.

the pattern $\frac{AB}{CD}$, for example, occurs four times in the total pattern, it is economical to represent it by the single symbol, a.

If a complex structure is completely unredundant—if no aspect of its structure can be inferred from any other—then it is its own simplest description. We can exhibit it, but we cannot describe it by a simpler structure. The hierarchic structures we have been discussing have a high degree of redundancy, hence can often be described in economical terms. The redundancy takes a number of forms, of which I shall mention three:

1. Hierarchic systems are usually composed of only a few different kinds of subsystems, in various combinations and arrangements. A familiar example is the proteins, their multitudinous variety arising from arrangements of only twenty different amino acids. Similarly, the ninety-odd elements provide all the kinds of building blocks needed for an infinite variety of molecules. Hence, we can construct our description from a restricted alphabet of elementary terms corresponding to the basic set of elementary subsystems from which the complex system is generated.

2. Hierarchic systems are, as we have seen, often nearly decomposable. Hence only aggregative properties of their parts enter into the description of the interactions of those parts. A generalization of the notion of near-decomposability might be called the "empty world hypothesis" —most things are only weakly connected with most other things; for a tolerable description of reality only a tiny fraction of all possible interactions needs to be taken into account. By adopting a descriptive language that allows the absence of something to go unmentioned, a nearly empty world can be described quite concisely. Mother Hubbard did not have to check off the list of possible contents to say that her cupboard was bare.

3. By appropriate "recoding," the redundancy that is present but unobvious in the structure of a complex system can often be made patent. The most common recoding of descriptions of dynamic systems consists in replacing a description of the time path with a description of a differential law that generates that path. The simplicity, that is, resides in a constant relation between the state of the system at any given time and the state of the system a short time later. Thus, the structure of the sequence, 1 3 5 7 9 11 . . ., is most simply expressed by observing that each member is obtained by adding 2 to the previous one. But

this is the sequence that Galileo found to describe the velocity at the end of successive time intervals of a ball rolling down an inclined plane.

It is a familiar proposition that the task of science is to make use of the world's redundancy to describe that world simply. I shall not pursue the general methodological point here, but shall instead take a closer look at two main types of description that seem to be available to us in seeking an understanding of complex systems. I shall call these *state description* and *process description*, respectively.

STATE DESCRIPTIONS AND PROCESS DESCRIPTIONS

"A circle is the locus of all points equidistant from a given point." "To construct a circle, rotate a compass with one arm fixed until the other arm has returned to its starting point." It is implicit in Euclid that if you carry out the process specified in the second sentence, you will produce an object that satisfies the definition of the first. The first sentence is a state description of a circle, the second a process description.

These two modes of apprehending structure are the warp and weft of our experience. Pictures, blueprints, most diagrams, chemical structural formulae are state descriptions. Recipes, differential equations, equations for chemical reactions are process descriptions. The former characterize the world as sensed; they provide the criteria for identifying objects, often by modeling the objects themselves. The latter characterize the world as acted upon; they provide the means for producing or generating objects having the desired characteristics.

The distinction between the world as sensed and the world as acted upon defines the basic condition for the survival of adaptive organisms. The organism must develop correlations between goals in the sensed world and actions in the world of process. When they are made conscious and verbalized, these correlations correspond to what we usually call means-end analysis. Given a desired state of affairs and an existing state of affairs, the task of an adaptive organism is to find the difference between these two states, and then to find the correlating process that will erase the difference.[22]

Thus, problem solving requires continual trans-

lation between the state and process descriptions of the same complex reality. Plato, in the *Meno*, argued that all learning is remembering. He could not otherwise explain how we can discover or recognize the answer to a problem unless we already know the answer.[23] Our dual relation to the world is the source and solution of the paradox. We pose a problem by giving the state description of the solution. The task is to discover a sequence of processes that will produce the goal state from an initial state. Translation from the process description to the state description enables us to recognize when we have succeeded. The solution is genuinely new to us— and we do not need Plato's theory of remembering to explain how we recognize it.

There is now a growing body of evidence that the activity called human problem solving is basically a form of means-end analysis that aims at discovering a process description of the path that leads to a desired goal. The general paradigm is: given a blueprint, to find the corresponding recipe. Much of the activity of science is an application of that paradigm: given the description of some natural phenomena, to find the differential equations for processes that will produce the phenomena.

THE DESCRIPTION OF COMPLEXITY IN SELF-REPRODUCING SYSTEMS

The problem of finding relatively simple descriptions for complex systems is of interest not only for an understanding of human knowledge of the world but also for an explanation of how a complex system can reproduce itself. In my discussion of the evolution of complex systems, I touched only briefly on the role of self-reproduction.

Atoms of high atomic weight and complex inorganic molecules are witnesses to the fact that the evolution of complexity does not imply self-reproduction. If evolution of complexity from simplicity is sufficiently probable, it will occur repeatedly; the statistical equilibrium of the system will find a large fraction of the elementary particles participating in complex systems.

If, however, the existence of a particular complex form increased the probability of the creation of another form just like it, the equilibrium between complexes and components could be greatly altered in favor of the former. If we have a description of an object that is sufficiently clear and

[22] See H. A. Simon and A. Newell, Simulation of human thinking, *in* M. Greenberger (ed.), *Management and the computer of the future*, 95–114, esp. pp 110 ff., New York, Wiley, 1962.

[23] *The works of Plato*, B. Jowett, trans., **3**: 26–35, New York, Dial Press.

complete, we can reproduce the object from the description. Whatever the exact mechanism of reproduction, the description provides us with the necessary information.

Now we have seen that the descriptions of complex systems can take many forms. In particular, we can have state descriptions or we can have process descriptions; blueprints or recipes. Reproductive processes could be built around either of these sources of information. Perhaps the simplest possibility is for the complex system to serve as a description of itself—a template on which a copy can be formed. One of the most plausible current theories, for example, of the reproduction of deoxyribonucleic acid (DNA) proposes that a DNA molecule, in the form of a double helix of matching parts (each essentially a "negative" of the other), unwinds to allow each half of the helix to serve as a template on which a new matching half can form.

On the other hand, our current knowledge of how DNA controls the metabolism of the organism suggests that reproduction by template is only one of the processes involved. According to the prevailing theory, DNA serves as a template both for itself and for the related substance ribonucleic acid (RNA). RNA, in turn, serves as a template for protein. But proteins—according to current knowledge—guide the organism's metabolism not by the template method but by serving as catalysts to govern reaction rates in the cell. While RNA is a blueprint for protein, protein is a recipe for metabolism.[24]

ONTOGENY RECAPITULATES PHYLOGENY

The DNA in the chromosomes of an organism contains some, and perhaps most, of the information that is needed to determine its development and activity. We have seen that, if current theories are even approximately correct, the information is recorded not as a state description of the organism but as a series of "instructions" for the construction and maintenance of the organism from nutrient materials. I have already used the metaphor of a recipe; I could equally well compare it with a computer program, which is also a sequence of instructions, governing the construction

[24] C. B. Anfinsen, *The molecular basis of evolution*, chs. 3 and 10, New York, Wiley, 1959, will qualify this sketchy, oversimplified account. For an imaginative discussion of some mechanisms of process description that could govern molecular structure, see H. H. Pattee, On the origin of macromolecular sequences, *Biophysical Journal* 1: 683–710, 1961.

of symbolic structures. Let me spin out some of the consequences of the latter comparison.

If genetic material is a program—viewed in its relation to the organism—it is a program with special and peculiar properties. First, it is a self-reproducing program; we have already considered its possible copying mechanism. Second, it is a program that has developed by Darwinian evolution. On the basis of our watchmaker's argument, we may assert that many of its ancestors were also viable programs—programs for the subassemblies.

Are there any other conjectures we can make about the structure of this program? There is a well-known generalization in biology that is verbally so neat that we would be reluctant to give it up even if the facts did not support it: ontogeny recapitulates phylogeny. The individual organism, in its development, goes through stages that resemble some of its ancestral forms. The fact that the human embryo develops gill bars and then modifies them for other purposes is a familiar particular belonging to the generalization. Biologists today like to emphasize the qualifications of the principle—that ontogeny recapitulates only the grossest aspects of phylogeny, and these only crudely. These qualifications should not make us lose sight of the fact that the generalization does hold in rough approximation—it does summarize a very significant set of facts about the organism's development. How can we interpret these facts?

One way to solve a complex problem is to reduce it to a problem previously solved—to show what steps lead from the earlier solution to a solution of the new problem. If, around the turn of the century, we wanted to instruct a workman to make an automobile, perhaps the simplest way would have been to tell him how to modify a wagon by removing the singletree and adding a motor and transmission. Similarly, a genetic program could be altered in the course of evolution by adding new processes that would modify a simpler form into a more complex one—to construct a gastrula, take a blastula and alter it!

The genetic description of a single cell may, therefore, take a quite different form from the genetic description that assembles cells into a multi-celled organism. Multiplication by cell division would require, as a minimum, a state description (the DNA, say), and a simple "interpretive process"—to use the term from computer language—that copies this description as a part of the larger copying process of cell division. But such a mechanism clearly would not suffice for the differentiation of cells in development. It appears more natural to conceptualize that mechanism as based on a process description, and a somewhat more complex interpretive process that produces the adult organism in a sequence of stages, each new stage in development representing the effect of an operator upon the previous one.

It is harder to conceptualize the interrelation of these two descriptions. Interrelated they must be, for enough has been learned of gene-enzyme mechanisms to show that these play a major role in development as in cell metabolism. The single clue we obtain from our earlier discussion is that the description may itself be hierarchical, or nearly decomposable, in structure, the lower levels governing the fast, "high-frequency" dynamics of the individual cell, the higher level interactions governing the slow, "low-frequency" dynamics of the developing multi-cellular organism.

There are only bits of evidence, apart from the facts of recapitulation, that the genetic program is organized in this way, but such evidence as exists is compatible with this notion.[25] To the extent that we can differentiate the genetic information that governs cell metabolism from the genetic information that governs the development of differentiated cells in the multi-cellular organization, we simplify enormously—as we have already seen —our task of theoretical description. But I have perhaps pressed this speculation far enough.

The generalization that in evolving systems whose descriptions are stored in a process language, we might expect ontogeny partially to recapitulate phylogeny has applications outside the

[25] There is considerable evidence that successive genes along a chromosome often determine enzymes controlling successive stages of protein syntheses. For a review of some of this evidence, see P. E. Hartman, Transduction: a comparative review, *in* W. D. McElroy and B. Glass (eds.), *The chemical basis of heredity*, Baltimore, Johns Hopkins Press, 1957, at pp. 442–454. Evidence for differential activity of genes in different tissues and at different stages of development is discussed by J. G. Gall, Chromosomal Differentiation, *in* W. D. McElroy and B. Glass (eds.), *The chemical basis of development*, Baltimore, Johns Hopkins Press, 1958, at pp. 103–135. Finally, a model very like that proposed here has been independently, and far more fully, outlined by J. R. Platt, A 'book model' of genetic information transfer in cells and tissues, *in* Kasha and Pullman (eds.), *Horizons in biochemistry*, New York, Academic Press, forthcoming. Of course, this kind of mechanism is not the only one in which development could be controlled by a process description. Induction, in the form envisaged in Spemann's organizer theory, is based on process description, in which metabolites in already formed tissue control the next stages of development.

realm of biology. It can be applied as readily, for example, to the transmission of knowledge in the educational process. In most subjects, particularly in the rapidly advancing sciences, the progress from elementary to advanced courses is to a considerable extent a progress through the conceptual history of the science itself. Fortunately, the recapitulation is seldom literal—any more than it is in the biological case. We do not teach the phlogiston theory in chemistry in order later to correct it. (I am not sure I could not cite examples in other subjects where we do exactly that.) But curriculum revisions that rid us of the accumulations of the past are infrequent and painful. Nor are they always desirable—partial recapitulation may, in many instances, provide the most expeditious route to advanced knowledge.

SUMMARY: THE DESCRIPTION OF COMPLEXITY

How complex or simple a structure is depends critically upon the way in which we describe it. Most of the complex structures found in the world are enormously redundant, and we can use this redundancy to simplify their description. But to use it, to achieve the simplification, we must find the right representation.

The notion of substituting a process description for a state description of nature has played a central role in the development of modern science. Dynamic laws, expressed in the form of systems of differential or difference equations, have in a large number of cases provided the clue for the simple description of the complex. In the preceding paragraphs I have tried to show that this characteristic of scientific inquiry is not accidental or superficial. The correlation between state description and process description is basic to the functioning of any adaptive organism, to its capacity for acting purposefully upon its environment. Our present-day understanding of genetic mechanisms suggests that even in describing itself the multi-cellular organism finds a process description—a genetically encoded program—to be the parsimonious and useful representation.

CONCLUSION

Our speculations have carried us over a rather alarming array of topics, but that is the price we must pay if we wish to seek properties common to many sorts of complex systems. My thesis has been that one path to the construction of a nontrivial theory of complex systems is by way of a theory of hierarchy. Empirically, a large proportion of the complex systems we observe in nature exhibit hierarchic structure. On theoretical grounds we could expect complex systems to be hierarchies in a world in which complexity had to evolve from simplicity. In their dynamics, hierarchies have a property, near-decomposability, that greatly simplifies their behavior. Near-decomposability also simplifies the description of a complex system, and makes it easier to understand how the information needed for the development or reproduction of the system can be stored in reasonable compass.

In both science and engineering, the study of "systems" is an increasingly popular activity. Its popularity is more a response to a pressing need for synthesizing and analyzing complexity than it is to any large development of a body of knowledge and technique for dealing with complexity. If this popularity is to be more than a fad, necessity will have to mother invention and provide substance to go with the name. The explorations reviewed here represent one particular direction of search for such substance.

28

Journal of Economic Literature
Vol. XXX (September 1992), pp. 1382–1415

Hierarchy: The Economics of Managing

By ROY RADNER

AT&T Bell Laboratories and New York University

This paper was prepared for the Marshall Lectures, Cambridge University, October 25–26, 1989. I am grateful to C. V. Kuh for helpful discussions and suggestions during the preparation of this paper, and to U. Pagano and two referees for comments on a previous draft. The views expressed here are those of the author, and not necessarily those of AT&T Bell Laboratories.

1. Introduction

ONE HUNDRED YEARS AGO, at the time of the publication of Alfred Marshall's *Principles of Economics*, the typical British or U.S. firm was a small enterprise, managed by the owner, and perhaps a few assistants. There were, of course, larger enterprises, such as railroads, mines, and shipyards, but even in those firms relatively few persons specialized in the activity of managing. In the United States, according to Thomas K. McCraw (1984, p. 64),

Although the profound economic movement that has become known as the "rise of big business" began with the railroads in the 1850s, it continued to move forward, in vastly expanded form, causing revolutions in manufacturing and distribution. These changes occurred between about 1880 and 1920. Prior to this period, no single manufacturing enterprise, indeed no entire manufacturing industry, had attained sufficient size to affect masses of people. Before the 1880s, even major factories customarily employed no more than a few hundred workers. . . . Yet, within a single generation after 1880, all this changed. By 1890, each of several large railroads employed more than 100,000 workers . . . and in 1901, the creation of the United

States Steel Corporation climaxed a $1.4 billion transaction. This sum, which far exceeded the imaginations of most contemporary citizens, became a symbol of the new giantism in the American economy.

According to Joan Robinson, "Marshall had a picture, based on observation, of the family business in British manufacturing industry. . . . He observed that in many cases the fortunes of a business are bound up in the life of a family. An individual sets it going and it prospers, but by the third generation its vigor is lost" (Robinson 1977, p. 1324). On the other hand, Marshall was not unaware of "big business."

And as with the growth of trees, so it was with the growth of businesses as a general rule before the development of vast joint stock-companies, which often stagnate, but do not readily die. . . . Nature still presses on the private business by limiting the length of life of its original founders, and by limiting even more narrowly that part of their lives in which their faculties retain full vigor. And so, after a while, the guidance of the business falls into the hands of people with less energy and less creative genius, if not with less active interest in its prosperity. If it is turned into a joint stock-company, it may retain the advantages of division of labor, of specialized skill and machinery: it may even increase them by a further increase in its capital; and under favorable conditions it may secure a permanent and prominent place in the work of production. But it is likely to have lost so much of its elasticity and progressive force, that the advantages are no longer exclusively on its side in its competition with younger and smaller rivals. (Marshall 1920, p. 316)

The economies of today's industrialized nations are dominated by giant firms, each with thousands or even hundreds of thousands of employees. For example, the largest private firm in the world, General Motors, has more than 700,000 employees. In such firms, more than a third of the employees may be working full time in activities that are part of—or support—the management process. Thus, quantitatively as well as functionally, "managing" has become a significant activity in our economy.

This phenomenon has not escaped the attention of our colleagues in schools of business and management, where many courses are devoted to the subject. The pure science of economics, however, has been slower to focus on this phenomenon, and pure theory even slower. The picture of the firm in most economic textbooks, and in much current economic research, is still that of a unitary "entrepreneur," bent on maximizing profits. But there is also a growing body of research that views the modern firm as an *organization* of economic agents. There are two aspects of this relatively "new look" that I shall discuss here: (1) the sense in which *the large business enterprise is a small economy* (and sometimes not so small), and (2) the *central role of managing* in that economy. More particularly, I have set myself three tasks:

1. to convince the reader that managing is an activity worthy of economic analysis;
2. to review some insights that economic theory has provided into the

economics of managing, and thereby also to persuade you that this activity is amenable to economic analysis; and
3. to sketch a number of theoretical problems waiting to be solved.

There is also a subtheme in my paper, namely, the significance of hierarchy. Large firms are widely perceived to be organized hierarchically, whatever that means precisely. Indeed, a well-known book opposes "markets" and "hierarchies" as the predominant forms of modern economic organization, the latter, of course, referring to the organization of firms (Oliver Williamson 1975). Students of management are well aware that many interactions in a typical firm are not organized hierarchically, even if the formal organization chart looks that way. Nevertheless, it is an important principle of organization, both in its prevalence and in the prevalence of attempts to circumvent it. So in addition to the three tasks I have just described, I shall focus on the question: *What is the economic significance of hierarchy in the organization and management of large firms?*

It will be seen, then, that my topic falls under the heading, the theory of the firm, but falls far short of encompassing the whole of that subject. In particular, I shall have nothing to say about why firms are owned by stockholders rather than workers or customers or the state, or how stockholders' voting rights should be exercised, or when one should expect vertical integration to take place. I shall be pleased if what I have to say has some interesting implications for these issues, but I leave it to other occasions, or even other investigators, to make the inferences. I suspect that, when it comes to the economics of managing large firms, capitalist, socialist, cooperative, and labor-managed firms have much in common, and it is that common element I hope to stress here.

Here, then, is a brief outline of my paper. To begin, I shall show you a few statistics to try to persuade you that managing has become a significant economic activity. Given the size of modern firms, and given the bounds on individuals' capabilities for information processing and decision making—"bounded rationality," if you like—it is obvious that the labor of managing must be divided among many persons in the firm. Although not inevitable, it is not surprising that this division of labor is accompanied by specialization, as with other kinds of labor. I shall use the general term *decentralization* to describe the division of labor of managing among several persons in a firm. As we shall see, this decentralization takes many specific forms.

First, *the processing of information must be decentralized*, i.e., divided among many persons. I shall use some ideas from computer science to argue that many information-processing activities in a firm can be accomplished efficiently by a hierarchical structure. Of course, in order to define "efficiency" I shall have to be precise about what is being economized.

Second, the "management sector" of the firm makes vast numbers of decisions, and bases these decisions on vast numbers of observations, or information variables. It is not economical for all decisions to be based on all the information available to the firm; that is to say, different decisions will typically be based on different sets of information variables. Put another way, different decision makers in the firm will typically have different information. I shall call this the *decentralization of information*. In principle, one could have decentralized information processing without the decentralization of information, but in large firms we see both. The efficient decentralization of information is the subject of the *theory of teams*.

Third, all the members of a firm will not have exactly the same goal. Indeed, even if no one were greedy or lazy, members would still be likely to disagree about what is best for the firm. With the decentralization of information (and of information processing), and a divergence of interests among the members of the firm—i.e., with the *decentralization of incentives*—goes a loss of control. Even if they wanted to, members of the firm could not credibly bind themselves to reveal information honestly or to follow prescribed decision rules. We do not need the theory of games to predict that misrepresentation and moral hazard are likely to lead to inefficiencies, but recent research on principal-agent and partnership models yields some theoretical understanding of the extent to which clever mechanism design and the exploitation of long-term relationships can remedy these inefficiencies. On the other hand, it is just in the context of models of sequential decision making under incomplete or imperfect information—not to mention bounded rationality—that the inadequacies of the present state of noncooperative game theory are most mercilessly exposed. Furthermore, I know of no theoretical research to date that compares the relative efficiency of hierarchical and nonhierarchical organizations within a common model.

Finally, I shall have to admit that research to date has not provided an adequate explanation on economic grounds alone of the conditions under which one expects to see a hierarchical organization of business firms. In fact, the explanation of hierarchy may in many cases be more sociological and psychological than purely "economic" in the mainstream sense. Furthermore, one sees in the current management literature articles that call for a less hierarchical organization of business, whatever that might mean. I suspect that, for economists to contrib-

TABLE 1

1988 "FORTUNE 500" U.S. INDUSTRIAL CORPORATIONS
WITH MORE THAN 100,000 EMPLOYEES

	Empl. in 1000s	Sales Rank
1. General Motors	766	1
2. IBM	387	4
3. Ford	359	2
4. General Electric	298	5
5. Pepsico	235	26
6. United Technol	187	16
7. Philip Morris	155	10
9. Boeing	147	19
9. Chrysler	146	7
10. Eastman Kodak	145	18
11. DuPont	141	9
12. Digital Equipment	122	30
13. McDonnell Douglas	121	25
14. Westinghouse	120	27
15. RJR Nabisco	117	20
16. Goodyear	114	32
17. Xerox	113	22
18. Rockwell International	112	28
19. Allied Signal	110	29
21. General Dynamics	103	41
21. Motorola	102	52
22. Pillsbury	102	70
23. Exxon	101	3

Source: Fortune, Apr. 24, 1989.

TABLE 2

TWELVE LARGEST EMPLOYERS AMONG THE 1988 "FORTUNE
500" NON-U.S. INDUSTRIAL CORPORATIONS

	Country	Empl. in 1000s	Sales Rank
1. Coal India	India	670	335
2. IRI	Italy	418	4
3. Siemens	W. Germany	353	7
4. Daimler-Benz	W. Germany	339	5
5. Philips	Netherlands	310	13
6. Unilever	U.K./Nether-lands	291	11
7. Fiat	Italy	277	8
8. Hitachi	Japan	264	6
9. Volkswagen	W. Germany	252	10
10. CGE	France	204	24
11. Steel Auth. India	India	201	216
12. Nestlé	Switzerland	198	14

Source: Fortune, Apr. 24, 1989.

2. Managing in the Economy

Here are some statistics about the largest firms in the world, and about the fraction of the labor force devoted to the activity of managing. Although these few statistics hardly constitute a systematic study, I hope they will persuade the reader that a significant fraction of the industrialized labor force is employed in rather large firms, and that a significant fraction—perhaps more than 40 percent—is devoted to the activity of managing. In fact, the latter fraction has grown steadily during the past century.

Table 1 shows the largest 23 employers among the 1988 "Fortune 500" United States industrial corporations, the ones with at least 100,000 employees. The largest of these is General Motors, with 766,000 employees, which makes it the largest private industrial corporation in the world. Incidentally, the last time I checked, General Motors had about as many employees as there are persons employed in manufacturing in the Netherlands! Table 2 shows the largest 12 em-

ute to that discussion in a scientific way, we shall have to modify our model of economic behavior, not merely—as is beginning to happen on a small scale—to take account of bounded rationality, but also to enrich our model of human motivation.

Let me interject here a note on the style of this paper. I shall not burden you with any formal mathematics, except for some tables and graphs. But I want to emphasize that I shall be talking primarily about the contributions of *formal theorists*, not of historians, astute observers, or even informal theorists. Hence you must be prepared to deal with a number of abstract ideas, even if they are deceptively clothed in the English language.

TABLE 3

1988 "FORTUNE 500" U.S. INDUSTRIAL CORPORATIONS

Employees	Non-U.S.	U.S.	Combined
≥ 200K	11	5	16
≥ 100K	44	23	67
Median	19.2K	—	—
Mean	37.8K	25.4K	—
Total	18.9M	12.7M	—

Source: Fortune, Apr. 24, 1989.

TABLE 4

U.S. ESTABLISHMENTS AND EMPLOYEES BY EMPLOYEE SIZE CLASS, 1986

Establishments with number of employees at least	Percentage of establishments	Percentage of employees
1000	0.1	12.9
500	0.2	19.8
100	2.0	44.1
20	12.4	73.3

Source: U.S. Dept. of Commerce 1989, p. 512.

ployers among the 1988 "Fortune 500" industrial corporations outside the United States; the smallest of these, Nestlé, has almost 200,000 employees.

Table 3 provides some summary statistics about both U.S. and non-U.S. "Fortune 500" industrial corporations. We see that altogether there are 16 firms with more than 200,000 employees, and 67 firms with more than 100,000 employees. In all the "Fortune 500" non-U.S. industrial corporations, the median employment is 19,200, and the mean is 37,800. In the corresponding 500 U.S. firms, the mean is 25,400.

We are clearly dealing with some very large firms here, but how representative

are they? I cannot answer this directly but U.S. government statistics on *establishments* (rather than firms) give an indirect answer. Table 4 shows that establishments with at least 1000 employees account for almost 13 percent of the employees but only 0.1 percent of the establishments. Similarly, 0.2 percent of establishments have at least 500 employees, and account for almost 20 percent of all employees. Of course, the typical large firm will have more than one establishment under its management.

We should not be surprised if the management of such large enterprises re-

TABLE 5

U.S. FULL-TIME WAGE AND SALARY WORKERS, 1987

(MILLIONS)

	Male	Female	All
Managerial and professional	11.6	9.3	20.9
Technical and related support	1.5	1.3	2.8
Admin. support, incl. clerical	3.1	11.1	14.2
Total managing	16.2	21.7	37.9
Total employees	47.2	33.7	80.8
Managing	34.4%	64.4%	46.9%

Source: U.S. Dept. of Commerce 1989, p. 406.
Note: Not all sums and percentages appear consistent, because of rounding.

quires a lot of effort and resources. For example, AT&T currently has about 300,000 employees; of these, about 125,000 or 42 percent, are classified as "exempt from the provisions of the Fair Labor Standards Act" which is roughly equivalent to having a managerial rank. Now some of these "exempt" employees are salespersons, attorneys, and scientists; on the other hand, many "nonexempt" personnel are doing secretarial and clerical work, as well as maintenance of the buildings that house administrators and corporate staffs. A more global picture is reflected in the next table. In 1987 there were approximately 81 million fulltime wage and salary workers in the U.S.; of these about 47 percent were engaged in occupations that probably formed part of the activity of managing, either as managers or in support of the management effort. Incidentally, Table 5 also reveals that women make up more than half of the workforce devoted to managing, but also suggests that more than half of managers in the narrow sense are men (the latter statement is confirmed by other sources).

The next table shows how the fraction of the labor force devoted to managing has increased since the beginning of the century, from about 12 percent in 1900 to more than 43 percent in 1980. (Recall that the corresponding figure for 1987 was 47 percent, although the data are not exactly comparable. In constructing Table 6, I was able to make use of relatively detailed occupational classifications.)

I have been unable to extend the last table to years before 1900, but it is possible to trace the growth of the *clerical* workforce from 1870 to 1970, which is shown in Figure 1. This figure shows the percentage that "clerical and kindred workers" made up in the total labor force, starting from less than one percent in 1870, and rising to about 18 percent in

TABLE 6
MANAGING IN THE U.S. LABOR FORCE, 1900–1980

	Managing (millions)	Total Experienced Labor Force	Percent Managing
1900	3.4	29.0	11.6
1910	5.6	37.3	15.1
1920	7.8	42.2	18.5
1930	10.2	48.7	20.9
1940	11.5	51.7	22.2
1950	16.3	59.0	27.6
1960	20.9	68.0	30.7
1970	30.7	79.8	38.5
1980	45.6	104.1	43.8

Sources: U.S. Bureau of the Census 1975; 1984, V.1, Ch. D, Part 1, Sec. A, Tables 253–310.

1970. It is also interesting that, although the percentage of clerical workers who were women started out very small, it had passed the 50 percent mark in 1940, and was almost 74 percent in 1970.

I shall become more precise about what I mean by managing in the next section.

3. Managing, Decentralization, and Hierarchy

What is managing? In a nutshell, we might say that it is "figuring out what to do," in contrast to "doing it." This was expressed more eloquently in 1921 by Frank Knight, who stressed the importance of uncertainty and the role of the entrepreneur as a specialist in decision making:

> When uncertainty is present, and the task of deciding what to do and how to do it takes the ascendancy over that of execution, the internal organization of the productive groups is no longer a matter of indifference or a mechanical detail. (Knight 1921, p. 268)

By an extension of this point of view, the managing activity of a firm might be visualized as contained in a large "black

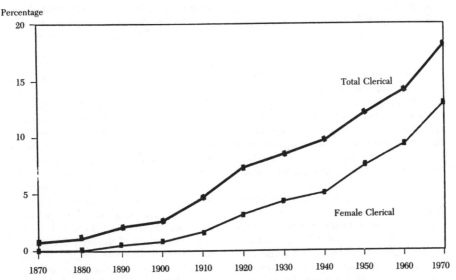

Figure 1. Clerical and Kindred Workers in the U.S. Labor Force, 1870–1970
Sources: U.S. Bureau of the Census 1943, Table XXI, p. 100.

box," into which are periodically fed observations about the firm's environment and the results of its past actions, and out of which come decisions for actions the firm is to take: inputs, outputs, choice of technique, etc. In the modern firm this black box is no longer a single entrepreneur, but is a complex organization including many specialists of different kinds.

At this point, I should say that I am aware that no job in a firm, no matter how routine, is completely devoid of decision-making activity. The blue collar worker on the most routinized assembly line must repeatedly make decisions about how to handle nonstandard situations, and in particular when to call one to the attention of the supervisor. On the other hand, sales managers, in addition to managing their salespersons, often spend considerable amounts of time with clients, engaged in selling, and thus

in "doing." Nevertheless, in a large firm it is a useful approximation to divide activities between managing and doing.

Notice that I have used the word "managing" rather than the word "management." In ordinary parlance, the latter word has two meanings: (1) the act of managing, and (2) the collection of persons in the firm called "managers." The first meaning can be "what managers do," or it can have a more general connotation. What do managers do? Here is a partial list:

1. observe the environment and results of past actions
2. process and communicate information
3. make decisions
4. monitor the actions of other firm members
5. hire and fire
6. train and teach

7. plan
8. solve problems
9. exhort, persuade, set goals and values

These are things that would naturally fall under the rubric of managing. In addition, many managers engage in other activities that look more like "doing;" for example, they try to persuade the financial community that the company stock is a good investment, they negotiate loans, they interact with customers and regulators, etc.

In carrying out their (management) activities, managers usually receive help, from staff, secretaries, clerks, equipment, buildings, people who operate and maintain the equipment and buildings, etc. All of these activities and resources I include under the heading of *managing*. In all but the smallest firms, the activities of managing are carried out by more than one person, a phenomenon I have called the *decentralization of managing*.

Activities 1–4 in the above list are usually part of our economic models of statistical decision making and game theory, although we do not usually explicitly consider the resources devoted to them in our "production" or "payoff" functions. Activity 5 (hiring and firing) may also be included in a model of explicit or implicit labor contracts. Training and teaching is sometimes renamed the "production of human capital."

The seventh and eighth activities, planning and problem solving, begin not to fit so comfortably into our standard model. Planning and problem solving might be identified with the choice of strategy, but these activities are not usually modeled as requiring the expenditure of economic resources. (In this connection, where do the activities of research and development fit in?) Finally, the last item makes us downright

uncomfortable; in the standard model, peoples' preferences and beliefs (or in the jargon of decision theory, their utility functions and prior probabilities) are exogenously given.

By the *economics of managing* I shall mean the consideration of the resources that go into the activity of managing, and the ways in which different organizations of managing do a better or worse job of economizing those resources and producing good results. To study seriously the economics of managing, one must face squarely the boundedness of rationality of economic decision makers. This phenomenon has long been recognized by theorists, if rarely acted upon. One need not go to critics of modern decision theory, such as Herbert Simon, to find an acute awareness of the boundedness of rationality. In his book, *The Foundations of Statistics* (1954), Leonard J. Savage provided economic theory with the most complete and coherent model of rational economic behavior under uncertainty (in single-person decision problems), but in the same book he emphasized the limitations of the theory as a realistic basis for the description—or even *prescription*— of rational behavior. In his chapter on "Preliminary Considerations on Decision in the Face of Uncertainty" he comments on the dilemma of decision theory that is reflected in the two proverbs, "Look before you leap," and "You can cross that bridge when you come to it:"

Carried to its logical extreme, the "Look before you leap" principle demands that one envisage every conceivable policy for the government of his whole life (at least from now on) in its most minute details, in the light of the vast number of unknown states of the world, and decide here and now on one policy. This is utterly ridiculous, not—as some might think— because there might later be cause for regret if things did not turn out as had been anticipated, but because the task implied in making such a decision is not even remotely resembled by human possibility. It is even utterly beyond our power to plan a picnic or play a game of chess in accordance with the principle, even when the world of states and the set of available acts to be envisaged are artificially reduced to the narrowest reasonable limits. (p. 16)

(Later in the book, Savage tried to explore some conditions under which out of the grand decision problem of life one could, with approximate accuracy, isolate smaller and more manageable decision problems, but—as I think he recognized—this effort was not entirely successful.)

From a philosophical point of view, it might be argued that an analysis of the economics of managing that is based on the hypothesis of bounded rationality is doomed to failure as a bootstrap operation, or an infinite regress. After all, one way to translate "the economics of managing" is "the management of managing!" This point of view is taken by Pavel Pelikan (1989), who argues that the scarcity of what he calls "economic competence" makes it impossible to determine whether firms are organized to use economic competence efficiently.

Although I might agree with this point of view in principle, in the practice of theorizing I believe that some progress can be made with a more modest and pragmatic approach. Thus, in Section 4, I shall take the point of view that a management organization does implement *some* kind of decision function—or behavior—and that 'it is interesting to inquire as to what organization structures do this efficiently, i.e., economize on the resources needed to implement the given class of decision functions, given a particular model of the boundedness of rationality. In Section 5, I push this a little farther: given that information processing is costly, what strategies for economizing on information are effective in reducing the amount of information actually used without unduly reducing

its effectiveness (value)? In particular, *it is interesting to inquire whether—or under what conditions—there are increasing returns to scale in information-processing and in the use of information.*

Now that I have given some idea of what I mean by the economics of managing, I should explain the remaining word in my title: "hierarchy." Although this is a word that can be given a unique abstract—or mathematical—meaning, in the context of this paper it will take on several different concrete meanings. At the risk of losing part of my audience, I shall start out with the abstract meaning; in fact I shall start by defining a more general concept, that of a *tree.* (I fear that the mathematical name may be misleading, since it corresponds more or less to the botanical object with the same name, but upside-down!) Formally, a *tree* is a collection of objects, together with a relation among them, to be called here "superior to." This relation has the following properties:

1. Transitivity—if A is superior to B, and B is superior to C, then A is superior to C.
2. Antisymmetry—if A is superior to B, then B is not superior to A; in this case I shall say that B is *subordinate* to A.
3. There is exactly one object, called the *root,* that is superior to all the other objects.

I shall say that A is the *immediate superior* of B if there is no object that is "between" A and B in the relation. A fourth property required of a tree is:

4. Except for the root, every object has exactly one immediate superior.

Figure 2 shows a tree with 5 objects, The root is at the top! Notice that not all the objects in the tree need be

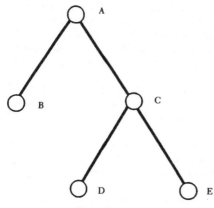

Figure 2. A tree

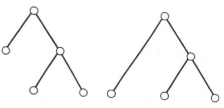

Figure 3. The same tree organized in levels in 2 different ways

"comparable;"[1] for example, B is not superior to D, nor is D superior to B.

In everyday language, the word hierarchy not only connotes an upside-down-tree-like structure, but also an assignment of rank or level. By a *ranking* of tree I shall mean an assignment of a number (rank) to each object such that:

1. if A is superior to B, then it has a higher rank (larger number);
2. if A and B have the same rank, then they are not comparable, i.e., A is not superior to B, nor is B superior to A.

I shall adopt the convention that the lowest rank is 1.

I can now define a *hierarchy*; it is a ranked tree. I note that there may be more than one way to rank a tree (in a way that satisfies properties 1 and 2 above); Figure 3 illustrates this. The hierarchies in Figure 3 look like organization charts (for a small organization!). With this interpretation, the relation "superior to" is that of formal authority. In this paper, I shall be discussing other kinds of hierarchies, as well. In fact, the

first kind of hierarchy I shall consider is one that represents an organization of tasks or work.

In his article, "The Architecture of Complexity" (1962), Herbert Simon gives a wide-ranging discussion of the significance of hierarchy in the structure of complex systems. I shall have to be satisfied here to quote from his parable of the two watchmakers (called Tempus and Hora), which he uses to introduce his discussion of the evolution of complex systems:

> The watches the men made consisted of about 1,000 parts each. Tempus had so constructed his that if he had one partly assembled and had to put it down—to answer the phone, say— it immediately fell to pieces and had to be reassembled from the elements. The better the customers liked his watches, the more they phoned him and the more difficult it became for him to find enough uninterrupted time to finish a watch.
> The watches that Hora made were no less complex than those of Tempus. But he had designed them so that he could put together subassemblies of about ten elements each. Ten of these subassemblies, again, could be put together into a larger subassembly; and a system of ten of the latter subassemblies constituted the whole watch. Hence, when Hora had to out down a partly assembled watch to answer the phone, he lost only a small part of his work, and he assembled his watches in only a fraction of the man-hours it took Tempus (Simon 1981, ch. 7, p. 200)

The theme of this parable is repeated in "The Science of Design":

> To design . . . a complex structure, one powerful technique is to discover viable ways of

---

[1] In mathematical jargon, a tree is a partially ordered set, but need not be completely ordered.

decomposing it into semi-independent components corresponding to its many functional parts. The design of each component can then be carried out with some degree of independence of the design of others, since each will affect the others largely through its function and independently of the details of the mechanisms that accomplish the function. (Simon 1981, ch 5., p. 148)

Here the hierarchical structure of the system is a reflection of the process of design, rather than the process of construction, although the two aspects might well be related. In fact, design is a particular case of problem solving, and as Simon (1981, p. 206), points out "we can take over the watchmaker parable and apply it also to problem solving." The idea is that a problem is decomposed into subproblems such that, if each is solved then the original problem will be solved. Each subproblem can then be further decomposed, etc., resulting in a hierarchical structure of problems.

Simon's watchmaker parable involved the hierarchical organization of work by a single person. In what follows, it will be useful to have in mind another illustration, which involves the allocation of work among many persons. With apologies to Henry Mintzberg (1979, pp. 1–2), I shall call this the parable of the firm. This firm has two major divisions, Manufacturing and Marketing, plus a Corporate Office (I have deliberately refrained from calling this last the corporate headquarters). The Manufacturing Division contains many production units, some of them spatially separated, and not all of them producing the same product. The Corporate Office performs a number of "overhead-type" activities, including services that are used by both of the other divisions, like payroll and financial accounting, legal services, research and development, etc. As I have described it, one can define a hierarchy in the firm by the relation "is part of." Thus a production unit is part of the Manufacturing Division, which is in turn a part of the firm as a whole. But I have said nothing about any hierarchical organization of authority. In particular, one could imagine that the Corporate Office is simply a service organization, with the task of supplying certain services requested by the two main divisions, but without any authority over them.

One might expect that the organization of work in the firm—in Simon's sense—would have a powerful influence on the way the decentralization of managing is organized. In particular, would a hierarchical design of the processes of production lead to hierarchical management? Some aspects of this will be explored in the following sections, but I can reveal right now that, from a purely theoretical point of view, this is still an open question, and that a full exploration will require substantial additional research. For recent theoretical discussions of the organization of work in modern manufacturing see Masahiko Aoki (1990) and Paul Milgrom and John Roberts (1990).

4. Decentralization of Information Processing

Although managers in a firm have many different functions, one of their most important functions is that of processing information. We might think of the information processing part of the firm as one huge decision-making machine, which takes signals from the environment and transforms them into actions to be taken by the "real workers." Of course, as I already pointed out, every worker on an assembly-line or lathe, and every salesperson in the field, makes many decisions every day that are not precisely dictated by management and that has always been so. The point I am making here is that in the modern corporation a large part of the information processing activities are highly *decentralized*, i.e., assigned to a large number of persons in the corporation who specialize in these activities. This is so, even though corporations are thought to be highly centralized from the point of view of authority and supervision.

It is the main theme of this section that hierarchical structures, which are usually thought of as the epitome of the centralization of authority, are also remarkably effective in decentralizing the activities of information processing. As we have seen, the decentralization of information processing is dictated by the large scale of modern enterprises, which makes it impossible for any single person to do it all. Thus the limited capacity of individuals for information processing implies that this activity uses significant amounts of scarce resources, including people, and hence information processing would appear to be a natural object of economic study. On the other hand, it is the computer scientists, more than any others, who have specialized in studying how effectively to organize the resources used in information processing. The present section, then, is on the boundary between economics and computer science. (For bibliographic notes, see the end of this section.)

The economist may have noted that I used the word "effective" rather than "efficient." This is because computer scientists—who are more like engineers than economists—are generally concerned with improving things, rather than with proving that something is optimal under some unrealistic and restrictive assumptions. In this sense, the focus of the present section is more like that of computer science than that of mainstream economics. On the other hand, since my concern is with a human information processing organization rather than with a physical computer or network of computers, my focus is a little different than that found in the current literature on computer science.

Various aspects of the processing of information are costly, and therefore should be "economized:"

1. the observation of the data about the environment.
2. the capabilities and numbers of the individual processors (persons, equipment).
3. the communication network that transmits and switches the data (both original and partly processed) among the processors.
4. the delay between the observation of the data and the implementation of the decision(s).

The last aspect, delay, is costly to the extent that the delayed decisions are obsolete (e.g., not timely).

In fact, computer scientists have been largely concerned with delay, that is, the time it takes to compute a particular function. Here I shall give equal attention to economizing the number of processors. I do not here consider the cost of communication; this has, I think, some empirical justification in human organizations. The problem of "information overload" is apparently particularly acute in modern times, and is a reflection of the relative cheapness of communication compared to processing (digestion) of information.

Also, in the present section I take the amount of environmental data as given, but in fact it should be an endogenous variable, determined by the balance between its cost and its value. This consideration is, however, deferred to the next section.

I shall now consider explicitly two paradigms of the transformation of environmental signals into decisions: (1) linear decision rules, and (2) pattern matching.

In the first, the decision is a linear function of the environmental signals. This corresponds, in particular, to the typical processing of accounting information. Numerical data are rescaled to common units, like dollars or minute-miles, and then added up. Thus we may think of the calculation of a linear function as occurring in two stages: (1) each variable is multiplied by its respective coefficient (conversion to a common unit), and (2) the resulting products are added up (aggregation). The items to be aggregated might well be vectors, not just numbers, so that the coefficients are matrices. The decentralization of computing the linear function is dictated by the fact that the number of items to be added (numbers or vectors) is very large.

In the second paradigm, the decision maker, i.e., decision-making organization, compares the "pattern" of data about the environment with the members of a finite set of reference patterns, picking the one that is "closest" in some sense. To each reference pattern corresponds a decision, so that the problem of choosing a decision is reduced to the calculation of the closest reference pattern. For example, the data and reference patterns might be represented as vectors in a space of very large dimension, and the measure of closeness might be ordinary Euclidean distance. This dimension is so large that no single processor can handle an entire vector at once. Each huge vector will, therefore, have to be divided up into smaller component vectors for processing. In fact, we can imagine that the original observations themselves are on the component vectors, rather than on the entire vectors.

It is interesting that both "addition" and "finding a minimum" are associative operations,[2] and thus lend themselves naturally—as we shall see—to decentrali-

zation, or what the computer scientist would call *parallel computation* (Jacob Schwartz 1980). In fact, from a formal point of view these concepts are the same in the context of information processing.[3]

These considerations lead me to consider the following problem: Given N items to be added, and P processors, arrange and program the processors to add the N items in minimum time. Here, for "add" we can read any associative operation, and the "items" are anything amenable to the associative operation. As I have stated it, this problem is not well defined, because I have not been precise about what a processor is. In what follows, a *processor* is an object with an *in-box*, a *register*, and a *clock*. Time is measured in cycles; in one cycle a processor can take one item from its in-box and add it to its register. From each processor there may be one or more one-way communication links to other processors. At prescribed times, a processor can also send the contents of its register to the in-boxes of other processors to which it is directly linked, and then re-initialize its own register to "zero;" this can be done in any cycle without additional elapsed time. Finally, there is a particular processor that, at a designated time, sends out the contents of its register as the result of the computation, i.e., the grand total. The set of processors and links will be called a *network*. The *program* prescribes the original assignment of the items to the several processors' in-boxes, and the times of communication and final output. The number of cycles used to perform the computation will be called the *delay*.

I can now restate the problem: *arrange*

---

[2] A binary operation, say ∗, is associative if $(A * B) * C = A * (B * C)$. Addition, multiplication, minimum, maximum, set-union, and set-intersection are all associative. The operation "x to the power y" is not.

[3] Another computer science term for decentralized processing is "distributed computation." In the computer science literature, the terms "parallel" and "distributed" connote different sets of research problems (and usually different researchers), but both are concerned with what I have called decentralized information processing.

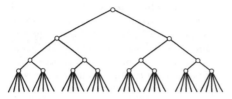

Figure 4. A hierarchical network with 15 processors, 40 items, and delay 11

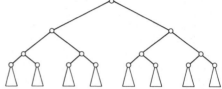

Figure 5a. Regular hierarchy before reduction

the given P processors in a network, and program the network, so as to add the given N items with a minimum delay,

Figure 4 illustrates a hierarchical network, with 15 processors indicated by circles, and 40 items. The links joining the processors are to be understood as pointing upward. One processor is the immediate superior of another if there is a direct link pointing upward from the second to the first. The successive levels in the diagram indicate the ranks, of which there are 4. Here is the way the program works. The 40 items are originally assigned equally to the processors of the lowest level (rank 1). This is indicated in figures by the 5 lines coming up into each of the 8 lowest-levels processors. The computation starts with each first-level processor adding its 5 items into its register. At the end of the 5th cycle each first-level processor then takes 2 cycles to add its items and send its partial sum to its third-level immediate superior, etc. At the end of 11 cycles the single fourth-level processor (the root of the tree) puts out the grand total of the 40 items; thus the delay is 11.

As we shall see, the minimum achievable delay is actually 8, not 11. Indeed, we shall also see that one can achieve the same delay, 8, with fewer than 15 processors, namely 8.

I shall say that a *network is efficient* for a given number of items if the number of processors cannot be decreased without increasing the delay, or vice versa. Thus the network in Figure 4 is not efficient. By extension, I shall say that *the*

pair *(P,C) is efficient for N items* if there is a network with *P* processors that is efficient for *N* items and adds them with a delay equal to *C*.

Although the hierarchical network of Figure 4 is not efficient, one can show that hierarchical networks are sufficient to attain efficiency, in the following sense: *For any number of items, N, and any pair (P,C) that is efficient for N, there is a hierarchical network with P processors that can add the N items in C cycles.*

I shall show how to construct such efficient hierarchies, but first I need to introduce some terminology. The hierarchy in Figure 4 has a symmetric appearance. I shall call a hierarchy *regular* if (1) all the immediate subordinates of any processor are at the next lower level and (2) at each level above the first, all members of the same level have the same number of immediate subordinates. All of the processors at one level that are the immediate subordinates of the same processor at the next higher level will be called a *cadre.* The hierarchy in Figure 4 is not only regular, but each cadre has two members. (In general, however, in a regular hierarchy cadres at different levels need not be of the same size.)

I can now describe how a regular hierarchy can be "reduced" so as to decrease both the total number of processors (*P*) and the delay (*C*). I suppose we start with the *N* items allocated equally (or as equally as possible) among the lowest-level processors. Figure 5a shows the hierarchy of Figure 4, but with each group

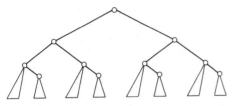

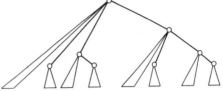

Figure 5b. Regular hierarchy after 1 stage of reduction

Figure 5d. Regular hierarchy after 3 stages of reduction (final)

of 5 items at the bottom replaced by a triangle, or "fan." The reduction will be done in stages; at each stage we reduce the amount of idleness in the network. At stage 1, we eliminate one member of each cadre at level 1, and assign its items to its corresponding immediate superior. Figure 5b shows the result of applying the first stage of reduction. As there were originally 4 cadres at level 1, 4 processors have been eliminated at level 1, reducing the total number of processors from 15 to 11. Each second-level processor now has 5 items plus 1 first-level processor assigned to it.

I shall call the items and/or immediately subordinate processors assigned to a processor its *predecessors*. Let R denote the number of levels in the hierarchy. The reduction procedure is completed in stages as follows: at stage r < R, one processor is eliminated from each level-r cadre, and its predecessors are assigned to its immediate superior at level r + 1.

Figures 5c and 5d show the second and third stages of reduction for the hierarchy of Figure 5a. The number of processors has been reduced from 15 to 18, and the number of cycles from 11 to 8. Although there is still some idleness in the network, no further increase is efficiency is possible.

There is, however, something odd about Figure 5d, at least as a picture of an organizational hierarchy. We see that the top ranking processor has immediate subordinates at all levels. In fact, a similar phenomenon is repeated at each lower level. Reporting through skipped levels is not unheard of in corporate hierarchies (in fact, at AT&T this is called "skip-level reporting"), but the practice does not seem to be as widespread as the above reduction process would suggest.[4]

I shall now give the solution to the problem previously posed. Recall that, for integers N and P, N mod P denotes the remainder after dividing N by P. To add N items with P processors, the minimum delay is given by the following formula:

$$\text{Min } C = \lfloor N/P \rfloor + \lceil \log(P + N \text{ mod } P) \rceil,$$

where the brackets $\lfloor\ \rfloor$ denote rounding down to the nearest integer, the brackets $\lceil\ \rceil$ denote rounding up to the nearest integer, and the logarithm is taken to the base 2. Furthermore, this minimum de-

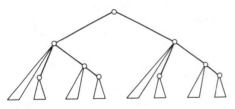

Figure 5c. Regular hierarchy after 2 stages of reduction

[4] Figure 5d is somewhat misleading because in the original hierarchy each cadre had only two members. If we had started with larger cadres, then the relative importance of skip-level reporting would have been smaller.

TABLE 7

MINIMUM DELAY (C) FOR ADDING 40 ITEMS

P	MIN C	
1	40	*
2	21	*
3	15	*
4	12	*
5	11	*
6	10	*
7	9	*
8	8	*
9	8	*
10	8	
11	8	
11	8	
12	7	*
13	7	
..	..	
20	7	
..	..	
40	7	

Source: see text.

P = number of processors.

* denotes an efficient network

lay is attained by a hierarchy of the type that one gets from reducing a regular hierarchy, as described above. Indeed, it is attained by reducing a regular hierarchy whose cadres originally all have size two! (Note that the hierarchy of Figure 5a does have this property.)

Table 7 illustrates this formula for $N = 40$ and P varying from 1 to 40. A one-processor hierarchy is the slowest, with a delay of 40 cycles. The minimum delay is 7 cycles, and can be attained with 12 processors; the use of more processors will not further reduce the delay. Thus a network with more than 12 processors is not efficient for 40 items. Similarly, we see from the table that networks with 9, 10, and 11 processors are not efficient, either, since a delay of 8 cycles can be attained with 8 processors. Thus, although the formula gives the minimum number of cycles for any number of pro-

cessors, not every pair (P,C) generated by the formula is efficient. Figure 6 shows a graph of Table 7, and illustrates the same phenomenon. For very large numbers of items, however, these inefficiencies will not be very significant unless the number of processors is too large. For example, Figure 7 shows a plot of the minimum delay vs. the number of processors for $N = 10,000$; inefficiency does not become a significant problem until the number of processors exceeds 2000 (approximately). (Note that the scales on both axes of Figure 7 are logarithmic.)

Figures 6 and 7 illustrate the tradeoff between delay and number of processors. This tradeoff is a reflection of the tradeoff between serial and parallel processing. With few processors, there is little parallel processing of the items at the first level, which causes a large delay. Many processors permit much parallel processing, which reduces the delay.

I must now address a fact about real organizations I have thus far ignored, namely, that typically new data about the environment will be coming in periodically, with the consequence that new decisions must be calculated periodically. (Computer scientists sometimes call this the *systolic mode*.) This can cause a problem for our highly efficient reduced hierarchies if the new data arrive too frequently. The reason is that, in an efficient reduced hierarchy, *the highest ranking processor is busy all the time*. Thus, if the time between periodic arrivals of new data—or as I shall call them, new *cohorts* of data—is less than the delay in computing each sum, then the backlog of unprocessed cohorts, and the delays in the calculation of the corresponding sums, will also increase without bound. In this case, the successive decisions will become unboundedly obsolete! (Notice that this problem does not arise in a regular hier-

1398   *Journal of Economic Literature, Vol. XXX (September 1992)*

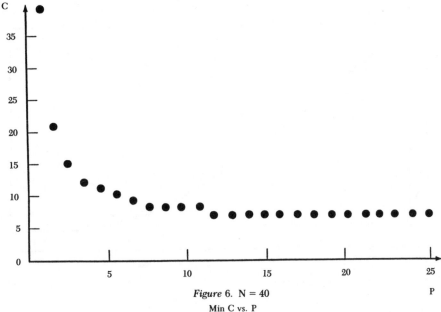

Figure 6. N = 40

Min C vs. P

archy unless the time taken by one *level* exceeds the time between cohorts.)

Timothy Van Zandt (1990) has recently solved the problem of constructing efficient networks for the systolic mode. Roughly speaking, one assigns an efficient "one-shot" tree to each incoming cohort; as processors are successively freed up from working on one cohort, they are assigned to the next available cohort. (This is not quite correct, however; paradoxically, one can usually further reduce idle time and average delay by adding some processors to the efficient "one-shot" tree!) Typically, the total number of processors, P, will be larger than the number of processors assigned to any one cohort, say Q. Although a simple formula for the minimum delay is not available for the systolic mode, the following pair of equations determines an approximation to the efficiency frontier:

$$C = (N/Q) + \log(Q),$$
$$P = (N + Q - 1)/T,$$

where a new cohort arrives every T cycles, and is processed by Q processors (on the average). (These equations are exact in those cases in which all idle time has been eliminated, which, however, is usually not possible. In any case, the equations provide a *lower bound* on all feasible pairs (P,C).)

As one varies Q between 1 and N, one traces out the $P - C$ efficiency frontier (approximately). In fact, one can get quite close to this frontier with a symmetrical hierarchy, as follows. The network is made up of one or more groups of "preprocessors" and a single "overhead" tree, which is symmetric. Each incoming cohort is assigned to one group of preprocessors; as each group finishes its task of preprocessing it sends its par-

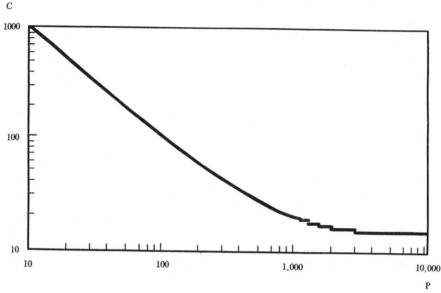

Figure 7. N = 10,000

Min C vs. P

tial sums to the overhead tree and then turns to the next available cohort. The overhead tree is designed so that it can handle the successive groups of partial sums without creating a backlog. I call the resulting network a "preprocessing overhead tree" (POT). Figure 8 shows the (P,C) points corresponding to selected POTs, superimposed on the graph of the approximate efficiency frontier. One sees that the POTs are close to efficient except when P is large.

I turn now to the question of returns to scale. What, exactly, should we mean by this? Although I have referred to the processing delay as "costly," it is probably more in conformity with the economic concept of a production function to regard delay as a "quality" of the output—the answer—with the processors and the items to be processed as the inputs. From this point of view, the above

equations tell us two things. First, as the second question shows, the number of processors, P, must increase at least in proportion to N, the number of items to be processed. Second, and more striking, the first equation shows us that, as the number of items increases, the delay, C must also increase; even if the number of processors is unlimited, the minimum delay is $(1 + \log N)$. Thus we have decreasing returns to scale in a very strong sense.

Is there any escape from this dismal conclusion? If we recall that the purpose of the information processing is to provide information for decision making, then we might ask: what are the returns to scale from the use of the information, taking account of the fact that the information must be processed before it can be used? Unfortunately, the answer to this question will depend upon the par-

1400   *Journal of Economic Literature, Vol. XXX (September 1992)*

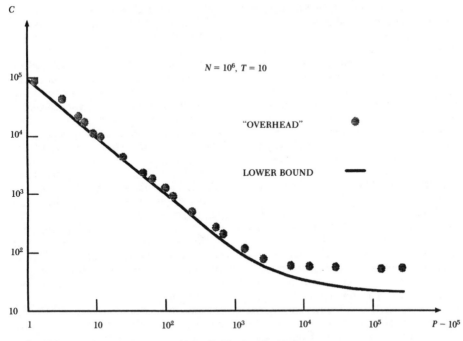

Figure 8. The Systolic Mode

ticular decision problem for which the information is used. In particular, it will depend upon: (1) the statistical properties of the environment and the observed data, and (2) the functional form that describes how the loss due to an incorrect decision depends on the "decision error." It remains to be seen whether something useful and general can be said about this problem; from a series of examples it would appear that one can get anything from decreasing to increasing returns to scale, depending on the assumptions that one makes about the decision problem. More detailed discussions are provided by Radner (1989) and Radner and Van Zandt (1992).

Now to summarize this section of my paper. In the context of a decision-theoretic model of the firm, I have represented managers and their helpers

as individual information processors of limited capacity, and using ideas from computer science I have explored the efficiency of different "architectures" for the network of manager-processors. Here "efficiency" is measured in terms of (1) the number of processors and (2) the delay between the receipt of information by the organization and the implementation of decisions. The tradeoff between these two "costs" is achieved by varying the degree of *parallelism* in the network of processors relative to the amount of *serial* processing done by individual processors. The first important conclusion is that *efficiency can be achieved by hierarchical networks*. The second is that, if one regards the delay as the quality of the output, then there are decreasing returns to scale in a strong sense, namely, one cannot maintain constant quality indefinitely as one increases the number of items to be processed, even if the processors are free. However, if one considers the value of the information that is processed, in the context of a particular decision problem, then it appears that—depending on the decision problem—one can get anything from decreasing to increasing returns to scale,

I conclude this section with a few bibliographic notes. As I noted above, two strands of literature have influenced the ideas presented here, one from economics, and one from computer science. Thomas A. Marschak and C. Bartlett McGuire (1971) were probably the first to propose the model of a finite automaton as a formalism of the notion of a boundedly rational decision maker. The model of a decision-making organization as a network of information processors was explored by Jacob Marschak and myself (1972, ch. 9), but our analysis was concerned more with the decentralization of information than of information processing. In a similar spirit, Thomas A. Marschak and Stefan Reichelstein (1987) studied conditions under which a "hierarchical" structure of decision making would be efficient in a broader set of structures. In their model, every processor is also responsible for the final decision about some action variable, and the only cost of processing is that of communication. Their analysis derived some conditions under which hierarchy would be preferred, but I shall not attempt to summarize their results here. Two papers of Michael Keren and David Levhari (1983, 1989) provide an alternative way to look at the problem of minimizing the costs of information processing in an organization. In the "economics strand," the current research of Stanley Reiter and Kenneth Mount is most closely related to the present paper, and I have benefited from exposure to that research in conferences (Mount and Reiter 1982)

and in their draft manuscript, "A Model of Computing with Human Agents" (1990). Their focus is primarily on the computation of equilibria of resource allocation mechanisms, and on the tradeoff between the delay and the amount of information required to be communicated. The latter is measured, roughly speaking, by the dimension of the space of messages utilized in the allocation mechanism.

Thomas A. Marschak (1986) and Jacob Marschak and Roy Radner (1972, ch. 7) studied the effect of delay on the value of decisions, particularly in the context of decentralization of information. As pointed out above, the cost of delayed decision may not be simply proportional to the delay; the functional form of the dependence of cost on delay will depend on the intertemporal statistical properties of the stochastic process of environmental data.

From the "computer science strand," the reader familiar with the article, "Ultracomputers," by Schwartz (1980), will recognize how heavily I have relied on the ideas in that paper. I have also benefited from the paper by Clyde Kruskal et al. (1988).

Recently, some game theorists have used the automaton model to explore how the boundedness of rationality might alter the predictions of Nash equilibrium theory, especially in sequential games (see Ariel Rubinstein 1986; Abraham Neyman 1985; Ehud Kalai and William Stanford 1988; Dilip Abreu and Rubinstein 1988; and the references cited there). In most of these explorations, however, the boundedness of a player's rationality is expressed only by a bound on the number of states of the automaton, a direction that is quite orthogonal to the one taken here.

5. Decentralization of Information

In the previous section, I focused on the process of producing a decision from a large amount of data, so large that the information processing task of producing the decision had to be divided up—decentralized—among a number of separate processors. The decision was the output of a single processor, for example, the top of the hierarchy.

In a firm, there are many, many different decisions to be made, and it is totally impractical for them to be put out by the same processor, and as a function of the same information. This situation, in which different decisions are based on different information, I shall call the *decentralization of information.*

In principle, the same network could be used to compute different decisions from different sets of incoming data (using, of course, different programs). But in practice this never happens for all of the decisions in a firm. We sometimes read of an executive who tries to decide everything, is unwilling to delegate any decisions to subordinates, but the point of such stories is that these executives get into trouble. Even such stories exaggerate; *no executive can truly decide everything in a timely fashion!*

The same limitations that prevent any one person from deciding everything also make it uneconomical for all decisions to be based on the same data. We observe that firms take in enormous amounts of data every day, but most decisions are based on a very small part of it, and the reason may seem obvious. For most decision problems, a relatively small amount of information enables one to make a fairly good decision, if the information is chosen wisely. On the other hand, the information required for a good decision is typically different for different decision problems.

Let me illustrate this in the context of the "parable of the firm' (Section 3). A small decision about the maintenance of a machine can be made quite well based on information local to the produc-

tion unit; similarly, a good decision about the order in which to visit customers can be made on the basis of information local to the sales office. On the other hand, a decision to change the rate of production should be based, in part, on information about conditions at other production units, as well as on information about demand for the product. But even in this case, completely detailed information about all other production units and all sales units is not really needed; certain aggregate measures will be adequate.

The efficient use of information in an informationally decentralized organization is the subject of the *theory of teams,* an early development in the formal theory of organization. This theory, originally proposed by Jacob Marschak, has also been taken up by applied mathematicians in the area of decision and control theory (Jacob Marschak and Radner 1972; McGuire and Radner 1986; Ki H. Kim and Fred W. Roush 1987; for an elementary exposition, see Radner 1986). In the theory of teams, efficiency is evaluated in terms of an overall organizational goal or objective function (e.g., profit in the case of the firm). The focus is on (1) the incomplete and heterogeneous[5] dissemination of information among the several decision makers (i.e., informational

---

[5] A note on terminology: it has become common to use the term "asymmetric information" for what I have here called "heterogeneous information" or "informational decentralization." This is unfortunate, as the following example shows. Suppose that there are two decision makers, A and B, and that A costlessly observes information X, whereas B costlessly observes Y. Consider three different information structures: (1) A's decision is based on X alone, and B's on Y alone, i.e., there is no communication; (2) B communicates Y to A and then A's decision is based on X and Y, while B's is based on Y alone; (3) there is complete communication, so that A and B each base their decisions on X and Y. In ordinary as well as mathematical parlance, one would normally say that information structures 1 and 3 are symmetric, whereas 2 is asymmetric. On the other hand, in structures 1 and 2 information is decentralized or heterogeneous, whereas some current authors would call it "asymmetric."

decentralization), (2) the characterization of decision functions that are optimal, given that decentralization, and (3) the comparison of alternative (decentralized) information structures, under the assumption that each one will be used efficiently. In this theory, no attention is paid to the private incentives of the individual decision makers, who might as well be computers. In this sense, the theory of teams occupies a middle ground between the theory of decision for a single person and the theory of games.

This is not the place to review systematically research on the theory of teams. However, I want to call attention to two propositions that are relevant to my previous discussion of information processing and hierarchy.

First, under certain regularity conditions, for a given structure of information each decision maker's optimal decision function will be approximately linear in his information; to put it another way, linear decision rules will be approximately optimal.[6] This provides a justification of the analysis in Section 4 of the processing of information using associative operations. Recall the conclusion there that—under certain conditions—efficient processing could be achieved by hierarchical networks. In the situation I am now discussing, with decentralized information, the implication is this: for each decision maker, there is an efficient hierarchy to calculate his decision as a function of his peculiar information. *But these hierarchies will typically be different for different decision makers, since different decisions will be based on different sets of original data items.* When we think about this situation carefully, we see that the formulation of Section 4

[6] Important exceptions to this proposition can arise when one person's information is about other persons' actions; this was first shown by Hans Witsenhausen (1968), who independently formulated a team-theoretic framework.

was not really adequate to consider the problem of efficient information processing in a team. It rarely will be efficient to use a different network for *every* decision, or even for every decision maker. On the other hand, in all but the very smallest organizations, there will be different networks for different sets of decisions and decision makers. In fact, empirical studies of "informal organization" have shown this to be universally true (Arnold S. Tannenbaum 1966 and Mintzberg 1989 on "adhocracy"). As far as I know, there has been no formal analysis of the general question of how to organize processors of given capabilities to compute a *number of different decisions functions* in an economically efficient manner, i.e., the *team-theoretic analogue* of the problem discussed in Section 4.

The second proposition I shall discuss has to do with what is sometimes called "management by exception." By this I mean a behavior in which the value of an observed variable or pattern is reported to a superior only when it is "exceptional" or "unusual." For example, the maintenance status of equipment in a particular production unit would not be reported to the production vice president (except possibly at infrequent periodic intervals) unless there were a massive breakdown that threatened to upset the planned production schedule. Theoretical studies, as well as practical experience, suggest that management by exception is a powerful device for economizing on the use of information in an organization (Jacob Marschak and Radner 1972, ch. 6). On the other hand, those theoretical studies did not explicitly integrate team theory with the new model of decentralized information processing of Section 4. Notice that, with management by exception, the number of items to be processed in any cohort of data is not constant, but will fluctuate randomly from one cohort to the next. The effect of this is that there will be *stochastic queues* of items in the in-boxes of the processors, rather than a regular flow, and hence the decision delays will also be stochastic. Similar analytical problems arise in the study of telecommunications networks, especially data networks, and one hopes that similar methods will be useful here. (For further recent research in the spirit of team theory see Jacques Crémer 1980; John Geanakoplos and Milgrom 1991; and Raaj K. Sah and Joseph E. Stiglitz 1986.)

6. Decentralization of Incentives

I have argued that, in any but the smallest firms, no one person has all of the information relevant to the firm's activities. It follows that no one person can completely control all of those activities. This is so even in firms that are described as highly "centralized." From this fundamental observation, it follows that individual members of the firm will have some freedom to choose their own actions. If in addition, there is some divergence among the members' goals or objectives, then one can expect some inefficiencies to arise in the firm's operations. The theoretical analysis of these inefficiencies, and the possible remedies by means of organizational design, are the subject of the present section.

In this discussion, I shall concentrate on the members of the firm who do have some freedom of action, and I shall therefore call them *agents*. If the behavior of the agents is "rational" in the sense typically used by economists and decision theorists, then the appropriate formal model would appear to be the theory of games, especially games of incomplete information, as developed in the past two decades (John Harsanyi 1967–68; Roger Myerson 1985). Furthermore, the relationships among members of a firm are

typically long lived, calling for an analysis in terms of dynamic games.

Two special paradigmatic models have arisen in the game-theoretic analysis of the firm. In the first, which I have elsewhere called a *partnership*, the agents act together to produce a joint outcome (e.g., output or profit). This outcome can be observed by the several agents, but they cannot directly observe each others' actions, nor do they completely share each others' information. In the most general—and realistic—case of this theoretical model, the outcome is also influenced by random variables that are only partially observed, if at all. The incompleteness of the information leads to what the statisticians call a "confounding" of the sources of variations of the outcomes, making it difficult to assign responsibility to the individual agents for the occurrence of unsatisfactory outcomes. It is this confounding that leads to organizational inefficiency, if the goals of the agents are not identical. In particular, the agents can engage in what is colloquially called "free riding."

The so-called "principal-agent" model provides a second paradigm, which may be relevant to hierarchical organization. In the simplest principal-agent model, there are two players. The first, the *principal*, performs no immediately useful actions himself, but monitors the activities of the other player, the *agent*, whose actions, together with the (stochastic) environment, determine the outcome. In the standard model, this outcome is a number, like money. The principal can observe neither the agent's action nor the stochastic environment, but both players can observe the outcome. Thus we again have a situation in which the confounding of the sources of variation of the outcome makes it difficult to correctly assign to the agent responsibility for the occurrence of satisfactory outcomes. However, the phenomenon of free riding on others is absent. The principal is restricted to rewarding the agent according to the outcome, and then retains the residual for himself. In a more elaborated version of the model, the agent and the principal may each have some information about the environment, but their information is not the same. In addition, the principal may have partial, but not complete, information about the agent's action.

Thus there may be two different sources of inefficiency in the principal-agent relationship. The first, called *moral hazard,* refers to the fact that the principal cannot accurately monitor the agent's actions, and hence experiences a loss of control over the agent. The second source exists when the agent knows something the principal does not, leading to *misrepresentation* or *adverse selection.*

In fact, most organizations combine aspects of both the partnership and principal-agent models. A hierarchy of authority can be thought of as a cascade of principal-agent relationships, each supervisor acting as a principal in relation to his subordinates, and as an agent in relation to his own supervisor. On the other hand, in most cases the valued outcomes of organizational activity depend on the joint actions of several agents, as in the partnership model, so that the assignment of individual responsibility for specific outcomes—as required by the principal-agent model—may not be justified. Unfortunately, I am not aware of significant progress on more comprehensive theoretical models of the firm that combine these two submodels in a systematic way.

In a less formal way, economists have long recognized aspects of principal-agent relationships in the firm. Adam Smith (1776, vol. 2) took a dim view of the relationship between the shareholders and the board of directors and/or senior management. After describing the difference between a joint stock company and a "private copartnery," he goes on to offer this opinion of joint stock companies:

> The trade of a joint stock company is always managed by a court of directors. This court, indeed, is frequently subject, in many respects, to the control of a general court of proprietors. But the greater part of those proprietors seldom pretend to understand anything of the business of the company, and when the spirit of faction happens not to prevail among them, give themselves no trouble about it, but receive contentedly such half-yearly or yearly dividend as the directors think proper to make to them. The directors of such companies, however, being the managers of other people's money rather than of their own, it cannot well be expected that they should watch over it with the same anxious vigilance with which the partners in a private copartnery frequently watch over their own. Like the stewards of a rich man, they are apt to consider attention to small matters as not for their master's honor, and very easily give themselves a dispensation from having it. Negligence and profusion, therefore, must always prevail, more or less, in the management of the affairs of such a company. It is upon this account that joint stock companies for foreign trade have seldom been able to maintain competition against private adventurers. (pp. 264–65)

Smith certainly understood the incentive problems inherent in the principal-agent relationship. On the other hand, it appears that this judgment of joint stock companies was too pessimistic. What would he have thought of the "Fortune 500?"

Frank Knight (1921) called attention to the principal-agent relationship between the entrepreneur and his workers. Here he focused on the allocation of risk between the entrepreneur and the worker. He argued that important characteristics of social organization can be traced to

> the system under which the confident and the venturesome assume the risk or insure the doubtful and timid by guaranteeing to the latter a specified income in return for an assignment of the actual results . . . With human nature

1406   *Journal of Economic Literature, Vol. XXX (September 1992)*

as we know it, it would be impractical or very unusual for one man to guarantee to another a definite result of the latter's actions without being given the power to direct his work. And on the other hand the second party would not place himself under the direction of the first without such a guarantee. . . . The result of this manifold specialization of function is the enterprise and wage system of industry. Its existence in the world is the direct result of the fact of uncertainty. (pp. 269–70)

The allocation of risk in the presence of moral hazard is, in fact, one of the dominant themes of the contemporary principal-agent literature. The term "moral hazard" itself arose in the insurance industry, and the first formal economic analysis of moral hazard was probably given by Kenneth J. Arrow (1963) in his paper, "Uncertainty and the Welfare Economics of Medical Care."

The standard principal-agent model typically *assumes* that the principal is neutral towards risk and the agent is averse to risk. In such a context it is easy to see the conflict between insurance and incentives. Since the outcome of the agent's action is also influenced by random factors beyond his control, and he is averse to risk, he would like to be insured against this uncertainty. Since the principal is risk-neutral, an optimal allocation of risk requires that the principal bear all of it, i.e., that the agent's compensation be independent of the outcome. In this case, the agent would get a fixed compensation (wage), and the principal would get the outcome minus this fixed payment. However, with a payment independent of the outcome, the agent would have no incentive to try to make the outcome higher than lower. For example, if the outcome depends on the agent's "effort," and the agent is lazy, then the agent will not be likely to put in an optimal amount of effort; to induce the agent to put in the optimal effort, his compensation would have to depend on the outcome. Thus there can be no

scheme for sharing the output between the principal and the agent that simultaneously induces the optimal effort and fully insures the agent against risk.

Although this argument may sound plausible, I have not defined what I mean by "optimal," nor have I been precise about my theory of the behavior of the principal and agent in this situation. Because some readers may not be familiar with game theory, I shall take a little space to be more precise. I shall describe the principal-agent situation as a two-move game. The principal moves first, announcing a *compensation function*, namely, a schedule that determines the agent's compensation for each possible outcome. The agent moves second, choosing his action. The outcome is then determined as a function of the agent's action and some unobserved random variable. (Put another way, the probability distribution of the outcome depends on the agent's action.) The outcome is then observed by both players, and the agent is compensated by the principal according to the previously announced compensation function. The resulting utility to the principal is the difference between the actual outcome and the compensation that he pays the agent. This expresses the assumption that the principal is neutral towards risk. The resulting utility to the agent depends both on the action he has chosen and on the compensation that he receives, in a way that represents his aversion to risk. Each player is interested in maximizing his own *expected* utility. In this game, the principal's *strategy* is the same as his move, namely the announced compensation function, but the agent's strategy is a decision-rule that determines his action corresponding to each alternative compensation function that the principal could announce.

An *equilibrium* is a pair of strategies, one for the principal and one for the agent, such that:

1. Given the announced compensation function, the agent chooses an action that maximizes his own expected utility.
2. Given the optimizing behavior of the agent, the principal chooses a compensation function that maximizes his own expected utility.

In the formulation of a principal-agent model one typically adds one or both of the following constraints on the compensation function that the principal may announce. First, the compensation function must enable the agent to attain (ex ante) an "acceptable" expected utility. This constraint can be interpreted as requiring that the principal must offer the agent an expected utility at least as large as what the agent could obtain in other employment. Second, the agent's compensation is bounded below by some exogenously given bound. This second constraint recognizes that the agent's wealth is finite, and so the agent cannot be compelled to pay the principal arbitrarily large amounts of money (negative compensations).

A pair of strategies is defined to be *Pareto optimal* or *efficient* if no other strategy-pair yields one of the players more expected utility and yields the other no less. A basic proposition of principal-agent theory is that, with the above assumptions and some additional "reasonable" conditions, *an equilibrium is not efficient*. Here is a sketch of the argument. First, I shall argue that, since the principal is neutral towards risk, and the agent is averse to risk, in an efficient strategy pair the agent's compensation must be independent of the outcome. Suppose, to the contrary, that different outcomes led to different compensations, and let w be the *expected compensation*. Since the agent is averse to risk, he would be better off if he used the same action but received a fixed compensation

equal to w. The principal, on the other hand, would be no worse off in this new situation, since he is neutral towards risk. (Indeed, if one wanted to make both players strictly better off, the principal could pay the agent a fixed compensation slightly less than w.)

On the other hand, a strategy-pair in which the agent's compensation does not depend on the outcome typically cannot be an equilibrium, unless by coincidence the action that the agent most prefers is also part of an efficient strategy-pair. For example, if increasing the probability of higher outcomes requires more "effort" by the agent, and the agent prefers less effort to more, then if the compensation is independent of the outcome the agent will have no incentive to exert any effort at all! *The incentive requirements for equilibrium, therefore, will typically be incompatible with the conditions for efficiency.*

An exception to the basic proposition occurs if the agent is neutral towards risk and is sufficiently wealthy. (The principal may be risk-neutral or risk-averse.) In this case, an efficient equilibrium is obtained if the principal sells the agent a "franchise" to the enterprise, that is, the agent pays the principal a fixed fee, and then keeps the entire outcome.[7]

Are there any remedies for the inefficiency of equilibrium in the principal-agent relationship? One possible remedy is for the principal to expend resources to monitor the agent's action (and, more generally, his information and environment). Whether this will improve *net* efficiency will depend, of course, on the cost of monitoring. The prevalence of de facto decentralization suggests that accurate and complete monitoring of agents' actions and information in all but the

---

[7] Up to this point I have been discussing what is called the "static" or "one-period" model. For a thorough treatment of this model with moral hazard, see Sanford S. Grossman and Oliver D. Hart (1983).

1408 *Journal of Economic Literature, Vol. XXX (September 1992)*

smallest firms is too costly to be efficient, or even practicable.

Another remedy for the inefficiency of equilibrium may be available if the principal-agent relationship is a long-term one. The long-term relationship is usually modeled by game theorists as a situation in which the one-period situation is repeated over and over again.[8] These repetitions give the principal an opportunity to observe the results of the agent's actions over a number of periods, and to use some statistical test to infer whether or not the agent was choosing the appropriate action. The repetitions also provide the principal with opportunities to "punish" the agent for apparent departures from the appropriate action. Finally, the fact that the agent's compensation in any one period can be made to depend on the outcomes in a number of previous periods (for example, on the average outcome over a number of periods) provides the principal with an indirect means of insuring the agent, at least partially, against random fluctuations in the outcomes that are not due to fluctuations in the agent's actions. Thus, the repetitions provide an opportunity to reduce the agent's risk without reducing his incentive to perform well.

Although this remedy is in some sense available, game theory does not unequivocally predict that the players will adopt it. I want to explain this statement more carefully, because it is related to a basic problem that game theory has in dealing with long-term relationships. In the repeated game, each player's strategy is a complex object. Thus the principal's strategy is a sequence of decision rules that he uses to determine the agent's compensation in any one period as a function of all of the previous outcomes. Likewise, the agent's strategy is a sequence of decision rules that determines his action in each period as a function of his past observations of the process (outcomes and compensations). In principle, the players' strategy spaces are very large and include very complex strategies.

It may come as no surprise, then, that a *repeated principal-agent game typically has infinitely many equilibria.* One of these equilibria consists of the simple repetition of the (inefficient) one-period equilibrium. Others may be more efficient. Indeed, one can show that, under reasonable conditions, *the less the players discount future utility, the closer the most efficient equilibria will be to full efficiency; in the limit, when they do not discount the future at all, there will be fully efficient equilibria.* On the other hand, game theory itself gives no reason why the players would end up in one equilibrium rather than another.

Unfortunately, I have no space to discuss the game-theoretic treatments of partnerships, except to say that the results are qualitatively similar (although there are some interesting differences): (1) equilibria of the one-period game are typically inefficient, (2) there are many equilibria of the repeated game, some of them more efficient than the one-period equilibrium (or equilibria), and (3) with lower discount rates, more efficient equilibria become available. I should point out that, in addition to moral hazard, another potential source of inefficiency in a partnership is the phenomenon of *free riding* (Radner 1991).

I have thus far said little about misrepresentation, except to mention it as another source of inefficiency. Unfortunately, I shall have no space to discuss this important topic, either. (For an elementary exposition, see Radner 1987; for recent references, see Nahum D. Melumad and Reichelstein 1989.)

It is time to ask: What has game theory

---

[8] For a rigorous treatment of repeated principal-agent games see Radner (1985, 1986b), and the references cited there.

contributed to our understanding of the economics of managing, and especially the decentralization of incentives? On the positive side, it has illuminated in a rigorous way the sources of the inefficiencies that we can expect to arise with the decentralization of incentives. It also suggests how long-term relationships can be exploited to improve efficiency, especially if the agents in the firm do not discount the future too heavily. Although these results have been derived in very special models, similar results appear in other branches of game theory, and so we could reasonably expect that they are fairly robust.

If we look at the matter in more detail, however, the theoretical analysis remains somewhat disappointing. Principal-agent-like relationships certainly obtain between the shareholders and the board of directors, between the board and the management, and between management and the workers. But each of these groups is not a single player, and the strategic interactions are potentially much richer and more complex than a two person principal agent model can represent.

Moreover, if we look at individuals in the firm, especially in the managing sector, it is rare that we find a person whose output can be realistically measured in money or any other one-dimensional variable. Indeed, it is well known that within the firm it is usually difficult to attribute a definite output to any single member. On an informal level, we can certainly expect to find the pernicious effects of moral hazard, misrepresentation, and free riding in these more complex situations, but we look to game theory to take us beyond the level of informal and intuitive understanding.

I have already alluded to the infinite multiplicity of equilibria that one typically finds in repeated-game models of long-term relationships; one says in these

cases that *equilibrium is indeterminate*. This means that game theory does not provide sharp predictions of behavior in these situations. One can imagine elaborating the game theory models to describe processes of learning, adaptation, and evolution, and the corresponding influences of "history," but research of this kind is still in its infancy (David Canning 1989, and Drew Fudenberg and David Kreps 1989).

Finally, we lack a comprehensive model in which we can explore the relative efficiency of different organizational structures. For example, it is not yet possible to compare the efficiency of partnerships and principal-agent relationships because the two models make completely different assumptions about the possibility of imputing outcomes to individuals.

Although, as an economist, I am disappointed in the contribution that game theory has made thus far to the economics of managing, as a practicing game theorist I am not discouraged by the challenge of what remains to be done. But for the time being, game theory has not provided us with an "economic" explanation of the conditions under which we could expect the hierarchical organization of authority and incentives to occur.

7. Loose Ends

In this section I will take up some topics that do not yet fit neatly into any economic theory of managing, but probably ought to be taken seriously as we go about developing that theory. The first of these is "coordination," a term so common in writings about organization that you might well wonder why I have waited so long to mention it. According to the *Shorter Oxford English Dictionary*, (p. 1855) one definition of coordination is:

Harmonious combination of agents or functions towards the production of a result; said especially in Physiology of the combined action of a number of muscles in the production of certain complex movements.

I suppose "harmonious" in our context would mean "good," or even "optimal," so that coordination would mean "making several decisions that are jointly optimal."

If that were all there were to it—which may well be the case for many authors—then I need not have mentioned the word "coordination" at all. But let me propose two more special, and related, meanings. In a team, where we have a well-defined notion of optimality, there may be several different optimal combinations of decisions. In particular, different assignments of persons to jobs may be equally good. For example, in repairing a leaky dike, it will be important to get the right number of sandbags in the right places, but it may not matter just who fills bags with sand and who carries which bags. As volunteers arrive at the dike to offer their services, there will be a coordinator who assigns them to their respective tasks and locations. A second—and related—interpretation would be applicable to a (noncooperative) game in which there are several equilibria. A coordinator might play the role of persuading the players to focus on a better equilibrium rather than on a worse one. However, here the situation is more complicated. If there are several essentially different Pareto optimal equilibria, then there will be a conflict of interest among the players concerning which equilibrium should be implemented (this is, of course, what I mean by "essentially different"). The job of a coordinator now must include, not only the identification of Pareto optimal equilibria, but also the resolution of the conflict inherent in the choice among them.

I have written as if coordination requires a single person to do it, but that is not generally so. Indeed, under the

rubric "mechanism design," game theorists have studied how to design metagames, or how to redesign the original game, so that the equilibria will be Pareto optimal. An example is the Groves-Vickery-Clarke mechanism, which has in particular been applied to the problem of allocating resources to the production of overhead-type activities within the firm.[9]

Mintzberg (1989, p. 101) lists three ways in which work is coordinated in organizations, the third constituting in itself four different methods:

Mutual adjustment.
Direct supervision and authority.
Standardization
    of work processes,
    of outputs,
    of skills and knowledge,
    of norms.

Only the second, direct supervision, would seem to imply hierarchy. The first, mutual adjustment, suggests an equilibrium of a game. The standardization of work, outputs, and skills, suggests decision rules (or strategies or behavior) that are generally expected and accepted, which again has an equilibrium flavor.

In the standardization of norms, we seem to be leaving the confines of economic theory and game theory, in which the tastes and beliefs of the agents are taken as given. In their popular book, *In Search of Excellence,* Thomas J. Peters and Robert H. Waterman (1982) stress the importance of values and "corporate culture." One of the most important tasks of leadership (another popular organization term I have neglected) is said to be the formation and maintenance

[9] See (Theodore Groves and Martin Loeb 1979). For recent contributions to the study of "incentive-compatible" mechanisms, see (Groves, Radner, and Reiter 1987, especially ch. 2). For an elementary exposition in the context of the firm, see (Radner 1986a).

of values in the firm. At the beginning of Chapter 9 they write:

> Let us suppose that we were asked for the one all-purpose bit of advice for management, one truth that we were able to distill from the excellent-companies research. We might be tempted to reply, "Figure out your value system." Decide what your company *stands for*. What does your enterprise do that gives everyone the most pride? Put yourself out ten or twenty years in the future: what would you look back on with greatest satisfaction? (p. 279)

Far from assuming that employees come to the firm with given goals, Peters and Waterman devote their whole Chapter 3 to the heading, "Man Waiting for Motivation;" the "leader" (boss, management) is going to play a crucial role in supplying that motivation. (Lest the reader think that this is just an isolated example of "pop management wisdom," I want to assure you that this theme appears in many management texts and monographs on the sociology of organizations.) However, to pursue this topic in any depth would require a serious look at what has been written about the psychology—and social psychology—of human motivation, and I have neither the space nor the expertise to do that here.

8. *Conclusion*

In summary, I hope that I have persuaded the reader that managing has become a significant activity in the economies of industrial nations. Not only is the activity significant, but large numbers of persons are specialists in managing or in activities that support managing.

The large size of many modern firms, and the limited capacities of individuals for observation, communication, information processing, and decision making are factors that have contributed to this phenomenon. These limitations lead to the decentralization of information processing, and of information, and hence

to the de facto decentralization of power and incentives. This is so even in firms that are said to be highly "centralized."

I have sketched some of the contributions of recent research in economic theory to our understanding of the economics of managing, by which I mean the consideration of the resources that go into the activities of managing—especially the human resources—and the ways in which different organizations of managing do a better or worse job of economizing those resources and produce better or worse results.

I described a model of decentralized information processing that incorporates in a limited way some bounds on individual processing capacities. Using this model, I could assess the relative efficiencies of different network structures, including hierarchical ones. Also, within this model, decentralized information processing exhibits decreasing returns to scale.

I also described Herbert Simon's suggestive discussion of the hierarchical organization of work, and I sketched some implications of such an organization for the efficient decentralization of information. Here further research is needed to integrate the analyses of the decentralization of information processing and the decentralization of information.

The theoretical analyses of principal-agent and partnership models, especially in their dynamic versions, have given us some rigorous insights into the loss of control and efficiency due to the decentralization of incentives, but I had to admit to disappointment in the progress that has been made thus far. In particular, game-theoretic treatments typically leave us with a serious multiplicity of equilibria, and hence with indeterminate predictions of behavior. Also, there seem to be no substantial analyses of comprehensive models in which we can explore—from the incentive point of view—the relative efficiency of different structures of managing.

With regard to hierarchy itself, what have we learned from economic theory? The most positive and definite result was the one about the efficiency of hierarchies for information processing (Section 4). But this is precisely the area in which we know, empirically, from the study of "informal organization," that firms are *not* predominantly hierarchical. At least, if there are hierarchies embedded in the patterns of information processing, there are many overlapping ones; *in fact, this is predicted by the theory of the decentralization of information* (Section 5).

On the other hand, in the area of incentives where hierarchies of authority and supervision seem most evident in reality, economic theorists—and their colleagues, the game theorists—have not provided an incisive comparative analysis of both hierarchical and nonhierarchical forms of organization.

Now the absence of a comparative analysis is not the same as a negative analysis that shows that there is no economic justification for hierarchies of authority. However, it does tempt one to speculate about noneconomic—or partly noneconomic—explanations of such hierarchies.

One possible explanation is both economic and historical. Small owner-managed firms were authoritarian because the owners wanted to maintain control over their assets. As the firm grew, the authoritarian pattern was repeated at successive levels as managers were added who were not themselves owners, perhaps just in imitation of the pattern that was already there. However, if nonhierarchical management were in fact more efficient than hierarchical management, then why weren't such structures eventually adopted *within* the management sector, while maintaining the authority of the owners as a group over the management as a group?

In fact, there has been growing criticism of purely hierarchical structures of authority in firms, not only from the left, but also mainstream analysts, consultants, and managers themselves. One example is the "matrix management" movement, in which a single hierarchy of authority is replaced by two or more overlapping—and sometimes conflicting—hierarchies (Stanley M. Davis and Paul R. Lawrence 1977). A second example is the recent spurt of interest in "flat organizations," which—although formally hierarchical—have very few levels, and give each supervisor so many subordinates that effective authoritarian control becomes impossible (Peter Drucker 1988; Allan Cox 1989). A third line of thought asserts that activities in large modern firms have become so interdependent—whatever that means precisely—that de facto hierarchies of power no longer exist, and that power is exercised by mutual adjustment, persuasion, exhortation, and leadership, rather than by virtue of office alone. For an exciting discussion of organization structures that are neither hierarchies nor neoclassical markets—and the challenge to economic theory that they represent—I recommend two recent papers by Michael Piore (1989a, 1989b) on research that he has been doing for the International Labor Organization.

Going farther afield, one might find the roots of authoritarian hierarchies in human personality itself, as described by Theodor Adorno et al (1950) in *The Authoritarian Personality*, and by Erich Fromm (1941) in *Escape from Freedom*. After all, we grow up in authoritarian families, and many aspects of our society recreate and perpetuate these hierarchical structures. From this point of view, it should not be surprising that most employees feel most comfortable in hierarchical firms.

All of this takes me far from my own field of expertise, and also far from the comfortable haunts of mainstream economic analysis and game theory. But rather than withdraw to safer ground, I am going to leave us in these dangerous precincts, in the hope that some of the more daring—and probably younger— theorists will be tempted to venture out from the citadel of general market equilibrium, and try to build some solid structures here, too.

REFERENCES

In addition to works cited in the text, the following list of references includes items that may be useful for further reading.

ABREU, DILIP AND ARIEL, RUBINSTEIN. "The Structure of Nash Equilibrium in Repeated Games with Finite Automata," *Econometrica*, Nov. 1988, 56(6), pp. 1259–82.

ADORNO, THEODOR W. ET AL, *The authoritarian personality*. NY: Harper and Row, 1950.

ALCHIAN, ARMEN A. AND HAROLD, DEMSETZ. "Production, Information Costs, and Economic Organization," *Amer. Econ. Rev.*, Dec. 1972, 62(5), pp. 777–95.

Aoki, Masahiko. "Toward an Economic Model of the Japanese Firm," *J. Econ. Lit.*, Mar. 1990, 28(1), pp. 1–17.

ARROW, KENNETH J. "Uncertainty and the Welfare Economics of Medical Care," *Amer. Econ. Rev.*, Dec. 1963, 53(5), pp. 941–73.

———. *The limits of organization*. NY: Norton, 1974.

BARNARD, CHESTER I. *The functions of the executive*. Cambridge, MA: Harvard U. Press, 1938.

BECKMANN, MARTIN J. *Tinbergen lectures on organization theory*. Berlin: Springer-Verlag, 1983.

BUTTRICK, JOHN. "The Inside Contract System," *J. Econ. Hist.*, 1952, 12(3), pp. 205–21.

CANNING, DAVID. "Social Equilibrium." Unpub. ms. Pembroke College, Cambridge, 1989.

CHANDLER, ALFRED D., JR. *The visible hand*. Cambridge, MA: Harvard U. Press, 1977.

CLARK, JOHN M. "Economics and Modern Psychology," *J. Polit. Econ.*, Jan. 1918, 26(1), pp. 1–30.

Cox, ALLAN. "Managing without Hierarchy: Even 'Flat' Companies Need Leaders," *New York Times*, Aug. 20, 1989, 138, Sect. 3. p. F3.

CRÉMER, JACQUES. "A Partial Theory of the Optimal Organization of a Bureaucracy," *Bell. J. Econ.*, Autumn 1980, 11(2), pp. 683–93.

DAVIS, STANLEY M. AND LAWRENCE, PAUL R. *Matrix*. Reading, MA: Addison-Wesley, 1977.

DRUCKER, PETER E. "The Coming of the New Organization," *Harvard Bus. Rev.*, Jan./Feb. 1988, 66(1), pp. 45–53.

"The Fortune 500," *Fortune*, Apr. 24, 1989, 119(9), pp. 354–76.

"The Fortune International 500," *Fortune*, July 31, 1989, 120(3), pp. 279–318.

FROMM, ERICH. *Escape from freedom*. NY: Rinehart, 1941.

FUDENBERG, DREW AND KREPS, DAVID. "A Theory of Learning, Experimentation, and Equilibrium in Games." Unpub. ms. Economics Dept., Massachusetts Institute of Technology, Cambridge, MA, 1989.

GALBRAITH, JAY. *Designing complex organizations*. Reading, MA: Addison-Wesley, 1973.

GEANAKOPLOS, JOHN AND MILGROM, PAUL. "A Theory of Hierarchies Based on Limited Managerial Attention," *J. Japan. Int. Economies*, Sept. 1991, 5(3), pp. 205–25.

GILBOA, ITZHAK AND SAMET, DOV. "Bounded Versus Unbounded Rationality: The Tyranny of the Weak," *Games and Economic Beahvior*, Sept. 1989, 1(30, pp. 213–21.

GROSSMAN, SANFORD J. AND HART, OLIVER D. "An Analysis of the Principal-Agent Problem," *Econometrica*, Jan. 1983, 51(1), pp. 7–45.

GROVES, THEODORE AND LOEB, MARTIN. "Incentives in a Divisionalized Firm," *Manage. Sci.*, Mar. 1979, 25(3), pp. 221–30.

GROVES, THEODORE; RADNER, ROY AND REITER, STANLEY, *Information incentives, and economic mechanisms: Essays in honor of Lenoid Hurwicz*. Minneapolis, MN: U. of Minnesota Press, 1987.

HARSANYI, JOHN C. "Games with Incomplete Information Played by Bayesian Players," *Manage. Sci.*, 1967–68, 14, pp. 159–82, 320–34, 486–502.

HART, OLIVER. "An Economist's Perspective on the Theory of the Firm," *Columbia Law Rev.*, Nov. 1989, 89(7), pp. 1757–74.

HESS, JAMES D. *The economics of organization*. Amsterdam: North-Holland, 1983.

KALAI, EHUD AND STANFORD, WILLIAM. "Finite Rationality and Interpersonal Complexity in Repeated Games," *Econometrica*, Mar. 1988, 56(2), pp. 397–410.

KEREN, MICHAEL AND LEVHARI, DAVID. "The Internal Organization of the Firm and the Shape of Average Costs," *Bell. J. Econ.*, Autumn 1983, 14(2), pp. 474–86.

———. "Decentralization, Aggregation, Control Loss, and Costs in a Hierarchical Model of the Firm," *J. Econ. Behav. Org.*, Mar. 1989, 11(2), pp. 213–36.

KIM, KI H. AND ROUSH, FRED W. *Team theory*. NY: Halsted Press, 1987.

KNIGHT, FRANK H. *Risk, uncertainty, and profits*. Cambridge, MA: Houghton Mifflin, 1921; reprinted by Kelley and Millman, New York, 1957.

KRUSKAL, CLYDE P. ET AL. "A Complexity Theory of Efficient Parallel Algorithms," *Theoretical Computer Science*, Mar. 1990, 71(1), pp. 95–132.

LINHART, PETER B.; RADNER, ROY AND SATTERTWAITE, MARK A. "Introduction: Symposium on Noncooperative Bargaining," *J. Econ. Theory*, June 1989, 48(1), pp. 1–17.

LINHART, PETER B. ET AL. *Bargaining under incomplete information*. NY: Academic Press, 1992.

MARRIS, ROBIN. *The economic theory of managerial capitalism*. NY: Macmillan, 1964.

MARRIS, ROBIN AND WOOD, ADRIAN. *The corporate*

economy. Cambridge, MA: Harvard U. Press, 1971.

MARSCHAK, JACOB AND RADNER, ROY. *Economic theory of teams*. New Haven, CT: Yale U. Press, 1972.

MARSCHAK, THOMAS A. "Computation in Organizations," in MCGUIRE AND RADNER 1986, ch. 12. pp. 237–82.

MARSCHAK, THOMAS A. AND MCGUIRE, C. BARTLETT. "Lecture Notes on Economic Models for Organization Design." Unpub. ms. Graduate School of Business Administration, U. of California, Berkeley, 1971.

MARSCHAK, THOMAS A. AND REICHELSTEIN, STEFAN. "Network Mechanisms, Informational Efficiencies and the Role of Hierarchies." Unpub. ms. Graduate School of Business Administration, Stanford U., Dec. 1987.

MARSHALL, ALFRED, *Principles of economics*. London: Macmillan, [1890] 1930.

MCCRAW, THOMAS K. *Prophets of regulation*. Cambridge, MA: Harvard U. Press, 1984.

MCGUIRE, C. BARTLETT AND RADNER, ROY. *Decision and organization*. 2nd. ed. Minneapolis, MN: U. of Minnesota Press, 1986.

MELUMAD, NAHUM D. AND REICHELSTEIN, STEFAN. "Value of Communication in Agencies," *J. Econ. Theory*, Apr. 1989, 47(2), pp. 334–68.

MILGROM, PAUL AND ROBERTS, JOHN. "The Economics of Modern Manufacturing: Technology, Strategy, and Organization," *Amer. Econ. Rev.*, June 1990, 80(3), pp. 511–28.

MINTZBERG, HENRY. *The structuring of organizations*. Englewood Cliffs, NJ: Prentice-Hall, 1979.

———. *Mintzberg on management*. NY: Free Press, 1989.

MIRRLEES, JAMES. "The Optimal Structure of Incentives and Authority within an Organization," *Bell J. Econ.*, Spring 1976, 7(1), pp. 105–31.

MOUNT, KENNETH R. AND REITER, STANLEY. "Computation, Communication, and Performance in Resource Allocation." Paper presented at the CEME-NBER Decentralization Seminar, U. of Minnesota, Minneapolis, May 21–23, 1982.

———. " A Model of Computing with Human Agents." Unpub. ms. Center for Mathematical Studies in Economics and Management Science, Northwestern U., Evanston, IL, June 1990.

MYERSON, ROGER B. "Bayesian Equilibrium and Incentive Compatibility: An Introduction," in *Social goals and social organization*. Eds.: LEONID HURWICZ, DAVID SCHMEIDLER, AND HUGO SONNENSCHEIN. Cambridge: Cambridge U. Press, 1985, pp. 229–59.

NEYMAN, ABRAHAM. "Bounded Complexity Justifies Cooperation in the Finitely-Repeated Prisoners' Dilemma," *Economics Letters*, 1985, 19, pp. 227–29.

PELIKAN, PAVEL. "Evolution, Economic Competence, and the Market for Corporate Control," *J. Econ. Behav. Organ.*, Dec. 1989, 12(3), pp. 279–303.

PENZIAS, ARNO A. *Ideas and information*. NY: Norton, 1989.

PETERS, THOMAS J. AND WATERMAN, ROBERT H. JR.

In search of excellence. NY: Harper & Row, 1982.

PIORE, MICHAEL J. "Corporate Reform in American Manufacturing and the Challenge to Economic Theory." Unpub. ms. Massachusetts Institute of Technology, Cambridge, MA, 1989b.

———. "Work, Labor, and Action: Work Experience in a System of Flexible Production." Unpub. ms. Massachusetts Institute of Technology, Cambridge, MA, 1989b.

PORTER, GLENN. *The rise of big business, 1860–1910*. NY: Crowell, 1973.

PRATT, JOHN W. AND ZECKHAUSER, RICHARD J., eds. *Principals and agents: The structure of business*. Boston: Harvard Business School Press, 1985.

RADNER, ROY. "Repeated Principal-Agent Games with Discounting," *Econometrica*, Sept. 1985, 53(5), pp. 1173–97.

———. "Teams," in McGuire and Radner 1986, ch. 10, pp. 189–215.

———. "The Internal Economy of Large Firms," *Econ. J.*, 1986a, 96 (Supplement), pp. 1–22.

———. "Repeated Moral Hazard with Low Discount Rates," in *Uncertainty, information, and communication: Essays in honor of Kenneth J. Arrow*. Vol. 3. Eds: WALTER P. HELLER, ROSS M. STARR, AND DAVID A. STARRETT. Cambridge, MA: Cambridge U. Press, 1986b, pp. 25–63.

———. "Decentralization and Incentives," in GROVES, RADNER, AND REITER 1987, ch. 1, pp. 3–47.

———. "The Organization of Decentralized Information Processing." Unpub. ms. AT&T Bell Laboratories, Murray Hill, NJ, 1989.

———. "Dynamic Games in Organization Theory," *J. Econ. Behav. Organ.*, July 1991, 16(1–2), pp. 217–60.

RADNER, ROY AND VAN ZANDT, TIMOTHY. "Information Processing in Firms and Returns to Scale," *Annales d'Economie et de Statistique*, June 1992, 25/26, pp. 265–98.

ROBINSON, JOAN. "What Are the Questions?," *J. Econ. Lit.*, Dec. 1977, 15(4), pp. 1318–39.

RUBINSTEIN, ARIEL. "Finite Automata Play the Repeated Prisoners' Dilemma," *J. Econ. Theory*, June 1986, 39(1) pp. 83–96.

SAH, RAAJ K. AND STIGLITZ, JOSEPH E., "The Architecture of Economic Systems: Hierarchies and Polyarchies," *Amer. Econ. Rev.*, Sept. 1986, 76(4), 716–27.

SAVAGE, LEONARD J. *The foundations of statistics*. NY: Wiley, 1954.

SCHWARTZ, JACOB T. "Ultracomputers," *ACM Transactions on Programming Languages and Systems*, Oct. 1980, 2(4), pp. 484–521.

SIMON, HERBERT A. "The Architecture of Complexity," *Proc. Amer. Philosophical Soc.*, Dec. 1962, 106(6), pp. 467–82; reprinted as Ch. 7 of SIMON 1981, pp. 192–229.

———. *The sciences of the artificial*. 2nd ed. Cambridge, MA: MIT Press, 1981.

SMITH, ADAM. *The wealth of nations*. 1776; reprinted by the U. of Chicago Press, Chicago, IL, 1976 (Cannan Edition).

SOLOMONS, DAVID. *Divisional performance: Mea-*

surement and control. NY: Markus Wiener, 1965.

TANNENBAUM, ARNOLD S. *Social psychology of the work organization.* Belmont, CA: Wadsworth, 1966.

U.S. BUREAU OF THE CENSUS. *Sixteenth census of the United States: 1940. Population. Comparative occupation statistics for the United States, 1870–1940. A comparison of the 1930 and the 1940 census occupation and industry classifications and statistics; a comparable series of occupation statistics, 1870 to 1930; and a social-economic grouping of the labor force, 1910 to 1940 . . .* Washington, DC: U.S. Dept. of Commerce, 1943.

———. *Historical statistics of the United States: Colonial times to 1970, bicentennial edition,* *Part 2,* Washington, DC: U.S. Dept. of Commerce, 1975.

U.S. BUREAU OF THE CENSUS. *1980 census of population.* Vol. 1. *Characteristics of the population.* Washington, DC: U.S. Dept. of Commerce, 1981.

U.S. DEPT. OF COMMERCE. *Statistical abstracts of the U.S.* Washington, DC, 1989.

VAN ZANDT, TIMOTHY. "Efficient Parallel Addition." Unpub. ms. AT&T Bell Laboratories, Murray Hill, NJ, 1990.

WILLIAMSON, OLIVER E. *Markets and hierarchies.* NY: Free Press, 1975.

WITSENHAUSEN, HANS S. "A Counterexample in Stochastic Optimum Control," *SIAM J. Control,* Feb. 1968, 6(1), pp. 131–47.

29

Strategic Management Journal, Vol. 17(Winter Special Issue), 63–76 (1996)

MODULARITY, FLEXIBILITY, AND KNOWLEDGE MANAGEMENT IN PRODUCT AND ORGANIZATION DESIGN

RON SANCHEZ
Graduate School of Management, University of Western Australia, Nedlands, Western Australia, Australia

JOSEPH T. MAHONEY
College of Commerce and Business Administration, University of Illinois at Urbana—Champaign, Champaign, Illinois, U.S.A.

This paper investigates interrelationships of product design, organization design, processes for learning and managing knowledge, and competitive strategy. This paper uses the principles of nearly decomposable systems to investigate the ability of standardized interfaces between components in a product design to embed coordination of product development processes. Embedded coordination creates 'hierarchical coordination' without the need to continually exercise authority—enabling effective coordination of processes without the tight coupling of organizational structures. We develop concepts of modularity in product and organization designs based on standardized component and organization interfaces. Modular product architectures create information structures that provide the 'glue' that holds together the loosely coupled parts of a modular organization design. By facilitating loose coupling, modularity can also reduce the cost and difficulty of adaptive coordination, thereby increasing the strategic flexibility of firms to respond to environmental change. Modularity in product and organization designs therefore enables a new strategic approach to the management of knowledge based on an intentional, carefully managed loose coupling of a firm's learning processes at architectural and component levels of product creation processes.

INTRODUCTION

Daft and Lewin identify the 'modular organization' as a new paradigm that has as its premise 'the need for flexible, learning organizations that continuously change and solve problems through interconnected coordinated self-organizing processes' (1993: i). This paper investigates approaches to *managing knowledge* in a firm's product-creation processes that facilitate specific forms of 'coordinated self-organizing processes'

capable of improving a firm's *strategic flexibility* to respond advantageously to a changing environment (Sanchez, 1993, 1994b, 1995). To do so, we investigate concepts of *modularity* in both product designs and organization designs.

We explain how advanced technological knowledge about component interactions can be used to fully specify and standardize the component interfaces that make up a modular product architecture, creating a nearly independent system (Simon, 1962) of 'loosely coupled' components. We then suggest that just as some work may be coordinated by specifying standard operating procedures (Cyert and March, 1963) that govern *processes* directly, much work in product devel-

Key words: coordination; knowledge management; modularity; strategic flexibility

CCC 0143–2095/96/S20063–14
© 1996 by John Wiley & Sons, Ltd.

opment may be coordinated by specifying standardized component interfaces that govern the *outputs* of component development processes. In essence, the standardized component interfaces in a modular product architecture provide a form of *embedded coordination* that greatly reduces the need for overt exercise of managerial authority to achieve coordination of development processes, thereby making possible the concurrent and autonomous development of components by *loosely coupled organization structures* (Orton and Weick, 1990). Thus, using technological knowledge to create *modularity in product designs* becomes an important strategy for achieving *modularity in organization designs*.

This paper is organized in the following way. The next section builds on Simon's (1962) notion of 'nearly decomposable' systems by proposing that product designs and organization designs follow the fundamental principles of decomposition.

We then investigate modularity in product and organization designs. We suggest that although organizations ostensibly design products, it can also be argued that *products design organizations*, because the coordination tasks implicit in specific product designs largely determine the feasible organization designs for developing and producing those products.[1]

The following section considers how learning processes create *information structures* in product development processes, and it evaluates the characteristic information structures and resulting learning efficiencies of three models for organizing product development processes: sequential development, overlapping problem solving, and modular product design.

We conclude by suggesting that the emerging prominence of modular product designs is being accompanied by new knowledge management strategies (Grant, 1993; Sanchez, 1996c) that allow product creation to be carried out more effectively through flexible, 'modular' organization structures.

NEARLY DECOMPOSABLE SYSTEMS

A complex system—whether product design or organization structure—consists of parts that interact and are interdependent to some degree. Simon (1962) argues that *hierarchy* is an organizing principle of complex systems, which are essentially composed of interrelated subsystems that in turn have their own subsystems, and so on.

This paper applies Simon's (1962) *structural* conception of hierarchy in complex systems to the analysis of product designs and of organizational processes for developing new products. In so doing, we use a more general conception of 'hierarchy' than that usually invoked in organizational economics and strategic management (e.g., Mahoney, 1992b, 1992c; Williamson, 1975), where hierarchy typically denotes subordination to an *authority* relationship. Our interest here, however, is in understanding hierarchical systems for creating new products in which there is *little or no overt exercise of managerial authority.*[2]

In this discussion, 'hierarchy' refers to a decomposition of a complex system into a structured ordering of successive sets of subsystems, in the manner suggested by Simon (1962)—i.e., a partitioning into relationships that collectively define the parts of any whole. We suggest that hierarchy, in this structural sense, may be a feature of both designs for products and designs for organizations that create products (Sanchez, 1995, 1996b).

Simon (1962) further defines a *nearly decomposable system* as one in which interactions among subsystems are weak (but not necessarily negligible). The interactions between the divisions of a multidivisional organization are representative of a nearly decomposable system (Mahoney, 1992a; Williamson, 1975). The tasks within a multidivisional firm are intentionally designed to require low levels of coordination so that they can be carried out by an organizational structure of quasi-independent divisions functioning as *loosely coupled subsystems* (Weick, 1976).

An important property of this structural hierarchical decomposition is that the impacts of

---

[1] Product design should be recognized as a strategic activity with important economic implications. A 1986 study at Rolls-Royce suggested that design determines 80 per cent of the final production costs of 2000 components, and General Motors executives maintain that 70 percent of the total cost of manufacturing truck transmissions is determined in the design stage (Whitney, 1988).

[2] In fact, Radner (1992: 1392) poses the question 'Would a hierarchical design of the processes of production [necessarily] lead to hierarchical management?' In effect, what we are suggesting in this paper is that specific forms of hierarchical designs of processes *need not* be accompanied by hierarchical management.

environmental disturbances may be localized within specific subsystems, increasing the survivability and adaptability of the overall system in a turbulent environment (Orton and Weick, 1990). Extending these insights to product designs and organizations that create new products, we suggest that new approaches to decomposing and structuring product designs have enabled the adoption of more structurally decomposed—and thus more adaptable—organization designs for creating products.

MODULARITY IN PRODUCT AND ORGANIZATION DESIGNS

Product designs differ fundamentally in the degree to which a design has been decomposed into 'loosely coupled' vs. 'tightly coupled' components. The degree to which components are loosely coupled or tightly coupled in a product *design* depends on the extent to which a change in the design of one component requires compensating design changes in other components. *Modularity* is a special form of design which intentionally creates a high degree of independence or 'loose coupling' between component designs by standardizing component interface specifications. This section explains how modular design achieves the loose coupling of component designs and in the process creates an *information structure* that can provide *embedded coordination* of loosely coupled component development processes (Sanchez, 1995).

Modular product designs

A component in a product design performs a function within a system of interrelated components whose collective functioning make up the product. Relationships between components are defined by the specifications of inputs and outputs linking components in a design,[3] and a complete

[3] Note that tight or loose coupling of components in a product *design* is different from tight or loose coupling in an actual (usually physical) product. A personal computer design, for example, may have loosely coupled components in that different microprocessors or hard disk drives may be substituted into the computer design without requiring a redesign of the other components. Nevertheless, the components in the physical computer will be tightly coupled in the sense that all components must function properly for the computer to function as a system.

set of component interface specifications constitutes a *product architecture* (Abernathy and Clark, 1985; Clark, 1985).

Traditional engineering design follows a methodology of constrained optimization, which tries to obtain the highest level of product performance within some cost constraint or the lowest cost for a product meeting a minimum performance constraint. This design methodology typically leads to product designs composed of highly integrated, tightly coupled component designs. Specifications of input and output interfaces between components must therefore reflect the idiosyncratic characteristics of each tightly coupled component design. As a consequence, *processes for developing tightly coupled component designs require intensive managerial coordination*, since a change in the design of one component is likely to require extensive compensating changes in the designs of many interrelated components. Thus, product designs composed of tightly coupled components will generally require development processes carried out in a *tightly coupled organization structure* coordinated by a managerial *authority hierarchy*, an organization design typically achieved within a single firm.

Some firms, however, are now using an alternative design methodology that intentionally creates loosely coupled component designs by specifying *standardized component interfaces* that define functional, spatial, and other relationships between components that, once specified, are not permitted to change during an intended period in a product development process. The 'intended period' during which standardized component interfaces are not permitted to change may range from key stages in the development of a new product architecture (Cusumano and Selby, 1995) to the entire commercial lifetime of a product family (Sanchez, 1995). Standardizing component interface specifications during a period of time allows processes for developing component designs to become loosely coupled, because they can be effectively coordinated simply by requiring that all developed components conform to the standardized component interface specifications.[4]

[4] Specifying standardized interfaces to create loosely coupled components allows each component within a product design to be treated as a 'black box' (Wheelwright and Clark, 1992) by the product developing firm. In developing new car models, many car makers now provide their suppliers with only a 'black box' specification of the (standardized) functional,

66   *R. Sanchez and J. T. Mahoney*

Thus, controlling the required *output* of component development processes by standardizing component interfaces permits effective coordination of development processes without the continual exercise of managerial authority. The specifications for standardized component interfaces provides, in effect, an *information structure* (Radner, 1992) that coordinates the loosely coupled activities of component developers.

A *modular product architecture* (Sanchez, 1994a; Ulrich and Eppinger, 1995) is a special form of product design that uses standardized interfaces between components to create a *flexible* product architecture. In modular product design, the standardized interfaces between components are specified to allow for *a range of variations* in components to be substituted into a product architecture. *Modular components* are components whose interface characteristics are within the range of variations allowed by a modular product architecture. The modular architecture is *flexible* (Sanchez, 1995) because product variations can be leveraged by substituting (Garud and Kumaraswamy, 1993) different modular components into the product architecture without having to redesign other components. This loose coupling of component designs within a modular product architecture allows the 'mixing and matching' of modular components to give a potentially large number of product variations distinctive functionalities, features, and/or performance levels (Sanderson and Uzumeri, 1990; Sanchez, 1994a; Ward *et al.*, 1995).

Modular product architectures can be an important source of *strategic flexibility* (Sanchez, 1995) when they enable a firm to respond more readily to changing markets and technologies by rapidly creating product variations based on new combinations of new or existing modular components. The standardized component interfaces of

a modular product architecture also enable the coordination of a loosely coupled organization structure linking geographically dispersed component developers. Thus, a firm may be able to use a modular product architecture to coordinate a global network (Kogut and Bowman, 1995; Kogut and Kulatilaka, 1994) or 'constellation' (Normann and Ramirez, 1993) of component developers and suppliers to source a broad range of component variations, thereby further enhancing the ability of the firm to leverage new product variations. In this way, 'loose coupling [within a product architecture] facilitates continuous change' (Spender and Grinyer, 1995) by improving the ability of a firm to generate new product variations. As Table 1 indicates, modular product architectures that allow mixing and matching[5] of modular components are now appearing in diverse product markets (Sanderson and Uzumeri, 1990; Sanchez, 1991).

Modular organization designs

Specifying the required *outputs* of component development processes permits those processes to be partitioned into tasks (von Hippel, 1990) that can be performed *autonomously and concurrently* by a loosely coupled structure of development organizations. In effect, the *information structure* provided by the standardized component interface specifications of a modular product architecture provides a means to embed coordination of loosely coupled component development processes. The information structure of a modular product architecture thus provides the 'glue' of embedded coordination that allows a loosely coupled development organization to achieve syntheses (Spender and Grinyer, 1995) in the form of developed products.[6]

---

spatial, and other interfaces of the required component, leaving the actual design and development of the component to the supplier (Clark and Fujimoto, 1991). This design principle is also evident in software development, where object-oriented programming methods require that each component of a program be written by software developers who have no knowledge of the code used by other developers in writing their program components. Decomposition of program design allows a regime of 'information hiding' among program component developers (Parnas, 1972) analogous to 'black box' component development in the automobile industry. (For further discussion of standards and interfaces, see David and Greenstein, 1990).

---

[5] Shirley (1990) investigates the potential for product designs using modular components to provide a large number of product variations while reducing overall manufacturing costs. We suggest that modularity in product design creates many options for product variations in the form of feasible combinations of modular components, some of which may be drawn from a 'design library' of existing components. In this regard, leveraging product variations from modular designs is a specific expression of Kogut and Zander's (1992) 'combinative capabilities' in the context of creating new products.

[6] In a more general sense, embedded coordination is the coordination of organizational processes achieved by any means other than the continuous exercise of managerial authority and may include, for example, clan coordination through tradition (Ouchi, 1980). We thank the editors for bringing this point to our attention.

Table 1. Examples of products with modular designs

Products	Form of modular product design	References
Aircraft	Common wing, nose, and tail components allow several models to be leveraged by using different numbers of fuselage modules to create aircraft of different lengths and passenger/freight capacities (used by Boeing, McDonnell-Douglas, and Airbus Industries).	Woolsey (1994)
Automobiles	Automakers have long used many basic modular components specified by the Society of Automotive Engineers.	Nevins and Whitney (1989)
	Some automakers use common (modular) components in many different models. Also, the Taurus platform design is leveraged to provide a basis for the Taurus and Mercury Sable sedans and wagons and for the Ford Taurus Windstar minivan.	*Automobile* (1994)
	Ford is converting its auto and truck engines to modular engine designs with high levels of common (modular) parts. The 4.6 L V-8 introduced in 1992 was Ford's first modular engine.	*Ford Engineering World* (1990)
	Chrysler's LH car designs are modular. Several models have been leveraged from common power train and engine components. The interior of each model is composed of four easy-to-install units that arrive ready-built from separate suppliers. The Chrysler Neon uses numerous modular assemblies.	Tully (1993)
Consumer electronics	Over 160 variations of the Sony Walkman were leveraged by 'mixing and matching' modular components in a few basic modular product designs.	Sanderson and Uzumeri (1990)
	Several upgraded models of Sony HandyCam video cameras were leveraged from an initial system design by successively introducing improved modular components.	Sanchez (1994a)
Household appliances	General Electric leverages several models of dishwashers by installing different modular doors and controls on common assemblies of enclosures, motors, and wiring harnesses.	Sanchez and Sudharshan (1993)
Personal computers	Personal computers often consist largely of modular components like hard disk drives, flat screen displays, and memory chips, coupled with some distinctive components like a microprocessor chip and enclosure.	Langlois and Robertson (1992)
Software	Software designs are creating modules of routines which can be combined to create customized applications programs.	Cusumano (1991)
	Software designers attain modularity through loose coupling. The objective is often to minimize coupling—i.e., to make modules as independent as possible. Loose coupling between modules signifies a well-designed system. Modular programming (1) allows one module to be written without knowledge of the code in another module (a decomposition using an 'information hiding' regime), and (2) allows modules to be reassembled and replaced without design of the whole system. Separating *action* (what the module does) and *logic* (how the module accomplishes the action) is a 'composite' approach to software engineering that has been deployed by NASA and GTE, among others.	Parnas, Clements and Weiss (1985)
	Software for designing application-specific integrated circuits (ASICs) provides modular circuit elements which can then be linked together to provide the specific functionalities needed to customize an ASIC for a specific product application.	von Hippel (1994)
Test instruments	Philips created a flexible chassis for receiving modular components which permit the configuration of large numbers of specialized oscilloscopes for testing various kinds of electronic products.	*Electronics* (1986)
Power tools	Black and Decker designed its entire line of power tools in the 1980s to incorporate a high degree of common modular components.	Utterback (1994)

A loosely coupled product creation organization in which each participating component development unit can function autonomously and concurrently under the embedded coordination of a modular product architecture appears to correspond closely to Daft and Lewin's notion of *modular organizations* 'that continuously change and solve problems through interconnected coordinated self-organizing processes' (1993: i). A firm using a modular product architecture to coordinate development processes has a means to quickly link together the resources and capabilities of many organizations to form product development 'resource chains' that can respond flexibly—i.e., broadly, quickly, and at low cost (Sanchez, 1995, 1996b)—to environmental change.

MODELS FOR MANAGING KNOWLEDGE AND LEARNING IN PRODUCT CREATION

Product development projects can be thought of as 'programmed' innovation in which firms create new products by applying existing knowledge and creating new knowledge about components and their interactions. To create the information structure of fully specified and standardized component interfaces in a modular product architecture requires a high level of architectural knowledge (Sanchez, 1996c; Wright, 1994) about how components function and interact in a product. To the extent that a firm has inadequate knowledge of components and their interactions, creating a new product architecture requires learning by experimenting (Baldwin and Clark, 1994) with new component designs and alternative arrangements of components.

Innovation during product development may therefore involve (i) creating new information about the functions components can perform, which implies learning about components *per se*, or (ii) creating new information about the ways components interact and can be configured, which implies learning about product architectures (Henderson and Clark, 1990). Extending the notion of learning at component and architectural levels, Figure 1 identifies four modes of learning—radical, architectural, modular, and incremental—that can occur in product innovation processes (cf. Henderson and Clark, 1990).

Research in strategy has often emphasized the challenges to organizations of 'radical' learning (Dewar and Dutton, 1986). More recently, attention has also been paid to the importance of 'architectural' learning (Morris and Ferguson, 1993; Henderson and Clark, 1990). Significant benefits may also be realized, however, by effectively leveraging new products based on 'modular' or 'incremental' forms of learning that can take place within an existing product architecture (Sanchez, 1995, 1996b). All these forms of learning are vital to organizational renewal and development, but not all processes for learning during product development are equally efficient. This section considers ways in which processes for architectural, modular, and incremental learning during product development may be managed to improve the efficiency of both component and architectural levels of learning.

Much recent research into improving the effectiveness and efficiency of product development has focused on processes of knowledge creation and information transfer in product creation projects (e.g., Clark and Fujimoto, 1991; Wheelwright and Clark, 1992). The product creation process generally consists of product concept development, feasibility testing, product design, component development processes, pilot production, and final production (Takeuchi and Nonaka, 1986). We now analyze more closely three alternative approaches to creating knowledge and transferring information in product design and component development processes: 'traditional' sequential development, overlapping problem solving, and modular product development.

'Traditional' sequential development processes

The 'traditional' model of product design and development follows a sequential staging of design and development tasks (Takeuchi and Nonaka, 1986), as suggested in Figure 2(a). In this model, after defining the product concept, design and development tasks are sequenced so that technology and component development tasks with the greatest need for new knowledge and with the greatest impact on other component design and development tasks are undertaken first. As the firm develops new technical knowledge about components and their interactions at each stage, it makes component design decisions and

Learning about Component Functions and Designs

	Moderate	Significant
Moderate	**Incremental Learning at the Component Level** Incremental learning through component development leads to limited functional improvements and design variations in components used within an existing product architecture.	**Modular Learning at the Component Level** Learning about new kinds of component technologies leads to significant changes in feasible component functions and designs that can be accommodated within an existing product architecture.
Significant	**Architectural Learning** Learning about new product market opportunities leads to new product architectures based on changes in the ways existing kinds of components are combined and configured in product designs.	**Radical Learning at Architectural and Component Levels** Learning about new market opportunities and new product and component technologies leads to major changes in both kinds of components used and ways components are configured to form a product architecture.

Learning about Component Interactions and Configurations

Figure 1. Modes of learning in product creation processes

communicates new information about component interface specifications that allow the next stage of component design and development tasks to proceed. This process is repeated at each stage of development until all components and their interfaces are fully specified. Thus, a critical feature of the sequential development process is that the information structure of component interface specifications—i.e., the new product architecture—is the *output* of the design and development process.

Recent research has made evident the likelihood of breakdowns, losses, and delays in information flows when product development processes are organized as a sequence of development tasks (e.g., Clark and Wheelwright, 1993). A sequential ordering of design and development tasks, for example, typically results in recursive information flows that often slow the development process, as suggested by the information feedback flows in Figure 2(a). A sequential process is also likely to 'lose information' as development proceeds from one stage to the next, because the information and assumptions underlying upstream design decisions may not be transferred intact to downstream stages of development. Technical incompatibilities between interdependent compo-

nents may then actually be 'designed into' downstream components.

We suggest here that in addition to these well-known effects, the incomplete information structure of an *evolving* product architecture also has profound implications for feasible approaches to organizing this kind of development process. Because the information structure of an evolving product architecture is incomplete and indefinite until all stages of component development are completed, the desired outputs of specific component development tasks cannot be fully specified before beginning development. Coordinating incompletely specified but interdependent development tasks will require managerial adjudication of many technical and financial issues likely to arise between component development groups. The authority hierarchy needed to manage a sequential development process requires, in effect, the *tightly coupled organization structure* of a single firm or a firm with strong ties to a 'quasi-integrated' group of dependent component suppliers (Nishiguchi, 1994; Sanchez, 1995).[7]

---

[7] A further argument for the necessity of carrying out sequential development processes within a single firm is the difficulty of contracting for component development services when the

70   *R. Sanchez and J. T. Mahoney*

Overlapping problem solving

An alternative model for managing product development organizes the sequential development processes of Figure 2(a) into staggered but overlapping stages, as shown in Figure 2(b). Overlapping development stages make possible greater sharing of current information through processes of *overlapping problem solving* (Clark and Fujimoto, 1991; Clark and Wheelwright, 1993) that link closely interrelated component design and development tasks. Overlapping problem solving, which is often carried out in a team-based organizational structure (Takeuchi and Nonaka, 1986), improves information flows between overlapping development tasks, as suggested by the information feedbacks in Figure 2(b), allowing some interrelated component development to proceed more quickly and reducing information losses between stages.

Although it offers improvements over a sequential development process, an overlapping problem solving process also has an evolving information structure (i.e., product architecture) and thus also requires intensive managerial coordination of incompletely specified development tasks within the boundaries of a single firm or within a small group of quasi-integrated component developers. Clark and Fujimoto (1991), for example, have observed that development projects using overlapping problem solving are more successful when they are managed by a 'heavyweight project manager' who has the *authority* to make design and specification decisions and adjudicate disputes between development groups.

Modular product design

Modular product design follows a new model for managing learning and knowledge in product creation processes. In contrast to the evolving information structures characteristic of the sequential and overlapping problem solving models, a modular product design process creates a complete information structure—i.e., the fully specified component interfaces of a modular product architecture—that defines required outputs of

component development processes *before* beginning development of components. To fully specify component interfaces in a modular product architecture, a firm must have, or have access to, advanced *architectural* knowledge about relevant components and their interactions.

When a firm can use advanced architectural knowledge to specify a new modular architecture within which development of modular components can take place, learning at the modular or incremental levels through developing new and improved components may be improved by being *intentionally separated* from and made only *loosely coupled* to processes for creating new architectural knowledge. Moreover, processes for learning at both levels may become more efficient.

Improved component-level learning

When learning through the development of individual components can take place within the stable information structure of a fully specified product architecture, learning inefficiencies due to breakdowns, losses, and delays in information flows between component development activities can be avoided. In effect, adopting a modular design process allows learning at the component level to be 'insulated' from disruptions by unexpected changes in product architecture during development projects.

Because fully specified component interfaces allow component-level learning processes to be carried out *concurrently and autonomously* by geographically dispersed, loosely coupled development groups, as suggested in Figure 2(c), a firm may be able to combine its capabilities more readily with those of an extensive network of component developers, thereby increasing the absorptive capacity of the firm (Cohen and Levinthal, 1990) and its potential for realizing the full *combinative capabilities* (Bartlett, 1993; Kogut and Zander, 1992) of the firm's current architectural knowledge. Decoupling architectural and component levels of learning may therefore allow a firm to be more effective in exploiting its current stock of architectural knowledge (March, 1991). After the initial round of concurrent component development suggested in Figure 2(c), a developing firm may use the stability of a modular product architecture to accelerate network-based development of new kinds of 'mix

---

performance of a contractor would be difficult to assess, given the high degree of dependence of each development group's work on the effort of other development groups (Alchian and Demsetz, 1972; Ouchi, 1980).

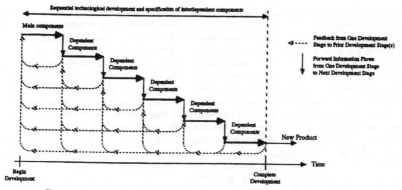

Figure 2(a): Sequential Organization of Product Development Processes

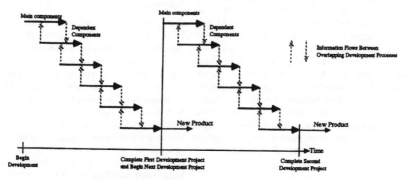

Figure 2(b): "Overlapping Problem Solving" Approach to Product Development

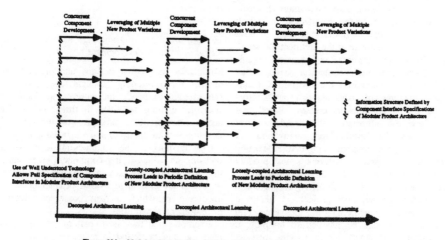

Figure 2(c): Modular Organization of Product Development Processes

Figure 2. (a) 'Traditional' sequential organization of product development processes (b) 'Overlapping problem solving' approach to product development (c) 'Modular' organization of product development processes

and match' modular components for leveraging product variations.

A modular product design process may therefore enable a firm to accelerate its *learning about markets* by enabling the firm to leverage many different variations of a product more quickly and at reduced cost. In effect, allowing more focused component-level learning within a current product architecture may facilitate an evolutionary process of real-time market research (Sanchez and Sudharshan, 1993) that supports accelerated creation of market knowledge in an enterprise (Baldwin and Clark, 1994). The decoupling of architectural and component learning processes may also create a more efficient environment for involving suppliers and customers in 'localized learning' in developing specific components. Boeing's use of a modular design process in developing the 777 aircraft (Woolsey, 1994), for example, created a decoupled component-level learning environment that facilitated the involvement of Boeing's lead customers in developing improved designs for key components which directly affect customers' use of the 777. Use of modular product architectures to achieve a managed separation of architectural and component learning may therefore provide a framework that supports expanded involvement of lead users (von Hippel, 1988) in product development.

Improved architectural-level learning

The loose coupling of learning at the component and architectural levels may also improve architectural learning processes. Henderson and Clark (1990) suggest that organizations tend to lose their abilities to innovate at the architectural level, because over time organizations develop organizational structures and information channels that are focused on component-level activities. Compartmentalization of organizations and information around components creates 'filters' that block flows of information that would suggest opportunities for architectural innovation. A further set of concerns about architectural learning arises from the 'project' nature of most product development processes. The time-sensitive, high-pressure environment which often characterizes new product development projects is likely to impose severe constraints on the time and resources which can be devoted to learning at the 'architectural' level. Using specific product

development projects as the *context* for creating new technical knowledge may therefore lead to an excessive focus on incremental (and perhaps modular) learning which can be applied immediately to current development needs. Learning at the architectural level, when intentionally decoupled from learning at the component level, may become more open to technological and market change, less dominated by the near-term demands of component-level learning during development projects, and thus less suceptible to falling into patterns of myopic learning (Levinthal and March, 1993).

Using modular product architectures as mechanisms for coordinating organizational learning

The process of periodically revising or creating a new modular product architecture provides an important coordinating mechanism for periodically linking loosely coupled processes for learning at architectural and component levels. Learning at the architectural level may suggest advantageous changes in components compatible with a current product architecture (i.e., opportunities for modular learning), as well as possibilities for significant changes in both components and product architectures (opportunities for radical innovations). Periodic redefinitions of modular product architectures may therefore provide a 'programmed' opportunity for reconnecting and coordinating architectural and component-level learning.

The shifting focus of knowledge management in modular product development

Modularity in product designs and organization designs for developing products may lead to a fundamental shift in the nature and focus of strategic learning activities in firms. Firms that create new products through modular product development are likely to place increasing emphasis on learning at the architectural level, while focusing and intensifying component-level learning in one or a few key components of subsystems that are critical to overall product performance and in which a firm possesses superior development capabilities.

Examples of this new pattern of 'modular learning' can be found in a growing number of industries, from high-tech to industrial. As an example of the latter, we cite Venkatesan's (1992) analysis of product competition in the earth-moving equipment industry. Venkatesan (1992) discusses the product architecture of a backhoe/loader—a complex mechanical system composed of a number of subsystems of components such as hydraulics, drive train, chassis, ground-engaging tools, vehicle electronics, operator cab, and engine. Venkatesan (1992: 101–103) describes the process of deciding which components and subsystems will become the focus of a firm's own learning efforts and which the firm will manage by using its architectural knowledge to define modular component interface specifications:

> The first thing to decide is what subsystems will be indispensable to the company's competitive position over subsequent product generations. This choice will vary from company to company and ultimately drive product differentiation. . . . [W]hen capable subsystem suppliers exist, it is not so important to be able to design and manufacture the sub-system in-house as it is to have *the ability to specify and control the performance characteristics of the subsystem.* [italics added for emphasis]

Venkatesan's (1992) observations suggest that much strategic learning is now directed at improving a firm's architectural knowledge needed to control the specifications of subsystems and components in a modular product architecture. This kind of architectural learning is becoming a strategically important means for assessing and coordinating an extended network of component development capabilities in other organizations (Sanchez, 1996d; Sanchez and Heene, 1996). As more firms begin to use modularity not just to create greater product variety, but also as a new framework for aggressive strategic learning and more effective knowledge management, new innovation dynamics are being created whose implications for technology-driven competition invite further investigation.

CONCLUSIONS

A useful tool for management and organization science is to make use of the world's redundancy to describe the complexity of our world as simply as possible (Simon, 1981: 222). The principle of the decomposability of systems deepens our understanding of the architecture of complexity, whether the system in question is physical, biological, social, or economic. Our effort to understand more fully the potential for *intentionally decomposing* complex products and organizational phenomena into loosely coupled subsystems suggests an approach to gaining new insights into the structure and dynamics of changing product markets and evolving organizational forms.

Extending the principle of decomposition, this paper has suggested that the creation of modular product architectures not only creates flexible product designs, but also enables the design of loosely coupled, flexible, 'modular' organization structures. Embedding coordination in fully specified and standardized component interfaces can reduce the need for much overt exercise of managerial authority across the interfaces of organizational units developing components, thereby reducing the intensity and complexity of a firm's managerial task in product development and giving it greater flexibility to take on a larger number and/or greater variety of product creation projects.

Adam Smith (1776) showed early insight into the importance of managing knowledge by suggesting that a firm organized around processes based on the specialized *content* of knowledge may gain efficiencies in producing physical products. Here we make an analogous argument about knowledge-intensive work: organizing a firm around specialized *processes for creating and applying* knowledge can lead to important dynamic efficiencies in the production of *intellectual* products in the form of new product and component designs and technologies.

We expect that the knowledge management processes of product-creating firms pursuing greater dynamic efficiencies will become increasingly focused on the codification of architectural knowledge about component interactions needed to specify modular product architectures and on using that architectural knowledge to coordinate loosely coupled modular organization structures for component and product development. In general, while firms may develop specialized knowledge about some strategically important modular components, we expect firms to undertake internal development of fewer components, as more product-creating firms learn how to use modular architectures to source more components through loosely coupled networks of component suppliers.

Growing strategic use of modularity as a framework for more effective strategic learning and knowledge management may result in increasingly dynamic product markets. These are likely to be characterized by expanding interactions among modular development organizations through 'quick-connect' global electronic networks (Sanchez 1996a). The consequences of this new modular creation environment will be previously unattained levels of product variety and change.

Discontinuities in product technology (Tushman and Anderson, 1986) lead to changes in the *content* of product markets—i.e., to new kinds of products made by new organizations. This paper, however, has described the rise of modular product design as a recent discontinuity in *coordination technology* (Sanchez, 1996b) that is leading to changes in the *processes and structures* of product markets—i.e., to new kinds of product development processes carried out by new forms of product development organizations. Thus, the possibilities for adapting new coordinating technologies and knowledge management processes based on modularity concepts are making it possible as never before for *organizational form* to become a variable to be managed strategically.

Finally, this paper concludes that the increased flexibilities that can result from the embedded coordination of standardized interfaces in modular architectures may not be limited to product development processes. The flexibilities to be derived from the standardized interfaces of modular architectures also appear to be attainable in the design of marketing, distribution, and other processes. Thus, we suggest that standardizing interfaces in modular system architectures of many types may be a new dominant design for achieving increased flexibility and interorganizational connectivity among broadly de-integrating organizations.[8]

ACKNOWLEDGEMENTS

The comments of Kathy Alexander, Stephen Bowden, Charles Galunic, Philip Gorman, Rob Grant, Jim Hagen, Kathryn Rudie Harrigan, Doug Johnson, Dong-Jae Kim, Bruce Kogut, Georgine Kryda, Arie Lewin, James Mahoney, Mark Pruett, Tom Roehl, Anju Seth, J.-C. Spender, Devanathan Sudharshan, Greg Winter, and especially Carliss Baldwin on earlier drafts are gratefully acknowledged. All remaining errors are the authors' responsibility.

REFERENCES

Abernathy, W. J. and K. B. Clark (1985). 'Innovation: Mapping the winds of creative destruction', *Research Policy*, **14**, pp. 3–22.

Alchian, A. A. and H. Demsetz (1972). 'Production, information costs, and economic organization', *American Economic Review*, **62**, pp. 777–795.

Automobile (August 1994). '1995 SAAB 900SE turbo coupe', pp. 97–98.

Baldwin, C. and K. B. Clark (1994). 'Modularity-in-design: An analysis based on the theory of real options', working paper, Harvard Business School, Cambridge, MA.

Bartlett, C. A. (1993). 'Commentary: Strategic flexibility, firm organization, and managerial work in dynamic markets'. In P. Shrivastava, A. S. Huff and J. Dutton (eds.), *Advances in Strategic Management*, Vol. 9. JAI Press, Greenwich, CT, pp. 292–298.

Clark, K. B. (1985). 'The interaction of design hierarchies and market concepts in technological evolution', *Research Policy*, **14** (5), pp. 235–251.

Clark, K. B. and T. Fujimoto (1991). *Product Development Performance: Strategy, Organization, and Management in the World Auto Industry*. Harvard University Press, Boston, MA.

Clark, K. B. and S. C. Wheelwright (1993). *Managing New Product and Process Development*. Free Press, New York.

Cohen, W. M. and D. A. Levinthal (1990). 'Absorptive capacity: A new perspective on learning and innovation', *Administrative Science Quarterly*, **35**, pp. 128–152.

Cusumano, M. A. (1991). *Japan's Software Factories: A Challenge to U.S. Management*. Oxford University Press, New York.

Cusumano, M. A. and R. W. Selby (1995). *Microsoft Secrets: How the World's Most Powerful Soft-ware Company Creates Technology, Shapes Markets, and Manages People*. Free Press, New York.

Cyert, R. M. and J. G. March (1963). *A Behavioral Theory of the Firm*. Prentice-Hall, Englewood Cliffs, NJ.

Daft, R. L. and A. Y. Lewin (1993). 'Where are the theories of the "new" organizational forms? An

---

[8] We observe, for example, that modularity in product designs can facilitate modularity in manufacturing processes as well as in development processes. In industries whose product designs are typically most modularized (e.g., personal computers), production, assembly, and servicing of components are commonly carried out by globally dispersed, loosely coupled organizations.

editorial essay', *Organization Science*, **4** (4), pp. i–vi.

David, P. A. and S. Greenstein (1990). 'The economics of compatibility standards: An introduction to recent research', *Economic Innovation and New Technology*, **1** (1), pp. 3–41.

Dewar, R. D. and J. E. Dutton (1986). 'The adoption of radical and incremental innovations: An empirical analysis', *Management Science*, **32** (11), pp. 1422–1433.

Electronics (7 April 1986). 'How Philips sweated the cost out of its new scopes', pp. 39–41.

Ford Engineering World (1990). '4.6 L V-8 is Ford's first modular engine', **15** (3), pp. 1–4.

Garud, R. and A. Kumaraswamy (1993). 'Changing competitive dynamics in network industries: An exploration of Sun Microsystems' open systems strategy', *Strategic Management Journal*, **14** (5), pp. 351–369.

Grant, R. (1993). 'Organizational capability within a knowledge-based view of the firm', School of Business Administration Working Paper Series, STRAT-2277-03-1293, Georgetown University.

Henderson, R. M. and K. B. Clark (1990). 'Architectural innovation: The reconfiguration of existing product technologies and the failure of established firms', *Administrative Science Quarterly*, **35**, pp. 9–30.

Kogut, B. and E. H. Bowman (1995). 'Modularity and permeability as principles of design'. In E. H. Bowman and B. Kogut (eds.), *Redesigning the Firm*. Oxford University Press, New York, pp. 243–260.

Kogut, B. and N. Kulatilaka (1994). 'Operating flexibility, global manufacturing, and the option value of a multinational network', *Management Science*, **40** (1), pp. 123–139.

Kogut, B. and U. Zander (1992). 'Knowledge of the firm, combinative capabilities, and the replication of technology', *Organization Science*, **3** (3), pp. 383–397.

Langlois, R. N. and P. L. Robertson (1992). 'Networks and innovation in a modular system: Lessons from the microcomputer and stereo component industries', *Research Policy*, **21** (4), pp. 297–313.

Levinthal, D. A. and J. G. March (1993). 'The myopia of learning', *Strategic Management Journal*, Winter Special Issue, **14**, pp. 95–112.

Mahoney, J. T. (1992a). 'The adoption of the multidivisional form of organization: A contingency model', *Journal of Management Studies*, **29** (1), pp. 49–72.

Mahoney, J. T. (1992b). 'Organizational economics within the conversation of strategic management'. In P. Shrivastava, A. S. Huff and J. Dutton (eds.), *Advances in Strategic Management*, Vol. 8. JAI Press, Greenwich, CT, pp. 103–155.

Mahoney, J. T. (1992c). 'The choice of organizational form: Vertical financial ownership versus other methods of vertical integration', *Strategic Management Journal*, **13** (8), pp. 559–584.

March, J. G. (1991). 'Exploration and exploitation in organizational learning', *Organization Science*, **2** (1), pp. 71–87.

Morris, C. R. and C. H. Ferguson (1993). 'How architecture wins technology wars', *Harvard Business Review*, **71** (2), pp. 86–96.

Nevins, J. L. and D. E. Whitney (eds.) (1989). *Concurrent Design of Products and Processes: A Strategy for the Next Generation in Manufacturing*. McGraw-Hill, New York.

Nishiguchi, T. (1994). *Strategic Industrial Outsourcing: The Japanese Advantage*. Oxford University Press, Oxford.

Normann, R. and R. Ramirez (1993). 'From value chain to value constellation: Designing interactive strategy', *Harvard Business Review*, **71** (4), pp. 65–77.

Orton, J. D. and K. E. Weick (1990). 'Loosely coupled systems: A reconceptualization', *Academy of Management Review*, **15** (2), pp. 203–223.

Ouchi, W. G. (1980). 'Markets, bureaucracies, and clans', *Administrative Science Quarterly*, **25**, pp. 120–142.

Parnas, D. L. (1972). 'On the criteria to be used in decomposing systems into modules', *Communications of the ACM*, **15**, pp. 1053–1058.

Parnas, D. L., P. C. Clements and D. M. Weiss (1985). 'The modular structure of complex systems', *IEEE Transactions on Software Engineering*, **11**, pp. 259–266.

Radner, R. (1992). 'Hierarchy: The economics of managing', *Journal of Economic Literature*, **30**, pp. 1382–1415.

Sanchez, R. (1991). 'Strategic flexibility, real options, and product-based strategy', Ph.D. dissertation, Massachusetts Institute of Technology, Cambridge, MA.

Sanchez, R. (1993). 'Strategic flexibility, firm organization, and managerial work in dynamic markets: A strategic options perspective'. In P. Shrivastava, A. S. Huff and J. Dutton (eds.), *Advances in Strategic Management*, Vol. 9. JAI Press, Greenwich, CT, pp. 251–291.

Sanchez, R. (1994a). 'Towards a science of strategic product design', paper presented at the Second International Product Development Management Conference on New Approaches to Development and Engineering, 30–31 May, 1994, Gothenburg, Sweden.

Sanchez, R. (1994b). 'Higher order organization and commitment in strategic options theory: A reply to Christopher Bartlett'. In P. Shrivastava, A. S. Huff and J. Dutton (eds.), *Advances in Strategic Management*, Vol. 10B. JAI Press, Greenwich, CT, pp. 251–291.

Sanchez, R. (1995), 'Strategic flexibility in product competition', *Strategic Management Journal*, Summer Special Issue, **16**, pp. 135–159.

Sanchez, R. (1996a). 'Quick-connect technologies for product creation: Implications for comeptence-based competition'. In R. Sanchez, A. Heene and H. Thomas (eds.), *Dynamics of Competence-based Competition: Theory and Practice in the New Strategic Management*. Elsevier, Oxford.

Sanchez, R. (1996b). 'Strategic product creation: Managing new interactions of technologies, markets, and organizations', *European Management Journal*, **14** (2), pp. 121–138.

76   *R. Sanchez and J. T. Mahoney*

Sanchez, R. (1996c). 'Managing articulated knowledge in competence-based competition'. In R. Sanchez and A. Heene (Eds.), *Strategic Learning and Knowledge Management*. Wiley, Chichester.

Sanchez, R. (1996d). 'Integrating technology strategy and marketing strategy'. In D. O'Neal and H. Thomas (eds.), *Integrating Strategy*. Wiley, Chichester.

Sanchez, R. and A. Heene (eds.) (1996). *Strategic Learning and Knowledge Management*. Wiley, Chichester.

Sanchez, R. and D. Sudharshan (1993). 'Real-time market research: Learning-by-doing in the development of new products', *Marketing Intelligence and Planning*, **11** (7), pp. 29–38.

Sanderson, S. W. and V. Uzumeri (1990). 'Strategies for new product development and renewal: Design-based incrementalism', working paper, Center for Science and Technology Policy, Rensselaer Polytechnic Institute, Troy, NY.

Shirley, G. V. (1990). 'Models for managing the redesign and manufacture of product sets', *Journal of Manufacturing and Operations Management*, **3** (2), pp. 85–104.

Simon, H. A. (1962). 'The architecture of complexity', *Proceedings of the American Philosophical Society*, **106**, pp. 467–482.

Simon, H. A. (1981). *The Sciences of the Artificial*. MIT Press, Cambridge, MA.

Smith, A. (1776). *An Inquiry into the Nature and Causes of the Wealth of Nations*. The Modern Library, New York.

Spender, J.-C. and Grinyer, P. H. (1995). 'Organizational renewal: Top management's role in a loosely coupled system', *Human Relations*, **48** (8), pp. 909–926.

Takeuchi, H. and I. Nonaka (1986). 'The new new product development game', *Harvard Business Review*, **64** (1), pp. 137–146.

Tully, S. (8 February 1993). 'The modular corporation', *Fortune*, pp. 106–114.

Tushman, M. L. and P. Anderson (1986). 'Technological discontinuities and organizational environments', *Administrative Science Quarterly*, **31**, pp. 439–465.

Ulrich, K. T. and S. Eppinger (1995). *Product Design and Development*. McGraw-Hill, New York.

Utterback, J. M. (1994). *Mastering the Dynamics of Innovation: How Companies Can Seize Opportunities in the Face of Technological Change*. Harvard Business Press, Boston, MA.

Venkatesan, R. (1992). 'Strategic sourcing: To make or not to make', *Harvard Business Review*, **70** (6), pp. 98–107.

von Hippel, E. (1988). *The Sources of Information*. Oxford University Press, New York.

von Hippel, E. (1990). 'Task partitioning: An innovation process variable', *Research Policy*, **19** (5), pp. 407–418.

von Hippel, E. (1994). 'Sticky information and the locus of problem solving', *Management Science*, **40** (4), pp. 429–439.

Ward, A., J. V. Liker, J. J. Cristiano and D. K. Sobek (1995). 'The second Toyota paradox: Delaying decisions can make better cars faster', *Sloan Management Review*, Spring, pp. 43–61.

Weick, K. E. (1976). 'Educational organizations as loosely coupled systems', *Administrative Science Quarterly*, **21**, pp. 1–19.

Wheelwright, S. C. and K. B. Clark (1992). *Revolutionizing Product Development: Quantum Leaps in Speed, Efficiency, and Quality*. Free Press, New York.

Whitney, D. E. (1988). 'Manufacturing by design', *Harvard Business Review*, **66** (4), pp. 83–91.

Williamson, O. E. (1975). *Markets and Hierarchies*. Free Press, New York.

Woolsey, J. P. (April 1994). '777', *Air Transport World*, pp. 22–31.

Wright, R. W. (1994). 'The effects of tacitness and tangibility on the diffusion of knowledge-based resources', *Academy of Management Best Papers Proceedings*, pp. 52–56.

Name Index